Modern Branch Libraries and Libraries in Systems

by

Eleanor Frances Brown

The Scarecrow Press, Inc.

Metuchen, N.J.   1970

Dedication

For Marie Simpson
who gave such valuable assistance
in this "labor of love"

Table of Contents

Page

v

List of Illustrations

vii

ix

x

xi

xii

xiii

xiv

xv

Introduction

I have endeavored to do two things in this volume: first, to give an over-all survey of branch library work and the problems connected with establishing branch service, building branches, and operating them; second, to gather together in one volume a summary of the thinking and writings of prominent figures in the library world who are knowledgeable in the extension field. Original sources have been used to a great extent, including some excerpts from letters and from speeches at library conferences.

I have included material, especially in regard to branch buildings, that could be found in periodical articles in order to save the time of librarians, board members, or architects who might wish to find as much branch material as possible within the covers of one book. Much of the material should be of assistance to member or affiliated libraries that have joined systems and in many areas, are taking the place of the traditional branch.

To include everything that might or should be included would require much more than one volume; thus the greatest task has been one of selection. The study of outside sources was confined to the literature of the United States, Canada, and other English-speaking countries. An effort has been made to present varying opinions and to include examples of buildings and practices from various parts of the country. Until there has been much more research on a scientific basis than can be found at present, positive recommendations cannot be made concerning many branch building or operational procedures. Certain points that have proven themselves by experience over the years are brought out as fact. Examples would be recommending branch locations in shopping centers and opposing them in school buildings, changing from old-fashioned hand charging methods to modern photocharging or other automatic systems that save many steps, and certain principles of building that have emerged quite clearly as desirable and practical. Many fine photographs were received. The response to requests for material was generous and widespread. Librarians are like that. I wish to thank all of those who contributed photographs, information, or opinions. This book is the work of many, gathered and put together by one.

Chapter 1

Then and Now: Historical Development

The first public library branch in the United States, according to Milton Byam, was established nearly one hundred years ago, in 1871 in Boston, the Commonwealth of Massachusetts having passed enabling legislation which permitted the establishment of libraries "with or without branches."[1] This seemed to presuppose some previous experience with branches, but the only earlier record concerns the Manchester (England) Public Library which was established in 1851 and had five branches by 1866.

For most of the rest of the century the function and objectives of public libraries were not defined professionally. Their development was more or less haphazard and was based on casual interpretation of year-to-year needs. By 1890, however, the trend toward branches was very evident. The public library movement at that time was not publicly supported but was maintained chiefly by philanthropy, by social organizations, and by individuals who cooperated to share books or to lend them to the poor.[1]

Some of the early philanthropic libraries had branches. The New York Free Circulating Library, established in 1878, operated eleven branches until it incorporated into the New York Public Library in 1901. The West Side Circulating Library, founded in Chicago in 1869, had several branches within a few years of its establishment. About the same time circulating libraries were increasing in a number of cities, and these too had branches. A discussion in Library Journal, January, 1898, mentions the Free Circulating and Aguilar Library Systems of New York, the Boston, Philadelphia, Enoch Pratt (Baltimore), and Pratt Institute (Brooklyn) libraries as having branches.[2]

Social and philanthropic libraries promoted the development of branch libraries and were often the beginning of circulating

19

branches as opposed to the reading room type. This was particularly true if the parent library had been a reference center only, as was true of the Newberry and John Crerar Libraries in Chicago.

Boston took over the Summer Library Association of East Boston to establish its first branch, while the Chicago Public Library took over the existing Hyde Park Lyceum in 1891. Cincinnati and Providence also absorbed existing community private libraries to establish branches. In 1901, Mrs. Blackstone presented the Chicago Public Library with its own first circulating branch, in memory of her husband. Boston also received some direct gifts to benefit its branch system. The number of branches has shown an interesting pattern of fluctuation. The 1960 American Library Directory reported 3,625 branches in city, county and regional systems. The number reported in 1964 was 3,376, a drop of 249. The 1968-69 Directory, however, reported 3,833, showing a 457 increase. The trend to build fewer and larger branches as older, more inactive branches were dropped, undoubtedly influenced the change in 1964. With the 1964 change in the Library Services Act to permit financial aid for construction, the building of both branch and central libraries took an upward swing. Should federal and state funds no longer be available at some later date, this fact, combined with the trend toward larger branches, may well cause the total figure to decrease again.

The best-known philanthropy, of course, is that of Andrew Carnegie, who gave approximately 1900 library buildings to the United States and Canada alone between 1897 and 1917, many of which were branches. He offered 65 branches to New York City at a cost of $5,200,000; 30 to Philadelphia, 3 to East Orange, 8 to Pittsburgh, and 10 to Cleveland, among others. Although the pattern of architecture through those years has sometimes been a drawback to the development of modern buildings, a big impetus was given to public support by Carnegie insistence that any community receiving a building must provide a site and must also agree to furnish an annual operating budget of at least ten per cent of the amount of his gift.

Figure 1. A typical interior - Carnegie Library
Branch - early 20th century (Montclair Free
Public Library, Montclair, New Jersey).

Lewis W. Hine, photographer

The contract with the Carnegie Corporation which had to be
signed by any city accepting a building indicated minimum support
and suggested minimum standards. Library hours, privileges and
services were thus more or less standardized as they could have
been in no other way. Individual communities, however, were not
idle during all this time. Oakland, California established its first
branch in 1878; Boston had achieved 15 branches on its own initiative by 1901. Cleveland opened its first branch in 1892; Buffalo,
in rented quarters, in 1901; and Providence in 1906.

During the early part of the century and on into the 20's
and 30's many branches were to be found in city halls, converted

Figure 2. A typical exterior, Carnegie type of architecture. Upper Montclair Library Branch, Montclair
Free Public Library, Montclair, New Jersey, opened 1913.

F. F. Brown, photographer

Figure 3. By contrast: Modern branch of the Los Angeles
Public Library--Sherman Oaks Branch, opened May, 1962.

Figure 4. THEN: West Elmira Branch of the Steele Memorial Library of Chemung County, New York, located in Elmira, typical of many opened in remodeled residences or wings of a town hall or other civic building during the early years.

Figure 5. NOW: The West Elmira branch as it appeared after completion of the new building in 1965.

Photographer: Lon Mattoon
Elmira, New York

Figure 6. Floor Plan, West Elmira Branch.

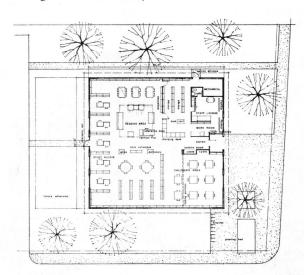

private residences, or in conjunction with other civic buildings such
as museums.   This type of combination is still used occasionally
where economy is a prime factor.   It did not prove successful in
many cases in the past and sometimes delayed for long periods the
erection of larger, more adequate quarters.

The disadvantages of a multiple-floor arrangement, so often
found in converted residences reserved by gift or bequest, were the
difficulty of supervision and of proper staffing.   Problems of adequate heating arose when branches were placed in buildings that
were not used for other purposes at night and over weekends.
Dependence upon public philanthropy for sites, buildings, or furnishings held down services and often resulted in a branch being located
where it could not attain its best use.   Dependence upon outside
sources also tended to make governmental jurisdictions slow to assume their proper burden of public support and thus slowed the
development of much-needed branches.

High ceilings increased heating costs in cold climates, and
dark woodwork and monumental appearance of the buildings did not
add to their warmth and inviting appearance.   Some so-called

"branches" were merely deposit stations by today's standards. Within existing limitations, however, many branches were fairly effective.

From the period 1890 to about 1910 there was a trend, in certain sections of the United States, to include public library branches in school buildings. This occurred primarily in the central part of the country. Libraries in Indiana, Missouri, and Michigan were definitely affected. In most large cities, such as St. Louis and Indianapolis, this relationship was broken years ago. A few cities in Indiana have just in recent years divided the two types of service. In Kansas City, Missouri, a major political battle was recently fought in an attempt to get the public library system out of the school buildings and out of the jurisdiction of the school board.

The first business library supported by taxes was opened Oct. 1, 1904 as a branch of the Newark (New Jersey) Public Library, of which John Cotton Dana was librarian at the time. [6] The first year's budget was approximately $1500.

Although the social and philanthropic libraries did a great deal to promote the development of branches, the original branches developed from the attempts by pioneer librarians to provide some sort of service outside the main library through revolving collections. A library established a few deposit stations. These soon became inadequate and a better traveling library system was developed, with collections changed more frequently or supplemented according to demand. As particular sections of a city grew more rapidly, the schools in these sections needed book services; children mobbed the traveling libraries or bookmobiles when they came once a week or less often. The next step was a branch library with permanent book stock and staff. [3] Bookmobiles were an advance over fixed deposit stations since, in general, they carried many more books and usually had a better-trained staff. As traveling branches they served an important purpose and are still doing so; permanent branches, when bookmobile usage showed the need, were an even greater advance.

The deposit stations, too small to be considered true branches as we think of them today, but often mistakenly called so, developed in the late 1800's and first half of the 1900's. Many of these were only delivery stations; others were in industrial locations, homes, hospitals, or other institutions.   Some of these stations, Herbert Goldhor points out in Practical Administration of Public Libraries, have not proved successful or efficient and have either disappeared from the scene or now have only a special and limited role.   But for approximately 75 years the use of branch libraries to reach out into the community to serve those who would not or could not come to a central library has been the backbone of public library extension.[4]

Prior to World War II the remarkable growth in branches was justified by the limitations of both public and private transportation. The proliferation of branches was made easy in these earlier years by the relatively low cost of buildings and of personnel to staff them.   Furthermore, the relatively low standards of library services in those times defined the branch library as a kind of neighborhood reading room and the branch was not expected to meet either the qualitative or the quantitative standards of service supplied by a strong central library.[5]

Kenneth R. Shaffer, in a study entitled Design for Tomorrow, produced for the Bridgeport, Connecticut Public Library in 1966, has this to say concerning the development of branches:[5]

> Frequently the only resemblance of the branch library
> to its central parent was in the physical design of the
> building, which, likely as not, was a copy of its monu-
> mental parent in miniature.   New England towns and
> cities are still characterized by multitudes of branch
> libraries of this vintage, frequently located as close
> as three-quarters of a mile from each other and which,
> in 1966, drain off fiscal support for good library
> service.   Often such libraries are imbedded in the
> cultural folklore of their neighborhoods, and until this
> psychological resistance can be overcome, these small,
> temple-like structures cannot be torn down.
>
> The climate which characterized branch library develop-
> ment until World War II has undergone an abrupt and
> complete change.   For the first time, during the past
> quarter century, our concepts of the branch library as
> a vehicle for library extension has become a matter of
> careful scrutiny and evaluation.   In the post-war years,
> many public library systems have discovered that their
> accumulated investment in satellite branches was no
> longer fiscally possible nor justifiable in terms of the
> kinds and levels of library services which are acceptable

to their communities. In large metropolitan centers, the
high per capita costs of branches have militated against
the establishment or continuance of a branch unless it
serves a population of from 40,000 to 65,000. [5]

Mr. Shaffer goes on to point out that the changes in patterns
of library extension are not only economic. While greater building
costs and higher salaries for personnel may be determinants in many
communities, the main consideration is the limited quality of service
which may be imposed upon library patrons through proliferation of
small branches. Today every city and neighborhood throughout the
country is characterized by a high level of mobility. It is no longer
necessary to have a library within walking distance of every citizen.
The small branch is giving way to strong regional branches serving
large areas. Related to these factors is the truism that small,
weak branches with diminutive book collections, lacking personnel of
high quality, and with limited programs and services, generally do
not justify themselves by public use. Libraries which are strong in
book collections, a well-trained staff and a variety of high-quality
services, are economical and justify the tax dollars spent upon them
by proportionately higher use.

County libraries with their many branches comprise a later
development than those in urban areas, although there were early
experiments in widely separated sections. The first county library
originated in Washington County, Maryland, just before the turn of
the century; by 1905 it had a horse-drawn vehicle on the road distributing books. In 1911 Washington County had a motorized pioneer
bookmobile or traveling branch in operation. Development of county
libraries with their community branches came first and most effectively in the Middle and Far West where areas to be served were
bigger and more sparsely settled.

On a larger scale, this trend paralleled that of the branch
library movement in urban centers. A county system was established
in Cincinnati, Ohio in 1898. The same year Van Wert County, in
the same state, set up a headquarters building. The most successful and widespread early service appeared in California. James
Gillis, the California State Librarian, started, about 1909, to make

books available throughout the state by a type of traveling extension service. Gradually, county libraries with branches in many smaller towns and cities were established. California and New York now have extensive networks of county and regional libraries with branches or federation member libraries throughout these states. Development in practically all of the states has followed these patterns.[3]

Notably in New York State and in the far western State of Montana, according to Milton S. Byam,[1] library systems gather together on a county or population basis a number of independent libraries in a cooperative pattern of shared centralized services much like those available to branch libraries. These are known as federations, and since these provide the same types of service as do branches, should be considered in connection with them. In Canada municipal libraries usually have fine central buildings and extensive branch systems. Numerous new branches have been built in the last few years, with many of them in Ottawa, Vancouver, and Calgary established in shopping centers.

The place of the branch library has been firmly established. Although in many areas it may be advantageous to build branches only when the population served will be from 40,000 to 65,000, as Mr. Shaffer suggests, it seems that there will be a place for some years to come for branches serving from 25,000 to 40,000 population. Each community will have to decide this matter upon the basis of need, demand, and economics. However, there is no question but that the present growth pattern is toward larger and better-equipped regional branches, both urban and rural. In urban situations some of the regional services may parallel those of the central library, and there are a few instances in the United States where a large new branch has surpassed the central library in readers and circulation.

Regional branches have also been set up in large county or regional systems and may serve as the bookmobile and/or extension headquarters for the entire system. In several sparsely-settled states such as New Mexico, the State Library agency has set up its own branches at strategic points.

Today's problems center around the improvement of branch services through better locations, more modern buildings, optimum hours, determining the best distances between agencies, building better book collections, providing more ample staffing, and finding better methods of reaching the great unreached segments of population in each branch area.

The image of the modern branch library is in refreshing contrast to the small, poorly-stocked central library stepchild of a few decades ago. Networks of community branches tailored to fit their neighborhoods or small towns, many of them large and dynamic activity centers offering vigorous and varied service programs, have become an accepted "must" for progressive library systems.

Since the days of lending only books and a few tattered magazines, the modern branch has enlarged its resources to include phonograph records, art prints, films, maps, pamphlets, and tapes. It may also provide listening equipment, microfilm viewers, copy machines, rental typewriters, pen dispensers, and other convenient items for the public.

Today's effective branch is ideally a cultural center for the community. Adult groups can meet in a comfortable auditorium; children can gather for reading clubs and story hours, puppet shows, and films; patrons in general may attend library-sponsored lectures, music programs, travel talks, movies, Great Books or Great Ideas sessions, Story League meetings, or various other activities. Furthermore, the modern branch is providing the traditional services, including reference, in greater depth and with greater efficiency. However, many branches have not achieved this status, and this is no time for complacency.

Such enriched programs as those described furnish information, recreation, inspiration, and mental stimulation. These branches typify the broader objectives of general library service in a modern age, objectives which must grow increasingly broader and more socially significant if branches are to play their proper role in the total library picture. There is no better bargain for the taxpayer's dollar. To maintain this highly desirable situation library administrators must consistently study the need and demand

Figure 7. Kenwood Branch Library, Cedar Rapids
Public Library, Cedar Rapids, Iowa,
as it appeared in 1930.

Figure 8. The greatly-enlarged Kenwood Branch, Cedar Rapids Public Library, Cedar Rapids, Iowa. This branch, twice remodeled and enlarged since 1930, is now thoroughly modern in every respect, even has a drive-in service window, first in Iowa and one of the few in the country.

Figure 9. Before improvement by remodeling, a view of the interior of the Kenwood Branch.

Figure 10. Interior of Kenwood Branch today.

for branches. Furthermore they must keep informed on new developments, equipment, and services. In many cities the War on
Poverty is producing interesting experiments to find ways to make
libraries meaningful to the less educated and otherwise disadvantaged
segments of our population. As one example, a federally-subsidized
program in Venice, California, a branch of the Los Angeles Public
Library, has attracted widespread attention and publicity because of
its method of approach. The project director, Don Roberts, has
attempted to meet the so-called "hippie" or "flower-children" groups
on their own grounds. A special attempt was made, from the first,
to understand and appeal to these young people. Here is a notable
example of fitting a branch to its community since Venice is heavily
populated with the hippie group. It is on the outskirts of Santa
Monica by the sea, part of Los Angeles but hardly in that sprawling
city. It is a suburban slum and summer resort town. The poverty
pocket of Venice, about 45 square blocks in area, is inhabited main
ly by Negro and Mexican-American families who moved in during
the Depression and the post-war years as the town was gradually
deserted by its wealthy residents. It has a small art community,

is a haven for mixed marriages, and is occasionally visited by
groups like the Hell's Angels.

The City of Los Angeles Public Library allocated part of its
$500,000 Library Services and Construction Act grant in 1965 to this
multi-ethnic area in order to try to reach the non-readers.   Three
community librarians (adult, young adult, and children's) plus a
clerk, were added to the regular staff and a generous materials
budget was allowed, these all being drawn from the federal grant.
Several articles have appeared in library literature on this project
since that time.

There are many factors which have affected and still are
affecting the development of branch libraries in regard to size,
location, number, design and service.   These are:

1. One of the most potent is the greatly increased mobility
    of the family through automobiles, freeways, and better
    traffic patterns, making distances between library
    agencies much less important and permitting fewer and
    larger branches with better collections, longer hours,
    and more staff.

2. The decentralization of business from downtown centers
    to shopping centers has created focal points where people
    come in large numbers, where there is plenty of park-
    ing space and greater convenience.   Libraries have been
    quick to take advantage of this fact by locating branches
    in or near shopping centers.

3. The change in educational approach from almost total
    dependence upon textbooks to wide use of outside en-
    richment and reference material has made the provision
    of general informational service to students, not neces-
    sarily on the "research in depth" level, but generous in
    amount and widespread in content, a highly important
    aspect of service.   The handily-located branch has as-
    sumed an increasingly important role in meeting this
    need.

4. The improved and increased aids to library building
    planning have made possible branches which are more
    functional, more enticing, and more adaptable.   Archi-
    tects, library directors, and extension heads constantly
    find more help at hand for good branch planning in
    library literature and practical experience.

    There is no reason today why any good library system
    cannot produce a well-located, usable, attractive branch
    building by making use of all available resources for

ideas. There have been excellent books, institutes on
library architecture, programs at library conferences
the annual architectural issue of Library Journal, and
increased awareness of specialized library needs on the
part of many architects. Good buildings obviously make
possible better service.

5. There has been a change in the educational background
    of the populace. As the educational level has risen so
    has interest in reading. Branches become more neces-
    sary and the content of branch collections is affected.
    City people demand more than one central building for
    library service, and they read more and better materials.

6. Population shifts seem to increase as people move out
    from concentrated inner-city residential neighborhoods
    to subdivisions and fringe areas at a considerable dis-
    tance from downtown sections. This movement has
    created new need for geographically scattered branches
    in large cities and for more community branches in
    rural areas. Suburbs grow by leaps and bounds. Busy
    bookmobiles become too busy to serve outlying metro-
    politan areas or small communities properly. They are
    superseded by branches. The network grows apace.

7. The very size and complexity of departments of many
    large central libraries is bewildering to many people.
    They prefer the informality of their own neighborhood
    library center, the ease with which they can find the
    material they seek, and the friendliness of a small
    staff they can easily get to know. Thus, in all but the
    most culturally deprived neighborhoods or communities,
    demand for library service within easy driving distance
    grows until something is done about it.

8. As cities grow, the formation of new traffic patterns
    may make a former branch location unfeasible and cre-
    ate a demand for a new modern branch. Likewise, the
    decay or deterioration of a neighborhood can make a
    branch superfluous but cause the building of one or more
    modern branches in housing centers or spreading suburbs.

9. The advent of Federal Aid for construction, as contained
    in The Library Services and Construction Act of 1965,
    has been a vital influence to increase the number of
    branch libraries. Library services to people in poverty
    areas, the economically and culturally disadvantaged,
    have improved as a result of other Federal programs
    in the anti-poverty war. A case in point is the Latin-
    American Library of the Oakland, California, Public
    Library, established with Federal Funds. This is a
    specialized example, but many communities took advantage

of Federal aid to build additional branches in areas in which they were needed. A summary of Federal aid requested for building construction will be found in Chapter 14.

10. Probably the most obvious reason for the spread of branches has been the general population growth of the country as a whole.

11. Still another factor is one which has often been given as a cause of decreasing use of public libraries, namely, the growth in number and quality of school libraries. While it is true that when a new school library is established, a public library in the area may show a temporary decrease in circulation of children's and young people's books, it has often been found that in the long run the school library may serve as a stimulus to reading and to public library use. Reading begets reading. School librarians have often more time to work with slow readers, to know their student patrons, and to work with them as reading counselors. Such librarians usually stimulate young readers to use the public library as well. Some new readers may well be gained in this fashion.

12. The difficulty and mounting expense of parking in downtown areas, at or near central libraries, often militates against their use and helps the growth of branches where parking is ample and free, and the surroundings are usually more attractive.

13. The increasing tendency for central libraries in urban centers to become research centers with a higher concentration of in-depth material and reference aids is increasing the importance of and dependence upon the community branch as a center for general individual and family reading. Thus they should increase in number and importance.

14. With the great increase in number of titles published yearly, particularly in the field of children's books, libraries must give more attention to children's services and more space to children's collections in order to include even the best books.

15. The general explosion of knowledge: 90 % of the world's scientists who have ever lived are living today. This is the blossoming time of our accumulated knowledge. Young and old are trying to assimilate more of this knowledge. It means more and larger libraries with more seats and more specialized personnel. Central libraries cannot handle the demands alone. Branch libraries will continue to grow in size and value as sources of information.

16. There is more leisure time. Also the older age group
    increases along with those of elementary school age.
    The special needs of these age groups will demand in-
    creasing library time and attention. More leisure means
    more reading.

17. The increasing sense of social responsibility on the part
    of librarians promotes a move to reach out into the un-
    reached areas of city or county. This requires more
    outlets.

Perhaps the most important factor in development of the
modern branch is the tendency to develop each particular community's individuality so that its branch is not a facsimile of the
central library. No two neighborhoods are identical, and the successful branch is one that is based upon a thorough knowledge of
the area served. The matter of individual branch development to
fit the community will be discussed further in Chapter 5, Organization: Relationship to the Central Library or Headquarters, and
Chapter 6, Tailoring the Branch to the Community.

Enrichment of services is being found particularly in those
small, independent libraries which have become members of a
system, assuming some branch functions but losing none of their
local autonomy. Services have also widened and improved when
independent libraries have cooperated for certain specified services.
Such areas of cooperation may be centralized processing or centralized cataloging, information retrieval, pooled book or supply
purchasing, subject specialties, a storage center for older materials or for valuable or out-of-print materials for which there is
only occasional demand; the sharing of bookmobiles, or the sharing
of professional specialists. All such cooperative arrangements can
only result in improved services for all libraries concerned.

The literature dealing with branch libraries has been notably
limited in the present century, even though branches have been an
important factor in metropolitan library development for almost a
hundred years. Aside from a paper by Lowell A. Martin in 1940
on the purpose and administration of branches in large city libraries; a little over a chapter in Wheeler and Goldhor's book Practical
Administration of Public Libraries; slightly more consideration in
Roberta Bowler's Local Public Library Administration; some

discussion in Dorothy Sinclair's Administration of the Small Public
Library; and a number of articles in library periodicals, including
an issue of Library Trends in April, 1966, too little attention has
been given to branch libraries, their history, scope, function, and
operation.

There is one full-length book, Branch Libraries, by A. D.
Mortimore, published in 1966 by Deutsch. It deals with English
libraries. Some of the best material is to be found in branch
surveys made by leading librarians. These, however, usually
refer to specific cities or areas. Several unpublished theses also
provide material.

Among recent studies and surveys which may be especially
helpful are the following:

Changing Patterns: A Branch Library Plan for the Cleveland
Metropolitan Area, a report to the Cleveland Public Library and the
Cuyahoga County District Library, by the Cuyahoga County, Ohio
Regional Planning Commission.

Investigation to Determine the Most Efficient Patterns for
Providing Adequate Library Service to all Residents of a Typical
Large City, by Leonard Grundt. Thesis for the Ph. D. , Rutgers
University, 1965. A summary entitled "Branch Library Inadequa-
cies in a Typical Large City" appeared in Library Journal, v. 90,
no. 17, p. 3397-4001, Oct. 1, 1965.

Branch Library Service for Dallas, by Lowell A. Martin.
The Library, Dallas, Texas, 1958.

Branch Libraries, a Long-Range Development Plan, by the
Roanoke, Virginia Dept. of City Planning and the Roanoke Public
Library Board. The authors, 1963.

Design for Tomorrow, by Kenneth Shaffer. Bridgeport,
Connecticut, Bridgeport Public Library, 1966.

Study of Branch and Bookmobile Needs for the City of
Victoria, British Columbia, Canada, by Rose Vainstein, Victoria
Public Library, 1962.

Comparison of Branch Library Services in Three Seattle Communities, by Jane F. Waldron. Thesis for the M. S. in Library
Science, University of Washington, Seattle, 1957.

Neighborhood Library Service, by Frederick Wezeman. Des Moines Public Library, Des Moines, Iowa, 1959.

A Study of Branch Libraries, by Frederick Wezeman, for Lincoln City Library, Lincoln, Nebraska, 1967.

The above studies are concerned primarily with branches. General surveys and studies of large systems such as the Tulsa City-County System, Tulsa, Oklahoma, and the long-range development plan of the City of Phoenix, Arizona, also contain much material relating to branch development.

Notes

1. Byam, Milton. "History of Branch Libraries." Library Trends, 14 (no. 4): 72, April, 1966.

2. Rose, Ernestine. The Public Library in American Life. N. Y., Columbia University Press, 1954. p. 218.

3. Ibid, p. 35-36.

4. Wheeler, Joseph L. and Goldhor, Herbert. Practical Administration of Public Libraries. N. Y., Harper and Row, 1962. p. 410.

5. Shaffer, Kenneth. Design for Tomorrow. Bridgeport, Conn., Bridgeport Public Library, 1966. p. 37-38.

6. Kane, Joseph N. Famous First Facts. N. Y., H. W. Wilson, 1964. p. 342.

Chapter 2

Types and Definitions

There seem to be three general methods of designating
branches: by size, by function, and by organization. The term
"branch" has sometimes been loosely used in the past to describe
agencies of a central library which today would not be regarded as
branches but as deposit stations or sub-branches.

In order to clarify the differences we will attempt to define
these agencies. The changing concept of what constitutes a "branch"
has made the term as such almost obsolete. The word suggests in
its original botanical meaning a complete state of dependence upon a
central trunk as its source of life. Today's new branches--larger
(averaging 8,000 square feet or so as compared to 2,000-6,000
square feet a few decades ago), better located, better staffed, supplied with a more adequate book collection, and physically functional
and attractive,--have less dependence upon the central library for
resources, although they are still closely allied to it in organization
and financial support.

The modern branch must conceivably be able to survive quite
readily and with continued good service if operational support is still
available, even though the central library should burn down or be
changed over to a reference and information center. The main
weakness of most branches at present is their limited reference
facilities.

Although administrative policies and procedures stem from
the central library, the latter has occasionally been equaled or even
surpassed in actual size or service by one or more of its branches.
In the not too distant future we may expect that the majority of book
loans may be made from branches or service centers, while central
libraries, often marooned in a downtown location with little or no

parking, become centers for specialized reference and research for
the public and information centers for its community libraries via
telephone and teletype.   Actually, in such a case the term "branch"
should be replaced by the newer designations of "community library,"
"area library," or "member library."

Although still in good repute as far as city library systems are
concerned, the use of the term branch sometimes impedes the development of a new county or regional library system. Independent libraries,
treasuring their local autonomy, dislike the word as stressing their
dependence and decreasing their importance.   They prefer to think
of themselves as cooperating libraries or members of a federation.
Although their fears of being swallowed up or taken over by the headquarters library have usually proved unfounded, the most successful
and quickly-achieved larger systems formed since the Library Services Act first came into being have been those that used the "come
join us as a partner" approach.   Local pride which rebels against
the idea of becoming just one of many subsidiary branches is
assuaged by the invitation to join as a cooperative partner.

In metropolitan areas where library expansion goes on apace
and where new branches spread out naturally from an already existing central agency, this matter of terminology has seldom caused a
problem. But as far as county and regional systems are concerned,
the time seems ripe to adopt, as most federations have, a new
standard term for cooperating member libraries and to scrap the term
branch.   For want of a generally-accepted substitute, we shall be
forced to use the old term generally throughout this book when
referring to branches in the traditional sense.

The general term branch, as used here, includes any library agency which is part of and receives direction, services,
and support from a central library or headquarters.   A branch
is differentiated from a deposit station in that it is housed in its
own building or room--not necessarily its own property but
separate from any other type of operation;   it has a substantial
permanent book collection and a paid staff, and is open at regularly scheduled hours: North Carolina standards specify at least

30 hours a week. A good community branch will be open 45 to
60 hours per week. It is a major library unit.

> A Swedish visiting librarian called the American branch
> library the 'American library masterpiece,' its archi-
> tecture inspired by tradition, climate, and surroundings.
> All the branches he saw, he said, had 'an atmosphere
> of friendliness, an open door for the entire community,
> big and small, and an unconscious suggestion that inside
> one would meet a cultured hostess.'[1]

Edith Meyers says, in Meet the Future: People and Ideas
of Today,

> For a chance to try out ingenious ideas, for richly-
> rewarding personal contacts with people and books, and
> for the best possible preparation for even more responsi-
> ble library positions, nothing exceeds a branch library,
> nothing, that is, unless it may be a bookmobile.[1]

Now to define the various types by size:

1.   The regional branch, running generally from 12,000 to
65,000 square feet, acts as a resource and often as administrative
center for a group of smaller branches in a wide area surrounding
it.   One library, the Omaha, Nebraska, Public, has built a regional branch of 25,510 square feet.   One of the largest regional
branch systems in the nation was opened in the fall of 1963 when
Philadelphia's Northeast Regional Library, the first of five to be
erected, began operations. It was built at a cost of $1,198,377
and was expected to serve 500,000 residents in the area by 1980.
Sprain Brook regional Branch in Yonkers, New York has 65,000
sq. ft.   The Brooklyn Public Library calls its regional branches
District Libraries.   One was to be set up in each of Brooklyn's
larger communities.   Each would have a minimum collection of
50,000 volumes and necessary personnel.   Within these areas will
be satellite branches known as "family reading centers" staffed
entirely by non-professional personnel including the clerk in
charge--a senior clerk with title of "Center Manager." District
librarians would render complete and continuous consultation service.   The reading centers would be circulation agencies with
minimum reference collections, developed mainly for patron use.
Brooklyn reported success and satisfaction when the plan was in
its third year.   Regional branches are also sometimes called area
libraries.

2. A typical neighborhood or community branch, the next smaller unit, will range from 2500 to 12,000 square feet. In a few cases, branches as big as 20,000 square feet are not designated as or functioning as regional units. Branches under 4,000 to 5,000 square feet are being built less frequently today and are not recommended. Medium-sized community branches, which are the most common pattern in most cities, may be in rented quarters or in buildings of their own. They will offer as complete a service as possible within the limitations of budget and staff. For a detailed suggested service program for such a branch, see Chapter 11, The Service Program. In general, a good branch offers reference and other special services. It can be expected to produce a circulation of 75,000 to 300,000. Forty-five to fifty per cent of the book collection would be for adults. Minimum floor space would be about 8,000 square feet and it should serve around 30,000 persons. Such a branch may be located three to four miles from any other library service agency. Since the book ordering, cataloging, and processing are done at the central library, practically all staff time and effort at branches can be given to the public. Most users are repeaters who get to know the staff, and the staff gets to know them.

3. A sub-branch, still existing in some cities but rapidly fading from the scene, emphasizes the circulation of books, with little or no reference service. It is often in rented quarters, is open only 2 or 3 days a week for only a few hours, and is frequently in a remote neighborhood where the population is too limited to warrant the installation of a full branch. In practice, these have usually been staffed by untrained or non-professional assistants. Sometimes a staff member comes out from the central library on the appointed days. There is a minimal collection with the emphasis on popular reading. Thus, only partial branch service is given.

4. Deposit station: Not properly a branch, the deposit station has sometimes been referred to as such. It is usually in a strategic location such as a hospital, fire station, general store,

school, or even a well-situated private home, where a few boxes of books have been placed and are changed at regular intervals by the central library. Sometimes the books are shipped by mail. Deposit stations in homes, schools and stores are more often found in rural areas as part of county or regional service, although bookmobiles have in many areas made them unnecessary. Deposit stations may have a legitimate place in such locations as rest homes, hospitals, supermarkets, juvenile detention homes or other correctional institutions, or in special locations such as parks, neighborhood community centers, boys' clubs, airports, barber shops, beauty parlors, or bars, etc., where a special effort is being made to provide some service to people who would not come to a library building. Both the sub-branch and the deposit station attempt to provide a minimum of reading matter. It can hardly be called true library service. The many paperbacks available through commercial outlets are reducing the importance of this type of library extension agency.

5. Family Reading Centers or Book Distribution Centers: Recently there has been a trend back toward the sub-branch called a Book Distribution or Reading Center. They are mainly concerned with ready reference and circulation of popular books at the neighborhood level. In their ready reference service they differ from the older type sub-branch, and they specialize in popular books. They are an effort on the part of some city systems to fill a gap between the larger community or regional branches and to solve the problem of insufficient professional help to man regular branches. Reading centers chould serve a population of 10,000 or more. Non-urban centers should serve 3,000 or more people residing within a 1-1/2-mile radius. The Reading Center of Sheppard Memorial Library, Greenville, North Carolina, is located in a shopping center, in rented space. It has a fluid collection of about 6,000 volumes, 75 to 100 recordings, and a small basic reference collection which is used regularly. It is open 28-1/2 hours per week during the school months, 46 hours a week in the summer, and occupies only 1000 square feet.

Brooklyn's Reading Centers are mainly for recreational reading. They are the smallest branch units of all as far as physical size is concerned, but are branches rather than deposit stations, for they meet the requirements of a basic permanent collection, regular hours, paid staff, and separate quarters of their own.

6. Mobile branches: These can be subdivided into two types: A) The large truck-tractor type of van pulled by a detachable vehicle to a specified location and left for a half day, full day or more than one day as a portable branch. Such a mobile branch may carry as many as 5,000-7,000 books, have one or two reading tables, a browsing area, and extra materials such as magazines, recordings, films, pictures and pamphlets. It corresponds to a sub-branch open one or two days a week, but has the advantage of being able to take the place of several small permanent locations. Such a mobile branch would be used in locations where circulation is large but does not yet justify a permanent branch. B) The smaller, conventional type bookmobile which carries 1500 to 4000 books is self-propelled, as a rule, and visits far more stops for much shorter periods. This type of vehicle is much more maneuverable and can move more often, having stops of as little as 15 minutes to as much as half a day or more. A detailed discussion of bookmobiles is to be found in the author's 1967 publication, Bookmobiles and Bookmobile Service.[3] Mississippi uses a mobile unit to explore the need for a permanent branch or community library.

From the standpoint of function, branches may be classified as follows:

A. Those that serve a general public and attempt to provide a cross section of books and reference service in many subjects. These have already been described.

B. Specialized branches, with material or services in one or more related fields, such as the Denver Public Library's and the San Francisco Public Library's special business branches; the

Glendale (California) Library's Brand library for art and music; or the separate children's libraries maintained by a few city systems. These attempt to provide service in the center of the area where it will be used; this is the case with most of the business branches, which are located in the heart of a downtown business section.

A notable example of a specialized branch is the International Trade Library established by the Mobile (Alabama) Public Library in the fall of 1966. It is located at the International Trade Center of the Alabama State Docks and is a cooperative undertaking between the Trade Center and the Public Library System. The library provides professionally trained staff, while the Trade Center provides space, equipment and materials. It has a very specialized, complete and expensive collection of research materials covering all aspects of international trade. Its purpose is to help promote and expand trade through the Port of Mobile. Materials do not circulate except in special cases. Information is supplied in person, by letter, or by phone. A language laboratory has audio equipment for learning 20 languages. Free translating services are offered for German, French, and Spanish. The library is open week days from 9 a.m. to 6 p.m. Most of the library's service is given over the telephone and by letter.

There are three other specialized trade libraries in the United States--in New Orleans, Houston, and San Francisco--but Mobile's is the only one which is a cooperative venture with another agency.

The Jones Avenue Branch, a boys' and girls' library in Toronto, Ontario, Canada, formally dedicated during Young Canada's Book Week in November, 1962, is part of a developing trend by the city's library board to serve the recreational reading needs of children in public and private schools. The trend toward large regional libraries for adults in Toronto has made it more necessary to have special children's branches which could be reached on foot. The Jones Avenue Branch is centrally located in a heavily populated section within half a mile of two public schools and one private school. It is a long, one-story structure with many windows, fieldstone walls, and honeycomb recessed ceiling lighting. The story room is carpeted and features a Swedish-style fireplace with copper chimney hood.

The stately Brand Music and Art Branch of the Glendale Public Library, almost classical in its lines, stands on a slight hill in the midst of beautifully landscaped grounds. It is a veritable treasure house of phonograph records, scores, librettos, song collections, sheet music, and books on all aspects of music and art. Although it is not technically a branch since it serves all sections of the city, another very excellent example of a specialized outlet is the Latin-American Library established by the Oakland, California, Public Library in 1967 under a Federal grant. It is located in a rented glass-front, store building in the heart of the Mexican-American section. A large part of the collection is in Spanish and an effort is made to hire Spanish-speaking staff.

Certain specialized branches are further limited in the clientele they serve. For example, the Santa Clara County Free Library in San Jose, California, the Los Angeles County Library, and others, maintain branches in correctional institutions, children's shelters, hospitals, etc.

The school-housed public library branch is another distinct type. It has a dual function, since it serves both as a school library and public library.

School-housed public library branches may differ in organization, administration and support. Some are under the direct management of the school board. In other situations the school district may furnish the room, utilities, furnishings, and possibly some of the books, while the public library furnishes the personnel, most of the books and supplies, and some equipment, such as typewriters. In this case there may be dual administration, or all administration may be left to the public library.

In any event, the public library-school library combination has not usually proved satisfactory to either side. A survey by Ruth White[3] showed a preponderance of school and public library

staff people against the plan. Another survey of 132 cities of over
100,000 population in the United States, made by the Santa Ana
Public Library, Santa Ana, California, in 1968, brought 129 letters
strongly opposed to such combinations, and only six in which the
writers thought it was a good idea or might work.

Increasing availability of Federal funds for school library
development has made it possible for more schools to build up libraries of their own or to strengthen already existing school libraries and to become less dependent on public libraries for service.

The reasons why the combination is not recommended are
many and varied. For a complete discussion and listing of these
reasons, see Chapter 12, Choosing a Site.

A differing pattern of school-public library cooperation is to
be found in the Coalinga District Library in Coalinga, California.
The Coalinga Union High School District operates this library,
which serves both the schools and general public but is located in
a fairly new modern building of its own in a downtown location.
There is a branch in Huron, 20 miles away, and deposit stations
are maintained in hospitals, schools, a youth center and other
special locations. Coalinga is the only school district in California
at present operating a library of this type.

All of the foregoing are not special libraries but specialized
branches, because they maintain a working relationship with the
central library and are under its jurisdiction.

Branches in unusual locations:

Various experiments are being performed by some library
systems in placing small branches (in some cases actually deposit
collections) in hitherto unusual locations. These do not differ
sharply from larger branches in function except that their primary
purpose is to reach more people who are not at present using the
library and might not otherwise be aware of its services.

The Evansville Public Library and Vanderburgh County Public Library, Indiana, as far back as 1957, established a collection
in a new supermarket, using a 15-foot wall space and having

approximately 1000 books. The collection was that of a public library branch in miniature. There was no one in attendance; the
patron signed his name and address on the book card, dropped it
in a slotted box and wrote a four-week due date on the date due
slip. He could return the books to any library agency or drop them
in a box built into the booketeria. Once a day a library messenger
emptied the return box and picked up the book cards. There were
no overdue fines but notices were sent. Average circulation was
about 60 per day. This Bookateria has since been replaced by a
by a permanent branch.

The Nashville, Tennessee, Public Library put in a small
branch in the city's new airport in 1962. A librarian goes out two
or three times a week to supply new books and straighten up, but
the reading room is open 24 hours a day on the honor system. This
has been enthusiastically received by the public, according to a
report received in 1968. Losses have been negligible. [4]

Location of deposit collections in barber shops, bars, and
beauty parlors is being tried by the Brooklyn Public Library.

Cleveland Public Library has established a booth in the
Union Terminal, hub of commuter travel for the Cleveland area.
Open Monday to Friday from 7:30 a. m. to 7:00 p. m. , Saturdays
from 9:00 a. m. to 4:00 p. m. , it maintains a rotating collection of
2,000 books. Specific titles may be requested from the main library and picked up after 1:00 p. m. the next day. Borrowers must
have a Cleveland Public Library card and may return all system
books to that station. Fines are not collected at the booth.

Types of branches by organization may be divided as follows:
These categories are based largely on a discussion found in Roberta
Bowler's Local Public Library Administration. [5]

A. Single library system with community branches: In this
type no independent or autonomous libraries exist within a county or
service area covered by the system. One library serves as a
headquarters and central library for the city in which it is located,
providing service to the area residents through several (or a network of) branches. Examples of this type of branch organization

are the Kern County Library, Bakersfield, California, and the
Deschutes County Library, Bend, Oregon. In Kern County the library provided service in 1964 to the county's 291,984 residents
through 34 branches, 71 stations, and a bookmobile. The Deschutes
County Library, in a small county of only about 25,000 inhabitants,
serves through two branches, a half dozen deposit stations, some
schools, and a bookmobile.

B. Federated library system: In this system by the joint
action of the governing bodies involved, several libraries join together to coordinate certain responsibilities and provide specific
services on a cooperative basis. Each library also continues to
function independently, provides its regular services, and is administered by the local librarian and board. A system board or
similar special body is designated but is responsible only for those
services and financial aspects which relate to the cooperative program. This system has been very successful in New York and
Montana. New York, particularly, has many such systems.

C. Joint city-county system: Under this plan the county
contracts with the city's municipal library to provide county-wide
service. A single administrator operates the entire system with
bookmobiles and permanent branches as needed. Once the appropriation is made, the two budgets are often handled as a single
package. This permits greater administrative flexibility and insures maximum discounts, which come with volume book purchasing.
The Public Library of Stockton and San Joaquin County, California,
is an example of this type.

D. State Library branches: In their efforts to insure adequate state-wide public library service, several state agencies have
instituted supplementary or direct library service through regional
branches. These vary in organization and in the scope of services
offered. As a case in point, New Hampshire has four branch offices, which in effect makes the entire state a single library
system. New Mexico, too sparsely settled in most areas to justify
county or independent regional libraries, has divided the state into
geographical areas, each served by a regional branch of the State

Library.   In Tennessee there were, in 1964, eleven regional library centers.   Not all public libraries in this state are affiliated with the regional centers, and some others, notably the major metropolitan centers, have only a limited service relationship with the state's regional program.   All Hawaiian branches are operated as part of the State Library System.

E. Specialized regional library: Such a library may be an independent unit or may be a part of the State Library.   Alabama has the first state-wide regional library for the blind to have its own board of library trustees and a developed set of policies as well as a long-range program of service.   This five-year program includes a proposal for two branch libraries or "vision centers."

Member or Affiliated Libraries:

Independent libraries which join a federated or regional system are not branches in the traditional sense of the word but they correspond to true branches in giving local community service. In forming a federation and inviting existing libraries to join, the term branch, as previously pointed out, may be a problem and is therefore not ordinarily used.   The organizational pattern of true branches differs from that of federation members.   Local libraries of long standing, the board members of which fear for their local autonomy, are often willing or even anxious to work with other independent units in the area, with or through a central headquarters, cooperating in such matters as centralized information retrieval, centralized cataloging and processing, pooled purchasing, the services of public relations or other professional specialists, specialization in subject fields, and exchange of materials through inter-library loan.   However, they wish to retain control of their library's policies, operations, and budgets.

Such cooperative arrangements for specified services may lead to a more closely-knit system after mutual benefits are recognized, confidence has been developed, and local boards have realized that they need have no fear of being swallowed up by the larger unit.   Even if a federation moves into closer relationships

at a later time, the terms "member library," "cooperating library,"
or "community library" are more suitable and satisfying to all concerned than the term branch.

Where branches develop naturally as a city library grows
and reaches out into the community, the relationship is quite different, and the term branch is generally accepted.

The Lake County Public Library in the extreme northwest
corner of Indiana represents an unusual type of branch organization.
It was established as an independent library system in 1959 when it
discontinued its contractual arrangement for service from the Gary
Public Library. At that time the system consisted of eight branch
libraries (five owned, three rented), one bookmobile and two
trailers. The 125-square-mile district includes four townships and
part of two others, encompassing both rural and urban areas, but
for the most part consisting of suburban communities. It now has
fourteen library facilities and an administration center to serve a
population of 170,000. This library is unique in that the main library concept was discarded at the outset and the branch library
label was dropped in favor of community library. Fourteen community libraries have been built in less than eight years, and with
the completion of the new Reference Library-Administration Center
in 1969, an ambitious building program will have been accomplished.

Although a central technical service handles all ordering,
cataloging and processing for the Lake County Library, there is no
central book collection. From the beginning, the collection of
books and other library materials has been treated as a single unit
divided among the fourteen agencies. The collection is now nearing
250,000 volumes. Although a book collection will be built up in
the new Reference Library (capacity 50,000 volumes) the traditional
central library-branch library concept still will not exist. The
collection in the Reference Library will be primarily reference,
local history, Indiana History, and special circulating materials.

Book catalogs are used instead of card catalogs in all its
agencies. They are printed by LCPL's own data processing and
offset printing equipment on an annual schedule. A closed circuit

teletype network keeps all libraries in immediate and constant
communication with Library Center and with each other.

As Frederick Wezeman says,

> The term branch can be one of many things. It can be
> a regional center of a large city system with personnel
> and bookstock outranking many central city libraries. It
> can be small rented quarters in a little hamlet with a
> part-time untrained librarian and a meager bookstock,
> or it can be the average branch of a city system, where
> the trend is toward larger units with specialized person-
> nel, a larger book collection, and adequate reference and
> bibliographic resources. 6

The larger branch units known as regional or area or
district libraries illustrate the trend toward larger and better
facilities.   Chicago had them in the 1920's and 1930's.   Operating
as liaison agencies between central management divisions and the
smaller branches in their respective areas, they also provide resource centers to which patrons needing in-depth material can turn
without making a long trip in to a central library.

Regional branches maintain lines of communication between
the various central departments and they interpret policies and
procedures to the staff in the region.   They often supervise and
coordinate book collections, materials, personnel, and other services of the permanent and mobile branches in their area.   All of
their enriched resources are directed toward giving efficient and
satisfactory service to residents of the surrounding community.
They offer reference service to a greater extent than was possible
in the average branch of the past; audio-visual materials are stocke
in greater number and variety; the book collection is much larger,
and the staffs include specialists in children's and young adult services, adult services, and the various aspects of reference service.
There is more time, space, and staff for adult education activities,
sponsorship of cultural and special events, and general reader advisory service.   It seems quite certain that the coming years will
see an increase of regional branches in libraries large enough to
have a branch system.

Notes

1. Meyers, Edith. Meet the Future: People and Ideas in the
    Libraries of Today. Little, Brown, c 1964. p. 93-94.

2. Brown, Eleanor Frances. Bookmobiles and Bookmobile
    Service. Scarecrow Press, 1967.

3. White, Ruth. The School-housed Public Library: a Survey.
    American Library Association, 1963.

4. ----------. "Nashville Claims a First for its Airport
    Reading Room." Library Journal, v. 88, no. 1, Jan. 1,
    1963, p. 74.

5. Bowler, Roberta. Local Public Library Administration. Inter-
    national City Managers' Association, 1964. p. 32-34.

6. Wezeman, Frederick. "Better Branch Libraries." Minnesota
    Libraries. v. XX, no. 6. June, 1962, p. 170-171.

Figure 11.   Area or Regional Branch
Baltimore County Public Library, Towson, Md.
The Baltimore County North Point Area Branch is a well-
planned, functional unit of 24,500 square feet, located on the
corner of a busy shopping center. It seats over 100 patrons.

Architects: Smith and Veale
Size: 24,500 square feet
Costs:
          Building cost (includes some built-ins): $391,000
             Cost per square foot: $16.00.
          Site   85,000
          Landscaping: 3,000
          Fees: Architect: 23,500
              Miscellaneous   1,000
          Equipment and furniture (other than
             built-ins): (includes carpet).   63,149
          Total project cost: $576,175; cost per square foot: $23.52
Lighting: Recessed and surface-mounted flourescent, recessed
       incandescent.
Floors: Wool carpet (public areas); vinyl asbestos (staff areas);
       slate tile (lobby).
Heating: Gas-fired hot water/hot air.
Materials: Brick and cast stone.
Air Conditioning: Chilled water.
Adult reading area capacity: 100.
Bookmobile area: Operates as a bookmobile headquarters. Covered
       loading platform.
Books: Open shelf capacity: 76,000 volumes.
       Closed stack and storage capacity: 27,000.
       Total volume capacity: 103,000.
Parking: Uses parking facilities of the shopping center for a small
       annual fee based upon floor area of the branch.

Figure 12. Lounge area looking toward charge desk and
reference area. North Point Area Branch, Baltimore
County Public Library, Towson, Md.

Figure 13. Adult study area. North Point Area Branch,
Baltimore County Public Library, Towson, Md.

Figure 14. Bookmobile loading platform. North Point
Area Branch, Baltimore County Public Library,
Towson, Md.

Figure 15. Coalinga District Library, Coalinga, California.
This library may be considered a sub-division of the
Coalinga Union High School District, since the School District
operates it as a dual school and public library. It is not located in a school building but in a fairly new modern building
of its own in a downtown location. It has a branch in Huron,
20 miles away, and deposit stations in hospitals, schools
a youth center, and other special locations. Coalinga is the
only school district in California at present operating a library
of this type.

Figure 16. Brooklyn Public Library. Gravesend
Reading Center, 303 Avenue X, Brooklyn.

Credit: Jay Sharp, Photography

Figure 17. Brooklyn Public Library. Bay Ridge District
Library, 7223 Ridge Blvd. (at 73 St.) Brooklyn, N. Y. 11209

Photo credit: Publicity Photographers, Brooklyn, New York

Figure 18. Mobile Branch - Mississippi Library Commission. (Used as a temporary branch at Enterprise, Mississippi). The Mississippi Library Commission uses this unit in demonstration areas where communities might need help in making a decision on the location of a library building or whether a stationary library unit is justified. As a result of this temporary use Enterprise planned a permanent building of its own and the unit was moved in March, 1969.

Figure 19. Chapel Reading Center, New Haven Public Library, New Haven, Conn. This store-front reading center branch displays its wares enticingly to passersby and offers a varied service with emphasi on recreational reading.

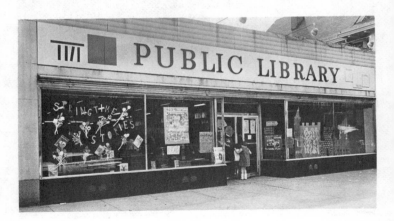

Affiliated or Member Library

Figure 20. AMORY PUBLIC LIBRARY, Amory, Mississippi

(Affiliated with Tombigbee Regional Library
Dedication Date: February 13, 1966)

Architect: Cooke-Douglass-Farr, Jackson, Mississippi
Type of Construction: New
Furniture and Equipment: Howell, Steelcase, Madison, Davis
Shelving: Republic Steel
Floor Area: 4,355 square feet
Seats in Reading Areas: 34
Book Capacity: 10,000
Seats in Meeting Room: 22

Costs: Site. $20,000
           Architect.   3,303
           General Construction   55,062
           Furniture and Equipment.   8,926
           Other.   923
                                                            $88,214

Financed: City of Amory, private donations, and Library Services
     and Construction Act

Construction Cost per Square foot $12.24

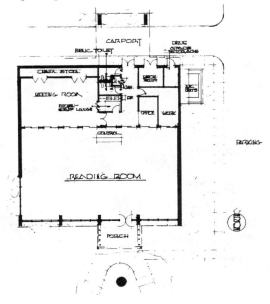

Figure 21. Amory Municipal Library. Amory, Miss.
A modern community library affiliated with the Tombigbee Regional Library System. Dedicated February 13, 1966.

Figure 22. Amory Municipal Library. Interior view.

Figure 23. Specialized Services. A very small sampling of the international and foreign publications available at the International Trade Library of the Mobile Public Library, Mobile, Alabama.

Figure 24. Specialized Branch. The International Trade Library of the Mobile, Alabama Public Library occupies a ground floor room in the International Trade Center of the Alabama State Docks.

Figure 25. A specialized Arts and Music Branch. The Brand Library of the Glendale Public Library system, Glendale, California contains 17,117 books, 11,460 phonograph records, and collections of framed prints, color slides, piano rolls, portfolios, and periodicals. There are three listening posts for records. In late 1968 the building was being enlarged from 5,000 square feet to 20,000.

Photo: Courtesy of Glendale Public Library

Figure 26. Youth Branch in Decatur, Alabama. This specialized branch of the Wheeler Basin Regional Library is in a quonset-type building belonging to the Decatur Junior Service League and is rented to the library for $1.00 a year and utilities. The League members helped staff the library for two years by giving volunteer service of members. It was opened in 1965 and will be used until a new regional library building can be constructed. This is a fine example of community cooperation

Figure 27. Jones Avenue Boys and Girls Branch. Toronto Public Library, Toronto, Ontario, Canada. Example of a specialized branch for children, opened in 1962, the Jones Avenue Branch circulated 42,500 books in 1967-68, carries a book stock of 11,500 volumes. It is an inner city location and the children are not readers, so many activities are initiated to attract children to the library. During 1967 there were 295 events, including story hours and puppet shows, and 368 class visits.

Figure 28. Jones Avenue Branch for Boys and Girls. View of the main circulation area from the story hour room.

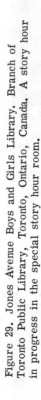

Figure 29. Jones Avenue Boys and Girls Library. Branch of Toronto Public Library, Toronto, Ontario, Canada. A story hour in progress in the special story hour room.

Figure 30. Reference-Library Administration Center. Lake County Public Library System, Griffith, Indiana. Architect's sketch of the new administrative center and reference library to be finished in 1969. This library has an unusual type of organization.

Figure 31. The Highland Community Library of the Lake County Public Library, Griffith, Indiana, is the largest (10,000 sq. ft.) of the 14 facilities, with a capacity of 37,700 volumes.

Chapter 3

The Role of Branch Libraries in a Changing Society

No discussion of branches could be complete without an attempt to define their current role. Here is a set of branch objectives adapted from those of one Southern California library.[1]

1. To become a community center for informational reading, recreational reading, and related cultural activities.

2. To provide both reference and general materials in the most frequently asked for subjects such as health, family life, child care, public and current affairs, science, literature, and the arts.

3. To provide specialized guidance in the use of books and related materials for all ages.

4. To work closely with the central library in meeting reader needs.

5. To have an attractive building, conveniently-arranged and efficiently-staffed to encourage maximum use.

6. To have a personality distinct from other branches by fitting itself to the community it serves. This is done by taking into consideration the character of the neighborhood in planning buildings, in setting hours, in selecting books, and in determining service and administrative policies.

7. To be so constructed and organized as to be expandable in size and services to meet growing needs.

8. To be located where people gather for shopping, and where adequate parking facilities are available.

9. To give the best possible service within the current limitations of budget, staff, and time.

10. To strive from year to year to plan and budget for increasing needs.

If a branch is well planned and well situated it can have great importance. Sometimes the total circulation of the two or three branches in a medium-sized city may exceed that of the central library. In cities of 100,000 or more, branches may do 45% of total system circulation; in cities of 1,000,000 or more, as much as 80%.

There are definite differences between a branch and a central library, most of which go beyond the matter of square feet of area. These are differences in patterns of service, purposes and use. Here is a list as noted by Edith Patterson Meyer:[2]

1. Since branches are not burdened with many routine duties performed at the central library, such as cataloging, processing, heavy mending, and book ordering, the staff has more time to give to the public.

2. As a result, the library atmosphere is more personal. Staff and patrons know each other better.

3. Branches are usually more heavily used by children than are central libraries.

4. A branch becomes an integral part of its neighborhood, often serving as a community activity center.

5. Because branches are smaller patrons can find material much more easily.

6. The book collections are more general, more limited, far less specialized. There will be many topics upon which there is no material.

7. Parking is usually less difficult at a branch because of its location away from a city center.

8. The branch can more closely fit its service program to the needs of its community because its community is more compact and communication is easier. The branch can relate its program to other neighborhood activities. It can play an important role in the already-existing groups.

This writer would like to add two more points to the foregoing:

9. Because of the closer relationship between patrons and staff more effective reading guidance is possible. Just how

Figure 32. A Branch Can Play a Vital Role
On opening day this branch had a total circulation of 9,132 books in 8
hours, the largest book circulation ever recorded for one day by an
American branch library. The jam was terrific, as this photo shows.

Opening Day of a New Branch
Feb. 29, 1964. Casa View Award-Winning Branch, Dallas
Public Library, Dallas, Texas

Photo by John Flynn for the Dallas Morning News

effective, of course, depends upon the personalities of the staff members and the availability of the specific materials needed for general guidance and bibliotherapy.

10. Branch librarians do not have as much freedom to fix policies and procedures or to set up innovative programs since they are part of a system and are usually subject to a certain amount of uniformity in system practices.

In an M. A. thesis written at the Catholic University of America in 1960, a study of the Pennsylvania Avenue Branch of the Enoch Pratt Free Library in Baltimore,[3] Mary Herispe concludes that the whole concept of librarianship in this type of under-privileged community must be more positive, almost more aggressive. She suggests a pilot project to investigate adult education activities in a blighted area.

Librarians are taking a new look at the place and function of branches. Reaching out into the community is the key word, a point so skillfully emphasized in the 1965 book, The Library Reaches Out, edited by Kate Coplan and Edwin Castagna.[4]

Wheeler and Goldhor[5] point out that there are two main theories of branch library function. The "Library Service Branch" emphasizes the branch as a smaller scale public library offering reference and other special services, as does the central library. The "Book Distributing Branch" theory assumes that branches should be mainly agencies for the circulation of popular books at the neighborhood level.

Both are valid since they apply to different types of branches, but there should be fewer of the small book distributing branches, and many more of the larger branches which can give informational service to adults and young people. The modern branch can operate under this latter concept without becoming a rubber stamp of the central library and following a rigidly set pattern which does not conform to the particular area served. A survey will make it possible to conform to the neighborhood rather than to a set system pattern.

The Des Moines, Iowa, Public Library has set forth the

following objectives or functions for its branches: that they be--

1. Symbols of the importance of books, reading, and learning.

2. Places of inspiration and education for all citizens.

3. Learning places for students.

4. A significant and important selling point to industry and business looking for an Iowa or Midwest location.

5. A public institution providing a tremendous return for the money invested, an information center for all who need it.

Figure 33. Story-Telling on the Stoops. The New Haven, Connecticut Free Public Library Reaches Out, as John Gitmore tells stories to a group on the street. After these sessions some of the children will follow him to the branch or neighborhood center.

Photo by Reggie Jackson

It is obvious that here the emphasis is upon the very practical aspects of value to the community.

Much emphasis is being placed on the role of the branch library in a changing society. The changes in our society which alter the role of our branches are:

1. Decentralization in urban living and in business.

2. A change in educational methods in our schools: emphasis on non-textbook materials as sources.

3. Increase of government programs in the U.S. to help the economically and culturally disadvantaged as well as the functionally illiterate. Head Start, Economic Opportunity, and Laubach are examples.

4. Improvement in branch construction, materials and methods.

5. Rising building costs.

6. The availability of Federal funds for construction grants: the Library Services and Construction Act, particularly.

7. The importance of the missionary aspect of branch service increases as we try to reach the great unreached. Increasing complexity of our society makes more and more demands on the individual's time. He will not make the effort to go long distances to the library. It must come to him.

8. Slum clearance and urban housing development which have brought rapid change in some city areas.

9. Rapid increase in school age population and number of schools being built, especially in suburban areas.

10. Increasing crime in both city and country, with parents reluctant to let children walk any distance to a branch.

11. The population "explosion."

12. The great increase in scientific and technological research and information.

13. The rapid increase in number of large shopping centers.

14. Increased tensions in everyday living.

15. The rising standard of living in America.

16. The rising popularity of paperback books.

17. The increased development of school libraries.

18. The emergence of the "New Neighborhood."

19. The new community center concept of the branch as against the traditional quiet study concept.

20. Changing patterns of mobility. People move more often.

21. Increase in number of automobiles.

22. Changing traffic patterns.

23. Automation and new equipment.

24. Demand for "convenience services."

25. The growth of bookmobile service.

26. Rising educational levels.

27. Increasing status of minority groups.

28. Dearth of library schools for professional training.

29. Occupational changes in our society.

30. Increasing amount of leisure for adults.

How does each of these points affect the present and future role of branches?

1. Decentralization in urban living has caused rapid increase in population of suburbs and new housing developments on the outskirts, adjacent to, or near larger centers. These areas grow so rapidly in many parts of the country that utilities and services cannot financially keep pace with them. There is a special need for branches in suburban areas, often unincorporated areas, outside city limits, and the task of providing them must fall to a county or regional library. Bookmobiles can often provide the needed service until the potential of the area and use of the bookmobile justify a branch. But in some areas there is no county or regional service available and there is a large gap between needed and available library service. When there is no governmental jurisdiction able to provide library service, such branch needs may pave the way for the formation of county or regional libraries or for provision of a branch by a neighboring city library under contract with the county. Such developing areas must be watched and tested for branch needs, but the actual branch may have to wait until after proper police, fire, sanitary facilities, streets and water supply have been provided.

As a result of decentralization, the use of branches in once progressive neighborhoods may decline, and these branches may be more effictive if moved out toward the city limits.

The decentralization of business from city centers to neighborhood shopping centers has created new and strategic locations for city branches. It has also provided good suburban locations for branches where financing and sponsorship is available through a county or regional library or a neighboring city library.

2. The change in educational methods has had a far-reaching effect on library branches. Far from being quiet neighborhood reading centers, most branches are now veritable beehives of reference service and reader guidance, mainly because of the needs of students. Some branch librarians are disturbed by this, others welcome it, while still others simply accept it. Whatever the attitude, the fact remains that branches are going to have to become larger, employ more reference staff, buy more sound reference and informational material, and be willing to cooperate with school libraries to the fullest extent in satisfying student needs. This in no way implies that a branch should try to replace the school library. Branch service to the student group must be of sufficient quality that students do not have to inundate the central library. Textbooks are only a starting point for student assignments. Few public libraries can handle the situation by themselves and cooperation with school administrators and school librarians is the keyword to success in meeting the needs of students.

3. The increase since 1965 of government programs aimed at helping the economically and culturally disadvantaged and the functionally illiterate, has special significance for branches because to reach these people it is usually necessary to go where they are. Branch staffs in certain sections of large cities, where there is a concentration of disadvantaged people, are faced with a great challenge to depart from traditional patterns, to reach out and mingle with these people, and to plan activities that will draw them into the library. Financial assistance to meet these needs has been available under the Head Start program, the Economic

Opportunity Act, the Older Americans Act, or from private movements like the Laubach literacy projects. Often the branch can
and should cooperate with other city, county, or special agencies
in the neighborhood, to work with these groups. Branches are
closer to the neighborhoods where the need is greatest, and can
often accomplish more than the central library agency. In some
areas libraries have set up special agencies, such as the experi-
mental Latin-American library of the Oakland Public Library in a
predominantly Mexican neighborhood, or the Pennsylvania Avenue
branch of the Enoch Pratt Free Library in Baltimore, or the
special programs of the young adult division of the Los Angeles
Public Library. Similar programs to work with Headstart, Economic Opportunity Groups, Senior Citizens, or with groups with a
language barrier are being undertaken by an increasing number of
branches in forward-looking libraries throughout the country, with
or without government aid.

    4. Improvement in branch construction, materials, and
methods has resulted in more attractive, more functional branches
which tend to attract more borrowers and to make staffing and
supervision less of a problem. Use of laminated beams and open
modular construction have given more flexibility of use, and have
made it possible to supervise large areas. One-story construction
at street level has removed problems of access for the physically
handicapped and for elderly citizens.

    5. Rising building costs have, of course, had an adverse
effect on branches. In many cases construction has been delayed
and many libraries which desperately need branches are trying to
get along with bookmobile service instead. This has been detri-
mental to service, since no bookmobile, no matter how large, can
adequately substitute for a good branch.

    6. The extension of the original Library Services Act to
the Library Services and Construction Act in 1964 made possible
branch construction in many areas where other local agencies or
local governmental authorities have combined forces in planning
and supplementing local financing. In some areas, unfortunately

where branches are most needed, opposition to use of Federal
funds for any purpose and unwillingness to meet necessary conditions have prevented use of the L. S. C. A. funds.

7. Along with the emphasis on reaching the poor and the
disadvantaged has come a strong emphasis upon reaching the great
number of unreached in our population who do not use the library
for other reasons. It may be a matter of distance, indifference,
or an unhappy library experience at some time. It may result
from inability to speak English or simply from ignorance of the
variety and extent of material to be found in libraries.

All librarians have had the experience of having a first-
time patron remark that he had not dreamed that the library had
such and such material or so many services available. The steps
that can be taken to correct this situation are: (1) Advertising the
branch and its services through every conceivable medium that
will reach the unreached; (2) Going out from the library to find
those people singly or in groups; and (3) making them feel, when
they have finally come for the first time, that the library is de-
lighted to have them and will welcome them back with open arms.

Some suggestions for getting non-library users into the
branch for the first time will be offered in Chapter X, which deals
with special activities and services. Suffice it to say at this point
that the branch library, with its smaller size, staff, and book collection, has a better chance to create an atmosphere of friendly informality and ease of use which will appeal to non-users than does
the large complex and impersonal central or headquarters library.

8. Slum clearance and urban housing developments have
brought such rapid changes in some cities that those responsible
for establishment of branches must anticipate such developments.
They must keep in constant touch with city, county, state, and
Federal agencies involved. Wholesale changes in a neighborhood
can radically affect the present or future status of an existing
branch and can influence the location of a proposed branch.

9. The rapid increase in population of school age and in the
number of schools being built, both in urban and rural areas,

creates two problems for branches: (1) accommodating large numbers of children and young people in children's and young people's sections, and (2) finding qualified personnel to work with these age groups and do adequate reference and reader advisory work with those old enough to need it.

The greatest shortage of library personnel seems to be in the field of children's librarianship; yet this is probably the most important area for establishing good library habits. More and more libraries are being forced to employ non-professionals with college education, a good knowledge of child psychology and experience in working with children, in lieu of trained children's specialists. Such people, hired often in a temporary capacity, should know children's books or have enough interest to take evening courses in children's literature and read children's books assiduously.

10. Increasing crime in city and county has made parents more reluctant to allow children to walk to a branch alone. The old precept of a branch within walking distance of every child has, therefore, lost much of its validity. This, coupled with the constantly increasing use of automobiles, has made it possible for branches to be farther apart and larger.

11. The effect of the population explosion is self-explanatory. Constantly increasing demands upon libraries where population increase is heavy usually make the construction of branches mandatory.

12. The amazing increase in scientific and technological knowledge has created a whole new field of demand. In order to give good service a branch must have a much stronger collection in science and technology than in the past, and must be prepared to deal with the reference demands in these fields. Children and young people particularly are much more knowledgeable about science than in the past and they make requests in terms that are often foreign to the average librarian. Branches must offer a more complete service in these fields because the central library or headquarters cannot possibly satisfy all the demands of a city

or county populace, and many residents cannot make the trip to a central library.

13. The popularity of the shopping center has been a great boon to branch library development. It has provided a center to which people come in great numbers and its parking space is usually unequaled in any other location. Locations in or near shopping centers have become the number one choice of most librarians when new branches are established. A more detailed discussion of this point will be found in Chapter 12, Choosing a Site.

14. Although the increased tensions to be found today, due to general world unrest, speed, wars, economic instability, and a host of conflicting stimuli assailing people from all sides, may seem to have little to do with branches, to this writer at least, there is a psychological relationship.

There is something very stable and secure about the relatively quiet atmosphere of a library, be it a branch or a large metropolitan center. Here the child or teenager, unable to study at home because of family noise, T.V., or emotional problems, finds a measure of peace. The older citizen, unable to cope with demanding or over-exuberant grandchildren, can steal away for a quiet afternoon of rest and reading. What matter if he dozes in the easy chairs in the browsing room or lounge area? He has found a haven in the library, and psychologically and socially this is important for any age.

Problems in everyday living arise with increasing frequency in our complex society. Reference departments, or perhaps just the informational books to be found in the circulating non-fiction stacks, help solve many of these problems. Books on practical psychology, relaxation, emotional anxiety, and religion give guidance and help to some readers. Although the modern branch may be a very busy place where the tomblike silence of former years does not prevail, most readers seem to become oblivious of the presence of others and live in a world of their own for a short while.

15. The rising standard of living in America has brought more education, more travel, more thirst for knowledge about

more things to the individual's expanded world.   Here the branch
library satisfies an obvious need, for it is often closer to the homes
and hearts of its area residents than is the more remote and formal
Central library unit.

16. The rising popularity and increased production of paperbacks has made it possible for many more people to own many more
books.   Reading inspires reading, and purchase of paperbacks often
leads to increased use of libraries.   Paperbacks likewise have made
it possible for libraries, including branches, to furnish greater quantities of titles in demand and a greater variety of titles for less
money and in less space.   Few progressive libraries today are
without a paperback collection of some sort and few of them treat
heavily used paperbacks as formally as they do hard cover books.
Only the more expensive or informationally fruitful titles are catalogued; in some cases paperbacks are not even processed but are
put on special shelves on a bring-one, take-one basis.   It has been
found that in many cases where junior and senior high school
English teachers and librarians encourage young people to belong to
paperback book clubs especially planned for these age groups, public library use by such groups increases.   Live branches in good
areas soon become overcrowded and the paperback collection can
be a decided asset.

17. For the same reason--that reading inspires reading--
and that good school librarians encourage their students to use the
public library, the development of better school libraries, spurred
in recent years by the availability of Federal funds, has brought
young readers to branch libraries in increasing numbers.   In some
areas the rise of school libraries has temporarily decreased
children's and young people's circulation in the public libraries,
but in the long run it has had a stimulating effect and is certainly
a boon to busy branches which otherwise could not and often cannot
cope with the increasing student reference load.

18. The "new neighborhood" as used here refers to the
residential areas around large shopping centers.   Little communities within cities have always existed, but the large shopping center

affords a hub or focal point which, in many cases, provides practically all the services a family needs, so that there is little
necessity to drive to a downtown business section. Thus a visit to
the central library in a central location may mean a special trip
and is less apt to be made. A branch in or near a shopping center
means an extra convenience for the average family. Thus branch
patronage often increases at the expense of the central library but
the main purpose of any library, getting books to readers, is
accomplished.

In some cities property owners have banded together in various neighborhoods under such names as "West Side Property
Owners' Association," "North Hill Improvement Society," or something similar. Often their purpose is to combat rising taxes, but
also it is often to encourage improvement of their respective neighborhoods. In either case, this group can be a powerful ally in the
establishment of branches or an antagonistic force to oppose it.
These groups must be approached and educated as to the value of
branches. Their cooperation must be secured; they cannot be
overlooked.

19. Tied in very closely with the "new neighborhood" is the
growing concept of the branch library as a community center for
its neighborhood, where all kinds of library-related activities may
draw people of all ages into the library. Sometimes it may seem
to the traditionalist as if some of the activities have little relationship to library business, but any activity can be book-related via
proper exhibits and short discussions, and any activity which brings
into the branch people who might not otherwise come, and exposes
them to its riches, is worthwhile.

20. Changing patterns of mobility can affect branches in
several ways. The growth of the mobile home type of living, war-
time booms in industry, and the mass movement of people into
certain fast-growing states such as California, Florida, and
Arizona, have created special problems in branch construction and
in financing. Also the movement from city to suburbs or open
country, already mentioned, has increased need for county and
regional branches in areas outside of a city library's tax area.

21. The increase in number of automobiles and the fact that many households have become two-car, or even three-car families, have made it possible to forget the old criteria item of a branch within walking distance of every child and concentrate on larger, more adequate branches spaced farther apart.

22. Changing traffic patterns can affect branch locations. New freeways can bisect a neighborhood to cut it off from a branch. New arterial streets create new traffic patterns away from formerly busy streets upon which a branch may be located. At the same time such changes may create suitable new locations for other branches.

23. Automation and new equipment have affected branches in the same way as all libraries. They have permitted even more centralization of routine processes at headquarters, such as circulation control records, registration records, book stock records, ordering of materials, etc., freeing branch staffs for more person-to-person work with patrons. They have speeded up service, eliminated many mistakes, and in the long run usually cut costs, although initial cost of equipment for the central system is high. Automatic charging methods have cut time-consuming steps from daily routines in a branch.

24. Because convenience equipment and services such as photocopying, pen machines, and pay telephones are found in increasing numbers in so many places, patrons look for and are finding such conveniences in their own libraries. It is quite conceivable that future branches might be expected to provide these three services plus many more, such as record players, coin-operated typewriters, paperback books for sale, and sale of such supplies as typing and notebook paper, carbons, or even lending of staplers. No library wishes to go into the stationery business, but requests for such supplies are so numerous that branches may have to keep them on hand and sell them in self-defense.

25. The growth of bookmobile service has provided a means for testing readership potential of future branch sites, a substitute service until a branch is needed and can be built, and a means of

providing a new branch with a ready-made clientele.   Patronage
will, of course, grow with the enlarged facilities.

26.   The rising educational level in the United States and its
impact upon all library service is self-evident.   Minority groups
are using libraries more.   The improving social status and standard
of living of these groups particularly involves libraries in the areas
where these people have congregated, and this is usually a branch
area.   Literacy movements, private and federally-financed, bring
more patrons to branches.   Some Federal programs are being
tailored especially for groups with a language barrier and branches
are formed particularly to help these groups (e.g. The Oakland,
California Public Library's Latin-American Library).   More branches
are needed in pockets of foreign settlement, and collections need
to be built up to meet the needs and interests of Mexican-Americans,
Puerto Ricans, Cubans and people of other non-English speaking
nationalities.   There is need for strengthening of collections of particular interest to Negroes as well as to the foreign-language groups.

27.   The dearth of accredited library schools for professional
training is obviously an inhibiting effect upon all library service but
especially in branches where children's specialists are so badly
needed.   The children's field is one in which many vacancies exist.
Good administrators of branch libraries are not easy to find, and
many branches are now headed by non-professionals in areas where
professionals are badly needed.   Many non-professionals are doing
excellent jobs, but there are few jobs that cannot be done even
better by someone especially trained for them.

28.   Occupational changes have been taking place very rapidly.   Machinery supplants unskilled workers; automation supplants
semi-skilled and skilled workers.   These people need to re-educate
themselves for other types of work.   While schools are usually the
answer, they turn to the library for supplementary material.
Branch use is increased, particularly in areas where there is much
industry. Specialized branches in business and industry are also
needed in increasing number.   Displaced workers often need help
in writing applications, producing resumes, and in how to conduct

themselves at interviews.

29. Increasing amount of leisure time due to shorter work weeks, the increase in number of retired people, longer vacations, prolonged strikes, and increased unemployment in certain areas, all create further demands upon branches. Much of the reading resulting from these causes will be recreational, but there will always be the demand for informational material from those who want to improve themselves in one way or another.

Some libraries are being forced into establishing small neighborhood reading centers, the purpose of which is to supply primarily recreational reading. These are usually in rented quarters and are staffed with non-professionals. In fact, the prime reason for establishing them is the fact that trained personnel is not available, and it is felt that by using such centers for recreational needs, trained staff can be available at the larger units (community and regional branches) to provide reference and reader advisory needs.

Ernestine Rose[6] says that libraries can act as a clearing house and coordinating agency in relation to other institutions in their own area. This, she feels, is natural and desirable, since nearly all social and educational programs need books and the specialized book knowledge which are a part of a library's equipment.

An alert and observing attitude, she points out, and constant awareness of current social needs, practices and problems on the part of the branch administrator, are essential for this type of service. Many types of social activity can be carried on most successfully by religious, welfare, or other institutions; whereas programs which include political, economic, or social discussion and reference (such as Great Books, Great Ideas, Great Decisions groups), as well as those in the literary or educational area, find their natural home in the library. It has the essential tools for implementing and interpreting such programs. [6]

Thus the role of the branch library must be ever-changing to keep up with current variations in its society. A static program

Figure 34. The Cultural Role of a Branch
New Haven Free Public Library. Meeting and concert, Senior
Citizens' Music Appreciation Club, Chapel Library Center, 1966.

Photo by Robert Perron, New Haven, Conn.

and slavish adherence to a narrow traditional role can rob any
branch of most of its vitality and effectiveness.

"The branch library, because of its participation in neighborhood life and staff acquaintance with library users," says Richard
Sealock, librarian of the Kansas City, Mo., Public Library, "has
a unique opportunity to relate its program to other neighborhood activities. It can play an important role in the already existing educational groups and can be closely related to the special programs
offered in the neighborhood. The branch can bring additional
program and educational offerings and resources, particularly if
the main library facilitates this service."[7]

"Ralph Ulveling of the Detroit Public Library stressed the
unique opportunity which the branch library has in the library
system. Branches are not service satellites of the main library
but 'have a definite educational responsibility... which is one of

providing for the educational self-improvement of individuals.' This responsibility cannot be discharged properly unless branch services are, in fact as well as in word, conditioned to separate the individual from the mass and to guide him competently into reading that will be beneficial to him. "[7]

These are interesting opinions but seem to give too much stress to the role of librarian as teacher and that of the branch as solely a means of education. The informational and educational function is continually assuming more importance, but branches have a role of furnishing recreational reading purely for entertainment and relaxation as well. This is more true of branches than of central libraries which are tending to become reference and information centers primarily.

Reading can be fun as well as educational. Let it remain so. The branch can act in both roles successfully, given the right staff and the right collection. The reading of adults cannot be guided in the same way as that of children and young people. The materials are there. The adult reader will choose what he wishes and will grow in the process. Our job as librarians is to see that the materials are available: serious, light, humerous, basic, entertaining, informational, educational, classic, and modern; the right book for the right person at the right time.

Notes

1. Santa Ana Public Library, Santa Ana, California. Branch Library Objectives. Compiled 1965.

2. Meyer, Edith Patterson. Meet the Future: People and Ideas in the Libraries of Today. Little, Brown, c 1964. p. 93-94.

3. Herispe, Mary. The Role of the Library in an Underprivileged Neighborhood. Thesis, M. A. degree, Catholic University of America, Aug. 1960.

4. Coplan, Kate, and Castagna, Edwin, editors. The Library Reaches Out. Oceana, 1965.

5. Wheeler, Joseph L. and Goldhor, Herbert. Practical Administration of Public Libraries. Harper and Row, c 1962. p. 411-41

6. Rose, Ernestine. The Public Library in American Life.
    Columbia University Press, 1954, p. 110.

7. Sealock, Richard B. Extending Library Services. In: Bowler,
    Roberta Local Public Library Administration. International
    City Managers' Association, 1964. p. 261.

Chapter 4

Factors Indicating Need for a Branch

How does one determine when there is sufficient justification for the initial expense of building a branch and the continuing expense of operating it? Every new branch will increase the total operational budget of the library system by $20,000 to $100,000 or more a year, depending upon the size of the branch and whether it is in rented quarters, a city or county-erected building, or possibly even a free facility. Since the original construction cost of a branch can be anywhere from $150,000 to $750,000 for a building ranging from 8,000 square feet to as much as 25,000 to 30,000 square feet, such an expenditure of tax funds should be made only after careful study of the need.

If the existing library system does not adequately serve all sections of a city, town, or rural area, some extension of services is undoubtedly in order, but the answer may lie in instituting or extending bookmobile service or strengthening an already-existing headquarters or other branch. Bookmobiles are widely used, not only to serve until patronage grows to a point where a branch is plainly indicated but also as a testing medium to see if immediate need for a permanent branch exists.

Alternatives to building a new branch, therefore, may include strengthening an existing library or libraries by building additions, increasing staff, and building up the book collection. The community might be better served by a single strong library offering in-depth service than by additional smaller collections at other locations. Sometimes the need may be for specialized services rather than more general service. Examples might be business or technical services, enlarged children's service, or a larger reference department.

Assuming that a question has arisen concerning the need for one or more branches, the following steps could help answer whether the time is ripe for such development:

1. Test the area with bookmobile service. If the bookmobile does an annual circulation of 100,000 or more, the need for a branch would seem to be self-evident. Potential branch circulation in such a case would likely range from 150,000 to 200,000. If the circulation on the bookmobile is between 75,000 and 100,000 it would be reasonable to assume that the larger and better facilities of a permanent branch would increase usage to well over 100,000 and perhaps to as much as 150,000. A temporary mobile-home type branch may be set up for longer periods to test for a permanent branch.

2. Calculate the potential service area. A branch may be expected to have a one-and-a-half-mile radius of maximum attraction and a two to three mile radius of influence, depending upon its size and the services offered. An often-used formula is:

90% of the children in a one-mile radius

50% of the adults in a mile to a mile and a half radius

50% of the children in a two or three mile radius

30% of the adults in a two or three mile radius.

Spacing between neighborhood branch libraries should generally be two to three miles. Estimate the potential circulation based upon this type of use.

3. Secure all possible information about the area being considered: total population, density of population, age levels, educational level, and economic level of the residents. A recent regular or special census, a survey by professional planners, or studies by the research staff of the local unit of government are sources of such information. Sometimes Chambers of Commerce make surveys, and graduate students in the social sciences or municipal government use such projects for theses. Such data will furnish clues as to probable use of a branch when testing out the area with a bookmobile is impossible, or will supplement bookmobile service as an indication of need for a branch.

Figure 35. Mobile Trailer Branch may be used to test for permanent branch locations.   A specially-built house trailer type
of mobile branch may be brought to a location and left for
months, possibly even a year or more to test potential usage
before determining whether a permanent branch is needed.

Photo: Courtesy of Flannigan Industries
Houston, Texas

4.   Check sources of books and book services already available in the area.   Such sources might include commercial lending
libraries, bookstores, school or college libraries, specialized libraries, or drug stores and supermarkets.

5.   If the apparent need is the result of oral or written
demands by residents of the area, the librarian, and possibly the
library board, should meet with spokesmen of the group or groups
concerned and discuss the reasons advanced. How many residents
of the area do the petitioning groups represent?   Is their demand
broadly based or merely the wishful thinking of a few?

6. A questionnaire could be circulated among residents of
the area. It should be very short, should be given out as these
residents visit the central library or bookmobile, and should simply
ask those answering to state frankly whether they would use a branch
in preference to the central library. It would be necessary to give
an idea of the size of the proposed branch and its book collection
before those questioned could give any kind of intelligent answer.
A faster and better method of circulating such a questionnaire would
be to carry it from door to door in the proposed community or send
it through the mail. The first method would be expensive, and few
libraries have the staff to do it. Mailing would be easier and
probably less expensive, but the percentage of returns would undoubtedly be less. The personal touch usually brings better results.
Boy Scouts might help with this. Of course, such queries can only
be one indication of need, for not all of those answering in the affirmative will really become steady users of a branch. Others may
divide usage between a branch and the central library, depending
upon their needs of the moment. Still others may use a branch
only occasionally.

7. Work with organized groups in the area to see whether
they feel a branch is needed and would be used. Enlist their aid
in making a neighborhood survey with block chairmen to gather
opinion in their own respective blocks, and a general chairman to
coordinate the block-by-block results.

A mimeographed three-page sheet of suggestions entitled
"It's Your Library: Branch Library or Bookmobile" issued by the
American Library Association, lists the following points to consider in deciding between branch or bookmobile service, assuming
that neither type of service is available:[1]

The Branch:

Advantages:

1. Permanent quarters, well-located, can provide convenience of access, parking facilities, library
   service always in one place, and regular service
   for longer periods of time.

2. Space can be made for all types of readers and
    various types of service.

3. Book supply, larger than possible in a bookmobile,
    may duplicate much of the main library's collection
    for general reading, but can also be planned to in-
    clude titles for special local needs.

4. Residents of the area will take pride in their library
    building and feel responsibility for its use and well-
    being.

Disadvantages:

1. Difficulty in securing desirable location.

2. Cost of buying (or renting) and maintaining quarters
    might be too large in proportion to its use and the
    size of the population to be served.

3. Need for duplication of book supplies and staff suf-
    ficient to give regular and specialized service.

4. Shifting population may require frequent change of
    location.

5. Small collections of books need constant refreshing, or
    users will feel they have "read everything." If the branch
    is of good size and the book collection fairly large, this
    point will not apply to any extent.

The Bookmobile:

Advantages:

1. One unit can serve several locations. Regular schedules
    may be arranged, with length of each visit sufficient for
    each locality. Service can be brought close to the people.
    Location of stops can be changed whenever necessary.
    Thus bookmobile service might be best in a neighborhood
    of rapidly shifting population or one in which commercial-
    ization is replacing residential use but some kind of ser-
    vice is needed. Permanent branches built in such loca-
    tions could be a waste of money and would have no future.

2. Size and type of bookmobile may be determined by
    probable use, to include space or shelving for books
    and other printed materials, films, recordings, etc.,
    as well as for borrowers and staff.

3. One collection of books can serve several neighbor-
    hoods and can be changed according to changing
    requirements of patrons. One staff is sufficient for

all local visits of the bookmobile. Cost of upkeep, as well as original outlay for purchase, is less than that necessary for a branch, building and operation both being taken into consideration.

4. A bookmobile is colorful, convenient for the general reader, attracts attention and stimulates use by new readers because of its mobility.

Disadvantages:

1. No specialized programs are possible; these must be held either at the central library or by arrangement at neighborhood meeting places such as churches, schools, recreation centers, etc.

2. Except in an exceedingly large unit, materials must necessarily be limited.

3. Service is available for each location for only a short period at infrequent intervals.

4. Study and research by patrons are not possible owing to limitations on space and materials. No tables and chairs can be included for reading on the spot.

5. Juvenile circulation usually outweighs adult circulation. Adults are reluctant to use a bookmobile constantly crowded with children and young people.

Standards for branch library buildings and for bookmobiles must be carefully studied. Can branch standards be met? A too small, sub-standard branch may offer little better service than a large bookmobile. Close cooperation should be maintained between the planning committee and local library authorities at all times, for it is the librarian, the staff, and the trustees who, through years of serving the community, can best advise on the expanding program. Outside planners, other individuals, and governmental researchers can provide the facts and opinions, but the final decision must rest with the library officials and administration.

North Carolina, long a leader in the field of extension via branches and bookmobiles, has a set of guidelines compiled in 1966 from five different sources. The list is prefaced by a discussion of when branches become necessary:

When are branch libraries needed?

A library serving a city of 25,000 to 50,000 will need
some book distributing agencies such as mobile library
stops but not a branch.

A city of 50,000 to 75,000 may be justified in operating
a distribution or reading center in areas geographically
remote from the central library.

A city serving a population of 100,000 may need one and
sometimes two service branches in addition to its main
library and bookmobile stops.

County and regional libraries may need to establish community branches in small towns where there are 3,000 or
more people living within a mile and a half radius.   In
sparsely populated areas, a branch of a regional system
is frequently established in the county seat, although it
may have less than minimum population. [2]

Wheeler and Goldhor are quite explicit in stating that "a
library serving from 25,000-50,000 population will need some distribution agencies such as classroom sets, bookmobile stops, or
deposit stations but not a branch." Many librarians, however, feel
that classroom sets are the obligation of school libraries, not
public libraries, and that deposit stations are too meager to have
much usefulness.   Wheeler and Goldhor concede that "a city of
50,000-75,000 may be justified in investing capital building costs
and part of its annual budget to operate a distributing branch but
cannot afford a staff of fully-trained librarians to do good reference
work." This is open to argument since the reference load has been
constantly increasing in most branches, even though circulation may
not have increased.   It is hard to imagine a modern, vital community branch not offering a measure of good reference service. [2]

"With almost universal ownership of automobiles," Wheeler
and Goldhor declare, "not more than one such branch is needed
for this population (50,000-75,000), though in exceptional cities
with high economic and educational background two or three
branches may do well.   But would that economically be the best
thing?" They suggest it might be better to wait until the city can
finance a larger service branch. [2]

Wheeler and Goldhor state that a branch is justified only when an objective survey shows that it will be assured a minimum annual circulation of 75,000, and preferably 100,000 books (of which 45 to 50% will be adult circulation), and that at least 10,000 adult informational questions can be expected to be answered each year.[2]

Lee B. Brawner, Assistant State Librarian, Texas State Library, points out that many libraries' budgets have been so wed to circulation statistics as a measure of performance that the circulation potential has often been the only criterion for establishing a new branch. This frequently meant that branches were only established in areas of the city with a middle to high educational and socio-economic background where high circulation would be guaranteed.

Fortunately, and due in large part to Federal poverty programs, public libraries are now willing to establish substantial branches in low educational and socio-economic areas. These libraries are utilizing specialized materials, staff and programming in an effort to generate even a modest circulation.[3]

Thus, some of the old standards for establishing a branch cannot be applied in a socially-oriented library system. The need to reach people, particularly the disadvantaged, is rapidly assuming prime importance as a criterion. The humanitarian aspect increasingly overshadows the practical fiscal factor. Persuading appropriating bodies to appreciate this fact can be a problem, since they are accustomed to using the old measuring sticks of circulation and registration as indicators of how well the money is being or will be spent. The fact that government money is available to help build branches and to carry out some of these welfare-type library programs is, of course, a telling argument with some appropriating bodies.

John C. Kountz, Library Systems Analyst for the Orange County Public Library, Orange, California, has designed a model for library resource allocation based on what he refers to as "constant" and "variable" features of the location to be served. This model has been in use at the Orange County Library since 1966.[4]

In answer to the question, "How are we to know when a community branch is needed?" Mr. Kountz's model responds in terms of population:

> .... although approximately 25,000 population is optimum, the transition from station to branch should be made at an earlier point in development; therefore 10,000 is suggested, especially if use velocity indicates a higher level of service.
>
> And for a larger service unit, an area or regional branch, a confirmed 20,000-25,000 population should exist.
>
> .... and/or the requirement for services beyond those available at a community branch. Such requirements can be based on the strategic location of the potential area branch with regard to expanded holdings for a group of community branches, or an advantageous location for basing bookmobile operations.

However, Mr. Kountz warns against the use of population alone and indicates that while

> .... thresholds for changing service levels can be established in terms of population for the purposes of long-range planning, as the lead time to implementation decreases, greater dependence on actual community developments is of extreme importance.

According to Dorothy Sinclair,[5] factors which make it advisable to consider a new outlet may include:

(1) The opening of a superhighway or freeway that cuts off half the people from easy access to the library.

(2) Annexation of an area.

(3) Natural growth of a city or county in population.

A small rural or county library is, of course, quite different from the urban library serving a compact community and usually requires a comparatively larger number of service points. A branch should not be considered, however, until all factors have been taken into account. These include:

1. Are there enough funds to provide a large enough building and collection to give efficient service? A small, inadequate branch, especially a first branch unit in a system, can be a disappointment to the public and may inhibit the building of future branches.

2. Are there enough funds available so that the central library collection or other branches do not find their collections weakened by dispersal of books and other materials?

3. Is there assured financing for proper operation and development of service as needs increase, remembering that a new branch increases costs of delivery service, packing and shipping (in the case of rural branches), record keeping, card catalog provision, and supervision, in addition to the routine costs of operation? The annual book budget will have to be substantially increased.

4. Have studies been made to determine whether a branch is the best answer? Would bookmobile service be more feasible? How about a mobile branch such as a double-width 50-or 60-foot house trailer which could be located semi-permanently and moved to another location later if conditions change?

All of this may sound as though branches are to be considered only as a last resort. This is not the case, but at least 50 per cent of the branches now existing in the United States have outmoded buildings and services because for too long branches were built in an established pattern and without sufficient study and analysis.

Libraries which are small enough to have only two or three professional staff members usually have neither the need nor the ability to establish a second outlet. However, public demand may arise in such cases, perhaps because of some unusual circumstance such as the growth of the community in a long thin line away from the library, possibly along a major highway. Establishment of a new shopping center in an outlying area may attract a number of residents away from the old shopping district or central business district in which the library is located. [5]

In the latter case it might be better to move the existing library to the new shopping area but frequently, service will still be needed in the older area. Serious thought may have to be given to a new outlet for outlying residents, but it may not be possible or practical for the local government in a city of 50,000 or under

to finance a branch library. One solution, and not often the first
to be thought of, is sometimes the simplest and best: cooperation
or agreement with a neighboring jurisdiction if it can provide a
convenient location for the citizens in question and if it has the
facilities and staff to extend service of a quality which the original
library feels is up to its own standard. [5]

The average librarian and library board will not have too
great a problem determining whether or not there is real need for
extension through branches. Their real problem will lie in figuring out how to finance the needed expansion, particularly in urban
areas where the tax base is eroding.

As was pointed out earlier in this chapter potential usage--
based upon a careful study of an area plus whatever evidence can
be derived from testing with a bookmobile, checking with school librarians, or establishing a temporary mobile branch--is the most
important factor in determining need for a new or permanent
branch. In order to make a reasonably accurate estimate, the
following additional factors should all be considered:

1.   Population
       a.   Size
       b.   Rate of growth
       c.   Distribution
       d.   Economic level
       e.   Educational level
       f.   Age levels
       g.   Racial origins
2.   Land area
3.   Geographic factors that isolate areas
4.   Cultural facilities and activities
5.   Industrial and business activity
6.   Educational facilities
7.   Transportation
8.   Military establishments
9.   Lakes and parks
10.   Religious life

    11.   Communications

    12.   Medical services

    13.   Recreational facilities

    14.   Entertainment.

Much of this information can be secured merely by driving around the area in question. Some of it will have to be secured from city planning, parks and recreation departments, and other areas of city government. Available surveys of the area or city or county as a whole should be checked. And there is always the person-to-person approach: talking to residents and business men, and asking questions.

The well-known authority on library buildings, Joseph L. Wheeler, said, in a letter to the author:

"In general, no city of less than 70,000 population should have any branch. Also, no city of less than 100,000, unless it has a budget of at least \$3.50 per capita and has one full-time trained reference librarian and ditto children's librarian per 16,000 population."

"The present objective of serving depressed areas is a worthy one, but branch buildings and collections are too expensive and the temptation to run a social center too great... Bookmobiles with longer schedules, including six nights a week, are effective and so much more economical. There's an element of action and excitement in bookmobile arrival, and the turnover (material per dollar) is so much greater that it seems to me hard to justify branches in these non-reading areas."[6]

Notes

1. American Library Association. It's Your Library. Branch Library or Bookmobile? Mimeographed. 3 pages. n.d.

2. Wheeler, Joseph L. and Goldhor, Herbert. Practical Administration of Public Libraries. Harper and Row, c 1962. p. 412.

3. Brawner, Lee B. Opinion expressed orally in speeches

4.   Kountz, John C. "Charting a Course in Charaymak: a
       didactic Tale with Overtones." ALA Bulletin, v. 61,
       no. 4. Apr. 1967, p. 407-08.

5.   Sinclair, Dorothy. Administration of the Small Public Library.
       American Library Association, 1965, p. 162-163

6.   Wheeler, Joseph L. Letter to the author dated March 10, 1969

Chapter 5

Organization: Relationship to Central Library or Headquarters

Systems, whether metropolitan or rural, may be either highly centralized in their administration and procedures or may permit considerable latitude in adapting rules and methods to fit the local situation.

According to an item in Library Journal, "The Brooklyn Public Library is going to try to allow greatly increased freedom to individual library units in order to foster a more sensitive response to local conditions."[1]

This is an example of a trend which has become increasingly apparent in other systems, one which seems to this writer to be highly desirable. If branches are going to meet the needs of their patrons there must be variances in procedures, collections, staffing, and even the physical aspects of the building, although such variances must be based on careful studies of the areas involved. Since no two neighborhoods, according to the sociologists, are identical, good library service cannot be fitted into a rigid pattern of policies and procedures established by the central library extension service or the library director and applied in blanket fashion to every branch in the system.

Along these lines, George Jefferson states: "A good relationship between the central library and the branch requires an administration that decentralizes initiative where local knowledge is important, and centralizes tasks that are repetitive or require uniformity throughout the whole system for some very important reason."[2]

Such adaptation to the immediate area of service has been helped in large city systems like New York, Brooklyn, and Los Angeles by the emergence of the regional or district branch. The central administrative load for a large network of branches becomes

too heavy.   Distances become too great for quick delivery of books
and other needed items.   The central headquarters becomes too
remote to be able to understand all the problems of a local area.
These are the kinds of factors which have led to the building of
large regional branches.   Such branches are at a good distance
from the main library, are spaced well apart, and furnish administrative and service centers for all the smaller branches in
their designated areas.   Since the regional unit is closer to the
individual branch and its area, and has fewer branches than the
central administration with which to work, it is easier for the
regional branch librarian and the individual branch librarians in
his region to plan together to meet more closely the needs of the
patrons in their respective areas.

The validity and economy of this kind of decentralization is
questioned by some.   The regional or intermediary branch, they
say, is feasible and sensible only in a city of 700,000 population
and with 20 or more branches.   One Los Angeles City branch, for
example, recently lent 800,000 books in one year.

In any good system, opponents of decentralization claim,
reference questions that cannot be handled at one agency should be
mailed or sent overnight directly to the central library.   Only at
central can the best reference service and the best collection of
books be found.   To shunt such requests to or through an intermediate point seems to be uneconomic and actually slows down the
operation.   If there are two or three such intermediary branches
the costs for materials and extra paperwork increases, for there
will still be some requests that have to be passed on to central.

In 1968 Baltimore County librarians (Towson, Maryland)
were given a chance to rate their administration.   A questionnaire
designed by Director Charles W. Robinson sought their opinions
on present administrative practices.   Among their complaints
were (a) Too little attention paid to branches; and (b) Lack of
participation by branch personnel in policy decisions.

The administration received good marks in a number of
other areas. Mr. Robinson reported to the staff: "We will now
proceed to attempt to correct the areas shown to be weak before

our administrative techniques become so fossilized that change is difficult or impossible." Copies of the questionnaire were available to interested libraries at the time of this writing. This system of questioning and attempting to correct known problems illustrates a healthy administrative situation as regards branch relationships with central.

So much emphasis is being placed today on reaching out into the community, with the branch seen as a cultural center tailored to fit the interests and needs of the area residents, that it seems logical to plan for certain differences of operation and to permit a competent branch librarian to perform her function as a coordinator between library and community unhampered by a rigid set of regulations from headquarters. Too often, though, branches are staffed with people who do not live in the area and who may have little in common economically and culturally with local residents. Such a situation is not desirable, but some areas yield few qualified people able to work in a branch. However, if the head librarian is competent, sympathetic, and anxious to fit the service closely to the population and its needs, she should have the freedom to develop a dynamic, neighborhood-oriented program that can produce results. There have been highly centralized systems where so many minute details are decided at the central library that the trained branch head becomes almost a robot, mechanically carrying out dictates from above. Creativity is stifled, service often misses the mark, and the library cannot reach into the hearts of the people.

Communication is of intense importance in branch-headquarters relationships. When a patron, through some error, fails to get back from central a book needed to meet a deadline, the branch tends to blame headquarters for being too slow; conversely, headquarters may blame the branch for not having made the request sooner or in the prescribed manner. There should be carefully defined avenues of communication between headquarters and branches, a perfect understanding as to procedures, and participation of branch personnel in meetings and training offered at the central library. Too often, branch staffs are made to feel like

stepchildren of the parent library because they are not asked to
participate in important staff meetings, in central social activities,
or in various other events.   Staff associations, particularly, should
be careful to see that branch personnel are made to feel an important part of the group, with ample branch representation among
officers, committee appointments, and other assignments.

Branch staff should visit central headquarters often enough
to be thoroughly familiar with the operations that bear a relationship to branch service.   Central staff concerned with branch matters should also be fully aware of what goes on at the branch end.
Exchange visits of this type make each group aware of the other's
duties and problems, and eliminate a great deal of friction or
criticism.

A fine example of staff preparation to insure good relationships between central and branch staff and a smoothly coordinated
operation at the branch, was the workshop on communication and
coordination held, before the branch library was completed, at the
Whittier Public Library, Whittier, California, on February 28, 1968.
This excellent program, directed by Margaret Fulmer, Librarian,
is reproduced here in its entirety as a guide for other libraries
which are beginning to expand into a branch program.   During the
meetings case studies involving problems in communication and coordination were presented and the staff was asked how they would
handle each problem.   These problems are also reproduced here
by permission of the Whittier Public Library.

Workshop on Communication and Coordination
In Preparation for Expanded Services Through the New Branch
Library. Whittier Public Library, February 28, 1968

9:00-9:45 a. m.   Goals and Organization for Library   All Staff
                       Service to the Public

9:00-9:05   Introduction to the Workshop
                       (Margaret Ward, State Library
                       Consultant)

9:05-9:15	Objectives, Policy and Program of the Whittier Public Library (Margaret Fulmer, Librarian, Whittier Public Library)	
9:15-9:45	How Departments Work Together to Achieve Objectives; The Branch Library as an Extension of Services (Panel of Supervisors)	
9:45-10:00	Coffee in the Staff Room	
10:00-11:00	Effective Communication in an Expanding Organization	First Group*
10:00-10:45	Methods of Communication, using circulation functions as examples --Group Discussion	
10:45-11:00	Film: More than Words	
11:00-12:00 noon	Repeat of above program on Communication	Second Group*
2:00-3:00 p. m.	Maintaining Coordination in an Expanded Organization	First Group*
2:00-2:30	Methods of Coordination, using reference functions as examples--Group discussion	
2:30-2:45	Channels of Communication as an Aid to Coordination--Group Discussion	
2:45-3:00	Summary of Workshop (Margaret Ward and Margaret Fulmer)	
3:00-4:00	Repeat of the above program on Coordination	Second Group*

*Approximately half the staff will attend the first session and half the second

Case Studies Involving Problems in Communication

In thinking of solutions to the problems presented here, try not to think about the mechanics of the procedure, but keep in mind the communication involved.   For instance:

a) How does the library patron feel? What information does she need so that she will understand the situation and accept the rules, and act on them in the future?

b) How do the actions of the desk assistant at the branch affect the staff at the central library and visa versa?

c) What does the desk assistant's supervisor need to know about the various problems that have arisen?

Mrs. Jones has been a regular patron of the Springdale Public Library for years. She has recently moved from the older part of town to the new section and has been looking forward eagerly to using the new branch library. Once established in the new neighborhood, she begins getting books there; but she finds that she still occasionally needs to use the larger collection at the central library. She checks out so many books that she does not always keep them separated and is likely to return all the books she has to whichever library she is visiting that day. She also sometimes forgets that her books are due, and receives overdue notices. She likes to keep up with the new books, and often reserves specific titles.

She always has so many problems that the staff rather dread to see her coming in the door. However, she is a great booster for the library; and, as a member of a number of community groups, has several times helped get citizen backing for a larger book budget. Also, she is so enthusiastic about her reading that the staff cannot help liking her.

Today she comes in with an armload of books, in a hurry because she is on her way to a meeting. She has books which have been checked out from both the central library and the branch.

Problem One

Among the items she is returning, Mrs. Jones has an envelope containing pamphlets. The charge indicates that six pamphlets have been checked out, but only five are in the envelope. The pamphlets are from the central building.

How do you, as desk assistant, explain the situation to Mrs. Jones? What information do you give Mrs. Jones? Who else has to be informed? When and how do you give this information?

Problem Two

Mrs. Jones has received an overdue notice from the central library. The book listed on the notice is not among those she has just deposited on the desk. She says she has returned this book and wants you "to straighten this out."

What action do you, a branch assistant, take? What problems in communication are involved?

Problem Three

For the meeting she is attending, Mrs. Jones needs a book she has borrowed previously from the branch, but a quick search shows that it is not on the shelf. She says she has to pass the main library in order to get to the meeting place and wonders if she can find the book there.

Remembering that Mrs. Jones is in a hurry, what procedure do you think best to follow? Why? Who has to be informed and what information does he or she need?

Problem Four

Mrs. Jones has with her a booklist. She says she got it at a Community Council meeting she attended the evening before, and it lists books she wants to take with her to the meeting, this afternoon.   You have not seen the list before, but note that it does have the name of the library on it, and that it states that the books on the list have been placed on a special reserve shelf at the central building for the use of the Community Council during the next two weeks.

What do you say to Mrs. Jones?

How do you get word to the central library that the branch staff is not receiving information it needs?

Problem Five

As she is about to leave, Mrs. Jones sees on the desk a book which has just been returned by another patron.   It is one she wants, and she says so.   A check of the reserve file shows that there are several reserves on it.   Mrs. Jones says, "I only want to take it to this afternoon's meeting to show to the other members of the group, and I'll return it tomorrow. Can't you let me have it on special loan?"

How do you explain the rule to Mrs. Jones? If this library is one which allows exceptions to rules in unusual cases, what information do you give to Mrs. Jones?   Who else is probably involved and what information should those persons have?

Case Studies Showing the Uses of Coordination

(Coordinate: to bring into common action, movement, or condition; to harmonize; to be or become coordinate so as to act together in a smooth, coordinated way. --Webster's Seventh New Collegiate Dictionary.)

Mr. Smith is a free-lance writer and publicity man who lives in the neighborhood served by the South Branch of the Springdale Public Library.   He maintains an office downtown and often stops by the central library during his lunch hour or on his way home from work.   He asks many reference questions both at the branch and the central library.   Here are some typical situations arising out of his requests:

Situation One:

Mr. Smith comes into the branch library late on a Monday evening and asks for technical information on the chemical composition and reactions of a certain type of plastic material.   This

is for copy he is writing for a small company, which has no
publicity man and has commissioned him to write a brochure to
mail to companies which are potential customers for the product.
    A check of the branch catalog and the magazine indexes
shows that the branch has no information technical enough for his
needs. It is near closing time and he would not have time to
drive to the central library building to get material from there.
You, as branch assistant, know that ten minutes before closing
time on a Monday evening is a time when the reference staff at
the central building has a line of patrons waiting for last-minute
service. Mr. Smith has a deadline to meet and wants the material at least by the time the central library opens the next morning.
    Consider how best to serve Mr. Smith. How best can you
get cooperation from the central library reference staff? How can
you give Mr. Smith good service without keeping other patrons
from being shunted aside?
    Consider the feelings of the central library reference staff.
Should there be a rule that no telephone reference calls be accepted from the branch during the last fifteen minutes before the library closes? If you, as branch assistant, think there should be
such a rule, how do you go about making the suggestion? If, as is
more likely, the central library reference assistant realizes this,
how does she go about making the suggestion?

Situation Two:

    Mr. Smith comes into the main library on a Monday even-
ing and says he is working on a feature article for the local newspaper on a type of paper cloth manufactured locally and needs
background material on the uses of this kind of cloth. He is about
to leave town and will be gone until Saturday evening. A check of
the catalog and magazine indexes reveals the fact that the library
does not own material on this subject. Neither the central library
nor the branch are open on Sunday. Mr. Smith, however, needs to
use the material on Sunday to meet a Monday deadline. His wife
probably cannot get downtown to the central library to get the
material when it arrives by interlibrary loan, because of being
confined to the house with a seriously ill mother. His ten-year-old
boy can call at the branch, though, to pick up the material.
    What action do you, as central library reference assistant
take?
    Who is involved in this problem?
    Who has to be notified, and what information does each
need?
    What sort of coordination does the central library reference
assistant have to accomplish? What sort of coordination does the
branch library reference assistant have to accomplish?
    What planning in the establishment of policies and procedures
had to be accomplished previously in order to make this coordination
possible?

Situation Three:
        Mr. Smith suggests that the library should own books on the sub-
ject of paper cloth. His contact with advertising companies has given
him inside information that there is to be a nation-wide publicity campaign on paper clothing, using television, radio, newspapers, and
magazines; and it is likely that there will be a call for material on this
subject from many people within the next month. What action should
you, as reference assistant, take as follow-up on this information?

Reading for the In-service Training Workshop

        In preparation for the workshop staff was asked to browse
through the following reading list and select the books and articles
of most interest to them.

Berelson, Bernard	Reader in Public Opinion and Communication. Free Press, 1953.
Bellows, Roger	Executive Skills, pp. 58-91. Prentice-Hall, 1962.
Bennis, W. G.	Changing Organizations. McGraw-Hill, 1966.
Drucker, Peter	The Effective Executive. Harper, 1967.
Kaufmann, C. B.	Man Incorporate. Doubleday, 1967.
Killian, R. A.	Managers Must Lead. pp. 228-239. American Management Ass'n. 1966.
Levenstein, Aaron	Why People Work. pp. 87-108. Crowell-Collier, 1962.
Lilienthal, D. E.	Management: A Humanist Art. Columbia Univ. Press, 1967.
Logan, Harlan	Are You Misunderstood? pp. 158-172. Funk, 1965.
McLuhan, H. M.	The Medium is the Message. Random, 1967.
McLuhan, H. M.	Understanding Media. McGraw-Hill, 1964.
Matson, F. W. and Montague, Ashley, eds.	The Human Dialogue. Free Press, 1967.
Morgan, J. S.	Getting Across to Employees. McGraw-Hill, 1964.
Pigors, Paul	Personnel Administration. pp. 74-97. McGraw-Hill, 1965.
Redding, W. C.	Business and Industrial Communication. Harper, 1964.
Roy, R. H.	The Administrative Process. pp. 159-182. Johns Hopkins Press, 1958.
Drucker, P. F.	"How the effective executive does it." Fortune, v. 75, no. 2, Feb. 1967. p. 140
Drucker, P. F.	"How to manage your time." Harpers, v. 233, Dec. 1966. p. 56.
Knowles, H. P. etc.	"Human relations and the nature of man." Harvard Business Review, v. 45, no. 2, March-April, 1967, p. 23-

Levine, Jules   "Getting started on a communications
                               program." The Office, v. 64, no. 5
                               Nov. 1966, p. 135-
Potter, Curtis   "Supervising, a look in the present."
                               Supervision, v. 29, no. 7. July, 1967.
Sandell, Roland   "Follow through to make plans work."
                               Supervision, v. 29, no. 2. p. 28. p. 10
Stern, Isadore   "Why communications break down."
                               Supervision, v. 29, no. 2. Feb. 1967,
                               p. 2.

        The branch for which Miss Fulmer prepared her staff so
carefully was the Whittwood Branch, opened early in 1968.   In
size, plan, and service program it approaches the ideal modern
branch.   It contains 10,000 square feet, expandable to 15,000 square
feet.   Parking spaces are provided for automobiles, motorcycles
and bicycles.   The air-conditioned building operates on one level,
is modern and functional, and has an inviting approach.   The interior plan and decor are attractive and colorful, characterized by
convenience and efficiency.   The branch contains five main areas:
children, adults, staff work area, the central circulation desk, and
the multipurpose room.   About 25,000 books are shelved in free-
standing stacks.   About 100 seats are provided, plus the children's
picture book benches.   When the building is expanded the book collection can be increased to about 50,000 volumes and the seating
capacity increased.   Total cost, including site, building and
furnishings, was about $500,000, to be paid from the city's general
capital fund.   Architect was Mr. William H. Harrison, F. A. I. A. ,
working with the staff of the Whittier Public Library.   Mr. H. J.
Perry, Jr. , was the interior specialist.

County Headquarters and Branches
        In an interesting article in the Library Association Record,
Geoffrey Smith, Deputy County Librarian of Hampshire, England,[3]
points out that the patron's opinion of a library is often affected by
an apparent lack of coordination between the library where he
selects his books and the administrative center from which the
service is organized.   Branch library staff may all too often give
as an excuse for a lack of new books some such statement as

"Headquarters has not sent any this week." At headquarters, the excuse for not being able to supply a certain title may be: "The book you want is at a branch library, and we can't get it back." Or, on a Saturday afternoon, if a branch reader asks a tough reference question, the staff response may be, "We are sorry, we could try on Monday, headquarters isn't open on Saturdays."

It is easy to blame someone else but when a reader has to go away unsatisfied, it is not the branch or headquarters that are at fault but the service as a whole. Branches and headquarters are parts of one service, and staff loyalty to that service should come before loyalty to the particular part of the system in which they work.

Mr. Smith describes varying interpretations of the function of headquarters. He refers to the highly centralized, authoritarian organization as the "big brother" type, where the branch manual tells how to hold the date stamp, and where to put the labels on the parcels; and the chief and headquarters staff insure that no local deviations are made. In this type of organization, headquarters "is always right."

The opposite extreme is when no one from headquarters is ever seen in the branches. Branch librarians are left to do as they like. They seldom, if ever, visit headquarters. In this situation, borrowing a book from another part of the county library system is regarded as a last and seldom-used resort; headquarters is always wrong, always to blame, and is thought of by the branches as second-rate and unhelpful.

What the headquarters should be, says Mr. Smith, is a natural center of the library service to which branches may look for leadership, help, encouragement, information, advice and, most important, service in meeting readers' requests. This presupposes a completely unselfish type of organization.

A library staff is made up of individuals each having his own personal opinions, ideals, and aims. Best results are obtained when they are treated as members of a team rather than as a staff to be directed, supervised or controlled. If this approach

is adopted with professionals who work mainly outside headquarters, the regional and branch librarians and librarians of
bookmobiles are more likely to exercise responsibility and
authority in providing the best possible service to patrons.

The function of headquarters should be to help them do this,
not tell them from afar how to do it in detail. This is not decentralization carried to the extreme that branch librarians must
sacrifice valuable time which should be spent serving the public in
order to cope with a mass of paperwork, form filling, keeping of
accounts, making estimates, etc. It is merely a way of encouraging the local librarian to use her own judgment for the sake of
better service and better public relations.

For example, book selection is often a headquarters function, but librarians in charge of branches and bookmobiles, who
are in direct touch with the needs of the communities they serve,
should select the books they want rather than accept what headquarters thinks their readers want. Headquarters should encourage librarians to provide a wide range of books and should help
branches revise their collections and make them more effective
and useful to readers.

Certain services can be most effectively, efficiently and
economically organized centrally, and these should be provided by
the headquarters library to the branches. Inter-library lending,
accounting, booklists, classification and cataloging, processing,
the more difficult mending, staff training, equipment and supplies,
reserve stocks, transport, technical and information service are
among the main services usually provided by the central agency.
However, headquarters must never forget they are services provided for the benefit of readers, not for the branch staff primarily or as ends in themselves. When a centralized service
head begins to feel that branch demands are excessive, without
relating these to community needs, the seeds of friction are
planted. The services provided are for the public; the branch is
only the intermediary. Branches actually ask little for themselves other than an occasional item for the staff lounge, a
special parking area for staff, or some such item.

Headquarters must insure that, while routines which directly affect public service and other branches in the system are uniform enough so that they do not confuse patrons who use more than one branch, they are also elastic enough to permit adaptation to individual community needs. It is also a headquarters responsibility to see that high standards of public service are maintained. Readers have a right to expect consistent treatment, and standard practices should be widely publicized. To permit one branch to answer reference questions by phone, for example, while another is prohibited from doing so, would be most damaging to the branch denied this service.

A positive attitude and a willingness to help and advise branch personnel is necessary, but there should be few occasions when arbitrary orders and directives are issued without personal contact between headquarters and branch personnel.

B. M. Charlton,[4] presenting the branch viewpoint in a companion piece to the Library Association Record article by Geoffrey Smith cited earlier, points out that the work of headquarters is much more oriented toward satisfying the needs of branches than is true in the opposite direction. He urges branch assistants in general to be legible, accurate, prompt, correct and courteous in letters to headquarters, and to provide specific and adequate information when requesting books from headquarters.

It is a fundamental responsibility of regional, area and branch librarians and their staffs, Mr. Charlton says, to achieve and maintain a deep and clear understanding of the character and needs of the area they serve, to make suggestions for the improvement of service in their areas, and if these are approved, to carry them out, to do something. He believes headquarters does listen to and make use of ideas from branches, although action on them may be hindered by library boards or county officials. The local staff should not give up easily, however.[4]

The headquarters obligation is largely one of coordination, Mr. Charlton believes. The branch staff should put themselves in the place of the borrower, who is their primary concern.

Branches must keep presenting suggestions to headquarters, Mr. Charlton insists.

Relations between headquarters and branches are a crucial factor in the success or failure of county libraries, according to Mr. Charlton. He says:

Headquarters expectations of branches:

1. Make the best use of book stock, staff, and facilities
2. Keep headquarters informed and play an active part in developing the service.
3. Be accurate, always on the lookout for improving the service to readers, for opportunities to publicize the services, for chances of better quarters, for criticism.
4. Most of all: provide a good, efficient, and professional library service.

Branch expectations of headquarters:

1. Help and encouragement, tangible and intangible.
2. Information. Branch staffs should be fully informed as to what is happening.
3. Clearly-expressed policy. Objectives should be plainly outlined.
4. Authority to match their responsibilities. Performance should not be hindered by lack of authority to carry out approved plans.
5. Staff training courses, exchanges, meetings, newsletters, and week-end conferences should be planned by headquarters to improve communication, develop skills, and provide coordination.
6. Headquarters should be a sounding board for reader comments and criticisms, and should carry them back to branches and provide constructive suggestions. [4]

Wheeler and Goldhor[5] point out that if a city has six or more branches, enough cost, personnel and traffic are involved to justify consideration of the need for a branch or extension division head. Two main questions are involved:

1. The relationship of the branch librarians with the chief librarian and other supervisory personnel.

2. The extent to which branches shall function on their own, or follow uniform practices set down for the whole system.

If there are five branches or less, these authors believe, the branch librarians should report directly to the director, or at least to the assistant director of the system, and no other supervisor is needed. In turn, the head of a regional branch could be responsible for any smaller branches, stations, bookmobiles, or deposits within his general section of the city. This latter arrangement, in cities of 300,000 or more, or in systems that extend for some miles, could apply not only to general supervision of the work of the smaller units but also to the filling of their more elementary book needs and to the loan of staff to cover emergency periods, vacations, etc.

Some feel that greater unity and closer feeling are engendered among staff members working in the same geographic area, producing better operating results than does central control from one point for all extension agencies.[5]

An example of an interesting type of organization is that of the Montgomery Country Library in Maryland. Each public library and bookmobile in the county system has an Advisory Committee whose members live in the area the facility serves. These committees are provided for in the Library Act to stimulate maximum citizen participation in library growth and activity.

Committee members are appointed by the Library Board for two-year terms that begin on October 1 of even-numbered years. More than 150 county residents serve on Local Advisory Committees. Committee duties as outlined in the Library Board bylaws are:

(a) To obtain advice and view from local citizens on library needs in the areas they serve and to report findings and recommendations to the Library Board.

(b) To make recommendations to the Board concerning construction of libraries in the areas they represent.

(c) To make recommendations to the City Council for filling vacancies on the Library Board.

Interpreting their duties broadly, the committees have been active in a variety of library matters and have made invaluable contributions. They have helped bring new libraries into existence by arousing citizen interest and petitioning the County Council. They

have spoken on behalf of library budgets at public hearings, and
have alerted the Board and Department to needs at existing facilitie
They also have undertaken such projects as enlisting the aid of a
garden club to landscape library grounds, raising funds to purchase
equipment, organizing clubs for library users, and meeting with
civic organizations.

Small Town Branches:

Small town branches may be part of a county system, a
regional system, or a federation.

If part of a county or regional system, a branch may have
one of two origins. It may have been an independent, already
established, village library begun by a women's club or other group
of public spirited citizens, which joined a system when a county or
regional system came into being; or it may have been established
after the county library was established. In the former case the
original local library board may still function, working in cooperation with the county board. In the latter case, there is not likely
to be a local board.

Those who favor a highly centralized system may decry the
existence of small community boards. It is this writer's opinion
and experience that local boards can be of value when worked with
tactfully and with due regard for the local influence of their members. These people know their own community. They know how to
get needed local support; they can recommend local people needed
for staff positions; they can help interpret county and regional
policies and procedures; and they can give the local branch or mem
ber library good publicity. In short, they can be an excellent liaison between the central administration and local officials and borrowers. It is true that they can also be a problem, human nature
being what it is, but care on the part of the central administration
in maintaining a good relationship can make the local board both
productive and helpful. Local pride in a library is an asset well
worth preserving.

Thus it might be wise to have local advisory boards appointed by town councils when a county or regional library is set up and

new community branch is formed. Starting from scratch, such
an advisory board would have full cognizance of its function and its
relationship to the board of the larger unit of which it is a part.
Problems would not be so likely to arise; yet the value of the local
contacts would be there to be utilized.

A local library which becomes a branch should not be made
over in the image of the central agency. Like the individual city
branch, each small town branch will have an individuality the better
aspects of which should be retained. This does not mean that old,
shabby, outdated books need be kept, or outmoded methods continued. It does mean that change should come slowly, that good
features should be retained, and that friendly, personal relationships
between the local librarian and the patrons should not be jeopardized.

An unusual type of organization exists in Vermont where
most of the small libraries could be considered branches of the
state agency. ALA speaks of small libraries in terms of a population figure of 35,000. Vermont has one city of that size; all other
communities are smaller. Because of the lack of strong community
libraries the state extension agency has developed a system of
agency regional libraries which provide supplemental book collections to community libraries and professional and technical help to
librarians and library trustees. The state agency hopes that this
necessary service will gradually be transferred to some of the larger
public libraries. But recognizing that the community libraries will
not be prepared to undertake this responsibility for some time, the
state agency has undertaken the construction of four regional libraries in recent years, and, at the time of this writing, hoped to
replace the present inadequate quarters of the fifth regional library
with a new building.

In the pattern of organization of the Tulsa (Oklahoma) City-
County system, all actions of the Tulsa City-County Library Commission require the approval of the Tulsa City Commission and of
the Board of County Commissioners. The functions of community
library boards and committees are to:

1. Serve as a liaison between the community and the city-
county library commission. It is the policy of the city-county

library system to adapt each library to the needs of its community.

2.   Continually promote and encourage the fullest use of eac
community library.

3.   Consult with the community librarian regarding the
progress of the library and opportunity for its continuing growth
and improvement.

Since major responsibility of the community committee or
board will be in connection with the opening of the library (recommending hours of service, serving as hosts for open house
occasions, etc.), it is not anticipated that this group will have a
formal organization or regular meetings.   It may be called a boar(
or a committee, and may be made up of three to seven members
depending upon the segments of the community which should be
represented.   The appointments should be made by the mayor of
each community, with suggestions coming from interested citizens.

The community librarian is directly responsible to the Chief
of Extension of the City-County System.   Her hours of service,
conditions of work, library routines, rules of the library, rate of
pay, are worked out by the administrative staff of the library
system and are maintained as uniformly as possible in all libraries
in the system.   Suggestions from the local library committee regarding any of these matters are welcomed and may be made throu₃
the librarian or directly to the library administration.

The responsibilities of the system administrator and the library commission are as follows:

1.   To finance the operation of the library, including salary
of the librarian, rent, utilities, janitorial service, equipment and
supplies, regular purchases of books and other materials.

2.   To establish system-wide policies regarding rules and
regulations, personnel policies, hours of service.   The administrative staff advises regarding the selection of books and other
materials.

The Chief of Extension is responsible for all library services to the public except those of the central library.

Branch and community libraries: 19 branches are located
strategically throughout Tulsa County to bring library services as

close to as many citizens as possible. Eight libraries in the smaller towns surrounding Tulsa are selected as community libraries.
Branches within the city limits are located close to shopping centers
and schools in order to be accessible to all patrons.

Uniform pattern throughout a state:

In South Carolina the libraries are organized on a county or
regionwide basis, and all branches or stations are full members of
the system. They operate under one board, with one staff, one
budget, and a unified program of service.

This type of organization is in contrast with New York State,
where most of the systems are made up of members or affiliates and
are not highly centralized. Most of the South Carolina library systems
hold staff meetings which include the branch librarians and which
are used for training purposes.

The South Carolina State Library has made a determined
effort to improve the level of reference service in the branches.
It has conducted a Book Collection Improvement Project designed to
raise the level of the material available at the branch level and to
give the librarians and branch personnel training in the use of their
new reference tools.

Regional Libraries (As part of a city system):

Purpose of the Regional System:

Regional libraries and librarians maintain lines of communication with the administrative offices and departments
at the Central Library, and interpret procedures and
policies to the staff in the region. They supervise and
coordinate book collections, materials, personnel and
other services of the branches in the area.

In addition to its administrative function, the regional
branch provides library service to the surrounding
community. All of its activities are directed toward
efficient and satisfactory use by the public. It attempts to fill the needs of those who seek information,
reading materials, audio-visual aids or other services
people expect from a modern public library.

A regional library should offer more to its patrons than
the community branch because of the greater size and

quality of the reference and circulating collections, the special services available, and the volume of business transacted. The larger staff should include specialists in children's work, young adult services and adult reference. The size of the staff should be sufficient to offer library assistance and support to cultural and educational organizations within its boundaries. Because of these added assets, the regional branch can extend superior branch library facilities to the immediate community.

Objectives of Regional Organization:

To help establish the library upon a more effective administrative foundation.

To provide for more equitable and efficient distribution of library facilities throughout the city and county.

To make more specialized library services readily accessible to outlying communities.

To develop a plan of service designed for a specific area.

To increase time for community involvement.

To improve the quality of book selection in size and specialization.

To make better and more effective use of personnel.

Following are examples of two regional organization patterns, one for a three-county and one for a six-county system, both involving cooperation among the counties concerned. Also presented is the pattern of organization of a city system (Denver) which has larger than usual regional branches, each with one or more branches under its jurisdiction.

Regional Systems with County Branches:

1.   Savannah Public and Chatham-Effingham-Liberty Regional Library.

This is a regional library, serving three counties, with the headquarters library in Savannah. Library agencies are:

1) In the city of Savannah: the Main Library, 2 full time branch libraries, 3 part-time branches in Negro public housing projects.

2) In Chatham County: 3 part-time branches in 3 small incorporated towns which are within 12 miles or less of the heart of Savannah and which are largely dormitory suburbs of Savannah; 4 bookmobiles to serve elementary schools outside the city limits, residential areas outside the city limits, and elementary schools and residential areas within the city but at some distance from an established library agency where the population is largely Negro.

3) In Effingham County: a part-time branch and a bookmobile.

4) In Liberty County: a part-time branch.

Administration of the part-time branches in the Negro public housing projects: Service in these agencies is a cooperative project of the public library and the Housing Authority of Savannah and Chatham County. The Authority furnishes and maintains quarters free and assists with publicity to the residents in the project. The library supplies books and magazines, public service staff, and overall planning, publicity, and general supervision. The libraries are available to residents in the community generally, but most of their users live in the housing projects.

Libraries of this type might fit into the neighborhood branch idea which many library planners have advocated in the past few years.

Administration of the part-time branches in small incorporated cities of Chatham County: None of the three cities has a population as big as 3,000 people, so full time branch service is not warranted.

The local city governments furnish and maintain quarters and pay local untrained people to be in charge of the public service. In one community there is an active group of volunteers who have backed up the library for more than 20 years by assisting with the public service, giving special publicity to the library, and presenting the library's needs to the city council at annual budget time.

The headquarters library supplies books, overall publicity and program planning, and general supervision.

Denver Public Library
Denver, Colorado

Library Commission

Librarian

- Public Information Office
- Book Selection Center
- Special Collections
- Western History Department

Director Technical Services
- Catalog Department
- Serials Division
- Book Preparation Unit

Director Administrative Services
- Personnel Office
  - Payroll
- Business Office
  - Switchboard
  - Guards
  - Book Procurement Unit
- Circulation and Registration Div.
  - Circulation Control Unit
- Data Processing Unit
- Print Shop
- Shelving Unit

Director of Public Services and Assistant Librarian
- Coordinator of Adult Services
  - Group Services
  - Extension Services
    - Office
    - Bookmobiles
    - Interlibrary Loan
- Coordinator of Children's Services
  - Children's Library
- Art and Music Department
  - Audio-Visual Center
- Literature and History Department
  - Genealogy Division
  - Young Adult Division

Region #1
- Park Hill Regional Library
- Warren Branch Library
- Montclair Neighborhood Library

Region #2
- Ross-Cherry Creek Regional Library
- Ross-Broadway Branch Library
- Byers Neighborhood Library

Region #3
- Ross-University Hills Regional Library
- Decker Branch Library
- Field Branch Library
- South Holly Neighborhood Library

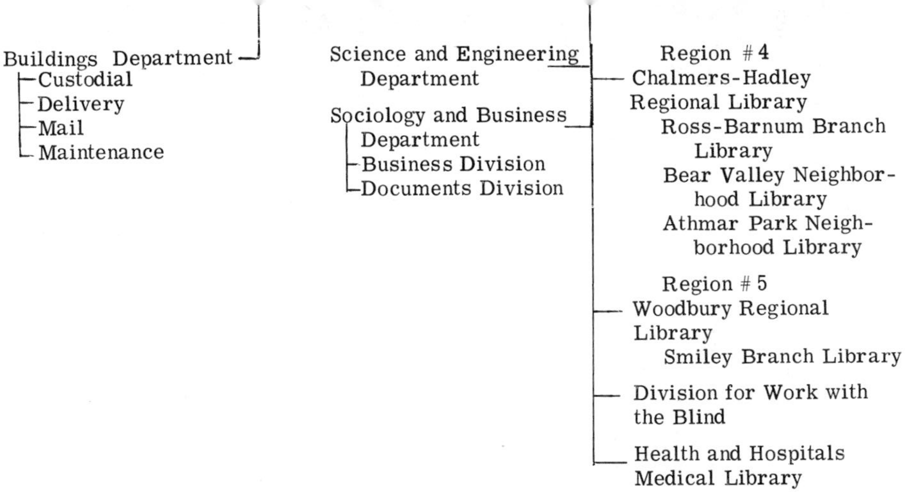

Buildings Department
- Custodial
- Delivery
- Mail
- Maintenance

Science and Engineering Department

Sociology and Business Department
- Business Division
- Documents Division

Region #4
Chalmers-Hadley Regional Library
Ross-Barnum Branch Library
Bear Valley Neighborhood Library
Athmar Park Neighborhood Library

Region #5
Woodbury Regional Library
Smiley Branch Library

Division for Work with the Blind

Health and Hospitals Medical Library

Figure 36: Example of an organizational pattern in a large system where there are regional branches, each with some responsibility for neighborhood branches within their respective areas.

2. White River Regional Library, Batesville, Arkansas

This is another fairly typical regional organization in a multi-county region and with a number of branches within the counties. The description would indicate a fairly high degree of centralization at the headquarters library.

White River Regional Library consists of six counties. According to Mrs. Terry Griffith, librarian, the policies followed, although not unusual, have proven very satisfactory.

All financial and statistical records and reports are pre-pared at the headquarters library. The branch clerks keep a daily circulation sheet which is mailed to the headquarters at the end of each month. One mill tax money is kept in each individual county. Warrants are prepared in headquarters for accounts payable in each county.

Branch clerks send requests to headquarters for material they cannot furnish locally. Book selection is done in headquarters with requests from branches given first consideration. Workshops for in-service training of branch clerks are held at intervals.

The bookmobile visits four of the counties once a month. These counties pay a fee toward expenses. The bookmobile librari-an and driver-clerk assist the branch clerks with problems and make special selections for them. The head librarian visits the branches on regular schedule and is "on call" at any time for emergencies.

When branch librarians are non-professionals the necessity for a greater degree of centralization becomes apparent, especially in the areas of book selection, budgetary control, and formation of policies. However, individual purchase requests and inter-library loan requests from the individual branches receive careful considera tion and are supplied whenever possible.

Wheeler and Goldhor[6] suggest that book selection at head-quarters should involve at least the branch librarian, and that her professional staff, in turn, should be involved in advising her at the branch level. The branch head, they believe, should be free to decide, within limits set by headquarters, but in line with his own thinking, what is needed for provision of the best library service in his community. The same philosophy should also apply in the selection of equipment and supplies.

Flexibility and branch autonomy are especially fruitful in the area of reader services. It would be unwise, for example, to lay down for all branches a uniform pattern for book promotion or adult film showings. What might be a great success in one neighborhood could be a complete failure in another. Uniformity should not be sought for its own sake. Experimentation should be allowed and encouraged in the branches. The branch head should be free, for example, to decide whether and how to use reader interest classification. One area in which individual branch selection is very important is that of pamphlets. Branch librarians should select these, as well as other vertical file material.

Headquarters, however, should be concerned with the ordering and processing of pamphlets, just as with books. As many as possible of the clerical and mechanical processes should be performed at the central library or headquarters for the sake of economy and to free branch personnel for public service. Two areas of borderline activity are book repairing and the sending of overdues. Whether only the very simple mending processes, none, or all types will be performed at the branches is a matter to be determined by the size of the branch staff, the methods used, and the efficiency of communication and delivery service between headquarters and the branches.

Many branch heads feel, and perhaps rightly so, that it is a waste of time and money, and slows down considerably the return of the books to circulation, when all mending has to be done at the central headquarters. The branch staff can mend tears and hinges and erase markings, as well as repair other minor damage very quickly in occasional spare moments, and can return the material to circulation much sooner.

The processing of overdues can be handled at the central library. Where there is every day or every other day delivery between the headquarters and the branches, sending records back

and forth becomes a relatively simple matter. There should, however, be an efficient system so that patrons who pay for fines or
lost books at an agency or department other than the one at which
the charge was incurred will have their record cleared promptly.

Nothing irritates a patron more than to pay an overdue or
lost book charge on a branch item and then be told that he cannot
take books at the Central Library, or vice-versa, because he still
owes an mount sufficient to place him in the "refuse service"
category. Clearances should be sent through daily if possible.

There is never a need to decentralize routine operations to
provide "busy work" for desk assistants in branches. A busy,
well-supervised branch will not lack work for its clericals, and
any agency which needs such busy work should be questioned and
analyzed. The two tests to apply in deciding whether any process
should be performed at headquarters or at the branches are:

1. Which plan will result in faster and better service for
the patrons?

2. Which plan is more economical in time and money for
the library system? Although both factors should be considered,
efficiency of public service should take precedence over economy.

There are two major advantages to centralization of
processes beyond the foregoing factors:

1. Specialization breeds competence.

2. Sufficient volume will justify use of machinery or
automation.

Communication has been repeatedly stressed as a means of
maintaining good relationships. Any branch system needs four
simple administrative devices to improve communication: (1) Frequent meetings of branch librarians to exchange views, seek assistance, receive information, and keep up to date; (2) a staff
bulletin or notices issued regularly; (3) A procedure manual worked
out jointly by the central extension staff and the branch heads;
(4) A truck pickup and delivery system, or an arrangement with a
local delivery company, for making daily (or at least every other
day) rounds of the branches.

Branches will also provide better service in filling patron reserves if the central library maintains a fluid collection of books on which branches may draw for temporary or long-term use and to which they can transfer books no longer needed at a branch but too valuable to discard. This constitutes a reservoir of material which can be called upon to fill occasional but important requests.

Branch withdrawals could also go into a central pool of withdrawals and duplicate gifts. From the gift collection could be drawn replacements of fiction or non-fiction out-of-print and otherwise not obtainable; only those volumes which were in good physical condition would circulate, other valuable out-of-print material which was needed only occasionally being retained in the storage collection. [6]

Decentralization

This chapter began with a reference to the Brooklyn Public Library and its changing attitude toward branch relationships.   In an article entitled "Big City Libraries: Strategy and Tactics for Change," [7] John C. Frantz, Director of the Brooklyn Public Library, said:

"This brings me to what is probably the most controversial suggestion I have to put forward: the selective decentralization of library policies and procedures to recognize and accommodate racial differences between specific neighborhoods.

"One of the things I learned when I went to Brooklyn was that there is no such place. It's just a useful abstraction, for Brooklyn is really a collection of very discrete neighborhoods with very distinct population, economics, social and racial characteristics, and very different reactions to, and needs for, libraries. To put all these neighborhoods into one program straitjacket strikes me as being something less than realistic. "

Mr. Frantz recognizes the administrative difficulties in policy decentralization and does not propose solutions, but he suggests that it is a more realistic approach to library service in branches.   In Brooklyn, therefore, a conventional library service

is being provided for conventional areas--such as Sheepshead Bay,
Midwood, and to some extent, Coney Island and Bay Ridge. For the
radically different kind of user a different and innovative approach
is being used. These innovations will be discussed in some detail
in Chapter 10, on "Special Activities and Services in Branches
Today."

The Brooklyn District Library program has changed the
system from a series of fully-staffed small, medium, and large
branches to a small number of district libraries with a complement
of reading specialists, each of these libraries being surrounded by
satellite neighborhood reading centers designed to be book-dispens-
ing agencies. The library kiosk idea would carry the pattern one
step further, getting the dispensing units out to places like subway
entrances and busy street corners at rush hours. [7] This pattern of
organization is being used in several other large cities.

In city systems branches are close enough together so that
in-service training programs, inter-branch meetings, and frequent
visits and conferences do not present a problem, providing the
system is well organized. In county systems distance, winter
weather problems, the expense of long distance calls, and the
greater diversity of communities can make coordination more difficult. In general, strong organizational patterns are needed to
insure a good and consistent standard of service. However, highly
decentralized exceptions which produce good service can be found.
One such system is described in Library Journal, in "Portrait of
a Library System: Country Style," in which Edward Overman and
Mary Anders present the distinctive organizational pattern of the
Knox County Library, Knox County, Tennessee. [8]

The Knox County system consists of a headquarters library,
12 community libraries, and 35 stations served by bookmobile. The
12 community libraries are staffed by local personnel, and collections ranged from 1,000 to 8,000 in 1962. What is distinctive
about this system?

1. It is highly decentralized. Each of the 12 community
libraries has its board, there are committees for the book stations,

and several hundred citizens are involved in some aspect of library affairs. The community boards do more than advise. They determine policy, in cooperation with the county library board, and select their librarian, with the county board reserving the right to veto if the person selected does not meet standards.

2. The community orientation is outstanding. The local librarians live a role of community service. They work with P. T. A. 's, home demonstration units, and church groups. They attend systematic in-service training conferences and workshops conducted with the help of staff members of the Library Science department of the University of Tennessee.

3. Community clubs and other organizations provide the buildings. Shelving, furniture, and movable equipment are ordinarily provided from county tax funds. Public funds are also used for maintenance and alterations. Many people and organizations thus have an attachment to the library.

4. Communication and community services are maintained at a high level through 200 library committees appointed by the various groups and organizations in the county. A directory is published by county headquarters each year with the names, addresses, and telephone numbers of committee members. Copies are mailed to more than 100 community organizations to aid them in communicating with each other. The library teams up with the University of Tennessee, Knox County, and the Council of Community Clubs to secure the publication of a citizens' handbook on the organization and operation of the government of Knox County, assuring wide distribution. Lay readers are used for book reviews in the Knox County Monthly Bulletin.

These are "peoples" libraries, exerting a definite impact on their respective communities. The Knox County organization is cited because it represents a highly commendable integration with the area it serves and provides a rarely equalled degree of communication between branches, among branches and organizations, and between branches and county government.

Decentralization can be an asset when the various units of a system can work together with such a degree of harmony and

communication. It can be a detriment to good service if there is
a lack of coordination and the various branches go off in all
directions at once. In such a situation centralization may be necessary for good service.

The Evansville Public Library, Evansville, Indiana, divides
responsibility and services between the Central building and the
branches. In some respects the organization is typical, being
quite centralized, but it has some interesting variations such as
channeling all book reserves through Central, pooling of all
juvenile books and records, and the use of one master story teller
to tour the branches.

Much of the branch activity is coordinated through offices
at Central Library. For example, substitute workers during vacations, vacancies or illness are sent from an office at Central;
long overdue book records are turned over to Central for settling;
all book reserves are channeled through a central clearing house
to be located through the union catalog for any patron in any part
of the city; all juvenile books and phonograph records belong to
one big pool collection and are assigned or re-assigned to branches
as needed.

All displays at Central and in each branch are worked out
by two full-time staff artists, relieving each branch of this worry
and freeing branch closets of the miscellaneous display items which
usually require special storage facilities. All pre-school story
hours, film showings, creative writing clubs, puppet clubs, book
discussion groups, etc., are co-ordinated by Central staff members
in cooperation with branch personnel. Evansville finds it better to
have one very good story teller tour the branches on a publicized
schedule than to insist on each branch librarian telling stories.

A three-man Book Order Committee, consisting of a branch
head, a professional worker from the Central Adult Information Department, and the Director or Assistant Director, meets weekly to
compile an approved list of books to be purchased, based on the
written book selection policy. This list is distributed to all department and branch librarians who commit their own funds for the

books they choose. They may elect to rent certain titles from the
American Lending Service, $2500 a year being budgeted for this pur-
pose. Two new branches had book allotments of $10,000 in 1968,
and approximately $100,000 in book funds went to establish basic
collections in each of these two branches.

The organization of the Hawaiian libraries is of interest because
branch libraries in Hawaii are actually direct branches of the State
Library System and are closely linked with school libraries.   Each
island has a central library, and they in turn are divisions or
branches of the state library.   They exercise supervision over the
branches and school libraries on their island.

The close relationship between school and public libraries
seems to have existed because the office of library services for
Hawaii is a division of the Department of Education.

Community libraries meet the most frequent needs of library
users with general resources and basic collections of classic and current reading material in subjects of general interest to all ages. School
libraries request appropriate materials from community libraries. The
regional libraries provide higher levels of information, reference service, and bibliographical resources, as well as more comprehensive
collections of both general and specialized interest. Six existing libraries with strong collections are designated as regional libraries
and one was being constructed in 1968.   The Hawaii State Library
serves as the research library, providing highly specialized research
materials and extensive collections of indexes, abstracting services,
back files of periodicals, microfilm materials, and government
documents.

Rating Chart for Branch-Headquarters Relationship

This chart, excerpted from A Survey of the Branches Service
of a Multi-County Library System prepared by the Mississippi Library Commission, Jackson, Mississippi, provides a handy means
for assessing relationship factors as they exist, and for the library
director, branch supervisor, and branch librarian to discuss possible improvements.

Relationship Between Branch and Headquarters

			Yes	No	Comment
A.	From Branch to Headquarters				
1.	Does the branch librarian know				
	a.	Names of counties in the library system.			
	b.	Names of the other branches in the library system.			
	c.	Chief librarian or the director of the system.			
	d.	Name of the assistant director.			
	e.	Name of Branch Supervisor.			
	f.	How the library gets its financial support.			
	g.	Names of the members of the library board of trustees of the library system.			
	h.	Names of the members of the local library board or committee, if any.			
2.	Does the branch librarian make regular visits to headquarters?				
3.	Does the branch librarian seem to understand the philosophy of the larger unit of service?				
4.	Does the branch librarian seem to appreciate the benefits of being part of a larger unit of service?				
5.	The branch librarian sends to headquarters:				
	a.	Monthly circulation record			
	b.	Monthly financial record			
	c.	Monthly narrative report			
	d.	Copies of all publicity about the library			
	e.	Intermittent reports of special events, problems, etc. via letter			
	f.	Intermittent reports of special events, etc. via telephone			
	g.	Intermittent reports of special events, problems, etc. via Branch Supervisor			
	h.	Notice of planned absences from the library			
	i.	Notice of emergency absences from the library			

6. What specific help does the branch librarian feel that she receives from the Branch Supervisor?

7. What help would this branch librarian like to have from headquarters or Branch Supervisor that she does not get?

B. From Headquarters to Branch   Yes   No   Comment

	Yes	No	Comment
1. Does the chief librarian or director visit the branch library?			
2. Does the Branch Supervisor make regularly scheduled visits to the branch library?			
3. Does the library system make provisions for regular staff meetings?			

    4. How does headquarters inform branch librarian of:
       a. Special events planned for the system?
       b. Interesting and unusual happenings throughout the system?
       c. New books received?
       d. Changes in policy?
       e. Changes in personnel?
       f. Changes in schedule?

    5. What specific help does the Branch Supervisor give the branch librarian?

Notes

1. Library Journal. Editorial. v. 93, no. 11, June 1, 1968. p. 2189.

2. Jefferson, George. Public Library Administration. Philosophical Library, 1966.

3. Smith, Geoffrey. "County Headquarters and Branches: The Headquarters Viewpoint." Library Association Record. v. 63, no. 4, April, 1961. p. 128-30.

4. Charlton, B. M. "County Headquarters and Branches: The Branch Viewpoint." Library Association Record. v. 63, no. 4, April, 1961, p. 128-30.

5. Wheeler, Harold L., Goldhor, Herbert. Practical Administration of Public Libraries. Harper and Row, c 1962. p. 417.

6. Ibid. p. 419-20.

7. Frantz, John C. "Big City Libraries: Strategy and Tactics for Change." Library Journal, v. 93, no. 10, May 15, 1968.

8. Overman, Edward S., Anders, Mary E. "Portrait of a Library System: Country Style." Library Journal, v. 87, no. 6, Mar. 15, 1962. p. 1084-88.

Chapter 6

Tailoring the Branch to the Community

The term "community" is defined in this chapter as a neigh-borhood area served by a city branch, or as a small town or open area in the country served by a rural branch or affiliated town li-brary. City branches will be considered first.

A commonly encountered attitude is that to insure good ser-vice in a neighborhood branch all that is necessary is to build an attractive building of adequate size, equip it with a good materials collection, staff it with a sufficient number of people, and open the doors. Library service, of a kind, will result from such hit-or-miss extension, and perhaps there will also be a respectable circu-lation, but the quality of service will be far below what it could and should be.

A careful survey of an area, based on past studies and cur-rent findings, together with certain criteria to be discussed under "Choosing a Site," will initially determine whether a proposed site is feasible for a branch. When a suitable site has been selected the community study should determine the type of collection, the kind of staff, the physical facilities to be provided, the service program and even the architectural style, function, and appearance of the buildings and grounds. At least ten factors should be studied and considered in relation to the proposed branch:

1. The Racial Composition of the Area: This is highly important. In a predominantly colored area, for example, there should be at least two, and possibly more, colored staff members. Books with Negro heroes and heroines or biographies of Negro leaders in all fields should be in the collection, the Negro's love of music, for example, should be reflected in a sizeable collection of good material in this field.

132

Where a large part of the population of an area is Mexican, or Cuban, many books in Spanish for the older generation who do not speak English, books for learning English, and books which emphasize the cultural heritage of Mexico or Cuba, their music, legends, and customs, should be stocked in generous supply. This general pattern should hold true with reference to any race or nationality which is substantially represented in the community. Contrary to the opinion that immigrants or Americans of old-world extraction prefer to forget their own language and customs and become thoroughly Americanized, it has been this author's experience that the majority of the so-called "foreigners" have a definite pride in their own country or ancestry and wish to preserve it for their children, together with adjustments to the American pattern of living.

2. The Economic Status of the People in the service area of any branch cannot be disregarded because it basically affects the educational status, standard of living, and recreational interests of the inhabitants. A branch in a culturally disadvantaged or poverty area would enjoy little popularity or use if its collection consisted almost entirely of scholarly books or reading geared to middle-class suburbia.

Such a branch should instead stock a large number of books for slow readers, including high-interest but low-vocabulary "stepping stone" material. Much adult non-fiction could well be on the junior and senior high school levels. Audio-visual material of all types, would be highly desirable. One reason that branches in poor areas are often little used is that not enough effort has been made to interest the potential readers at their current reading level, nor enough follow-up effort to raise that level, slowly and unobtrusively.

Non-users in such an area are a particular problem. A branch in a poor neighborhood should use every legitimate, known device to lure possible patrons into the library and to convert them to borrowers. Free movie programs, contests, special-incentive reading projects, story hours combined with games, music, puppets, and similar activities are in order. In culturally-disadvantaged and foreign or racial areas it is vitally important that the branch

library reach out into its community actively, continuously, and ex-
citingly if it is to accomplish its objectives.   This means a careful
selection of materials, staff, location, and activities, as well as
public relations lures planned to fit type of clientele.   A very successful program for reaching the unreached was instituted by Mrs.
Harriet E. Bard, librarian of the Morrisson-Reeves Library,
Richmond, Indiana, in the summer of 1964, before the widespread
government programs for poverty areas were in full swing. [1]   For
a description of this program, see the chapter on Service Programs
and Activities.

    3.   Business and Industries in the Area will influence strongly
the collection and activities of a carefully-planned branch.   How
large should the business collection be in comparison with the
central business collection?   Can local business men be induced to
call on the branch staff for ready reference information and material or will they rely entirely on the central library?   Can business
or industry personnel be persuaded to help advertise branch services through their employee organizations?   How can the branch
reach the children of factory workers, or busy employees who do
not realize that a library is not just a place for recreational reading and children?

    Obviously, the system's policy on centralization or decen-
tralization of services will largely determine the answers to some
of these questions, but in pre-planning a branch it is advisable to
discuss such questions with business executives and factory managers
in the area.

    There is another aspect to this type of contact.   A key
industry or business in a neighborhood may take sufficient interest
in the establishment of a branch to contribute money, furnishings,
or such items as landscaping, signs, or books.   In the City of
Fullerton, California, the Hunt Foods Foundation, one of the leading industries, actually donated the land and built a beautiful branch
near its plant, at a total cost of around $500,000.

    4.   The Age Levels and Ranges in any service area obvious-
ly have to be considered in determining the proportionate size

of the adult and juvenile collections, the amount of staff time to be devoted to children's or young people's services, and the amount of space allotted to the children's, young people's, and adult collections and activities.   In areas of lower economic level there are usually more children per family.   If no recent community survey is available, information as to age range and levels may often be secured from the local school district or individual schools.   Checking on the number and size of schools may also provide a good indication of the proportion of children and high school-age people in relation to the adult population.

5. The Strengths and Weaknesses of School Libraries in a neighborhood community are potent factors in planning a branch service program.   Are there libraries in all the schools?   Do the elementary schools have trained librarians or non-professionals? Are they part or full-time?   If part-time, are they teacher-librarians or outsiders brought in for a few hours each week?

How about junior and senior high schools in the area?   Does a visit to these libraries reveal well-chosen collections planned to supplement the school curriculum, or heterogeneous collections of fiction and non-fiction inferior to the collections in the neighborhood branch?   The writer is thinking in this connection of school libraries she has visited in which the Carolyn Keenes, the Cherry Ames, the Hardy Boys, and similar series donated by parents and children occupied much of the shelf space, with only a sprinkling of classics and recommended books in between.   This type of school library is diminishing in number, but too many remain.

If the schools are doing a good job of providing supplementary, school-oriented material, the public library branch can happily forego this task and concentrate on recreational reading and the normal proportion of factual material to be found in the average non-school oriented branch.   No public library should allow itself to become just another school library because the school libraries may be inadequate.   However, in some areas where there is an almost indissoluble organizational or political connection between school and public libraries, or where the public libraries are administered by a Board of Education, the ideal balance in collections cannot always be attained.

The content of the branch library's juvenile and young adult collections must, however, bear some working relationship to the quality and quantity of children's and young people's books available in neighborhood school libraries. Even though public library branches should not become extensions of school libraries, good public library-school library cooperation is important if the best results are to be attained by either library. School and public librarians should cooperate, for example, in avoiding duplication of highly-expensive reference sets or highly-specialized material.

6. <u>Library Facilities Other than School Libraries</u> may be available in the service area. There may, for example, be a county library headquarters located only a few blocks from a city branch. Some county headquarters provide lending and reference service to city residents as well as to those living outside of cities. While such an arrangement leads to duplication of effort it does exist in some communities, and in such cases city residents can use either library freely. A case in point was Klamath Falls, Oregon, where for years the city and county libraries were located only about a block apart but have now combined. As county and city libraries combine into systems, this problem will gradually diminish. Even in situations where no legal or federated connection seems possible, friendly cooperation between the librarians is important if either library is to operate at maximum effectiveness.

There is also the possibility that a specialized library may be located in the same area--a law library, art or music library, hospital library or armed forces library. Any of these can affect the potential use, service program, and collection of a public library branch.

Although the potential influence of a hospital library's collection on a public library's collection may appear to be slight, it can influence use because doctors, nurses and other employees, as well as patients, will have an ever-ready supply of reading immediately on hand at the hospital. They are not likely to use the services of the public library branch regularly, unless it happens to have a sub-branch offering library service to the hospital in lieu of a hospital-operated library.

A law library should not offer much competition to a branch, since few branches are likely to invest very heavily in expensive legal reference books. However, every branch librarian should be aware of the existence and general resources of a legal or any other special library in his or her service area, and if and when such facilities are available to the public.

The existence of a specialized branch such as the Brand Art and Music Branch of the Glendale Public Library, Glendale, California, usually means that the nearest branches, or perhaps all the branches in a city system, stock fewer books in these fields. In such cases other branches depend upon the specialized branch to supply all needs directly or via delivery of requested specialized materials to the other branch outlets.

Occasionally, large factories may provide a small library for their employees. Larger churches often set up a religious library for their parishioners. Public librarians have sometimes been unaware of the full extent of library resources within their service areas. In planning branch services a thorough analysis of the area is a desirable safeguard in this respect.

7. Organizations and Social Life can be an important factor. Some areas are over-organized, others have a dearth of clubs and social life. Where there are many organizations, public and private, such as women's groups, men's service clubs, hobby groups, etc., the branch library can be affected in many ways. For example:

A. A real need may exist for a small auditorium in the branch, to be used with or without charge for local meetings or events. Obviously, such a room should be included in the original building plans if preliminary contacts with area groups indicate that it would be used and appreciated. It can, of course, be planned as a later addition, if it is impossible at the beginning.

Sometimes a wealthy local resident will provide all or part of such a room as a memorial.

B. Branch personnel can offer their services to groups for book reviews, program planning, story telling, workshops and similar activities.   Such talks provide incentives to increased library use.

C. Organizations will often provide help, financial or personal, for worthwhile library projects.   Art groups can sponsor displays of paintings and crafts; club members who are specialists in one area or another (photography, weaving, horsemanship, etc.) can recommend excellent books in the fields they know best.   Most groups will be willing to help advertise the library's services if given suggestions and materials for doing so.

D. Organizations already existing in a neighborhood can provide representative members for forming a "Friends of the Library" group.

E. Where there is little worthwhile social activity a neighborhood branch can and should sponsor adult education activities such as Great Books or Great Discussion groups, if the caliber of the neighborhood warrants it, or story telling classes for parents and other adults, open houses, recruitment teas, public lectures, informal concerts, free travel movies or slides by local people, or any worthwhile activity which will draw people in and make them friends and users of the library.   Any branch that helps to fill a gap in neighborhood social activity is "reaching out" to the people in its service area.

8.   Recreational Interests of the Area are too often overlooked in book selection and in planning the service program.   Is there a roller skating rink in the neighborhood, a golf course, a riding academy, bowling alleys, a jujitsu or karate parlor, a public stadium for athletic events?   Are there lakes or streams nearby for fishing or boating, tennis courts, dance halls, public and/or private swimming pools, public parks with organized game program

What recreational interests predominate? Does the presence of
snow and ice in winter presage increased interest in books on ski-
ng or ice skating? These and other questions will be asked by the
alert branch librarian. The inescapable conclusion, again, is that
a good branch librarian and, for that matter, the general director
of a library system, must be thoroughly acquainted with the area
surrounding the proposed or established branch. What is in the
area? Who is in the area, and where are the groups and individuals to be used as key contacts? It is a complex task but an important one. A business promoter contemplating opening a business
in a new area rarely does so without inspecting, inquiring, and
analyzing the entire area of potential service before a location is
chosen. Libraries, in establishing branches, should be just as
painstaking and as thorough.

9. Cultural Levels and Interests. Is the area one that has
many artists, many musicians? Are the organizations on a fairly
high cultural level? Is there an interest in opera, or in the racial
culture of other lands? These factors are closely coupled with the
educational level of the area and with the availability of cultural
events. Does a local community college sponsor good plays, concerts, speakers, other programs? Are there adult evening classes
in local colleges or high schools that trigger requests for non-fiction
of the more thoughtful literary, psychological, or philosophical type?

10. Miscellaneous Factors: Other factors which may affect a
branch in its service program, security measures, or staffing, are
the crime rate of the area, the presence or absence of nearby police
protection, the nearness of a place to deposit monies taken in over
the desk, the harmony of appearance of buildings and grounds with
surrounding buildings or homes, and the transportation facilities in
the area. Can non-car owners such as elderly pensioners get to
the library by public transportation or must they always call a taxi?
All the factors listed affect the type of clientele, and they in turn
affect the building, service program, collection, and staff of a
branch.

The point to be emphasized is that the most successful
branches are planned after many diverse external factors have been

taken into consideration. Obviously, the size of a building and the extent of service are limited by available funds, but it is better not to provide branch service at all than to provide such poor service because of financial limitations that patrons receive a poor opinion of library service in general. This chapter is concerned only with environmental and human factors which influence branch planning. Building planning, based upon a previously planned service program, will be discussed in a later chapter.

The Rural Branch:

How do the foregoing ten factors influence the structure, staffing and program of a rural branch? As far as racial composition and economic status, age levels, cultural and recreational interest, organizations and social life, quality of school libraries or presence of other libraries are concerned, their application to and influence upon the rural branch are just as important as in a city.

Recreational interests may vary from those of city dwellers; the racial concentration may be less or more varied; other library facilities will be found less often; social life may be more limited and of a somewhat different nature; organizations will follow recreational, religious, and agricultural patterns; and agriculture, fishing mining, or lumbering are more apt to be the occupations influencing book collections and reference service. Service to varied businesse and industry will be more limited, except in those areas where industry is moving away from the outskirts of cities and into the smaller towns and open country where land is cheaper and expansion space more available and is often offered free to attract industry; taxes may be lower, and zoning restrictions less arduous. Rural branches may therefore find themselves faced with more reference demands from business and industry in the future.

An enterprising rural branch will make it a point to seek out industry in its area and offer special service to any company which does not maintain a library of its own. Even in the case of companies which do have libraries cooperation with the specialized

library should be offered. The basic human and environmental factors which influence a branch in its operation, structure, collection,
and staff should not vary greatly from city to country.

How does one proceed to make a study of a potential service
area? Or of an area in which the branch program does not seem to
be functioning effectively? Ideas for a community survey are suggested in the following outline of the public library administration
course at the University of Alabama:[2]

Why Study the Community?

A library fulfills its educational function by meeting the needs
of the people it serves. These needs must be discovered before
they can be met. One way of discovering these needs is to gather
various kinds of information about the community. But first it is
necessary to understand how this information is going to be useful.

Why Do We Need the Information?

a) to be able to know what books and other materials we
need to buy;
b) to enable us to set goals for planning our services;
c) to help us to plan special activities;
d) to enable us to develop an effective public relations
program;
e) to establish working relationships with other agencies and
organizations;
f) to give the staff insight and understanding about the community based on concrete knowledge;
g) to determine the library's educational role in the community.

What do We Look for?

a) the backgrounds of the people;
b) the kinds of jobs they hold;
c) how much money they are earning, spending, saving;
d) the organizations and churches they belong or do not
belong to;
e) the kinds of houses they live in;
f) the recreation they enjoy;
g) how old they are;
h) how much formal education they have had;
i) the opportunities they have for further learning.

Where Do We Go To Find Out?

a) to newspapers;
b) to census reports;
c) to town, city, county records;
d) to individuals;
e) to private and governmental agencies;
f) to organizations.

The facts about the community are related to the services of the library. These services are measured against the needs the study reveals, and future plans are built around this information.

To be more specific, what questions do we ask about the neighborhood we hope to serve or to serve better? The following is a sample outline for a community analysis. A service program can be based on its results. The proper physical facilities can be planned around the service program. Too often, the reverse procedure is used. The branch building is planned and the service program is then worked out to fit the facilities.

The Community: An Outline for an Analysis (based on Administration of the Small Public Library, by Dorothy Sinclair) [3]

Age Levels and Proportions:

How many children? Young adults? Older people? Foreign Language Groups?

Education:

How many with college degrees?
Other education levels? Or particular skills?
Adult Education groups?

Economic Facts:

Occupational patterns: industries, small businesses, farms, professions.
Workers: skilled, unskilled?
Changes: rural, urban, suburban?

Schools and Colleges:

Elementary: private, public, pre-school
Secondary
Junior Colleges, Technical Schools
Colleges and Universities

Community Habits:

Size and type of homes
Recreations
Shopping at home or in big cities
Major interests

Cultural Opportunities:

>Concerts, Art Exhibits
>Theaters, Museums
>Lectures
>Amateur Groups

Civic Interests and Problems:

>Patterns of community growth
>Needs for expanded facilities
>Matters of public concern

Churches:

>How many, what denominations?
>How large? With libraries?
>Is there a ministerial association?
>Weekly programs: Meetings, discussion groups, summer
>   programs for children?
>Has any church made a community survey?

Clubs and Organizations:

>Service clubs
>Special interest hobby groups
>Book and current affairs discussion and action
>Civic groups
>Senior citizens
>Scouts, etc.

Institutions:

>Hospitals
>Health Clinics
>Welfare institutions, penal institutions

Government--Levels and Patterns:

>Mayor, council: city manager
>Agencies: State, National, Extension (i. e. Farm Bureau,
>   Home Demonstration)
>Federal

Physical Features:

>Rivers, lakes, farm ponds, bridges
>Mountains, unusual terrain
>Highways
>Railroads, Airports

Unique, Particular, or Famous Features:

> e. g. Statue to the Bollweevil in Enterprise, new causeway in
> Mobile, TVA or Martin Dam, Guntersville Lake, Little River
> Canyon (Desoto Park), Chewacla State Park.

Is the area included in studies for industry, state planning board surveys, or Chamber of Commerce literature?

If a branch has had a good record of adult usage and then experiences a decline which cannot be traced to outside factors, here is a self-study outline adapted to branches which may help to discover the problem and make it possible to tailor the branch more closely to the community.

A Branch Self-Study[4]

The purpose of a branch self-study is to find how well the branch is doing in relation to the adult education goals of the library. The branch librarian, the library director and the staff work together to assess the service and to discover ways to improve its effectiveness. Studying the Community, published by the Community Project Headquarters Staff of A. L. A. , is highly recommended as a tool for community study.

The Library Administration and Branch Head Will Want to Explore Such Questions as These: Do the branch objectives include statement of purpose which indicates adult educational goals? Does the book selection policy reflect an emphasis on adult educational functions? Does any policy statement indicate under what circumstances the facilities of the branch may be used by the community?

The Staff Will Want to Explore Such Questions as These: Are the purchase practices of the library in accord with the book selection policy? Do the patrons complain about the book selection or the unavailability of many needed titles? Is the public relations program geared to educational objectives? Are there changes in routines and job assignments that can be made that will release more professional time to carry out the educational purposes of the library?

The information gathered should be interpreted by asking such questions as these:

If we Lack Materials Is It: (a) for want of funds? (b) for want
of attention to our goals? (c) for lack of knowledge of what is needed?

If Our Circulation Indicates Inadequate Use of Our Educational
Materials, Is It Because: (a) our materials are out of date? (b) we
are not buying in relation to our community's needs? (c) people do
not know that we have these materials?

If all Population Groupings in Our Community Are Not Proportionately Represented In Our Registration, Is It Because: our
services are not geared to several educational levels? our services
are not geared to the particular needs of certain groups? our public
relations do not reach all kinds of people? our hours of opening and
closing are not convenient for certain groups? our location is a
handicap? our staff is not convinced of the branch's responsibility
for meeting the educational needs of its own community?

If Our Users Are Not Satisfied, Is It Because: we lack appropriate materials? we are not providing adequate staff services?
we do not interpret the services of the library sufficiently?

The following is a sample of the background material used by
the City of Newport Beach, California in planning for a new branch
dedicated in 1968:

> To do an adequate job, the Library must know the com-
> munity, and the community must be aware of the Library
> and its services.

> City of Newport Beach
> Incorporated 1906 (no library) Population: 445
> Population growth:
> 1950 Official Census (1 library   12,120
>   2,200 sq. st.)
> 1960 Official Census (2 libraries--   26,564
>   total 6,000 sq. st.)
> 1966   (3 libraries--   40,060
>   14,028 sq. ft.)
> 1985   Projected
>   Population: 117,105

> Newport Beach is a development of well-planned manufac-
> turing, trade (wholesale and retail), finance, insurance,
> and real estate establishments. Among the five largest
> industries are Aeronutronics, a division of Philco, Hughes
> Aircraft, Rosan Incorporated, Lido Shipyards, and
> Western Canneries.

According to the United States Bureau of Census, Newport
Beach is among the highest in the county on the educational range. Statistics show that the years of education
for the male are 13.5 and an average of 12.8 for the
female. These figures are for the 1960 census, and the
educational standards have been considerably higher since
then, according to Mr. Al Bell of the Orange County
Census Bureau.

The cultural and educational institutions attended are the
University of California, Irvine; and Orange Coast Junior
College. Private schools (kindergarten through 12th grade
total 2,505 students, and 23,816 attend public K-12, making
total of 26,331 students from K-12.

The absence of school libraries places an increased burde
on the branch libraries at the elementary school level.
The defeat of the recent school bonds eliminated the projected plan for this function, and also for the high school
to maintain evening hours.

Forty-one (41) classes have scheduled monthly visits at
the 3rd and 4th grade level which enables each Newport
Beach child to have a library card at 9 years of age.

The Friends of the Library hold book discussion groups.
Several organizations are active in the fine arts field,
with art and music generally popular. Special interest
groups; professional men's and women's service clubs;
women's clubs; most of which call upon the library for
programs or for study materials. The library strives to
achieve a balance among the various group interests as
a primary goal.

Library statistics reflect: 9.5 books per capita are read
by our citizens. 20,603 citizens use the library.

In closing, let us quote from a statement by Lowell Martin
in his study, Branch Library Service for Dallas. Although this
statement was made more than ten years ago, it still holds true:

"By their very nature, branch libraries should each be individual and different. Each serves a distinct community with special
interests and needs, and effective branch service takes account of
such variations. A good branch library is an integral part of its
locality, not a stereotyped copy stamped out in a central office."

"Nonethelsss there are certain basic conditions and general
principles that apply throughout a branch system. Variations and
deviations from these principles will emerge as branches adjust to

heir localities, but as they do they should be reviewed to be sure
hey represent genuine adaptation and not deficiencies."[5]

Notes

.   Bard, Harriet E. "Reaching the Unreached". Wisconsin Li-
      brary Bulletin. v. 62: Jan.-Feb., 1966, p. 7-15; same in
      Library Occurrent v. 22: May, 1966, p. 31-37.

2.   University of Alabama. Course outline in Public Library
      Administration.

3.   Sinclair, Dorothy. Administration of the Small Public Library.
      American Library Association, 1965, p. 11-13.

4.   American Library Association. Library Community Project.
      Studying the Community: A Basis for Planning Library Adult
      Education Services. American Library Association, 1960.
      Mimeographed.

5.   Martin, Lowell A. Branch Library Service for Dallas. The
      Library. Jan. 1, 1958, p. 64.

Chapter 7

Staffing the Branch

The ability and personality of the head librarian have much
to do with the success of a branch library. Since branches are
smaller and their staffs are fewer in number than in a central library or headquarters, individual staff members and patrons come
face to face much more often. Patrons frequently prefer to use a
branch because of its informality, the more personal relationship
with staff, and the greater ease in finding books and other material.
It is important that staff be carefully selected to encourage and retain this type of rapport.

Since the branch librarian is directly responsible for staff
behavior and attitudes, qualifications and duties of this position
should be considered first. The man or woman given the leadership
of a branch should be a good organizer, supervisor, and politician,
the latter because it is necessary to please at least four, and possibly five different groups: the public, the staff, the central staff,
other branch heads, and the central administrative head or library
director. In the case of the librarian of a small community branch
affiliated with a system, the list includes the public, the staff, a
system staff and head, and a local library board to which she may
be directly responsible.

The branch librarian must like dealing with all ages, be
willing to work all kinds of odd hours in case of staff emergencies,
be capable of filling any position in her branch temporarily, be able
to participate in budget making, be able to cooperate with central
headquarters, know books, enjoy working with groups, be versatile,
tactful, and have executive ability. This is a formidable list of
qualifications, suggesting an ideal which few could match. However,
the degree to which the branch head is able to meet these qualifications will affect the branch library's success or failure.

The branch librarian's duties will vary, of course, depending on whether the branch is a county branch in a cooperative system, an average-sized urban branch serving 25,000 people or more, a large regional branch, or a very small village branch loosely affiliated with a county or regional library system. Primarily, however, the branch librarian must provide leadership in the development of an effective staff and service, build up branch services, help to select and evaluate the personnel, supervise the daily work program, coordinate activities with the central agency, encourage efficient performance by the individual staff member, correct shortcomings, and foster high morale within the branch. Specific duties, all or part of which any branch librarian may perform, include:

1. The branch librarian's _first_ job is to become a specialist on the community served by his agency by understanding its social relationships, background, and developing trends. This requires time to attend organization meetings, to talk with key people, and to attend meetings or appear on programs. It means working with the public in the library as well.

2. The second job is administration. This includes planning, directing, receiving and writing reports, making evaluations and operational studies; doing professional reading, personnel administration, public relations; carrying responsibility for building maintenance, the public service program, and possibly branch budgeting. It means doing all or part of the book selection, the staff scheduling, and the planning of the in-service training programs.

Physical separation from the main library inevitably places upon the branch librarian a greater responsibility than that carried by a department head at Central. The branch head must meet emergencies, make decisions, and interpret established policies without a group of her peers at hand to advise and encourage her.

3. If the branch librarian is a professional, and sometimes she is not, she will aid in the selection of the books and other materials for the branch by attending cooperative book selection meetings at the central library or system headquarters, by working from lists supplied from the central headquarters, or by accepting

choices made by Central and supplementing them with selections
based on her own community's special needs and interests. A professional librarian should always be given a voice in book selection.
No one at headquarters can possibly be as much aware of the every
day needs and demands of a branch clientele which may vary considerably from the clientele of another branch in a different area in
the same system.

Should the branch librarian be a non-professional and be
limited in her knowledge of books, as is the case in some small
community branches in rural systems, the headquarters book selection group may pass on all branch selections or provide basic selections.   The branch head who may know her community better than
her books should still be able to initiate buying suggestions.

One of the duties usually required of a branch head is to
make a monthly and annual report to the Extension Head, Branch
Supervisor, or Library Director, whichever is her immediate
superior.   Brevity is important, but no important matters should be
omitted.   Material should be topically arranged and in logical order.
Short sub-titles or topics in the left-hand margin help to highlight
the information and permit the reader to see at a glance what is
covered.

If a branch librarian is required to make regular reports, as
she should be, it is important that she keep notes on all important
facts, figures and events as they occur throughout the month.   Such
a practice insures that the report will be complete, aids brevity,
and gives more time for the final writing.

The busy supervisor will be grateful to the branch head who
can give her reports written in an interesting, entertaining style but
which are also succinct.   Studying some of the material written to
aid business executives in preparing good reports can be of assistan
to the librarian who would like to improve this technique.   Topics
which might be mentioned or discussed in a branch report include:

    a) Circulation for the month: brief comments and total figures
       Try to account for any sudden changes in circulation,
       either up or down.

b) Reference questions handled, including any unusual or difficult questions.
c) Trends in reading of patrons or changes in type of readers using the branch.
d) Booklists produced, displays arranged, posters, pictures, newspaper stories, other publicity activities during the month.
e) Service to special groups.
f) Personnel changes, if any.
g) In-service training activities of any type.
h) Librarian's and staff attendance at staff and professional meetings and workshops.
i) Noteworthy additions to the collection by gift or purchase.
j) Any rearrangement of shelves or library areas.
k) Any new or special services added.
l) Any new time-saving device, procedure, or equipment introduced.
m) Number of discards and additions to the collection. Any special weeding project.
n) Outstanding accomplishments of any staff member in or out of the library.
o) Community contacts made during the month outside of the library (visits to schools, playgrounds, hospitals, talk to organizations, book reviews given).
p) Progress of any special project underway at the branch.
r) Plans for the next month.
s) Long-range plans

Seldom would all of these topics be included in any one report, but the first two and the last two are usually routine inclusions. From time to time it will be expedient to mention outstanding needs, repeating these as often as necessary until some action is taken. The annual report will include the highlights of the monthly reports.

In order to write a complete report for her supervisor, the branch librarian needs information from the people on the branch staff. Here is a suggested form (from the Alabama Public Library Service) for keeping a record of the children's activities. This would be turned in to the branch head each month by the children's librarian.

Report of Children's Activities

_____Public Library,_____County

_____Reporting

Story Hour, _____, _____
_____, 197__.
Theme:_____
Attendance
Number of Children:_____.
Number of Adults_____.
Materials:
Titles of books talked about:_____

_____
Recording Used:_____
Overall number of books displayed and talked about:_____
Title of film used: _____
Activities:
Names of games played:_____
Stories told or read:_____
Poem(s) read or recited:_____
Others:_____
Comments: _____

The librarian in charge of a branch in a county or regional system,
an affiliated or member library:

Personnel or staffing problems of county and regional branch
es, as well as of system-affiliated libraries in smaller communities
differ somewhat from those of branches in city systems.   City
systems usually have less difficulty in securing professional head
librarians for branches, because city salaries are usually higher,
fringe benefits are better, and branches are larger.   Also, some
people do not wish to live in smaller communities.   Thus community branches in the so-called "rural" areas often have a higher
percentage of non-professional librarians.   Many of these are local
residents who have been librarians for many years, often before the
community library joined a system as a branch or federation
member.

An outsider brought in to head a small community branch
may not receive the same cooperation as the local resident, even
though the latter may not be as well qualified.   If professionals or

high-level sub-professionals are sent out from headquarters, they
need to have unusual tact, poise, skill, leadership and personality
in order successfully to manage an operation so close to the hearts
and minds of the local residents. They must get along with local
library boards, if those still exist, with the library staff, with the
"powers that be" in the community, with their superiors at headquarters, and with the patrons. Without the advantage of previous
residence in the community, this is no small task. Thus, if there
is a local resident who is qualified, who has the attributes of a
good librarian, and who knows the community, she may be the
best choice to head a county or regional branch or a library which
is a member of a federated system. The young, ambitious professional starting in a smaller branch may regard the assignment merely as a stepping stone and in some cases may not take
the trouble to acquire the necessary "feel" of the community.

The choice of a branch librarian in the small community
should be a painstaking process. It is not the place to put a welfare recipient.

There are small branches or community libraries in some
systems where the entire staff consists of one librarian and perhaps
one assistant, part- or full-time. In most cases the librarian will
be a non-professional and her duties will include the following as
outlined in the job description for a branch or community librarian
in a very small agency, in the Mississippi Library Commission's
Trustee Manual:[1]

Specific responsibilities:
1. Acts as good will ambassador for the library in the
   community or neighborhood.
2. Charges and discharges books and other material
   (when helper is not available).
3. Assists patrons in locating material and in using the
   library.
4. Makes personal contacts with clubs and groups in her
   area.
5. Contacts sick people and shut-ins. (Uses volunteer help
   such as Y-teens, Scouts, civic and church groups
   to help).
6. Encourages school class visits to the library.
7. Cooperates with school librarians in every way possible.

8.   Learns the collection and other resources of her
     branch.
9.   Scans all new books carefully before they are shelved.
10. Sees that shelves are kept in proper order. Reads
     shelves periodically or sees that they are read by
     her assistant.
11. Scans reserves and makes records of most requested
     types of books or titles. Also keeps in touch with
     reference requests to ascertain what reference books
     are lacking. Transmits these requests to whomever
     has the responsibility for ordering books for the
     branch.
12. Handles any complaints or special problems that arise.
13. Cooperates with local board (if there is one), local
     governmental jurisdiction, and system supervisors
     and staff for a smooth working operation in her
     branch or member library.
14. Attends system book order meetings and recommends
     titles for her branch.

Publicity:
1.   Sends news stories of library interest to local news-
     paper.
2.   Keeps attractive bulletin boards and other displays in
     the library.
3.   Plans displays outside the library (store windows,
     banks, real estate offices, barber shops, etc.).
4.   Actively seeks help from system consultant for
     publicity ideas.
5.   Gives book reviews and library talks at local
     organizations.

Routine duties:
1.   Makes regular written reports as required by the
     system headquarters.
2.   Sends out interlibrary loan requests for patrons.
3.   Keeps daily circulation records, reference tallies,
     and other statistics that are required or will be
     helpful.
4.   Sends or sees that overdue notices are sent.
     Occasionally makes home calls to recover unre-
     turned books where large sums or many books are
     involved.
5.   Registers new borrowers.
6.   Works with Friends of the Library group if one exists.
     Otherwise may form a group.
7.   Prepares or makes herself aware of all procedures
     and practices in the branch manual furnished by the
     system.
8.   Attends meetings and workshops as scheduled by system
     supervisors.
9.   Reads professional literature and attempts to keep up
     with new developments in the library world.

10. Sees that supplies are kept on hand and orders same
when depleted.
11. Supervises assistant or page and plans their work.
12. Sees that the library is kept looking clean and as
orderly as possible. Supervises janitor (may have
to do part of the work herself in very small units).

Duties of a Regional Branch Librarian
(As listed in the Tulsa (Oklahoma) City-County System)[2]

Nature of Work: This is administrative and professional
library work assisting the Chief of Extension in the management
of the branch libraries within a region.

Knowledges, abilities and skills: Previous professional and super-
visory experience.
Wide knowledge of the system organization, procedures, policy,
aims and service.
Skill in coordinating various branches and directing staff.
Initiative, resourcefulness, good judgment and tact.
Considerable knowledge of reader interest levels and a wide
knowledge of books and authors.
Ability to establish and maintain effective working relationships with
community groups, the public, and with other employees.

Desirable Experience and training: Experience in professional library
work including some experience in a responsible supervisory position; and graduation from an accredited college or university and
attainment of a graduate degree from an accredited school of library
science.

Description of Duties: Head librarian of regional branch.
Is familiar with the purposes of a regional library in order to formu-
late a service plan for the area.
Knows the community or area each branch serves within the region.
Immediately supervises the branches and personnel within the
specified region.
Advises and interprets library policies to branch librarians.
Schedules and supervises personnel within the region.
Holds regularly scheduled meetings at the regional library for branch
personnel.
Reviews merit evaluation sheets for all regional personnel before
sending to Chief of Extension.
Works periodically in each branch within the region to become
familiar with the book collections and the personnel.
Visits branches within the region at frequent intervals and sends
report to the Chief of Extension who will forward a list of
needed repairs, etc. to the people involved.
Reviews monthly reports from the branches within the region before
sending them to the Chief of Extension.
The Chief of Extension will continue to visit branches periodically.
Items which need to be discussed with branch librarians will

be first discussed with the regional librarian who will in
turn talk with the branch librarian.
All problems and suggested changes within a region should be made
known to the Chief of Extension who will make the final decision.
Makes written reports to her immediate superior.

Extension Head or Branch Supervisor:

The Extension Head and Branch Supervisor in a system are
not synonymous positions. Very large systems will have a Branch
Supervisor whose sole responsibility is branches; smaller systems
will combine the duties of branch and bookmobile supervision under
the title of Extension Head. As far as the branches are concerned,
however, the duties of either position will be quite similar. These
are included here because, although the Extension Head or Branch
Supervisor will work out of headquarters as a general rule, her
work is closely concerned with that of the branches, and her duties
are important in relation to those of the branch head.

As has been noted previously, the branch head's freedom to
make decisions, to establish procedures, and to hire personnel
will differ from system to system, but the tendency is toward allowing greater freedom in all but basic procedures. There is a
fine balance between the responsibilities of the branch supervisor
and the branch head. If it is a proper balance the relationship is
a cordial and stimulating one. If the supervisor is too conserva-
tive, too bound by tradition, or too dictatorial, the relationship can
be very unhappy. In general, the Extension Head or Branch Supervisor should do the following:

1. Assist the library director in planning for the establishment of new branches.

2. Make surveys of branch service in other places as to
costs, sites, size, book stock, number of employees, circulation,
etc. Read and study standards for branch construction and service.

3. Confer with branch head and give directions and suggestions regarding any problems. Personally handle and adjust
any complaints from branch staff concerning branch administration.

4. Assist in organizing and conducting in-service training
programs for staff of all branches.

5. Prepare monthly and annual narrative and statistical reports of the branch activities, using reports of the branch heads as a basis. Give these summary reports to library director.

6. Visit branches, observing work and service. Offer tactful suggestions for improvement.

7. Attend professional meetings and visit other libraries.

8. Interpret general library policy for all branches.

9. Assist with planning and writing of branch manual in cooperation with all branch heads.

10. Act as liaison person between branch head and library director to help secure extra help, equipment, or books needed during the budget year.

11. Conduct book order meetings in which all branch heads participate. May prepare lists.

12. Encourage the use of library resources through community and group contacts; participate actively in the observance of special weeks, such as Book Week or National Library Week.

13. Plan, recommend, and execute changes in organization approved by Director.

14. Make or assist branch head in making time and motion studies and work efficiency analyses. Recommend improvements growing out of these specialized studies.

15. Assist in preparing branch budgets or over-all extension budget which includes all branches. Confer with branch heads and library director before finalizing.

16. Assist individual branch heads in working out branch objectives and programs. Work out general objectives for total branch service.

17. Introduce new ideas and encourage branch heads and staff members to keep up with new developments in the library world through professional reading, attendance at workshops, taking classes in library science, etc.

18. May participate in programs or give book talks for outside groups. Branch librarians should do these things in their own areas; the supervisor might confine her efforts to areas where there are no branches or to all-city affairs.

19. Maintain files of pertinent information regarding buildings, book collection, operational techniques, any aspect of branch work.

20. As the administrator of branches under the direction of the Library Director, take final responsibility for decisions on important branch policy matters.

21. Stimulate and encourage the branch heads to know their community, to strive constantly to improve service, and to be original and creative.

The Extension Head or Branch Supervisor must have a wide knowledge of modern library organization, procedures, policies, aims, and services. He should have considerable ability in analyzing branch needs. Initiative, resourcefulness, good judgment, planning ability, and tact are important. In addition, considerable knowledge of reader tastes, a wide knowledge of books and authors, the ability to establish and maintain good working relationships with all branch heads, the library director, and fellow supervisors, and a knowledge of the area served by the system are necessary attributes. Desirable preparatory experience and training would include graduation from an accredited library school and several years of library experience in a supervisory or administrative capacity. Wheeler and Goldhor maintain that a branch supervisor is not needed in any library which has less than five large branches.[3] Five large branches plus bookmobile service could keep an Extension Head very busy, in this writer's view.

Need for a Branch Supervisor or Extension Head definitely exists if there are more than four or five units, whether bookmobiles or branches. If there is bookmobile service, such a position may be needed if there are only three branches. The position should be full-time, but if there are fewer than three units the position could probably be combined with one devoted to general public service supervision at the Central Library.

In most systems of any size there will be supervisors of children's services, adult services, extension services, and possibly young adult services. These specialists will work with the children's and young adult librarians and the head librarians at the branches. They should be policy makers and consultants, and should not administer details at the branches. The branch specialists need as much freedom as possible to develop the programs

within their own branches without receiving constant directives.
Too close supervision will dampen initiative and take the challenge
and fun out of the job for any staff member.

It creates difficulties for a branch librarian if the work of
staff members is supervised by two people whose opinions may differ.
The branch librarian should have the final decision on matters within her own branch, but she should cooperate with, actively seek the
advice of, and whenever possible heed the advice of the consulting
specialists from headquarters. The latter should serve in an advisory capacity, not in an administrative capacity within each
branch. If the supervisors from headquarters use the right
approach and achieve an understanding with each branch librarian,
there should be few problems. Any differences should be promptly
aired and settled. Merit ratings on specialized professional staff
members such as children's or reference librarians could well be
a joint responsibility of the branch head and the headquarters supervisor.

Much confusion seems to exist among the general public,
teachers, and even library boards as to what constitutes professional training or how to define "professional librarian." Some people
seem to be under the impression that a few library science courses
at a non-accredited institution, perhaps even one course, will produce a "trained" librarian. This thinking can be seen in some of
the courses offered in teacher-training institutions for school librarians wishing to meet state education department requirements
for varying minimum hours of credit. If professional standards
are to be maintained, the required degrees and kinds of training
need to be clarified and made more available to those who are concerned with hiring library personnel.

The acute shortage of professional personnel, however, has
forced many libraries to compromise, and this problem can only
be solved by an intensified program of recruitment for professional
staff and a continuing improvement in salaries and fringe benefits
competitive with other professional positions, particularly those in
the field of education.

Many branches are now staffed by non-professional head librarians who are doing an excellent job. These librarians may have come up through the ranks and have a fine background of experience in the system and in branch work, and some of them perform better than some professionals. However, when hiring new personnel every possible effort should be made to see that urban branches and community branches in county and regional systems are headed by fully-trained professionals. This is especially important where there are not enough branches to justify having an Extension Head or Branch Supervisor who will act as consultant. A few systems have solved the problem of professional supervision, at least partially, by having one professional head responsible for two of the smaller branches, spending about half of her time alternately at each.

Securing Non-professional Personnel:

Branches enjoy an advantage over a downtown or central library in the matter of staff recruitment. The branches can often secure housewives or students in the neighborhood, part or full-time. Occasionally a professional may live in the branch service area who has been out of active duty for awhile because of marriage or the need to stay at home with children. Many librarians prefer working in a neighborhood branch where parking is easier and traffic less congested, and where they can get to know their patrons better. If the branch is a new one, there is a special appeal about being in the new building and starting out with new services and new patrons.

If the branch is part of a large system the Personnel Officer for the system will attempt to fill positions in the branches, or, if the library is under a civil service system, the personnel officer for the city may do the hiring through the regular competitive examination system. Regardless of the method used, the branch librarian should sit in on the selection of staff or have the final decision concerning successful candidates who have passed the examinations. For it is the branch head who must work with the new person and who can judge how well he or she may be able to work with the existing staff.

If there are no candidates from the central library staff who wish to move out to fill branch vacancies and no eligible list from civil service examinations, the following are suggested as means of finding likely candidates for clerical or sub-professional positions:

1. Contact the nearest branch of the State Employment Office.

2. Contact teachers of library science classes for library assistants, sub-professionals, library technicians, or library aides. Courses to prepare library assistants are being offered in quite a number of the junior colleges in the United States at present.

3. Advertise in local newspapers but do not give the library name. Ask applicants to write a letter to a given box number, stating their qualifications, experience and education. This enables the librarian to weed out the obviously unfit without being deluged with applications or phone calls at the start.

4. Ask branch and headquarters staff for suggestions. They may know of qualified people.

5. Attend library workshops and conferences where there are likely to be quite a few non-professionals in attendance.

6. Contact local high schools and business colleges for people who will soon be graduating and looking for positions.

7. Check the "situations wanted" ads in local papers. Be wary of these if the local employment situation is good because there may be good reasons why the person has difficulty in obtaining a position.

8. Contact private employment agencies if all else fails.

Number and Classification of Staff Required:

The number and classification of staff required in a branch will vary with the size, services, and objectives of the branch. Branches may vary from a few thousand square feet to 65,000 square feet or more, and may offer services ranging from the semi-self-service policy of the Philadelphia Reading Centers which are staffed with one full-time and one part-time library technician,

to Philadelphia's Northeast Regional Branch which requires a staff
of 80, including 26 professionals, and staff needs will vary accordingly.   Even the use of standards based upon units of circulation or
units of population served cannot be applied without also taking into
account the many other differences that affect the degree and kind
of branch library service.

Some of these differences stem from racial, economic,
cultural, and educational factors in the community served.   Others
relate to such practical matters as the crime and juvenile delinquency rate, age levels, and special interests of the area.   (See
the chapter on "Tailoring the Branch to the Community.")

Is vandalism and violence a problem?   If so, the branch
may need one or more uniformed monitors.   Are there more young
people between the ages of 15-19 than any other age group?   If so,
services to young adults will need to be strengthened particularly,
as will reference services on the high school and college levels.
Does the racial or national character of the neighborhood indicate
the need for strengthening the Negro collection or for having a
Spanish-speaking staff member or two who can communicate easily
with patrons who do not speak English?

Perhaps the low economic level of the branch neighborhood
requires a special program for the disadvantaged.   Possibly the
presence of many businesses and industries in the service area of
a large or regional branch demands the services of a business
specialist on the staff.   All these and many more questions will
need to be asked and answered before the right kind of staff can be
assembled for a new branch or increased at an older branch where
circulation is booming.

Whatever number of staff becomes necessary and whatever
its composition, it is highly important that those selected be friendly
warm, approachable people who will create and preserve the informality and personal touch that so often distinguishes a smaller
agency from a large one. The regional branches that equal or surpass
many central libraries in size or services offered will find it harder to
know as many of their patrons, but the branch tradition of helpfulness
and friendliness can be fostered and maintained, nevertheless.

If the size of the branch justifies only two professionals, they should normally be the branch librarian and a children's specialist. When a third professional can be hired, many recommend a young adult specialist; this writer favors a reference specialist because of the increasing reference load in recent years. The children's librarian is usually qualified to assist teenagers as well as small children and can double as young adult librarian; whereas if the head librarian has to handle most of the reference load for lack of a reference specialist she will get little else accomplished.

Versatility is very important in a branch staff, because at vacation times, when sickness occurs, or when there is a temporary peak load in one particular aspect of the public service, any staff member may have to undertake another's work or assist at a job other than his own. In the small branch, especially, each staff member must literally be a jack-of-all-trades.

A master list of duties should be posted on the bulletin board in the workroom (see chapter on "Operational Techniques" and each staff member should have his own list. Responsibility for every task in the branch should be clearly assigned. The old adage, "Professionals should do professional work and clericals should do clerical work," becomes increasingly applicable as branch size and staff increases, but is rarely possible in the smaller branches where the head librarian and other professionals may find themselves doing whatever needs doing, simply because there is no one else to whom clerical or other functions can be delegated.

Certain sources of free or low-cost help have arisen in recent years and properly used, may help the branch staffing situation. These sources include:

1. Availability of trainee students from various library courses, including the library assistant courses being offered in many junior colleges. Many of these courses require field work, as do the accredited graduate library schools. Libraries, both branches and central, can cooperate with these schools to secure assigned trainees each semester. Some of this field work carries no stipulation of salary; other programs require that the student be

paid a nominal sum or that the library set up a trainee-pay program

2. The work-experience program in many high schools sends students out into the business and professional world to gain practic experience and try out various occupations. These are often superi or students. They are released from school to work about two hour per day and no pay is required. These people can shelve, file, work at the charging desk, mend, or do other tasks, but the work must be varied and some teaching is involved.

3. Youth Corps and Job Corps young people are paid at government expense and are assigned to various organizations or institutions which will cooperate with the program. This, again, is a learning situation, and they cannot be assigned to repetitive tasks which will teach them little. They can, however, do many simple jobs in a branch if these jobs are rotated. The Youth Corp program faced possible termination at the end of June, 1969, at the time of this writing.

4. Other government programs may offer part-time or full-time help. Since federal programs come and go, the interested branch librarian should check what is available locally, then confer with her supervisor or library director as to the possibilities of obtaining free or low-cost clerical and page help.

5. Under the terms of the Library Services and Construction Act, funds can be made available for improving services, and one method of improving services is adding staff. Any participation in LSCA benefits must be through system participation and must meet very specific conditions.

6. Although opinions differ as to whether volunteer help is worth the supervision time, many branches have found volunteer services well worthwhile. Friends of the Library members, Girl and Boy Scouts, Campfire Girls or interested housewives may be sources of such help. If not given tasks beyond their experience or ability, volunteer workers sometimes develop such an interest that they contribute many hours and provide a source of recruitment for future permanent positions. It is often easier for young people to work in their own neighborhood than to travel to a central library in a downtown location.

Until a branch librarian has explored all possible sources of free or low cost help, he has not done all he can to create a condition wherein purely clerical and page tasks can be delegated in order to free higher-level people for professional duties and better service to the public.

The Newark Public Library, Newark, New Jersey, found college students hired as library aides very useful in their special summer programs for children. One student was assigned to each children's room, her special function being to offer friendship, understanding, a listening ear, and encouragement. The individual child was her special interest but she was also assigned to work with small groups. Her main purpose was to help children increase their reading ability.

There should be a specific probationary period for all staff members. Civil Service regulations usually require six months or one year for supervisory personnel and sub-professionals, and six months for clerical employees. If a library system is not under city or county civil service the A. L. A. Statistical Standards for 1967 can be used as a guide. They recommend one year for professionals and sub-professionals, six months for clerical employees. [4]

On number of staff the A. L. A. Standards recommend one professional and two clericals for every 6,000 population served. This is merely a breakdown of the general recommendation of one full-time or equivalent staff member for each 2,000 population, made in the 1966 Minimum Standards for Public Library Systems. [4]

Wheeler and Goldhor state that a branch circulating 100,000 or more books per year should have five or six full-time employees other than the custodians, and including two or three professionals. [5] Dr. Frederick Wezeman has proposed, in a 1967 study, a staff of at least three professionals (specialists for children, young adults, and adults) and a minimum of three clerical staff members for a large branch of 12,000-14,000 square feet. [6] Thus we have examples of three different criteria used as a basis for determining number of staff: a) Number of population served;

b) Circulation; and c) Number of square feet in the building.   A
good approach might be not to use any one of these criteria alone,
but to take an average derived from applying each in turn.   In the
case of a new branch only estimated circulation could be used, so
that population in the service area and the size of the building
would be the best criteria.   Determining the required number of
staff, even using a combination of the above three criteria, is difficult because many other factors are likely to influence branch use.
Community characteristics affecting circulation have already been
cited several times.

The Fresno County Free Library, California,[7] suggests a
staff of six (two professionals, two library assistants, and two
pages) for a county branch serving a population of 5,000-10,000 and
having an annual circulation of 35,000-60,000.   This could also apply to a small community library which is a member of a system.
A branch of this size would be small by today's standards.

For a metropolitan area branch serving 10,000-25,000
people and circulating 60,000 to 100,000 books the same staff is
recommended in the Fresno County standards as for the smaller
county branch.[7]   The exact reason for this similarity is not given,
but we can assume that it is because the county branch, being
further isolated from the county headquarters, has to perform more
duties for itself.

For a large metropolitan area branch or regional headquarters, with a population of over 25,000 and a circulation over
100,000, Fresno County standards call for 10 people, (3 professionals, 3 library assistants, 4 clericals and pages).[7]

Contra Costa County Library, Pleasant Hill, California, has
in the past recommended 4 full-time staff or equivalents for each
15,000 annual circulation.   For communities of 7,500-25,000 population, 4-7 full-time staff, including two professionals, was recommended.   For populations over 25,000 Contra Costa County cited
a total of 8 full-time staff or equivalents, including three professionals.   These standards are now being revised.

While such matters as hours in the work week, vacations,
sick leave, retirement, and overtime pay will undoubtedly be

determined for branch employees by the policies of the city or county of
which their library is a part, some libraries, particularly community
agencies which have existed as independent units and then have joined a
system, have been able to regulate some of these matters through their
local library boards. In other instances, especially where there is no
civil service organization in the city or county, libraries have been allowed to follow special rules because of the long hours libraries are
open and the fact that they differ in many ways from other departments
and offices of the governing jurisdiction. The A. L. A. Addenda to the
Minimum Standards (1967)[9] recommends a 35-hour work week, no more
than two nights per week, and no more than two Saturdays a month.
They propose no less than 20 working days or four weeks of vacation for
professionals and 10 working days or two weeks for clerical employees,
and an extra vacation allowance for longevity. Another recommendation
is for three months' leave with pay for professionals after five years of
satisfactory service.

The annual branch staffing pattern survey made by the San Diego
Public Library has been a great service to the profession. Here are
their recent survey results as tabulated in March, 1969. [10]

Branch Library Staffing Pattern
Municipal Libraries Serving Populations Between 400,000 - 700,000

Municipal libraries in this report are: Boston, Dallas, Denver,
Indianapolis, Minneapolis, New Orleans, Pittsburgh, San Diego,
and Seattle. Only branches supervised by professional librarians are included. Subprofessionals listed in the survey are
persons doing professional work who do not have qualifications
normally required of junior librarians.

A - Circulation over 175,000
(Circulation shown in parenthesis)

ity & Branch	Libns. F. T. Equiv.	Sub- Prof. F. T. Equiv.	Clerks F. T. Equiv.	Pages Hours Weekly	Open Hours	Salary Branch Librn.
Dallas						
Casa View* (52,789)	4	1	7	200	42	805-1017
Hampton-Illinois (87,301)	4	1	6	150	42	744-939

A - Circulation over 175,000 (Cont.)

City & Branch	Libns. F.T. Equiv.	Sub-Prof. F.T. Equiv.	Clerks F.T. Equiv.	Pages Hours Weekly	Open Hours	Salary Branch Librn.
Lakewood (212,230)	4		3	75	42	744-939
Pleasant Grove (238,271)	3	1	4	100	42	744-939
Preston Royal (446,550)	2	3	6	125	42	744-939
Walnut Hill* (401,396)	4	1	6	123	42	805-101
Northlake (249,497)	3	1	3	58	42	744- 93
Denver						
Chalmers Hadley* (268,570)	5	1	2	60	51.5	734- 91
Ross-Cherry Creek* (244,786)	4	2	2	60	51.5	734- 91
Ross-University Hills* (340,080)	5	1	2	80	51.5	734- 91
Indianapolis						
Broad Ripple (286,801)	6	2.5	3	66	57	717-867
Emerson (207,401)	4	2	4	66	44.5	717- 86
Minneapolis						
Linden Hills* (203,409)	3	.4	4.6	60	49.5	730- 88
New Orleans						
Algiers (210,866)	3	1	2	52.5	60	710- 90
Pittsburgh						
Allegheny Regional (194,202)	6	4	8	268	75	720- 84
San Diego						
Benjamin (190,954)	3		2.6	42	48	663- 80
Clairemont (227,625)	3		3	42	48	663- 80
North Clairemont (274,775)	3		4.6	44	52	663-805
Pacific Beach (192,637)	3		2.6	42	48	663- 80

A - Circulation over 175,000 (Cont.)

City & Branch	Libns. F. T. Equiv.	Sub. Prof. F. T. Equiv.	Clerks F. T. Equiv.	Pages Hours Weekly	Open Hours	Salary Branch Librn.
Point Loma (177, 862)	3		2. 4	40	48	663- 805
Serra Mesa (202, 448)	3		3	42	48	663- 805
Seattle						
Ballard (214, 226)	4	. 4	1. 3	100	40	656- 782
Greenwood (176, 838)	3. 17		1. 5	90	40	656- 782
Lake City (269, 642)	5. 4	1	3. 1	88	40	782- 929
North East (315, 863)	5	1	4. 8	88	40	782- 929
Southeast (218, 120)	3. 5		2. 6	90	40	656- 782
University (231, 090)	4. 5		3. 65	94	40	782- 929

B - Circulation 150,000 - 174,999

City & Branch	Libns. F. T. Equiv.	Sub. Prof. F. T. Equiv.	Clerks F. T. Equiv.	Pages Hours Weekly	Open Hours	Salary Branch Librn.
Boston						
Roslindale	3	2	3	91	64	700- 850
West Roxbury	3	1	4	62	64	700- 850
Denver						
Park Hill*	4	2	2	40	51. 5	702- 877
Indianapolis						
Brown	4	1	2. 5	66	44. 5	717- 867
Pittsburgh						
Brookline	4		3	160	44	749- 843
San Diego						
College Heights	2		2. 4	40	48	663- 805
La Jolla	2		2. 4	40	48	663- 805
Seattle						
Columbia	3		1. 9	53	40	656- 782
Green Lake	2	1	. 6	52	40	656- 782
West Seattle	3	. 8	1. 8	93	40	656- 782

C - Circulation 125,000 - 149,999

City & Branch	Libns. F. T. Equiv.	Sub-Prof. F. T. Equiv.	Clerks F. T. Equiv.	Pages Hours Weekly	Open Hours	Salary Branch Libn.
Dallas						
Lancaster-Kiest*	4		4	100	43	805-101
Indianapolis						
Eagle	2	1	2	48	44.5	683- 83
Northeast	2		5	54	39.5	683- 83
Shelby	2	1	3	54	42	683- 83
Minneapolis						
Nokomis*	2	.28	3.29	39	49.5	730- 88
Walker	2	.49	3	36	49.5	730- 88
Pittsburgh						
Knoxville	2		3.5	106	45	749- 84
San Diego						
East San Diego	2		2	40	48	663- 80
North Park	2		2	40	48	663- 80
Seattle						
Henry	1.5	1	1	65	40	656- 78
Magnolia	2	1	.9	58	40	656- 78

D - Circulation 100,000 - 124,999

City & Branch	Libns. F. T. Equiv.	Sub-Prof. F. T. Equiv.	Clerks F. T. Equiv.	Pages Hours Weekly	Open Hours	Salary Branch Libn.
Boston						
Adams Street	2	2	3	48	52	700- 85
Codman Square	2	2	3	64	52	700- 85
Hyde Park	2	1	3	66	56	700- 85
Dallas						
Jefferson	2	1	2	58	42	744- 93
Oak Lawn	1	2	2	58	42	744- 93
Denver						
Ross-Barnum	2		1	30	33.5	642- 80
Woodbury*	4	.5	2	40	51.5	734- 91
Minneapolis						
Roosevelt*	2	.49	2.49	30	49.5	730- 88
Webber Park*	2	.49	3.75	30	49.5	730- 88
New Orleans						
East New Orleans*	3	1	2	52.5	50	710- 90
Latter*	1.8	1	1	35	60	613- 78

D - Circulation 100,000 - 124,999 (Cont.)

City & Branch	Libns. F.T. Equiv.	Sub-Prof. F.T. Equiv.	Clerks F.T. Equiv.	Pages Hours Weekly	Open Hours	Salary Branch Libn.
Pittsburgh						
Carrick	2		3	58.5	34	693- 810
Downtown	1	1	4	15	54.5	720- 843
Homewood	3	1	4	98	45	749- 843
South Side	3		3	85	48	749- 843
Woods Run	2		3	84	45	720- 810
San Diego						
Ocean Beach	2		1.6	32	48	663- 805
Seattle						
Queen Anne	2.5		1.2	40	40	656- 782

E - Circulation 75,000 - 99,999

City & Branch	Libns. F.T. Equiv.	Sub-Prof. F.T. Equiv.	Clerks F.T. Equiv.	Pages Hours Weekly	Open Hours	Salary Branch Libn.
Boston						
Mattapan	3		3	44	46	700- 850
South Boston	3	1	3	61	56	700- 850
Denver						
Field	1	1		20	33.5	642- 803
Smiley	2			20	33.5	642- 803
Indianapolis						
Broadway	2	.5	2	54	44.5	683- 833
Minneapolis						
Central Avenue*	2	.49	3.1	30	49.5	730- 888
East Lake	2	.2	2.49	20	49.5	730- 888
Hosmer*	2	.49	3.28	30	49.5	730- 888
North	2	.49	3.1	30	49.5	730- 888
Southeast*	2	.2	2.53	26	49.5	730- 888
New Orleans						
Gentilly*	1.8	1	1	35	27	613- 782
Nix*	1.8	1	1	35	60	613- 782
Smith*	1.8	1	1	35	50	613- 782
Pittsburgh						
Beechview	2		2	58	41	693- 810
East Liberty*	3		4	105	45	749- 843
Hazelwood	2	1	2	81	34	720- 843
Lawrenceville	2	1	3	72	41	749- 843
Mt. Washington	2		1.2	64	40	720- 810
West End	1	1	1	83	31	693- 810

E - Circulation 75,000 - 99,999 (Cont.)

City & Branch	Libns. F.T. Equiv.	Sub-Prof. F.T. Equiv.	Clerks F.T. Equiv.	Pages Hours Weekly	Open Hours	Salary Branch Libn.
San Diego						
Linda Vista	2		1	34	48	663- 80
Mission Hills	1		1	24	33	601- 69

F - Circulation 50,000 - 74,999

City & Branch	Libns. F.T. Equiv.	Sub-Prof. F.T. Equiv.	Clerks F.T. Equiv.	Pages Hours Weekly	Open Hours	Salary Branch Libn.
Boston						
Brighton	3		1	17	57	700- 85
Charlestown	2	1	3	37	46	700- 85
Connolly*	2.5	1	2	51	42	700- 85
Dorchester	4		.6	50	46	700- 85
East Boston*	2.5		2	25	46	700- 85
Egleston Square	3		2.5	36	48	700- 85
Faneuil	2		2	34	46	700- 85
Jamaica Plain*	2.5		2	37	56	700- 85
Lower Mills	3		2.5	42	46	700- 85
North End*	2.5		2	40	40	700- 85
Uphams Corner	3	2	1	32	44	700- 85
Washington Village	3		3	32	42	700- 85
West End*	2.5	1	1	44	48	700- 85
Denver						
Dahlia*	1	1	1	20	46.5	614- 76
Decker	2			20	33.5	642- 80
Ross-Broadway	2		.5	20	33.5	642- 80
Indianapolis						
East Washington	2		.6	36	39.5	683- 83
Minneapolis						
Franklin	1	.49	2.49	15	49.5	730- 88
San Diego						
Normal Hts.- Kensington	1		1	24	33	601- 69
Paradise Hills	1		1	24	33	601- 69
University Hts.	1		1	24	33	601- 69
Valencia Park*	2		1	34	48	601- 69
Seattle						
Fremont	1.8		.5	31	40	593- 69
Yesler	1	1.5	1	50	40	656- 78

G - Circulation 25,000 - 49,999

City & Branch	Libns. F. T. Equiv.	Sub. Prof. F. T. Equiv.	Clerks F. T. Equiv.	Pages Hours Weekly	Open Hours	Salary Branch Libn.
Boston						
Allston	3	1	1	38	46	700- 850
Mt. Bowdoin	1	1	2	28	42	700- 850
Mt. Pleasant*	1. 5		2	38	39	700- 850
Orient Heights*	2. 5		1	24	46	700- 850
Parker Hill	3		2	26	42	700- 850
South End	1	2	2	27	44	700- 850
Dallas						
Forest Avenue	1	2	1	30	42	642- 805
West	1	1	1	30	42	642- 805
Denver						
Warren	2	1	. 75	20	33. 5	642- 803
Indianapolis						
Brightwood	1	1	. 6	36	39. 5	683- 833
Haughville	1		1. 6	36	42	683- 833
Prospect	1	1	1	36	39. 5	683- 833
Rauh*	1. 6		1	36	44. 5	717- 867
Spades	1	1	. 6	36	42	683- 833
West Indianapolis	2		. 6	36	39. 5	683- 833
Minneapolis						
Bottineau	. 6	. 32	1. 74	15	39	730- 888
Sumner	1. 8		2. 29	15	49. 5	730- 888
New Orleans						
Alvar*	. 2	1. 1		17. 5	40	481- 613
Mayer-Broadmoor*	. 2	1. 1		17. 5	40	481- 613
Napoleon*	. 2	1. 1		17. 5	40	481- 613
Nora Navra*	. 2	1. 1		17. 5	40	481- 613
Pittsburgh						
Wylie	1	1	4	60	40	693- 810

H - Circulation under 25,000

City & Branch	Libns. F. T. Equiv.	Sub. Prof. F. T. Equiv.	Clerks F. T. Equiv.	Pages Hours Weekly	Open Hours	Salary Branch Libn.
Boston						
Memorial*	1. 5	2	1	16	35	700- 850
Indianapolis						
Riverside*	. 4		2	30	27. 5	717- 867
Pittsburgh						
Business	3. 8		2. 5	23	49. 5	810- 912

		Sub-				
	Libns.	Prof.	Clerks	Pages		Salary
	F. T.	F. T.	F. T.	Hours	Open	Branch
City & Branch	Equiv.	Equiv.	Equiv.	Weekly	Hours	Libn

H - Circulation under 25,000 (Cont.)

City & Branch	Libns. F. T. Equiv.	Sub-Prof. F. T. Equiv.	Clerks F. T. Equiv.	Pages Hours Weekly	Open Hours	Salary Branch Libn
San Diego						
Logan Heights*	1		1	17	33	601- 69
San Ysidro*	.4		.4	6	15	601- 69

Notes

Boston: Connolly and Jamaica Plain branches (F) are jointly administered by 1 librarian; the same holds for Memorial (H) and Mt. Pleasant branches (G) by 1 librarian; and for East Boston (F) and Orient Heights branches (G) by 1 librarian.

Dallas: Casa View, Walnut Hill (A) and Lancaster-Kiest (C) branches are bookmobile branches with three additional staff members over those shown here. The branch librarian is also in charge of bookmobile service. Circulation figures do not include bookmobiles.

Denver: Park Hill (B), Ross-Cherry Creek (A), Ross-University Hills (A), Chalmers Hadley (A), and Woodbury (D), are designated as Regional Libraries whose heads are also responsible for assigned branch libraries and neighborhood libraries in their regions. Dahlia branch (F) opened June 20, 1968; circulation group is an estimate.

Indianapolis: The same branch librarian administers both Rauh and Riverside branches (G) and (H) respectively.

Minneapolis: Beginning in September, 1968 branch library service was divided into two districts, and two district librarian positions (Grade V, 960-1181) were created. The position of branch librarian is being changed to that of community librarian (Grade II, 730-888) in a process of attrition. Some branches are still served by branch librarians Grade IV (873-1075) and branch librarians Grade IIIa (800-986). They are Nokomis (C), Roosevelt (D), Webber Park (D), Central Avenue (E), Hosmer (E), Southeast (F).

New Orleans: East New Orleans branch (D) opened October 23, 19 group assignment is based on estimated annual circulation Gentilly branch (E) had been on a renovation schedule since April 22, 1968 and open only 27 hours a week. Alvar, Mayer-Broadmoor, Napoleon and Nora Navra (all G) are designated neighborhood branches and are under supervisi of the branch librarians of major branches, Gentilly (E), Nix (E), Latter (D), and Smith (E), respectively.

Pittsburgh: Allegheny Regional branch (A), almost inaccessible to the public for a year due to an urban renewal program, closed its doors to the public September 23, 1968, opening one month later in rented quarters while the library building undergoes an extensive 2-year renovation. East Liberty branch (E) closed in early November 1968 in preparation for a move to a new building. It was scheduled to re-open February 1, 1969.

San Diego: One added Senior Librarian ($663-805) provides special programs for three branches in low income area: Valencia Park (F), Logan Heights, San Ysidro (H) branches.

In-Service Training of Staff

Among the causes of inefficiency is one which is in no way the fault of a new employee: lack of proper instruction, both at the outset and as the work progresses. Insufficient instruction may re-sult from a lack of written procedures, from assuming that the new staff member knows more about libraries than he does, or from not sufficiently defining individual duties so that each staff member knows what he is supposed to do. Any of these causes are the result of poor management by the head of the branch. Most important of all elements for success is the right introduction to the job.

The branch librarian should personally welcome each new staff member on his first day and conduct him on a tour of the branch, explaining the various areas, location of unusual material, and any special procedures or regulations to be emphasized. It is flattering to the new person to be welcomed and shown around by the person in charge and a cordial relationship may well be estab-lished from the outset between the branch head and the new staff member. The tour should be unhurried and should be followed by coffee in the staff lounge and an informal chat.

A part of the orientation program for a new staff member should be a visit to headquarters and to as many of the other branches as possible. The place of the branch and his new position in the whole library organization and activity should be carefully ex-plained to the newcomer. Although all this takes time from his work it will pay dividends in the end, in better understanding of the importance of that work and in a better feeling toward all those whom

he met and who took an interest in welcoming him. The amount of
explanation and number of visits to other parts of the system will
depend to some extent on the nature of the new person's position,
but an incoming page should have the same general introduction and
instruction concerning his own branch as a new assistant librarian
or other administrative staff member.

Harold Hamill, Los Angeles Public Library Director, suggests[11] that the three most important elements in "within the librar
training" of staff are: "1) Communication; 2) Comprehension;
3) Application. There must be a follow-up to all this introduction.
Time must be allowed for the instruction to be assimilated; then
when the new person has been on the staff for several weeks, or
even months, more intensive in-service training should be given."

A branch head can learn much from staff in the course of
training. Suggestions should always be welcomed and the channels
kept open to relay such suggestions as far up the line as necessary
A very necessary part of the orientation of a new staff member is
study of the branch manual which contains in written form the
policies, procedures, and personnel regulations of the system and
branch. In very large systems such as the Los Angeles Public Library, the policy, procedure and training manuals run to many volumes, giving the newcomer a thorough grounding in the history, ob
jectives, and operations of the entire system. Three branch manuals used in Los Angeles cover the library's technical services as
they affect branches, registration, ordering, circulation, cataloging
and binding.

One branch management manual includes such topics as:
Supervisors' guide for inducting and training new employees; Schedu
ing in branches; Assignment of duties in branches; Branch management checklist; Checklist of duties for use with new staff members;
Branch records, order and shipments;[2] Statements on service to
children and young adults. Manuals are kept up to date by amend-
ments, supplements and daily special bulletins.

If the library system does not furnish each branch or memb
library with a policy and procedure manual, the branch head will

igure 37: Librarians Ponder Questions at Orange County Library's In-
raining Program at County Headquarters. Participants in the Effect-
e Supervision Conferences, held from April 16 through June 18, 1968
ere 24 library staff members, mostly from branch libraries. The
range County Public Library, one of the country's largest, is located
 Orange, California.

ve to compile one for himself and submit it to his immediate
pervisor for approval or change. It should be done on loose-leaf
per to permit easy insertion of revisions, and points should be in
tline form, using the standardized designations of sections and not
ge numbers. The index can then refer to sections and sub-sec-
ons, and it is not necessary to renumber pages each time a change
 made and new pages added or subtracted. A detailed index at
e beginning of the book will help new people to find a point in a
rry when they are uncertain of some procedure and patrons are
aiting.

Topics which should be included in a branch manual are:

1. The objectives and service philosophy of the system as whole and the part the branches play in carrying out these objectiv and services.

2. A short history of the library system and the branch.

3. A welcome letter from the system administrator, head librarian and staff to new staff members.

4. An organizational chart of the library system showing lines of authority.

5. A similar chart for the branch.

6. A list of the Special services provided by the system a available to all branch patrons.

7. Circulation procedures of the branch.

8. Overdues, notices, fines, penalties, payments for damage, lost books, other charges.

9. Registration regulations.

10. What records are kept and why.

11. Lending rules and periods of loan.

12. Special collections in the branch and their locations. A special rules regarding them.

13. Regulations regarding conduct of patrons in the library. Some general principles of good discipline. How to handle serious problems of discipline.

14. What to do in case of emergency such as fire, a bomb scare, earthquake, or other serious disturbance.

15. General rules of conduct for staff members, such as "no chewing of gum in public service areas," perhaps no mini-skirts, consequences of being late, general good taste in dress. Attitude toward the public, etc.

16. Fringe benefits and other personnel matters, such as: vacation, sick leave, holidays, compensatory time, payment for overtime, group health and insurance plan, retirement system in-formation, staff association membership, whether or not the librar is on a state industrial accident insurance system, etc.

17. A list of the special activities or programs the branch sponsors for the public and how to make them known.

It is easier to incorporate the orientation information and
elcome into the regular policy and procedure manual if the system
anual is not already large and formidable. If it is, a smaller,
eparate orientation manual should be used, containing those items
bove which are primarily for new people and such extra information
s a list of nearby restaurants, parking information, names and ad-
resses of branches in the system, etc.

In-Service training meetings may be planned by a branch
pervisor or coordinator, using a common series of topics, but
ways in consultation with the branch head and with enough flexi-
lity so that individual branch meetings may be combined with the
egular staff meetings for that branch or so that special material
ay be inserted which will not be the same for all branches. If
e system does not have a branch supervisor, coordinator or ex-
nsion head to take part in planning such meetings or occasional
l-system workshops, the branch head must plan her own in-service
aining program. They should be held at least once a month, twice
possible. The best time is from 8 to 10 a.m., assuming that the
brary opens at 10, or from 8 to 9 if the library opens at 9 a.m.
the branch does not open until 12 noon or 1 p.m., the meetings
ay be scheduled at any time in the morning. As branch staff
embers are seldom all scheduled to be on duty at the same time,
may be necessary to call in some people especially for the meet-
g, granting them either overtime pay or compensatory time for the
ertime they put in. Staff members should not be asked to attend
aff meetings or in-service training sessions on their own time.

Suggested topics for in-service training meetings:

1. A series in which the various classes of reference
    books in the branch are reported upon by various
    members of the staff and discussed as to their or-
    ganization, content, and value as reference tools. The
    series could be ten sessions in length, one Dewey
    class being studied at each session. This will be a
    refresher for professionals, very helpful to non-
    professionals.

2. Telephone courtesy. Telephone companies have a special
    program on this, complete with movies and a very charm-
    ing demonstrator.

3. Professional library organizations and professional
    library literature.   Discuss membership in A. L. A. ,
    state library association, regional associations, city
    or county employees association, and staff association
    Discuss professional publications, how to use them,
    and how to get them--Library Journal, Wilson Librar
    Bulletin, Library Trends, Library Literature, Top of
    the News, etc.   Two meetings could be devoted to
    this, one to the literature, one to the organizations.

4. General desk performance and attitudes toward the
    public, especially for clericals and those who work at
    the charging desk, but also for readers' advisors and
    reference librarians.   Use Patrons are People as a
    basis or plan a skit or demonstration to illustrate
    certain points.

5. An overview of outstanding classics, adult and juve-
    nile, likely to be constantly requested by the public.
    A staff member who knows her books and authors
    saves much time in finding material without using the
    card catalog.

6. If a changeover to automatic charging is anticipated,
    staff will need careful preparation and discussion to
    insure easy acceptance and a smooth transition to the
    new system.   All advantages should be stressed and
    staff should be reminded that the new system may not
    seem faster until they have become fully accustomed
    to using it.

7. A discussion of how the system budget and branch
    budget is worked out.   A lack of understanding of how
    the library is financed often leads to criticism of the
    administration, city or county officials, etc. by the
    staff.   Many staff members, particularly those in the
    lower echelons, do not realize the problems involved
    in securing adequate budgets.

8. A capsule history of children's literature, broken dow
    into several lecture and study sessions and conducted
    by the system's most experienced children's specialis
    Outstanding books illustrating different periods in the
    development of children's material should be used as
    illustrations of periods and types.

9. A detailed explanation of the library's health and in-
    surance plan, with a representative from the company
    present to do the explaining and answer questions. A
    similar program can be given for the retirement sys-
    tem, with one of the state, county, or other retire-
    ment plan representatives making the presentation.

10. A brainstorming session in which all staff members are asked for suggestions for improvements in services or branch techniques.

11. A discussion of opportunities in the library field, presented by the branch librarian and professionals on the staff, to encourage non-professional members to continue their professional education.

12. Ideas for good public relations, newspaper news and features, special events, and how staff can help. Get an outside speaker if possible.

13. Staff ethics, loyalty to the branch, the organization, and the city or county.

14. Suggestions for making the branch more a part of the community or neighborhood.

15. Discussion of problem patrons; techniques for handling difficult situations gracefully.

16. School and public library relationships. How the branch can do a better job of cooperating with the schools. Get school librarians in on this if possible.

17. Student use of the branch. Problems and how to help solve them.

18. The library's book selection policy and how it was formulated. How to handle complaints from irate patrons about "dirty" books.

19. A frank discussion of good teamwork and how to get along with fellow workers.

20. If an efficiency study, work analysis, or time and motion study is to be made, carefully-planned discussion and explanation must precede it in a staff session so that staff members will understand why it is being done. Many fear such a project, thinking they will lose their jobs or be demoted because of the findings. Staff must be reassured and the workings of the project explained. This could usually be done in one meeting.

The Tulsa (Oklahoma) City-County Library System has an excellent staff orientation program which is used after specific instruction for the particular position has been given by the new employee's supervisor. The Tulsa program, easily adapted to any system, is given in two or three- 3-hour sessions.[2]

Outline for Staff Orientation Program
(Tulsa City-County Library System)

      All employees are instructed regarding their immediate area
of responsibility by their supervisors and/or division heads. In
addition, an understanding of the total system of operation is essent

      Each new employee will be required to attend the orientation
program. Clerical assistants, bookmobile drivers, and maintenanc
personnel will be involved in two 3-hour sessions. All other personnel will attend three 3-hour sessions. This in-service program
is designed to introduce the new staff member to the library system
its philosophy, table of organization, financing, and the broad-range
of its activities. Can be given once every month, every two months
oftener or less often, depending upon the total number of new employees in the system.

I.   First Session
     12:30 - 12:45   Why Libraries? - Objectives
     12:45 - 1:05   Film * "The Library Is"
      1:05 - 2:15   General introduction to the System
                   A.   Library's government
                   B.   Sources of revenue
                   C.   Pattern of administration
                   D.   Relationship of divisions
      2:15 - 2:30   Break
      2:30 - 3:00   Supportive Non-public Services
                   A.   Administrative Services
                   B.   Technical Processing
      3:00 - 3:30   Tour of Technical Processing

II.   Second Session
     12:30 - 1:00   Film - "Hottest Spot in Town"
      1:00 - 2:15   Public Services
                   A.   Central
                   B.   Extension
                   C.   Coordinator of Adult Services
                   D.   Coordinator of Children's Services
                   E.   Coordinator of Community Services
      2:15 - 2:30   Break
      2:30 - 3:30   Tour of Central Library. Work of each
                     department explained to the new people
                     by the department head.
                   A.   Business & Technology Department
                   B.   Reference Department
                   C.   Readers Services Department
                   D.   Circulation Department

III.   Third Session (Extension Services)
     12:30 - 2:00   Services and programs of branches and book-
                     mobiles, including visits to each branch and
                     the bookmobile headquarters. These should
                     be scheduled after the discussion session, ap-
                     proximately one hour for each branch.

It is possible to use federal funds, through a State Library, for financing an in-service training program. In 1968, the East Baton Rouge Parish Library, Baton Rouge, Louisiana, used this source to finance a program to provide improved service to the public through better trained personnel. The instructor conducted 12 training sessions, October through April, at the Mid-City Branch for 31 staff members of East Baton Rouge, West Baton Rouge, Point Coupee, and Assumption Parish Libraries. Expenses paid for those attending included costs of travel and of materials used.

In-service training meetings of such length as to be considered workshops are often held. In October, 1967, the Lake County Public Library, Griffith, Indiana, scheduled a week-long in-service training meeting conducted by J. L. Tinkle, adult education specialist of the Indiana State Library and the Vigo County Public Library, Terre Haute. The project was essentially participation training for 30 key staff members, designed to help them understand themselves and each other better and to work together as a team.

Staff discussion and participation were noticeably better after the training, and there was a keener awareness of the importance of fellow employees. A formal discussion period on a pre-selected topic has become an established part of the monthly community librarians' meetings. Lake County planned a follow-up week of training for a later date.

At the Gaston County Public Library, Gastonia, North Carolina, in-service library training is provided by the system and both personnel and branch library activities are under the direction of professional staff members. The branch personnel meet once a month at the main library for discussion and instruction. They also use this opportunity to select additional books and materials from the main library for their individual library units. In this county all branch libraries are staffed by non-professional librarians who are local residents.

Another interesting program is that conducted by the Vancouver Island Regional Library at Nanaimo, British Columbia. This regional library serves 17 branches, two deposit stations, and three

bookmobiles. Its in-service training includes a series of workshop
one-day in length, held in the more spacious branches. The purpo
is to acquaint the clerical branch librarians with reference materia
and how to deal with problems arising out of reference questions.
Held in various parts of the island, each workshop is attended by
12 to 20 people who are paid for their time and transportation. Th
reference librarian from headquarters organizes and runs these wor
shops. Librarians feel that the regularity of the workshops is a go
feature. General workshops are also held by this system, emphasi
ing organizational problems and solutions and informing staff of new
routines and such matters as the recent introduction of a new book
catalog.

Hazel Elks, Director of the Free Public Library of Elizabet
New Jersey, notes that the library began, in 1966, to participate in
programs sponsored by the local Office of Economic Opportunity.
These were: 1) Work training programs which varied in number of
participants, sometimes as many as 35 people; 2) Conducting a trai
ing program in which 25 older people were trained for various jobs
in the community. As vacancies occur in the library and money is
available, preference is given to hiring through this training group.

Because of insufficient professional staff in the branches, the
Vancouver Island Regional Library set up five areas with a professional librarian in each. These professionals each supervise about
three branches, advising and working closely with the clerical staffs
These area librarians do their own publicity, choose the books from
headquarters for the rotating collections in their branches, and in
general contribute their professional training to the success of the
units they supervise. It is an ideal arrangement, according to the
library director, and thus far highly successful. These area librar
ans are chosen for their youthful enthusiasm, most of them being
recent library school graduates who present a favorable and vital
image to the public.

City branch staff members can get together much more easil
for meetings than can county or regional branch staffs, who must
travel greater distances. However, since more branch librarians in

ural areas and small communities are non-professionals, the train-
ig meetings assume even greater importance than in city systems
here professional branch librarians are carrying on informal in-
ervice training every day.   City branch heads are likely to belong
) a staff association, to have access to specialists who can come
s often as called and on very short notice, and to be provided with
 branch manual in which uniform procedures and policies are
pelled out.   County or regional branches, and community libraries
hich have joined systems, will occasionally encounter more pres-
ure and more attempts to control their activities and procedures
y local authorities, organizations, and townspeople.   Specialists
ill be available from headquarters but rarely on short notice.
fore uniformity will be found among city branches than among rural
nd community branches in county and regional systems, the latter
eing more likely to have acquired some of the characteristics of
eir own communities.   City branches also vary widely but in
eneral they have been held more closely to uniform practices by
eir central agency.

Notes

Mississippi Library Commission, Jackson Mississippi.
    Trustee Manual.

Tulsa (Oklahoma) City-County Library System, Tulsa,
    Oklahoma. Policy and Procedure Manual.

Wheeler, Joseph L. and Goldhor, Herbert. Practical Ad-
    ministration of Public Libraries. Harper and Row, c 1962.
    p. 417.

American Library Association. Public Library Association.
    Standards Committee. Minimum Standards for Public
    Library Systems. 1966. p. 54. Statistical Standards.
    Addenda to same, 1967. p. 4.

Wheeler, Joseph L. and Goldhor, Herbert. Practical Admini-
    stration of Public Libraries. Harper and Row, c 1962. p.
    412-13.

Wezeman, Frederick. Study of Branch Libraries for the
    Lincoln City Library, Lincoln, Neb. 1967. p. 45-47.

Fresno County Free Library, Fresno, Calif. "Branch Standards."

8.   Contra Costa County Library, Pleasant Hills, Calif. "Branch Standards."

9.   American Library Association. Public Library Association. Standards Committee and subcommittees. <u>Minimum Standard</u> for Public Library Systems. 1966. <u>Statistical Standards,</u> Addenda to same, 1967, p. 4.

10.   San Diego Public Library, San Diego, Calif. "Branch Library Staffing Pattern." Mimeographed. March, 1969.

11.   Hamill, Harold, Director, Los Angeles Public Library, Los Angeles, Calif. "Selection, Training, and Staffing for Branch Libraries." In: "current Trends in Branch Libraries." <u>Library Trends</u>, April, 1966, p. 412.

12.   Elks, Hazel, Director, Free Public Library, Elizabeth, New Jersey. Letter to Author dated May 1968.

An unusually good source of material on staffing the small community library or branch is "The Library Staff" by June S. Smith, no. 4 in a series of pamphlets entitled <u>Small Libraries Project,</u> Library Administration Division, American Library Association. It is not cited specifically in this chapter, as most of the material applies to the small, independent library. However, much of the material can be used or adapted to any small library: branch federation member, or independent.

Chapter 8

The Collection and the Patrons

Throughout this volume we shall stress repeatedly the importance of fitting a branch library to its service area if it is to give truly effective service. Nowhere is this more true than in the selection and handling of the branch collection: books, periodicals, pamphlets, and audio-visual materials.

Materials collections in today's branches should increasingly reflect the librarian's awareness of social change. Fortunately, library policies, in many instances, seem to be moving, though perhaps too slowly, in the direction of more dynamic social action. The alert branch librarian, realizing that his library and his neighborhood or community are constantly changing, must not only fit his materials selection to this change and growth but must also look ahead to anticipate future changes and the needs which may arise from them. This requires keen observation, wide reading, and association with other vital agencies in the community.

A branch librarian's primary task is to help patrons use and appreciate books. To do this he must know the basic rules and tools of book selection and must recognize that age levels, income, economic trends, personality patterns, environment, and even seasons vary the interests and needs of his reading public.

Three factors not connected with community characteristics which influence book selection for any branch are: 1) Meeting the accepted standards for fiction and non-fiction, through the use of the usual book selection tools; 2) Non-duplication of specialized material available at the Central Library; and 3) Following the general book selection policy of the system. Unfortunately, these sometimes become restrictive factors, stressing uniformity at the expense of special community needs. The branch librarian should have some elasticity in book selection.

187

Support for the community need theory as the major factor
in selecting the book collection is provided by Mary Duncan Carter
and Wallace J. Bonk: "The selection of books for the branch will
be governed by the nature of the community each branch serves...
.....Thus there will be a variety of types of collections in the
various branches."[1]

The book selection policy of the Enoch Pratt Free Library
agrees with this premise: "It is around these community functions
that the average branch builds its permanent collections." The
policy also states, "each branch maintains a basic collection of
standard works in the major fields of knowledge."[2]

Interpretations of the branch collection in various surveys
refer to it as "actively changing," "useful," "containing fewer expensive books than the central library," "with a higher proportion
of recreational reading," and "with emphasis upon current reading
resources and materials used by students and children."

In current practice there appears to be general agreement
that the collection of the medium or large service branch should be
both recreational and educational and that neither quality should pre
dominate.   The emphases should be determined by the needs and
preferences of the people in the community.   The average library
patron cares nothing for theories of librarianship concerning the
composition of the branch collection.   He asks only: "Does the
branch give me what I need or want?   If not, does it make every
possible effort to borrow or buy it?"

In discussing types of collections it is necessary to distinguish
between the branch which endeavors to give as much service as pos
sible within the limitations of facilities, staff, and budget (the
service branch), and the smaller reading or distribution centers
used by larger systems to supplement the large area or regional
branches.   The service branch will offer reference and other
special services, a good proportion of non-fiction, a rather wide
range of fiction, and more books for children.   The reading center
aims mainly to circulate popular books at the neighborhood level,
and will be staffed usually by non-professionals.

A great deal has been written concerning the "well-rounded"
or "balanced" book collection.   Both terms are ambiguous, for
aside from the well-known classics in adult and children's books,
there is no one standardized list of books that can be used as a
measuring stick for all branches, even those of approximately equal
size.   The Standard Catalog Series comes the closest to furnishing
such a set of guidelines, but it, too, must be used with discrimination.

Even were such an ideal list of basic books for all branches
available, it would be in a constant state of flux, and extremely
difficult to keep up to date.   The branch book collection must be
measured against such factors as demand, reader satisfaction,
physical condition, timeliness, accuracy, and the opinions of the
experts.

How far shall the branch go in supplying ephemeral best-
seller fiction?   The quality of the reviews will help determine this,
of course, but many branches now satisfy much of the initial heavy
demand for best-sellers (fiction or non-fiction) through one of the
rental services such as American Lending Service or the Mc-
Naughton Service.   Although these services are not cheap, they may
be less expensive than buying and cluttering up shelf space with
multiple copies of books which may soon fade in popularity.   Since
most copies of rental books can be purchased by the library,
usually after about six months, for about 25 per cent of retail cost,
the end result, should demand continue, is more books for less
money, available at a time when they are most needed.   Whether
or not a rental service will be available to the branch will depend
largely on the policy of the system.

Most book selection policy statements seem to have originated
in an attempt to provide a defense of controversial books or to af-
firm a broad policy of intellectual freedom.   However, to be really
effective a good book selection policy should give a broad outline of
all types of material to be purchased, relating the types of material
to two basic factors: the characteristics of the community to be
served, and the goals of the particular branch or library.[3]

Figure 38: Book Selection Workshop at Cypress Branch,
Orange County Public Library, Orange, California
Participants were book selection people from branch libraries and
headquarters. Branch heads meet with the regional librarian once a
month and work from a suggested purchase list. However, branch
heads can bring up recommendations not on the list at each meeting.
The Orange County Public Library has two regional libraries at
present. Two more are planned.

No branch or member library can hope to meet all the
diverse requests it will encounter. The hobbyist always wants more
books on his particular hobby. The student will expect more mater
al in depth than any branch can provide. One patron will be
shocked at some of the modern novels; others will request the
latest sensation. The mystery fans will clamor for ever more
who-dun-its; and parents will wonder why the branch does not have
all the favorite books they read as children. A book selection
policy based firmly on the interests, occupations, educational at-
tainments, age levels, and preoccupations of the service area will
be more easily justified than any other type and will provide the

branch librarian, new or experienced, with guidelines for making her
selections, from the ever-increasing publishing output. [3]

Certain general principles, particularly those relating to controversial titles, will be the same for all branches, but policies
concerning general types of material should be tailored to the branch
and its area. Thus one all-inclusive policy for the system should
be supplemented with individual book-selection outlines for each
branch that shows special needs. Obviously the branch librarian
and her staff are best fitted to work out such a supplement. This
idea will seem revolutionary to the traditionalist who has held
branch policies and procedures to a standard pattern, but it is far
more in line with today's attempts to meet reader needs.

The advice of specialists in the community may be helpful
when no one on the branch staff has special ability in a particular
field, but ultimate responsibility cannot be delegated to the community. In a non-consolidated system, member libraries, board
and librarian, working together, will have to ask themselves the
following questions when framing their book selection policy:

How much weight should be given to public demand?

Should the library aim for a well-rounded collection?

How much depth is needed in subject collections?

How many books are necessary for different age groups? What
proportions of the collection?

Can the same standards be used for selection for different
age groups?

What shall the stand be on controversial books?

What basic tools of selection will be used? [3]

Help will be available from system headquarters. There are
also many books and articles available on the subject of book selection, and sample book selection policies may be obtained from other
libraries. In the field of children's books selection should closely
follow professional standards and a larger degree of uniformity
throughout the system is acceptable and usually desirable.

Among the specific community factors to be taken into consideration in building a good branch collection are the following:

1. The presence or absence of other libraries in the area and the types of books available in these libraries.

2. The number and types of schools or colleges in the area which will influence the volume of student demand.

3. Recreational interests of the community.

4. Racial origins of the residents.

5. Types and number of clubs and organizations.

6. Average income of the residents.

7. Age levels of the residents.

8. Educational levels.

9. Changing fads of the times.

10. Current political and social trends.

11. Religious groups in the community.

12. Businesses and industries located within the service area.

13. Occupations of the people.

14. Density of population.

As an example, a branch located in the heart of a Mexican-American neighborhood would need far more books in Spanish for all ages, books on learning English for foreigners, and material on the cultural heritage of Mexico than would a branch located in a downtown area patronized by only a few Mexican-Americans. A branch in a disadvantaged area would need more high-interest, low-vocabulary material, more books of practical help on baby care, sewing, and other aspects of homemaking, more purely recreational material, and many activities designed to motivate those who have not developed the reading habit. Interviews with branch librarians in Baltimore, Boston, Dallas, Detroit, Los Angeles, and New York reveal that these libraries are building different book collections and updating services to reach out to the ghetto dwellers and the so-called disadvantaged.

The character of the book collection will establish the type of service rendered, according to Richard Sealock:

Even the smallest branch can make a contribution to
popular, informal education with a carefully chosen collection.......... The provision of a branch book stock,
however, should be made with full understanding of the
resources of the much more convenient commercial outlets which emphasize light entertainment. Book selection
should consider the great amount of time former avid
readers of mystery stories and other light novels now
spend watching television. Public funds are too limited
to permit too much emphasis on such light fare when
television and the corner drug store book stand can do a
better job and this without the red tape of the circulation
desk and return procedure.

Individual branches with extensive service areas will find
a minimum of 30,000 volumes is desirable to meet the
demands. Another useful standard is two books per
capita based on the estimated service area. There will
be a few branches in geographical pockets where 20,000
volumes or less are sufficient. These figures will increase as variety and duplication expand the collection.
A regional branch will need at least 100,000 volumes,
particularly if it is to serve an area with many senior
high school or college students and meet the demand for
bound periodicals and other reference sets. A sub-branch
with a limited schedule should have 8,000 to 12,000 volumes. Any decrease in the figures given would only add
to the burden of books requested from the main building
reserve stock. Any interlibrary loans should be limited
to the occasionally-used item or to a book or subject sud-
denly but temporarily in demand. [4]

The question of how much duplication is justifiable in a branch
to meet student demand for frequently-assigned books is one which
occurs in all libraries, central or branch. Some librarians feel
this is the responsibility of the school library and that purchasing
such titles in large quantity deprives non-students of valuable titles
which they need. Others believe that students are so large a part
of the total body of users that every effort should be made to supply
such demand. One solution has been to purchase such titles in
paperback and in such quantity that there will nearly always be at
least one copy on the shelf. George B. Moreland, Director of the
Montgomery County Department of Public Libraries, Bethesda,
Maryland, has described an experiment[5] in which branch librarians
selected a minimum of ten copies of each of 60 titles from a master
list of 90. Instructions were given to branches to reorder in

multiples of five copies whenever the supply on hand was reduced
to three copies.   Paperback racks were supplied by the dealer
without charge.   Books were stamped for ownership only, pockets
marked with "PB" and pasted in; no other processing was done and
no cataloging.

> No limit was placed on the number of books charged out
> and overdues were not sent unless they appeared on the
> Regiscope film with other charges to the patron on that
> date.   A pencil mark was made on the pocket each time
> a book was returned, and it was found that the average
> number of circulations was ten before discard became
> necessary.
>
> From January 20, 1967, the duration of the experiment,
> the 11 branches participating (five for nine months, two
> for six months, and five for four months) purchased
> 21,821 copies of 122 titles (90 from the original list plus
> 32 added during the nine months) at a cost of $14,799 or
> an average of 68¢ per copy, including the dealer's 20
> per cent discount. [5]

When the project was completed, comments from the branch
librarians indicated it had been an unqualified success.   Following
this procedure in lesser or greater quantity, according to the size
of the library system and its budget, might well provide the answer
for those directors who feel that it is essential to supply the "in-
demand" titles on an always available basis.

"In regard to reference service the branch collection should
include reference and bibliographic materials adequate to supply
answers to the most commonly-asked questions.   It should also
contain circulating materials adequate to supply the most common
needs, and should, if necessary, be supplemented by a rotating
collection and inter-library loans from the central headquarters
library.   The circulating collection should represent a reasonable
balance among the adult, young adult, and children's material." [6]

When allocating funds among adult, young adult and children's
books, an often-used method is to base the allocation upon the percentage of total circulation for each age group for the previous
year.   This assumes that the collections are already fairly well
balanced and do not require special building up in one or more of
the three divisions.   Since some libraries do not keep a separate

circulation total for young adult books, but include them with either the adult or juvenile count, a two-way division based on previous circulation may be necessary.

In the larger branches the collection may be built with a view to the development of resources for a larger region. Proper consideration should be given to the materials available at the Central Library, and it is important that the branch librarian be well acquainted with the resources of the central agency. If each community branch stocks certain titles indigenous to its area, interbranch lending will be used frequently, in addition to central-to-branch lending. Branch librarians should therefore be fully aware of any subject specialization in other branches so that subject requests are not slowed up by sending them all unnecessarily through headquarters.

Few branches attempt to supply separate reference collections for young adults unless they are very large indeed. The Standard Catalog for High School Libraries, Standard Catalog for Public Libraries, the A. L. A. Basic Lists for Junior and Senior High Schools, the New York Public Library's annual Teen-Age list, and the current recommendations of Booklist, Library Journal and other standard tools are the best sources for building a young adult collection. The trend seems to be toward upgrading such collections by using many more titles selected from the adult shelves. One school of thought today does not believe in a special young adult section, but many librarians, this writer among them, believe that such a collection serves a useful purpose in bridging the gap between the use of the children's room and more or less unrestricted use of the adult collection. There is no question but that today's teen-agers are reading on a more sophisticated and mature level than their counterparts of the 40's and 50's. Books of greater social import, some of them controversial, are placed on high school reading lists. The alert branch librarian must meet this challenge and be prepared to supply such material, whatever her personal inhibitions.

In some systems, where the demand for mysteries, light love stories, westerns, and science fiction is still heavy, such demand is being met either by paperback collections of the best authors in these fields or by collections of hardbounds which rotate from branch to branch, giving each one a fresh supply of new titles at certain intervals. Demand for this type of material seems to be diminishing, undoubtedly due to the ease with which they can be purchased and because of the increasing fare of such material via television. The patron who regularly watches Gunsmoke, Bonanza, The Virginian, and other westerns on T. V. has less time or taste for western books.

Periodicals present branches with a real problem. Because of space limitations, many branch librarians would like to convert almost entirely to microfilm for past issues, keeping only about a one-year file of original issues. However, the average branch cannot afford a whole battery of microfilm readers, and microfilm viewing does not satisfy the patron who wants or needs to take the material home. The ideal situation would be to have both if space permitted, allowing the single periodical issues to circulate until worn out but assuring retention of all back issues on microfilm. The cost of converting back issues to microfilm, or rather of purchasing microfilmed files from one of the standard suppliers, is less than might be expected. If microfilm is nevertheless not possible and back issues are retained, most branches find it impractical to keep more than a five-year run. When space permits, magazines indexed in The Readers' Guide should be retained, for patrons may find back issues out or missing from the central library's files, and some patrons cannot make the trip to the central library. Periodicals are now used so much in reference that their importance cannot be overstressed.

Some branches confine their periodical files to titles listed in the Abridged Readers' Guide, but this seems a short-sighted policy. The branch may grow in use and find it difficult to expand back files later. Many high school libraries already carry the magazines listed in the Abridged Readers' Guide, and the student patron expects something more from a public library branch which serves all ages.

In branches, periodical selection, like book selection, is influenced by the character of the community served and the availability of space and funds. Although the Readers' Guide items should be priority purchases, titles not indexed should be on the subscription list if they satisfy special needs of the patrons in the service area. Branches refer patrons to the central periodical collection for more scholarly and specialized periodical references.

The newspaper collection should include all local papers, the nearest metropolitan daily and Sunday edition (or several, if there are several large cities nearby), the Christian Science Monitor, The New York Times, and The Wall Street Journal. Others will be added as needed. It is rarely possible to keep more than a one-month file of dailies or a six-months file of weeklies among out-of-town papers, but the local papers should be kept as far back as space allows, or should be sent to the central library for preservation or microfilming.

The following list of periodicals is suggested as minimum for a branch of 6,000-10,000 square feet. Since the minimum recommended for an 8,000 square foot branch is 100 subscriptions, it is suggested that the individual branch fill out this list with a dozen or so magazines particularly suited to its area's recreational interests or reference needs.

A.   Indexed in Readers' Guide

America	Current History
American Artist	Ebony
American Heritage	Electronics World
Americas	Esquire
Atlantic Monthly	Field and Stream
Audubon	Flying
Aviation Week and Space Technology	Fortune
Better Homes and Gardens	Good Housekeeping
Bulletin of the Atomic Scientist	Harpers
	Hobbies
Business Week	Holiday
Catholic World	Hot Rod
Changing Times	Ladies Home Journal
Christian Century	Library Journal
Congressional Digest	Life
Consumer Bulletin	Look
	Mademoiselle
Consumer Reports	Mechanix Illustrated

A.   Indexed in Readers' Guide (Cont.)

Motor Trend	Science Digest
Nation	Science Newsletter
National Geographic	Scientific American
Natural History	Senior Scholastic, with
New Republic	Scholastic Teacher
New Yorker	Seventeen
Newsweek	Sports Illustrated
Outdoor Life	Sunset
Parent's Magazine	Time
Plays	Today's Health
Popular Electronics	Travel
Popular Mechanics	U.S. News and World Report
Popular Photography	Vital Speeches
Popular Science	Vogue
Reader's Digest	Wilson Library Bulletin
Redbook	Writer
Saturday Review	Writer's Digest

B.   Not Indexed in Readers' Guide but Usually of Popular Interest

All Pets*	Life en Espanol
American Girl	Modern Maturity
Arizona Highways	Negro Digest
Booklist	Selecciones de Readers'
Boys' Life	Digest
Child Life	Surfer
Children's Digest	Teen
Family Handyman	Trailer Life
Highlights for Children	Western Horseman

*(In medium-sized or small branch preferable to taking specialized magazines on the various types of pets, such as cats, dogs, horses, etc.)

Periodicals may be mailed directly to the branch or may be received, checked in and processed at the Central Library. In a rural system it is best if the issues come directly to the branch; otherwise delays can occur and there is an extra transportation problem. In a city system, if it is the custom to reinforce magazines or place them in special covers, this will usually be done at headquarters before the magazines are sent out to the branches. Subscriptions will usually be handled through the central library on an overall bid system.

At least one currently published periodical title should be available for each 250 people in the service area. Branch and community libraries should not ordinarily attempt to build extensive back files of periodicals but should depend upon the headquarters collection if they cannot have them available on microfilm.

Prince George's County Library, Hyattsville, Maryland, has as its ultimate aim having each large branch offer a special emphasis on one particular subject area, i. e. , business, psychology, sociology, law, in addition to its basic collection. At present the larger branches offer special rooms housing Marylandia, a special collection on the American Negro, a horse racing collection, and a reference collection of children's literature for parents and teachers. Any patron interested in one of the special subjects can go directly to the branch where that collection is located and find all of the material in one place. Basic books in each of the special fields should, of course, be available at all branches.

Community libraries should organize their own pamphlet collections. Other non-book materials needed regularly should also be in the branch collection, but the local branch or community library should be able to draw on the larger collection of the system for supplementary material. It is assumed that patrons will be able to borrow from any branch or the central library and return the material to any branch or the central library. Material returned at a different agency should be promptly placed in the delivery bin for prompt sending to the agency from which borrowed. Information about the total holdings of the system should be readily available to each unit. Headquarters or the Central library should supply filmstrips, recordings, tapes, and films as needed by the branches for special requests, and to meet the needs of such special groups as the Laubach Literacy groups, the handicapped, the blind, and the individual specialist who for one reason or another cannot use the central library. The central library should make available the necessary supporting and bibliographic information, or access thereto, to locate facts and specialized resources in the area, the state, and the nation.

Materials used regularly in the branch should be in the collection in sufficient duplication to prevent unnecessary delays in

serving the needs of the community. The bulk of materials in the
smaller neighborhood libraries is expendable within ten years, but
withdrawals at any level should be offered to the next higher eche-
lon of resources (for example, the regional or area branch) before
being destroyed.

Most modern branch libraries now have phonograph record
collections, selection being influenced by record reviewing media,
available funds, and a compromise with popular demand. A too-
classically weighted collection will limit usage, as will a collection
too heavily weighted with ephemera. The branch should have the
best works by the best artists in many fields, as recordings of
good quality produced by standard companies. Spoken word recordings (plays, poetry, speeches), shorthand dictation records, records
for learning languages, novelty records such as sound effects, bird
songs; folk music, opera, symphonies, concertos, dance music,
vocal and instrumental should all be considered for inclusion.
Broadway musicals are especially popular. Lesser known works
can be requested from the central library. Since record manufacturers are now turning entirely to stereo reproduction, record collections should be predominantly of this type, although monaural
records of recent vintage should not be discarded. Many patrons
may still have monaural machines which cannot take stereo records.
How far the public library and its branches should go in supplying
records of the "new" music must at this point be the decision of
each individual system, in some cases, of each individual branch.
Where a special effort is being made to reach disinterested groups of
young people in a disadvantaged area, more latitude should be allowed.
Some libraries now have casettes and recorders.

Two lists of basic reference book selection tools, one for
community branch libraries and one for regional branch libraries,
have been prepared in a joint effort of the staffs of the Minneapolis
Public Library and the Hennepin County Library. They are available at a nominal price from the Minneapolis Public Library
Business Office, 300 Nicollet Mall, Minneapolis, Minnesota, 55401.
These two lists are combined on following page.

A Basic Reference Collection

     This list is a combination of two lists compiled by a joint committee of branch librarians from the Hennepin County Library and the Minneapolis Public Library. The basic consideration of the committee was the selection of titles to provide a well-balanced collection of reference materials which would satisfy general community needs. Specialized materials were considered the province of the Central Library upon which all branches may draw for information and to which all patrons may be referred. The list is not meant to be a static one but is to be updated and revised as publication of new materials and change in patron requests dictate.

     Titles marked with an asterisk in the following list are included only in area or regional libraries, which supplement reference collections of the community libraries with some of the more specialized materials needed to serve a larger area in greater depth, but draw upon and refer patrons to the more complete collections of the Central Library.

     Except where otherwise noted, all other titles are included both in the area or regional libraries and in community branch libraries of Hennepin County Library and Minneapolis Public Library which have adult book collections of 20,000 to 30,000 volumes.

General Works

Encyclopedias

Collier's Encyclopedia. Collier-Macmillan, 179.50 (price varies)
Encyclopaedia Britannica. Encyclopaedia Britannica, 229.00 (price
    varies)
Encyclopedia Americana. Grolier Corp., 218.00 (price varies)
World Book Encyclopedia. Field Enterprises, 114.00 (price varies)
    4 encyclopedias for each branch, purchased on rotating basis,
    one new encyclopedia each year.

Catholic Encyclopedia. McGraw, 1967.
Jewish Encyclopedia. Isidore Singer, ed. KTAV Pub., 1964, 81.95
General Encyclopedias in Print. S. P. Walsh. Bowker, 1966, 3.00

Yearbooks

Americana Annual. Grolier Corp., Annual, 12.00
Britannica Book of the Year. Encyclopaedia Britannica, Annual,
    8.00
Collier's Encyclopedia Year Book. Collier-Macmillan, Annual, 7.00
    One yearbook each year for five years.

Almanacs, Statistical Records, Etc.

Census of Population: 1960: Minnesota; U. S. Census Bureau.
    GPO, 1963, 1.50
Information Please Almanac. Simon, Annual, 2.95
*Negro in America; E. W. Miller. Harvard, 1966, 6.95
Reader's Digest Almanac. Reader's Digest, Annual, 2.50
Statesman's Yearbook. Little, Annual, 10.00
Statistical Abstract of the U.S.; U.S. Census Bureau. GPO,
    Annual, 3.75
*Whitaker's Almanack. Whitaker, Annual, 3.50
World Almanac. Doubleday, Annual, 2.75
*World Communications: Press, Radio, Television, Film. Unesco,
    1964, 11.00

Dictionaries

Funk and Wagnalls New Standard Dictionary of the English
    Language. Funk, 1963, 47.50
Webster's Third New International Dictionary of the English
    Language. Merriam, 1961, 47.50
    (Only one of the above in community branches)
English Language Dictionaries in Print; S. P. Walsh. Bowker, 1965,
    3.00
*Oxford English Dictionary; J. A. H. Murray. Oxford, 1933, 300.00
Webster's Seventh New Collegiate Dictionary. Merriam, 1965, 5.75

Language

Abbreviations Dictionary; Ralph DeSola. Meredith, 1964, 4.95
Acronyms and Initialisms Dictionary. Gale, 1965, 15.00
*American Language; H. L. Mencken. Knopf, abridged ed. 1963, 12.9
*American Thesaurus of Slang; L. V. Berrey & Melvin Van den Bark.
    Crowell, 1953, 15.00
*Dictionary of American Slang; Harold Wentworth & S. B. Flexner.
    Crowell, supp. ed. 1967, 7.95
*Dictionary of Contemporary American Usage; Bergen Evans.
    Random, 1957, 6.95
Dictionary of Foreign Phrases and Abbreviations; Kevin Guinagh.
    Wilson, 1965, 6.00
Dictionary of Modern English Usage; H. W. Fowler. Oxford, 1965,
    5.00
Dictionary of Slang and Unconventional English; E. H. Partridge.
    Macmillan, 1961, 17.50
Modern American Usage; Wilson Follett. Hill & Wang, 1966, 7.50
NBC Handbook of Pronunciation; J. F. Bender. Crowell, 1964, 4.95
*New Roget's Thesaurus in Dictionary Form; P. M. Roget. Putnam,
    1965, 4.50
Roget's Thesaurus of English Words and Phrases; P. M. Roget.
    St. Martin's, 1965, 6.95
Shorter Oxford English Dictionary on Historical Principles; 3rd ed.
    rev. by C. T. Onions. Oxford, 1944, Addenda 1955. 2 vols., 32.0
    (included in community branches only)

Webster's Dictionary of Synonyms. Merriam, 1951, 6.75
Wood's Unabridged Rhyming Dictionary; Clement Wood. World, 1943,
    7.50

Indexes

*Bibliographic Index. Wilson, Semi-annual, Annual & 3 year cum.,
    service basis (51.00)
*Bibliography of American Autobiographies; Louis Kaplan, comp.
    U. of Wis., 1961, 6.00
Biography Index. Wilson, Quarterly, Annual & 3 year cum., 15.00
Book Review Digest. Wilson, Monthly, Quarterly & Annual cum.,
    29.25
*Book Review Index. Gale, Monthly, Quarterly cum., 24.00
Cumulative Book Index. Wilson, Monthly, Semi-annual & 2 year
    cum., 50.00
Debate Index; J.R. Dunlap. Wilson, 2nd supp., 1964, 3.00
*Library Literature. Wilson, Quarterly, Annual & 3 year cum.,
    service basis (55.00)
*National Geographic Index. Underhill, 2 vols. & 2 suppls., 12.75
*N.Y. Times Index. Bowker, Semi-monthly & Annual, 125.00
Reader's Guide to Periodical Literature. Wilson, Semi-monthly,
    Annual & 2 year cum., 25.00
Speech Index. Scarecrow, 1935-1955, 8.50; Supp. 1956-1960, 5.00
*Vertical File Index. Wilson, Monthly, Annual cum., 8.00

Biographical Dictionaries

*Celebrity Register; Cleveland Amory, ed. Harper, 1963, 25.00
*Chamber's Biographical Dictionary; J.O. Thorne, ed. St. Martin's,
    1962, 15.00
Current Biography. Wilson, Monthly, 6.00; Yearbook, 7.00
Dictionary of American Biography. Scribner, 1958, 242.00
*Dictionary of Canadian Biography. U. of Toronto, 1966- , 15.00
    per vol.
Dictionary of National Biography. Oxford, 1953- , 250.00
*Hall of Fame for Great Americans; Theodore Morello, ed. N.Y.
    Univ., 1967, 6.00
*New Century Cyclopedia of Names; C.L. Barnhart, ed. Appleton,
    3 vols., 1954, 39.50
Webster's Biographical Dictionary. Merriam, 1964, 8.50
Who Was When? M.A. deFord. Wilson, 1950, 6.00
Who Was Who in America. Marquis, 4 vols., 1943-1961, 100.00
Who's Who. Macmillan, Annual, 27.50
Who's Who in the Midwest. Marquis, Biennial, 26.00
Who's Who of American Women. Marquis, Biennial, 26.50

Booklists and Catalogs

American Book-Prices Current. Am. Book-Prices Current, Annual,
    25.00; 5 year cum., 50.00
Basic Book Collection for High Schools. A.L.A. & N.E.A., 1963,
    3.00

Booklists and Catalogs (Cont.)

Book Bait. A. L. A., new ed. in prep.
Booklist and Subscription Books Bulletin. A. L. A., Semi-monthly,
    8.00
*Bookman's Price Index; Daniel McGrath, ed. Gale, vol. 2, 1966,
    32.50
*Bookman's Guide to Americana; J. N. Heard. Scarecrow, 3rd ed.
    1964, 10.50
Books For You; N. E. A. Wash. Square, 1964, .90
Books in Print. Bowker, Annual, 18.00
*Catalog of Reprints in Series; R. M. Orton. Scarecrow, 1964, 25.00
Catholic Booklist. Cath. Lib. Ass'n., Annual, 1.50
Doors to More Mature Reading. A. L. A., 1964, 2.50
Fiction Catalog. Wilson, 7th ed. 1960, Supp. 1961-1965, service
    basis (11.00)
Forthcoming Books. Bowker, Bi-monthly, 12.00
Gateways to Readable Books; Ruth Strang. Wilson, 1966, 5.00
*Good Reading. New Am. Lib., 1964, .75
*Guide to Reference Books; C. M. Winchell. A. L. A., 7th ed. and 4
    supps., 27.50
Historical Fiction; Hannah Logasa. McKinley, 1964, 8.50
Historical Nonfiction; Hannah Logasa. McKinley, 1964, 8.50
*How and Where to Look it Up; R. W. Murphey. McGraw, 1958, 16.50
Is My Old Book Valuable? E. L. Stern. Antiques, 1966, 2.00
Junior High School Library Catalog. 1965.
Paperbound Books in Print. Bowker, Monthly, Quarterly cum., 16.00
Patterns in Reading; Jean Roos. A. L. A., new ed. in prep.
Public Library Catalog. Wilson, 5th ed. 1968, service basis.
*Publisher's Trade List Annual. Bowker, Annual, 10.00
*Rare Bibles: An Introduction for Collectors and a Descriptive
    Checklist; E. A. R. Rumball-Petrie. Duschnes, 1963, 7.50
Reader's Adviser; Hester Hoffman, ed. Bowker, 1964, 20.00
Senior High School Library Catalog. Wilson, 9th ed. 1967,
    service basis.
Subject Guide to Books in Print. Bowker, Annual, 17.50
Subject Guide to Forthcoming Books. Bowker, Bi-monthly, 8.00
*Subscription Books Bulletin Reviews. A. L. A., 3 vols., 1956-1964,
    9.50
*Textbooks in Print. Bowker, Annual, 4.00
*Vocations in Biography and Fiction; K. A. Haebich. A. L. A., 1962,
    1.75

Library and Publishing Directories

*American Book Publishing Record. Bowker, Annual, 25.00
*American Library Directory. Bowker, every three years, 25.00
*Bowker Annual of Library and Book Trade Information. Bowker,
    Annual, 10.25
*Special Libraries Directory. Spec. Lib. Ass'n., 1966, 12.50
*Literary Market Place. Bowker, Annual, 7.45
Writer's Handbook; A. S. Burack, ed. Writer, 1964, 7.95
Writer's Market. Writer's Digest, Annual, 5.95

Government Publications

*Guide to U. S. Government Serials and Publications; J. L. Andriot.
   McLean, vol. 1, 1964, 16.00
Popular Guide to Government Publications; W. P. Leidy. Columbia,
   1965, 8.95
Price Lists of Government Publications. GPO, Irregular, Free
Selected U. S. Government Publications. GPO, Bi-weekly, Free

Quotations

Contemporary Quotations; J. B. Simpson. Crowell, 1964, 6.95
Familiar Quotations; John Bartlett, comp. Little, 1955, 10.00
Home Book of Quotations; B. E. Stevenson, ed. Dodd, 1959, 25.00
Macmillan Book of Proverbs; B. E. Stevenson, ed. Macmillan,
   1965, 25.00
Magill's Quotations from World Literature in Context; F. N. Magill,
   ed. Harper, 1965, 9.95
Standard Book of Shakespeare Quotations: B. E. Stevenson, comp.
   Funk, 1953, 7.50
*Treasury of Lincoln Quotations; Fred Kerner, ed. Doubleday, 1965,
   4.95
Treasury of Presidential Quotations; C. T. Harnsberger. Follett,
   1964, 6.95

Speeches

*Representative American Speeches; A. C. Baird, ed. Wilson,
   Annual, 3.00
Treasury of Great American Speeches; Charles Hurd, ed. Hawthorn,
   1959, 5.95
Treasury of the World's Great Speeches; Houston Peterson, ed.
   Simon, 1965, 7.50

Associations and Foundations

Encyclopedia of Associations. Gale, 1964, 3 vols., 62.50
Foundation Directory; A. D. Walton. Russell Sage Found., 1964,
   10.00

Directories

Directory of Post Offices; U. S. Post Office Dept. GPO, Annual,
   2.75
Polk's Minneapolis (Hennepin County: Minn.) City Directory. Polk's
   Biennial, 90.00
Polk's Minneapolis Suburban (Anoka, Hennepin and Ramsey
   Counties, Minn.) City Directory. Polk, Biennial, 50.00
Polk's Saint Paul (Ramsey County, Minn.) City Directory. Polk,
   Biennial, 90.00
Zip Code Directory; U. S. Post Office Dept. GPO, 1966, 7.00

Newspapers and Periodicals

Ayer Directory of Newspapers and Periodicals. Ayer, Annual, 30.00
*Foreign Press; J.C. Merrill. Louisiana State, 1963, 6.50
*Ulrich's International Periodicals Directory. Bowker, 2 vols. and
    supps., 15.00
*Willing's Press Guide. Willing, Annual, 7.00

Etiquette

Amy Vanderbilt's New Complete Book of Etiquette; Amy Vanderbilt.
    Doubleday, 1963, 5.50
Etiquette; Emily Post. Funk, 1965, 5.95
*Good Housekeeping's Book of Today's Etiquette; Louise Raymond.
    Harper, 1965, 5.95
*Navy Blue Book. Military Pub. Inst., Annual, 4.95
*Service Etiquette; B.J. Harral & O.D. Swartz. U.S. Naval Inst.,
    1963, 6.50

Names

*Baby Name Finder; J. E. Schmidt. Thomas, 1960, 10.50
Pet Names; J. E. Taggart. Scarecrow, 1962, 9.00
What to Name the Baby; Evelyn Wells. Garden City, 1953, 2.95
    (Community libraries only)

Current News

Facts on File News Reference Service. Facts on File, Weekly,
    120.00
*Facts on File Master Index. Facts on File, 4 vols., 1946-1965,
    200.00
*Public Affairs Information Service Bulletin. Public Affairs,
    Weekly, 100.00

Miscellaneous

American Book of Days; G.W. Douglas. Wilson, 1948, 6.00
American Negro Reference Book; J. P. Davis, ed. Prentice, 1966,
    19.95
American Nicknames; G. E. Shankle. Wilson, 1955, 7.50
*American War Medals and Decorations; E. S. E. Kerrigan. Viking,
    1964, 6.50
Chase's Calendar of Annual Events; H. V. Chase. Apple Tree Press,
    Annual, 1.50
Dictionary of Dates; Audrey Butler, ed. Dutton, 1964, 5.50
Encyclopedia of Superstitions; Edwin Radford. Dufour, 1961, 7.95
Famous First Facts; J. N. Kane. Wilson, 1964, 18.00
Guinness Book of World Records; Norris McWhirter. Sterling,
    1966, 3.95
Lasser's Your Income Tax. Simon, Annual, 1.95
Medicare; Sydney Goldberger. Oceana, 1966, 3.00

Nicknames of Cities and States of the U.S.; Joseph Kane. Scarecrow,
    1965, 7.50
Reader's Encyclopedia; W.R. Benet, ed. Crowell, 1965, 8.95
Robert's Rules of Order; H.M. Robert. Scott, 1956, 3.75
*Student's Guide to Military Service; Michael Harwood. Meredith,
    1966, 5.95
What Happened When? S.M. Merkin. Washburn, 1966, 6.95
Your Social Security; J.K. Lasser. Simon, 1966, 1.95

History and Geography

Atlases and Gazetteers

General World Atlases in Print; S.P. Walsh, comp. Bowker, 1966,
    3.00
Goode's World Atlas. Rand, 1964, 9.95
Historical Atlas; W.R. Shepherd. Barnes, 1964, 15.00
Historical Atlas: Ancient, Medieval and Modern; Ramsey Muir.
    Barnes, 1965, 16.00
Medallion World Atlas. Hammond, 1966, 19.95
Oxford Economic Atlas of the World. Oxford, 1965, 15.00
*Rand McNally Commercial Atlas and Marketing Guide. Rand, An-
    nual, 55.00
Rand McNally Road Atlas. Rand, Annual, 1.95
*Times Atlas of the World. Houghton, 1955-1959, 5 vols., 125.00
*Times Index-Gazetteer of the World. Houghton, 1966, 50.00

Geography

*Glossary of Geographical Terms; L.D. Stamp, ed. Wiley, 1961,
    12.50
Larousse Encyclopedia of World Geography. Odyssey, 1965, 19.95
Webster's Geographical Dictionary. Merriam, 1964, 8.50

American History

Album of American History; J.T. Adams. Scribner, 6 vols.,
    1944-1961, 81.00
Atlas of American History; J.T. Adams, ed. Scribner, 1943, 16.50
Chief Executive: Inaugural Addresses of the Presidents...;
    F.L. Israel, ed. Crown, 1965, 4.95
Civil War Dictionary; M.M. Boatner. McKay, 1959, 15.00
Dictionary of American History; J.T. Adams, ed. Scribner, 7 vols.,
    98.00; Index vol. inc. supp., 1963, 12.50
Documents of American History; H.S. Commager, ed. Appleton,
    1 vol. ed., 1958, 6.75
Encyclopedia of American Facts and Dates; Gorton Carruth.
    Crowell, 1962, 6.95
Encyclopedia of American History; R.B. Morris, ed. Harper, 1965,
    8.95
Encyclopedia of the American Revolution; M.M. Boatner. McKay,
    1966, 17.50

American History (Cont.)

Facts About the Presidents; J. N. Kane. Wilson, 1959, 6.00
Gopher Reader; Gopher Historian. Minn. Hist. Soc., 1958, 3.00
*Growth of the American Republic; S. E. Morison & H. S. Commager.
    Oxford, 2 vols., 1962, 30.00
*Guide to Historical Literature. Macmillan, 1961, 16.50
*Guide to the Diplomatic History of the U. S.; S. F. Bemis & G. G.
    Griffin, Peter Smith, 1965, 12.50
*Harvard Guide to American History; Oscar Handlin. Harvard, 1954,
    12.50
Historical Statistics of the United States, Colonial Times to 1957;
    U. S. Census Bureau. GPO, 1960, 1.00; Continuation 1962 and
    revisions
Minnesota: A History of the State; Theodore Blegen. Univ. of Minn.,
    1963, 8.50
Oxford Companion to American History; T. H. Johnson, ed. Oxford,
    1966, 12.50
*State of the Union Messages of the Presidents: 1790-1966; F. L.
    Israel, ed. Chelsea, 3 vols., 1966, 45.00

American Government

*American Counties; J. N. Kane. Scarecrow, 1962, 11.00
*Biographical Directory of the American Congress, 1774-1961. GPO,
    1961, 11.75
Book of the States. Council of State Govts., Biennial, 13.00
Cases in Constitutional Law; R. E. Cushman. Appleton, 1963, 8.95
*Congressional Quarterly Service. Cong. Quart. Service, Weekly,
    120.00, includes Congressional Quarterly Almanac (Annual).
Congress and the Nation. Congressional Quarterly Service, 1965,
    27.50
County and City Data Book; U. S. Census Bureau. GPO, 1962, 5.25
Diplomatic List; U. S. Dept. of State. GPO, Quarterly, 1.25
Encyclopedia of U. S. Government Benefits. W. H. Wise, 1965, 7.95
Foreign Consular Offices in the U. S.; U. S. Dept. of State. GPO,
    Annual, .35
Foreign Service List; U. S. Dept. of State. GPO, Quarterly, 1.75
How to Become a Citizen of the U. S.; Am. Council for
    Nationalities Service. Oceana, 1963, 2.50
*Immigration Laws of the U. S.; F. L. Auerbach. Bobbs, 1961 &
    supp., 15.00
Leading Constitutional Decisions; R. E. Cushman. Appleton, 1963,
    3.50
Legislative Manual. Minn. Sec'y. of State, Biennial, Free
Minneapolis Ordinance Code. Mpls., 2 vols., 1960, Free
Minnesota Statutes. West, 2 vols., 1965, 40.00
*Municipal Year Book. Internat'l. City Managers' Assoc., Annual,
    10.00
Official Congressional Directory; U. S. Congress. GPO, Annual, 3.00
United States Code. GPO, 14 vols. and supp., 93.00
U. S. Government Organization Manual. GPO, Biennial, 2.00

World History

*Cambridge Ancient History. Cambridge, 12 vols. of text, 5 vols.
    of plates, 150. 00
*Cambridge Medieval History. Cambridge, 8 vols., 140. 00
Concise Encyclopedia of Archaeology; Leonard Cottrell, ed.
    Hawthorn, 1960, 15. 00
Encyclopedia of World History; W. L. Langer. Houghton, 1952, 10. 00
*Harper's Dictionary of Classical Antiquity; H. T. Peck. Cooper
    Square, 1962, 25. 00
Larousse Encyclopedia of Modern History; D. M. Dunan. Harper,
    1964, 20. 00
*New Cambridge Modern History. Cambridge, 7 vols. of 14 planned,
    9. 50 each
Oxford Classical Dictionary; M. Cary, ed. Oxford, 1949, 14. 50
Shorter Cambridge Medieval History. Cambridge, 1952, 2 vols.,
    17. 50 (community libraries only)

History and Government of Foreign Nations

*Modern Governments; Harold Zink. Van Nostrand, 1966, 8. 50
Political Handbook and Atlas of the World. Harper, Annual, 7. 50
Worldmark Encyclopedia of the Nations; Mosche Sachs, ed. Harper,
    5 vols., 1965, 49. 95
Africa: A Handbook to the Continent; Colin Legum. Praeger, 1966,
    18. 50
African Encounter. A. L. A., 1963, 1. 50
*West Africa Annual. Int. Pub. Serv., Annual, 15. 00
*Year Book and Guide to East Africa. Rand, Annual, 3. 00
*Year Book and Guide to Southern Africa. Rand, Annual, 3. 00
Asia: A Handbook. Praeger, 1966, 25. 00
Australian Encyclopedia. Mich. State, 1958, 125. 00
Modern Encyclopedia of Australia and New Zealand; V. S. Barnes.
    World, 1964, 25. 00 (community libraries)
Canadian Almanac and Directory. Pitman, Annual, 12. 50
Canada: the Official Handbook. Canada Bureau of Statistics, annual,
    2. 50 (community libraries)
Encyclopedia Canadiana. Grolier, 10 vols., 1965, 149. 50
Europa Yearbook. Int. Pub. Serv., 1 vol. only, Annual, 25. 00
Britain: an Official Handbook. British Info. Service, Annual, 6. 00
British Political Facts, 1900-1960; D. E. Butler & Jennie Freeman.
    St. Martin's, 1963, 9. 50
Illustrated English Social History; G. M. Trevelyan. McKay, 4 vols.,
    1949-1952, 34. 00
Atlas of Soviet Affairs; R. M. Taaffe & R. C. Kingsbury. Praeger,
    1965, 4. 00 (community libraries)
McGraw-Hill Encyclopedia of Russia and the Soviet Union; M. T.
    Florinsky. McGraw, 1961, 23. 50
Atlas of Latin American Affairs; R. M. Schneider & R. C. Kings-
    bury. Praeger, 1965, 4. 00
South American Handbook. Rand, Annual, 4. 95

Wars

Chronology, 1941-1945 (vol. 47 of U. S. Army in WWII).
    U. S. Dept. of the Army, 1960, 4. 75
Cold War: A Book of Documents; H. L. Trefousse, ed. Putnam,
    1965, 5. 95
Great War: 1914-1918; Cyril Falls. Putnam, 1959, 5. 95
*Guide to the Battlefields of Europe; David Chandler, ed. Chilton,
    2 vols. , 1966, 10. 95
*History of United States Naval Operations in World War II; S. E.
    Morison, Little, 15 vols. , 1949-1960, 112. 50
*Military History and Atlas of the Napoleonic Wars; V. J. Esposito
    and J. R. Elting, eds. Praeger, 1964, 19. 95
Two Ocean War; Samuel Morison. Little, 15. 00 (community
    libraries only)
War: A Concise History, 1939-1945; L. L. Snyder. Messner, 1960,
    7. 95

United Nations

Everyman's United Nations. U. N. , 1964, 5. 00
*Statistical Yearbook; U. N. Int. Doc. Service, Annual, 12. 50
*United Nations Documents Index. U. N. , Monthly, 28. 00
Yearbook of the United Nations. Columbia, 1964-66, 16. 50

Political Science

American Political Terms: An Historical Dictionary; Hans Sperber
    and Travis Trittschuh. Wayne Univ. , 1962, 14. 50
National Party Platforms, 1840-1960. Univ. of Ill. , 1961, 10. 00
    Supp. , 1964, 1. 95
*Political Science: A Bibliographic Guide to the Literature; R. B.
    Harmon. Scarecrow, 1965, 8. 75
*Statistical History of the American Presidential Elections; Svend
    Petersen. Ungar, 1963, 9. 50

Flags

Flags of the World; E. M. C. Barraclough. Warne, 1965, 10. 00
History of the U. S. Flag; M. M. Quaife. Harper, 1961, 4. 95

Law

Black's Law Dictionary; H. C. Black. West, 1966, 11. 00
Guide to Everyday Law; Samuel Kling. Follett, 1965, 5. 95
Law Digests; Vol. 4 of Martindale-Hubbell Law Directory. Martin-
    dale-Hubbell, Annual, 25. 00

Genealogy and Heraldry

Boutell's Heraldry; Charles Boutell. Warne, 1963, 10. 00
Searching for your Ancestors; G. H. Doane. Univ. of Minn. , 1960,
    3. 95

Miscellaneous

Air Force Bases. Stackpole, 1965, 5.95
Bibliography of Civil Rights and Civil Liberties; A. D. Brooks.
  Civil Lib. Educ. Found., 1962, 1.95
Foreign Affairs. Faxon, Quarterly, 6.00
Guide to Army Posts. Stackpole, 1963, 3.95
How Did it Begin? R. Brasch. McKay, 1966, 5.50
Indians of North America; H. E. Driver. Univ. of Chicago, 1961,
  10.95
Names on the Land; G. R. Stewart. Houghton, 1958, 6.00
Official Hotel Red Book and Directory. Am. Hotel Assoc., Annual,
  7.50
Science and Humanities Index. Wilson, Quarterly, Annual cum.,
  service basis (12.00)

Literature

American Literature

American Authors: 1600-1900; S. J. Kunitz & Howard Haycraft, eds.
  Wilson, 1938, 8.00
American Authors and Books, 1640 to the Present Day; W. J.
  Burke, ed., rev. by I. Weiss. Crown, 1962, 8.50
American Novel, 1789-1959; A Checklist of Twentieth Century
  Criticism; D. L. Gerstenberger. Swallow, 1960, 4.75
American Treasury, 1455-1955; Clifton Fadiman, ed. Harper,
  1955, 8.95
Best Loved Poems of the American People; Hazel Felleman, ed.
  Doubleday, 1936, 3.95
Bibliography of American Literature; Jacob Blanck, comp. Yale,
  4 vols., 1955-   , 80.00
Cambridge History of American Literature; W. P. Trent, ed.
  Macmillan, 3 vols. in 1, 1954, 9.95
Library of Literary Criticism: Modern American Literature;
  Dorothy Nyren, ed. Ungar, 3rd ed. 1964, 12.50
Literary History of the United States; R. E. Spiller, ed. Macmillan,
  3rd ed. 1963, 12.50; Bibliographical Supplement, 1964, 12.50
Minnesota Writers; Carmen Richards, ed. Denison, 1961, 4.95
Oxford Book of American Verse; F. O. Matthiessen. Oxford, 1950,
  7.00
Oxford Companion to American Literature; J. D. Hart. Oxford,
  4th ed. 1965, 12.50
Reader's Encyclopedia of American Literature; M. J. Herzberg, ed.
  Crowell, 1962, 12.95
Recent American Literature; D. W. Heiney. Barron's, 1958, 4.95

English Literature

Age of Fiction: The Nineteenth Century British Novel; F. R. Karl.
  Farrar, 1964, 6.00
British Authors before 1800; S. J. Kunitz & Howard Haycraft, eds.
  Wilson, 1952, 8.00

British Authors of the Nineteenth Century; S. J. Kunitz & Howard
  Haycraft, eds. Wilson, 1936, 8.00
*Cambridge Bibliography of English Literature; F. W. Bateson.
  Cambridge, 5 vols. 1941-1957, 45.00
Cambridge History of English Literature; A. W. Ward & A. R.
  Waller, eds.   Cambridge, 15 vols., 1949, 85.00
Complete Concordance of Shakespeare; John Bartlett. St. Martin's,
  27.50
Concise Cambridge Bibliography of English Literature; George Wat-
  son, ed. Cambridge, 1958, 4.95 (community libraries only)
Concise Cambridge History of English Literature; George Sampson,
  ed. Holt, 2nd ed. 1962, 6.50
*English Novel, 1578-1956: A Checklist of Twentieth Century
  Criticisms; Inglis Bell & Donald Baird. Swallow, 1959, 3.00
Library of Literary Criticism of English and American Authors;
  C. W. Moulton, ed. Peter Smith, 8 vols., 1901-1905, 80.00
Library of Literary Criticism: Modern British Literature; R. A.
  Temple and Martin Tucker. Ungar, 3 vols. 1965, 35.00
New Century Handbook of English Literature; C. L. Barnhart &
  W. D. Halsey. Appleton, 1956, 12.00
Oxford Book of English Verse, 1250-1918; Arthur Quiller-Couch, e⟨
  Oxford, 1939, 8.50
Oxford Book of Nineteenth Century English Verse; John Hayward,
  comp. Oxford, 1964, 10.00
Oxford Companion to English Literature; Paul Harvey, comp.
  Oxford, 1946, 10.00

Poetry (other than only American or British)

Anthology of World Poetry; Mark Van Doren, ed. Harcourt, 1936,
  8.75
Concise Encyclopedia of English and American Poets and Poetry;
  Stephen Spender & Donald Hall, eds. Hawthorn, 1963, 15.00
Encyclopedia of Poetry and Poetics; Alex Preminger, ed. Princeton
  1965, 25.00
Explicator Cyclopedia, Vol. 1 Modern Poetry; J. E. Whitesell.
  Quadrangle, 1966, 10.00
Granger's Index to Poetry. McClurg, ed. 5, 1962, 65.00; Supp.,
  1960-1965, 35.00
Home Book of Modern Verse; B. E. Stevenson, ed. Holt, 2nd ed.
  1953, 10.00
Home Book of Verse, American and English; B. E. Stevenson, ed.
  Holt, 2 vols., 9th ed. 1953, 30.00
Masterpieces of Religious Verse; J. D. Morrison. Harper, 1948, 7.95
Modern American Poetry and Modern British Poetry; Louis Unter-
  meyer, ed. Harcourt, rev. ed. 1962, 11.00
*New Rhyming Dictionary and Poet's Handbook; Burges Johnson.
  Harper, rev. ed. 1957, 5.00
*Oxford Book of Christian Verse; Lord David Cecil, ed. Oxford,
  1940, 5.50
*Oxford Book of Light Verse; W. H. Auden. Oxford, 1938, 5.00
Oxford Book of Modern Verse, 1892-1935; W. B. Yeats. Oxford,
  1936, 6.00

Poems that Live Forever; Hazel Felleman. Doubleday, 1965, 4.95
Poetry Explication; J. M. Kuntz. Swallow, 2nd ed. 1962, 4.75
Poetry Handbook: A Dictionary of Terms; Babette Deutsch. Funk,
    rev. ed. 1962, 3.95

World Literature

Cassell's Encyclopedia of World Literature; S. H. Steinberg, ed.
    Funk, 2 vols. 1954, 25.00
Columbia Dictionary of Modern European Literature; Horatio Smith,
    ed. Columbia, 1947, 12.50
Concise Encyclopedia of Modern World Literature; Geoffrey Grig-
    son, ed. Hawthorn, 1963, 15.00
Contemporary Authors. Gale, 4 vols. per year, 25.00
Crowell's Handbook of Classical Literature; Lillian Feder.
    Crowell, 1964, 6.95
Cyclopedia of Literary Characters; F. N. Magill, ed. Harper, 1963,
    9.95
Cyclopedia of World Authors; F. N. Magill, ed. Harper, 1958, 8.95
European Authors; S. J. Kunitz, ed. Wilson, 1966
German Men of Letters; Alex Natan. Dufour, 3 vols. , 1962-1963,
    20.00
Masterpieces of Catholic Literature in Summary Form; F. N. Magill,
    ed. Harper, 1965, 9.95
Masterpieces of Christian Literature in Summary Form; F. N.
    Magill, ed. Harper, 1963, 9.95
Masterpieces of World Literature in Digest Form; F. N. Magill, ed.
    Harper, 3 series, 1952-1960, 30.00
Oxford Book of Ballads; Arthur Quiller-Couch. Oxford, 1910, 5.50
Oxford Companion to Classical Literature; Paul Harvey, ed.
    Oxford, 1937, 4.50
Oxford Companion to French Literature; Paul Harvey & J. E.
    Haseltine, eds. Oxford, 1959, 13.00
*Reader's Digest of Books; H. R. Keller. Macmillan, rev. ed.
    1936, 9.95
Twentieth Century Authors; S. J. Kunitz & Howard Haycraft, eds.
    Wilson, 1942, 12.00; 1st supp. , 1955, 10.00

Drama and Theater

*Biographical Encyclopedia and Who's Who of the American Theatre;
    Walter Rigdon, ed. Heineman, 1965, 82.50
Digest of 500 Plays; Theodore Shank. Crowell, 1963, 5.95
Digests of Great American Plays; John Lovell. Crowell, 1961, 5.95
*Dramatists' Guide to Selection of Plays and Materials; Gail Plum-
    mer. W. C. Brown, 1963, 3.50
Globe Playhouse; J. C. Adams. Barnes, 2nd ed. rev. 1961, 8.50
Guide to Great Plays; J. T. Shipley. Public Affairs, 1956, 10.00
*Guide to Critical Reviews; J. M. Salem. Scarecrow, pt. 1, 1966,
    4.50
History of the American Drama; A. H. Quinn. Crofts, 2 vols. 1943,
    1947, 14.00

Drama and Theater (cont.)

*Index to the Best Plays Series. Crofts, 2 vols., 7.00
Index to Full Length Plays, 1895-1944; R. G. Thomson. Faxon,
    2 vols., 1946, 1956, 15.00; Continuation, 1944-1964, N. O.
    Ireland, 1965, 8.50
Index to One-Act Plays; Hannah Logasa & Winifred Ver Nooy,
    comps. Faxon, basic vol. and 5 supps., 45.00
Index to Plays in Collections; J. H. Ottemiller. Scarecrow, 4th ed.
    rev., 1964, 9.50
Modern American Playwrights; Jean Gould. Dodd, 1966, 5.00
New Theatre Handbook and Digest of Plays; Bernard Sobel, ed.
    Crown, 8th ed. 1959, 5.95
Oxford Companion to the Theatre; Phyllis Hartnoll, ed. Oxford,
    2nd ed. 1957, 13.00
Play Index. Wilson, 2 vols., 1953, 1963, 19.00
Reader's Encyclopedia of Shakespeare; O. J. Campbell. Crowell,
    1966, 15.00
Shakespeare Commentary; A. E. Baker. Ungar, 2 vols. 1957, 15.00
*Shakespeare Companion; F. E. Halliday. Schocken, 1964, 10.00
Shakespeare's England. Oxford, 2 vols., 1916, 12.80
*Stubs: The Seating Plan Guide. Tobin, Annual, 1.00
*Theatre Language, a Dictionary; W. P. Bowman & R. H. Ball.
    Theatre Arts, 1961, 6.95

Short Stories

Short Fiction Criticism, 1800-1958; Jarvis Thurston. Swallow, 1959
    4.00
Short Story Index; Dorothy Cook & I. S. Munro, eds. Wilson, basic
    vol. and 3 supps., 1953-1964, 38.00
Twentieth Century Short Story Explication; W. S. Walker. Shoestring
    basic vol. and 2 supps., 1961-1965, 17.00

Mythology

Bulfinch's Mythology; Thomas Bulfinch. Crowell, rev. ed. 1962,
    5.95
Classic Myths in English Literature and in Art; C. M. Gayley, ed.
    Blaisdell, rev. ed. 1939, 6.95
Dictionary of Classical Mythology; J. E. Zimmerman. Harper, 1964,
    4.95
*Dictionary of Mythology, Folklore and Symbols; Gertrude Jobes.
    Scarecrow, 2 vols. 1964, 50.00; Index, 10.00
Dictionary of Phrase and Fable; E. C. Brewer. Harper, 8th ed. rev.
    1964, 7.50
Encyclopedia of Classical Mythology; A. R. A. van Aken. Prentice,
    1965, 5.00
Folklore in America; T. P. Coffin & Hennig Cohen, eds. Doubleday,
    1966, 4.95
Funk and Wagnalls Standard Dictionary of Folklore, Mythology and
    Legend. Funk, 2 vols., 1949-1950, 20.00

Larousse World Mythology; Pierre Grimal. Putnam, 1965, 25.00
*Mythology of All Races; J. A. MacCulloch, ed. Cooper, 13 vols. 1964.
    150.00

Foreign Language Dictionaries

Cassell's Italian Dictionary. Funk, 7.50
Cassell's New French Dictionary. Funk, 7.50
Cassell's New Latin Dictionary. Funk, 7.50
Cassell's Spanish Dictionary. Funk, 7.50
English-Russian Dictionary; V. K. Muller. Dutton, 7th ed. 1959,
    9.95
Greek-English, English-Greek Dictionary. Follett, 7.50
*Latin Dictionary; E. A. Andrews, rev. ed. by Charlton Lewis &
    Charles Short. Oxford, 1955, 12.80
McKay's Modern Norwegian-English, English-Norwegian Dictionary.
    McKay, 6.50 (community branches only)
McKay's Modern Swedish-English, English-Swedish Dictionary.
    McKay, 4.00 (community branches only)
New Cassell's German Dictionary. Funk, 7.50
*Norwegian-English Dictionary; E. I. Haugan. Univ. of Wis., 1966,
    12.50
*Russian-English Dictionary; A. I. Smirnitski. Dutton, 1967, 8.95
*Swedish-English Dictionary; Karl Kaerre. Heinman, 2 vols., 20.00

Miscellaneous

*American Dialects; Lewis Herman. Theatre Arts, 1959, 8.50
American Journalism; F. L. Mott. Macmillan, 1962, 8.95
*Author Biography Master Index; J. M. Ethridge, ed. Gale, 1965,
    28.00
Complete Toastmaster; H. W. Prochnow. Prentice, 1960, 4.95
Essay and General Literature Index. Wilson, Semi-annual and
    Annual cum., 16.00
*Film Daily Year Book of Motion Pictures. Film Daily, Annual,
    20.00
Film Goer's Companion; Leslie Halliwell. Hill & Wang, 1965, 7.50
*Foreign Dialects; Lewis Herman. Theatre Arts, 1943, 8.50
*History and Bibliography of American Newspapers, 1690-1820;
    C. S. Brigham. Archon Books, 2 vols., 1962, 13.75
*History of American Magazines; F. L. Mott. Harvard, 4 vols.,
    1930- , 39.00
*International Dictionary of Literary Awards; Jane Clapp. Scribner,
    1963, 15.00
*International Film Guide; Peter Cowie, ed. Barnes, Annual, 2.95
International Motion Picture Almanac. Quigley, Annual, 8.00
International TV Almanac. Quigley, Annual, 8.00
Literary and Library Prizes; O. S. Weber. Bowker, 1963, 8.50
Oxford Dictionary of Nursery Rhymes; I. P. Opie. Oxford, 1951,
    10.00
Reader's Guide to Literary Terms; Karl Beckson. Farrar, 1960,
    4.95

Miscellaneous (cont.)

Standard Book of Letter Writing and Correct Social Forms;
    W. E. Watson. Prentice, 1958, 6.95
Study of the Types of Literature; M. I. Rich. Appleton, 1937, 4.40
    (community branches only)

Science and Technology

General

AAAS Science List for Young Adults. Am. Assoc. for the Adv. of
    Science, 1964, 2.50; Supps.
*American Men of Science: Physical and Biological Sciences.
    Bowker, 6 vols., 1965-1967, 150.00
*Applied Science and Technology Index. Wilson, Monthly, Annual
    cum., service basis (242.00)
Asimov's Biographical Encyclopedia of Science and Technology;
    Isaac Asimov. Doubleday, 1964, 8.95
Harper Encyclopedia of Science; J. R. Newman, ed. Harper, 4 vols.
    1963, 40.00
*Index to Scientists of the World; N. R. Ireland. Faxon, 1962, 12.00
*McGraw-Hill Basic Bibliography of Science and Technology.
    McGraw, 1966, 19.50
*McGraw-Hill Encyclopedia of Science and Technology. McGraw,
    1960, 1965 yearbook, 16 vols., 219.50
McGraw-Hill Modern Men of Science. McGraw, 1966, 19.50

Agriculture and Gardening

*Agriculture Yearbook. U. S. Agriculture Dept., Annual, 2.75
*Biological and Agricultural Index. Wilson, Monthly, Annual cum.,
    service basis (103.00)
Encyclopedia of Gardening; Norman Taylor, ed. Houghton, 1963,
    9.95
Gardener's Book of Plant Names; A. W. Smith. Harper, 1963, 5.95
Poisonous Plants of the U. S. and Canada; J. M. Kingsbury. Prentice,
    1964, 13.00
Wildflowers of North America; R. S. Lemmon. Hanover, 1961, 9.95

Anatomy

Gray's Anatomy of the Human Body; C. M. Goss. Am. Bk. Co.,
    1966, 17.50

Automobiles

*Glenn's Auto Repair Manual; H. T. Glenn. Chilton, Annual, 9.95
*Glenn's Foreign Car Repair Manual; H. T. Glenn. Chilton, 1966,
    17.50
Motor's Auto Repair Manual; Motor Magazine. Wehman, Annual,
    9.95

Aviation and Space

Aerospace Age Dictionary; Clarke Newlon. Watts, 1965, 5.95
*Aerospace Power; Charles Coombs. Morrow, 1966, 4.95
*Jane's All the World's Aircraft. McGraw, Annual, 42.50
Man in Space Dictionary; Martin Caidin. Dutton, 1963, 6.95
    (community branches only)
Space Age Dictionary; Charles McLaughlin, ed. Van Nostrand,
    1963, 7.95

Electricity and Electronics

*American Electricians' Handbook; C. C. Carr, ed. McGraw, 1961,
    17.50
Broadcasting Yearbook. Broadcasting Pub., Annual, 5.00
*Modern Dictionary of Electronics; R. F. Graf. Sams, 1963, 6.95
NFPA Handbook of the National Electrical Code. McGraw, 1966,
    12.75
*Terminology Handbook; Communications-Electronics. Public Af-
    fairs, 1965, 7.00

Engineering

*Civil Engineering Handbook; L. C. Urquhart. McGraw, 1959, 21.50
*Mechanical Engineer's Handbook; L. S. Marks. McGraw, 1958, 25.00
*Metals Handbook. Am. Soc. for Metals, 2 vols., 1961, 40.00

Formulas

Henley's 20th Century Book of Formulas. Books, Inc.,1957, 5.00
*National Formulary XL. Mack, 1965, 10.00
*Pharmacopoeia of the U.S. of America. Mack, 1965, 12.50

Health and Medicine

Book of Health; R. L. Clark. Van Nostrand, 1962, 16.50
*Current Therapy; H. F. Conn, ed. Saunders, 1966, 13.00
Dorland's Illustrated Medical Dictionary. Saunders, 1965, 13.00
Drugs in Current Use; Walter Modell. Springer, Annual, 2.75
*Hospitals. Am. Hosp. Assoc., 1966, 3.50
Modern Drug Encyclopedia and Therapeutic Index. Donnelly, 1965,
    19.00
*Psychiatric Dictionary; L. E. Hinsie. Oxford, 1960, 17.50
Stedman's Medical Dictionary. Williams, 1966, 14.00

Mathematics

Handbook of Mathematical Tables. Chemical Rubber Co., 1964, 7.50
International Conversion Tables; Stephen Naft. Duell, 1961, 7.95
*International Dictionary of Applied Mathematics. Van Nostrand,
    1960, 25.00

Nutrition, Food, Cooking

Complete Round the World Cookbook; Myra Waldo, ed. Doubleday,
    1954, 4.95
*Dictionary of Nutrition and Food Technology; A. E. Bender.
    Butterworths, 1965, 9.50
Food Values and Calorie Charts; J. G. Szanton. Fell, 1965, 2.95
*Food Values of Portions Commonly Used; Charles & Helen Church.
    Lippincott, 1963, 4.50
Joy of Cooking; I. S. Rombauer. Bobbs, 1962, 6.50
*Larousse Gastronomique. Crown, 1961, 20.00
Menu Dictionary: Polyglot. Hayden, 1961, 5.00

Animals

Field Guide to the Mammals; W. H. Burt. Houghton, 1964, 4.95
Living Mammals of the World; Ivan Sanderson. Doubleday, 1955,
    12.50
*Mammals of the World; E. P. Walker. Johns Hopkins, 2 vols.
    and bib. , 1964, 37.50
Modern Dog Encyclopedia; H. P. Davis. Stackpole, 1958, 13.50

Biology

*Collegiate Dictionary of Zoology; R. W. Pennak. Ronald, 1964, 8.50
Encyclopedia of the Biological Sciences; Peter Gray, ed. Reinhold,
    1961, 20.00

Birds

*Audubon Land Bird Guide; R. H. Pough. Doubleday, 1949, 4.50
*Audubon Water Bird Guide; R. H. Pough. Doubleday, 1951, 4.50
*Check-List of North American Birds. Am. Ornith. Union, 1957,
    8.00
Field Guide to the Birds; R. T. Peterson. Houghton, 1947, 10.95
New Dictionary of Birds; A. L. Thomson, ed. McGraw, 1964, 17.50

Amphibians

Living Fishes of the World; E. S. Herald. Doubleday, 1961,12.50
Living Amphibians of the World; D. M. Cochran, Doubleday, 1961,
    12.50

Chemistry

*Encyclopedia of Chemistry; G. L. Clark, ed. Reinhold, 1966, 25.00
Handbook of Chemistry and Physics. Chemical Rubber Co. , Annual,
    17.50

Insects

Field Book of Insects of the U. S. and Canada; F. E. Lutz. Putnam,
    1948, 3.95

Astronomy

Field Guide to the Stars and Planets; D. H. Menzel. Houghton, 1963, 4.95
*Flammarion Book of Astronomy. Simon, 1964, 22.95

Rocks and Minerals

Field Guide to Rocks and Minerals; R. H. Pough. Houghton, 1953, 4.95

Textiles

Modern Textile Dictionary; G. E. Linton. Meredith, 1963, 18.50

Trees

*North American Trees; R. J. Preston, MIT Press, 1965, 2.95
Shrub Identification Book; G. W. D. Symonds. Barrows, 1963, 15.00
Tree Identification Book; G. W. D. Symonds. Barrows, 1958, 12.50
*Trees and Shrubs for the Northern Plains; D. G. Hoag. N. D. Inst. for Reg. Studies, 1965, 12.50

Miscellaneous

Audubon Nature Encyclopedia. Curtis, 12 vols., 1965, 44.95
Fieldbook of Natural History; E. L. Palmer, McGraw, 1949, 11.95
Glossary of Data Processing and Communications Terms; Honeywell, Inc. Wellesley Hills, 1965, 1.00
How To Clean Everything; A. C. Moore. Simon, 1961, 3.75
How-To-Do-It Books. Bowker, 1963, 7.50
Index to Handicrafts...; E. C. Lovell & R. M. Hall. Faxon, 1st vol. and 3 supps., 1936-1965, 32.50
*Jane's Fighting Ships. McGraw, Annual, 42.50
*Materials Handbook; G. S. Brady. McGraw, 1963, 17.50

Social Sciences

Religion

American Catholic Etiquette; K. T. Fenner. Newman, 1961, 5.95
*American Jewish Year Book. Jewish Pub. Soc. of Am., Annual, 6.50
Butler's Lives of the Saints. Kenedy, 4 vols., 1956, 39.50
Christmas Customs Around the World; H. H. Wernecke. Westminster, 1959, 3.50
Complete Concordance to the Bible (Douay); Newton Thompson. Herder, 1945, 17.50
Dictionary of Saints; Donald Attwater, ed. Kenedy, 1958, 4.50 (community branches only)
Dictionary of the Bible; James Hastings, ed. Scribner, 1963, 15.00
Dictionary of the Bible; J. L. McKenzie. Bruce, 1965, 17.95

Religion (cont.)

Documents of the Christian Church; H. S. Bettenson, ed. Oxford,
    1963, 3.50
Encyclopedia of Religion; Vergilius Ferm, ed. Philos Lib., 1964, 10.00
*Exhaustive Concordance of the Bible; James Strong. Abingdon,
    1958, 15.75
*Guide to the Catholic Sisterhoods in the U.S.; T. P. McCarthy.
    Cath. Univ. of Am., 1964, 4.50
Handbook of Christian Feasts and Customs; F.X. Weiser, Harcourt,
    1958, 4.95
Handbook of Denominations in the United States; F. S. Mead.
    Abingdon, 1965, 2.95
*Historical Atlas of Religion in America; E. S. Gaustad. Harper,
    1962, 8.95
History of Witchcraft and Demonology; Montague Summers. Univ.
    Bks., 1956, 6.00
Holy Bible; Revised Standard Version.
Holy Bible; King James Version
Holy Bible; Douay Contrafraternity
Holy Scriptures According to the Masoretic Text. Jewish Pub. Soc.
    of Am., 1955, 5.00
Home Book of Bible Quotations; B. E. Stevenson. Harper, 1949,
    8.95
*Interpreter's Bible. Abingdon, 1951-1957, 12 vols., 89.50
*Interpreter's Dictionary of the Bible. Abingdon, 4 vols., 1962,
    45.00
Koran; George Sale, tr. Warne, 2.50
National Catholic Almanac. St. Anthony's Guild, Annual, 2.10
Nelson's Complete Concordance of the Revised Standard Version
    of the Bible. Nelson, 1957, 15.00
*Official Catholic Directory. Kenedy, Annual, 17.00
Oxford Annotated Bible with the Apocrypha. Oxford, 1965, 10.50
Papal Encyclicals in their Historical Context; Anne Fremantle, ed.
    New Am. Lib., .95
Rand McNally Bible Atlas; E. G. H. Kraeling. Rand, 1956, 8.95
*Religions, Mythologies, Folklore; K. S. Diehl. Scarecrow, 1962,
    12.50
6000 Years of the Bible; G. S. Wegener. Harper, 1963, 7.95
*Small Sects in America; E. T. Clark. Peter Smith, 3.25
*Twentieth Century Encyclopedia of Religious Knowledge (Schaff-
    Herzog). Baker Bk. House, 2 vols., 1955, 15.00
Westminster Historical Atlas to the Bible; G. E. Wright. West-
    minster, 1956, 7.50
Yearbook of American Churches. Nat'l. Council of Churches of
    Christ in the U. S., Annual, 7.50

Sociology

Dictionary of the Social Sciences; Julius Gould & W. L. Kolb, eds.
    Free Press of Glencoe, 1964, 19.50
*Encyclopedia of Social Work. Nat'l. Assoc. of Social Workers,
    3 year intervals, 12.50

Sociology (cont.)

*Golden Bough; James Frazer. St. Martin's, 13 vols. , 1955, 100.00
*Mental Measurements Yearbook. Gryphon, 6 year intervals, 32.50
New Golden Bough; James Frazer. Macmillan, 1960, 10.00
National Directory on Housing for Older People. Nat'l. Council on
    the Aging, 1965, 5.00
*Public Welfare Directory. Am. Pub. Welfare Assoc. , Annual,
    15.00

Education

American Junior Colleges; E.J. Gleazer, ed. Am. Council on
    Educ. , 1963, 10.00
American Universities and Colleges; A. M. Cartter, ed. Am.
    Council on Educ. , 1964, 15.00
Baird's Manual of American College Fraternities; W. R. Baird,
    Banta, 1963, 8.00
Barron's Profiles of American Colleges; Benjamin Fine. Barron's,
    1964, 8.75
*College Blue Book; C. E. Burckel. Burckel, 3 vols. , 1965, 36.00
Comparative Guide to American Colleges; James Cass & Max
    Birnbaum. Harper, 1965, 8.95
*Complete Guide to the Accredited Correspondence Schools; Alice
    Fleming. Doubleday, 1964, 1.95
*Dictionary of Occupational Titles; U. S. Employment Service, GPO,
    2 vols. , 5.00
Directory for Exceptional Children. Porter Sargent, 1965, 7.00
Education Directory; U. S. Office of Education. GPO, 4 pts. ,
    .30-.65 each
*Education Index. Wilson, Annual, service basis (172.00)
Handbook of Private Schools. Porter Sargent, Annual, 10.00
How to be Accepted by the College of Your Choice; Benjamin Fine.
    Appleton, 1965, 6.95
*How to Prepare for College Entrance Examinations; S. C. Brownstein.
    Barron's, 1962, 5.75
*International Handbook of Universities and Other Institutions of
    Higher Education; H. M. R. Keyes, ed. Int'l. Assoc. of Univ. ,
    1965, 13.50
Lovejoy-Jones College Scholarship Guide. Simon, 1964, 4.95
Lovejoy's College Guide. Simon, Biennial, 6.50
*Lovejoy's Prep School Guide. Harper, 1963, 5.95
Lovejoy's Vocational School Guide. Siomn, 1963, 5.95
Occupational Literature: An Annotated Bibliography; Gertrude
    Forrester. Wilson, 1964, 8.50
Occupational Outlook Handbook;   U. S. Labor Statistics Bureau.
    GPO, Annual, 4.50
*Patterson's American Education. Educ. Dir. , Annual, 25.00
*Scholarships, Fellowships and Loans; S. N. Feingold. Bellman,
    2 vols. , 20.00

Sports and Games

Cokesbury Game Book; Arthur Depew. Abingdon, 1955, 2.95
Cokesbury Party Book; Arthur Depew. Abingdon, 1955, 3.50
Encyclopedia of Sports; F. G. Menke. Barnes, 1963, 15.00
Goren's Hoyle Encyclopedia of Games; C. H. Goren. Hawthorn,
    1960, 5.95
New York Times Sports Almanac. Watts, Annual, 2.95
Sports Rules Encyclopedia; Jess White. National Press Pub.,
    1961, 7.50
Story of the Olympic Games; John Kieran. Lippincott, 1965, 6.95

Psychology

*Comprehensive Dictionary of Psychological and Psycho-Analytical
    Terms; H. B. & A. C. English. McKay, 1958, 10.75
Dictionary of Psychology; James Drever. Penguin, 1953, 1.25

Philosophy

Dictionary of Philosophy; D. D. Runes. Philos. Lib., 1963, 6.00
*Encyclopedia of Philosophy. Macmillan, 1966, 219.50
Masterpieces of World Philosophy; F. N. Magill, ed. Harper, 1961,
    9.95
Who's Who in the History of Philosophy; Thomas Kiernan. Philos.
    Lib., 1965, 6.00

Business and Economics

Best's Insurance Guide with Key Ratings. Best, Annual, 8.75
Business Dictionary; L. C. Nanassy & William Selden. Prentice,
    1960, 5.00
*Business Periodicals Index. Wilson, Monthly, Annual cum.,
    service basis (299.00)
*Commodity Yearbook; Commodity Research Bureau. Author,
    Annual, 16.85
Consumer Price Index: Minneapolis; U. S. Bureau of Labor
    Statistics. Chicago, Monthly, Free
Consumer Price Index: U. S. City Average; U. S. Bureau of Labor
    Statistics. GPO, Monthly, Free
*Dictionary for Accountants; E. L. Kohler. Prentice, 1963, 14.95
Economic Almanac. Nat'l. Ind. Conf. Board, Irregular
Facts and Figures on Government Finance. Tax Found. Inc.,
    Annual, 3.50
*Investor's Dictionary; J. K. Low. Simon, 1964, 4.95
*Investment Companies; Arthur Wiesenberger. Annual, 32.00
*International Yellow Pages. Annual, 20.00
McGraw-Hill Dictionary of Modern Economics; Douglas Greenwald.
    McGraw, 1965, 14.75
*Market Guide. Editor and Publisher, Annual, 10.00
*Middle Market Directory. Dun & Bradstreet, Annual, 75.00
*Million Dollar Directory. Dun & Bradstreet, 2 vols., Annual, 158.50

Minnesota Directory of Manufacturers. Minn. Dept. of Admin., in
    prep.
*Moody's Manual of Investments. Moody's Inv. Service, 5 vols.,
    Annual, 415.00
*Paper Money of the U.S.; Robert Friedberg. Sterling, 1964, 12.50
*Poor's Register of Corporations, Directors and Executives.
    Standard & Poor, Annual, 96.00
*Scott's Standard Postage Stamp Catalogue. Scott, Annual, 13.50
*Secretary's Handbook; S.A. Taintor. Macmillan, 1958, 5.95
*Sources of Business Information; E.T. Coman. Univ. of Calif.,
    1964, 8.50
*Standard Directory of Advertisers: Classified Ed. Nat'l. Reg. Pub.
    Co., Annual, 85.00; Geographical Ed., Annual, 34.00
Standard Handbook for Secretaries; L.I. Hutchinson. McGraw, 1956,
    6.95
*Survey of Buying Power. Sales Management, Annual, 6.00
*Statistics Sources; Paul Wasserman, ed. Gale, 1962, 15.00
*Tax Guide for Small Business; U.S. Internal Revenue Service.
    GPO, Annual, .50
Thomas' Register of American Manufacturers. 4 vols. plus index,
    Annual, 20.00
Your Federal Income Tax. GPO, Annual, .50

Art

General

*Art Index. Wilson, Quarterly, Annual and 2 year cum., service
    basis (330.00)
Art Through the Ages; Helen Gardner. Harcourt, 1959, 11.75
Catalogue of Colour Reproductions of Paintings - 1860 to 1965.
    Unesco, 1966, 7.00
*Dictionary of American Painters, Sculptors and Engravers; Mantle
    Fielding. Carr, 1965, 28.50
Dictionary of Art and Artists; Peter and Linda Murray. Praeger,
    1966, 14.95 (community libraries only)
Dictionary of Contemporary American Artists; Paul Cummings.
    St. Martin's, 1966, 17.50
*Dictionary of Modern Painting; Carlton Lake & Roger Maillard, eds.
    Tudor, 1964, 8.95
*Dictionary of Modern Sculpture; Fernand Hazan. Tudor, 1962, 7.95
Dictionary of Pronunciation of Artists' Names; G.E. Kaltenbach.
    Art. Inst. of Chicago, 1938, .75
Fine Art Reproductions of Old and Modern Masters. N.Y. Graphic,
    1965, 25.00
*Guide to the Collecting and Care of Original Prints; Carl
    Zigrosser and C.M. Gaehde. Crown, 1965, 3.00
Harper History of Painting; D.M. Robb. Harper, 1951, 14.50
Picture Book of Symbols; Ernst Lehner. Tudor, 1956, 3.50
*Praeger Picture Encyclopedia of Art. Praeger, 1958, 17.50
Symbols, Signs and Their Meaning; Arnold Whittrick, Branford,
    1960, 12.00

General (cont.)

*Who's Who in American Art; D. B. Gilbert, ed. Bowker, 1965,
    22. 50

Architecture

*Architecture of America; J. E. Burchard & Albert Bush-Brown.
    Little, 1961, 15. 00
History of Architecture on the Comparative Method; B. F. Fletcher.
    Scribner, 1961, 17. 50

Costume

Costume Through the Ages; James Laver. Simon, 1964, 4. 95
Five Centuries of American Costume; R. T. Wilcox. Scribner,
    1963, 6. 50
Historic Costume for the Stage; Lucy Barton. Baker, 1961, 8. 95
Mode in Costume; R. T. Wilcox. Scribner, 1958, 8. 95
Western World Costume; C. G. Bradley. Appleton, 1954, 6. 50
World Costume; Angela Bradshaw. Macmillan, 1961, 12. 00

Furniture

American Furniture; Helen Comstock. Viking, 1962, 17. 50
Encyclopedia of Furniture; Joseph Aronson. Crown, 1965, 8. 50
Furniture Treasury; Wallace Nutting. Macmillan, 3 vols. , 1928-
    1933, 27. 00

Antiques

Antiques and Their Current Prices; E. G. Warman. Warman, 1965,
    6. 95
Complete Encyclopedia of Antiques; L. G. Ramsey, ed. Hawthorn,
    1966, 25. 00
Dictionary of American Silver, Pewter and Silver Plate; R. M. &
    T. H. Kovel. Crown, 1960, 5. 95
Dictionary of Antiques and the Decorative Arts; L. A. Boger & H.
    Batterson. Scribner, 1957, 15. 00
Dictionary of Marks: Pottery and Porcelain; R. M. Kovel. Crown,
    1953, 3. 00
Early American Pressed Glass; R. W. Lee. Lee, 1960, 10. 00
Nineteenth Century Art Glass; R. W. Lee. Barrows, 1952, 5. 00
Price Guide to Pattern Glass; R. W. Lee. Lee, 1963, 5. 00

Coins

Catalogue of the World's Most Popular Coins; Fred Reinfeld.
    Doubleday, 1965, 7. 50
*Catalog of Modern World Coins; R. S. Yeoman. Whitman, 1964, 4. 00
*Coins of the World, 1750-1850; W. D. Craig. Whitman, 1966, 6. 00
*Guide Book of U. S. Coins; R. S. Yeoman. Whitman, Annual, 1. 75
Handbook Of U. S. Coins. Whitman, Annual, 1. 00

Museums, Galleries, etc.

*American Art Directory. Bowker, every 3 years, 22.50
Museums Directory of the U.S. and Canada. Am. Assoc. Of
    Museums, 1965, 8.00
*Museums, U.S.A.: A History and Guide; Herbert & Marjorie Katz.
    Doubleday, 1965, 6.50

Music

General

American Popular Songs; David Ewen, ed. Random, 1966, 10.00
Baker's Biographical Dictionary of Musicians; rev. by Nicolas
    Slonimsky. Schirmer, 1958 with 1965 supp., 25.00
*Book of World Famous Music; J.J. Field. Crown, 1966, 12.50
*Complete Book of Light Opera; Mark Lubbock. Appleton, 1963, 12.95
Complete Book of the American Musical Theatre; David Ewen. Holt,
    1959, 7.50
Complete Book of 20th Century Music; David Ewen. Prentice,
    1959, 10.00
Concise Oxford Dictionary of Music; P.A. Scholes. Oxford, 1964,
    7.00
*Dictionary of Hymnology; John Julian. Dover, 1957 reprint, 17.50
*Dictionary of Music and Musicians; George Grove. St. Martin's,
    10 vols. including supp., 1954, 142.50
Encyclopedia of Jazz; Leonard Feather. Horizon, 1960, 15.00
Encyclopedia of Popular Music; Irwin Stambler. St. Martin's, 1965,
    10.00
Great Composers: 1300-1900; David Ewen, ed. Wilson, 1966, 10.00
History of Western Music; D.J. Grout. Norton, 1960, 8.95
*Index to Biographies of Contemporary Composers; Strom Bull.
    Scarecrow, 1964, 9.75
*Index to Songbooks; Robert Leigh. Leigh, 1964, 4.95
International Book of Christmas Carols; Walter Ehret & G.K. Evans,
    eds. Prentice, 1963, 12.50
International Cyclopedia of Music and Musicians; Oscar Thompson,
    ed. Dodd, 1964, 35.00
*Introduction to Contemporary Music; Joseph Machlis. Norton, 1961,
    10.75
*Jazz Lexicon; R.S. Gold. Knopf, 1964, 5.95
Music Festivals of the World; D.G. Stoll. Pergamon, 1964, 3.75
*Music for the Piano; James Friskin. Rinehart, 1954, 5.00
*Music Index. Info. Service, Inc., Monthly, Annual cum., service
    basis (195.00)
Musical Instruments: A Comprehensive Dictionary; Sibyl Marcuse.
    Doubleday, 1964, 17.50
National Anthems of the World; Martin Shaw & Henry Coleman, eds.
    Pitman, 1963, 12.50
*New Oxford History of Music. Oxford, 3 vols. of 11 vol. work,
    11.50 each
*Our American Music; J.T. Howard. Crowell, 1965, 12.95

General (cont.)

*Oxford Companion to Music; P. A. Scholes. Oxford, 1955, 25.00
 Popular American Composers; David Ewen, ed. Wilson, 1962, 7.00
*Popular Music; N. Shapiro. Adrian, 2 vols., 1964-65, 32.00
*Rudiments of Music; J. Castellini. Norton, 1962, 5.50
 "Variety" Music Cavalcade, 1620-1961; Julius Mattfeld. Prentice,
    1962, 15.00

Opera

Concise Oxford Dictionary of Opera; J. H. Rosenthal & H. J.
    Warrack. Oxford, 1964, 6.50
Crowell's Handbook of World Opera; F. L. Moore, comp. Crowell,
    1961, 7.50
Kobbe's Complete Opera Book. Putnam, 1963, 10.95

Ballet

Balanchine's Complete Stories of the Great Ballets; George
    Balanchine. Doubleday, 1954, 6.95
*Dictionary of Modern Ballet; S. J. Cohen, ed. Tudor, 1959, 7.95

Folk Music

*Bibliography of North American Folklore and Folksong; Charles
    Haywood. Peter Smith, 2 vols., 1951, 12.50
*English Folksongs from the Southern Appalachians; Cecil Sharp.
    Oxford, 1960, 15.00
*Folksingers and Folksongs in America; Ray Lawless. Duell, 1960,
    10.00
 Folk Songs of North America; Alan Lomax, ed. Doubleday, 1960,
    8.50
 Folksongs of the World; Charles Haywood. Day, 1966, 12.50

The A. L. A. Statistical Standards, Addenda to Minimum
Standards for Public Library Systems, 1966, [7] suggest "that the
proportion of juvenile holdings in the total system should range
from a minimum of 25 per cent to a maximum of 40 per cent."
However, "when the total collection is distributed through many
facilities, the proportion which is juvenile should be increased. No
more than one-half of these should be new titles. In general,
two-thirds of the annual additions for children should be replacements or duplicate copies of older books. Even the largest
systems should not exceed 1,000-1,200 new titles annually. A
minimum of 80 per cent of the juvenile materials requested should

be available locally without having to resort to inter-library loans."

The Statistical Standards suggest that the following percentages of adult non-fiction titles requested should be available locally
without inter-library loan:[7]

Population Served	Percentage of Adult Non-fiction Material Locally Owned
Under 10,000	35-50%
10,000-24,999	50-65%
25,000-49,999	65-80%
50,000-99,999	80-95%

Percentages should be calculated proportionately to the
population served. Most branches, unless they are regional or
area branches, will serve populations of from 10,000 to 50,000.
The last listing above could apply to a large regional or area
branch.

Many library systems in line with the trend toward larger
and fewer branches, are constructing buildings with book capacities
as high as 50,000-60,000 volumes. A survey made in 1960 and
cited by Wheeler and Goldhor showed that book collections in 162
branches in 61 library systems had much smaller collections than
might be expected, the median group having 5,000 to 6,000 volumes, and the modal group, 10,001 to 20,000. [8]

In an article in Library Trends, Meredith Bloss describes
a sampling he took of 371 branches in 40 cities of over 100,000
population in 17 states.[7] He reported that 121 branches, or 33
per cent, had fewer than 15,000 volumes; 147 branches, or about
40 per cent, had 15,000-25,000 volumes; 103 listed 26,000 or
more, with 13 of the latter listing 50,000 or more.[9]

Such a sampling taken in 1969 or 1970, just a few years
later, would undoubtedly reveal a considerable rise in the number
of books in branch collections. Federal aid to city systems in
recent years, larger buildings, and increased book budgets have
helped build collections closer to desirable standards, but there is
still much room for improvement.

Methods of allocating book funds to branches are extremely varied. Everything from wear and tear on the books to circulation may be used as criteria. There is little or no uniformity from library to library. Here is a field ripe for study and research, particularly to determine which methods will result in the best collections for each branch.

Methods of book selection for branches are almost as varied as methods of book fund allocation. Although agreeing in theory that branch librarians know best what their libraries should have, many directors are not giving branch heads enough voice in selection. In some systems choices are made first by the central library staff, and branch librarians may recommend titles or may choose their books from lists already prepared at headquarters. Sometimes the branch librarians attend regular book review and selection meetings of all those engaged in the book selection process. Often they are given an opportunity to examine book selection tools ahead of time and to make recommendations. In his sampling, Mr. Bloss found that about half the libraries he queried prepared lists "for branches only" and some broke them down into books for large, medium, and small branches. In some libraries, branch librarians made all decisions regarding purchases for their respective branches.

Where a committee from the central library selected branch books there were few instances where all branch librarians were members of the committee. In the case of children's material, the supervisor or head of children's services for the system was very often given more authority to make the decisions.

Reference books for branches are often purchased by the Central Reference Department, with additional volumes or sets purchased automatically when deemed suitable for branch use. [9] It would certainly seem that in this case the advice of the head librarian or branch staff member most responsible for reference work should be sought.

No matter how determined an individual librarian may be not to let his or her personal tastes influence book selection it happens more often than many would like to admit. This works to the disadvantage of the library if the librarian in question buys a disproportionate number of books in his favored field or happens to have an unusual hobby which will have little public appeal. On the other hand, if the librarian's field of interest happens to be a popular one, the specialized knowledge he or she possesses may result in purchasing material which can be recommended to patrons with confidence and enthusiasm. Actually, the librarian with many hobbies and interests is in a better position to do a good job of book selection than one whose interests are limited. The ideal combination for good branch book selection would seem to be:

1. A librarian well trained in the use of the best selection tools.

2. A librarian who studies the branch service area and knows its needs, who talks with patrons about their preferences and makes occasional reader interest surveys, who gets out into the community to feel its pulse and know its preferences.

3. A system with a democratic method of book selection which assures the branch librarian a strong voice in selection for her own branch.

4. A written book selection policy for the system, with supplements for special branch situations.

5. Careful consideration of reader requests for purchase.

What Patrons Read

Among subjects which many libraries find impossible to keep available in sufficient numbers are Civil Service examination books, high school equivalency test material, books on improving reading skills, material on preparing job resumés, house plans, hypnosis, flying saucers or unidentified flying objects, books of prophecy, the art of self-defense (karate and judo), sex hygiene, narcotics, cook books, capital punishment, hot rods, Supreme Court discussions, witchcraft, how to do term papers, raising small animals, occupations, Shakespearean plays (when assigned to classes), and literary criticism.

In a survey of reader interests conducted at the Buena Park (California) District Library several years ago, 100 patrons, 26 men and 74 women, answered lengthy questionnaires which included a question on the types of books borrowed most frequently. The headquarters library of the district where the survey was made would correspond in size and book collection to many of today's larger branches. Here are the results:

17 reported reading mysteries, westerns and science fiction most frequently

25 reported other popular fiction

12 reported classics, modern and standard

5 reported art and music

10 reported science and technology

3 reported psychology

5 reported philosophy and religion

3 reported drama, poetry, and criticism

10 reported biography, history, and travel.

Although this may not be a typical pattern, it is interesting to note that only a little over 40% of the patrons preferred fiction. Biography, history and travel have been reported in first place among non-fiction classes in other surveys as well, and the only possibly surprising element in this survey was the fact that the classics won out over science and technology. A survey taken elsewhere might well reveal more interest in science and technology and less in the classics. One factor tending to influence this would be that schools are now placing increasing emphasis on science and technology.

At the same time, most English teachers requiring students to make book reports or undertake supplementary reading are moving away from traditional classics and now include more contemporary works such as Gone with the Wind, Catcher in the Rye, and the novels of Hemingway, Steinbeck, and Orwell.

Weeding

Maintenance of a book collection is as important as good selection. Nothing identifies poor management so obviously as shabby, outdated books, worn and outdated pamphlets, scratched or cracked phonograph records in the collection. All types of branch materials should be mended or discarded when it becomes necessary, and standards of appearance should be established that will be consistently maintained. Staff members who work at the circulation desk and receive returned books should be taught how to recognize possible mends and discards. There should be a bin or shelf at the desk into which this material can be put.

At frequent intervals these materials should be examined by the branch librarian. Decisions on what to discard or mend should not be left to clerks, except obvious cases of simple tears, loose hinges, pencil marks to be removed, or similar minor problems.

Frequent surveys of the shelves are also necessary to catch books that have not circulated in a long period or which are no longer useful. In a branch manned by a non-professional head librarian assistance in weeding may be available from the branch supervisor or other professional staff member. Well-organized systems will have a central mending department to which all difficult mending will be sent from branches.

One of the hardest lessons many branch librarians have to learn is to discard rigorously. A good branch head will, however, lay aside for further checking any items which may have historical or rare book value, or out-of-print and perhaps irreplaceable items which should be rebound or kept in reserve storage for use when needed. The advice of the branch supervisor, head of extension services, or other Central authority should be asked before any item which might have special value is discarded.

Regular inventories, now generally outmoded as being too expensive and time-consuming, formerly brought to light most books in need of discarding and possible replacement. Because few inventories are now made, examining the shelves and enlisting the aid of desk clerks to find shabby or outdated books becomes

even more important. In general, the criteria for discarding in a
branch are the same as for any library, except that a larger library may have several copies of a much-used book, where a
branch may have only one. In such a case the central or larger
unit might discard rather than go to the expense of rebinding,
whereas rebinding would be the only way of preserving the volume
for the branch.

It usually does not pay to rebind the average-sized book if
it is still in print and can be purchased for $5.00 or less. All
candidates for discard should be checked against Books in Print if
they are still needed in the collection. Old copies which cannot
be rebound can be brightened up with one of the colorful covers
carried by library suppliers for this purpose. All new books
should come to the branch equipped with Plasti-Kleer or similar
plastic covers, since these covers not only preserve the new appearance and retain the dust jackets but can also protect the books
from wet weather, stains, and surface damage.

The Branch Patrons

There have been many studies of library users and of their
reasons for coming to a library but few studies of non-users and
their reasons for not coming to libraries. The present trend
among libraries to reach out to the non-reader makes this sort of
information doubly valuable.

In 1965 the Regional Planning Commission of Cleveland and
Cuyahoga County, Ohio, in cooperation with the staffs of the
Cleveland Public Library and the Cuyahoga County Library System,
made an exhaustive study, the results of which were published in
a report entitled Changing Patterns. [10] Two thousand households,
including some 6,400 persons, were contacted in door-to-door
interviews and asked a lengthy series of questions regarding their
use or non-use of libraries.

The sampling of households was designed so the data would
be representative of the population in the metropolitan area as a

whole.   It was found that slightly less than one-half (45. 9%) of the respondents used some kind of library in the six weeks period prior to the interview.   Virtually all of this group had used some public library but over half had also used a school or other type of library.   The public library was more popular than the school library, even though youths were the most active users.

Among children and young people (ages 5-19) 80. 2% of those interviewed had used a public library within the six-week period, in contrast with only 23. 6% of adults interviewed.   These users visited branches, the Cleveland Public Main Library, or the bookmobile.   Among users of branch libraries, 68. 9% were young people and children.   This compared with a 76. 3% figure arrived at in a one-day at-the-library survey.

Among those interviewed, 51. 5% had not used a library in the designated period of six weeks.   Adults comprised the majority, 86. 2%.   Among all adults interviewed, 73. 8% had not used a library in six weeks; whereas only 17. 9% of the children and young people had not been library users.   Reasons for non-use and statistics on frequency of reading are given in the following tables:

Reasons for Non-Use

	No. of Persons	No Need	Too Busy	Have Own Library	Inconvenient Location of Library	Uninterested	Physical Disability	Buy Books Needed
All Non-Users	3,383	50.8%	41.3%	10.8%	5.4%	2.3%	2.8%	1.2%
Adult Non-Users	2,926	50.9%	44.6%	11.6%	4.6%	---	---	---
Children Non-Users	457	50.1%	19.9%	6.1%	10.5%	---	---	---

Frequency of Book Reading	Per cent of Users	Per cent of Non-Users	Total Per cent
Regularly	81.9	18.1	100
Often	47.5	52.5	100
Seldom	29.7	70.3	100
Never	15.5	84.5	100

		Had a Need within a Year		Action Taken		
All	No. persons	No	Yes	Used Pub. Lib.	Used Other Lib.	Did Nothing
All Non-Users	3,383	77.14%	22.86%	79.3%	10.01%	10.69%
Adult Non-Users	2,926	78.92%	21.08%	81.8%	8.37%	9.78%
Children Non-Users	457	65.10%	34.9%	70.3%	16.5%	13.25%

It was found that completed education through the 11th grade did not add significantly to the likelihood of using a library, but any education beyond the 11th grade did. The difference in percentage between the 0-8th grade group and the 9-11th grade group was insignificant. There seemed to be no significant differences in per cent of use by persons in the junior high school, senior high school, or college.

The at-home survey also checked use of particular agencies. Among children questioned, 68.9% used branches, 63.3% used the main library in Cleveland, and 85.2% used bookmobiles. Children clearly used more than one agency. Adults showed 31.1% branch use, 36.7% central library use, and 14.8% bookmobile use.

The contrast between users and non-users of the library in the amount of book reading was interesting: 81.9% of users read books regularly, as opposed to only 18.1% of the non-library users. As might be expected, only 15.5% of library users never read books, as compared to 84.5% of the non-users.

Among the 2000 households contacted in the door-to-door survey it was found that 60.5% of the homes read magazines regularly, 12.9% never read magazines, 17.7% read them occasionally, and 8.6% seldom. Newspapers were read regularly by 78.6%; 7.3% never read them; 9.3% read newspapers occasionally, and 4.4% seldom.

Among the 2,000 households, 12% did not buy or receive any magazines per month; 43.7% received 3-6 magazines per month; 20.8% brought or received 6 or more magazines per month; and 22.7% received one or two magazines.

More precise information about branch user patterns was sought through a survey of patrons on one day, Monday, October 25, 1965. All visitors were given questionnaires. The 21 branches in the survey included branches in these locations: major shopping center, minor shopping area, store groupings, single-family residential area, multi-family residential area, school building, civic or institutional, shopping and institutional, and mixed. There were one to 5 libraries in each environment. The following information emerged from this study:

	Age of Branch Library Users				
Age	0-14	15-19	20-24	25-64	65 and over
Per cent	51. 8%	24. 5%	3. 1%	19. 9%	0. 8%

        The predominantly young users went to the library for school
and reference work but personal pleasure was also given as a
reason.   Adults used the branches primarily for personal or pleasur
purposes.   Where the proportion of youthful users was high, circulation per capita was, on the average, lower.   Adults most often
combined shopping with library trips, or stopped at the library wher
going to or from work.   Ninety per cent of the people were satisfie
with the location of the branches, 10% were dissatisfied.   Satisfactio
or dissatisfaction seemed to hinge primarily on the proximity of the
branch to the user's home. [10]

Sample form for making a branch-use survey   Date_____
by means of individual interviews   Time of Interview
                                       _____

Public Branch Library Research Questionnaire
Cleveland and Cuyahoga County Library Systems
Regional Planning Commission

Please fill out this short form. It will take you about four minutes. The
information will be kept confidential. Its purpose is to help maintain
good public library service and provide needed information for recommending improvements. This research is designed to find out more
about the public's library habits and to record some of your opinions
regarding public libraries. Please ask the person who gave you this
form for any assistance you may need.

1. Your Home Address:
    Number and Street_____

    City or Village_____

2. a) Sex   Male ( )   Female   ( )

    b) Age Group:

        14 or Younger ( )   20 Thru 24 ( )   65 or Older ( )
        15 Thru 19   ( )   25 Thru 64 ( )

3. How did you come to this library? (Check only one)

    Walked all the way   ( ) Drove and Parked at the
    Rode bicycle all the way   ( )   Library   ( )
    Used Bus or Rapid   ( ) Drove and Parked_____
    Rode with a friend or   blocks away from library ( )
        family   ( ) Other (specify)_____   ( )

4. a) What services are you using today? (Can check more than one)
        Taking out or returning books and Magazines   ( )
        Reference Materials   ( )
        Other (specify)_____   ( )

    b) For what are you using the library? (Can check more than one)
        To get information for personal use   ( )
        To get information for school use   ( )
        To get information for job use   ( )
        Reading for pleasure   ( )
        A place to study your own books   ( )
        Other (Specify)_____   ( )

5. About how often do you use this library? (Check only one)
    Twice a Week or More ( )   About once a month   ( )
    About once a week   ( )   Infrequently   ( )
    About every two weeks ( )   (Specify)_____   ( )

Sample form for making a branch-use survey
by means of individual interviews (Cont.)

6. Do you find this branch conveniently located for your use?
    (Check only one)   Yes ( )   No ( )

    If Yes, Why? (Can check more than one)
            It's close to shopping   ( )
            It's close to school   ( )
            It's close to home   ( )
            It's close to work   ( )
            It's close to transit stops( )
            It's close to city/village
                hall   ( )
            Parking is usually easy
                to find   ( )
            Other (Specify)
            _____   ( )

    If No, Why? (Can check more than one)
            It's too far from shopping   ( )
            It's too far from school   ( )
            It's too far from home   ( )
            It's too far from work   ( )
            It's too far from transit
                stops   ( )
            It's too far from city/
                village hall   ( )
            Parking is usually hard to
                find   ( )
            Other (Specify)
            _____   ( )

7. Do you have other suggestions about location or use of the
    library? (Please write your suggestions on the back of this
    questionnaire)

Sample of reader interest survey form which could be handed out to branch patrons

Reader Use Survey

_____branch of the Library exists to serve your needs. Please help us serve you better by checking the following questionnaire. Do not sign your name. When completed, please leave the sheet at one of the library desks.

1. Male_____ Age: 12-21____ Education:
   Female_____ 22-60____ Elementary school_____
   Total 61 up____ Junior high school_____
   High school_____
   Occupation_____ Junior college_____
   _____ College_____
   Graduate work_____
   I am now a student in_____

2. I live in_____Other City_____Unincorporated area_____
   To get here I traveled: 0-1 mile_____ 1-2 miles_____ 2-3 miles_____
   3-4 miles_____ 5 miles or more_____

3. I usually come by car____bus____taxi____walk____other_____

4. I parked within one-half block____1 block____2 blocks or more____

5. I am here today to: Check out books____records____other_____
   Read in the library_____other reason_____
   Use reference material_____
   Attend meeting in multi-purpose room_____

6. I am interested mainly in: Fiction____Non-fiction____Both____
   Records_____Magazines_____
   Newspapers_____

7. I rate the adult book collection: Excellent__Good__Fair__Poor__
   (young adult) __   __   __   __
   (children's) __   __   __   __

   I would like to see more books on these subjects_____
   _____

8. The service at this branch is: Excellent___Good___Fair__Poor___
   The service could be improved by_____

9. Please express your opinion on how your branch library can be of more service to your neighborhood. (Use back of page if more space is needed.)

A Baltimore study of student use has indicated several important factors:[11] "Almost two-thirds of the library service to students, both in number of books supplied and number of hours of use, comes from the public library....

"Analysis of student library use indicates that present-day teaching at the secondary level assumes the availability of a substantive subject collection, containing extensive holdings of books and magazines. School libraries do not serve this function except to a limited extent, and would not do so even if doubled in size. In some way subject collections of scope and depth must be made available to students, or methods of teaching must be modified.

".... Student readers express a preference for using the public library..... The reasons for this preference are: (1) more adequate collections in the public libraries, (2) more suitable hours of service, and (3) fewer restrictions and controls in use.

"Since the neighborhood distribution of branches frequently places them in relative proximity to school buildings, these branch will carry a heavy proportion of the public library system's total service to students. This service will supply supplementary readings, encyclopedias, technical material, periodicals, and books assigned for reviews or reports. The evening hours of the branches will encourage the use of the reference collection by students regardless of its size.

"Although recent years have seen an almost insupportable pressure by students on the limited facilities of most branch libraries, in general almost all would agree that this is a desirable step in the young person's search for school materials. He becomes adept in the use of larger collections and additional reference sources and is prepared at least in part for using the special collections of the main library when that becomes necessary.

"Since school libraries are hard pressed to maintain collections sufficient for the expanding academic program, there will be a growing use of other libraries. This expanding use will be one more reason for the public library to re-evaluate its standards for branches and come up with plans for more effective units. Broader emphasis on nonfiction, heavier duplication of titles, and an increase in the size of the reference collection, including pamphlet material, must be considered as necessary. Periodical files must be included in branch library collections. There seems to be no reason for the public library to avoid this important segment of its work; therefore, adequate provision should be made to accommodate this pressure. In the long run, it will also make possible better service to adult patrons. "

Cities seeking to provide adequate facilities for student use, and to mitigate the problems arising from heavy use of public libraries by students, should study the Baltimore report carefully since it is the most comprehensive investigation in this area. The Baltimore study showed that over one-half of the patrons in the adult sections, branch and main, were high school or college students. Student reading needs are so extensive and numerous that both the school system and the public library must be mobilized to meet the demand.

Book Buying for New Branches

Book buying should start two or three years ahead of the opening of a new branch if at all possible. This assures the books being available, processed and ready for the shelves when the branch opens. It also eliminates a big increase in the system book budget in the same year as the building cost, since the initial collection cost is spread out over several years. There is nothing worse than to open a new branch with too few books, too many bare shelves, or too many shabby volumes from other agencies in the system.

Here is a suggested program for a series of in-service meetings on book selection, involving as many branch librarians as possible. It was used by the Tulsa (Oklahoma) City-County System and is reproduced exactly, except for references to the specific library and staff members.

In-Service Seminar
on
Book Selection and Acquisition
4 sessions, 8:30 - 11:30 a. m.

Suggested Participants:

All members of the Book Coordinating Committee
As many of the Department Heads of Central and book selection
    network as can attend.
Also, at least one representative of each group of branch libraries.
It is realized that library schedules and previous commitments will
prevent attendance by some of those designated. The seminars will
be most profitable for all if the staff responsible for book selection
and acquisition can be represented as well as possible.

I.   Principles of Selection

    A.   Advance preparation
        Read the system Selection Policy and be prepared to
        discuss its revision.

    B.   General Discussion
        1.   Review of Principles
            a. Demand versus quality
            b. Censorship and the controversial book
            c. Do the same basic principles apply at all
               levels?
               1. Adult-Young Adult-Juvenile?
               2. Central versus branches and bookmobiles?
               3. Circulation versus reference?
        2.   General discussion of the Book Selection Policy
            after which the group would be sub-divided and
            portions assigned for review and editing before
            the 4th meeting. At the final session, any major
            changes recommended would be reported and all
            sections turned over to the editor for final typing,
            collating and binding.

II. Selection aids and reviewing tools available in the System
      How can they be most effectively used?
      Notable books project - How do we participate?

All of the Book Selection Aids currently received will be assembled.

The purpose, strength and weaknesses of these will be discussed by a panel.

1. Basic Aids
   Standard Catalog, Essay Index, Fiction Catalog, etc.
2. Current Professional Aids
   Library Journal, Booklist, Choice, Kirkus.
3. Reviewing tools
   New York Times, Saturday Review, New York Review of Books, Chicago Tribune.
4. Foreign Selection Tools
5. Special Subjects
   Science
   History and Biography
   Fine Arts

Following discussion, departments and individuals will be assigned responsibility for checking each on a regular basis.

III. Major strengths and weaknesses of the System Collection.
Prior to this session, a spot check of items called for which could not be supplied would be made. Also, a composite list of all items on reserve anywhere in the System would be prepared.

A. Strengths
1. Each department would report briefly on subjects or items of strength or unique interest and/or pressing need. A summary for the branches and bookmobiles would also be included.
2. Each would outline a plan for continued development and filling gaps.

B. Coordinating Resources
Plans for merging collections AL Level

C. Weeding, binding, mending - principles and procedures

IV. Acquisitions
1. The Greenaway Plan
   How it works - Strengths of publishers included - Types of publishers omitted
2. The Jobbers - Who are they? What are the problems?
3. Direct order versus Jobber - What is the Difference? In service? - In cost?
4. How can the book selection expedite the work of acquisitions?
5. The paper back - How best used?

A concise, general book selection policy is outlined in the Mississippi Library Commission's <u>Trustee Manual,</u> and is useful for affiliated and member libraries formulating their own selection policy or for branch librarians who have been given a voice in forming one for the system.

Book Selection Policy

Historically, the American Public Library was developed as an agency for free, informal education of individuals. Its stated objectives are the enrichment of personal life and the promotion of enlightened citizenry.

It is the policy of the _____ Library to select books and materials which provide a general circulation and reference service to adults, young people and children.

This library's policies of book selection have been formulated to implement the following objectives:

1. Selection and purchase of books for both present and potential readers.

2. Consideration of the makeup of the area and the communities served.

3. Provision of a good collection on local and state history and authors.

4. Concentration on a collection of books that will grow in value over the years rather than on just numbers of books for temporary use.

5. Recognition of demand as a factor without abandoning other stated principles of selection. On a limited budget, duplication of titles is a luxury that a library can ill afford. The demand for popular fiction can be served primarily through a library lending agency.

6. Selection of materials which tend toward the enrichment and development of life, with emphasis on authoritativeness, factual accuracy, effective expression, significance of subject, sincerity of the author's purpose and responsibility of the author's opinions.

7. Selection of materials that meet high standards of quality in content, expression and format; that are related to basic standards of selection, purpose and

need; that include recreational materials for their contribution to the development and wholeness of the
individual.

8. Selection of materials that will enable the library to
provide individualized service for every person who
comes to it.

9. Purchase of textbooks or school curriculum materials
only when the information needed cannot be secured in
other books.

10. Selection of materials which will enable each citizen to
form his own opinions. Books on controversial subjects
will be judged on their factual authority and competence
in presenting their viewpoint. Since the public library
serves all the people, all sides of an issue must necessarily be presented.

11. Selection of serious works which present an honest
aspect of life or of some human problem for their
positive values. Books selected for children and young
people will have the additional criteria of guiding and
developing their reading tastes.

Gifts will be judged on the same basis as purchased material. They are accepted without commitment as to final
distribution or housing.

Ultimate responsibility for book selection, as for all library
activities, rests in the Director, who operates within the
framework of policies determined by the Board of Trustees.
Staff members, particularly branch librarians, are to be
consulted on the needs of their communities and are encouraged to make suggestions. Requests from readers will
also be considered.

Date Adopted_____

_____
Secretary, Board of Trustees

Each branch should have a subscription to the main selection
tools for reference in case of complaint and for suggestions for
initiating orders. In case of a patron's protest it is often necessary to show him the reviews upon which the selection was based.
These will often justify the purchase since it is assumed that
selections are based, among other things, upon authoritative
reviews. The main selection tools (for current selection) assuming

that the branch has access to The Standard Catalog Series and the
A. L. A. basic lists, are:

> A. L. A. Booklist
> Bulletin of the Center for Children's Books
> Library Journal
> Top of the News
> Virginia Kirkus Service
> Horn Book
> Saturday Review
> School Libraries
> School Library Journal (not necessary if the combined
>   edition of Library Journal is purchased)
> Wilson Library Bulletin
> Choice
> N. Y. Times Book Review

> Note: The A. L. A. Bulletin, Wilson Library Bulletin and
> Library Journal are three major professional publications
> no branch should be without.

A suggested gift acceptance policy is outlined in the Mississip
pi Library Commission's Trustee Manual. The form follows:

> The Board of Trustees welcomes gifts of money, reading
> materials and time to the library. The support given the
> Library from public funds is necessarily limited and the
> addition of contributions, books, and volunteer help could
> do much to raise the standards and to improve the service
> of the library.

> Such gifts must fit into the overall program of the Library
> if they are to be of maximum value to the Library and
> bring satisfaction to the donor that the best possible use
> has been made of his gift.

> * * * * *

> Reading Materials. Gifts of books and other reading materi
> als are very welcome and can easily and readily represent
> a real contribution to the Library particularly in its begin-
> ning stages when building the book collection is a matter o
> great concern and heavy financial demands.

> The Board is glad to have gifts of books and reading ma-
> terials with these understandings:

> 1.   They must become the property of the Library and
>   the Board must be entitled to whatever disposition
>   of them will fit into the Library's service pattern.

2. They must fit into the Library's standards of book selection as to usability, content and physical condition.

3. No gifts can be accepted with any specific restrictions, like shelving in specified areas or restricted to use by certain people.

4. Gifts may be designated for certain branches (in fact, each town is encouraged to help build up its basic collection) on these two conditions:

   a. They must be sent to headquarters for sorting, classifying and processing to secure uniformity of form, accuracy of records and analysis of the book collections.

   b. It is understood that any book in any library throughout the system, regardless of source or ownership, may be used for special request by any unit of the system. The total resources of the Library are available to every reader in the area. The basic principle upon which the Library is established is complete fluidity of the book collection and 100% accessibility to any volume anywhere in the system for any reader.

5. Gift plates indicating the donor's name will be put in any gift volumes where the donor so desires.

6. Memorial volumes are especially welcomed by the Library. It is suggested that persons desiring to memorialize their loved ones in this way consult with the Library staff for suggestions and procedures. The Library has a special system of handling memorial books that will be explained when the occasion arises.

Time: The staff of the Library is very limited and there are many services which interested citizens could help the Library to give. Some of them include conducting story hours and discussion groups; writing news releases and book reviews; making talks for and about the Library and the books it contains; assisting in circulation during rush hours in the branches and on the bookmobile; helping to keep the book collection in good repair; providing displays which relate to reading and cultural matters of general community interest.

The Board solicits such help and requests that any persons who wish to assist the Library in this valuable way contact the Director and plan with her for the most effective use of such assistance.

Money. The Library is a public institution and as such
receives the mainstay of its support from public funds.
This does not mean that much more money is not needed
to approximate national standards for public library service and the Board welcomes any contributions from
individuals or organizations, provided the use for which the
donor designates the money fits into the general operational policies of the Library.   It is obvious that a purely
public institution could not accept gifts that would be contrary to the service philosophy of the institution or contrary to the laws under which it operates.

It is equally obvious that gifts to public libraries can be
of permanent and lasting value to a community and the
Board covets the opportunity to discuss gifts with any
individual or organization which desires to help the Library

> Adopted by the Board of Trustees
> of the_____
> as an official policy of the Library
> on:_____

The following offer especially helpful advice on book selection
and the drafting of a book selection policy.   The libraries listed
have good written book selection policies.

a)   Books, Articles, etc.

American Library Association, Co-ordinating Committee
on Revision of Public Library Standards, Public
Library Service. Chicago: ALA, 1956.

American Library Association, Public Libraries Division,
"Book Selection; Proceedings of a Work Conference,"
The PLD Reporter, No. 4, (Oct. 1955).

University of California School of Librarianship. The
Climate of Book Selection. Berkeley, 1959.

Carter, Mary Duncan, and Bonk, Wallace J. Building
Library Collections. 3rd Ed. Scarecrow Press, Inc.,
1969.

Wheeler, Joseph L. and Goldhor, Herbert, Practical
Administration of Public Libraries, N.Y.: Harper &
Row, c 1962.

Reid, Douglas. "Drafting a Written Book Selection
Policy," Wilson Library Bulletin, September, 1960.

Notes on the Institute on Building Book Collections,
sponsored by the school of Library Science, USC,
March 10, 1961 (by LC).

b) Book Selection Policy Statements: (Secure latest addresses
    from American Library Directory)

Enoch Pratt Free Library, Baltimore, Maryland.

Des Moines Public Library, Des Moines, Iowa.

Augusta-Richmond County Public Library.

Buffalo Public Library, Buffalo, New York.

Onondaga Library System.

Los Angeles County Public Library, Los Angeles,
California.

Los Angeles Public Library, Los Angeles, California.

San Francisco Public Library, San Francisco, California.

Berkeley Public Library, Berkeley, California.

Glendale Public Library, Glendale, California.

Santa Ana Public Library, Santa Ana, California.

One of the best articles on the subject of the book collection
is "The Branch Collection," by Meredith Bloss, which appeared in
the July, 1966, issue of Library Trends.

Notes

1. Carter, Mary Duncan, and Bonk, Wallace J. Building Library
    Collections. 3rd ed. Scarecrow Press, 1969, p. 15(?)

2. Enoch Pratt Free Library, Baltimore, Md. Book Selection
    Policies. 3rd ed. , 1963, p. 7.

3. Sinclair, Dorothy. Administration of the Small Public Library.
    American Library Association, c 1965. p. 90-99.

4. Sealock, Richard B. "Extending Services" in: Local Public
    Library Administration. International City Managers' As-
    sociation, c 1964. p. 237-274.

5. Moreland, George B. "Operation Saturation." Library Journal,
    v. 93, no. 10, May 15, 1968. p. 1975-79.

6. Tulsa City-County Library System, Tulsa, Oklahoma.
    Policy Manual. May, 1967. Sect. 7:3.1.

7. American Library Association. Statistical Standards, Addenda
    to Minimum Standards for Public Library Systems, 1966.
    Approved June 29, 1967. 4 p. leaflet.

8. Wheeler, Harold L. and Goldhor, Herbert. <u>Practical Admini-</u>
    <u>stration of Public Libraries</u>. Harper and Row, c 1962. p.
    414.

9. Bloss, Meredith. "The Branch Collection" <u>Library Trends,</u> v.
    14, no. 4, April, 1966, p. 422-432.

10. Cleveland and Cuyahoga County Library Systems. Regional
    Planning Commission. <u>Changing Patterns: a Survey of</u>
    <u>Reading Habits.</u> Conducted by Fuller, Smith, and Ross, Inc.
    Dec. 1965.

Chapter 9

Operational Techniques

Routine operations such as the charging system, registration methods, inter-library loan policies, methods of handling overdues, book selection, length of loans, overdue charges, lost book payment, teacher loans, mending methods, and procedures for obtaining supplies and equipment are usually standardized for all branches in a system and conform to those of the central or headquarters library. The philosophy underlying this is consistency and equal treatment of all patrons, economy of operation, and ease of transferring personnel from one branch to another without a new break-in period. Member libraries affiliated with systems may, however, have more flexibility in these matters. Increasingly, too, librarians of urban branches are being given more freedom to work out creative activities and procedures adjusted to the type of community.

A healthy trend is that system directors are encouraging branch librarians to present more original ideas for improvements affecting the entire system, and branches are increasingly being used to try out new methods before introducing them into the system as a whole. Branch librarians should, therefore, be aware of new procedures and be constantly on the alert to offer operational suggestions that will save time and money for all of the branches and possibly the headquarters library as well.

Opening Hours:

The hours the branch will be open to the public will vary according to the size of the branch and its staff. Thus they may not be standardized for the system as a whole. The Branch Library Staffing Pattern Study issued by the San Diego Public Library in

251

March, 1969 showed the following averages and ranges of hours
open for various-sized branches of municipal libraries serving populations between 400,000-700,000 (Boston, Dallas, Denver,
Indianapolis, Minneapolis, New Orleans, Pittsburgh, San Diego,
and Seattle.) Only branches supervised by professional librarians
are included. The chart below is adapted from the San Diego Annual Survey. For complete results of the San Diego Branch Library
Staffing Pattern Survey, see the Appendix.

No. of Branches	Size (Circulation)	Average hours open	Range of hours open
27	A. Over 175,000	46.9	40-75
10	B. 150,000-174,999	48.4	40-64
11	C. 125,000-149,999	44.4	40-49.5
18	D. 100,000-124,999	47.3	34-60
21	E. 75,000- 99,999	43.3	27-60
24	F. 50,000- 74,999	43.2	33-57
22	G. 25,000- 49,999	41.4	33.5-49.5
5	H. Under 25,000	32	15-49.5

Study of the above chart reveals a rather strange anomaly.
Although circulation in the A group of branches is seven times as
large as in the G group, the average number of hours open varies
by less than six hours per week. The range differences are also
much less than might be expected. The listing indicates that amount
of budget, number of staff, and community demand have a much
greater influence upon the total number of hours a branch is open
to the public than does the size of the operation as measured by
circulation.

Two years earlier than the above, the 1967 Staffing Pattern
Survey made by San Diego revealed the following:

No. of Branches	Size (Circulation)	Average hours open	Range of hours open
24	A. Over 175,000	45.0	40-75
14	B. 150,000-174,999	46.4	40-65
11	C. 125,000-149,999	47.3	40-57
16	D. 100,000-124,999	44.6	33.5-57
25	E. 75,000- 99,999	44.2	31-57
24	F. 50,000- 74,999	42.2	32-53
19	G. 25,000- 49,999	38.1	15-47
4	H. Under 25,000	30.3	15-45

In six out of the eight size groups the average number of
hours open increased slightly in the two year period; in only two did
the hours decrease. The range of hours continues to be puzzling,
for some city systems seem to have all branches open the same
number of hours regardless of the size of the branch or the annual
circulation. Thus, in Dallas, Texas, the Casa View Branch which
circulated 452,789 books, as shown in the San Diego survey, was
open the same number of hours as the Lakewood Branch which
circulated 212,230 books.

Comparing his own library's opening hours to the equivalent
circulation range in the San Diego charts will enable the branch librarian to determine whether or not his own branch is in line with
other branches of similar size, as judged by circulation. Most
standards seem to agree that branches should provide service to the
public a substantial part of six days per week, the hours to be
selected upon the basis of maximum potential use. Setting the
opening hours for a new branch can be a problem, however, because
it is not always possible to determine maximum potential use at the
outset, except in the case of a new building replacing an old building.
Experience has shown that circulation at a branch can double or
triple when new, attractive buildings are built and are furnished with
an adequate book collection.

The Public Library Section of the Louisiana Library Association produced a Standards Statement for Louisiana Public Libraries
in 1964 which included the following recommendation for branch hours
of public service:

Population	Hours per Week
3,000- 9,999	40 minimum
10,000-24,999	48 minimum
25,000-49,999	56 minimum
50,000-99,999	64 minimum
100,000 and over	72 minimum

Scheduling

Scheduling is an important branch administrative duty. Many
staff members prefer not to work on Saturdays, so the fairest

method is to rotate the Saturday work. How often Saturday duty
will occur depends on the size of the branch, the number of people
required on Saturdays on the average, and what special activities,
if any, take place on that day.

In many branches Saturday is a big day for the children. For
very small children it may be the only day their parents can bring
them in. The Story Hour or other children's programs may occur
on Saturday. It is highly desirable that the children's librarian be
present on Saturdays unless there is another staff member who is
qualified to work with the children and who can alternate with her.
Saturday work could perhaps be made a condition of employment.
However, few branch librarians would insist on this if it meant
losing a good children's specialist. A conscientious children's librarian will perhaps want to work every Saturday, knowing that is
the time when she can best reach the children who are her main
concern.

The author has found the form on the next page to be one
of the simplest and most practical of any she has seen for scheduling working and desk hours. At a glance it is possible to see, on
one sheet, who is scheduled to work each day and who is assigned
to the main and subsidiary desks at each hour of the day. If there
is a separate children's desk the letter "C" or "J" may be used
after the staff name to indicate this assignment. The space for
each hour of the desk schedule can be adjusted in size according
to the number of staff likely to be assigned. The busiest daytime
hours are usually after school, from about 3 or 3:30 p.m. to 6 p.m.
It is well to schedule extra desk people at that time, since one or
two may be kept very busy just checking out and receiving books,
while at least one (professional if possible) should be available to
assist the patrons with reference or other questions. A separate
and clearly marked reference or readers advisor's desk is helpful,
since clericals at the circulation desk are usually not equipped for
reference and reader guidance. Assignment to the reference or
readers advisor's desk can be indicated by an R after the staff name
on the schedule.

Desk Schedule

Hours	Monday	Tuesday	Wednesday	Thursday	Friday	Saturday
9-10						
10-11						
11-12						
12-1						
1- 2						
2- 3						
3- 4						
4- 5						
5- 6						
6- 7						xxxxx
7- 8						xxxxx
8- 9						xxxxx

Working Schedule

Branch librarian			Children's Librarian	Library Assistant	Library Clerk I	
Mon.	9-12	1-6	Mon.	Mon.	Mon.	Mon.
Tues.	8-12	1-5	Tues.	Tues.	Tues.	Tues.
Wed.	Off		Wed.	Wed.	Wed.	Wed.
Thur.	9-12	1-6	Thur.	Thur.	Thur.	Thur.
Fri.	8-12	1-5	Fri.	Fri.	Fri.	Fri.
Sat.	8-12	1-5	Sat.	Sat.	Sat.	Sat.
Total	40 hours					

Library Assistant II	Library Clerk II	
Mon.	Mon.	Mon.
Tues.	Tues.	Tues.
Wed.	Wed.	Wed.
Thur.	Thur.	Thur.
Fri.	Fri.	Fri.
Sat.	Sat.	Sat.

If staff members rotate working on Saturdays, several such schedules, numbered 1, 2, 3, 4, etc. should be prepared with the Saturday changes shown and another day off assigned for the Saturday staff members. These are placed on the bulletin board the week they apply and can be used over and over. Special schedules will be needed during vacation periods. The form should be duplicated in quantity, ready to fill in for any special schedules needed.

With this type of desk schedule, using the alternates for Saturday, it is not necessary to make a new schedule for each week or month, as is so often done. Temporary changes during vacations or illness can simply be penciled in lightly on the schedule and erased when the need is over. Schedule making can be very time consuming if new ones are made frequently. Staff members like to know what they can count on from week to week.

Another device is to place the initials O. C. after the name of a second or third staff member, indicating that this person is "on call" for certain busy hours and is to go to the desk and help when needed or summoned. This eliminates tying up at the desk more people than are needed at any given moment.

Should the branch be open on Sunday afternoons, the general city or county personnel ruling will determine whether staff members who work will be paid time and a half or double time, or given equal, one and a half, or double the compensatory time off. Should compensatory time be the normal practice, the staff member should be given, insofar as possible, his choice as to which day of the week he will take off. In order to rotate the Saturdays, several schedules should be made out, differing only in the lineup for Saturday and the assignment of days off for the Saturday worker. If possible, staff members should not be scheduled on desk duty for more than two hours at a stretch.

Charging methods and equipment

Urban branches will usually be required to use whatever charging system is in use at the central library. In rural branches, there may be more flexibility and the rural or small community branch may have some choice of charging method. The librarian, therefore, should have a knowledge of the methods best adapted to branch operation and should explore the feasibility of converting to whatever method will save time and money and improve service to patrons.

Basically, methods of charging can be divided into six main types: 1) Manual or hand charging, now used in fewer libraries each year; 2) Visible record, a cumbersome system which requires considerable time and space; 3) Mechanical, such as the Gaylord charging machine and the new Demco charger; 4) Thermographic, in which the charge is reproduced by a heat process; 5) Audio, a method in which the book charge is spoken aloud and recorded on a phono record or tape; 6) Photographic (Regiscope, the Recordak Starfile

Microfilmer, or Micromizer) in which the charge is recorded on microfilm. The photographic system seems to be gaining more rapidly in popularity than other systems.

Branches are occasionally used by systems heads to try out new systems. Choice of a system for a new branch will usually depend upon the following factors:

1. The system being used in the rest of the library system.

2. Whether the budget will stand the heavier initial cost of setting up an automatic system. This can run quite high the first year, depending upon the system selected.

3. Whether the equipment has operated satisfactorily in other branches.

4. The nearness of repair and servicing facilities.

5. Most important of all: the efficiency of the new method in relation to the current method being used. How much time will be saved? How do operational costs compare? How about speed of service to the public?

By use of a mechanical or other automatic system which records the name and address of the borrower rather than a registration or library card number, the time-consuming process of looking up names and addresses for overdues can be saved. Using a photographic system also saves arranging, counting and filing circulation or book cards each day and the slipping of books when returned.

Although most branches or affiliated member libraries will not be able to afford computer sorting of the transaction cards, larger systems often arrange for this to be done on county or city equipment and can extend this facility to branches if it is considered desirable. For those who do not have data processing equipment available, numbered transaction sheets are obtainable. When books are returned the transaction cards are pulled from the pocket and the corresponding number is checked off on the sheet. The numbers remaining after a certain period indicate the overdue books. It is then necessary to refer to the film to determine the borrowers' names and addresses. Sorting the transaction cards back into

Figure 39: The new Recordak Starfile Microfilm Camera brought out in early 1969 is a photocharging method apt to become very popular. The camera is small, light, and uses very low wattage, making it suitable for either branch or bookmobile, as well as central libraries.

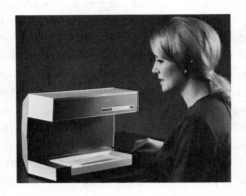

Photo by Eastman Kodak Co.

Figure 40:   The Standard Model Regiscope "B"

The most commonly-used of the Regiscope models at this writing was the Standard model. It is widely used in the United States, Great Britain and other countries.

Photo: Regiscope of America

Figure 41: THE MICRO-MIZER, light, fairly inexpensive, with removable magazine for film loading, was at last report being tested by its manufacturer for bookmobile and general use. These machines have been used in Pasadena, California branches.

Figure 42
Dickman and Sysdac Charging Machines

DICKMAN CHARGING MACHINE,
MODEL 500

SYSDAC

Figure 43. Demco Charging Machine

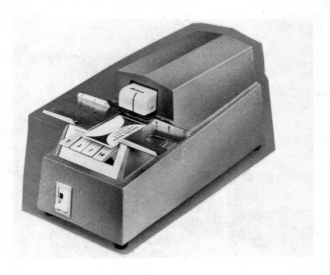

numerical order to be used again is a tedious hand job when computer sorting is not available.   Nevertheless, the initial cost of
purchasing the charging machine, transaction cards, and cabinets
for card storage is usually more than offset by subsequent savings
in time.   Staff members relieved of purely routine duties can give
added time to the public.

    A branch should normally have a circulation of 100,000 or
more annually before any type of automatic charging is justified.
Transaction card systems, whether using hand or machine sorting,
are rarely more expensive in the long run than the older methods,
and may be less expensive.   Contra Costa County Library, Pleasant
Hill, California, installed a microfilm charging system at all of its
branches which had 100,000 annual circulation or more, or which
anticipated such a circulation.   At each camera location the time of
at least one full-time clerk was saved. Personnel at Contra Costa
felt that the use of the cameras virtually eliminated errors, cut
costs, and speeded up operations.   Handling of overdues was also
greatly simplified.   One Southern California library circulating

400,000 books annually found a saving of 102 hours per week in staff time after changing to a transaction card system.

If a branch still uses a method of charging that requires arranging, counting, and filing book cards in circulation trays at the desk, time used for counting can be saved by using a small, inexpensive metal gauge which will do a remarkably accurate job. It is usually obtainable at office supply houses.

If one charging machine is used at a central checkout desk for both adult and juvenile books, as often happens at a branch or small library, and a separate circulation record is desired, a small hand click-counter can be kept beside the charging machine. After determining whether juvenile or adult circulation is usually heaviest the click-counter is used to record whichever is the smaller. Assuming that the adult circulation is smaller, the total recorded on the click-counter is subtracted from the total recorded by the charging machine at the end of each day, and the remainder will give the total juvenile circulation. Many libraries today, however, have decided to keep only a single total for circulation, taking spot checks if they wish to determine the trends in either total. The click counter must be used consistently for either the adult or juvenile circulation and cannot be used interchangeably or the record becomes confused.

Registration of borrowers

An increasing number of libraries are dispensing with registration. A driver's license, credit card, or other positive identification is used to check out books or the borrower may be issued a library identification card after establishing his identity. With photocharging, if the borrower has an identification card and forgets it, a temporary slip with his name and address may be provided free or for a small service charge (usually 10¢). This is photographed along with the book and transaction cards. If a driver's license, social security card or other usually carried identification is used instead of a library card there is no problem. Advantages of the no-registration system are:

1. Several steps are saved (typing the name and address on the registration card), filing the registration cards, and pulling them again when the registration has expired).

2. There is no need to maintain extra file drawers behind the desk or in the desk. Cost of the files and the space used are both saved.

3. Cost of the purchased or locally-printed registration cards is saved. These are 3x5 stiff card stock as a rule. A temporary paper registration slip is usually filled out by the patron but destroyed as soon as the card is issued. In the case of children it is kept until the borrower's card has been returned signed by the parent.

4. The library card is issued immediately.

References as given on registration cards have proved to be of doubtful value in the past. Their main purpose was to trace people who moved without returning books. By the time the library has sent routine notices, a bill, and possibly an attorney's letter, the patron is usually gone, and even if a new address is known, efforts to recover the books are usually futile, unless the branch wishes to become involved with skip tracers, search warrants, police recovery, collection agencies, or small claims court.

The authority to dispense with registration at a branch would, of course, come from headquarters and would depend upon whether or not it was deemed desirable to eliminate it throughout the system

Branch patrons often ask the staff to keep library cards on file for them (if library cards have been issued). This is an inadvisable practice which, if it is done for one patron, should be available to all. The added work of having to stop and pull the borrower's card from the file each time he wants to check out books, then return the card to the file again, slows up service and requires added filing space at a crowded charging desk. Once this procedure has been started it is difficult to drop it. The best rule is not to start it at a new branch. If it has been a long-standing practice the librarian should attempt to bring it to a close by returning the cards as the patrons come in, explaining regretfully that due to staff

shortages and the need for speeding up service at the desk, holding
cards for safekeeping will no longer be possible. Most people will
be reasonable about the matter. A few patrons may protest, and
the librarian will have to deal with them tactfully. Cards left in the
file after a certain period can be mailed to the patron's last known
address. If they are returned undelivered, this presents an opportunity to clear the registration files of people who have moved away,
died, or ceased to use the library within the three or five year
registration period.

Record keeping

Statistics and record keeping should be held to a minimum.
Few systems today require detailed breakdowns of circulation. The
majority still keep separate adult and juvenile figures but some libraries maintain only a single circulation total, taking spot checks
when they deem it necessary to know the proportion of adult and
juvenile usage, or the trend of fiction versus non-fiction. It is important to weigh the value of every record kept to ascertain whether
or not the time consumed in keeping it is justified by the use to which
the figure will be put.

If registration files are maintained, they should be kept up to
date by pulling expirations on a regular basis, preferably at least
once a month. If fines are charged, a file of 3x5 cards, arranged
alphabetically by the name of the patron, should be maintained at
the charging desk. This file should record all charges--fines, the
price of unreturned books, damage assessments, or any other unpaid
amounts--and should be checked as books are charged out. This
helps to hold down loss from perpetual offenders who do not return
books, continue to take out more, and run up large amounts of debt.
It also helps to collect fines promptly. Most patrons would rather
be reminded currently of a fine they owe than to be told about it a
long time after the charge was incurred. A number of libraries
that have dropped fines have reported that the rate of return is as
good or better than if fines were levied. The Douglas County Library

and its branches in Roseburg, Oregon, have never charged fines.
Should fines not be charged, a record of other charges, such as for
lost and unreturned books, still has to be kept and checked regularly.   Other sources of income in a branch, in addition to fines,
include payment for lost books, damage charges, reserve charges,
and charges for issuing duplicate cards when a borrower's card has
been lost.   If a card has been forgotten, a small charge of five to
fifteen cents may be made for making out a temporary slip so that
the patron can still check out material.

It is desirable to have a small but strong safe for locking
funds up at night, unless the Central library messenger collects the
money daily for deposit with Central funds. Careful records of income and refunds are usually required to be kept at each branch,
as well as the details of how any petty cash allotted to the branch
is spent.   Receipts are usually required for all petty cash expenditures, all of which should be authorized by the branch librarian

Records should be kept on branch activities to document the
staff work load and the success or failure of particular services or
facilities.   These records, useful for monthly or annual reports,
include details on attendance at story hours, at summer reading
projects and library-sponsored meetings, and occasional spot checks
of the number of people using reference facilities at various times
of the day or evening.   One important record to demonstrate increasing work load is the number of reference questions handled.
It is not necessary to record the actual questions, unless they are
unusual, in which case recording them may serve as a finding guide
for other staff members if they recur.   A simple tally of the total
number of questions asked and satisfactorily answered may also
indicate whether additional reference material is needed.

Such performance records are valuable to branch heads and
system directors in planning budgets and services, in writing
reports, in justifying staff increases, in scheduling staff assignments,
and in building the reference collection.

Certain standard records will be required by the Central
Library.   However, there is no reason why any branch librarian

should not keep additional records which she feels will be useful
for her own guidance. The main point is simply to be absolutely
sure that any record kept will have real value in improving service.

Multi-Purpose or Meeting Rooms

Policy regarding the use of multi-purpose or meeting rooms
in branches is usually set by the central library or headquarters.
Member libraries may make these decisions themselves. In either
case there should be a written, clearly-stated set of rules and they
should be applied consistently and without discrimination. There is
no one standardized set of regulations for use of library meeting
rooms and community controversies over this matter have sometimes reached serious proportions. To avoid such controversy, some
libraries prefer not to have meeting rooms, but this is a short-
sighted policy. A meeting room is much appreciated by the neighborhood or community and can enhance the library image. The
majority of libraries restrict free use of meeting rooms to public
or club meetings or events where no admission is charged. Many
do not permit use of such rooms by political organizations or by
organizations thought to be subversive. The criteria in such cases
may be difficult to define and to apply. The American Civil
Liberties Union has been known to step into the picture when an
organization is refused use of meeting rooms and the matter can
become difficult. The branch librarian should protect herself by
insisting on a written policy from headquarters. Organizations using
the room should also be expected to make good any loss or damage
resulting from their use, such as broken dishes, stains on furniture,
breakage of furniture unless due to natural wear and tear, or other
miscellaneous damage. In some branches a small fee is charged to
cover cost of heat, light, and janitor service. It is better not to
promise regular use of the room to any organization until it has
been determined how its members treat the room after a few trial
meetings.

Scheduling use of meeting or all-purpose room should be in
the hands of one staff member and a careful chart should be kept so

that there are no scheduling conflicts. Two groups arriving at once
to use the same room, because of an error in scheduling, can caus
a great deal of ill-will. A calendar with large spaces for recordin
the name of the organization and person responsible for the arrange
ment is one of the best methods. This chart should be kept beside
the phone. It is imperative that requests be submitted to the centr
authority at the main library if there is any doubt about the eligibility of a group to use the room.

A good meeting room should have available a large blackboar
of the easel folding type, a film strip projector, slide projector,
large wall screen, public address system, unbreakable plastic dishe
stainless steel silverware, a large 30-40 cup percolator, pots and
pans, and a small range-sink-refrigerator combination. Larger
branches may also own a movie projector. There should be a set
of written rules regarding the use of all equipment.

The kitchenette area of the all-purpose room should be
separated from the remainder of the area by a plastic or wood accordion door, or should be in a small separate room. There shoul
be a sufficient number of folding chairs for a capacity audience, and
if the room is also used for story hours, cushion pads or small
chairs used for this purpose should be kept in a nearby storage are

The branch head must see to it that someone, usually the
president or chairman of an event or group, is held responsible for
lights being turned off, exit doors locked, electric range turned off,
and any other equipment left in proper order. The outside exit doo
should be of the self-locking type. The branch custodian may be
responsible for such checking, but this is not always the case.

In the case of an affiliated or member library in a system,
the local board will probably pass on who is to use the library mee
ing room and under what conditions. All staff members should be
aware of the rules, where to find them, and how to explain them in
the most tactful way. It may seem that undue emphasis has been
given to this matter of meeting rooms, but, as mentioned before,
some libraries have encountered so many problems with them that
their librarians do not favor their inclusion in a branch building.

Many of these objections can be overcome if policies are clear and rules are just.

Matters pertaining to staff

For the comfort of staff and maintenance of good staff morale, staff lounge and rest rooms should be equipped with every possible convenience, including a studio couch or davenport for any staff member who does not feel well.

Branch staff should be encouraged to belong to and take an active part in the general staff association of the system and should also belong to any city or county employees' association. They should be allowed time, whenever possible, to attend workshops, professional meetings, and training sessions outside the library. Staff rules for borrowing should be carefully outlined and strictly adhered to. Staff members are usually not charged fines, so they owe it to their patrons not to keep books out for long periods, particularly those in considerable demand.

Books should always be checked out by staff in the same manner as by the public. They should receive overdue notices, and should be subject to discipline if they do not respond. Staff members' taking books home without checking them, and keeping them for long periods, has caused a problem in many a library. Some libraries require staff members to reserve books in their turn along with the public and do not permit new books to be checked out by a staff prior to their being put in circulation. The branch librarian will need to judge how strict such regulations must be, depending upon the extent of the problem. Within this writer's experience, when one branch staff member was separated from the library employment for health reasons, a visit to her home revealed 3 almost new in-demand books that had never been checked out. This is an extreme case, but it can and does happen. This person was a trusted employee who had been with the library for 25 years.

Story hours

Weekly story hours are desirable if a professional story
teller is available. Some branches offer two story hours, one for
pre-schoolers, usually on a weekday morning, and the other for
children aged about 6 to 10, usually during after-school hours or
on a Saturday. Some years ago, the Saturday morning hour was
almost standard procedure, but more recently, a number of activities have impinged on this time and attendance may suffer. Catholic
Catechism or Lutheran confirmation classes are often held on
Saturday mornings. Some theaters hold special shows for children
on Saturday morning or early afternoon. Music lessons or doctor
and dental appointments often conflict. Parents go to nearby cities
or large shopping centers and take the children with them, or week-
end trips take families out of town. Some branches have found a
mid-week after-school hour more satisfactory.

On the other hand, some children lack transportation to
come to story hours on week days when fathers are not at home,
or if mothers work. Each branch will have to experiment with
various times according to the activities taking place in their own
service areas, but story hours are important and should be held.
The programs, of course, can be varied--stories, films, recordings, creative drama, finger plays, games, puppet shows, magic
demonstrations, etc. The cardinal principle for any story hour or
other program is that it be book and library oriented. It is not
an entertainment hour solely, but a device for interesting children
in books. Thus there should be appropriate displays of related
books in the story telling rooms; the story-teller should mention
other similar stories, should find out how many of those in attendance have library cards, should talk a little about the fun of
owning and reading books.

Branches should make use of the specialists and supervisors
available through the central headquarters for help in planning
children-oriented programs and in providing story-telling talent.

Discipline in a Branch

A number of branches, especially some in ghetto and low economic neighborhoods, have found it necessary to employ uniformed monitors to keep order in the evenings. Retired policemen or firemen, or anyone strong enough to cope physically with a serious offender if necessary, make the best monitors. The choice of a monitor should be made very carefully, for some, by their very manner, arouse hostility and cause problems that would not otherwise occur. In potentially troublesome neighborhoods at least one male staff member or special monitor should be on hand each evening the library is open, and if possible, women staff members should never be left completely alone after 6 or 7 p.m. This is especially true if the branch is located in or near a park, or if the parking lot for staff cars is at the back of the building in a poorly-lighted area or is invisible from the street.

As far as general discipline is concerned, the old rule of never saying anything unless you mean it applies in full force. If a student council is working with the branch head, a code of conduct should be drawn up by a committee of students and submitted to the branch for approval. After approval, it should be enforced consistently, and should be posted prominently in several places. It may also be issued in mimeographed form and given out as needed. It is highly important that the branch staff be consistent in their enforcement of the rules. Branches have had to be closed at times because of discipline problems and vandalism. However, the majority of young people respect firmness and like having a comparatively quiet place to study and read, away from T.V. and from the noise and confusion of some of their homes. It is necessary to be firm yet pleasant, to enforce rules without arousing hostility. Occasional in-service training sessions should be held to discuss and demonstrate how to deal with various problem situations. If a situation gets beyond control, of course, there is no other solution but to call the police. Sometimes it is only necessary to let the troublemakers hear the call being made, and they are out of the building before the police arrive.

Recovery of Unreturned Items (See overdue book survey in Appendix):

The increasing rate of loss in public libraries has prompted many librarians to consider more drastic means of recovering un- returned books and other library materials than have been employed in the past.   If no response is secured after the usual notices and attorney letter have been sent to recalcitrant borrowers, some li- braries have submitted claims through the small claims court, have put the account owed into the hands of collection agencies, or have sent messengers to homes to recover unreturned materials.

Due to staff shortages and the higher cost of postage, a num- ber of libraries now send only one overdue notice.   The second notice is a bill.   The third will be a letter from the city attorney, county prosecutor or district attorney, calling the patron's at- tention to the law regarding the non-return of city or county property and carrying a veiled threat of prosecution.   The problem is that often, by the time the notices have reached this stage, the patron has moved away and left no address.   Branch librarians are in a somewhat better position to deal with the problem of unreturned books because they know their patrons better; they can secure in- formation more easily about patrons who have moved, and with fewer patrons than the large central library, they may be able to spot perpetual offenders earlier and to restrict or cut off their bor- rowing privileges.   Accurate and currently maintained records on fines and lost book charges also aid control.

The main problem, however, is not the books that are checked out and not returned, but the books that "walk out the door" without benefit of checkout.   Unless the branch has an exit turn- stile at the charging desk, through which all patrons who leave the library must pass, this situation is difficult to control.   Various security measures have been tried.   Several electronic devices are on the market which ring a bell, flash a light, or otherwise signal when a patron tries to leave with a book that has not been checked out.   Three such systems are: the Sensormatic, a micro-wave radio signal device; the Checkpoint, an electronic, solid state system; and the Sentronic, also an electronic detection device using magnets inserted into the books. Cost of installing these devices, for two units, was as follows in late 1968: Sensormatic, first year costs for leasing the equipment and purchasing supplies for 15,000 books was $5,462, with annual costs after the first year of $4,950. The Checkpoint system cost $8,090 for the first year and $4,090 per year thereafter for the same number of books. The Sentronic cost was $6,950 the first year, $3,450 annually thereafter for ten years, after which the library would own the equipment and costs would be $1,150. Obviously, branch loss would have to be very high to justify such costs, and few libraries had installed these systems in 1968. The systems are not completely foolproof. The theory is that the detection devices do not need to be installed in all books but only in the most valuable books and in enough others so that the public believes they are in all books. Cost of installing them in all books would in most branches be prohibitive. In time, prices may be lowered and the machines may be made more invincible.

Division of staff duties: Work simplification studies

Every branch, regardless of how small, should have a master list of duties posted on the bulletin board in the workroom. It should be in two forms: 1) The complete list of duties in alphabetical order, with the name of the staff member responsible following each item; 2) The names of the staff members with a list of the individual duties under each name. The individual duties can be listed in order of priority. The first list enables the branch librarian to check quickly who is supposed to be doing a particular task. The second list shows each staff member exactly what his responsibilities are. Each staff member should also have a copy of his own duties at his desk for quick reference.

Misunderstanding, duplication, and encroachment on the duties of another can be avoided when everything is written down. Having staff members keep task lists for a two-week period once a year or so will enable the branch librarian to determine whether some are

spending too much time on lesser duties at the expense of more
important matters, whether the jobs being done are all commensurate with the person's job classification, and whether some tasks are
being performed that could be shortened or eliminated altogether.
This is a better method of determining whether duties are being
performed in the most efficient manner than standing over the employee and observing each motion.   Most people are nervous under
detailed observation.

A simple form is used.   All activities are recorded even if
they are only of a few minutes duration.   If several people do the
same task at various times, they should use the same terminology
in describing it.   The question may arise: why do this if an exact
list of duties and assignments already exists?   The task list breaks
down each duty into its component parts and reveals whether or not
it is being done in the easiest and quickest way.

After the task lists have been kept for two weeks (10 working days), the staff member adds up the total time used for each
task, since many are repetitive, figures the percentage of total time
used for that particular task and then ranks the tasks in the order
of time used, with the one taking the most time in first place and
so on down.

At this point the branch librarian or head of the member
library analyzes the summary sheets and as a result may be able
to eliminate some steps, shorten others, rearrange duties to more
closely match abilities, save unnecessary steps by rearrangement
of the work room or charge desk, or in one way or another save
time and money while increasing efficiency.   Staff members, as a
rule, do not like task lists.   The head librarian should assure them
that no one will lose his position, be demoted, or be subjected to
criticism because of them.   Conferences at the time the final task
lists are turned in may reveal that some staff members are doing
tasks they dislike; whereas others would like these same tasks. The
conferences also afford an opportunity for each staff member to suggest improvements or changes in his own assignment of duties.

In the assignment of duties, of course, insofar as possible,
professional staff should be given professional duties, and non-

professional staff duties commensurate with their training and experience. The good branch head makes every effort within the limitations of her budget and available man-hours of staff time to achieve this goal.

When scheduling vacations and compensatory days off the branch head must be sure that all noon hours, dinner hours, and desk hours are covered by alternates. There should be several substitutes available either through a system pool or through a branch list of neighborhood people qualified to act as substitutes.

Friends of the Library

Friends of the library groups can be a great asset to a branch. They can also be a problem. Generally, however, they form a valuable link with the community and are worth forming and sponsoring. Friends' activities have helped many a branch to secure extra equipment, books, furnishings, or art work the budget could not provide. They have provided resource people to assist in the celebration of Book Week, National Library Week, or library anniversaries, and have helped spearhead campaigns for new buildings.

The Friends can raise money through book sales, teas, or special programs, and they can usually be counted on to provide volunteers to help the children's department with summer reading program parties, Christmas parties, or story hours.

The secret of a good Friends of the Library group is finding enough projects to keep members busy and give them a sense of accomplishment. Many a group has died on the vine because the branch did not really seem to need them. Working with them takes some of the professionals' time, but it pays off in good community relationships and other fringe benefits. Whether or not a group is a problem may also depend upon the officers the members elect. A poor and ineffective leader can set the tone for the entire group. Likewise, a too-aggressive or domineering president can kill initiative or arouse resentment among members.

Some branch heads unashamedly admit pulling strings to get
the best leaders into office, but the library staff should not seek to
control the group or it may lose its effectiveness as a lay group
which represents the community.

Cooperation with the Schools

The professional branch staff must actively seek cooperation
with the schools in the area and with all school librarians. As a
rule school people are too busy and too harassed to take the initiative. The branch should offer library instruction to classes, invite
groups in for special weeks, displays, or programs for children
and young people.   Professional staff must be willing to provide occasional consultant service to schools which have libraries but no
librarians, or to those with teacher librarians who need help. This
can be overdone, however, to the point where it might impinge upon
branch duties and also militate against the school system providing
funds for a full-time school librarian.

The Policy Manual

Many systems, especially those which are highly centralized,
provide branch manuals of policies and procedures, as well as information for new employees. In some branches, a supplement to
the system manual is needed to inform employees concerning individual branch procedures, neighborhood characteristics, and special
branch collections and facilities.

Included in the policy and procedure manual should be city or
county regulations for all employees concerning vacations, sick leave
holidays, overtime and overtime pay, compensatory time, leaves of
absence, health insurance, retirement, special regulations for part-
time employees, and any other personnel matters.   A branch library
will have a copy of the system's procedure and policy manual; a
member or affiliate library's procedures and policies will probably
be based upon those of the city or county in which it is located

rather than those of the system or jurisdiction. In the latter case, having the local policies in written form is particularly important since they will differ from library to library within the system.

Other matters which should be included in the manual, whether it is an all-system or an individual branch production, are policies regarding fines, lost books, refusal of service to patrons, patrons' use of non-pay phones, closing announcements, clarifying the difference between a reference or reader advisory question and a directional question for purposes of recording, renewals, vacation loans, receipts, reserve procedure, loan periods, checking out of rental books, any special procedures with paperbacks, policy regarding gift books, what to do in case of emergencies (fire, earthquake, bomb scare, accident), regulations regarding the use of the meeting room, overdue procedures if handled at the branch; use of record players, microfilm viewers, rental typewriters, any other special equipment; discard policies, teacher loan policy, interlibrary loan policy and procedure, distributing mail, tours of the library, library instruction procedure, the work-experience program to obtain student help, Youth Corps, Job Corps workers; snags, staff meetings and in-service training meetings, suggestions regarding good discipline, possibly suggested standards of dress and personal habits. Use a loose-leaf format so that changes are easily made.

Interlibrary loans

One staff member should be in charge of all requests for material from the Central library, the State Library, or other libraries in the system. If the branch works under a regional branch, requests may be channeled through the region. Unless the branch has a book catalog of system holdings it will have to channel all requests through the Central Library. There should be free exchange of materials within a system, and no reluctance on the part of one branch to lend an only copy of a title to another branch. Interchanging freely is one of the advantages of belonging to a system.

Staff Meetings

Staff meetings to discuss new regulations, operational problems, proposed changes, and new developments in the library world should be held regularly, at least once a month, and twice if possible. Every other meeting can be devoted to branch business and discussion; the alternate meetings to in-service training sessions. If the library opens at 10 a.m. the best meeting time is from 8:30 to 10 a.m. One hour is seldom quite long enough, especially if new books received at the branch are laid out and briefly examined or commented upon along with other matters. Staff members who come early for such meetings can be given the time off at noon or at closing time.

Time and Trouble Savers

It is important that branch librarians and staff members do not get bogged down in internal operations to the point where public service suffers. If operational procedures threaten to infringe on the quality of public service, it is time to insist on more staff and a closer analysis of operations. Here are a few miscellaneous suggestions for saving time and improving service:

1. Use all possible volunteer help and talent for setting up exhibits, celebrating special weeks, doing simple tasks in the branch. Enlist the help of Friends of the Library, Boy Scouts, Girl Scouts, Campfire Girls, Work Experience Students, Job and Youth Corps employees. The last two programs are for paid helpers, but the library does not foot the bill.

2. Have enough signs directing patrons to various sections, explaining the card catalog, advertising programs, so that the staff will not have to answer too many directional or elementary questions when they could be assisting patrons with more difficult problems.

3. Provide a photocopying machine to cut down on vandalism (students tearing out pages or stealing books from which they need only an excerpt).

4. Shelve ready reference books behind the charging desk to save steps and time when phone calls come in or people ask this type of question at the desk. At a branch desk, assistants must often handle such questions when no reference librarian is available.

5. If permission can be secured from the system headquarters count the circulation every other day instead of every day if you are still using a system where circulation must be counted by hand.

6. Devise printed or mimeographed forms for every possible use, to save writing time.

7. Arrange workroom desks, tables, chairs, and supplies for the best work flow and convenience of those working in the room. Supplies should be nearest the points where they will be used rather than all in one place.

8. Make one staff member responsible for seeing that all desk supplies are replenished well before they run out and that needed supplies are secured from the central headquarters in good time.

9. Investigate the possibility of eliminating borrowers' cards and of using drivers' licenses or other means of identification instead. Member libraries may be able to do this more easily than branches in centralized systems.

10. Have a list of busy work tasks for staff to do during slack moments at the desk.

11. Analyze and simplify steps in handling discards, rental books to be returned to McNaughton or American Lending Service, registration records.

12. Dispense with inventories unless system policy requires them. Most libraries now inventory seldom or not at all.

13. Work out printed or mimeographed routines for library instruction at various levels for the different age groups.

14. Keep clippings of book reviews or have the Book Review Digest available for patrons.

Book Drop Problems

In February, 1969, the Long Beach (California) Public Library Courier[2] carried a comment, reprinted from the local news-paper, about a patron's concern for damage to books returned through branch library book drops.   The writer and her family were ...."distressed to see the new book hit the floor with a thud, spread open, and stop with its pages bent under it." She wondered if a slide or conveyor belt would be helpful. A thoughtful gentleman who read the comment came up with a solution to at least part of the problem and made a special trip to tell the librarian about it. "Simply put a strong rubber band around the book to keep it from spreading open," he said.

Other methods of curing the problem of the book hitting the floor with a thud when put through book drops that open into the building are:

Place under the inside opening of the chute a large piece of thick foam rubber at least four inches thick and about five by five feet.   This affords protection for a wide area even if the books bounce or slide.   The foam mat can be rolled up and stored during the day.

Place beneath the inside opening of the chute a book cart on casters that depresses on springs as the weight of the books ac-cumulates.   As the top descends the pile of books remains on top and subsequent books do not have far to drop.   These carts are fairly expensive and have the disadvantage that when they are full all the books spill over onto the hard floor.   An advantage of the depressable cart, if not too many books come in so that it over-flows, is that the books can be wheeled to the central desk for the return process; with the foam pad all books must be picked up individually and loaded onto a standard book cart.

A portable slide which hooks on to the inside of the chute and comes clear to the floor could also be used, but it would probably have to be custom made and would be rather bulky and heavy to move back and forth twice a day.   The best procedure is

to encourage patrons to return books, if possible, during the hours
the library is open.   Book drops encourage unpaid overdue books
and cannot help but cause more wear and tear on the books, regardless of the equipment used.

Notes

1.   San Diego Public Library. Branch Library Staffing Pattern Study.
       March, 1969. 9 p. mimeographed.

2.   Long Beach Public Library, Long Beach, California. The
       Courier. February, 1969, p. 1.

Chapter 10

Special Activities and Services in Today's Branches

Some of the activities in branch libraries today might well
shock the austere librarian of earlier days. Yet these activities
have in many cases revitalized branch service as nothing else
could have done, and they have reached groups and individuals with
whom branches formerly had little contact.

No longer do large city branches cater only to the prosperous elements of society, the so-called intellectuals and upper middle class. Many of these readers have moved to the suburbs, and
the neighborhood library has new customers: the inner city's poor
and ghetto-bound. Only those branches remaining in quiet residenti
areas in smaller cities where less change has taken place have
missed the impact of the changing metropolitan social scene. [1]

The new patrons--Mexicans, Puerto-Ricans, Negroes, and
whites of many nationalities--want practical material or material
that is related to their own cultures. They want easy-to-read information on how to repair a car; how to cook economical,
balanced meals; how to paśs a literacy test; or how to care for a bab
They may want novels in Spanish, or books about Negro history.
They want activity in the library that makes it easy and informal
and makes them feel at home. [1]

Outreach programs in branch libraries in Washington, D. C.,
New Haven, Detroit, Brooklyn, Boston, Los Angeles, Baltimore,
and New York City, among others, include such events as these:

1. Phoebe, a film which deals with pre-marital pregnancy.

2. Discussion groups for mothers while children are at
pre-school story hours.

3. Story hour programs and books that feature Negro
children as heroes.

4. A discussion for parents on how to help children with school work and how to brighten the home (Detroit).

5. Karatê and judo demonstrations (Los Angeles).

6. Rock and roll concerts (New York City).

7. Celebration of Negro History Week (Detroit).

8. A nine-week black history course given by an all-Negro faculty (Dallas).

9. An Afro-American art exhibition, which was praised by the Negro community newspaper (Dallas).

10. A tour of Morgan State College for young people (Baltimore).

11. A steel band concert at a New York Latin-American community branch.

12. A "black is beautiful" program honoring Dr. Martin Luther King Jr. and Malcolm X (Venice Branch, Los Angeles Public).

13. Talks given by outside speakers at these libraries have included such subjects as the new developments in mathematics, music, Negro history, careers, charm, love and the facts of life, and health. Former drug addicts have been invited in to talk about their experiences.[1]

Boston, according to Carolyn F. Ruffin,[1] requires its branch librarians to join their community inter-agency councils. In fact, most of the big city libraries work with other agencies in inner-city community councils. Library representation at Council meetings helps to demonstrate to agencies other contributions the library can make to their over-all programs.

Libraries are putting book deposits in Head Start offices and demonstration libraries in the headquarters of citizen-action groups. In Santa Ana, California, the public library's summer outreach program places books in all the city parks, and uses volunteers to put on a combination music, games, story hour, and book talk program at bookmobile stops, the programs ending with the children going onto the bookmobile in small groups.

Many library systems are making their branches true community centers by encouraging them to become meeting headquarters for a wide variety of organizations. For example, the Tulsa, Oklahoma, City-County Library System had the following groups meeting in branch libraries during 1967-68: Homemakers' Extension groups, senior citizens, Artists Guild, Newcomers, Jaycees, Mothers' March of Dimes, Cub Scouts, Boy Scouts, Flower Guild, Garden Club, Boxby Public Works and Board of Trustees, Civic Club, Teenage Republicans, managers of community baseball teams, Business and Professional Women, Alpha Rho Tau Art Association, Great Books Group, Tulsa Dog Training Association, Hobby Club Workshop, Little League Baseball managers, Art Association, Tops Club, Cub Scout leaders, Civic Planning Committee, Girl Scout Service Team, Tulome Study Club, American Association of University Women, Beta Sigma Phi, Night Writers, Gladiola Garden Club, Eastern Star Study Groups, Jaycettes, Tulsa Jr. Charity Horse Show Association.

Other groups were: Xi Kappa Phi, Sweet Adelines, Oil Capitol Dog Club, District Council of Northeast Camp Fire Girls, Blue Birds, Chas. Page High School Parent-Teachers Association, Veterans of Foreign Wars Auxiliary, Pioneer Historical Club, Sand Springs Art Association, Little League Baseball Mothers, Dept. of Public Welfare Group, Bacone College Extension classes, National Alliance of Postal and Federal Employees, Neighborhood Citizens' Council, Zeta Phi Beta Sorority, Elite Ladies Inc., Social and Cultural Group, Voters' Registration Committee, North Tulsa Association of Real Estate Brokers, Mable Lynch Civic Club, Disabled American Veterans, Vista Craft Class, Camp Fire Institutes and Counselors' Workshop, Tulsa County Legislative Delegation, Gilcrease Quarterback Club, Lion Tamers, Sage Garden Club, Heart Fund Coffee Group, McClure Y. M. C. A., North Tulsa County Development Association, Orange Foothills Garden Club.

This long list is presented for several reasons: to emphasize the fact that a branch with a multi-purpose meeting room has a decided advantage in becoming a community center; to show the great diversity of interests represented; and to point out the publicity value for the library in having all these people come to its building, even though they may not enter the library proper at all on their first visit.   Those who come for meetings will at least know where the branch is, will come within speaking distance of its resources, will be impressed with the community service offered by what is usually a free meeting place, and may return in future to become regular library patrons.   The library has an opportunity for further publicity in arranging exhibits of appropriate books in the meeting room.   Few groups object to such a procedure.

One Tulsa Branch, Seminole Hills, had 19 different groups meeting in its building; the Nathan Hale Branch had 15.   The total of 92 organizations meeting in system libraries is impressive.   It is apparent from the great variety of organizations, ranging from cultural clubs to dog training groups, that these branches are sharing more fully than many in the life of their service areas. They are undoubtedly also making many new friends.

Some branches have instituted tutoring programs in remedial reading and English for non-English speaking patrons.   Rules and regulations printed in Spanish are helpful to some of these patrons. Detroit's Monteith Branch tries to attract more patrons from its community with non-bookish activities such as talent shows.   One show offered to teenage audiences a rock band and a one-act play written and performed by a 15-year old girl.

Other uncommon branch activities have included movies shown on the side of a van parked in a housing project, a trip to a Baltimore Oriole baseball game, provision of Erle Stanley Gardner's books in Spanish.   In Los Angeles, with federal help, teams of specialists were added to branch library staffs at Lincoln Heights, Venice, and the central region of the city to find ways to enable the library to help meet community problems.   Library specialists work cooperatively with existing community organizations and agencies.   Book deposits, displays, and library materials have been placed in such outlets as the Watts Skill Center for Adult Vocational Training.   Material on crafts, sculpture, painting, and allied

Figure 44: Chairmen and members of the Anderson County Home
Demonstration Club Reading Program work hard to master the techniques and absorb the inspiration needed for promoting better reading
in their clubs. Meeting held at Clinch-Powell Regional Library Center,
Clinton, Tennessee. Reading improvement clinics are now being
featured by a number of branch libraries.

subjects was loaned to the Watts Tower Art Center. Los Angeles
Green Posts, sponsored by the Office of Economic Opportunity, are
the scene of library-sponsored discussions of such topics as "The
Natural Look."

In Baltimore, where the Enoch Pratt Free Library has been
under contract with the Community Action Agency, small branches or
library rooms were set up in 16 of the 29 community centers located
in row houses, stores, or ground-level apartments in housing
projects.

In New York the North Manhattan and South Bronx Branch
Projects have made funds available for activities such as exhibits
of Afro-American art, photography exhibits from Ebony Magazine,
and a "black is beautiful" photo show. One such exhibit drew hundreds of visitors in mid-July of 1967, despite the library's lack of
air conditioning.

Art exhibits used in the Tulsa City-County System rotate on a two-months basis among the 19 branches, under the coordination of the Chief of Extension Services, the staff artist, and an art consultant committee made up of representatives of organizations participating in the collections. Local exhibits in the county towns and from schools adjacent to the city branches are encouraged.

The Appleby Branch of the Augusta-Richmond County Public Library, Augusta, Georgia, has presented, since 1955, a weekly musical program during the summer months. It is held on the library grounds and is arranged and managed by the library. Largely musical, the programs also include lectures and dramatic readings. Known as "Evenings in the Appleby Garden," the programs attract several hundred listeners and are given by local performers who receive only a modest fee. In case of rain the program is moved to the library's spacious verandah.

Although actually a specialized branch, the Biblioteca Latina, opened by the Boston Public Library in 1968, is housed in a Spanish Speaking Center, where Headstart, employment, tutorial, and similar activities share quarters. The Center is sponsored by the Roman Catholic Church, Archdiocese of Boston. The library, with Spanish-speaking help from the neighborhood and some voluntary help, has run film showings, had story hours, and has gone out to housing projects. The library's main concern, however, is Spanish books, pamphlets, recordings, and periodicals.

The Latin American Library of the Oakland Public Library, although not technically a branch since it serves the entire Spanish-speaking population of the city, is operating under a federal grant which, it was hoped, would be extended to June, 1970. The library is housed in a store front building which was formerly a little-used conventional branch. This library has a Spanish-speaking staff, and a collection predominantly in Spanish but with much material of interest to non-Spanish speaking people. Books and magazines, records, films and film strips are stocked, and programs are provided which are of interest both to those who speak Spanish and to those who do not. The programs include story hours in Spanish and English, film programs, musical programs, and discussion groups.

Figure 45:
   Cooperation with Government Programs an Increasing Trend
Four and five-year olds act out a toy soldier storybook character in
Memphis Public Library's "Early Childhood Awareness" program
(OEO-sponsored, through Community Action Council).

The Latin American Library has the further objective of
assisting those agencies and individuals working in behalf of the
Spanish speaking people in the community.   To this end it is acquiring published and unpublished materials that will be particularly
useful to these groups and individuals.   Services, funded under the
Library Services and Construction Act, have been offered to the
more than 40,000 Spanish speaking residents of the City of Oakland.
For meetings and programs the library uses the auditorium of the
Melrose Branch.   Attractively decorated and furnished to provide an
atmosphere of colorful and comfortable informality, the library is
proving popular with its many users.

An outstanding specialized program is that of the Venice
Branch of the Los Angeles Public Library, where Don Roberts,
bearded librarian who established very successful rapport with

his disadvantaged and "hippie" clientele, used many types of popular programs to attract patrons. Venice is a poverty area and a center for the "way-outers." The library sponsored combo bands, outdoor games on the grounds, off-beat publicity, and a high degree of personal guidance to interest children and young people, many of whom were not formerly readers. Other activities included chalk drawing on the sidewalk, a concert of unusual oriental instruments, puppet shows, a celebration of the Mexican Cinco de Mayo Holiday, and films.

Leys Institute, a branch of the Auckland, New Zealand, Public Library, has developed as community activities a gymnasium club, boxing club, debating group, library club, gardening club, chess club, orchestra, nature study club, and folksinging club--all attached to the library and all very active and enthusiastic. The Auckland Library has also developed "improver's collections" for slow and backward readers and for those for whom English is a second language. These collections are available in the system wherever needed. All branches have a lending service of art prints. Auckland City Council, incidentally, provides a central library, nine branches, and a mobile library for its 151,000 inhabitants. Few American cities could equal that coverage.

A number of central and branch children's departments today provide a program for parents while children are being entertained at story hours. The adult programs may take the form of a speaker, a book discussion, a presentation by a library staff member on how to choose children's books for the home library, or some other book-related program. At Boston's Roxbury Branch, however, such non-library subjects as nutrition, better schools, and the community tutoring program are presented at parent programs during story hours.

Programs highlighting Negro culture, heritage, achievements, and problems are being introduced in many central libraries and branches. Art displays by Negro artists and book displays by Negro authors are gaining in number and emphasis.

September coffee hours, afternoon teas, or special welcome meetings to acquaint new teachers with branch services are becoming

more common. These are sometimes followed up with a workshop
in service to students for both public and school librarians. A
notable series of these was sponsored by the Southern Maryland
Regional Library Association.

The Lexington Park Branch of the Southern Maryland
Regional Library Association puts on a special Halloween Costume
party and invites all the children of the community. About 350
children responded in 1967. A special Christmas party and program, which may include stories, a play, carollers from local
singing groups, or movies, is usually attended by about 500
children and their parents. Puppet shows put on by the same
library draw about 250 children. During the summer this branch
always sponsors a series of programs around a central theme such
as fairy tales, nature, animals, or Hans Christian Andersen. Attendance runs about 350. Fifty to 100 parents attend programs
presented for them at the same time.

Lexington Park Branch also offers special programs for the
mentally retarded, a service which "just grew," according to Mrs.
Mary R. Moses, coordinator of children's services, partly because
the special education center is located next door to the library.
Every juvenile program held is put on separately for the retarded
groups. Each retarded group and "trainable class" visits the library once a week, and the librarian makes it a point to talk with
each child and help him select a book.

Children's programs in the Boston Public Library branches
include, in addition to the usual activities, creative drama, creative writing, and puppetry (the art of making and handling puppet
shows). Boston has had excellent response from its "Never too
late Group," open only to those over 65, and organized at the
central library and several branches. The program ties in a
speaker or film with a book-centered interest. Professional staff
act as consultants and resource people. This is typical of a growing trend to provide special activities for senior citizens on an
organized basis. Other special programs sponsored by Boston Public
are an investment series with speakers from local investment firms,
programs on community problems, and local history.

Figure 46: Library Sponsors Tour of Historic Sites for Senior Citizens. A group leaves the Upper Montclair Branch of the Montclair, New Jersey Public Library, in spite of cold and snow. Several dozen attended the tour.

Such topics as drug addiction, police dogs, mock trials, and karate are presented in programs planned by members of the Boston Public Library's Young Adult Council, made up of representatives from different schools. They also furnish reviews of young adult books for a publication issued by the library.

Another Boston branch activity which is not very common is the regularly-scheduled Pre-School Class, often held in double sessions because of heavy demand. Operating somewhat like a nursery school or kindergarten, the children sing, play action and finger games, listen to recorded music or stories, do coloring, or have rhythm bands. Frequent change and contrast in what is done maintains the unflagging interest and enthusiasm of the children. Some programs include a short break for the enjoyment of tiny lollipops

and cookies to restore depleted energy. Books are arranged all
about the children, and time is scheduled for the children to
examine them.

    "Thus at a very tender age," says an article in the Boston
Public Library News, "the child is introduced to the library. If
the benefits and enthusiasms evident in children in Pre-School
Classes are an indication, these children will eagerly support and
participate in library activities in the future."

    To appeal to the "hip" crowd, Boston Public puts on pro-
grams like one given in April, 1968, at the Jamaica Plains Branch,
when Paul Williams, the 19-year old founder and editor of Craw-
daddy, talked to the gathered throngs about folk and rock music.
The invitation in the Boston Public Library News for this event was
written in hip language: "Groovin' at J. P. ," "The Hip Crowd is invited to make the scene," etc.........

    Citizens of San Antonio and Bexar County, Texas, are able
to pick up the phone and order library books which are then mailed
directly to their homes under a grant made to the San Antonio
Public Library by the Council on Library Resources. The $22,500
experiment was to determine the feasibility of ordering books by
mail as a regular feature of public library service. The service
is extended to individuals without library cards but excludes individuals owing fines on overdue books. As far back as 1933, the
Montclair, New Jersey, Public Library inaugurated a service for
the home delivery of books. Western Union originally made the
deliveries at 10¢ per book, but in 1937 the service was taken over
by a commercial firm and has continued satisfactorily to date. The
price has now gone up to 25¢ per package of one to four books. In
1966, 3,030 packages of books were delivered in this way, and
another 500 were mailed to out-of-town borrowers. The peak
months are March, October, and November. Borrowers purchase
reserve postcards at 25¢ per card and either mail them in or
bring them to the library. If the borrower wishes, he may leave
a deposit of $2.00 or more, and the library checks against this
fund as reserves are sent out. The borrower is notified when the
amount of deposit is below 50 cents.

A survey of home delivery service, made by Robert T. Jordan in 1967,[2] cited home delivery service by the Minneapolis Public Library, but this is not very heavily publicized and is used only to the extent of about 125 books per year. The patron is charged for insurance and postage, 30-35¢ per package of one to a few books. A borrow-by-mail service was started in December, 1966, for all residents of the five counties of the Pioneer Library System in western New York. The Fair Lawn, New Jersey, Public Library will mail books for a ten-cent charge paid when books are reserved. No major library has ever offered free home delivery service,[2] but many regional and county libraries will mail out books to patrons in rural areas who are not near a branch, sometimes charging the postage one way, sometimes charging no postage and including stamps for return of the books. A factor in the availability of mail service in the future may be the recent rise in the library book rate, which greatly increases costs for any library providing this service on a large scale.

For branches in the so-called "disadvantaged" areas the Brooklyn Public Library suggests that each agency recruit a library host or hostess from the indigenous residents. This host or hostess greets the new user and offers friendly, personal assistance in finding and borrowing material. This plan supplements and supports the community coordinator program which gives librarians freedom to walk the streets, knock on doors and encourage people to come into and use their branch facilities. The Community Coordinator program has had considerable success in making such initial contacts.[3] A small van also goes out from the Brooklyn Public Library into the most congested districts, puts out loan material and materials for sale onto the sidewalk, and refers people to the nearest branch for other services. Brooklyn is seeking much closer identification than in the past with multi-purpose or information centers, or with what have come to be known in New York as "little city halls." There is a proliferation of efforts by various city agencies to get information about programs, benefits, opportunities, employment, training classes, etc. to the people. The librarian,

with his special skills, could coordinate and make more valuable this
kind of information. Whether these skills are practiced inside or out
side the library building is of less importance than that they are
called into play to reach the people who need them the most. [3]

Librarians at both the main library and the branches of the
Mobile, Alabama Public Library phone patrons to announce the arrival of new books that may interest them. The circulation of
framed art prints is no longer a rarity at central libraries, but
all branches of the Macomb County Library System, Mount Clemens,
Michigan, loan custom-framed art prints, in full color, with no
deposit and no charge, as the result of assistance from a federal
grant. Borrowing is restricted to adults or to children accompanied
by adults. The loan period is one month, but overdue charges are
50¢ a day and prints are limited to one per family.

Large-type books for handicapped patrons of all ages are find
ing their way increasingly into branches and member libraries. The
people who need them most, however, the old or the poorly-sighted,
are often unable to get to the library to check them out. A great
deal of publicity and a link with a shut-in delivery service by the
Friends of the Library, Boy Scouts, Girl Scouts, Campfire Girls,
or mail service from the library may be necessary to assure the
best possible use of large-print material. Some branches that have
stocked them heavily have been disappointed with their use, because
some patrons object to the size and weight of the books.

A few main libraries and branches lay out on tables those
older issues of magazines which they are no longer keeping for reference and give them away to patrons. One advantage accruing from
this is that a student needing pictures for scrapbooks can secure
magazines to cut up without mutilating library copies which are to
be retained. A disadvantage is that it is sometimes difficult for
children or others to distinguish between the library copy to be returned and the issues they may keep.

Central libraries and branches are increasingly surmounting
city and county regulations concerning the sale of government
property, and many now hold used-book sales, annually or more

Figure 47:   Musical Program in a Branch

The Egleston Square Branch of the Boston Public Library presents a
musical program sponsored by the Library and the Home and School
Association of Henry Higginson District.   Typical of related cultural
activities increasing in number and importance as part of branch
services.

often, to get rid of surplus gift books and discards.   The public
likes these sales, and the library benefits by increasing its book
fund, unless it is required to turn the proceeds in to the city or
county general fund.   In the latter case, however, the money received may still be credited to the library fund.   Books range in
price at these sales from 5¢ to $5.   They can be arranged on tables
by price, a 5¢ table, a 10¢ table, etc., with a special table for
items over $1 or for sets.   In some communities surplus magazines
can also find a market at these sales.   Another device is to auction
the books by the box, but this method usually produces less income.
Often, such sales are conducted by the Friends of the Library and
the money is used to purchase books or some needed item not provided for in the library's budget.

The Brooklyn Public Library has placed basic reference books
books on sports, short stories, books on child care and psychology,
and cook books, in bars, beauty parlors and barber shops, with surprising success.   The Nashville Public Library placed a small
branch in the busy Nashville Airport.   Two million people pass
through this airport in one year.   The door to the reading room was
taken off the hinges, and the room is never closed.   A librarian
goes two or three times a week to take new books and straighten
up, but during most of the 24 hours the room is completely unat-
tended.   The losses resulting from this open-door policy have been
negligible.   Light bulbs and ash trays are hard to keep, and a table
disappeared, but among books only the Bible (placed in the room by
the Gideons) and a volume entitled The Story of the Bible regularly
disappear.

The "Librarian for a Day" program of the Memphis Public
Library, a recruiting device, has been extended to the branches and
to all types of libraries in the area.   The purpose was to acquaint a
student, through a special visit to the library, with the purposes and
functions of the library service and to encourage student interest in
librarianship as a profession.

The Open Shelf Department of the Boston Public Library
maintains an outdoor reading room under canvas in the courtyard of
the Central Library from June 1 to September 29.   An interesting
addition to story hour programs is an annual picnic held at the
Egleston Square Branch in Boston for all "alumni" of the Pre-School
Story Hours.   The program includes games, stories, and the re-
newing of acquaintances.

"Early Childhood Awareness" was the name given to a program of the Memphis, Tennessee, Public Library, under which a
team including one children's librarian, one adult librarian, one
general assistant, and a part-time projectionist went to branch libraries in disadvantaged neighborhoods twice daily to conduct a story
hour for the four and five-year-old children and a simultaneous program for the parents.   When a branch library was not available the
meetings were held in YMCA's, YWCA's, public housing meeting

halls, and other similar public places, once every week for each
neighborhood.   Thus ten neighborhoods could be served.   The
parents' program consisted of films on child care, household management, consumer education, and other such practical subjects.
Other programs were scheduled in cooperation with welfare agencies,
social workers and teachers.

At the end of each twelve-week period each child was awarded a paperback book for his own home bookshelf. In the proposed
nine-month project, three such books per child were awarded.
Parents were encouraged to buy an occasional 50-cent book for their
own children but the three gift books were awarded regardless of
whether the parent contributed.   From September 1966 to May,
1967, 405 children and 164 adults took part; 1432 books were loaned
and 5 free books were given to each child.   The program was
dropped for lack of funds.

Branches have been located in rented store buildings, in city
halls, in converted residences, in fire stations, and of course in
their own buildings, but seldom in mobile homes.   Enterprise,
Alabama has, however, set up a branch in a neat white mobile home
with a large, clear sign announcing its identity.   The purchase of
single or double width mobile homes for such a purpose offers an
opportunity to try out a branch location without the commitment of
a permanent building; yet such a vehicle provides more space and
book capacity than a conventional bookmobile.   A mobile home can
be a substitute until an adequate branch is built.

More unusual yet is the community branch created from a
converted railroad car in Terre Haute, Indiana. [4] Brought from
Indianapolis and set up in a largely Negro community, run by the
community young people in the way they chose, with all the help and
advice needed furnished by the Terre Haute Public Library, the
project generated city-wide enthusiasm and interest, according
to Edward N. Howard, Terre Haute Library Director.   Private
companies, an architect, labor unions, service agencies, and other
public agencies all worked together to establish the neighborhood
library.   A section of track was donated by the Milwaukee Railroad.

The car was brought to Terre Haute in three sections, was moved
several blocks to the Hyte Community Center, and was then set up
again in its original condition. [4]

Weatherford Branch of the Custer-Washita-Dewey Library
System, with its service center at Clinton, Oklahoma, hosts a
"Newcomers' Coffee" every two months for new residents of the
community.

The Tulsa (Oklahoma) City-County Library sponsored a series
of lectures through a grant from the National Endowment for the
Humanities.   One of the lecturers was Dr. James Farmer.   At the
time of his appearance the library held a "black book fair" in the
Seminole Hills Branch, which is located in an almost all-Negro community.   This was a selling fair with books supplied by a local book
store.

Bar Harbor Branch of the Massapequa Public Library, Massapequa, New York, offers a varied Sunday afternoon program from
October to May which is especially family-oriented.   Included are
feature-length films, short films, piano and other instrumental
recitals, lectures, and many types of popular programs.

The Savannah, Georgia, Public Library and Chatham-Effingham-Liberty Regional Branch conducted a noontime book review
program for some 20 years at its downtown branch.   The program
was used not only for highlighting significant books but to introduce
new community leaders to Savannah by using them as book reviewers, and to back up important events in the community by having
books reviewed in pertinent fields (e. g. a recent program on
oceanography when local leaders were trying to arouse interest in
connection with the development of a new local ocean science
facility).   A file of possible speakers is maintained and people who
have been particularly good reviewers are suggested for repeat
performances to groups asking the library for help with programming.

The Cleveland Avenue Branch of the Montgomery, Alabama,
Public Library has sponsored Conversational Clinics for young adults
and for adults.   This branch has also presented a group discussion

of LSD and other drugs, accompanied by a 30-minute film and a talk by an agent in the state's Division of Drug and Narcotic Control. Branches need more of this type of aggressive, socially-important program if they are to meet the challenge of community needs.

Program planners' institutes, for representatives of clubs and organizations, sometimes held annually, are an excellent method of getting in touch with and keeping in touch with various elements of the community. One library holds a number of such institutes in its various branches.

Among other activities which have taken place in branches or have been included in "reaching out" programs of branches are the following:

1. Street corner story telling. The story teller goes into a neighborhood, gathers an audience and starts performing. He then tries to get the children to go with him to the library to see the books.

2. Block parties.

3. Giving training in story-telling to housewives, teachers, or any interested patrons who will attend a series of lessons given by a library staff member.

4. Classes in reading improvement, for better comprehension or greater speed.

5. Doll shows or general hobby shows held in and sponsored by the branch.

6. Informal instruction in preparation for civil service examinations.

7. Programs for new citizens, with films to acquaint them with this country. Sometimes accompanied by talks by the consuls from the various countries represented.

8. Classes preparing candidates for citizenship examination.

9. Foreign language conversation groups.

10. Drama reading or creative writing groups.

11. A number of branches are working up special collections for the functionally illiterate and are working closely with Laubach Method teachers and government agencies in reaching this group of people.

New bases for developing group activities in branches are now discernible.   They are: 1) The material itself (the most prevalent); 2) National or world-wide concern; 3) Special needs and interests of the individual community.

The latter is the most important and the least reported in surveys on this subject.   Attention to this criterion is usually characterized by library cooperation with one or more agencies or organizations in the community.   There are many sources for dis-covering community needs and all of these should be tapped by the enterprising branch librarian.   Sources include:[6]

1. Community studies.
2. Discussion groups and town meetings.
3. Affiliation with coordinating councils.
4. Cooperation with and use of area communication media: newspapers, television, radio.
5. Program planning institutes and leader training courses.
6. Maintaining files of data on organizations, their objectives and programs.
7. Staff participation in a diversity of organizations.
8. Involvement in adult education programs.
9. Assignment of staff as institutional and group resource people.
10. Accumulating experience record of the library community consultant, neighborhood coordinator program. [6]

Among the community groups and individuals to contact for suggestions and help are:

1. Head Start agencies.
2. Adult literacy projects.
3. Other anti-poverty programs.
4. Leaders in adult and young adult continuing education activities of churches, schools, and other agencies.
5. Neighborhood coordinators.
6. Credit and consumer cooperatives.
7. Union councils.
8. Government field representatives such as Home Demonstra-tion Agents, County Agricultural Agents.

Figure 48: Training Outreach Workers to do Story Hours

Outreach workers from the Eastside Neighborhood Center of the Greater Jacksonville Economic Opportunity, Inc. were trained under the direction of the Eastside Branch librarian to do story hours and picture book presentations during the summer of 1967.

Emerson's Photo, Jacksonville, Fla.

9. Area committees of human resources.

10. Lay advisory committees for mental health and special education.

11. Senior Citizens' organizations.

12. Visiting nurses and rural health agencies.

13. University extension instructors and advisors.

14. Men's and women's service clubs.

15. Chambers of Commerce.

16. Other departments of city or county government.

17. Property Owners' Associations, taxpayers' leagues, civic betterment groups, and special groups organized for a specific purpose.

In all of the newer activities and programs techniques are minimized; human needs and interests are stressed. The library is constantly in touch with the social scene and the bonds of tradition are cast aside.

Other special services or activities found in branches include

A special play pen with toys and muslin books in the story hour room where women can leave babies while selecting books.

A special shelf of baby books for fathers. They may browse freely without having to ask for the material.

A pet show for children. The only requirement for entering a pet is having a library card.

A men only hobby show, as put on very successfully at the Barrington, Rhode Island, Public Library.

Notes of welcome sent to new key people in the county or city such as school principals, ministers, theater managers, city managers, newly elected councilmen or members of county commissioners, etc., inviting them to come in and get acquainted. Enclose a folder on the library's services.

Holding a Farmer's Day at a rural branch. Special displays of books on all phases of agriculture, talk by a leading agriculturist refreshments, a good color movie on some interesting phase of agriculture, displays and bulletin boards all keyed to agriculture of the area. If in season, a display of very large melons, turnips, tomatoes, or other prize-type products with the name of the grower.

A religious workshop for ministers during National Library Week to acquaint them with the library's resources in religion.

A good-neighbor program on Sunday afternoons once a month. Book reviews, music, and movies. A chance to meet neighbors on a day of leisure.

If the branch has a Friends of the Library Group that desires an activity or project to keep them interested, the following may offer possibilities:

Working up a speaker's bureau of Friends' members, on library topics (This group must be well informed and be good speakers).

Figure 49:   Story Hour in a Park
           Newark Public Library, Newark, New Jersey

Figure 50:   Talk About Personal Attention!

Two story hour mothers entertain a youngster with stories at the Mesa
Verde Branch of the Orange County Public Library, Orange, California.
Story hour mothers sometimes help the children's Librarian in the
selection of stories for the children's story hour. The branch is located
in Costa Mesa, California.

Photo by Rey Yap

Giving film preview programs.

Issuing publicity for a proposed building campaign. Campaign
ing by telephone just before a bond election.

Giving an author reception, dinner, tea, or luncheon.

Helping with letter writing on any special library project.

Putting on a used book sale for the benefit of the library.

Assisting with summer reading project activities and final
party for the children.

Sponsoring a Story League and assisting the story-telling
program, after proper instruction.

Putting on a coffee, duplicate bridge, or other money earning project to purchase some item of needed equipment for the
library.

Campaigning for old magazines to replace missing issues in
the library's files.

Assisting with easy volunteer work in the library, such as
simple mending, sorting magazines, etc.

Giving a Christmas party for the children.

Sponsoring a series of lectures.

Assisting with an anniversary celebration.

In a small branch, perhaps helping to paint or redecorate
furniture or walls.

Making art posters to advertise branch programs if such are
not provided by the central library.

Notes

1.   Ruffin, Carolyn F. "The Not-so-Silent Inner City Branch
     Library." No. 1 in a series: "Libraries that Care." Abridge
     by permission from the Christian Science Monitor, c 1968.
     The Christian Science Publishing Society. All rights reserved
     Sept. 7, 1968.

2.   Jordan, Robert T. Home Delivery Library Service. Wilson
     Library Bulletin. v. 42, no. 4. Dec. 1967, p. 403-405.

3.   Frantz, John C. "Big City Libraries: Strategy and Tactics for
     Change." Library Journal. v. 93, no. 10. May 15, 1968.
     p. 1968-70.

4. Library Journal. News Item. v. 94, no. 3, Feb. 1, 1969, p. 488.

5. Warncke, Ruth. "Library Objectives and Community Needs." in: Group Services in Libraries. Library Trends, v. 17, no. 1. July, 1968, p. 8-10.

6. Gregory, Ruth W. Search for Information About Community Needs. in: Group Services in Public Libraries. Library Trends, v. 17, no. 1. July, 1966. p. 15-16.

Chapter 11

The Service Program--Basis for Building

No branch building can be intelligently planned unless the program of services has been worked out previously. No program of services can be intelligently planned that is not based upon thorough study of the potential area to be served (see Chapter 6).

No librarian could or should work out a service program alone. In the case of a branch, the director of the system, staff members (extension service and branch people), and possibly an outside consultant should all be involved. It is too soon to involve the architect. Before he can begin to plan he must know what activities will take place, the potential readership, minimum space requirements, proposed size of staff, size and type of materials, etc.

In a city system with other branches, branch librarians will be of considerable help in pointing out mistakes in past buildings and the problems that may have arisen because of them. These people are on the firing line. They not only cope with space and design problems themselves; they hear patron and staff comments, and their advice can be very valuable. Branches of poor design or with inadequate space are very often the result of involving too few people in the preliminary planning.

Assuming that a thorough study has been made of the area to be served, formulating the service program really precedes the selection of an exact site, for its size and location must fit the service program, the branch aims, and objectives.

A few of the questions those planning the service program must ask and answer include:

1. Will it be desirable to sponsor meetings in the building? If so, what size and type of meeting room will be needed?

2. Will there be pre-school story hours, story hours for the first few grades? If so, there must be provision for the children's chairs to be stacked and stored somewhere.

3. How much will be stocked in the way of audio-visual materials? Will the branch circulate records, films, framed or unframed prints, projectors? Special shelving for records will be needed; listening tables or listening rooms will be needed if records are to be loaned; special housing will be required for films and prints.

4. How much reference service will the branch attempt to provide and how extensive will the reference collection need to be? How much need will there be for indexes to magazine articles and the supporting back numbers of periodicals? How many of the magazines listed in Readers' Guide will be stocked? How many saved? Or will the branch use only the Abridged Readers' Guide and the magazines it indexes? Storage space and accessibility are important factors here.

5. How many staff members will there be at the outset and to take care of anticipated growth? How many will need private offices; how many can be in a common workroom?

6. How heavily will the branch plan for displays and exhibits? How many bulletin boards will be needed? If there is no meeting room, will there need to be an area equipped for hanging art prints or photographs for special displays? Will display cabinets be needed? Wall mounted or free-standing?

7. What type of charging will be used? This will determine design of the charging desk, location, and space to be allocated.

8. For best work flow what will be the relationship of the various areas of staff activity?

9. For best supervision and patron convenience what will be the best arrangement of furnishings and book stacks? This has a strong relationship to design and floor layout. A round or octagonal building, for example, may solve some supervision and staffing problems.

10. What circulation (rough estimate) is anticipated? This

primarily affects size of building, of course, and relative size of area given over to circulation activity.

    11. What type of heat will be used? This affects utility area and janitor's quarters.

    12. Will convenience services be offered to the public--renta typewriters, photocopying machines, pen or pencil machines, microfilm viewer, public telephone booth? If so, space and/or booths must be provided for.

    13. How extensive will the children's area need to be? Will there be a special young adult section with separate collection?

    14. Will the public use a card catalog? Or will there be a book catalog? The latter would take less space, obviously.

    15. How many newspapers will be displayed on racks? How much storage should be allowed for back numbers?

    16. Will the public be provided with a lounge area? An outdoor reading patio?

    17. How much parking space for cars will be needed? How many bicycle racks?

    18. How many reading tables will be provided? Will the branch expect or cater to heavy use by students? If so, more seating space will be needed. Should there be a special work-reference area for non-student adults?

    19. How many special collections will need to be shelved? Can they be shelved within the regular collection or will some separation such as an alcove be needed?

    20. Is library instruction to school classes to be offered and encouraged? If so, the reading room must offer seating space for at least 35-40 at one time.

    21. How extensive an adult education program would the bran hope to undertake? If several activities are planned, such as Great Books Discussions, Story League, Great Ideas, etc., a conference room must be provided.

    22. Will the children's area have separate rest rooms?

    23. What ultimate book capacity should be planned for, taking into account provision for at least 20-30 years' growth? Will

the service area of the branch grow with a larger population of
higher density of 40,000 to 50,000, or will such growth be taken
care of by additional branches, the capacity of each branch being
planned to service 30,000-35,000 people? A decision must be
reached as to whether the branch is to be a medium-sized, 8,000-
10,000 square foot building to serve the 30,000-35,000 population
range, or a larger regional branch to serve 50,000 or more.

The service program of any branch should aim for the ideal
and for close adherence to standards. The number one requirement
to reach these goals is sufficient funding. If funds available for a
branch are too low to insure a good standard of service, it is better to delay construction until an adequate building and operation are
possible. Poor service will gain no friends for the library. On
the other hand, few branches can attain an absolute ideal, and if a
reasonably good service is possible, branch building should proceed.
Reasonably good service is better than no service at all, but the
idea that any service, no matter how poor, is better than nothing
is not valid.

A study made in 1957 by Jane Waldron[1] compared branch
library services in three separate neighborhoods of a large city
system. Its purpose was to determine how well the services provided by the three branches related to their communities. The results showed that, although the three neighborhoods differed greatly
in their interests, the three branches tended to identify more with
the large system of which they were a part than with the particular
communities in which they were located.

None of the three buildings was really patterned to fit the
architectural character of the district. Library staffs were found
to be generally indistinguishable from branch to branch. The three
areas were each occupationally and economically different, and the
study concluded that staff members should be more compatible with
the individual communities through personal and professional qualifications such as training, special interests, age, sex, and work experience. In the matter of branch collections, only minor differences were apparent, and it was recommended that guides to the

Figure 51:   Playing the Part

Orange County Public Library's West Garden Grove Branch Librarian, Mac Teverbaugh, in ship officer costume welcomes the first
batch of young patrons aboard the library on the opening day of Dr.
Doolittle's Voyagers Summer Reading Program.   The Branch is
located in Garden Grove, California.

Photo by Rey Yap

collections, displays, and exhibits should show greater distinction
among the three branches.

These branches have since been greatly improved, but
similar situations still exist in many larger systems where there
has been little evaluation and updating of services.

Reference to Chapter 6, "Tailoring the Branch to the Community"; Chapter 10, "Special Services and Activities"; and Chapter
8, "The Branch Collection and the Patrons," will help in working
out a service program based upon all available information about the
neighborhood concerned.

City Branch Service

The children's program of a typical branch will include story hours, summer reading programs, possibly a year-round reading club, and special programs planned for special occasions such as Book Week and National Library Week. Colorful and attractive bulletin boards are needed, as are occasional displays of new books, and special collections of picture books, a parent's shelf, and perhaps a special or a permanent display of Newbery and Caldecott award-winning books.

Reader's advisory service will be available part of the time but rarely at all hours except in quite large branches. Medium-sized and smaller branches usually are unable to staff the children's room with a trained librarian during all the hours the library is open. With today's modular construction the children's room is usually not separate but may be set off from the remainder of the public area by low shelving or partially set off by being placed in an alcove. Often there is no separate charging desk and all books, adult and children's, are handled at one central desk. A trained children's librarian should certainly be available within the children's area during the after-school hours and evening hours. One advantage of the open type of interior construction is that the children's area is accessible at all hours the library is open and may be used by both parents and children during the morning and evening hours. Larger branches may prefer a separate children's room so that the children's activities do not impinge upon the adult need for relative quiet. Such an arrangement requires more staff and may even decrease the hours the children's books are available.

Library instruction for visiting school classes should be carefully planned to suit varying grade levels. Instruction should be interspersed with games to test what has been taught, a short book review, or a 10 or 12-minute film. Mixing pleasure with instruction will make the library visit seem less like school and will make the children more interested in coming back on their own. A written series of lessons may be used, but quizzes or tests should be varied from year to year. Special programs should be planned

during the November Book Week, and many branches are now planning children's programs, as well as adult programs, in celebration
of National Library Week. Special or unusual activities are discussed in greater detail in Chapter 10.

A young adult alcove or corner is still in favor in the majority of libraries although many have eliminated separate sections in
the last few years and the trend seems to be in that direction. Librarians who are against young adult sections feel that it is a
mistake to make a distinction between young adults and adults, that
teenagers prefer to be regarded as adults. A special section, these
librarians believe, emphasizes the separation from adulthood and is
resented by some young people. If there is a young adult section
in a branch it should, in any case, be adjacent to or in the adult
section of the branch rather than in or near the children's area.
Much has been written on this topic in recent years, and ample
references can be found in Library Literature.

Youth councils drawn from junior and senior high schools in
the area, with one or two representatives from each, can be very
helpful to a branch librarian in keeping in touch with teen tastes and
needs. Youth councils have held some very illuminating discussions
concerning the library's failure to meet their needs; they make good
suggestions for book selection; in some communities they have drawn
up codes of conduct for students in the library and have helped
publicize and even enforce such codes. A council gives young
people a feeling of being represented, of having their advice sought
and their desires given fair consideration. Giving the restless,
modern teenager a job with some responsibility, on a volunteer
basis, has proved to be one of the best methods of getting them
interested in the library and its activities and objectives.

Meeting rooms are no longer a luxury but a must for most
branches. Libraries which have not included meeting rooms in
their branch plans in the last 10 to 15 years have usually regretted
it and resolved to include them in future branches. The Los
Angeles Public Library found itself in this situation. The tendency
today, however, is to refer to these rooms as "multi-purpose" or

Figure 52: Story Hour for Children from the Child Care Center
Jacksonville Public Library Branch, Jacksonville, Florida

Emerson's Photo

"all-purpose" rooms, since they are used for many more activities
than just meetings.   Such a term also seems to provide more justification for the extra expense.   Smoking areas or rooms are offered
in some branches; reading patios, sometimes combined with the
smoking area, are to be found in temperate climates.   More space
is being given over to bulletin boards and displays.

Service to shut-ins has become of increasing concern and is
often handled in branch areas by the Friends of the Library, Boy
Scout, Girl Scout, or Campfire groups.   Service by children or
young people presents a problem, however, as many parents are
reluctant to send children and young people into strange homes or
strange neighborhoods.   Thus any such delivery by minors must be
in the daytime, in safe areas, and with the full consent of the
parents.

Figure 53:   The Role of a Branch Library Broadens
              Special Activity at New Haven Free Public Library's
                    Library Neighborhood Center
         Scene from a skit - "Library Centers are What's Happening,"
                    Brookview Library Center, Spring, 1967.

Photo by Robert Herron, New Haven, Conn.

        Reference demands upon a branch today are more intensive
than in the past, due to the increasing complexity of technology,
industry, and the new education.   Most branches need larger reference collections than formerly, and more professional staff to handle
the volume of everyday reference demands.   There must be a private
or direct line to the central reference department for referral of
problems beyong branch resources, and in some larger systems the
branch will be linked to central by teletype.   Questions which are
not immediate and cannot be answered by the branch itself, should
be relayed to the central agency through the branch delivery system,
with excellent communication maintained throughout the entire system
In many branches the reference load keeps increasing although circulation may grow little or even show some loss.

Extensive special collections are rare in branch libraries but the changing school curriculum has encouraged the addition of special sections on such topics as "Literary criticism." These can be helpful both to the student and the librarian, particularly if subject and title analytics are made to lead to specific writers and specific works within general books of criticism or in collected works. Branches will do this on a smaller scale than a central agency, but those that do can save a great deal of staff time otherwise spent searching through indexes, tables of contents, or complete volumes.

Another special collection that has proved popular in some libraries is a senior citizen category with some such title as "The Golden Years," "Your Leisure Years," or "Senior Citizen's Section." In this grouping are placed books dealing with retirement, health, investment and finance, travel, hobbies, retirement homes and centers, and other subjects of particular interest to those over 50 or 60.

Browsing areas with special interest categories are found in many branches, even the smaller ones, with books of popular appeal grouped in such categories as "Your home and family," "Other Lands, Other People," "Science and Invention," "Hobbies," "Adventure," "Interesting Lives," "Your Funnybone," etc. A browsing corner should be equipped with easy chairs, side tables, hopefully a carpet and pictures, and other features which would contribute to an informal, homelike atmosphere.

Some librarians object to the traditional separation of mystery, western, and science fiction collections on the basis that patrons get into a reading rut and tend to overlook material in other subjects. It is really not the prerogative, however, of librarians to try to change adult reading tastes, so if patrons prefer having mysteries, westerns, and science fiction in special collections, why not?

Cooperation with neighborhood organizations is very important in planning services to meet special needs. If there are many organizations, program aid will become a major branch responsibility. Special interest groups and hobby groups will need special bibliographies and booklists. Furnishing book reviews and speakers for clubs

Figure 54: Opening day of the 1968 Summer Reading Program at the Mesa Verde (a branch of the Orange County Public Library). The turnout is so large that some parents who come to register their children in the reading club volunteer their services to ease the load of the library staff.

Photo by Rey Yap

Figure 55: Orange County Public Library's Fountain Valley Branch Children's Librarian, Mrs. Judy Clark, registers youngsters at the "Doctor Dolittle's Travel Bureau".

Photo by Rey Yap

in the area is a worthwhile branch service which helps advertise the library as nothing else can. Through such contacts the librarian gets out into the community instead of waiting for the community to come to him.

Rural Branch Service:

A rural branch, depending upon size, may find it necessary to combine the children's and young adult programs, since a young adult specialist is less likely to be available than in city branches. In reference service a rural or small town branch should be even more self-sufficient than a city branch because of the greater distance from headquarters.

The same convenience services can be offered by a small town or rural branch as are offered in the urban branch if demand warrants. There is less likely to be as much demand, however, since the population served will usually be smaller, so the cost of each convenience service must be justified. Some of the services such as rental typewriters, pen machines, and copying devices are self-supporting or may even return a small profit to the branch, providing the volume is sufficient.

It is often possible for a small town or rural branch to cooperate with other county or town agencies in providing certain added facilities such as a public rest room with lounge, or an art gallery or museum. Use of one building to house more than one facility can be an economy and provide mutual use stimulation, if the combination is one which is compatible. A recreation hall for teenagers, for example, with the attendant noise and activity, as well as the danger of vandalism, would not be a good combination for the library.

The rural library has an opportunity to provide exhibits and displays at county fairs, state fairs, meetings of Granges, 4-H Clubs, and Home Demonstration Units. Its services to these groups and other rural organizations can be wide and varied under an imaginative branch administrator.

We are concerned here chiefly with services to the public, but it should be pointed out that if there is no centralized processing or cataloging available in a county or regional system, each rural branch will have to make space and staff provision for these functions.

Service to teachers has always been a large factor in both adult and juvenile department work loads. Branches with limited juvenile collections may have to refer requests for special teacher loans for classroom use to the central children's department. Loan of one book per child or some round number such as 15, 20, or 25 books per room to one teacher, if the collection permits, are a much-appreciated branch service where neighborhood schools are still in the process of developing their own school libraries.

Public library service to schools has been a controversial question over the years. At present the accelerated development of school libraries under federal assistance has lessened the need for supplementary room collections issued to teachers, but where these are needed to supplement meager school library collections, the branch should, if possible, supply the books and cooperate with teachers and school officials. The source of the books is not as important as getting them to the child.

To recapitulate, two basic considerations apply in planning a service program for a new library or in reviewing an existing program. The first is to obtain all possible information about the community or neighborhood to be served, either through existing surveys and studies or by making an informal survey for specific library purposes. The second basic consideration is the resources of the library system: available funds, staff, and time.

The Mississippi Library Commission, in 1958,[2] worked out a chart for surveying branch services in a regional library system. This chart can be used, with suitable modifications, for branches in a city, county, multi-county, or regional system. It is presented herewith as an example of one way in which to analyze branch services and perhaps highlight areas needing improvement.

Figure 56:   Book Talk with Refreshments

Bixby Branch of the Tulsa, Oklahoma City-County Library System
sponsors a book talk, complete with refreshments.

A Survey of the Branch Services of a Multi-County Library System

I. General Information

Name of Library_____
Town_____County_____Library Tele
                                                    phone no. _____
Population: Total in Town_____White___Colored_____
                    Mexican-American_____Other_____
Sources of Information for this Report:
    Person(s) interviewed at Branch library:_____
    Branch Supervisor_____
    Chief Librarian of System_____
    Statistical records used_____
Date of Compiling this Report:_____

II. Branch Library Staff

Name	Position	Age	Highest Formal Educational Attainment	When First Employed by Library

Recommendations:

III. Service Schedule

	Mon.	Tues.	Wed.	Thurs.	Fri.	Sat.	Sun.	Total Hrs. Open
A. M.								
P. M.								
Total Hours Open								

Recommendations:

IV. Physical Facilities

A. Building

		Good	Fair	Bad	None	Comment
1.	General appearance of the building on outside					
2.	General appearance of the building on inside					
3.	General housekeeping practices					
4.	Lighting in building					
5.	Heating system in building					
6.	Cooling system in building					

		Good	Fair	Bad	None	Comment
7.	Arrangement of the books on the shelves					
8.	Sign on outside to identify library					
9.	Signs to direct traffic to the library					
10.	Sign on outside of building to indicate hours of library					
11.	Arrangements for returning books when library is closed					
12.	Size of library quarters in relation to the community needs					

B. Physical Equipment

		Does library have (yes or no)	Enough of it? Big enough?	In what condition?	Does library need it?
1.	Shelving, stationary (not adjustable)				
2.	Shelving, adjustable				
3.	Filing cabinet (for subject information file)				
4.	Reading tables for adults				
5.	Small reading tables for children				
6.	Chairs for adults				
7.	Chairs for children				
8.	Telephone				
9.	Charging (or loan) desk				
10.	Librarians desk (other than loan desk)				
11.	Work room				
12.	Work tables				
13.	Filing cabinet (for business records)				
14.	Typewriter				
15.	Storage cabinet for supplies				
16.	Card Catalog case				
17.	Staff room				
18.	16 mm Film projector				
19.	Slide projector				
20.	Record player				
21.	Meeting rooms (for discussion groups, etc.)				
22.	Waste basket				
23.	Mechanical charging equipment				
24.	Bulletin boards				
25.	Other display equipment (letters, etc.)				

C. Recommendations:

V. Library Materials

A. Books
_____ Total number of books in the branch
_____ % of this library's book collection is adult books
_____ % of the adult books in this library is non-fiction
_____ % of the total number of books in this library is children's
        books
_____ % of the adult fiction collection consists of westerns,
        mysteries and light love stories
Does the branch need weeding?_____

_____
                      (Comment on condition)
_____ new books sent to branch during past 12 months
_____ books sent to fill special requests during past 12 months
_____ total children's books added to branch during past May and
        June
_____ books returned from branch to headquarters during past
        12 months

B. Non-book material

Number of magazines the library subscribes to_____
Number of newspapers the library subscribes to:
        Daily_____ Weekly_____
Branch subscribes to: Readers Guide_____Abridged R. G. _____
                       None_____
Titles of magazines kept for reference use:

_____   _____

_____
What is the policy regarding the keeping of back issues of
magazines?_____
Are magazine files complete?_____
                         ****
What provision does the library make for pamphlets ?_____
        Keep in vertical file?_____
        Shelve in pamphlet boxes?_____ If so, where?_____
        Place in magazine racks?_____If so, in what order?_____
Does the library maintain a clipping file?_____
Does the library maintain a picture file?_____

C. Organization of materials

    1. Does this library have a shelf list?_____
    2. Does this library have a catalog?_____
    3. Are the books classified according to the Dewey Decimal
        System?_____
    4. Are the books neatly and clearly lettered on the spine?___

	Library gives this service	Library does not give this service	Library would like to give this service	what does most to keep the library from providing this service? (Answer this only if there is a circle around the x in column 3)

VI. Library Services

1. Finds information for people who come into the library (reference)				
2. Answers reference questions on the telephone				
3. Borrows books from headquarters when the library does not have a book or material on a subject				
4. Takes reservations for books that the library owns but which are out at the time				
5. Sends word to patrons of new books that have arrived (books that patrons did NOT necessarily ask about)				
6. Maintains a "reader interest" file				
7. Renews books by telephone				
8. Has regular story hours for children. Has a summer reading club				
9. Has groups of children come to the library to learn how to use library				
10. Has regular school classes coming to the library for reading and study				
11. Lends collections of books to teachers who come into the library				
12. Gives instruction in the use of the card catalog				
13. Sends articles to the newspapers				
14. Has newspaper reporters visiting the library				
15. Sponsors or gives a radio program				
16. Sponsors or gives a TV program				
17. Sends out news releases of other radio and TV library programs or programs about books and reading				
18. Sets up book displays outside the library				
19. Maintains attractive displays in the library				

	Library gives this service	Library does not give this service	Library would like to give this service	What does most to keep the library from providing this service? (Answer this only if there is a circle around the x in column 3)
20. Sends books to some patrons by mail				
21. Serves people in hospitals				
22. Serves people in jails				
23. Serves people in industries (actually at the plants themselves)				
24. Gives advice and counsel on reading to the blind				
25. Prepares special reading lists for individuals				
26. Furnishes reading lists and biographies in quantities				
27. Provides patrons with special reading lists (like Home Demonstration, etc.)				
28. Gives help in program planning to clubs and other groups				
29. Some member of the library staff gives talks, etc., for programs				
30. Takes or sends books to meetings of organizations				
31. Sponsors or conducts discussion groups				
32. Advises people on their personal book purchases				
33. Advises schools on their book selection and purchases				

VIII. Library Procedures and Techniques	Yes	No	Comment
1. Is there a staff manual of procedures and techniques for the library system?			
2. Is there a method for regular revision of the staff manual?			
3. Are books renewable?			
4. Can books be renewed by telephone?			
5. Can a book be renewed without bringing the book to the library?			
6. Can a book be renewed for a second time?			

                                            Yes   No   Comment

7. Can a patron check out a book
    while having out an overdue
    book?
8. Are patrons notified
    systematically of overdue books?
9. What happens when a patron asks for a book which is in the
    branch collection but is out in circulation?
10. What happens when a patron asks for a book or subject
    material which is not in the branch collection?
11. What happens when a patron asks a reference question
    which the branch librarian cannot answer?
12. What methods are used by the branch librarian to transmit
    special requests to headquarters?
13. What methods are used by headquarters to send books to the
    branches to fill special requests?
14. Under what conditions would a patron be refused a book by
    the library?
15. What books are restricted to use in the library?

16. What method is used to inform the public of the library
    rules?
17. Is there a fair and consistent application of these rules to
    all users of the library?

Recommendations:

_____

_____

IX. Participation by Branch Librarian

A. In Book Selection   Yes   No

1. Does the branch librarian participate in the
    selection of new books for the system?
2. Does the branch librarian participate in the
    selection of books sent to branch by
    headquarters?
3. Does the branch librarian have the following
    book selection tools in the branch library?
    a. Standard Catalog for Public Libraries
    b. Children's Catalog
    c. ALA Booklist
    d. Book Review Digest
    e. Buying List of Books for Small Libraries
    f. Reader's Choice from Wilson Library
        Bulletin
    g. Cumulative Book Index
    h. Books in Print
    i. Paper Bound Books in Print
    j. Publishers' Weekly

		Yes	No	Comment
k.	Retail Bookseller			
l.	Virginia Kirkus			
m.	Basic Reference Sources (Shores)			
n.	Bookman's Manual (Hoffman)			
o.	Guide to Reference Books (Winchell)			
p.	Saturday Review of Literature			
q.	New York Times Book Review			
r.	New York Herald Tribune Books			
s.	Book reviews from local papers			

B.   In Professional Activities Outside the System

1. Does the branch librarian belong to the State Library Association? (insert name of state if desired)

2. Does the branch librarian belong to the regional Library Association? (insert name of regional association)

3. Does the branch librarian belong to the American Library Association?

4. Did the branch librarian attend the meeting of the _____ Library Association held in:
   a. _____ in _____
   b. _____ in _____
   c. _____ in _____

5. Did the branch librarian attend these in-service training sessions?
   a. _____
   b. _____
   c. _____

C.   In Community Activities
(Draw a circle around the X that applies in each case)

	Library belongs as an institution	Librarian belongs as an individual	Librarian attends its meetings	Library helps with its program	Comment
1. A rural group (Farm Bureau, home demonstration)					
2. Community Development Organization					
3. Local Chamber of Commerce					
4. A service club (Pilot, B&PW, Altrusa, Rotary, Lions, Jaycees, Exchange, Civitan, etc.					

	Library belongs as an institution	Librarian belongs as an individual	Librarian attends its meetings	Library helps with its program	Comment
5. A woman's club (Federated, Garden Club, etc.)					
6. An educational group (PTA, League of Women Voters, A. A. U. W. , Delta Kappa Gamma)					
7. Other (specify) _____ _____ _____					

D. Recommendations:

_____

_____

X. Summary, Comments, and Recommendations

This Survey Guide was prepared by: Mississippi Library
                                     Commission
                                     405 State Office Building
                                     Jackson, Mississippi

One section of the Mississippi chart, No. 7, "Relationship between branch and headquarters, " has been deleted here and added to Chapter 5: "Organizational Relationships. "

Here is a sample service program as worked out by the Extension Section of the Santa Ana Public Library[3] in order to plan for a proposed new branch:

Branch Library Service Program
(for a proposed branch of 8000 square feet)

Basic philosophy: Each branch shall be considered as a small community library giving service to the fullest possible extent compatible with its budget and staff within its service area, the service area being defined as an area approximately two miles of radius from the branch location or approximately four miles in diameter, said area being a probable but not a limiting factor.

It is believed best to have fewer large branches of 8000-9000 square feet serving 25,000 to 35,000 people than many small branches with limited collections, staff, and other resources.

The following detailed program is necessary to carry out the above aim:

The Book and Materials Collection

I. Book Collection: Each branch should have a minimum of 15,000 volumes basic book stock to open and should build up to the ultimate capacity of 55,000-60,000 books as population and demands grow.

II. Magazines: 50-60 magazines, the most-used titles indexed in Readers' Guide should be provided and should be retained for 10 years back of the current date.

III. Newspapers: At least five newspapers, including the two local papers and the New York Times and Wall Street Journal should be available. The local papers should be retained for at least a year, others for one or two months.

IV. Audio-Visual materials: The circulation of phonograph records will be introduced as soon as feasible. Therefore provision for listening space and storage of a collection should be made for future use. There should also be space available should it be deemed desirable to add other audio-visual materials later.

V. Pamphlets: A core collection of pamphlets should be provided in the most-used subjects, but an extensive collection of newspaper clippings and pamphlets will very likely be impossible due to time and space limitations.

VI. Special collections: A browsing area similar to the one at the Central library is deemed desirable. A Y. P. or special teen-age section should be included. The usual special collections of mysteries, westerns, and science fiction should be maintained as separate from general fiction. Consideration should be given to the setting up of other special sections such as a Parents' Shelf, a Senior Citizen's Corner, etc.

VIII. McNaughton Service should be provided for current material, as at Central Library.

Special Activities Facilities:

A special "Library Activities" room should be included seating no less than 75 persons to be used for Story Hours, adult education groups such as "Great Books" sponsored by the Library, art and other displays, National Library Week activities, meetings.

Catalog:

Both the adult and children's department should have complete catalogs for readers' use, but the policy in regard to a shelf list will follow that of the Central Library.

Staff:

I. A. L. A. Standards call for one full-time staff member for each 2,000 population served. On the basis of serving our minimum of 25,000 people this would call for 12-1/2 persons on a branch staff. However, we are thinking in terms of 7-1/2 persons at the present time with added staff as needed.

II. Two professionals, a Head and a Children's librarian, should be included.

Children's Activities:

     I. Story hours: A story-hour, preferably weekly, should be a regular part of the children's program, possibly a pre-school as well as a school-age hour. Provision for a place should be made. If a special activities room is included in the building plans this problem will take care of itself.

     II. Library instruction: Usually given to visiting school classes, this is an important way to get youngsters into the library, to acquaint them with its facilities, to help them to be better library users, a boon to staff as well as the young borrowers. Folding chairs, to serve double duty for the activities room and library instruction, should be provided, and the reading room should be so arranged that a class of 35-40 children can be seated and worked with to the best advantage.

     III. The children's room should be a separate unit with its own entrance and with a solid partition separating it from the adult area for the best comfort, convenience, and quiet of all concerned. It should be large enough to provide plenty of space for expansion of the collection, should have low shelving, adequate storage space for exhibit materials, wall-to-wall carpeting, and its own rest rooms for both boys and girls.

Charging and Other Mechanical Operations:

     I. Provision should be made for mechanical photo charging from the first, the charging desk being arranged with this in mind. Centralized mending of all but the simplest mending tasks will be used; therefore elaborate storage facilities and space for mending will not be required. However, the workroom should have running water and some counter space. Processing of books will be performed at the Central Library.

Custodian and Gardener:

     I. Such services will undoubtedly be provided by the City Staff, but adequate provision must be made in the building for storage of janitor supplies, the proper type of heating and air conditioning, and storage of equipment used in maintenance.

How About Adult Education Activities?

     I. It is hoped it would be possible for each branch to foster Great Books or Great Decisions Groups for adults and young people, art displays, Teen-age Book Council, other worthwhile activities, making the inclusion of a special activities room almost a must.

Delivery Service and Communication:

     I. Daily or tri-weekly delivery service should be maintained between the branches and Central Library. A two-trunk phone system should be installed to avoid interference and a bottleneck on incoming and outgoing calls.

How Extensive Will the Reference Service be?

     I. The branch should have a large enough reference collection to be able to handle the bulk of general requests, excluding highly technical-type questions which will have to be referred to Central. The branch should attempt to meet the day-to-day needs of its adult and student patrons whether in recreational or informational material.

How Much in the Way of Extras?

     I. Should economy be a strong factor, such extras as patios may have to give way to more important structural and interior features. Art work, statuary, murals, dispensing machines, can be provided if donated by local groups, as well as special furniture items that would not otherwise be bought. Comfort should, however, be a guiding factor, along with usability or function, the latter being the most important factor. Comfort and beauty are usually associated, so function should not blind our eyes to the need for inviting appearance and comfort of our patrons and staff. Staff rooms and offices should be large enough; staff privacy will result in higher work output.

Notes

1. Waldron, Jane. Comparison of Branch Library Services in
    Three Seattle Communities. Thesis. M. S. in Library
    Science, University of Washington, 1957. 137 p.

2. Mississippi Library Commission. A Survey of the Branches
    Service of a Multi-County Library System. Mississippi
    Library Commission, Jackson, Mississippi. 15 p.

3. Santa Ana Public Library. Branch Library Service Program.
    Nov. 1968.

Chapter 12

Choosing a Site

The importance of location in determining the success of a library is emphasized repeatedly in library literature today. Tax money that creates a beautiful, well furnished building, adequately stocked with books and provided with a competent staff, is nevertheless poorly spent if the location is such that the branch will not be well used. The city, county, or library board that attempts to acquire a site simply because it is cheap and without regard to its utility, is doing the community a disservice.

The City Planning Commission of New York has stated: "It must not be assumed that people will search out the library. The library must be brought to the people. In this it is different from a school to which it is frequently compared when sites are discussed. Children are compelled to go to school, but people are merely invited to go to a library."

The following general principles should be considered in locating branch libraries:

1. Every effort should be made to locate branch libraries so that they are accessible to the population they will serve initially and for at least the next 30 years. That span of time is deemed necessary for the most constructive expenditure of funds. The site should be large enough to allow for later expansion of the building without infringing on needed parking space.

2. Economical planning calls for branches to serve from 25,000 to 35,000 people. In some large metropolitan areas these figures are being revised upwards, with regional branches planned to serve 50,000 to 75,000 people. Both the area covered and the concentration of population should be weighed in determining locations. Areas with high-rise apartments will provide a much higher level of potential use than an area comprised principally of conventional city lots and single-family residences.

331

3. Branches should be some distance from the Central Library, whose greater resources in material and staff will draw users from a wide radius.

4. A prominent, easily accessible location is required to attract a large number of people. This means a place where people naturally converge: in the heart of a shopping center or neighborhood business district, rather than in a remote location such as a park or quiet street. Past experience has shown that parks or wooded areas are unsuitable; use is rarely heavy, cars cannot be parked close in to the building, and there is danger of a delinquency problem at night. The location, if not in a shopping center or mall, should be on an arterial street, well-lighted, and easily reached by public transit or automobile.

5. Branch libraries should not be adjacent to or across the street from a school, but it is desirable to have them near or in the general neighborhood of several schools.

6. The location may be expected to have a one-mile radius of maximum attraction and a two to three mile radius of influence. This applies to a medium-sized branch, 6000-10,000 square feet in size. A larger or regional branch would have a larger sphere of influence. Depending upon the services offered, the medium-sized branch may expect:

90% of the children in a one-mile radius;

50% of the adults in a one-mile radius;

50% of the children in a two-or-three-mile radius;

30% of the adults in a two-or-three mile radius.

Traditionally designated by one, two, or three-mile radius formulae like the above, branch service areas are subject to modification because of limiting elements such as major thoroughfares and other man-made objects, natural barriers such as rivers or ravines, traffic patterns, and by an analysis of registration and circulation statistics from other branches in similar neighborhoods. A pat formula like the above may yield an average, but other factors must be considered when estimating potential usage and when determining a location. In a low-economic area the usage indicated above would be much too high; in a high economic area with every educational and cultural advantage, use could be much higher. Analysis of a proposed location might well show an irregular-shaped pattern with difficult-to-serve areas interspersed, which might best be served by a bookmobile or smaller branches in leased quarters.

7. In general, spacing between branches should be at least three miles. Larger branches can be four to five miles apart.

8. The location should be on or near an important traffic intersection and on a well-traveled thoroughfare. Since most shopping centers are so located, a shopping center location will solve this problem. If being actually in the shopping center is impossible, a site as near to it as feasible should be selected. According to Kenneth R. Shaffer, "Library use suffers 10% for every city block that it is distant from a high traffic commercial and business center."[1]

9. The branch should be clearly visible to people as they walk or drive in their normal rounds of activity.

10. A branch location should be such that people of all racial and national backgrounds feel free to use the facilities.

11. Locations in school buildings or on school grounds are definitely not recommended. Adults and family groups will make very limited use of such a location.

12. The site must be large enough for a suitable building and adequate parking. As far back as 1958, Lowell Martin suggested that a building of 9,000-10,000 square feet needs at least 12,000 square feet with walk and approaches, a delivery point with a driveway, and parking space for a few staff cars, plus of course the legal distance from property lines. Thus a minimum of one-half acre should be provided, and if parking is needed, another half acre. At least 150 feet of frontage is recommended for the most functional and attractive layout.[2]

13. Branches should be near sizeable residential districts.[3]

14. Branch locations should be accessible, as far as possible, to children coming alone to get books. This is not easy in the light of present traffic conditions but should be kept in mind.[2]

15. Proximity of other library services must be considered.
The nearness of the site to a boundary or boundaries between cities
or counties, unless joint agreement has been reached for provision
of service to peripheral areas or a reciprocal borrowing agreement
has been made with the adjacent cities or county, can be a problem.

16. What is the probable future of the site? Is there a possible slum clearance program? Are special zoning changes in the
offing? What residential developments are planned? Is the neighborhood likely to suffer blight within a predictable period?

17. What are the architectural possibilities? Shape of the
site is a governing, often a limiting, factor. Occasionally the challenge of an awkward shape has led to architectural attractiveness.
On the other hand, it may pose a real problem in providing a convenient, serviceable building.

18. The proposed site should be tested ahead of time for
potential usage by setting up a bookmobile stop at the nearest possible spot or by renting quarters on a short lease.

19. The ground should be level enough to allow building at
ground level unless leveling is financially possible. Having steps
is inconvenient, outmoded, and makes it difficult for handicapped
people to use the library.

20. The location should be based upon a careful survey of
the community in the potential service area, including density of
population, age levels of the residents, racial composition and
origins, occupations, educational level, economic level (average income), number and kind of schools in the area, number and kinds of
other library facilities, commercial book outlets, total population,
rate of population growth, etc. Most of this material can be obtained from city and county planning departments, or from surveys
by hired consultants.

21. Avoid a location within a single, compact housing development. In a letter dated August 16, 1968, Mrs. Jean Godfrey, chief
librarian of the branch library system of the New York Public Library, said of this type of location: "New York Public Library has
had considerable experience with the location of branch libraries

within housing developments.   Where possible we have relocated these branches, since local residents of the area who do not live in the developments tend to regard them as solely for the use of people within the developments.   When one of our branch libraries was moved from its former quarters within a housing development to new quarters on a main thoroughfare in the same neighborhood, its circulation tripled almost immediately. "

22. In the northern hemisphere a site permitting the architect to place the front facade on the north is usually considered best; east frontage is second choice. [3]

23. Where strong winds and cold weather are serious problems the front should be on the sheltered side and the layout of the site should make this possible.   When a site does not permit this placement, a protective but basically aesthetic design should be constructed.   An open design concrete-block wall is often used. South and east frontages are preferred in southern states. [3]

24. Zoning and building restrictions should be studied carefully before land is purchased. [3]

25. The underground features should be determined such as the condition of the soil and rock.   Test borings should be made. If a basement is to be built the matter of underground water table is important.   The building must have uniform foundation material to carry the heavy load of books.   Homogenous rock stratum or uniform soil condition provides the best base. [3]

26. If the building is not to be air conditioned and windows must be opened for ventilation, a plot should be purchased which will permit some isolation from outside noises.   A site adjacent to noisy surroundings should be avoided where possible. [3]

27. If schools and colleges are in a single direction from the business center, the branch could be on the school side of the business center, since the students will be moving between it and the schools. [3]

28. In campaigning for a bond issue or purchasing several sites at once from capital improvement funds, it is well to include representative locations in various parts of the city, even though

some sites will be held for future branches. If the people must
vote on a bond issue which includes only one location in a city
with few or no other branches, opposition may arise from residents
of the other sectors of the city. Site controversies have caused
problems in many a library system. It is important to try to
reconcile political pressures and practical desirable locations without yielding to pressure to purchase a site which will be undesirable
from the library's viewpoint.

29. At times it may be advisable to rent quarters rather
than build. Where the future of a neighborhood is uncertain; when
it is impossible to build a branch in a desired shopping center or
mall; or when a branch is desperately needed and there are no
funds to build, a rental or term-lease plan is the only answer.
A leased location should be selected as carefully as a site for a
building. The only difference in the case of renting is that the long-
range future of the area need not be of such great concern.

30. Specialized branches will require specialized locations.
A branch catering to Spanish-speaking people should, of course, be
in the very midst of the area in which they live and very definitely
in connection with commercial business streets or shopping centers.
This type of branch, like the Latin-American branch of the Oakland,
California Public Library, is set up for a certain purpose and location here is of even more importance than for a general branch.
Oakland has used rented quarters in a former store building. A
children's branch which serves only children and young people would
be another example of a special-clientele branch, the site for which
deserves even more than usual care in choosing.

31. If it is possible to secure a site which has natural
beauty in the way of trees, shrubs and adjacent surroundings, without sacrificing any of the more practical prerequisites, this is highly desirable. A rocky or hilly contour would not be a defect if it
does not interfere with a level building or adequate parking. Such
a contour might be at the back or side of the lot.

As to size, Wheeler and Goldhor recommend that: "A branch
circulating 100,000 or more books a year should have about 8,000

square feet of floor space, of which at least 7,000 should be on the
main floor at sidewalk level, with about 75 seats for adults and
young adults, and 50 for children. "[4]

The site should be a minimum of 25,000 square feet to provide room for an 8,000 square foot building and adequate parking.
However, to insure space for future additions, 30,000 to 35,000
square feet should be allowed. Where rapid growth of population is
expected this figure should be increased to 40,000-45,000 square
feet.

In some communities, city officials, planners, librarians,
library boards and architects still need to discard some outworn
concepts about branch locations. Among these are that a library
belongs in the center of a city park surrounded by trees and flowers,
that it should be on a quiet residential street, or that each branch
must be within walking distance for children. The question of combining a branch with a school library and locating it in a school
building is still raised occasionally, although much less often than
in the past. A few planners still think of the library as a monumental building with a heavy facade and classical lines to express
its cultural function.

For a master's thesis on The Location of Branch Libraries
in a County Library System, Margaret Ramsay[5] studied the Contra
Costa County Library System and suggested that locational considerations are more important to women than men because men are
more mobile. The effective service area of the library is closely
related to the activity area of the center in which the library is
located. The importance of a town as an activity center does not
necessarily depend upon its size, and a town which is important as
a center for one type of activity may not necessarily be important
for other types of activities. It seems clear, the Ramsay study
states, that:

> 1. The location of library service points should be
> determined in relation to the activity patterns of the
> readers rather than to general standards of distance.

2. Any assessment of the use of a service point must take into consideration the advantages of the location, the standard of service that can be established, and the extent to which the readers use alternative services.

3. The needs of the readers cannot be considered collective ly, as the needs of each reader group vary widely.

4. The needs of the readers must be re-assessed frequently as the activity patterns and library use patterns change.

The rural librarian is faced with the problem of providing library service for people scattered over a wide area, living in many cases in villages too small to support library service points, or on individual farms. It is very difficult to achieve an adequate coverage of the area while maintaining service of a satisfactory standard.

The Ramsay study showed that about 50% of the readers com- bined library use with other activities, and of these, 60% combined library use with shopping. Only people 14 years of age and over were included in the study. A questionnaire was issued to 25 of the county library's service points: 14 of the 15 branches then existing, and 11 of the 24 stations. The period covered was one week, and 1,593 returns were tabulated. This study was made over ten years ago but it is included because it is one of few dealing with county library service point locations.

Why Parks Are Undesirable as Sites for Libraries:

1. A good park site is not a good library site. Libraries in well-traveled locations such as shopping centers achieve a greater attendance and turnover of books per tax dollar expended. Most parks are in quiet, isolated areas away from main arteries of traffic.

2. The functions of parks and libraries are different. Active sports, spectator events, craft programs, and other recreational activities are noisy, distracting mass programs which interfere with the study, reference, and quiet reading activities of a library.

3. Sometimes parks attract "odd balls," transients and de-
linquents. This could make such sites unsafe for women and
children during evening hours when the library would be open.

4. Library practice in many cities tends to confirm the un-
desirability of branches located in parks. California cities which
have avoided park sites for branches include: Santa Monica,
Anaheim, Riverside, Los Angeles (since 1957), Long Beach, San
Diego, Glendale, and Pasadena.

5. The trash, litter, and food remnants which accumulate in
parks may create extra problems of physical maintenance in a park-
located library.

6. The type of events which take place in parks frequently
attract many cars, leaving little or no parking space for library
patrons.

In connection with this topic an article entitled "Danger
Stalks our Parks" will be of interest.[6]

Should Public Library Branches Be Located in Schools?

A national study, published by A. L. A. in 1963, The School-
Housed Public Library--A Survey, by Ruth White, was based on
questionnaires sent to 154 public libraries located in schools. This
objective report makes no recommendations but summarizes the
replies of librarians who have had first-hand experience with the
combination. Among points brought out in the study were:

1. 72 per cent opposed placing public library branches in
schools; 14 per cent thought the location was possible under certain
conditions; 7-1/2 per cent were non-committal; only 6-1/2 per cent
were in favor.

2. Library literature of the past twenty years has been almost unanimously opposed to the combination.

3. Combining school and public libraries is not new. It was
tried more than a hundred years ago and is now outmoded. The
trend for years has been away from this combination.

Studies and correspondence have shown that many large

cities have abandoned the combination in favor of separate school
and public libraries.   School-housed public library branches in some
cases were just as expensive as separate facilities, and were
psychologically and physically unsatisfactory.   Among cities which
have discontinued school-housed public libraries are Fresno, Stockton, Santa Barbara, Oakland, San Diego, and Los Angeles in
California; Wichita, Kansas; Minneapolis, Minnesota; Grand Rapids,
Michigan;   Toledo, Ohio;   Providence, Rhode Island; Atlanta,
Georgia; and Racine, Wisconsin.   Kansas City, Missouri, and Flint
Michigan, are currently working on eliminating this arrangement in
their cities.   Several of these cities dropped the idea of combined
facilities as far back as the 1940's.

In 1968 the Santa Ana Public Library Director, Howard
Samuelson, conducted a survey in which he asked librarians in all
cities in the United States with populations of over 100,000 for an
evaluation of their experience with school-housed branches.   If they
had no direct experience, they were asked for their views on the
subject. [8]

Some 130 answers were received, and only four librarians
felt that the combination was desirable or feasible.   Of the four,
only two felt it was a good idea in general; two thought it might
work out under certain optimum conditions.   These included the
public library's location in a separate wing of the building, or on
the ground floor; or having a separate, outside entrance.

Thus 97 per cent of those replying to Mr. Samuelson's in-
quiry were against school-housed branches.   About 70% of those replying had had experience with such a situation and some of these
felt very strongly on the matter.   In recent years school officials
have largely concurred in favoring separate school libraries.

In the face of such evidence and opinion it would appear that
city officials, library or school board members, interested citizens,
or librarians who favor the combination public library-school library
branch are placing seeming economy ahead of successful service and
are not considering the end result.   The supposed economy turns out
in most cases to be a myth.   Studies have shown that the cost per

ook circulated is actually higher in most cases in school-housed
ranches because of the small circulation achieved. Circulation has in-
reased by as much as four or five times when public library branches
ave been removed from school buildings. Frederick Wezeman made a
tudy in 1965 of Combination School and Public Libraries in
'ennsylvania. [9] Here are exceprts from his report:

> In 1965 there were about 25 combination school and public li-
> braries in the State of Pennsylvania. After State Aid for li-
> braries was established, after one year of experience with
> state aid for combination libraries, the State Library, after
> much consideration and deliberation among its own staff, and
> consultation with the Director of School Libraries in the
> Department of Public Instruction, recommended to the Ad-
> visory Council on Library Development that state aid be
> denied to all combined public-school libraries. Reasons
> were as follows:
>
> 1. Efforts to obtain proper records were discouraging.
>   It was difficult, and at times almost impossible, to
>   identify the "public library" part of the combination
>   library operation.
>
> 2. The combination libraries tended to be predominantly
>   school libraries and it was difficult to have the state
>   aid channeled only into public library improvement.
>
> 3. The possibility of obtaining public library state aid
>   money encouraged towns and school boards to think in
>   terms of combination libraries rather than working
>   toward the provision of good public and school
>   libraries.
>
> 4. The majority opinion of professional librarians in both
>   the school and public library fields is against com-
>   bined library facilities.
>
> At first glance, the idea of a school library also serving
> as a public library is an appealing one. To many com-
> munities anxious to save needed tax dollars, the possibility
> of having one institution fulfill two separate and important
> functions appears to be an excellent way 'to kill two
> birds with one stone.' Those who contemplate such a
> move greatly overemphasize any possible economies, and
> more seriously, often overlook the deficiencies in library
> service--both to the school and to the community--that
> usually result.

Reasons Why Public Library Branches Should Not be Located in Schools

They Differ in:	Public Library	School Library
A. Approach	Recreational reading given much more attention. Public librarians averse to being teacher-disciplinarians.	Mainly reference usage, a type of teaching involved. School librarians need to have time to work closely with all teachers, attend curriculum meetings, etc.
B. Specific Purpose (Philosophy and Aims)	Serves as an information and recreational reading center for the community. Meeting rooms provide a place for adult library-related activities, story hours, etc.	The philosophy and aims of the school determine the library's policies, materials, activities and services. Space for meeting rooms is not available and activities are restricted.
C. Methods of Operation and Organization	Voluntary and informal use by public. Separate and distinct institution with own governing authority and budget.	More rigid discipline and much required usage. Often a study center and an integral part of the school system.
D. Public Served	All ages - pre-school through oldsters.	Limited age group.
E. Materials Collection	Wide range of reading and reference suitable for all ages and tastes. Often mature subjects not suited for children and young people. Limited duplication.	To meet the needs of the curriculum, mainly curriculum enrichment with some recreational reading. Some material must be duplicated in quantity.

F. Staff	Branch librarian has broad, general training, usually a professional library degree, emphasis on adult education, public library problems of administration, varied services. May have no teaching background.	School librarian can often be hired with as little as 9-12 semester hrs. of library science. Special training includes educational psychology, practice teaching, school library problems and materials. Is considered a member of the instructional staff.
G. Location	Public libraries need to be at or near shopping areas and busy intersections. Public library branches need to be readily accessible.	Schools are usually in residential, less crowded and safer traffic areas. School libraries are often on second floors, or in center of school building, may be hard to find.
H. Costs of Operation	Public library branches usually show lower costs per book circulated because circulation is much higher in relation to total cost.	School libraries do not have to be so concerned about book circulation costs as costs are usually merged with entire school operational costs. Public rarely knows separate school library costs.
I. Hours Open	A public library branch should be open evenings, Saturdays, and during the summer.	Most school libraries close at 4 p.m. or thereabouts, five days a week. Adjustment to longer hours is often difficult due to heating, lighting, and janitor problems.

Reasons Why Public Library Branches Should Not be Located in Schools (Cont.)

They Differ in:	Public Library	School Library
J. Facilities Provided	A public library branch needs a workroom, staff room, and rest rooms, as well as special areas for small children and for reference.	Most school libraries are in one large room.
K. Use by Children from Other Schools (Particularly Parochial Schools)	Children from other schools are apt to regard the public library branch as a supplementary school library. Some parochial schools do not like to have their students go to other schools for service.	A school library is for its own school and the children like it because it is their own. A pride is engendered. Children and teachers prefer not to have others coming in to use the resources.
L. Effect on Growth of Good school Libraries	Having a public library branch in a school hinders the development of a good school library expressly geared to students' needs.	School libraries should be financed and developed by the school districts. They often will not take these steps as long as they can get public library service at small cost.

In those rare cases when, for some reason, political or otherwise, a public library branch-school combination seems inevitable, the following suggestions may help to insure as satisfactory a relationship as possible:

1.   The school should provide adequate parking for adult patrons during school hours.

2.   The school should provide branch quarters on the ground floor, with an outside entrance, and preferably in a separate wing.

3.   The school should provide adequate space for books, services for readers of all ages, and expansion for future growth.

4.   The space provided should be soundproofed and away from the gymnasium, auditorium, and cafeteria.

5.   Arrangements for heating, lighting, and janitorial service must be made so that the library can operate normally during off-school hours and weekends.

6.   If possible a separate heating and air-conditioning system should be provided.

Obviously such arrangements can be made more easily when the combination library is being set up in a new school building.

What can the library administrator do to help such an arrangement?

1.   Before establishing the branch, have a clear-cut understanding in the initial contract concerning the allocation of administrative responsibilities as between the library and the schools.

2.   Resist all efforts to turn the branch into a school library.

3.   Schedule the hours of service to meet the needs of the entire community.

4.   Make no binding commitment that would prevent withdrawal at a later date.

5.   Insure that the library area is reserved for the exclusive use of the library. The space should not be allocated to textbook storage or an audio-visual center for the school.

6.   Provide a large enough staff to serve both adults and students when classes are in session and during rush hours.

7. Guarantee an arrangement and program to permit school use of the library without interfering with adult use. Class visits are, of course, to be expected. They would also be encouraged in a non-school-located branch.

The chief restriction to good adult service is the limited space usually available for readers, books, and staff work areas. But the psychological limitations of a school location may be the most serious factor.

Who should choose the branch site? In most cases, the decision falls to the Library Board of Trustees, with the advice and help of the library director, the opinions of both being based on care ful studies of the neighborhood concerned. (See the chapter on Tailoring the Branch to the Community). If the library has a book-mobile and has been using it to test library usage in a possible branch area, the circulation shown will be one of the strongest factors to consider.

The true function of the city or county public works and planning departments in site selection is to provide information on foreseeable population trends, proposed routes of arterial traffic, superhighway plans, bus transit, and proposed developments in industry, retail centers, etc.

An architect may be concerned that too much is being spent for the site, since this can reduce the amount available for the building. Others may be unduly concerned about the exterior appearance of the building and not give sufficient enough thought to functional interior features. However, architects with experience in library planning are more likely to realize the value of a strategic site and the need for a functionally efficient building.

Joseph L. Wheeler's classic monograph, The Effective Location of Public Library Buildings,[10] shortened and edited by Herbert Goldhor in 1957, is based on solid fact, surveys, a study of the current literature at the time of writing, and many years of actual experience of choosing locations for a number of public libraries.

Ninety per cent of the librarians polled at that time, over

ten years ago, believed, and a multitude of cases indicate, that
every new public library, central or branch, should be located in
the center of a major pedestrian and shopping area. Several
studies have shown that only about one-fourth of the adults using
libraries make a special trip by auto to do so. The majority use
is in connection with other downtown or neighborhood shopping area
errands or business.

Even though the cost of the site may be much greater than
anticipated, even as much as 50% of the building cost, it is poor
economy in the long run to save on location at the expense of
potential use. It would be better to save on building costs than on
site costs.

In some communities, when site controversies arise, the
uninformed may suggest a popular vote to decide the matter, ignor-
ing precepts by stating that "no rule covers all cases". This is a
short-sighted escape route to avoid facing facts and to try to save
money. One misconception of the past is illustrated by Frank Lloyd
Wright's comment, "Let's have good libraries with a pleasant home-
likeness, not big ones."[11] Today's thinking is toward fewer and
larger branches, and no town, city, or county can afford to follow
this advice if it wishes to spend the taxpayer's money wisely.

Wheeler points out emphatically that although librarians are
logically in a position to have sounder opinions than anyone else in
the community as to where libraries should be located, public officials, citizen groups, real estate men, planners, newspaper
editors, and many others often ignore experienced opinion and advice, and offer unsound, illogical proposals, bringing heavy pressure to bear to choose locations which could be and have been
disastrous for the library's service to its community. The experienced advice of bankers, school administrators, hotel men, and
industrial engineers in regard to the location of their specialized
buildings should not be ignored,[12] nor should the advice of librarians on the location of libraries.

Many cities and counties pay too little and act too late in
acquiring sites. Strategic locations for branches should be bought

as early as possible, before prices rise. Exceptions to this rule
will be areas growing so rapidly that the future population patterns
of a neighborhood are uncertain, or where there is danger of
deterioration of a neighborhood in the foreseeable future. A proper
study of growth trends and population data should reveal such possibilities.

Shopping centers as locations:

      A majority of librarians in the United States choose sites in
or near shopping centers when new branches are being considered.
Library literature reveals many opinions and considerable evidence
that branches so located are very successful. In connection with a
site study in Tucson, Arizona, in 1963,[13] sixteen cities were asked
to indicate their experiences with shopping center locations. Support
for shopping centers was overwhelming. The Dallas, Texas, Public
Library has one of the most successful branch systems in the
country. Library Director Lillian M. Bradshaw is quoted in a
newspaper column in the Dallas Herald of November 25, 1968, as
follows:[14]

> Up until about 1960 Dallas had not built any new branches
> for decades, so we learned from the mistakes of others
> who had put branches in parks and quiet places. Their
> libraries were not used. Eight new branches have been
> constructed since 1960 and four new ones are being
> planned in the current Crossroads Bond Program, almost
> all in or close to shopping centers.
>
> We could buy a piece of land and get it cheaper or even
> get it free, but you will find your unit cost for circulating
> a book going pretty high; in a busy center, more people
> will utilize the facility, meaning a cheaper cost and edu-
> cational exposure to the most people.

      Mrs. Bradshaw then explained that the price tag on one site
alongside commercial and near residential property was $75,406.50.
      In a letter written November 4, 1968, Hoyt R. Galvin,
Director of the Public Library of Charlotte and Mecklenburg County,
Charlotte, North Carolina, said:[15]

> I am developing a conviction that most branch libraries
> serving urban communities should be in leased space in

shopping centers, and preferably in mall type shopping
centers. Experience with branch libraries in shopping centers is too limited to provide conclusive data, but the
limited experience plus the retailing record in shopping
centers underwrites the conviction. Library-owned buildings
immediately adjacent to shopping centers with space especially designed for library purposes may serve as effectively,
but being within the shopping center and its traffic lanes
appeals to my judgment as the best means to reach more
people with library services.

Since space in a shopping center may be hard to find, every
effort should be made to plan the branch quarters into shopping
centers before they are built, as integral parts of the plot plan and
architectural design. This should be possible, in many cases,
because the newer centers in the planning stage seek participation,
and where there is competition among centers they have often
welcomed the drawing power of a service organization such as a
branch library. If the city or county government has a policy
against renting or leasing quarters (which will usually be built by
the developer or promoter to library specifications), there is sometimes vacant land adjacent to the center which can be purchased. But
it will be expensive. Methods of setting up shopping centers vary,
but usually a corporation or promoter constructs the various stores
and they are available only on a lease basis.

It is not always costly to acquire a shopping center site, and
some have even been donated. In the Arizona Librarian, W. R.
Henderson, Director of the Phoenix Public Library, stated:[16]

... if cost-conscious city fathers in other towns jump to
the conclusion that Phoenix has been paying a high price
for its branch library sites, they are on the wrong
track. Two of the one-acre library sites were donated to
the City by two of the shopping center developers involved.
Of the other three one-acre sites mentioned, two were sold
to the City by the shopping center developers concerned at
a fraction of the market value. The fifth site had to be
acquired from a private owner because the adjacent shopping center had already built to the capacity of its property
before City officials came looking for the library site.

If shopping center branches are rented, as the majority are,
Claude Aubry[17] points out that they are more economical to operate
than any conventional branch. In a shopping center branch, the only

expenses (beyond service, staff, supplies, and books) are the rent,
a salary to a part-time maintenance man, electricity and water.
When the space was rented for Ottowa's Carlingwood Branch the
Library Board paid for the installation of the lighting fixtures, the
interior decoration, and the shelving.

To compare usage with that of conventional branches, Carlingwood is about one-fourth the size of any of the other Ottawa
branches in conventional locations. Carlingwood doubled the circulation of two branches located in library buildings and exceeded the
circulation of the largest branch (South) by 8,861 books during the
summer after its preparation for library use. While this is too
small a branch by present-day standards, having been rented in 1961,
and containing only 1,933 square feet, Mr. Aubry believes that it
offers certain advantages other than its heavy use:

1. If the rent is reasonable, it is more economical to
operate.

2. It does not require capital expenditure or interest thereon.

3. There are no maintenance troubles since the landlord
must take care of these.

4. There are no parking problems.

5. It brings the books where people are.

6. It provides, through one branch, service to a widely-
scattered population and to remote districts, thus helping to avoid
multiplying branches. Note: This would be true in a very large
shopping center where people come from a considerable distance or
where there are few, if any, other shopping centers. It would not
be true where shopping centers are smaller and spaced closer
together.

7. It saves time and gas for families who can shop and get
their books on the same trip.

Joseph Wheeler, on the other hand, sees certain possible
difficulties in a location in a suburban shopping center.[18] These
include: 1) the high cost of a permanent site on a 10-year rental
contract; 2) The temptation to take a second-rate location near or
just around the corner from the shopping center; 3) Many people

who come are outside the taxing district and might have to be refused books; and 4) Not all shopping centers have been unqualified successes.

What then are the advantages of branch locations in or near shopping centers? To review them briefly:

1. They place the library where the people come.

2. They solve the parking problem for branch libraries.

3. A shopping center developer may be willing to furnish quarters rent free or at smaller-than-usual cost, making it possible to have some branches that could not otherwise be provided.

4. The area around the library will be well-lighted, well-protected because of close business neighbors, and safer because traffic in a shopping center moves more slowly than on a busy street itself.

5. A shopping center location has been determined by careful survey data, almost guaranteeing library success from the start, without the time and trouble of a particular library survey.

6. A shopping center location is easily accessible to a diversity of ages, races, and nationalities without the artificial barriers of surrounding homes of residents of a certain economic level.

7. A branch placed in a shopping center is less likely to find itself left high and dry in a neighborhood which has changed from residential to purely commercial. Shopping center developers have studied trends and choose neighborhoods which are apt to remain permanently residential.

Where specifically would a branch be most successful given a choice of locations within a shopping center? In A Survey of the Fort Worth Public Library Branch Requirements,[19] made in 1959, Harry Peterson advises: "Look for grocery stores and drug stores, the places people patronize daily. Cleaning establishments, beauty parlors, and appliance shops are better than no stores, but they do not generate the same daily traffic that the grocery stores do. Usually the best spot is near a chain grocery. These organizations check a location carefully before they open an outlet. They rarely make mistakes; consequently the library can benefit by following their lead."

Figure 57: Crescenta Valley Branch, Glendale California, Public
Library is combined with a fire station to form a coordinated, attractive building. The sign indicates where the branch section begins and
continues to the right.

Photo by Marvin Rand
Wonderland Park, La.

Opened: April 3, 1961.
Architects: Frank E. Mosher and Associate, Richard A. Ohmert.
Size: 7,147 square feet in a 21,800 square foot building.
Costs:

Expenses for blue prints, specifications, bonding, newspaper bid notices, engineering services, fire insurance, office supplies:	$ 2,733.47
Original construction:	323,780.00
Change orders:	2,865.00
Construction per square foot: $14.98.	
Library furniture:	10,661.00
Steel shelving:	13,123.00
Miscellaneous furniture (including signs and rugs):	6,911.92
Parking lot contract:	7,525.00
Sprinkler system:	3,582.00
Architect's fee:	26,131.60
Site:	752.50
Landscaping	375.00
Total	$398,440.49

Cost per square foot: $18.27.

Note: This branch is combined with a fire station and city administrative offices, occupying 7,147 square feet in a 21,800 square foot
building. The costs given above are for the entire building.
Type of construction: Brick masonry and reinforced concrete.
Lighting: Fluorescent, luminous ceiling.
Ceiling: Acoustical tile and plaster. Meeting room capacity: 75
Book capacity: 25,000 volumes. Heating and ventilating: Combination
30 tons of refrigerated air conditioning and warm air heating by
gas-fired hot water boiler.

Combinations of branch libraries with other civic buildings have been tried in a number of places. Whether or not this is successful depends, of course, on the location in relation to the factors already discussed in this chapter and whether the facility with which the branch is being combined is a popular one. The Glendale Public Library, Glendale, California, has a successful branch, Crescenta Valley, combined with a fire station. This is a 7,147 square foot branch opened in 1961.

Here are the advantages and disadvantages of such a combination:

Disadvantages:

1. Fire trucks dashing out of the station to answer alarms, and the drivers of automobiles who like to follow fire trucks to see where the fire is located, can create a traffic hazard for children going and coming.

2. The noise of fire sirens can be a disturbing influence for a study situation in the branch reading room.

3. Annexing a branch library to another building immediately cuts one entire wall out as a possibility for expansion. It would have to be a very large lot to accommodate a fire station and an 8,000 square foot or larger branch, and to allow for expansion of either or both facilities. Few such large locations are likely to be available where they would be needed.

4. The criteria for a good location for a fire station and a good location for a branch library have little in common. Fire stations must be spaced at certain distances apart to serve certain areas, irrespective of neighborhood. Libraries may be badly needed where no need for a fire station exists, or where a fire station is already located and has no room for an addition. For either department to have to wait until a dual need exists in a certain area might take years.

Advantages:

1. Since the two facilities share a common lot and a common wall the cost of the combination building may be considerably less than

for two sites and two buildings.

2. Having the fireman so close, especially in problem
neighborhoods, is a comfort to women librarians on duty, particularly at night when discipline problems are apt to arise. There
is little danger of vandalism.

3. Insurance costs are apt to be less, due to the proximity
of the fire station.

4. Since firemen have much free time while awaiting fire
calls, their help can be enlisted for various small tasks in the
library when the custodian is not available.

5. Children find fire stations fascinating and the station
will act as a drawing card for them.   They may then become library borrowers.

It is obvious that some of the arguments on both sides, as
advanced by various proponents of either plan, are weak.   This
will probably not be a common combination, and library directors
and planners will have to decide its merits upon the basis of the
individual location and conditions.   In general, it may be said,
however, that it is unwise to try to combine a branch library with
any other facility which for one reason or another will weaken the
library service.

Parking Requirements:

As the number of automobiles increases, adequate parking
becomes more and more of a problem in site selection.   But if the
branch is to be heavily used, sufficient parking is vital.   Today,
very few patrons visit a library on foot except school children or
those who live very near the branch, and some senior citizens who
do not drive cars and must depend upon public transportation,
taxis, or walking.

A space at least nine or ten feet wide by 20 feet in length
is needed to park the average-sized car.   Branches that locate in
shopping centers do not have to solve the knotty problem of how
much space to allocate to staff and patron parking, but for further
discussion we shall assume at this point that such a location is not
available.   It must be remembered that if the library is only near,
not in the shopping center, its patrons do not have the right to use

the shopping center parking space.   Here are some parking space
formulae:

One approach is to provide one car stall for every 250 square
feet of the building.   Thus, an 8,000 square foot building would require a minimum of 32 stalls; a 12,000 square foot building would
require a minimum of 48 stalls, etc.

The Los Angeles County Library suggested this method of
determining parking: compute the expected peak-hour patronage for
one week.   Get the daily average and divide that figure by two to
arrive at a valid estimate of minimum spaces for patrons, exclusive
of employees.   The past experience of existing branches or branches
in other libraries in similar locations should be used to arrive at
estimates for peak-hour figures for future branches.

Specifications for the Contra Costa County branches in
California called for 40 stalls for a 4,000 to 8,000 foot branch, 100
spaces for a 10,000 to 14,000 foot branch.   The maximum of 100
spaces would be quite difficult to provide for a 10,000 square foot
branch in an expensive site area, but it should be secured if at all
possible.

Edwin Castagna, when director of the Long Beach, California,
Public Library, suggested 30 spaces for an 8,000 square foot
branch.

In planning a parking layout it is important to figure out the
amount of space needed for an average car to back out and turn.   A
fairly common error is to place parking rows too close together,
creating problems in backing out of the space.   This also creates
an additional traffic hazard.

Guy Garrison, in Library Quarterly,[20] listed some recent
public library branch location studies by city planners.   These may
prove useful to library administrators and boards trying to determine
locations.   Public libraries have relied increasingly on the services
of city and county planners.   Here are some examples:

1. 1970 Library Plan. Tucson, Arizona City-County Planning
    Department. 1964. 62p.

2. Branch Libraries; a Long-Range Development Plan. Dept. of
    City Planning and Roanoke Public Library Board,
    Roanoke, Virginia, 1963. 25p.

Figure 58: Layout for parking 33 vehicles. 20,000 sq. ft. site; 6,000 sq. foot branch.

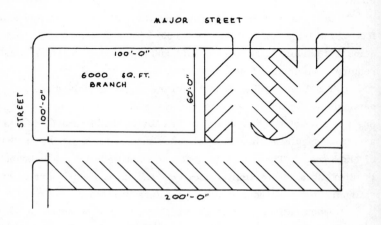

Figure 59: Layout for parking 25 vehicles, spaces 9x20'. For 8,000 sq. ft. branch on a 22,500 sq. ft. site.

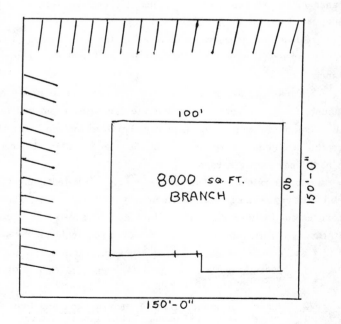

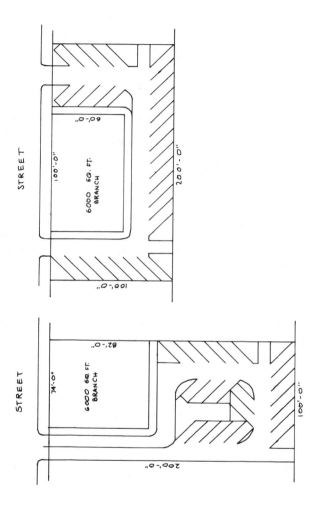

Figure 60: Parking layouts for 6,000 sq. ft. branch on 20,000 sq. ft. site. Left arrangement accommodates 23 vehicles, above, 29 vehicles.

3.   Branch Library System Expansion Study for Houston Li-
     brary Board. Houston, Texas City Planning Commission,
     1965. 30p.

4.   Report on a Branch Library System for Hamilton County
     Ohio. Cincinnati. Hamilton County Regional Planning
     Commission, 1964. 24p.

5.   Library Study: Dayton Area. Dayton, Ohio. City Plan
     Board, 1964. 19p.

6.   Los Angeles Master Plan: Public Libraries. (Los
     Angeles) City Planning Department, 1963. (mimeographed
     with added blueprint maps and charts.)

7.   Comprehensive Plan. Tulsa, Oklahoma. Metropolitan
     Area Planning Commission.

Other studies were made in Phoenix, Arizona in 1961; Nashville and Davidson County, Tennessee in 1961; Spokane, Washington in 1962; and Knoxville, Tennessee in 1963. Some communities
have taken advantage of the Urban Planning Assistance Program of
the Urban Renewal Administration to have library location studies
made. Changing Patterns: a Branch Library Plan for the Cleveland-
Metropolitan Area was done by the Cuyahoga County, Ohio Regional
Planning Commission in 1966 for the Cuyahoga County District Library and the Cleveland Public Library. It is a 162-page
document.

Despite their prevalence, branch site studies by planning
agencies seem to be little known by librarians and sparsely represented in library science collections. One reason is that they are
not listed in Library Literature, Vertical File Index, or Public Affairs Information Service and are seldom, if ever, reviewed in library periodicals. Even when such studies are listed somewhere,
supplies of them are soon exhausted. State Library agencies
should, however, have copies of the best-known studies available
on interlibrary loan.

Planners, unfortunately, too often accept circulation figures
as the only criterion of service. Branch libraries are not chain
store outlets, and the problem of locating or relocating them is not
solved solely in terms of volume of business. Yet until librarians

develop better measures of the utility of branch service, they should
not be surprised if city or county planners give too much attention
to circulation.

Notes

1. Shaffer, Kenneth R. Design for Tomorrow. Bridgeport Public
   Library, Bridgeport, Conn.

2. Martin, Lowell. Branch Library Service for Dallas. Dallas
   Public Library. Dallas, Texas, 1958. p. 64.

3. Galvin, Hoyt R. and Van Buren, Martin. The Small Public
   Library Building. Unesco. 1959, 1962. p. 48-50.

4. Wheeler, Joseph L. and Goldhor, Herbert. Practical Administration of Public Libraries. Harper and Row, c1962,
   p. 412.

5. Ramsay, Margery. The Location of Branch Libraries in a
   County Library System. Thesis for the M.S. degree in
   Library Science, University of California, Jan. 1958.
   Chapter IX, p. 120-135.

6. Grafton, Samuel. "Danger Stalks our Parks." McCall's,
   Oct. 1963. Condensed in Reader's Digest, July, 1964, p.
   114-117.

7. White, Ruth. The School-Housed Public Library: a Survey.
   American Library Association, 1963.

8. Santa Ana Public Library, Santa Ana, California. The School-
   Housed Branch - A Situation Survey. The Library, Santa
   Ana, California, 1968.

9. Wezeman, Frederick. Combination School and Public Libraries
   in Pennsylvania. A Study with Recommendations. Pennsylvania State Library, August, 1965.

10. Wheeler, Joseph L., Goldhor, Herbert, editor. The Effective
    Location of Public Library Buildings. University of
    Illinois, Urbana, Occasional Papers. no. 52, July, 1958.
    p. 2.

11. _____. Ibid, p. 5.

12. _____. Ibid, p. 8.

13. Anderson, John F. "Episode in Tucson." Southeastern Librari-
    an. Summer, 1964. v. 14, no. 2, p. 108-109.

14. Bradshaw, Lillian M. "City Beat: Library Lesson Learned," by Jerry McCarty, staff writer. The Dallas Herald, Nov. 25, 1968.

15. Galvin, Hoyt R. Letter written to author Nov. 4, 1968.

16. Henderson, W. R. "Plant a Library in a Shopping Center?" Arizona Librarian, Spring, 1967, p. 7-9.

17. Aubry, Claude. The Shopping Center Branch Library: A Brief Report. Ontario Library Review. v. XLV, no. 1, Feb. 1961. p. 17.

18. Wheeler, Joseph L. The Effective Location of Public Library Buildings. University of Illinois, Urbana. Occasional Papers. no. 52. July, 1958, p. 33.

19. Peterson, Harry A. Survey of the Fort Worth Public Library Branch Requirements. Washington, D. C. 1959. p. 54-55.

20. Garrison, Guy. Some Recent Public Library Branch Location Studies by City Planners. Library Quarterly, v. 36, no. 2, April, 1966. University of Chicago Press, p. 151-155.

Chapter 13

Pre-planning for a New Branch
or Group of Branches

How does branch planning differ from the planning of a
central or main library? Many general principles of good library
planning are the same, but among the differences to be considered
are the following:

1. A branch rarely has to provide space, desks, typewriters, and supply storage for the cataloging and processing of
books, since these processes are usually carried on at the central
library. If the central library is overcrowded, it is possible for a
technical services section to be located in a new, large branch
built with this in mind, but examples are few and far between. A
member library joining a federation or cooperative system might
conceivably continue to do its own cataloging and processing. However, since one of the reasons for joining is to be able to share in
cooperative cataloging, central processing, or central purchasing,
even formerly independent libraries may no longer have to carry on
these behind-the-scenes processes and can take this into account
when planning new buildings.

2. Branches generally have a higher proportion of juvenile
and young adult borrowers. Thus their services, space, equipment,
and staffing in children's services and young adult areas must be
planned with this in mind, and a larger proportion of the total space
given over to these services and collections than would be the case
in a central library.

3. Since land used for branches is almost always less expensive than downtown or central locations used for main library
buildings it is possible to provide much more space for parking at
less cost. Thus space at least two and preferably three times the
square footage of the building itself should be acquired for a branch.

361

Parking space at downtown locations is either very limited or non-existent for most central libraries.

4. Landscaping may become an important item at a branch; whereas it may be a very minor item at a downtown central library or may be entirely lacking. With the possibility of a moderate setback from the street, extra perimeter area or strips between parking rows, branch planners have an opportunity to provide a more attractive setting through expert landscaping. Sufficient allowance for this must be made in estimating costs.

5. Since a central library will draw a diversity of patrons from all over a city or county it cannot tailor its collection, physical facilities, or staff to fit the special requirements of any one particular area or neighborhood of city or county. A branch can and should plan its service and branch building to provide the best possible service for its own particular type of service area. This calls for a detailed knowledge of the service area in question.

6. A central library is usually situated in an area of business buildings of many types and styles of architecture. Therefore, no one particular style or type is called for in building. A branch, however, even though located in a shopping center, will be surrounded by a residential neighborhood with dwellings which may not vary greatly in property value, character, and architectural period. A branch should conform as much as possible to this prevailing tone, for it will be met with much more favor than if it were conspicuous because of some radical departure in architectural design. The feelings and tastes of the people who must live around or near a branch building must be considered.

7. In planning storage and custodial quarters in a branch the matter of how these services will be provided must be considered. The average central library will find itself in a city setting using the services of one or more full-time custodians and/or gardeners who will require considerable space for their tools and larger equipment and supplies. A branch may be supplied with such services by a centralized city public works department, parks department or other governmental unit or may use part-time

contractural services and find such elaborate facilities unnecessary. Minimum space should always be provided, however, in case the branch grows and the arrangement changes.

8. Warm, inviting colors, carpeted floors, convenience equipment, a meeting room, facilities for exhibits and varied library-related activities, are of even more importance in a branch because it will serve a smaller group of people more often in a more informal, family-oriented manner. The more this informal, homelike atmosphere can be created, the more successful the branch will be in serving as a neighborhood cultural and recreational center.

9. In a city the majority of residents will know the location of the central library, but branch exteriors should be especially well-lighted at night and should have large, impressive, and attractive signs easily visible to passersby so that locations may be seen and remembered.

10. Since there will be more space on branch grounds not occupied by the building it is essential that parking and other areas on the site be brightly lighted at night to prevent or restrict vandalism and criminal acts.

11. Since downtown locations are already zoned commercial, few locations for new central buildings provide a problem. However, when a location for a branch is being chosen it is important to check zoning laws, building code requirements, and any possible building restrictions on the site being considered. If an architect has already been hired, he will assist with such an investigation. In cases where the site is acquired ahead of building and there is no architect available as yet, the library administrator or proper city department must perform this task.

The Building Program:

Before the architect is engaged, the library director, the branch librarian (if one has been hired or is to be transferred from elsewhere in the system) and other branch heads should develop a program of requirements or a building program based

upon the previously-worked out service program. The Library
Board of Trustees will become involved in branch planning if the
system is small and this is a first branch; sometimes they are involved regardless of size. System supervisors of adult services,
children's and young adult services, reference services, circulation,
and any other departments should have a place on the planning team.

The building program should indicate area by area, room by
room, what is needed, graphically, and in a most elementary
fashion. Such schematics are helpful to the professional architect,
as they give him a head start which can save time in learning the
special problems of the area to be served. At this point good communication between architect and library officials is highly important.

The service program, the physical characteristics of the site
and its location, the climate, exposures, architectural ambience of
the neighborhood--each considered in its proper perspective--can
influence the total design. No two communities or neighborhoods
will be exactly alike.

There are two types of building programs: 1) a program
based upon a service program and planned for one specific library
building or branch; and 2) A long-range building program which is
part of a master plan of development for a city library or system
and which includes several new library buildings.

In this discussion (adapted from "Preparing a Program for
the Design of a Library Building" by Stanley B. Carman,[1]) we are
concerned with the first type, a specific building program for a
model branch of 8,000-10,000 square feet, which is the size proposed for the City of _____ branch to be constructed in the
_____ section of the city. (Description of site can be more
definite if desired).

An architect cannot possibly write a building program because he does not know the plan of service the library has for the
particular building under consideration. The librarian is the only
one who knows what is required, and is obligated to furnish the
architect with a program. A consultant from the outside can sometimes examine the problem more objectively, but librarian,

consultant (if there is one), staff members, and board members should all be called upon to serve as resource people and sounding boards while the program is being drawn up. The program includes:

1. A statement of the ends the building is to serve. This should be written only after a thorough study of the community. Is the community growing? What collections will receive greatest use? Are there changing economic factors? What is the place of the branch in community plans for future development of civic and cultural activities?

2. We have to determine what a building is going to do and how it is going to do it. This constitutes a service program to be made out before the actual building program can be formulated. Study the situation in terms of functions to be fulfilled, readers, books, working areas, movements of people and materials, meeting rooms, service to children, service to young adults, to the general reader-browser, and reference service. Also to be considered are: availability of materials for the patron, open stack storage, controlled stack storage such as reference and magazines, specially sized tables, chairs, shelving for special-sized little people, how we will control reader use; can one main desk serve; will there be a separate service area for reference; will there be any processing in this building; what will the work flow be?

After we have determined such questions as the above we are ready to decide on actual building specifications, division of areas, total size, amount of parking, built-in equipment to be included in the building contract, floor coverings, etc. Questions to be asked to determine the building program are:

1. Quantity factors: How many people will likely be using each area? How many volumes will be housed in each area? How many square feet for the children's area? How many tables and chairs of what type must be accommodated for study and reference-reading areas? Will there be study carrels? If so, more space is needed in reference and reading area.

2. Relationships: Examine the extent and relationship of each function or element of the building to all others with which it is in any way connected. This aspect is particularly important; otherwise awkwardness and extra

steps may be involved for staff and public. The functions
can be put on paper as overlapping circles. Examples:
charging desk, card catalog, reading room relationships.
Work with the public should have prior claim. The active
part of the book collection should be housed on open
shelves. Staff room and work room should be located
where they will occupy a minimum of space needed for
public service but should be planned for interrelation,
orderly flow of work, and economical administration.
The service desk should provide easy supervision of the
public entrance.

3. Pitfalls: Avoid library jargon. The architect is not
a librarian. Requirements must be in particular and
specific terms. Speak up and out. Eschew false
modesty. Be firm and determined. The librarian may
have to be diplomatic with his board, but this is when he
can say anything and everything to the architect and be
respected for it. However, do not rush to sketch out a
nice large rectangle, adding and labeling special rooms
and areas, thus usurping the role of the architect and
encumbering him with preconceived notions.

4. General: Building should be both practical and
beautiful. It should further the emotional, intellectual,
and spiritual values the library wants to serve.

5. Method: Keep an orderly file of notes, memoranda
and tentative sketches, as well as memos of agreements,
disagreements and understandings with the architect. This
crystallizes ideas, pushes the work forward, and helps
prevent oversights and misunderstandings later. Cooperation is the keynote, between librarian and consultant, librarian and staff, librarian and board, and between all
members of these groups. Examine as many other
building programs as possible, but keep always in mind
that what may be good for another community or area is
not necessarily good for your community or neighborhood
and that the building must be planned specifically for that
area or community.

6. Order of events:

1. Assemble as much information as possible about the
area in which the building is to be built, through a survey or already existing material.

2. Plan a service program suited to this area. See
"Service Program."

3. Cooperatively plan a building program, following
steps 1 through 5 above.

4. Work with the architect on design and plans.

5. Keep in touch with the construction as it proceeds, but always work through the architect.

To be more specific, the building program should contain at least the following information:

I. Size and description of the area to be served, based on surveys if such are available. If no general surveys are available, the city or county planning department should have separate data which can be combined for the description of the service area. This material should have been available previously for it is needed in relation to site selection and the writing of the service program. Include such items as:

Total estimated population of service area	Owner occupancy of homes
Density of population	Type of housing (single family or multi-housing)
Racial origins of population	Educational level of residents
Median Income	Schools, colleges in the area
Median age	Other sources of books, libraries or bookstores
Commercial establishments and shopping centers in the area	

II. Objectives of the branch briefly stated.

III. Estimated potential usage of the branch, by age groups.

IV. Quantity factors: Total seating space in building, total book capacity, staff requirements (number and training) hours open to the public and periodical storage capacity.

V. Maintenance factors for buildings and grounds. Which of the following will be used? Outside contractor, individual branch custodian, part or full time, gardener.

VI. Volumes capacity by separate areas: adult, young adult, reference, children's.

VII. Exterior requirements.

VIII. Interior requirements (wall finish, materials, floor covering, heating and air conditioning or ventilating, telephone connections, electric plug-ins, type of shelving--whether built-in wall shelving or purchased separately).

368   Modern Branch Libraries

IX. Relationships of interior areas.

X. Location and type of control unit (circulation desk).

XI. General type of building: number of stories, number of square feet, frontage on street, building material to be used.

XII. Space and furnishing required for each individual area: adult reading room, reference area, adult browsing or lounging area, conference room or rooms, young adult area, boys and girls' section, workroom, staff room and staff restroom, all-purpose room (meetings, etc.), public rest rooms and janitor utility room, librarian's office, exhibit or display facilities, parking area, entrance corridor or foyer outside all-purpose rooms, periodical storage area.

In a larger system the branch building question may embrace the possibility of more than one branch. A comprehensive program of branch building may be contemplated either because of expressed demand or as the result of a survey. In the case of a comprehensive plan the following questions should be asked and answered by a careful marshalling of facts: [2]

1. How many branches are really needed?

2. What size and type should they be?

3. How should space be divided in each? How much area for shelving, for study and reading, for storage, for office and work space, for special services?

4. Are the requirements such that the same service program and building design can be used for more than one branch? Meeting individual community needs should not be sacrificed for the sake of saving costs by uniformity. However, in some cases, neighborhoods may be similar and a uniform plan may be feasible.

5. How should reading room space be apportioned among the various age groups and kinds of readers?

6. Should there be a meeting room? If so, should it include space and facilities for:
      Art displays
      Theatrical productions
      Cooking facilities
      Storage of folding chairs
      Projection booth and equipment
      A completely separate entrance?

7. Is it desirable or possible to have branches open all day on Saturday? On Sunday?

8. Is it practical and desirable to include bulletin boards and display windows? How many and what size?

9. Where are the best locations? How far apart? (See the material on site determination, Chapter 12).

10. How much parking space should be provided?

11. How many professionals and how many clericals will be needed to staff the new branches? Where can they be secured?

12. How many hours of public service should be provided for maximum service?[2]

Finding answers to these questions is not easy. They must be based on a combination of past use patterns in other branches, staff estimates of what will happen, and any survey material on the areas concerned. Again, having a uniform service program is a mistake. If good service is to be given, individual programs must be developed.

Working with the Architect

If it is impossible to find an architect who has actually built other branch libraries, then at least an effort should be made to find someone who is a library user and who is willing to work closely with library director, staff, and board to produce a building that is functional as well as beautiful. Mistakes in building design, size of grounds, or choice of location can be frustrating and expensive. Therefore, plans should never be rushed through but should evolve as the result of reading and study, observation, group decisions, past experience, and the employment of the right architect.

Roberta Bowler points out in Local Public Library Administration[3] that the expansion of present branch services into more extensive library systems must be planned in relation to existing facilities. A thorough re-examination of all facilities in the light of community changes, shifting population, development of new shopping centers, and changing transportation patterns would give a

Figure 61: Margaret Fulmer, Whittier, California Public Library
            Director, and Architect William Harrison put their
            heads together for a planning session for Whittier
            Public Library's first branch.

fundamental base for re-evaluation of the existing system and point
to the need for various additions or changes.

> To assist in this re-evaluation libraries should rely on
> the local city or county planning commissions. Examples
> of basic planning documents may now be seen which in-
> clude the library as one element. The growth of branch
> systems in the past has too frequently been achieved with-
> out consideration of basic, broad plans for the city or
> county. The work of the local planning agency should be
> a vital force in planning all phases of future expansion.
>
> An example in which a planning commission has included
> the library was found in the Comprehensive Plan, Tulsa
> Metropolitan Area (Tulsa, The Commission, 1960). This
> study places the library's situation against a total picture
> of the city's social and economic situation.[3]

As a result of the relationship established between library
growth and the total city-county metropolitan area concept, the
Tulsa City-County Library System has experienced remarkable
development in a short period of time.

Assuming that the branch development plan has been viewed in relationship to general city or county master plans of development, the architect must also be made aware of this relationship. What are the qualities to look for in an architect? William Lyman of Jickling and Lyman, Architects, Birmingham, Michigan, expresses an architect's own view of this important question in the A. L. A. publication, Libraries Building for the Future. [4] He lists:

1. Vivid imagination.
2. No reputation for architectural stunts.
3. Understanding the meaning of humility.
4. Having a genuine concern for people.
5. Ability to lead but not dominate.
6. Having respect for tradition.
7. Having respect for the limitations imposed and the opportunities afforded by nature.
8. Having respect for the owner's practical needs or requirements.
9. Possessing broad interests.
10. Furnishing a record of satisfactory performance. Talk with previous clients and contractors, particularly contractors. They are a good source of information.

To these we might add two points brought out by George Jefferson in Public Library Administration: [5]

11. Ability to achieve unity of the building in line with the purpose and any special features or problems.
12. Ability to achieve intrinsic harmony with the surroundings within the limits of cost and site size and shape.

Be wary of the polished salesman. For many architects the planning of a branch library comprises a minor assignment, for they are accustomed to planning mainly larger, more elaborate, and more expensive buildings. It is well to check whether in past assignments the firm has taken as deep an interest and done as good a job with small buildings as with large. Sometimes a new firm or a young architect just starting may more than make up in enthusiasm, zeal, and conscientious application to the job for what is lacking in experience. Such a firm or architect may also be more flexible in ideas and cooperation with librarians, board members, and city planners.

The qualities listed do not define the exact duties of the architect. These are as follows: [6]

1. Helping to plan the interior of the building. The library officials take primary responsibility for this.

2. Designing the exterior.

3. Considering materials and methods of construction.

4. Preparing plans and specifications.

5. Furnishing cost estimates.

6. Advertising for bids.

7. Helping with preparation of the contract.

8. Checking to see that the building meets all legal and local building requirements.

9. Supervising construction. Instructions to the contractor should come from the architect, not the librarian.

10. Advising on any problems which may arise after the building has been completed.

The librarian and architect should, if possible, go together to visit other branches and should strive for an understanding of each other's problems. [6]

The librarian and staff will, in many cases, have worked out a tentative floor plan which they believe will best carry out the service program they have formulated. This should be shown to the architect very early, probably even before he has been definitely engaged. He may point out certain technical difficulties which the layman not versed in building construction will not have thought of. The library officials must be open-minded about necessary modifications, and the architect must be open-minded about accepting as closely as possible a floor plan which he did not create. An architect not versed in library operations cannot be aware of the necessary locational relationships which must exist among the various areas for efficiency and the best service to the public. Thus the process of working with an architect, particularly in relationship to a branch or branches which may have special needs differing from those of a central library, must involve a good deal of give and take.

After the architect has seen the service program, the building program, and any preliminary floor plans developed by the library staff, he will prepare his first ideas and suggestions based on these statements and plans. At this point proposals are free and fluid and changes are readily made. After final plans and blueprints have been prepared, and especially after construction has started, changes are difficult and expensive. Therefore it is highly important that last-minute changes be avoided and that both sides be very sure before the final plans are prepared.

Ten Steps for Achieving a Successful Library[8]

Organization: Trustees, Building Committee, Librarian, Consultant. Outline their responsibilities. Prepare Community Survey to appraise requirements.

Architect: Select an Architect who is concerned about Library design--one who has designed successful public structures and understands both technical and cultural implications of the project. Select one who can work successfully with groups of people.

Site Selection: Evaluate potential sites in relation to community growth and cultural activities. Secure topographic survey and corollary considerations: drainage, utilities, noise, sun, wind, etc.

Program: Define cultural requirements and library philosophy. Determine desired character of structure, location on proposed site, parking requirements, meeting rooms, display facilities, area relationships, patios, provisions for future expansion.

Cost Projection: Obtain reliable cost estimates on land, building, architect, engineering, inspection, tests, landscaping, furniture, moving and financing.

Schematics: Area and site relationship plan giving consideration to previously determined physical and philosophical requirements. No detail.

Preliminary plans: These define proposed floor plan, elevations, furniture layout. Preliminary specifications of materials and cost estimate should be provided with these plans.

Contract Documents: Should clearly define contractor's area of responsibility and provide cost and completion

clauses. Complete documents protect the community
from legal and on-job difficulties. Plans and specifications must be clear and comprehensive to avoid possibility of misinterpretation. They must be approved by
several agencies before bidding can proceed.

Bidding period: Usually three weeks. Plans and specifications that are easy to bid and build from will insure a
fair and equitable price.

Construction: During this period (construction time
depends primarily on magnitude of project) Trustees,
Building Committee, Librarian and others involved should
plan logistics of moving in, acceptance and dedication
program.

A number of libraries throughout the country have prepared
building programs for one or more branches. These may be borrowed from the American Library Association Professional Library
on inter-library loan. Available at recent listing were:

Branch libraries of Cincinnati and Hamilton County, Ohio

Branch Libraries of Dayton, Ohio

Branch Libraries of Houston, Texas

Branch Libraries of Los Angeles, California

Branch Libraries of Miami, Florida

Branch Libraries of Phoenix, Arizona

Branch Libraries of Queens Borough, New York:
  Laurelton Branch
  Vleigh Branch
  Howard Beach Branch
  Pomonok Branch
  Rockdale Village Branch
  Far Rockaway Branch

Donald G. Mitchell Memorial Branch, New Haven,
  Connecticut

La Retama Branch, Corpus Christi, Texas

Magnolia Branch, Seattle, Washington

North Tampa Branch, Tampa, Florida

Poplar-White State Branch, Memphis, Tennessee

Regional Library System, Free Library of Philadelphia,
  Pennsylvania

Richard B. Harrison Branch, Raleigh, North Carolina

Not included in the A. L. A. list were the following building programs which the author was able to secure on request from the libraries concerned.   These may also be available on inter-library loan:

      Sanger Branch Library Building Program, Fresno County
          Free Library, Fresno, California.

      Burnett Branch Library Building Program, Long Beach,
          California (also Lakewood Branch).

      Building Program of the South-Area Regional Branch
          Library of the Sacramento City-County Library System,
          Sacramento, California.

      A Building Program for the North End Branch Library, San
          Bernadino Public Library, San Bernadino, California.

      Program for the Architect for the Branch in East Whittier
          of the Whittier Public Library, Whittier, California.

Danger Signals in Planning

In planning a branch many mistakes can result from the thinking of librarians, trustees, or architects inexperienced in building libraries.   Here are a few that have been made, as reported by Keyes D. Metcalf in an article entitled "Hindsight in Planning Library Buildings."[9]

> 1. Too much intensity of light. Quality is more important than intensity. There are more complaints about glare and shadow than about too low intensity.

> 2. Too much glass with resulting high intensity of temperature around the outside walls of the building, making necessary high intensity in other parts in order to avoid too great a contrast. In hot weather the heat intake through glass plus that from high intensity lighting can seriously complicate the air-conditioning problem.

> 3. Direct sunlight is bad for books.

> 4. Glass windows or doors so placed and so clear that they are not noticed can cause absent-minded persons, as well as others, to run into them, often with serious consequences; 6000 persons are said to be hospitalized each year by walking through unnoticed glass doors.

Client-Architect Relationship[7]

Librarian	Architect
1. Should feel responsible	Feel Responsible
To give all facts (needs) at first.	To understand facts--not alter facts.
To have concern for right facts.	To create a library out of needs.
To consider large relationships first.	To consider first things first.
To remember that drawings cost money.	To remember that poor planning costs library money.
2. Know your place in the program	Know your place in the program
Librarian is source of information-- not the architect.	Architect should accept information--he is not the librarian.
Take whatever time it requires.	Don't rush the librarian.
Stay with the architect.	Don't get way ahead.
3. Know your area and limitations	Know your area and limitations
Evaluate old and new ways.	Evaluate old and new ways.
Don't carry over old ways that don't work.	Don't force new ways that may not work.
Know your community.	Accept community needs.
4. Communicate	Understand
Use words, not sketches (save sketches until later)	Use sketches, not salesmanship.
Make a written program.	Know the program as presented.
5. Understand sketches	Understand response
Respond in words, not sketches.	Respond in words and sketches.
Don't accept poor results.	Be able to justify your decisions, without seeking the aesthetic veil to avoid reality.
Don't take good results for granted.	

6. Have no preconceived ideas
   Give facts, requirements, needs.
   Use diagrams if you must.

7. Be open, flexible, objective
   There are many ways to solve a problem
   if the facts are all given.

8. Stick with decisions
   Don't make decisions with half the facts.

9. Don't assume architect is infallible
   Verify his words and ideas.

10. Don't be overpowered
    Architects are just people with the
    usual foibles.

11. Don't be oversold
    Remind architect of some mistakes--
    preferably his own. This induces
    humility which is much needed.

Have no preconceived ideas
   Use only real facts not current
   cliches or fads.

Be open, flexible, objective
   There are many design solutions.
   Don't be a prima donna.

Observe decisions
   Don't freeze the design with half the facts.

Don't assume librarian is infallible
   Verify his or her words and ideas.

Don't overpower
   After all--we aren't God.

Don't oversell
   A librarian convinced against his or her
   will is soon unconvinced.
   Have humility--it helps understand
   problems.

5. It is a mistake to omit air-conditioning because a complete system is more than a cooling device. It includes heating, cooling, humidifying, dehumidifying, filtering, and ventilating for complete air treatment.

6. Water fountains should be so installed that paneled walls or books are not spattered and damaged when the fountains are turned on.

7. Ceiling construction can interfere with stack lighting. A waffle ceiling or ribbed columns can play havoc.

8. Two entrances placed in such a way that the library is used as a passageway by people going to other buildings.

9. Buildings planned for vertical additions but in such a way that they are unduly expensive or difficult to expand.

10. Buildings planned, placed, or both so that they cannot be added to.

11. With modular plan and low ceilings you simply have to be sure that all heating and ventilating systems work right. You do not have light and air wells and you cannot use windows for ventilation. You can be hopelessly trapped in one of the deep, fine modern buildings with nothing working mechanically. [9]

12. Fire and other exits poorly controlled either architecturally or by nearby supervisor. Result: considerable loss of books. [10]

13. Locations of some staff and public telephones so that phone conversations are disturbing to patrons.

14. Cool white fluorescent tubes used instead of warm white. The latter produce more and softer light.

15. Electrical outlets poorly related to their greatest use because of late decisions on furniture placement, including bookstacks, exhibit cases, staff desks, etc.

16. Light switches too available to public and not available to library staff and janitor when they leave the building.

17. No ramps or on-grade entrance provided for the physically handicapped.

18. Poor relationship between public service desks and the supporting staff workroom, resulting in poor efficiency in operation and less service to the public.

19. Not enough flexibility in bearing walls, plumbing, air conditioning and electrical systems to avoid "road blocks" for future changes in the building.

20. Poor diffusing lenses on light fixtures contributing to glare.

21. Failure to tilt lower shelves of book stacks for best visibility of titles.

22. Building exterior facing materials which are expensive and/or difficult to maintain.

23. Poor location for public service desk in relation to entrance and/or exit.

24. Meeting room that cannot be shut off from main library after closing time to permit continued use by groups.

25. Use of an electrical heat activator for the fire alarm system recommended instead of automatic sprinkler system. Water does too much damage to books.

26. Having too cheap an air-conditioning system or one of insufficient capacity results in a poor system always needing repair. Costs more in the long run.

27. Placing mechanical equipment room, with compressor, etc. too close to reading rooms, resulting in noise and vibration being heard.

28. Inadequate provision for landscape sprinkler system and for hose bibbs at outdoor walls and patios.

29. Foolproof key stops not provided in public toilet rooms for plumbing fixtures. Taps left on can flood.

30. Some air ducts insufficiently sound baffled to prevent noise from meeting rooms, staff offices, workroom, etc. being carried out into public areas.

31. Carpeted floors with separate backing are a mistake since it is much more difficult to insert a satisfactory patch if damage is done to a carpet. A high quality 100% continuous filament nylon carpet with vulcanized rubber backing containing a carbon additive is the best all-round floor covering for libraries.

32. Recesses often are forgotten for entrance door mats. If not recessed people will stumble over them.

33. Hard floors often carried into areas where noise should be kept to a minimum, stack areas for example.

34. Some building interiors include very bold colors in large areas in permanent building materials, as well as in large painted walls. These greatly limit the colors which can be used initially and in future furnishings and equipment.

35. Placement of standing stacks to obscure visibility control. Place on diagonal.

36. Radiant heating in cement slab floors has advantage of air movement being less violent, no smoking of walls or ceiling, no return air grills needed in valuable wall area. Warm or cool air travels directly under the slab and enters the room at the perimeter. Be sure to use best grade copper tubing; otherwise if a leak occurs, repairs are very expensive.

37. Some flat ceilings of certain materials cause echo. Sloping ceilings prevent echo. However, avoid too high ceilings for waste of light and heat.

38. Consider use of many round tables instead of rectangular in reading room. More people can get around a round table in same space, also staff can walk diagonally to certain areas and save as much as 30% walking distance.

Furniture mistakes:
1. Casters used on desk chairs, book trucks, and typewriter stands are often of black rubber. If left to stand for any length of time on vinyl or asbestos-vinyl tile, discoloration of the tile will result.

2. Don't use chairs with metal legs. They make excessive noise when struck against each other.

3. Don't use glides too small. They result in carpet damage. Glides at least 1-1/4-ins. in diameter should be used or else ball-type rollers.

4. If the shelving contract and carpet contract are not included in the general contract, separate contracts can delay the project or make it difficult to decide who is responsible for determining damage to walls, floors, etc.

5. Include paving, off-street parking areas in the general contract. Problems arise otherwise concerning the condition of the subgrade at the time the paving contractor begins his work, as compared to when he made his bid. [10]

Besides these general mistakes which may cause problems for staff and for library patrons, specific, if unintentional, architectural and equipment barriers have sometimes been created to prevent or inhibit the use of branches by those who are handicapped. Larry K. Volin aptly points these out in an article in Library Journal,[11] in which he also stresses the number of handicapped in the population. Since 1962 these figures have undoubtedly increased, with the Vietnam war as a contributing factor. In 1962 Mr. Volin stated there were:

> More than 5,000,000 persons with heart conditions which prevented many from climbing stairs; 250,000 confined to wheelchairs; 200,000 wearing heavy leg braces, and 139,000 with artificial limbs. For these people many libraries had the following barriers:
>
> 1. Telephone booths or aisles too narrow for a person in a wheelchair or with leg braces.
>
> 2. Telephones, tables, or water fountains located in such positions as to make them inaccessible to the ambulatory handicapped.
>
> 3. Telephones or record players with no amplifying device for the hard of hearing.
>
> 4. Rooms with narrow doors a wheel chair, or persons with leg braces, cannot go through.
>
> 5. Rest rooms with unsuitable facilities.
>
> 6. Stairways instead of ramps.

A free copy of a booklet entitled Making Buildings and Facilities Accessible to and Usable by the Physically Handicapped is available from the President's Committee, Washington, D.C., Committee on Employment of the Handicapped.[11]

A good architect should be willing to look over such lists as these and be anxious to profit from the mistakes made by others. While all branches may not be able to provide all of the special facilities needed for the handicapped, many could probably arrange for at least some of them, and it is certain that those affected would be most grateful.

One of the best articles written on the subject of the library

staff, library board, architect relationship is "Mr. Architect,
Listen," by J. Russell Bailey. [12]   It contains some noteworthy
general principles of planning:

> 1. The architect should not use the library job to
> experiment with pet ideas. Communities may sometimes
> wish their library to fit its neighboring buildings in style
> and decor.
>
> 2. The plan should attempt to meet the needs of tomorrow
> for automated libraries. Extra floor space should be pro-
> vided for future electronic equipment in the workroom, and
> space in the floor and ceiling construction for system
> connections.
>
> 3. The plan should be useful and capable of reasonable
> additions in 20-50 years. It should be able to convert
> some areas from book space to reader space as micro-
> film or microfiche supplant back files of periodicals and
> cooperative information retrieval systems replace bulky
> reference collections.
>
> 4. The architect should design from the inside out. The
> architect must not feel that the outside is his problem
> and the inside is entirely the librarian's problem. Both
> must be done cooperatively. The building should be
> designed as a whole.
>
> 5. The plan should consider traffic pattern for pedestri-
> ans, automobiles, the crippled, book return, bookmobile
> or extension traffic (should the bookmobile work out of
> the branch), receiving traffic, multi-purpose room traffic,
> maintenance and trash collection facilities; all of these
> influence function and design.
>
> 6. It is better for both librarian and architect if there
> are no preconceived convictions which cannot be modified
> when the planning team is brought together.
>
> 7. A librarian, donor, or city official who may wish to
> dominate the building design can be and at times is as
> dangerous as the egotistical, completely self-sufficient
> architect could be.
>
> 8. First impressions are important. Make the entrance
> a feature which inspires confidence in the high quality of
> design to follow. In a hot climate use a shaded entrance;
> in a cold, wet climate, a roof over the entrance. In
> almost any climate there should be a covered entrance
> with sufficient paved space around it.
>
> 9. There should be a place for bicycles, motor scooters,

motorcycles.   Screen this area from view with a decorative concrete or stone wall.

10. A sculptor can enrich an entrance wall if funds or a memorial gift can be secured.

11. Landscaping should be attractive.   Use warmth and color to liven up the green.

12. The building should provide minimum maintenance and long wear.

13. The vestibule should be large enough to take care of peak loads of people in inclement weather.

14. Lights and foyer should show off the library to the best advantage.

15. The interior environment should set the patron at ease.   It should be informal and comfortable.

16. Reading areas should be so well integrated with library materials that there is a minimum of distance and traffic between the book and the reading location. A variety of reading spaces and areas seem to serve best.

17. Use color and contrast to overcome monotony.[12]

The following additional points are taken from basic principles of planning listed by the Los Angeles Public Library:[13]

18. Interior arrangement and design should allow maximum supervision of the area.

19. Interior arrangement and design should provide minimum walking for staff.

20. Design should provide maximum theft control with:
        Location and number of exits
        Controlled access
        Separate charging area and desk with turnstiles.

21. The collection should be in orderly sequence. Design and location of stacks should make this possible.

22. Art display areas should be arranged to require minimum supervision.

23. A separate entry inside the main entry will minimize noise and filter out dust.

24. Flexibility achieved through an open, unobstructed plan, movable partitions or minimum columns or walls in the center is best.

25. A minimum amount of glass should be used to avoid heat cost, glare, noise, and distractions. [13]

26. At least two times the area of the branch building should be secured for a site, preferably three times as much.

Three unusually good articles to provide help on the planning process are:

Dickenson, D.W. "Building Together: the Architect and the Librarian." Library Association Record, v. 65, Dec. 1963, p. 440-445.

Broome, E.H. "Telling Him." Library Association Record. v. 65, Dec. 1963, p. 44-45.

Harrison, K.C. "The Librarian and the Architect." Library World, v. 61 (717) March, 1960, p. 177-80.

A library would seldom bring in an outside building consultant for assistance in planning a single branch, but in the case of long-range planning for a system of branches the services of an outside consultant have often been used. Should such a consultant be engaged, it is important that he be brought into planning for the entire project at the very beginning, during the initial consideration of whether or not to build and to what extent. He can make a survey of the library as a basis for programming and can assist with the preparation of the building program without actually writing it. He should assist in the selection of sites or recommended sites and may even be consulted as to the selection of an architect. It is always regrettable when a city or county insists on hiring a local architect because he is local although he may not be as well qualified as an outside architect.

Libraries wishing to follow trends in branch size and volume capacity, number of reader seats provided, equipment cost, site cost, architects who are building branches, and cost of buildings per square foot are advised to consult the data on some 88 new branches constructed in the fiscal year 1968-69 as contained in the article by Hoyt Galvin and Barbar Asbury in Library Journal, Dec. 1, 1969, "Public Library Building in 1969." [14] This kind of data will be published annually from now on.

Checklist - Planning Branch Library Buildings

Item	1970	1980	1990	2000	2010	Comments
Population Served						
Estimated circulation						
Initial bookstock						
No. of periodicals stocked						
No. of years to be kept						
Staff:						
No. of professional						
No. of clerical						
No. of page						
Full-time equivalent						
of total staff						
Hours of public service						
Size of building-total						
Adult reading space						
Juvenile reading space						
Multi-purpose room						
Conference room						
Work Room						
Staff room						
Lavatories						
Librarian's office						
Seating capacity:						
Adults						
Juveniles						
Public meeting room						
Telephones needed						
Lighting adequacy						
(Candlefoot measurements)						
Type of heating						
Type of ventilation						
Air conditioning type						
Outside exhibit cases						
Inside exhibit areas						
Parking for cars						
Parking for cycles						
Signs						
Other						

The above chart may be useful in planning for the future as well as
the present since it provides space for estimates for 40 years into
the future at ten-year intervals. Only a daring soul will attempt
to predict as far as 2010 or after, but for some time planners have
been advising planning library buildings that will include possible
expansion for at least thirty years. Much too often, no provision
is made for additions to a building and it becomes crowded and inadequate a few years after erection. Due to a restricted site no
expansion may be possible.

1.   Carman, Stanley B. "Preparing a Program for the Design of
     a Library Building." Minnesota Libraries, V. XX. no. 6,
     June, 1962. p. 163-165.

2.   Hamill, Harold. "The Los Angeles Public Library--Reaching
     Out to a City of 459 Square Miles." In: The Library
     Reaches Out, compiled and edited by Kate Coplan and
     Edwin Castagna. Oceana, 1965. p. 82.

3.   Bowler, Roberta. Local Public Library Administration. Inter-
     national City Managers' Association, 1964. p. 263.

4.   Lyman, William. "Preliminary and Final Drawings, Bidding
     and Construction." In: Libraries Building for the Future,
     American Library Association, c 1967. p. 39-40.

5.   Jefferson, George. Public Library Administration. Philo-
     sophical Library, 1966. p. 58.

6.   Bowler, Roberta. Local Public Library Administration. Inter-
     national City Managers' Association, 1964. p. 282.

7.   Russell, Thomas J. "Client-Architect Relationship." Excerpt
     from address given at the California Library Association
     Conference, 1963, San Francisco, Calif.

8.   Russell, Thomas J. Ten Steps for Achieving a Successful
     Library. Mimeographed sheet, 1 p. n.d.

9.   Metcalf, Keyes, D. "Hindsight in Planning Library Buildings."
     In: Libraries Building for the Future, American Library
     Association, 1967, p. 7-8.

10. Fickes, Eugene W. "Mistakes that Have Been Made in Recent
     Library Buildings." In: Libraries Building for the Future,
     American Library Association, c 1967, p. 17-19.

11. Volin, Larry K. "Architectural Barriers." Library Journal,
     v. 87, no. 21, Dec. 1, 1962. p. 4396.

12. Bailey, J. Russell. "Mr. Architect, Listen." Library Journal,
     v. 90, no. 21, Dec. 1, 1965, p. 5147-51.

13. Los Angeles Public Library. "Basic Principles of Planning
     Needs of the City of Los Angeles Public Library."

14. Galvin, Hoyt R. "Public Library Building in 1969." Library
     Journal, v. 94, no. 21, Dec. 1, 1969, p. 4370-4387.

Chapter 14

Costs and Methods of Financing

One of the most helpful compilations to appear in a long time
was the statistical report on new public library buildings by Hoyt Galvin and Barbara Asbury, which appeared in the December 1, 1968 issue
of Library Journal[1] and again on December 1, 1969. Included in the
1969 issue were facts and figures on 88 branch buildings newly constructed in the fiscal year ending July 1, 1969. Eleven of the remodeling projects reported were branches.

For purposes of this volume only branch information is quoted,
although the Galvin report also includes central libraries, system headquarters and various combinations. Since the building picture includes
all states in the Union it is possible not only to arrive at average costs,
sizes, and other pertinent items, but to compare the same as to various sections of the country. The approximate rise in costs from 1968
to 1969 is also indicated.

Average cost per square foot of the new branches was $24.54,
as compared to $20.50 in the 1968 report. Remodeling costs on 11
branches ran considerably less in 1969, averaging $12.14 as compared
to $21.19 in 1968. This figure is not significant, however, as it
simply indicates less elaborate alterations.

Average square footage of the new branches for the period ending July 1, 1969 was 8,834, up 566 square feet from the 1968 average
of 8,268. The range of sizes was even greater than in 1967-68, ranging
from a low of 792 square feet to a high of 42,200 square feet. The
number of branches in each size range, and the average cost of furnishings and equipment for each size range are shown on the following page.

Size of Branch	No. of Branches	Average Cost of furnishings & equipment
1,000- 3,999 sq. ft.	11	$ 6,159
4,000- 6,999 sq. ft.	25	$ 17,136
7,000- 8,999 sq. ft.	20	$ 26,597
9,000-11,999 sq. ft.	16	$ 32,164
12,000-15,999 sq. ft.	7	$ 41,307
16,000-23,999 sq. ft.	5	$ 56,766
*24,000-29,999 sq. ft.	1	$ 63,972
*30,000-39,999 sq. ft.	1	$ 70,775
*40,000-49,999 sq. ft.	1	$ 102,844

*   These figures given although they apply to only one branch and cannot be considered average. Only new branches, remodeling or additions, or systems headquarters combined with a branch are included.

New Branches Constructed from July 1, 1968 to June 30, 1969

Community	Project Cost	Bldg. Area	Construc. Cost	Sq. Foot Cost	Equip. Cost	Site Cost	Other Costs
Abbeville, Ala.	$ 129,044	4,135	$110,668	$26.76	$11,335	owned	$ 7,041
Rogersville, Ala.	100,076	4,300	80,501	18.72	11,348		8,227
Phoenix, Ariz.	274,000	10,000	230,600	23.06	38,400	gift	5,000
Phoenix, Ariz.	224,000	6,600	142,000	21.52	27,000	$ 33,200	21,800
Bryant, Ark.	37,500	2,304	27,900	12.12	2,077	5,000	2,523
Jacksonville, Ark.	214,360	10,000	152,860	15.29	18,641	30,000	12,859
Baldwin Park, Calif.	486,625	15,320	344,971	22.52	56,808	49,004	35,841
Burney, Calif.	49,525	2,200	37,057	16.84	5,723	owned	5,745
Cudahy, Calif.	17,514	4,500	NA	NA	17,514	NA	NA
Diamond Bar, Calif.	14,500	2,400	NA	NA	14,500	NA	NA
La Puente, Calif.	388,163	10,458	240,669	23.01	39,599	70,875	37,020
Montebello, Calif.	18,776	5,500	NA	NA	18,776	NA	NA
Orange, Calif.	260,000	7,600	155,000	20.39	55,000	40,000	10,000
San Diego, Calif.	184,256	5,200	136,967	26.34	6,645	23,232	17,412
San Jose, Calif.	251,368	9,080	167,272	18.40	25,994	16,000	42,102
San Lorenzo, Calif.	401,000	11,970	327,810	27.38	47,000	gift	26,190
Santa Rosa, Calif.	270,400	7,840	197,000	25.12	14,700	36,300	22,400
Wasco, Calif.	123,038	4,400	95,895	21.79	12,463	5,680	14,000
Whittier, Calif.	596,122	10,404	273,453	26.28	43,349	279,320	33,798
Woodside, Calif.	197,091	4,500	99,643	22.14	23,650	40,000	33,798
Yucaipa, Calif.	155,304	8,284	128,717	15.53	7,542	owned	19,045
Boulder, Colo.	124,316	4,400	85,316	19.39	13,000	22,000	4,000
Jefferson Co., Colo.	259,765	11,605	210,781	18.16	39,235	gift	9,749
Fairfield, Conn.	541,400	15,455	451,300	29.20	34,900	owned	55,200
New Haven, Conn.	329,000	7,500	221,775	29.56	30,976	45,142	31,107

New Branches Constructed from July 1, 1968 to June 30, 1969

Community	Project Cost	Bldg. Area	Constr. Cost	Sq.Foot Cost	Equip. Cost	Site Cost	Other Costs
Coral Gables, Fla.	$ 1,050,500	$28,446	$746,105	$26.22	$63,972	$107,000	$133,423
Lehigh Acres, Fla.	69,947	3,024	45,826	15.10	9,139	10,000	4,982
Ormond Beach, Fla.	116,715	7,500	100,000	13.13	15,215		1,500
Tampa, Fla.	210,000	7,300	153,000	20.95	22,000	19,450	15,550
Winter Garden, Fla.	145,898	5,152	96,220	18.68	14,855	24,000	10,823
Riverdale, Ga.	150,852	6,400	115,500	18.05	8,317	17,465	9,570
Chicago, Ill.	452,053	13,715	319,422	23.29	44,318	61,887	26,326
Evansville, Ind.	279,970	10,500	205,556	19.58	27,654	22,650	24,110
Hobert, Ind.	276,908	10,000	223,340	22.33	15,000	34,948	3,620
Sioux City, Iowa	338,649	12,000	293,065	26.14	25,000	owned	20,584
Roeland Park, Ka.	436,153	16,554	356,420	21.54	45,873	owned	33,860
Chauvin, La.	32,225	1,456	26,700	18.34	5,525		
Farmerville, La.	167,393	6,886	108,772	15.79	28,004	21,000	9,617
Franklinton, La.	192,451	7,876	143,016	18.15	16,679	22,000	10,756
Houma, La.	325,000	11,972	199,162	16.64	30,000	60,000	35,838
New Orleans, La.	553,880	13,500	462,657	34.27	55,262	owned	39,961
Baltimore Co., Md.	76,000	20,000			76,000	lease	
Bowie, Md.	1,005,656	42,200	851,122	20.16	102,844	gift	51,690
Burnie, Md.	757,227	20,200	463,400		63,869	38,279	191,679
Hancock, Md.	47,360	2,200	36,383	16.53	7,438	gift	3,539
Kensington, Md.	502,450	16,896	297,000	17.58	52,250	147,200	6,000
Odenton, Md.	330,107	9,381	257,000	27.39	21,700	26,107	25,300
Grand Rapids, Mich.	104,325	5,500	88,325	16.06	16,000		
Biloxi, Miss.	163,153	7,067	136,994	19.38	24,920	1	1,238
Sumner, Miss.	13,423	792	11,254	14.21	1,865	owned	304
Webb, Miss.	13,795	792	11,254	13.21	1,865	gift	676

East Prairie, Mo.	61,133	1,848	46,136	24.96	5,920	gift	9,076
Port Reading, N. J.	204,728	4,500	172,149	38.25	27,538	gift	41,041
Bronx, N. Y.	467,812	16,524	440,532	26.66		owned	27,280
Bronx, N. Y.	453,123	7,630	320,160	41.96	39,263	55,200	38,500
Brooklyn, N. Y.	582,295	7,550	306,584	40.60	45,000	22,711	208,000
Brooklyn, N. Y.	550,197	7,601	345,857	45.50	31,340	55,000	118,000
Honeoye, N. Y.	53,677	2,500	46,000	18.40	2,700	1,700	3,277
Manhattan, N. Y.	479,111	8,410	398,404	47.37	41,820	owned	38,887
Queens, N. Y.	362,547	5,600	283,149	50.02	25,398	4,150	49,850
Queens, N. Y.	379,415	7,500	332,798	44.36	28,996	1,621	16,000
Queens, N. Y.	373,432	7,510	310,999	41.41	29,963	14,970	17,500
Rochester, N. Y.	462,940	16,405	373,658	22.77	45,480	18,400	25,402
Carthage, No. Car.	163,158	6,900	124,601	18.06	20,459	10,010	8,088
Siler City, No. Car.	209,852	7,300	123,067	16.86	31,285	35,000	20,500
Youngstown, Ohio	172,819	5,040	120,579	23.92	20,558	22,350	9,332
Pateau, Okla.	155,770	7,000	139,200	19.88	6,510	gift	10,060
Glenside, Pa.	458,666	9,300	338,700	36.81	37,735	49,899	32,332
Philadelphia, Pa.	463,825	12,518	381,487	30.47	25,959	25,863	30,516
Philadelphia, Pa.	453,677	11,407	371,732	32.59	21,177	25,299	29,469
Pittsburgh, Pa.	1,036,059	33,000	837,347	25.37	70,775	65,136	62,801
Charleston, So. Car.	193,935	6,520	117,365	18.00	25,258	38,160	13,152
Seneca, So. Car.	99,952	4,940	73,797	14.93	11,872	7,581	6,702
Nashville, Tenn.	233,000	8,000	172,953	21.60	14,701		45,346
Amarillo, Texas	289,017	11,314	205,790	18.18	46,500	4,061	32,666
Houston, Texas	173,374	5,700	125,000	21.96	12,000	27,624	8,750
Houston, Texas	264,009	9,642	201,800	20.92	36,000	12,609	13,600
Houston, Texas	295,550	9,000	199,400	22.16	45,000	40,500	10,650
Houston, Texas	105,135	5,000	77,910	15.58	14,702	gift	12,523
San Antonio, Texas	165,947	5,900	137,000	23.22	16,194	12,753	
San Antonio, Texas	153,369	5,800	137,845	23.76	15,524	gift	
San Antonio, Texas	181,018	8,108	161,595	19.93	19,423	gift	

New Branches Constructed from July 1, 1968 to June 30, 1969

Community	Project Cost	Bldg. Area	Construc. Cost	Sq. Foot Cost	Equip. Cost	Site Cost	Other Costs
Luray, Va.	76,814	3,000	50,000	16.66	10,000	16,814	
Norfolk, Va.	271,108	7,300	219,957	30.13	36,029		15,122
Virginia Beach, Va.	161,075	6,000	112,945	18.82	32,709	8,482	6,939
Bothell, Wash.	334,323	9,100	255,637	28.09	22,311	20,000	36,375
Omak, Wash.	150,452	5,300	114,309	21.57	14,226	10,000	11,917
Seattle, Wash.	271,556	7,600	210,161	27.65	20,582	gift	40,812
So. Charleston, W. Va.	348,756	10,426	202,220	19.39	59,522	71,650	15,364
Branches Enlarged and Remodeled							
Grossett, Ark.	50,000	3,678	41,030	11.16	4,367	gift	4,603
Smackover, Ark.	36,052	2,200	12,905	5.87	8,300	13,000	1,847
Albany, Ga.	11,034	4,500	9,890	2.20		owned	1,144
Thomasville, Ga.	54,400	2,338	46,000	19.67	8,000	owned	400
Ida Twp., Mich.	1,850	324	1,230	3.79	620	owned	
Taylor, Mich.	169,829	4,400	144,829	32.91		owned	
Zeeland, Mich.	7,920	1,625	4,414	2.71	3,506	25,000	
Barker, N. Y.	11,200	1,200	11,200	9.33		owned	
Abbeville, So. Car.	58,823	3,876	45,371	11.71	4,724	gift	8,728
Mercer Island, Wash.	170,828	8,490	104,600	12.32	13,460	14,800	37,968
Port Orchard, Wash.	27,917	1,275	27,885	21.87		owned	32

The following list of ten branches built in Southern California between 1967 and 1969 illustrates costs in an area in which labor costs are among the highest in the nation. Costs would be relatively lower in most other sections. Note the size of the 1969 Los Cerritos Branch of the Los Angeles County Free Library, 39,000 square feet, making it one of the very large branches in the U.S.

Kern Co. Free Library
Wasco Branch	1968	4,416 sq. ft.	$ 95,500

Los Angeles County Free Library
Baldwin Park	1969	16,000 sq. ft.	$337,521
East Los Angeles	1967	15,455 sq. ft.	462,750
Los Cerritos	1969	39,000 sq. ft.	1,379,134
Pico Rivera	1969	6,910 sq. ft.	177,640

Orange Public Library
Taft Branch	1969	7,874 sq. ft.	255,145

San Bernardino County Free Library
H. M. Rowe Branch	1968	6,000 sq. ft.	87,868

San Bernardino County Free Library
Yucaipa Branch	1969	7,500 sq. ft.	124,595

San Diego County Free Library
Oak Park Branch	1969	5,200 sq. ft.	161,000

Whittier Public Library
Whitwood Branch	1969	10,404 sq. ft.	500,000

Here are estimated percentages of building costs which may be taken as a rough guide. The one list affords a flat estimate of division of costs; the other provides a range:

General construction	57%	General construction	60-65%
Lighting, heating, air conditioning, and plumbing	13%	Electrical wiring and fixtures	7-11%
Movable equipment and built-in shelving	20%	Heating and air conditioning	10-14%
Architect's fees	8%	Architect's fees	6-10%
Unallocated for unexpected extras	2%	Plumbing and plumbing fixtures	2- 7%
	100%		

Since items are combined differently in the above lists percentages differ. Plumbing and plumbing fixtures will be proportionately higher for small buildings than for large. Architectural fees will vary, depending upon the amount of supervision of construction to be done by the architect, the amount of detailed design, and whether the architect is involved in the design and selection of furnishings and equipment.[2] It is wise to avoid division of responsibility whenever possible and to have the entire project under the direction of the architect. The only departure from this principle may be in the matter of landscaping, since a specialist in this field can usually do a better job.

Since landscaping costs are not mentioned in the above lists, it is assumed they are included under general construction or unallocated funds. Usually, however, they are included as a separate item. Paving or blacktopping the parking area must also be considered, unless the branch is to be located in a shopping center.

Based on the cost figures given in the Dec. 1, 1969, Library Journal,[1] there is considerable variation in average building costs in the various sections of the United States. These averages within the number of cases included in each are as follows:

1968-69 Fiscal Year

Northwest states	-	$25.77 per square foot
Southeast states	-	19.32 per square foot
Middle states	-	20.38 per square foot (belt extending north and south)
Southwest states	-	21.66 per square foot
Northeast states	-	32.08 per square foot

All costs given in this chapter should be revised upwards by the reader on the basis of from 10-12% per year for each year after the 1968-69 fiscal year that the inflationary upward spiral continues.

As a general rule the architect will be able to supply fairly accurate cost estimates to be used before bids can be obtained. Sometimes, however, it is necessary to have approximate cost estimates before an architect is hired or available. Cost factors that will influence the estimate to be made by the library administration, library board, and city or county officials are:

    1. Size of building.

    2. Style of architecture.

    3. Materials used, whether simple and inexpensive or lavish and rare.

    4. Amount of art work or sculpture, other "extras."

    5. Whether carpeted.

6. Whether air-conditioned.

7. Size of grounds and amount of landscaping proposed. [3]

Usually, detailed cost estimates on the building will not be required before acquisition of a site, but if the site is to be included in the cost estimates, it should be remembered that it is often necessary to pay one-third to one-half as much for the land as for the construction of the building.

Even if the annual operating cost of the branch is assumed to be only one-fourth of the cost of the building, the operation of the library service within 20 years will have been five times the cost of the building. In view of this it becomes a waste of community resources to operate a branch on an inferior site. [3]

It is important to be able to estimate accurately costs of construction versus lease-purchase plans or straight rental of quarters, to be able to figure costs of furnishings and equipment, and to estimate annual operational costs once the branch is established. The latter will pose a considerable problem, since the exact amount of use cannot be determined accurately in advance, but careful study of the area to be served and experience in other branches will provide some guidelines. The main point is that the operational budget should be elastic enough to allow for the unexpected. Among the unexpected factors which may not be determined in advance are emergency breakdowns in new equipment (these may or may not be covered by guarantees or contractor); how well the air conditioning and heating equipment will function and at what monthly average cost; and much greater volume of use than expected, requiring more personnel, more supplies, and more services from the central library.

Under-estimating of branch building costs, furnishings, equipment, and architect's fees can result in one or more of the following, according to Keyes D. Metcalf:

1. The whole project may have to be postponed or given up entirely.

2. The size of the building may have to be reduced so that it is inadequate from the day it is finished.

3. The quality of construction may be compromised, with

unfortunate results and increased maintenance costs.

    4. Considerable areas may be left unfinished, meaning that a large percentage of the construction cost was involved with no corresponding usable space. [4]

    One of the mistakes often made in long-range financial planning, where the construction of several branches is included over a period of from five to twenty years, is not allowing enough increment to take care of increasing costs from year to year. Although there is a remote possibility that costs can drop in case of an economic recession, the chances are much greater that they will increase.

    Except in the case of large city or regional systems where huge bond issues are passed to permit construction of branches in rapid succession, using a 10-12% annual cost of building increase is the only safe way to assure adequacy of long-term financing. If Library Journal continues to present an annual survey of building costs like these first excellent compilations, libraries everywhere will have facts upon which to base cost trends and will not have to rely upon a 5 per cent assumed increase. The Architectural Record also publishes a monthly tabulation of average building costs throughout the country for several types of building construction. Although not confined to libraries, this data may offer help in determining cost trends in any given area.

    Assuming that the preliminary building program for a new branch has been completed and careful cost estimates made, how shall construction be financed?

    In planning for branches, the plans can be based on the known available funds. However, it is preferable to plan for actual needs, and to try to justify whatever additional money may be required. The plans can always be scaled down if necessary, but the presentation of an attractive, functional plan to officials and public may sometimes open doors to extra financing such as a memorial gift.

    The cost analysis can be made by the architect and planning team after the plans have been approved. It is extremely important to have a graphic architectural drawing, a model, and a sample floor plan as selling points if there is to be a bond issue before the voters. [5]

   If a site has not yet been selected and its cost is to be included in the bond issue, be sure to allow for appraisal fees, value of the land, brokerage fees, surveying, subsurface testing (if unusual conditions are likely to occur), and utility extensions or relocations, such as water lines, sewers, and electrical equipment. If the site has been selected, most of these costs can be accurately determined. [5]

   It is customary and wise to add about 10% of total construction costs as a contingency fund to cover unforeseen requirements, changes in plans at the last minute, and costs which run higher than estimates. [5]

   Sources of building funds vary from state to state and are governed by state statutes. The local government usually has the delegated authority for public financing. The constitution or statutes of the individual states will determine, for example, the amount of bonding power. [6]

   1. Bond issues. This is the most common source of funds, the bonds being retired over a long period by an increase in property taxes. The bonding law must be strictly followed so that the sale of bonds can be accomplished without the delay of court cases. A bond issue becomes a public debt with attendant interest costs. [6]

   The pros and cons of including libraries in general bond issues or "package deals" which include other civic improvements have often been debated. If the other issues accompanying the library project are popular the library item may ride the wave of such popularity and have a better chance of passing. On the other hand, recent trends have been to vote down bond issues calling for large expenditures in some areas, in which case a bond issue for library development alone might well have a better chance.

   The attitude of a newspaper or newspapers can make or break a bond issue's success. A special problem that can arise with branch financing is that if a branch program is just beginning or if there are large areas of a city or county without branch service, each unserved area feels that it should be the one to have the first branch, even though surveys may have indicated otherwise.

For example, if a first branch is proposed for the northeast section of a city, residents of that section may vote for it overwhelmingly, but if the residents of the other three sections resent this choice of location or feel the issue is of little interest to them, the proposition may go down to defeat. For this reason, proposing a program of several branches in various parts of city or county may be more likely to succeed, even though it involves a great deal more money.

To succeed, even in prosperous times, a bond issue must be preceded by intensive campaigning, publicity to inform and persuade and the cooperation of and endorsement of many organizations. Very large bond issues for library construction of branches have been passed in recent years in King County, Washington (King County Library, Seattle); in Los Angeles (Los Angeles Public Library), and Lake County, Indiana (Lake County Library, Griffith).

2. Special Tax: The next most common method of financing library construction is the special library building tax, generally authorized and levied in the same manner as the library's operating tax. In some cases it is limited as to rate as well as to the length of time it can be in effect. The main objection to this method is that the yield cannot be totally realized until the very end of the special taxing period. Unless the assessed valuation of the property against which the tax is applied keeps rising gradually, rising construction costs could make the originally-estimated yield inadequate, especially if there is rising demand from a growing populace. [6] This type of tax often has to be voted upon by the people in order to increase a millage rate limited or set by a city charter. Thus, like a bond issue, it may require an intensive pre-vote campaign to be successful.

3. Accumulation from current operating funds: In a few states it is possible to save and use current unused operational funds toward the cost of a building. Both library and finance authorities are apt to disapprove of this method because it violates

the principle of public finance that requires each class of expenditure to be separately authorized. It is a very slow method, and costs tend to rise to such an extent while the fund is accumulating that there may be only enough to purchase a site or remodel an old building when the need becomes acute. [6] There is also the disadvantage that a librarian and Board may skimp on the current service program in order to save money for building.

4. Capital Improvement Fund: Most cities or counties of any size include a rather large capital improvement section in their annual budgets. If the needs of the library system for expansion through branch construction have been sufficiently impressed upon the citizenry and public officials, items for branch sites or construction, furnishings, and equipment can be included in the general capital improvement program and passed as a part of the annual budget decided by the appropriating body. If the city council or county board of commissioners are sympathetic to library requirements, this is often the least complicated method of securing funds.

5. Memorials and bequests: Memorial gifts of funds for a building and bequests through wills are another common source. However, only those gifts which do not carry restrictive stipulations that would hamper proper and adequate service should be accepted. It is common practice to name a branch given in honor of some individual according to the wishes of the donor.

Gifts have become more common in these days of high income taxes, for gifts to non-profit public institutions such as schools and libraries are tax deductible. Attractive leaflets for distribution to lawyers and to the general public have been devised by many libraries. They serve as reminders to people who might not otherwise think of libraries, and they may aid lawyers in counseling clients who are making their wills or seeking tax shelters.

Another form of gift from a private individual or corporation is that of land for a site or donation of free rent in a shopping center. Donation of land is not uncommon; donation of free space or land from a corporation or shopping center developer does not happen often, but it has happened several times in recent years. It would indicate that such donors consider the addition of a branch library to their commercial complex to be an asset.

Forsyth County Public Library System, Winston-Salem, North Carolina, built one branch within the past three years on property donated by the developer. Greenville County Library, Greenville, South Carolina, acquired its Fountain Inn Branch in this manner. When the Friends of the Library sought funds throughout the community they approached one of the local industries, and the industrial firm decided to present a building to the town on a town-owned site. In Fullerton, California, in the early 60's, a beautiful $550,000 branch building was built by the Hunt Foods Foundation. It surpasses the main library in luxury and general appearance.

There have been many examples of community effort in raising money or materials, time, and labor to build branches in smaller communities. The Jaycees in Simpsonville, South Carolina (Greenville County Library System) became interested in helping and secured all of a building, only half of which had previously been occupied by the library. The Jaycees raised funds to remodel and voluntarily helped with the work. The Garden Club sponsored the landscaping. On May 5, 1968, the opening was held and the whole community visited the library. This is a good example of community cooperation.

One unusual source of financing was when the Richfield, Minnesota, city council unanimously voted $100,000 for the construction of a library building, the funds to be appropriated from profits of the municipal liquor store. The Los Angeles Building standards for new branches were used as criteria, and final total costs came to $151,263 for a one-story and basement building with 6300 square feet on each level. The basement was to be finished later for a civic meeting room. [7]

A need for branch library expansion and a lack of public funds motivated the Wichita City Library Board of Directors to send out a questionnaire[8] to 126 libraries, to see if private funds have ever been used for branch library expansion and initiation; 93 libraries replied.

Figure 62.   Hunts Food Foundation Library, Fullerton, California

This 10,000 square foot branch of the Fullerton Public Library was built as the gift of the Hunts Food Foundation, a Fullerton Industry. The amount of $485,000 contributed by the Hunt Foundation covered full costs of design and construction of the library building, three acres of land and part of the costs for landscaping and furnishings. $175,000 was for paving and parking area. The building was dedicated Sept. 12, 1962.

Figure 63. Main Reading Room, Hunts Food Foundation Library Branch of the Fullerton Public Library, Fullerton, California

Note generous bulletin board area at top of each section of low shelving. There is an attractive all-purpose meeting and exhibit room included in this building.

The Board was most interested in examples of branch location and expansion in shopping centers. The size of the cities replying varied from 20,000 population in Rutland, Vermont, to approximatel 2,800,000 in Los Angeles. Later, a follow-up questionnaire was sent to the 34 libraries which rented in shopping centers. It contained nine questions designed to find out whether a branch library is regarded by business men as a desirable agency which is instrumental in bringing business to a shopping center. Here were the results:

1. Five libraries responded that store spaces had been donated in shopping centers by the promoters. Four of these said the promoters had donated space separate from the store groupings.

2. A savings and loan association in Seattle, Washington, built a branch for the Seattle Public Library. The library pays $250 a month rent.

3. Developers built a 3500 square foot branch for Detroit in 1947.

4. Private interests built a branch for the Orange County, California, Library in Westminster, following the library's specifications.

5. Two sites, valued at $40,000 each were given to the El Paso Public Library.

6. In 3 of the 5 shopping centers space was donated through the action of the merchants in the shopping area.

7. A shopping center developer in Richmond, Virginia, donated 42,000 square feet to the library.

8. Philadelphia bought through the Redevelopment Authority 6000 square feet for half the open market value.

9. Four libraries reported being given store space for one or more years free, then being charged rent: Atlanta, Georgia, and Springfield, Missouri, 10 years each; Austin, Texas, partially free rent; and Newark, New Jersey, free rent in two department stores.

The second question asked was: "If you rent store space in shopping areas, what is your rent and for what square footage?"

Thirty-four libraries rented space in shopping centers. The
average rent per square foot for the country as a whole and for
certain geographical sections was as follows in 1964 (Increase by
5 to 10% for 1969):

```
United States as a whole    --    $1.58 per square foot
New England--Insufficient data
Middle Atlantic States      --    $1.75 per square foot
South                       --    $1.96 per square foot
Midwest                     --    $1.48 per square foot
Southwest                   --    $1.60 per square foot
Rocky Mountains--Insufficient data
Pacific Coast               --    $1.57 per square foot
```

The next question, "How many branch libraries do you have
as a result of a financial gift?" revealed that 40 of the 93 reporting libraries had received branch gifts, in whole or in part. When
asked whether the gift came from an individual, family, mercantile,
or industrial corporation, the respondents replied that the Andrew
Carnegie foundation had given the most, as might be expected, 81
branch libraries. However, there was a total of 141 gifts, many
cities having received more than one donation. Families made
bequests for 20 branches; individuals for 14; industrial corporations
for 6; mercantile corporations for 3; and other sources, such as
school boards, government agencies, and neighborhoods, 17. The
average amount of such gifts was over $61,000. Twenty-one of
the libraries receiving gifts said they had named or would name
the libraries after the donors.

As a result of the Wichita survey a property owner offered
to build the library a branch building at square foot cost, about
70¢ less than they were then paying per square foot for a branch
in that part of the city. Wichita's first new branch in seven years
began operation in January, 1963, in rented quarters in the largest
shopping center in Southwest Wichita. It was made possible through
joint efforts of the shopping area owners, other tenants of the
center, and interested residents, including strong support from
Parent-Teacher groups. The center owners are giving the branch
a reduced rent plus free utilities and have offered to make land
available at a below-market price when the time comes for the

branch to be enlarged. Another property owner offered the library
a piece of land for $5000 less than he is asking commercially,
and merchants of a shopping area in a nearby annexed area of
Wichita gave free utilities for the bookmobile and expressed an
interest in having a branch library located there.

Andrew Geddes, writing of the experience of the Queens-
borough, New York, Public Library in meeting its housing
problems,[9] states that New York City had a tremendous building
backlog after World War II, which placed a severe strain on the
city's capital budget program. Beyond that, however, some people questioned placing substantial amounts of money in city-owned
branches which might face obsolescence and loss of use, as had
earlier Carnegie buildings. The city wanted to interest private
investors in constructing buildings which the library would occupy
on long-term leases. They realized the buildings had to be of a
type readily convertible to commercial use. To make the program
financially possible the costs of design and construction could not
approach those of a city-owned agency.

Many people feared that the program would lead to more
inadequate store-type buildings, but this has not been the case.
Instead, the program has made the system a vital part of the
borough and has enabled it to keep up with population increase.
Such a plan also allows for much flexibility, the keynote of today's
service. The plan works, as outlined by Mr. Geddes, in two
ways:

> (1) Approach the owner of a desirable site and suggest
> he construct a building according to library specifica-
> tions. After receiving the "specs" and determining
> costs, the owner submits a proposed rental charge and
> a suggested lease period--usually 15 or 20 years, with
> renewal options. This proposal is referred to the city
> and the appropriate departments negotiate with the owner
> on final terms. After agreement is reached, the owner
> constructs the building to fit requirements.
>
> (2) Find a suitable vacant store in a shopping area. The
> library, owner, and the city reach an agreement on
> suitable terms, and the owner remodels the quarters to
> fit requirements.

Both methods were found to be highly satisfactory. These are
2000 to 8000 square foot branches. Nine branch libraries so relocated up to 1961 each had at least a 40% increase in use, with
some having more than 100% increase. Advantages of the lease
plan as Mr. Geddes sees it are:

1. Economy of full-branch service;
2. Faster expansion rate for population increase;
3. Location of branches at points of maximum convenience;
4. Flexibility to relocate any agency if things change. [9]

Federal Funds:

After the Library Services Act of 1956 broadened in 1964 to
become the Library Services and Construction Act, federal appropriations became an important source of building funds for both
central buildings and branches. State agencies administered the
federal money and libraries or library systems applying for aid
were required to meet certain conditions, including partial local
funding. Title I of LSCA provided for new or extended services;
Title II for building construction.

Since the availability of federal funds varies from year to
year as laws, budgets, and appropriations change, it is impossible
to summarize in a volume of this kind the amounts or kinds of
funds available at time of publication. In April, 1969, President
Nixon's budget sent to Congress contained drastic cuts in library
programs, including no funding at all for Title II of the Library
Services and Construction Act (the building funds).

Major cuts in the Elementary and Secondary Education Act
funds, which appear to be inevitable, may return an insurmountable
burden of student use to the public library systems and their
branches.

There are other government programs which have been used
by a few communities in the past to help build libraries. These
included the Public Facilities Loan Program, 1962, which made it

possible for a community with a sound financial base to sell general bonds at a reasonable interest rate. The Accelerated Public Works Program, another possibility, provided 50% of the cost of a proposed project if the local community would finance the other 50% without too much delay. Since the purpose of the Accelerated Public Works Program was to provide employment at the local level, a condition was that the project must start construction within 120 days after receipt of funds.

Programs for the disadvantaged and those with language difficulties have provided funds for outreach activities, often through branches, or for setting up specialized libraries such as the frequently-cited Latin American Library of the Oakland Public Library System. Interested librarians should obtain the latest facts and figures, and information as to the availability of programs, from their state library agencies, working with and through their own system administrators. Germaine Krettek's "Washington Report" in the A. L. A. Bulletin serves to keep the library world up to date on federal bills and appropriations affecting libraries.

There are a few local communities where there is much resistance to the use of federal or state aid to libraries. One argument that might move such objectors is to point out that the money has already been appropriated and will be spent by other communities. The reluctant community officials or library boards might as well have their share of such funds since their state and federal taxes will be used to help support the program whether they like it or not.

Certain less obvious programs such as the Economic Opportunity Act, the Appalachian Program, and the Older Americans Act for senior citizens offer possibilities for supplementing branch personnel and development of special programs and collections for the aged. These programs are usually worked out in cooperation with other community agencies through the central headquarters of the library system. The nine regional offices of the Department of Health Education and Welfare, Library Services and Educational Facilities, Division of Education, are a good source of information on federal programs, in addition to the state library agencies.

State Funds:

Many states now have state aid for libraries in one form or another, a number of such programs having developed out of the necessity for matching funds under the Library Services Act and its successor. Each state agency makes its own libraries fully aware of these possibilities.

Many branches have been and are being built with the aid of state and federal moneys. The following breakdown for sources of building funds used in 1968-69 was reported by Hoyt Galvin:[10]

Federal funds	$21,917,716.
State funds	769,004.
Local funds	58,973,470.
Gift funds	4,154,104.
Total	$85,814,294.

Thus, while the largest single source of funds was still local, the Library Services and Construction Act accounted for nearly one-quarter of the total.

Leasing:

The Baltimore County Public Library now leases ten of its sixteen branches. Some buildings presently leased are the result of immediate branch needs in excess of the County's ability to raise capital funds through bond issues due to an authorized debt ceiling; however, such funds have been more available recently because of less demand for them by the schools.

Four of these leased facilities were designed and constructed originally as libraries. One of the four, Pikesville, was built as a community library and health center by a local non-profit holding corporation. After a number of years the branch is now inadequate in every way, needing a 7,000 square foot addition and extensive renovation if it is to continue service as an effective library. Remodeling will take place shortly after the building is given to the county by its present owners.

Another leased branch is both a community library and health center. The library's 8,000 square feet is a pleasant, well-lighted and adequately arranged branch with a meeting room. The branch is now leased at a square foot cost of $1.90 per year. The contract is for ten years with a five-year option for renewal. The library and county pay all taxes and maintain the building's interior. The combination of a library and health clinic has not interfered with library activities.

The Cockeysville Branch was originally leased as a 3,000 square foot library in 1961. The community grew rapidly and circulation rose by over 400%, making the branch very inadequate. A new lease was executed and an 8,000 square foot addition was constructed. Cockeysville is now one of Baltimore County's most pleasant branches featuring carpeting in all public areas, a meeting room and a large storage area. The new 15-year lease (with no renewal options) agrees to a yearly cost of $1.75 per square foot.

Figure 64:   Entrance and Building Front, Cockeysville Community Branch, Baltimore County Public Library, Towson, Md.

This is an 11,000 square foot branch, occupied on a 15-year lease with no renewal options at a yearly cost of $1.75 per square foot. It features carpets in all public areas, a meeting room, and a large storage area. Circulation has grown over 400% since 1961.

The Orange County (California) Public Library had 24 branches in 1968 but owned none. All were either built by the community where they are located or are leased. Lease arrangements vary according to size and location of the branch. Rental cost on the nine leases varied from $10 to $20 a square foot, and the leases were usually for five or ten year periods.

Lease-Purchase Plans:

The most ambitious leasing project of the Baltimore County Public Library involves a 20,000 square foot building recently constructed. This library, located in a shopping center, will be leased for a minimum of 25 years at an annual square foot cost of $2.20. The lease includes a renewal option for an additional 10, 15, or 25 years at a cost of $1.50 per square foot. The bonus of this lease, however, is the option to purchase the library at the end of the original lease period for $200,000. This provides the advantage of opening now a much needed facility that could not be built by the county for several more years, without the disadvantage of no tangible asset after the lease expires. The Baltimore County Library prefers to erect county-owned libraries but will certainly accept a leased facility when factors such as a changing community, unsettled traffic patterns, or the lack of capital funds present a problem.

Lease-purchase plans must necessarily include a long-term lease agreement with a private developer or corporation. The latter constructs a building, usually to the library's specifications, and then provides a lease at a figure which eventually permits the library, as a department of the city or county, to assume ownership. A rather unusual lease-back plan is that entered into by the New York Public Library and the Riverdale Neighborhood and Library Association for the construction of its Riverdale Branch.[11]

Robert L. Bien, architect for the building and a consultant to the New York Public Library, states that to relieve the New York Public and the City of New York of the expenditure of public funds, the Riverdale Neighborhood and Library Association purchased the land, using funds donated for the purpose by the

Figure 65. Riverdale Branch, New York Public Library

A beautiful branch built under a unique lease-purchase plan which will permit the library and the City of New York to assume ownership at the end of 20 years. This is an example of a branch planned to fit the attractive and scenic residential neighborhood which it serves. The Riverdale Neighborhood and Library Association assisted with the financing.

Photo: New York Public Library
Architect: Robert L. Bien, A.I.A.

Cleveland L. Dodge Foundation. The Association then arranged for a 20-year mortgage with the First National City Bank as trustees for certain pension funds, secured by the property and by the completely net lease from the New York Public Library. The bank also provided construction financing. The new building and land are leased to the New York Public Library for the 20-year period, at the end of which, the mortgage having been paid off and the cost of the project having been recovered by the Association, the library will assume ownership of both land and building. This form of financing is quite common in industry, but it is believed that this is the first time it has been used by two educational and civic organizations to accomplish a mutually desired objective.

Lease-purchase plans and straight long-term leases are used in a number of libraries throughout the country. This seems to be a growing trend, inasmuch as libraries desire branch locations in shopping centers and often can get such locations in no other way. The straight rental or lease arrangement has an advantage in a location which may change status and require a move later, or in an area where population is growing so rapidly that some sort of service is imperative but where finances do not permit immediate construction of a suitable branch. In such a case a short-term lease is preferable. Some cities or counties do not favor leasing because of the continuing cost over a long period and because advantage cannot be taken of construction aid from state and federal sources. Where a developer or private investor can be found who will build exactly the kind of building the library wants, usually of the type with potential for later conversion to other uses, the rent-lease plan is better than taking quarters already built but which are not particularly suitable for library use. The distinction should be clear between the lease-purchase plan which eventually means ownership of the property, and a straight rental or lease plan which does not carry such a provision.

In Roanoke, Virginia, a Long Range Development Plan prepared by the Roanoke Department of City Planning and the City Library Board showed comparative figures for construction versus leasing which gave a small financial edge to the rental plan. [12] Comparative costs of rented quarters and city-owned property revealed that the library could rent quarters for a medium-sized branch within a crossroads mall for $2,000 per year. By comparison, a building of 3,000-3,500 square feet would have cost $75,000 to build, plus maintenance costs of $300 per year over a 40-year period, for a total of $87,000. Renting quarters for the same period would cost $80,000 with all maintenance provided. Whether or not this is the case in other communities would depend upon the relative costs of land, building materials, labor costs, and architectural fees in relation to rental rates in the location being considered. Hoyt Galvin has this comment on renting: [13]

> We may have built our last branch library building.
> Since 1962 our expansion has been through renting space
> in shopping centers. The rental cost appears high on
> the surface, but it puts the library where the people are

going for food and fiber. We have had renewable five-
year leases. On April 22, 1968, we opened in a 4,200
square foot retail space in the Tryon Mall Shopping
Center. This will be our first experience in a mall-
type shopping center. The Chain Store Age, a bible of
the shopping center industry, indicates the shopping
center of the future is the mall type.

The disadvantage is that the annual rental cost keeps
space used to a minimum, but at the end of a lease
period the library can move if the shopping center is
not successful. I am convinced that a branch in a
shopping center will be successful if the shopping center
is successful. [13]

The cost figures on branch buildings which combine with
extension service headquarters and provide a base for bookmobile
service are more difficult to assess since fewer buildings of this
type are to be found. However, the 12,000 square foot John F.
Kennedy Branch of the Muncie, Indiana, Public Library, is one
example. It was built in 1964 at a cost of $146,000 for the
building and $20,000 for furniture and equipment. [14]

Some 5,000 square feet are branch area; 5,500, extension
headquarters; 1,500, bookmobile garage. The garage is so arranged that the two bookmobiles can drive in at one end and out
the other. [14] Since the building was completed in 1964, the figures
given here should be updated by adding approximately 5% per year
since that time. The exterior uses stone veneer over single concrete block construction. The interior has tile flooring, Estey
steel shelving, fluorescent lighting, and is completely air conditioned.

The Vista Branch of the San Diego County Library is
another combination of community branch and bookmobile headquarters. Detailed information concerning this excellent branch
can be secured from the San Diego County Library or from the
County Building Department, County Court House, San Diego.

In comparing building costs one encounters a lack of
standardization in reporting. One building's square foot cost may
include shelving; others do not. Air conditioning is included in
some totals and not in others. Carpeting is sometimes included
in the construction cost, sometimes in the furnishings and equipment total. Comparisons become almost meaningless unless

exactly the same items are included in cost tabulations.

Factors influencing costs are:

1.   Types of material used;

2.   Competition among contractors;

3.   Prevailing wage scales;

4.   Amount of construction going on in a particular area;

5.   Season of the year;

6.   Variations in costs of material based on availability and shipping costs;

7.   The complexity of the building (round or octagonal shapes, for example, are usually more expensive than a conventional rectangular or square building).

In his 1966 study, Design for Tomorrow,[15] Kenneth Shaffer recommended the following as an area or regional branch, with cost estimates, for Bridgeport, Connecticut.

> This regional branch (Northwest) will serve a total population, as of the 1960 census, of about 42,187 persons. This branch would supersede the present North Branch and should be programed for at least 40,000 volumes, with a multi-purpose room seating at least 120, and with a bookmobile service facility sufficiently generous to provide docks for two bookmobiles and a light truck. The bookmobile facility should include space for a bookmobile collection no less than from 20,000 to 25,000 volumes plus necessary working areas. The following tables estimate the necessary size of this building and, in terms of present levels, an estimate of its cost.
>
> Estimate of size of building
>
> | | |
> |---|---|
> | Entrance and control | 1,000 sq. ft. |
> | Adult books & reading (25,000 vols.) | 5,300 |
> | Children's books and reading | |
> | (15,000 vols.) | 3,000 |
> | Multipurpose room | 1,200 |
> | Work, staff, and office areas | 2,000 |
> | Utility space | 500 |
> | Bookmobile service | |
> | Docks for 2 bookmobiles & truck | 1,300 |
> | Bookstock & working area | |
> | (20,000 - 25,000 vols.) | 2,500 |
> | | 16,800 sq. ft. |

Estimate of costs

Cost of site & site preparation	$ 50,000
Construction of 16,000 sq. ft. at $23.	386,400
Air conditioning (10%)	38,640
Furnishings & equipment (15%)	57,960
Contingency	30,000
	$563,000

It should be noted that the cost of site and site preparation is a general estimate and in no way should be considered as a precise indication of the value of prime
business real estate. (Bridgeport, Conn.)[15]

Note also that there is a sizeable amount allowed for a contingency fund. This is a necessity, for there are always unexpected items, or last-minute changes. The latter, of course, should
be held to a minimum, and avoided altogether if possible.

Operational Costs:

To ask "What is the annual cost of operation for a branch?"
is like asking "How large is a dog?" There are more than a
score of factors which will influence costs. All of these should be
taken into consideration when trying to work out tentative operational costs for a new branch. If the new building is in a system
which has other fairly new branches of similar size, equipment,
and circulation load, there is little problem, since a basis of comparison is available. The following will influence costs:

I.   Physical size of branch. Affects:
     a. Heating and air conditioning cost. Electricity and
        gas bills.
     b. Floor maintenance.
     c. Janitorial labor.
     d. Number of staff required for supervision of public
        areas.
     e. Exterior maintenance costs.
     f. Cost of janitor supplies.

II. Anticipated circulation. Affects:
     1. Number of staff required. Part-time hours for
        paging, etc.
     2. Library supplies needed
     3. Size of book budget, periodical, and audio visual
        materials budgets.

III. Whether or not a meeting or all-purpose room is
     included affects:
1. Utility costs.
2. Repair and maintenance of equipment such as pro-
     jectors, cooking range, refrigerator, public
     address system, etc.
3. Janitorial labor costs for cleanups after meetings
     and other activities.

IV. Anticipated rate of book loss if no security system
     is installed, or in spite of it. Affects:
1. Amount of book budget allocated for replacements of
     standard titles, missing magazines, other
     materials.

V. Size of building site. Affects:
1. Water bill.
2. Labor costs for janitor or gardener.

VI. Whether certain services not included in the annual
     budget are provided by the city or county. These
     could be grounds care by the park department,
     custodial service by a central public works depart-
     ment, utilities, or general maintenance if such ser-
     vices are included as a part of an annual rent paid
     from the library system budget to the department
     providing the special services.

VII. Amount of glass in the building. Affects:
1. Heating costs.
2. Need for drapes or shades.

VIII. Whether the floors will be carpeted or will have a tile
     finish. Affects:
1. Janitor labor cost.
2. Janitor supplies such as wax or cost of cleaning
     carpeting.

IX. Height of ceilings. Affects:
1. Heating costs.
2. Lighting costs. More illumination means higher
     electrical consumption.

X. Whether lighting is incandescent or fluorescent. Affects:
1. Electric bills.

XI. Whether there is an air-conditioning unit. Affects:
1. Gas or electric bills or both.
2. Cost of repairs for general maintenance and
     breakdown.

XII.   Type of furniture (material used). Affects:
   1. Cost of cleaning chair and davenport coverings. Cloth
       upholstery to be avoided. Naugehyde or similar
       covering easier to maintain.
   2. Maintenance of table tops. Formica or similar
       material preferred to plain wood, which is
       subject to more vandalism, requiring frequent
       refinishing.

XIII.   Type of landscaping: Number of trees, shrubs, and
       flowers. Affects:
   1. Gardener or custodial labor.
   2. Water bills.
   3. Costs of fertilizer and replacement of plants or
       shrubs as needed.

XIV.   Exterior building surface and roofing material. Affects:
   1. Painting, pointing of bricks, or cleaning of
       concrete.
   2. Staining or otherwise treating wood shingles, preserv-
       ing tar coating on flat roofs, or other roof
       maintenance.

XV.   Number and types of machines in operation, such as
       photocharging equipment, microfilm viewers,
       typewriters, adding machines, duplicating equipment,
       dispensing machines, projectors, etc. Affects:
   1. Servicing and repair costs.
   2. Replacement costs.

XVI.   Publicity activities and special activities such as
       celebration of National Library Week, booklists
       issued, Friends groups, entertainment activities
       requiring refreshments, special equipment for the
       blind, adult education activities sponsored by library,
       outside talks given by staff, etc. Affects:
   1. Possible fees for speakers.
   2. Travel mileage for staff.
   3. Printing costs.
   4. Staff time for sponsoring activities.

XVII.   Extent to which mending is done in the branch. Affects:
   1. Cost of mending supplies.
   2. Personnel cost for a part-time mender.

XVIII. Hours open. Affects:
   1. All building maintenance costs and utilities.
   2. Staffing cost.

XIX.   Other aspects of service, such as extent of reference
       service provided. Affects:
   1. Size of book budget.
   2. Staffing costs.

Here are some estimates of annual operational costs:

1) For an 8000 Square Foot Branch:

Staff:		1969		1974	
Branch librarian	$	8,500	$	10,000	
Prof. children's librarian		7,200		8,800	
Library clerk II		5,800		6,600	
2 clerk-typists at $5400		10,800		12,000	(at $6,000)
2 pages full time at $4000		8,000		10,000	
100 hours page help per month		2,100		2,900	(add 24 hrs. per mo.)
Substitute help		300		400	
Total staff		42,700		50,700	
Custodial service, 1/2 time		3,700		4,000	
Utilities		3,800		4,000	
Telephone		300		400	
Books and other library materials		10,000		12,000	
Magazines and newspapers		400		600	
Supplies and equipment		500		600	
		18,700		21,600	
Totals	$	61,400	$	72,300	

2) For a 12,000 Square Foot Branch:

Salaries - Library Staff	1969	1974	
Branch Librarian	8,500	10,500	
2 Professionals at $7,000	14,000	17,000	(2 at $8500)
6 Clerical employees at $4,000	24,000	28,800	(6 at $4800)
	46,500	56,300	

Library Materials			
Books - 3500 at 5.00	17,500	24,500	
Reference and Bibliography	1,500	2,500	
Magazines - 100 at 7.00	700	900	
Newspapers	120	200	
Pamphlets	500	650	
Binding	800	1,000	
Total	21,120	29,750	

Maintenance - Utilities - Supplies			
Maintenance - heating, lighting janitorial	14,500	16,000	
Telephone, supplies, postage	3,500	5,000	
Total	18,000	21,000	
Totals	$ 85,620	$ 107,050	

Here is the actual record of annual costs of operation for five branches of the Bridgeport, Connecticut, Public Library in 1965-66, as reported by Kenneth R. Shaffer in Design for Tomorrow, A Study of Extension Services of the Bridgeport Public Library:[15]

Size in Square feet	Branches	Salaries	Books, periodicals and binding	Other*	Total	Circ.	Cost per circ.
8,192	North	$ 28,913	5,663	3,180	37,756	135,930	.277
8,371	East	27,827	5,189	5,168	38,185	159,598	.239
10,938	Sanborn	20,485	3,662	5,644	29,793	59,890	.497
7,577	Newfield	20,260	4,204	4,333	28,797	62,736	.459
7,546	Black Rock	16,950	4,639	3,220	24,810	52,410	.473
	Hospitals	6,607	1,034	none	7,641	17,155	.445

*   Fuel, electricity, repairs, custodial, furnishings and equipment

All of these branches were built between the years 1918 and 1932.

Figuring costs in an established branch:

When questions arise as to whether any branch in a system
is producing enough circulation to justify its cost of operation, the
most significant figure will be the cost per book circulated. Regardless of other factors, this is one unit of cost that can be compared from branch to branch, if the comparison is based upon a
norm of efficiency and is made within one system where all factors
affecting costs will be similar. To compare cost per book circulated in a New York City branch with a similar figure in Salt
Lake City, Utah, or Seattle, Washington, would not be a fair comparison.

Experience has proved that the larger the branch and the
more adequate its services, the lower the circulation cost per book.
Thus it is poor economy to have many small branches. A small
building may be cheaper to build in the first place, but its lower
circulation will usually result in a higher operating cost per book
circulated, so that the actual cost to the taxpayer is in the long
run greater in terms of results.

A few years ago any figure in excess of 25¢ per book circulated reflected an inefficient operation. Today the figure is likely
to be much higher. It can be determined for any given system by
dividing the circulation of the three highest producing branches into
their annual total costs of operation.

In calculating staff provisions and costs the statistical
standards of the Public Library Association's Minimum Standards for
Public Library Systems, which comprised an addenda to the basic
standards and which were approved June 29, 1967, state that the
following provisions should be met:

> For every 6,000 population served there should be one
> professional and two clericals. A 35-hour work week,
> five days a week, should be a standard, but in no case
> should the work week exceed 40 hours. There should be
> no more than two evenings a week, no more than two
> Saturdays per month. A wage differential should be pro-
> vided for evening and Sunday schedules. There should
> be a minimum vacation of 20 working days vacation for
> professional staff and 10 working days for clerical staff,
> with recognition of longevity in service by increase in
> vacation allowance. A three months' sabbatical or leave

with pay is recommended for professional staff for every
five years of satisfactory service.[16]

The committee which produced the statistical standards recognized the need to identify the subprofessional role, but was unable
to suggest a ratio between professional and subprofessional.   It
recommended a study to establish the optimum ratio for such staffing for various types and sizes of libraries.[16]

Comparison of costs of two extension patterns:

In comparing the traditional urban pattern of one central
library and a good many small and medium-sized branches spaced
fairly close together, with the plan of a few large area branches
plus a network of small reading centers, Leonard Grundt,[17]
comments:

> Estimated cost figures indicated that the establishment
> of a regional library system with a few large regional
> libraries to serve all age groups (but primarily adults
> and young adults) and many small neighborhood libraries
> to serve primarily children, would have made possible
> adequate service to all age groups at a lower cost than
> was possible with an adequate traditional branch system.
> Each regional library would have had 15,500 square feet
> of floor space, seats for 100 adults and young adults,
> seats for 50 juveniles, a meeting room, a book stock of
> 95,000 adult and Y.A. titles, 15,000 titles for children;
> a staff of four professionals and 5.5 non-professionals.
>
> Each neighborhood library would have had 3,500 square
> feet of floor space, seats for 50 children and 10 adults
> and young adults, a meeting room, a book stock of
> 12,000 children's volumes and 3,000 adult and young adult,
> a staff of one professional and two non-professionals. A
> regional library network of this kind with 27 outlets
> would have been about $6,000,000 less costly than to
> establish an adequate traditional branch system with the
> same number of units.[17]

Also considered must be operating costs.   To operate the
regional system it was estimated that an annual expenditure of
about $1,058,000 would be required.   To operate the same number
of units in the traditional branch system would cost $1,664,000 if
the branches were strengthened to adequacy, or $1,190,571 to
furnish service through the same units as those which were now
inadequate.   Not only would the new regional pattern be less

expensive, Mr. Grundt concludes, but adults would have adequate resource centers closer at hand without having to depend upon only one large main library center which would be at a greater distance from their homes.

Apparently Mr. Grundt's conclusions are valid, for urban branch development today is moving more and more toward the pattern of larger area branches plus smaller neighborhood centers.

Notes

1. Galvin, Hoyt R. "Public Library Building in 1969." Library Journal, v. 94, no. 21. Dec. 1, 1969, p. 4370-4387.

2. Galvin, Hoyt R. and Van Buren, Martin. The Small Public Library Building. Unesco, 1959, p. 55.

3. Ibid.

4. Metcalf, Keyes D. "The Use of Hindsight in Planning Library Buildings." In: Libraries Building for the Future. American Library Association, 1967, p. 4.

5. Jenkins, Joseph H. "Programming and Financing Library Buildings." In: Libraries Building for the Future. American Library Association, 1967, p. 35-39.

6. Bowler, Roberta, ed. Local Public Library Administration. International City Managers' Association, 1964, p. 145-46.

7. Young, Helen A. "County Branch for Richfield--Liquor Store Profits Finance." Library Journal, v. 86, no. 21, Dec. 1, 1961, p. 4112.

8. Water, Richard. "Free Space: Can Public Libraries Receive It?" American Library Association Bulletin. v. 58, no. 3, Mar. 1964, p. 232-34.

9. Geddes, Andrew. "Leasing Our Way." Library Journal, v. 86, no. 21, Dec. 1, 1961, p. 4088-4090.

10. Galvin, Hoyt R. "Public Library Building in 1969." Library Journal, v. 94, no. 21, Dec. 1, 1969, p. 4387.

11. "Leaseback Financing for New York Public Library's Riverdale Branch." The Bookmark, v. 25, no. 2, Nov. 1965, p. 56-58.

12. Roanoke, Virginia. Dept. of City Planning, and Roanoke Public Library Board. Branch Libraries, a Long-Range Development Plan. The Authors. 1963, 25 p.

422 Modern Branch Libraries

13. Galvin, Hoyt R. Letter to the author, April 4, 1968.

14. "John F. Kennedy Branch." Focus on Indiana Libraries, August,
    1964, v. XVIII. no. 3, p. 36.

15. Shaffer, Kenneth R. Design for Tomorrow: A Study of Extension
    Services of the Bridgeport Public Library. Bridgeport,
    Connecticut in 1965-66. p. 64-65.

16. American Library Assoc. Public Library Assoc. Addenda to
    Minimum Standards for Public Library Systems, 1966.
    American Library Association, 1967. Addenda June 29,
    1967.

17. Grundt, Leonard. Branch Library Inadequacies in a Typical
    Large City. Resume of a doctoral thesis: "An Investigation
    to Determine the Most Efficient Patterns for Providing
    Adequate Library Service to all Residents of a Typically
    Large City," Rutgers. The State University, 1964. 340 p.
    Research conducted in 1962-63.

Chapter 15

Building the Branch

A functional plan, sound construction, and a warm, inviting appearance are the three fundamental requisites in building a branch. The newer components and methods available to the building industry make these qualities easier to achieve today than in the past.

For purposes of review, there are six main steps in the building of a new branch.

1. Development of a written service program by the library staff.

2. Development of the detailed physical facilities, furnishings and equipment necessary to carry out the service program. This is the building program and should involve the joint effort of library director, branch staff, architect, and possibly the library board.

3. The architect's development of the schematic design, and the detailed specifications for bidding.

4. The opening of bids and awarding of the contract.

5. The actual erection of the building by the contractor under the supervision of the architect.

6. Final checking and acceptance of the building by the governmental unit involved (city or county) and its representatives (the library board and library administrator).

There are two different types of building programs: 1) Planned for one specific branch; 2) A long-range program which is part of a major plan for library development and includes a number of new branches to be built over a stated period of time. For the long-range program or for a large and expensive single branch an outside consultant may be called in, but for most single branches the building program is formulated by the librarian and his staff. If an architect has already been engaged he may become part of the planning team at this point. In this discussion we are concerned only with the program for a single branch.

No one can plan a proper building program without a previously-worked out description of the services to be offered. The service program will have answered such questions as what kind of area will be served; how many readers will be accommodated in seating areas; what size of collection will be provided for; how many periodicals will be received and how far back they will be kept; whether or not back issues will be microfilmed; how much of the technical work will be done behind the scenes at the branch; whether there will be lounging areas, a special young adult section, an all-purpose room; how reader use will be handled and controlled, etc.

The building program now takes each aspect of service and breaks it down into the physical facilities, furnishings and equipment needed. The service program is reviewed in greater detail and related to the building aspects. Here is a general outline for construction of a building program:

1. Review characteristics of the area to be served.

2. Review a list of the services to be offered.

3. State the branch objectives.

4. Give estimated potential usage: annual circulation to be expected at the outset, and anticipated reference use.

5. Describe the general size and type of branch building desired.

6. Give approximate size and description of each area of service (adult, young adult, children's). List furnishing and equipment needed for each.

7. Give approximate size and description of each staff area: workroom, staff lounge and rest room, circulation desk and reference desk, if separate. State total number of staff members who will be working when the branch opens. Librarian's office should be carefully described as to size, equipment, and convenience of arrangement and location.

8. Give approximate size and description of utility areas (heating and air conditioning, public rest rooms, storage, janitor's

closet, electrical equipment area).

9. Describe stack area, book capacity desired, size and number of standing shelving units, dimensions and type of wall shelving and where located.

10. Describe all-purpose room, give approximate size, expected uses, equipment needed, seating capacity desired.

11. List exterior requirements such as building sign, bicycle rack, parking capacity, flood lights, sprinkling system, other appurtenances to building.   Give preferences as to exterior finish (rock or brick facing, stucco, concrete block, etc.) and building material.

12. List special interior requirements such as open, modular construction (no supporting columns), type of heating, air conditioning, lighting, plumbing, telephone connections needed, fire alarm system, exhibit areas, type of floor covering desired, wall finishes, colors to be used in decorating.

13. Discuss landscaping, how building and grounds will be maintained, paving of parking area.

14. Clinch your arguments by showing relationships of areas with respect to function, relationship of desired features to sound construction and inviting appearance, and how such a building can adequately carry out the service program.

The writer secured sample building programs for branches from 22 city and county libraries in 1968.   They varied from a bare outline of two or three pages to documents with as many as 40 or 50 pages.   Contra Costa County Library, Pleasant Hills, California, the Los Angeles Public Library, and the San Diego Public Library use elaborate and detailed building programs; where-as some libraries seem to leave the determination of most details to the architect.   It is this writer's opinion that a detailed building program based upon a dynamic service program and the joint effort of all key staff members is not only valuable to an architect but may avoid many costly mistakes, particularly if the architect has never built a branch library before.   Even experienced library architects need guidance in the exact needs of individual branches which may vary widely in their size and service program.

Pitfalls:

Avoid library jargon when constructing a building program. The architect is not a librarian. Requirements should be in particular and specific terms; otherwise more than one interpretation is possible. Be firm and determined, but do not rush to sketch out a nice large rectangle, adding and labeling special rooms and areas. This usurps the role of the architect and encumbers him with preconceived notions.

Method:

Keep an orderly file of notes, memoranda and tentative sketches, as well as memos of agreements, disagreements, and understandings with the architect while working with him. This crystallizes ideas, pushes the work forward, and helps prevent oversights and misunderstandings later. Cooperation is the keynote, between librarian and consultant, librarian and staff, librarian and board, and librarian and architect, as well as among these groups.

Examine as many other building programs as possible, but keep in mind that what may be good for another community or area is not necessarily good for your community or neighborhood and that the building must be planned specifically for that area or community.

Keep in touch with the construction as it proceeds, but always work through the architect. Be sure that a thorough check has been made before the building is finally accepted. Many a library has found after formally accepting a building that the first heavy rain revealed roof leaks, that the air conditioning did not work properly, even that the cement floor was not level. These and less serious problems can arise within the first year, and acceptance or no acceptance, a conscientious contractor would wish to remedy something that was obviously his fault.

There is a great deal that could be said about building a branch but space does not permit more than a small share of it. Several excellent books are available, and there is a great deal of

material in periodical form, including specialized articles on lighting, air conditioning, heating, floor coverings, relations of librarian and architect, and the advantages and disadvantages of the
various construction materials.

In this chapter we are concerned with the actual building
and the physical features that will make it attractive and functional.
We will discuss size, basic exterior and interior features, desirable but not essential features, building standards, materials,
lighting, heating and air conditioning, amount of glass, carpeting
versus other floor coverings, recommendations for individual
areas, present design trends, division of responsibility, and
mistakes to avoid. We shall also attempt to define that intangible
combination of features that may give a branch a very distinct
and pleasing personality of its own.

Size:

Probably the most important factor in building a branch is
that it be of an adequate size.   Literally hundreds of branches
have outgrown their quarters within the first few years of their
existence.   Do the plans provide sufficient area to perform efficiently the services which need to be performed? Do they provide for future growth? Unfortunately, it seems few library
systems are able to provide financing for buildings which will be
adequate for 25 to 30 years, a period which is often mentioned as
a desirable goal. Where population growth is slow it can be done;
where populations are doubling every five years or so, the problem
becomes almost insurmountable and can be met only by building
additional branches.   In building, space should be provided not only
for an increase in the number of users but for added services
which are evolving quite rapidly in today's library world.

The survey of library buildings, July 1, 1968 to July 1,
1969, made by Hoyt Galvin,[1] included figures on 88 new branches,
remodeling of 11, and 2 combination branch and system headquarters buildings.   The average square footage of the 88 new
branches was 8,834, but sizes ranged from as low as 792 square
feet to 42,200. Predictions have been made that, by the end of

Guidelines for Determining Minimum Space Requirements[2]

Population Served	Shelving Space (a)			Reader Space	Staff Work Space	Estimated Additional Space Needed (c)	Total Floor Space
	Size of Book Collection	Linear Feet of Shelving (b)	Amount of Floor				
	Vols.		sq. ft.	sq. ft.			
2,500-4,999	10,000 plus 3 books per capita for pop. over 3,500	1,300. Add 1 ft. of shelving for every 8 bks. over 10,000	1,000. Add 1 sq. ft. for every 10 bks. over 10,000	Min.500 sq. ft. for 16 seats. Add 5 seats per M. over 3500 pop. served at 30 sq. ft. per reader space	300 sq. ft.	700 sq. ft.	2,500 sq. ft. or 0.7 sq. per capita whichever is greater
5,000-9,999	15,000 plus 2 bks. per capita for pop. over 5,000	1,875. Add 1 ft. of shelving for every 8 bks. over 15,000	1,500. Add 1 sq.ft. for every 10 bks. over 15,000	Min.700 sq.ft. for 23 seats. Add 4 seats per M. over 5000 pop. served at 30 sq.ft. per reader space	500 sq. ft. Add 150 sq. ft. for each full time staff member over 3	1,000 sq. ft.	3,500 sq.ft. or 0.7 sq. ft. per capita whichever is greater

| 10,000 -
24,999 | 20,000 plus
2 bks. per
capita for pop.
over 10,000] | 2,500. Add
1 ft. of
Shelving for
every 8 bks.
over 20,000 | 2,000. Add
1 sq.ft. for
every 10 bks.
over 20,000 | Min. 1,200
sq.ft. for
40 seats.
Add 4
seats per
M. over
10,000
pop. | 1000 sq.ft.
Add 150 sq.
ft. for each
full-time
staff member
over 7 | 1,800 sq.ft. | 7,000 sq.
ft. or 0.7
sq.ft. per
capita,
whichever
is greater |
| 25,000 -
49,999 | 50,000 plus
2 bks. per
capita for pop.
over 25,000 | 6,300. Add
1 ft. of
Shelving for
every 8 bks.
over 50,000 | 5,000. Add
1 sq.ft. for
every 10
bks. over
50,000 | Min. 2,250
sq.ft. for
75 seats.
Add 3
seats per
M. over
25,000
pop. served | 1,500 sq.ft.
Add 150 sq.
ft. for each
full-time
staff member
over 13 | 5,250 sq.ft. | 15,000 sq.
ft. or 0.6
sq.ft. per
capita,
whichever
is greater |

(a) Libraries in systems need only to provide shelving for basic collection plus number of books on loan from resource center at any one time.

(b) A standard library shelf equals 3 linear feet.

(c) Space for circulation desk, heating and cooling equipment, multipurpose room, stairways, janitor's supplies, toilets, etc., as required by community needs and the program of library services.

1969, branches would average closer to 12,000-15,000 square feet as the concept of regional branches becomes more popular. Unless a community or neighborhood can justify at least a 6,000-8,000 square foot branch, bookmobile service or a family reading center would seem more practical.

Check List of Features of a Good Branch Library

Based on a medium-sized branch
8,000-12,000 square feet

(Many of these items apply to any size branch)

General

1.   Basic: The physical facilities should fit the program of library service.

2.   The building must be inviting on the outside and both attractive and functional on the inside.

3.   Build the branch on one level, unless it is a very large regional branch with a limited and very expensive site.

4.   Use open, modular construction with laminated or steel beams. Avoid interior columns that break up the look of spaciousness.

5.   Quality of materials and construction should not be sacrificed for economy.

6.   Avoid expensive, excessive use of large areas of glass. They are fast losing popularity because they increase the cost of heating and cooling, cut down on interior book capacity, are subject to vandalism or accidental breakage, require expensive insurance, and can create a glare problem.

7.   Investigate the new materials available: pre-cast concrete wall sections fabricated at the factory and trucked in to the site to be interlocked; all metal skins of aluminum, stainless steel, or bronze; wood in new and beautiful textures; natural stone in varied shades of veneers; decorative tile. Relate materials to budget and consult with architect. He is the materials expert.

8.   Round, parobolic, hexagonal, octagonal, or other odd-
        shaped buildings may be striking from an architectural
        standpoint but increase costs and are often wasteful of
        space.

9.   If the building must have a south or west exposure plan a
        large overhang, grille, or other means of shading the
        interior.

10.   Include at least a few feet of carefully-planned landscaping
        at the front and sides of the building to enhance the
        appearance.

11.   If picture windows are used, do not bring glass down to
        ground level but have a solid wall under it.

12.   Consider carefully before installing curb return boxes.
        Some branches have had to remove these because of
        vandalism. Burning objects, live mice, rats or snakes,
        garbage, even human waste have been thrown into such
        boxes to destroy or damage books. Check carefully with
        police on the past history of vandalism in the area.
        Return book deposits in the branch walls are preferable
        although not as convenient for the public.

13.   Have a large exterior, well-lighted sign bearing the name
        of the branch and the system. Signs should have non-
        removable letters. Letters that can be reached, even
        with a short ladder, have been pried or filed off and
        stolen in many branches. Use light letters on a dark
        background or the reverse.

14.   Have a functional floor plan and interior relationship of
        areas that will save time and steps.

15.   The building should blend with its surroundings.

16.   The branch should be so constructed as to be expandable
        in size.

17.   In planning future growth of branch libraries the following
        recommended standards are suggested: [3]

Population estimates of service area	7,500-25,000 people	Over 25,000 people
Building size	8,000-8,000 sq. ft.	9,000-26,000 sq. ft.
Parking facilities	40 cars minimum	65 cars minimum
Book capacity	15,000-37,000	38,000-100,000
Reader capacity	50-75 seats	75-200 seats
Hours open	62 hours per week	62-85 hours per week
Estimated annual circulation	100,000-200,000	Over 200,000
Staff, full-time equivalent	4-8 including 2 professional	8 or more, including 4 professional

18.   There should be structural strength sufficient to withstand the dead load of book shelving and to comply with building codes for use as a public building.

19.   The site should be at least twice the area of the branch, three times if possible.

20.   Be sure concrete floors are poured so that they are perfectly level.

21.   Use a direct expansion type of air conditioning.

22.   Have a drive-up window return for books if possible.

23.   Exterior walls should have accents of pleasing design such as rock work, brick work, planters, etc. to avoid plain, boxlike appearance.

24.   Include a fire alarm system of the non-sprinkling type.

25.   There should be look-in windows to provide passersby with the widest view of the library and its activities.   If only one is possible it should be in the boys' and girls' area.   Windows 15 to 20 feet wide should be large enough.

26.   Be sure that access to the building from parking lot during evening hours is well-lighted and relatively safe.

27.   Exterior walls should be of durable, easily-maintained
        materials.

28.   Have no stairs at entrances. If the entrance is above
        ground level use a sloping concrete ramp for the con-
        venience of the handicapped, especially those in wheel
        chairs.

29.   Have a refuse can area at the rear of the building,
        screened by fence or shrubbery.

30.   Include hose bibbs at convenient locations on each face of
        the building, where there is lawn or garden.

31.   Use floodlights to light front of building at night.   Colored
        lights enhance.

32.   Make approach and entrance as inviting as possible.

33.   Insure ample drainage if a flat roof is used.

34.   Glass entrance doors, if used, should be so constructed
        that no one can walk through them.   Have solid bottoms
        and rims.

35.   A small patio with a place for story-telling is a nice
        feature.   It can also be used as an outdoor reading
        room or smoking area for adults, since use for story
        hour will be occasional.

36.   Use tinted glass for windows or glass-front areas where
        there is likely to be any sun glare.

37.   Make ample provision for parking of bicycles and possibly
        several small motorcycles.   Screen this area from the
        street with decorative wall.

38.   Have brackets near the mechanical room for a 14 foot
        ladder.

39.   Black top parking area and provide stalls at least 9x20
        feet with plenty of back-out space.   Consult standards
        for number of parking places to provide in relation to
        size of building.

General Interior Features

40.   Have plenty of work space for staff.

41.   Have a minimum of space devoted to corridors.

42.   Include the following areas:

        Adult Reading room and service area
        Reference area
        Young people's section or alcove
        Children's area
        All-purpose room
        Charging desk and circulation area
        Standing stacks
        Small conference room or rooms
        Workroom for staff
        Staff rest room and lounge
        Janitor's closet
        Utilities room for heating and air conditioning equipment
        Place for electrical equipment
        Public rest rooms
        Librarian's office.

43.   Avoid having heavy, dark-colored beams on low ceilings.
        These give a feeling of pressing down, of being hemmed
        in, and look top heavy.

44.   Have cement floors in janitor and mechanical rooms, car-
        peting if possible in other areas. Debatable for meeting
        room.

45.   Have plenty of electrical outlets throughout for cleaning
        equipment and other necessary operations. Phone out-
        lets should be placed wherever desks will be placed.

46.   Use copper water pipe. Group plumbing for economy and
        efficiency. Long runs of pipe cause stoppage.

47.   Have book return facility planned as part of the building
        near main entrance or opening into workroom off parking
        lot.

48.   The only solid partitions should be those that enclose work
        space, all-purpose room, office, rest rooms, and
        utility areas.

49. If air-conditioning is not possible at first, be sure that equip-
     ment for heating permits conversion to double use for
     heating and cooling later or that there is ample room and
     provision for adding air conditioning.

50. Reader capacity should be 60-100 seats for 8,000-12,000
     square foot branches.

51. Book capacity should be 40,000 - 60,000 for 8,000-12,000
     square foot branches , more if possible.

52. All wood doors should be solid core. Put fire doors where
     necessary as indicated, by applicable codes.

53. Inside lights with the exception of the exit and night light over
     charging desk should be on a master switch which will turn
     them all off at once. Locate master switch near rear exit
     door from workroom.

54. Have a timer to permit lights at exits and parking area to shut
     off automatically.

55. Have well-distributed fluorescent lighting, approximately 50-70
     foot candles maintained at table levels; 60 foot candles are
     often recommended. Number of foot candles will vary with
     coloring of furniture and reflectance of table tops.

56. If flooring cannot be covered with wall-to-wall carpeting, use
     resilient tile.

57. Use washable finishes on lower painted surfaces.

58. All partitions between offices, workroom, and staff rooms
     should extend to the ceiling. Partial partitions are unsatis-
     factory because they do not exclude voices, typing noise,
     kitchen odors, etc.

59. Use only low book shelving to set off areas in the public ser-
     vice section of the building.

60. Have some type of "conversation piece," such as an acquarium,
     special mural, statuary of particular interest.

61. Do not provide interior floor-standing exhibit cases. Staff time
     is limited and exhibits need the professional look. They
     take up floor space and require a great deal of time to
     maintain. Confine exhibit case to one wall-type built in at
     the entryway.

62. Make liberal use of color in interior finishes, furnishings, and
     equipment. Use warm colors but not too vivid.

63. Be sure there is a pleasing, uncluttered vista as patrons enter
     the library.

64.   Plan stacks and wall shelving to provide the collection in
      orderly sequence.

65.   Have the Young People's area near the charging desk for ease
      of supervision and holding down loss and vandalism.

66.   The question of the location and access to the children's room
      reveals two schools of thought.   One argument is to place
      the children's area near the main charging desk and use
      the same street entrance and charging desk for the children.
      The other argument is to place the children's section as far
      from the adult reading room as possible, with its own
      separate entrance.   This does not necessarily mean cutting
      it off with solid partitions.   The advantages of using the
      same general area for children's section and charging desk
      are being able to use the same desk and charging machine
      for both, having the children's books available at all hours
      the branch is open, and using the same work space to sup-
      port both services.   Disadvantages are the unavoidable
      extra noise and confusion caused by children's activity near
      a quiet adult reading and reference area.

67.   If the branch has a phonograph record collection, some pro-
      vision should be made for listening equipment.   Some li-
      brarians prefer soundproof small rooms or booths for
      listening; others prefer listening tables out in the open
      where they can be easily supervised.   A branch, unless it
      is very large, will usually find it more practical to have
      the listening tables and earphones.   Booths are expensive
      to construct, and even though they are soundproofed, some
      sound will carry if listeners turn up the volume.   Booths
      cannot be moved, such a revision being costly.   However,
      if abandoned as listening rooms they make good typing or
      conference rooms.   If small rooms or booths are used for
      listening they must have glass walls from about three feet
      on up, for supervision from the central desk.   Listening
      tables are, of course, more expensive than the portable
      machines used in listening rooms.

68.   Provide plenty of clocks and wall outlets for same.   There
      should be an electric wall clock in each of the main public
      areas and in the workroom.   A small clock should be
      placed in the staff room so that staff can keep track of the
      length of coffee breaks.

69.   Use acoustical tile on all ceilings and at the top of high walls.
      The acoustical treatment must harmonize with the artificial
      lighting fixtures.

70.   Leave ample space for free movement of patrons around the
      reading room, in the area near the charging desk, and in
      the boys and girls section.

71. Have reader interest areas such as a browsing section, new books' shelf, parents' shelf, small lounge area near magazine racks or shelves.

72. The card catalog for adults should be located as near the charging desk as possible but also near the adult reading areas. Try to work out a compromise to provide a minimum of steps for both staff and public using the card catalog.

73. Arrange floor stacks for good visibility and supervision. A radial or fan-shaped arrangement, with its center opposite the desk, gives the best position for visibility.

74. The location of the charging desk and exits from special areas should provide some measure of control against theft of books.

75. A separate foyer or entryway minimizes noise and filters out dust.

76. Plan windows for maximum light and air, with easily operated catches. Today's trend is toward more improved artificial lighting, as it allows more wall space for shelving. High clerestory windows above the book stacks are used to some extent.

77. Provide magazine storage for about ten years' back files of magazines to be taken by the branch, unless it is provided with microfilm of back issues from the start. In that case provide storage for the microfilm and about one to two years back issues of magazines.

78. The workroom should have a minimum width of 17 feet, should be directly accessible from the librarian's office, parking area, adult reading room, and staff room.

79. Traffic pattern from main desk to librarian's office and workroom should be designed so as not to disturb patrons. All work-flow patterns should be worked out to save staff time and steps, and furniture and departments should be placed accordingly, not overlooking convenience of public.

80. Provide index table for Readers' Guide.

81. Don't forget some bulletin board wall space.

82. Be sure every extra feature will serve a useful purpose.

Special Area Features: Charging Desk

83. Charging desk suggested is U-shaped, facing into the library, entrance on one side, exit on the other for natural flow of traffic and efficiency in services.

84. If mechanical charging is used, provide storage for Keysort or
     IBM cards: six drawers or covered trays, 5'' vertical x 3''
     wide and 15'' long.

85. Design desk to provide proper space for automatic charging
     machine.

86. Allow 4-feet wide entrance and exit aisles on each side,
     defined by low shelving.

87. Combine book charging for all age levels at one main desk.

88. Built-in registration or other files save space at charging desk
     if registration files are used.

89. Provide ample bin for storage of mending as it comes in.

Special Area Features: Boys' and Girls'

90. Provide desk and reader advisory service by children's li-
     brarian in B&G area, whenever possible.

91. Children's catalog near librarian's desk and middle of room.

92. Separate rest rooms for boys and girls.

93. Storage for exhibits materials.

Parking Area

94. Provide ample parking facilities. Each stall would be at
     least 9x20 feet. Slope to drain from site but not into
     street.

95. Provide wood car bumper protection between building and park-
     ing area.

96. Reserve parking spaces for staff.

97. Three formulae suggested for computing parking needed are:
     1.   Estimate peak-hour patronage for one week and divide
          by two for an estimate of minimum spaces needed.
     2.   One car for every five seats in the library.
     3.   Contra Costa County suggests 40 spaces for 4,000-
          8,000 sq. ft. branch. On this basis an 8,000-
          12,000 sq. ft. branch should have 55-60 spaces.

98. It is preferable to have parking area at rear as lots are apt
     to be deeper and it is cheaper than acquiring that much
     more frontage on street. Have separate exit and entrance
     lanes, one on each side of building if lot permits.

99. Provide racks for parking bicycles. Screen or place in incon-
     spicuous and spare space.

Meeting Room

100. Meeting rooms must have access to public rest rooms when library is not open.

101. Must be able to close off meeting rooms from library proper at closing time.

102. Meeting rooms should have small kitchenette and cupboard facilities for serving refreshments but not full meals.

103. Meeting rooms should have storage space for chairs, projectors, other equipment.

104. Meeting room walls should be of material to afford easy mounting or hanging of pictures and exhibit material.

105. A meeting room for 100 to 150 people is suggested for a 10,000 sq. ft. branch.

Office for Librarian

106. Office should be a minimum of 100 sq. ft.

107. Should be directly accessible from workroom and adult reading room, in close proximity to charging desk. Glass wall from about 3 ft. up on wall facing main reading area.

108. Should contain adequate shelving for library literature and other materials.

Staff Room

109. Should be directly accessible from workroom.

110. Should provide lockers, wardrobe closet, exhaust fan, clock, 25" x 7" double sink with garbage disposal, stove and refrigerator unit combined. Should have rest room opening off of it.

111. Should be attractive and comfortably furnished.

112. Should include studio couch or davenport where staff can stretch out if not feeling well.

Toilets

113. Toilets need 135 sq. feet. Consider use of baffles or vestibule for privacy. Should be located off reading room if possible, easily supervised from charge desk. One set of standards suggests they be in an inconspicuous place to discourage use as comfort stations.

Equipment and Extras

114. Provide space for development of audio-visual section.

115. Provide conference rooms for 10-15 people.

116. Provide typing rooms if possible.

117. Provide janitor room: 100 sq. ft. with service sink, broom and mop racks, shelving, drain.

118. Drinking fountains usually expected by public. If found necessary, locate so as not to invite "water play" and not near any book shelves.

119. Use plastic no-mar tops on reading tables, charging desk and tops of catalog cases. Formica good. Austin-Baily Formica color tops.

120. Have some individual study carrels if possible. Strip type most economical.

121. Be sure to provide for oversize shelving and deep shelving for periodical room.

122. Figure out space for such conveniences as pen machine, public phone booth, copying machine if possible, in order to avoid constant requests from public to use phone, borrow materials, etc.

123. Give special attention to durability and comfort of chairs and coffee tables used in browsing and lounge areas.

124. Try to consider the needs of the handicapped, especially those in wheel chairs, when planning widths of doors, height of phone from floor, placement of rest room fixtures.

Here are some of the highlights in recent trends in branch buildings:

1. Round, hexagonal, square on square design. Not a marked trend as yet, but some examples are appearing on the branch scene.

2. Majority of recent branch buildings are flat roofed.

3. More security measures are being taken in design of charging desk and aisles in and out, with railings and sometimes turnstiles.

4. Young adult sections are merging with adult reading area and bookstacks. Trend is away from a separate section. Young people do not like to be set apart, prefer to be classed with adults.

5. Few fireplaces are included nowadays. The idea of making the library look like a quiet home is unreal and costly.

6. Less glass, more artificial lighting.

7. More progress in planning and designing has been made in the last 15 years than in the previous 50 years.

8. Larger branches where there is no regional branch.

9. Large regional branches and smaller satellites are an emerging pattern.

10. Use of exciting new materials for exteriors such as pre-fabricated concrete walls, interesting new textures and finishes inside and out.

A few points need further elaboration:

Color

Colors in a branch should be selected for their reflectance values and psychological effect. Restful pastel colors are best, as many people react unfavorably to bright or intense colors. Those in charge of a branch library usually want to enhance the sense of coziness and intimacy which can be the special charm of branches; interior finishes in warm tones tend to advance toward the observer, thus emphasizing this effect. On the contrary, cool colors seem to recede and can be used to give the illusion of more space.

The tendency nowadays is toward the use of more and more color everywhere where it is possible or feasible. This is probably still a reaction against the somber tones of early li-braries or the dark, almost forbidding colors and finishes. The gaiety, warmth and appeal to all ages are heightened by the generous use of colors in harmony.

Sound Control:

With the increasing use of branches by students sound con-trol has become even more important than in the past. Branches, particularly, need to control this problem because they traditionally have had a larger percentage of children and young people using the facilities than does a central library, especially if the latter is in a busy downtown section.

Though not noise sources in themselves, many interior materials actively contribute to the disturbing echoes and reverbera-tions by simply being sound reflectors. Since today's branches include larger open areas than the old-style buildings the problem is compounded.[4] There are three main ways in which the noise level can be at least partially controlled: by the use of wall to

A Guide to Ceiling Materials for Library Interiors [4]

Type	Summary Description	Acoustical Efficiency	Maintenance	Cost	Advantages
General	Incombustible materials offered in fissured, striated and embossed surface designs; conducive to numerous special effects through "custom" installation.	Excellent	Washable; can be repainted without damage to sound-absorption	Moderate to high material cost; moderate installation	Incombustible; Especially distinctive surface designs
Job-Assembled	Materials which are fabricated at job sites; usually incombustible, these can be assembled with special backing set into the basic units to feature best sound-absorption of all types	Superior	Washable; can be repainted without damage to sound-absorption	High material cost; medium to high installation cost	Superior sound absorption; ease of maintenance
Fire-Resistant	A ceiling material which offers rated fire protection; designed to check the spread of fire to areas above the ceiling	Excellent	Washable; can be repainted without damage to sound-absorption	High material cost; low installation cost	Fire-protective; adds to construction savings
Cellulose	Usually not recommended for areas in which fire codes require an incombustible material; a fibrous material available in a wide variety of surface designs--some with decorative prints in addition to perforations	Excellent	Washable; can be repainted without damage to sound-absorption	Low material cost; low to moderate cost of installation	Low cost; wide selection of surface designs; ease of installation

wall carpeting, by installing acoustical sound absorbing ceiling materials; and by the use of large expanses of textured drapes on
wall areas, as well as acoustical tile used on wall areas above wall
shelving.

Lighting:

The branch building standards of the San Diego (California)
Public Library suggest the following minimum average maintained
foot candle intensities for various areas: [5]

```
Reading room:
    Table tops for study notes  -  70 foot candles
    Fixed stacks                -  40  "       "
    Moveable stacks             -  70  "       "
Charging area                   -  70  "       "
Foyer                           -  20  "       "
Work room                       -  50  "       "
Staff room                      -  40  "       "
Toilet rooms                    -  30  "       "
Janitorial and mechanical rooms 20  "       "
Interior entry area             -   5  "       "
Parking lot    Brightness determined by location and nearness
                     to street lamps
```

The maximum brightness to average brightness ratio for
lumaires should not exceed 3 to 1.   Fluorescent fixtures, which are
mainly used today, should be generally furnished with cool white
lamps.   Standards and recommendations for light intensity were
found to vary somewhat when a survey of this material was made by
the author.   However, there was quite general agreement that 50-70
foot candles for the reading room area is best.

Some librarians do not favor fluorescent lighting, believing
that glare is harder to control. Others believe that incandescent
lights, which concentrate the light into a smaller space, create more
glare.   This author noted, in gathering building data on samples of
various-sized branches, that almost without exception the lighting
was fluorescent.   A few branches had a combination of incandescent
and fluorescent which should provide a happy compromise in some
situations.   In places where the lights are turned on and off frequently, fluorescent tubes do not last nearly as long; therefore a
wise procedure would seem to be to use incandescent lighting in
such areas and fluorescent lighting where lights will be left on
practically all day and evening.   The great advantage of fluorescent

light, of course, is that it uses less than half the current the incandescent uses and therefore produces less than one-half the heat
in producing the same intensity of light.[6] Fluorescent tubes have a
longer life, and they give greater flexibility. Disadvantages are
higher bulb replacement cost, higher installation cost, and the fact
that fixture changing may take more time.

Illuminated ceilings using fluorescent lighting are becoming increasingly popular. Their use instead of acoustical tile may well
be questioned as a factor in controlling noise, however. Where
air conditioning is installed, the fluorescent fixtures, producing
less heat, reduce the cost of running the air conditioning equipment.
It is important to remember that quality of light, not intensity, is
the keynote of good lighting. Both Keyes Metcalfe and Ellsworth
Mason, well-known library directors and building consultants,
argue that no more than 20 foot candles will produce sufficient illumination if the lighting is of the proper quality and type, but the
environment must also be right. When building a new branch or
remodeling, librarians should investigate the matter of lighting very
carefully, for nothing can contribute to the discomfort of patrons and
staff as much as poor or inadequate lighting, unless it is inadequate
heat. Care must be taken to see that fixtures and furniture have
non-glare surfaces, that flooring tile, if used, is flat-toned, and
that outside light does not conflict with artificial lighting.

Stack loads:

We have touched on the load-bearing capacity of the branch
building. Here are specifics: Be sure the architect and contractor
are meeting these standards:

> 12 pounds per square foot of flooring if the floor is steel.
> 45 pounds per square foot if the floor is of 3-1/2 inch concrete.
> 40 pounds (minimum) per square foot of aisle area for live load,
> people, and furniture.

Humidity:

Ideal humidity for book storage stacks, 55%. For reading and
work areas, 45%. Avoid different humidities in the same building

or condensation will develop.

Shelving:

In computing shelving capacity allow 6-8 books per lineal foot of shelving for adult books, 8-10 for children's books, as much as 12 for thin picture books.   At least one-third of each shelf should be left for flexibility in shelving.

Adult shelving: 6 feet, 8 inches to 7 feet.

Children's shelving: 5 feet for wall shelving.

Counter-height shelving: approximately 3 feet 8 inches.

Use low counter-height shelving for picture books in children's area, deep shelves.   Occasional dividers in three foot sections help.

The Branch as a Headquarters for Bookmobile Service:

Not everyone agrees on the desirability of using a branch as a headquarters for one or more bookmobiles, with their attendant staff and book collection, but a number of library systems which have central buildings in heavily-congested downtown areas are finding it expedient to make provision in one of the new branches for a bookmobile garage or loading area, workroom and office for the bookmobile staff, and shelving for the bookmobile collection. If there is more than one bookmobile they may be quartered at one of the larger branches in the area in which they operate.   The advantage is that the driver does not have to spend a great deal of time threading through heavy traffic at rush hours to get out to his stops in the morning and back again at night.   Also, sometimes the central library needs to expand into the space occupied by the bookmobile operation.

Harry N. Peterson, writing in his survey of the Fort Worth Public Library Branch Requirements in 1959, does not agree with this procedure.   He says:

> Branch buildings should not be designed as bookmobile
> headquarters... Properly placed branches should occupy
> premium space in or near shopping centers, where
> pedestrian traffic is heavy. Such land is too valuable to
> devote to extension activities and garage use.   These

functions can be housed in a cheaply-constructed building
in a peripheral location where land can be purchased for
$2,500 to $3,000 an acre, compared to $10,000 for half
an acre of improved land needed for a branch. It would
still be wiser to obtain one of the abandoned warehouses
in the downtown section to house the extension department
and the bookmobiles. This would be even less expensive,
and, because of the proximity to the main library, a far
better arrangement from the administrative point of view. [7]

Mr. Peterson overlooks the fact that the bookmobile would
still have to fight traffic to get out to the area it serves, also the
fact that few central libraries in large cities are located in or very
near the warehouse section of the city which is often a deteriorating
section and not safe for women employees in some cities. Extension employees are also entitled to the same warmth and comfort
as other library employees, and these are often lacking in cheaply
constructed buildings.

Remodeling:

Supermarket buildings available for sale or lease because the
market has moved make excellent conversions because they are so
often built without supporting columns, using instead laminated arched
beams and making possible the open, modular construction so suited
to a branch. Such a building is also usually supplied with ample
parking spaces and may have an attractive front of brick and large
glass windows or natural rock and glass. If the building is in or
near a commercial area of other businesses this is an added advantage. Libraries seeking branch sites but unable to build from
scratch should seriously consider the possibility of finding such a
building. Factories and former post offices also offer possibilities.

Vacant store buildings are popular for branch conversions,
but unless located in a shopping center are apt to have no parking
space available. Such buildings may also be deep and narrow, a
dimension which does not lend itself as well as other shapes to library use. A wide front with medium depth type of building may
make a very good branch, especially if parking is available behind
the building or nearby. Sometimes a vacant lot can be secured next
door or an old building can be purchased and razed to provide the
needed parking.

A theater, if the interior floor, which is usually sloping, can be leveled without too much expense, may make a good branch, because there may be adjacent parking. Odd-shaped roofs of theatres and churches may make a conversion prohibitively expensive. Large, older homes make poor branches because they are usually constructed with load-bearing walls. Tearing out these walls is impossible, and the branch would have many small divided areas difficult to supervise and heat. The home will also usually be on two or even three levels, not considered desirable except for very large branches.

One of the problems in remodeling for a branch is the unpredictability of costs. As an older building is torn into, hidden defects of plumbing, wiring, or general structure may come to light and create an unexpected expense. Also the walls of many older buildings do not have sufficient load-bearing capacity if wall-hung shelving is desired. An even more serious problem can be the strength of the floors, which may not be sufficient to hold book stacks.

If location, space and structural requirements of the building being considered for remodeling are all favorable, it will probably pay to remodel. However, check the following:

1. Exterior, particularly the facade, should be friendly, inviting, and unostentatious or be easily changed to give this impression. Does it have dignity without monumentality?

2. Is it possible to convert to a street level entrance if there is not already one? How expensive would this be?

3. Is the interior open and flexible enough? Can steel beams or columns be substituted for load-bearing walls that would have to be removed? Will the main floor, if it is a two-story building, be suitable for a public service area with an efficient layout? Can behind-the-scenes activities, staff areas, or meeting room be placed on another level? Residences are the most difficult to remodel because they are so cut up into many small rooms with load-bearing walls which cannot be removed. Upper floors are almost useless, and supervision from a central desk is impossible.

4. Remember that library books and shelving create heavy loads. Qualified engineers must inspect and evaluate the building

for load-bearing capacity.   Technical and professional experts should
answer the following questions:

a.   Floors. Are they solid, level, able to carry the
     weight? If of wood, is there rot, decay, termites?

b.   How is the building insulated if at all?

c.   Are plumbing pipes and fixtures adequate?

d.   Would heating and ventilating be satisfactory or will
     new equipment be necessary?   Can air-conditioning be
     installed?

e.   How about the electrical wiring?   Does it meet modern
     codes for public buildings?   Is there an adequate ser-
     vice entrance?   Enough outlets?   How many circuits?
     How expensive will it be to wire the building
     properly?

f.   Roof. Is it in good repair? Is there good drainage?
     Skylights? Is the roof outdated? Of what material?

g.   Foundation. Is it dry and solid? Is it sufficient
     support for heavy loads?

h.   If building is of masonry, is it in good shape? Are
     there concrete stair wells? Reinforced concrete
     interior walls? Are there elevator shafts? Where?

i.   Which interior partitions are load bearing? Which
     could be removed without injury to the building
     strength?

j.   How near does the building come to meeting building
     codes, fire and safety codes?

It is often harder to remodel an old building than to plan and
build a new one. The first thing to decide is whether it will pay to
remodel. Several factors might enter into this decision. If there
is a space shortage, yet a compelling reason for remaining at the
same location, and an addition to the building will suffice, as could
be the case with some of the newer buildings, the answer is
simple--remodel. If there is strong community sentiment to retain
an existing building such sentiment may be too strong to resist and
remodeling may be the only answer.

On the other hand, should the branch be mechanically
obsolete, too small, and needing modernization throughout, it would

probably be much easier and just as cheap to start all over. Here are steps in making a decision:

1. Prepare a written service program as with a new building. Set forth the space requirements.

2. For a small project the basic planning team would be the governing body (board in a member or affiliated library; library director in a centralized system), the architect, and the branch librarian. If it is a large, complex project, it may involve a consultant and engineering and construction specialists, especially if extensive alterations must be made to the mechanical aspects of the building.

3. As the architect translates the service program into sketches and plans it will become apparent whether it is feasible to remodel the existing building. [5]

If it is a question of procuring an already existing building and converting it to library use, the following criteria should be observed: [8]

> Location: Is it conveniently accessible to the largest number of people, close to parking, large enough for future expansion, on a prominent site, does it have a street level entrance, and is it correctly oriented?

> Size: Is it large enough to meet the space requirements for the service program and also permit expansion? Is the structure flexible in design?

> Strength: Are floors and walls strong enough to carry the weight of books?

Attractive and functional branches have been set up in remodeled buildings, but the building must be carefully chosen or it may be necessary to accept out-of-date materials and equipment such as plumbing and heating. So often a building is donated for a branch and the library administration and governmental authority are faced with the problem of either accepting or offending a locally wealthy and prominent citizen. It is better to refuse a kindly-intentioned offer than to accept a building which will be a hindrance to good library service for the area.

Cost of repair and maintenance over a 20-year period should be estimated and compared with similar costs for a new building before making a final decision.

   With certain buildings only the cost of remodeling the facade
may be involved.

   Good planning is the key to a successful conversion. If the
librarian does not have the kind of imagination that can visualize the
finished renovation, a library building consultant should be called in
Some remodeling has been unsuccessful because poor planning negate
the potential for success.

   Enlarging a branch gives the first chance to rectify major
faults in the plan arrangement of the old building. If there is
space in front of the building, as is the case with so many of the
older branches, a major enlargement is possible by removing the
old portico or facade and building a new and modern addition in
front. If the new part is high enough it will conceal the old. If
not, it may be possible to lower the old roof line or erect a false
roof at a pitch extended back over the old roof. Entrances can
sometimes be changed to another street.

   For further examples and photos of remodeling projects see
The Small Public Library Building by Joseph L. Wheeler (American
Library Association, 1962, p. 32-36).

   A difficult conversion which came out surprisingly well is
that of a former, very oddly-shaped theatre building, now a branch
of the St. Louis County Library, St. Louis, Missouri. The Directo
Stewart Smith, saw possibilities in the building when it was offered
for sale after a very short life as a theatre. Before and after
photos of this remodeling are shown on pages 451 and 452.

   Another challenging conversion for a small branch could
possibly be a service station. Some stations today are quite attractive, faced with rock or brick, built larger than formerly to
house lubricating and mechanical repairing facilities. A station may
be abandoned because of too much competition, failure of a lessee,
or for some other reason, and if it is not reactivated soon, the
owners might be willing to sell or lease. Many are owned by
major oil companies; others are privately owned. The advantage
would be a good corner site with considerable parking area. Some

Figure 66.   Before Conversion

La Cosa Theatre had a short life. St. Louis County Library purchased the building, which was not library-type architecture, made
of it a very interesting branch.

Figure 67.   After Conversion

Rock Road Branch, St. Louis County Library, converted from a
theatre. Parking space for 225 cars at the rear.

Figure 68. Interior View, Rock Road Branch, St. Louis County
Library, converted from a theatre. High peaked roof presented a few
problems.

former stations could possibly be enlarged. Many types of service
stations would not be suitable, however, particularly those of the
smaller, metal-shell type.

It must be stressed that throughout the building process the
librarian, and possibly some of the branch staff, will be working
closely with the architect. If there is a branch supervisor, she
will probably be the one most directly responsible for conferring
with the architect, but she should certainly work also in close cooperation with the branch librarian if the latter has already been
appointed.

The points and precepts in this chapter are given merely as
guidance for the librarian or supervisor who has not previously been
involved in building or remodeling a branch. He or she can ascertain whether the features of a good branch building are being

included, but to offer the list in its entirety to an architect would, in most cases, be a bad mistake. Architects feel, and rightfully so, that their business is planning buildings; they expect a certain amount of direction and help from the technician who will occupy the building, in this case the librarian, but they do not want to be told every small detail.

This chapter could not be more fittingly closed than by a quotation from an article by a great architect, Richard Neutra:[9]

> Whenever an architect is confronted with an assignment, there is only one centerpiece to be served. When it comes to libraries, the centerpiece is the reader, and the design is the reader-centered library...A library must be a refuge from all the humdrum flashes of our progress that take off our fenders in the traffic jam of our industrialized age. Quiet and lasting shapes, not novelty or fashion, must be the background of world literature and should tune the interior of the library to the needs of our sensitiveness, making it a soul-anchor place.

Notes

1. Galvin, Hoyt R. "Public Library Building in 1969." Library Journal, v. 94, no. 21, Dec. 1, 1969, p. 4370-4387.

2. Alabama Library Association. "Guidelines for Determining Minimum Space Requirements." Alabama Standards for Public Libraries by the Committee on Standards, Division of Public Libraries, Alabama Library Association, May, 1966.

3. City of Newport Beach, California, Public Library. Standards for Planning for Future Growth, 1967-68. Mimeographed.

4. Graybill, E. S. "Ceilings and Sound." Library Journal, v. 86, no. 21, Dec. 1, 1961, p. 4086-87.

5. San Diego, California Public Library. Branch Library Standards.

6. Metcalfe, Keyes D. Library Lighting. Library Journal, v. 86, no. 21. Dec. 1, 1961, p. 4081-85.

7. Peterson, Harry. Survey of the Fort Worth Public Library Branch Requirements. Washington, D.C. 1959, p. 52, 54, 55.

8. Doms, Keith. "Public Library Buildings." In: Bowler, Roberta, Local Public Library Administration. International City Managers' Association, 1964, p. 301-2.

9. Neutra, Richard J. "Centerpiece of a Library." Library Journal, v. 89, no. 21. Dec. 1, 1964, p. 4695-97.

Chapter 16

Samples of Modern Branches Built Within the Last 10 Years

The branches included in this chapter are drawn from various parts of the country, and from urban library systems, county and regional library systems, and independent libraries which have affiliated with systems as members or cooperating units.

For ease of study they have been grouped in four groups: (1) those having from 2,000 to 5,999 square feet; (2) those with 6,000 to 9,999 square feet; (3) those having 10,000 to 14,999 square feet; and (4) those with over 15,000 square feet.

The smaller units are included only as prototypes for very small existing branches which cannot enlarge much or at all but which may be interested in remodeling to improve appearance and function; and also for those communities which are determined to build a small branch regardless of today's trends. Branches at the upper end of this range, from 4,000 to 5,999 square feet, may be able to give fairly good service if linked up with a good system and if well staffed and provided with an unusually well-chosen book collection.

Since the average of all branches built within the one-year period of July 1, 1968 to July 1, 1969 was a little over 8,800 square feet, the medium group, from 6,000 to 9,999 square feet, is probably the most representative of today's branches. Most branches over 10,000 square feet now being built are area or regional branches in city systems, often with several smaller branches under their jurisdiction. This is especially true of those branches in the very large group, from 15,000 square feet on up. Several area branches built recently were 24,000 to 30,000 square feet, and the beautiful Sprain Brook Branch in Yonkers, New York, is an amazing 65,000 square feet.

Building data is not reported in an exact standardized form with precisely the same items of information for each branch, because the material came to the writer in many forms and in varying formats. An effort has been made, however, to report the essential items of size, costs, physical features, and outstanding points of each.

Small Branches
2, 000 to 5, 999 Square Feet
Arranged in order of increasing size

Figure 69.   Fletcher Hills Branch Library. San Diego County Library,
San Diego, Calif. View of charging desk area.

Location: 576 Garfield Avenue, El Cajon, California
Architect: Department of Public Works, Architectural Division.
Date completed: June, 1964.
Anticipated yearly circulation: 60,000.
Square feet of floor area: 2366; one level.
Parking spaces: Public: 8; staff: 2.
Costs:

Site	$	gift	
Construction cost	$	61,430.	
Heating, cooling	$	9,510.	(incl. in contract)
Built-in furniture	$	1,600.	(incl. in contract)
Total building cost	$	61,430.	
Other furniture & equipment	$	3,674.	
Landscaping & site work	$	2,582.	
Total project cost, approx.	$	78,800.	

Sources of funds: Budget appropriation and Federal grant.
Construction: Masonry exterior, wood roof, and interior partitions.
Lighting: Reading rooms: Continuous - suspended - fluorescent.
        Stacks: Fluorescent.
Floor coverings: Carpet.
Heating and cooling: Electric cooling. Gas heating. "Supreme-aire"
    12 ton weathercreator.

Figure 70.   Maben Public Library
Member, Oktibbeha County Library System
Maben, Mississippi

View of adult reading room and windows

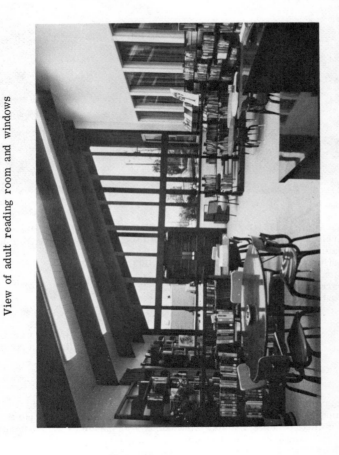

Figure 71.   Maben Public Library
            Member, Oktibbeha County Library System,
                      Maben, Mississippi

                Fine arts and meeting room

Location: Maben, Mississippi.
Building:
    Site $ 1,040.00
    Construction $ 45,915.00
    Furniture and equipment $ 4,370.00
    Costs per square foot $ 17.70
    Size (square feet)   2,446
    Book capacity   4,500
    Seating capacity   35
    Meeting room seats   40
Architects:
    Thomas O. Wakeman, AIA
    A. Neilson Martin, AIA
        Wakeman & Martin
        Starkville, Mississippi
General Contractor:
    Sam E. Oswalt
    Mathiston, Mississippi
Consultants:
    Miss Mary Love, Assoc. Dir. (now Dir., Miss. State Library
      Comm.)
    Miss Simmie Roberts, Construction Supervisor
    Mrs. Linda Harwell, Area Consultant
    Charles C. Harris, Building Consultant
    Toney Harris, Building Consultant
    Robert L. Grady, Construction Mechanic of the Mississippi
      Library Commission
Special features:
    Fine arts and meeting room
    Outside book return facility

Figure 72   Imperial Beach Branch
                         San Diego County Library
                          San Diego, Calif.

Location: 810 Coronado Avenue, Imperial Beach, California
Architect: Dept. of Public Works, San Diego County.
Date of completion: July 24, 1967.
Population served: 20,500.
Anticipated yearly circulation: 80,000.
Dimensions of site: 140x125 feet. Location: Corner in park across
        from civic center.
Size of building: 3,000 square feet.
Parking spaces: For public, 12; for staff, 3.
Costs:
            Site furnished by city of Imperial Beach
            Construction: $ 98,900
            Mechanical equipment:
                Heating and cooling: $ 8,000
            Built-in furniture:
                Charging desk: $ 3,000
            Other furniture and
              equipment (shelves, etc.) $ 2,850
            Landscaping and site work: $ 17,500
            Fees: $ 450
            County labor, equipment,
                contracts, and overhead $ 18,425.86.

Figure 73.   Imperial Beach Branch
                     San Diego County Library
                       San Diego, Calif.
                           Entrance

Figure 74.   Broken Arrow Branch
                        Tulsa City-County Library System
          Opened - December 1963. Charging Desk and Children's Area

Photo by Bob Hawks, Inc.
Tulsa, Oklahoma

Architect: Bob Hale
Consultants: Knoll Associates (interior).
Costs:
  Building cost (Including built-in equipment): $44,413; cost
   per square foot: $12.85; gross floor area: 3,455 square
   feet.
  Site $ 22,000
   sitework: included in building cost.
  Landscaping: $ 646.27.
  Fees: Architect: $ 3,028.41.
    Surveyors: Breisch $ 150.00
     Engineering Company
  Equipment and furniture $ 8,678.12.
   (other than built-in)
  Total project cost: $ 78,915.80
  Cost per square foot: $ 22.83
Lighting: Fluorescent.
Floors: Carpet in multipurpose room.
Heating and air conditioning: Forced air, gas.
Shelves and stacks: Amestack, Oklahoma Seating.
Library furniture: charging desk: architect designed, Central Mill.
 catalog cases: none, book catalog; exhibit cases: architect
 designed, Oklahoma Fixture; tables: Steelcase.
Books: Open shelf capacity: 11,250 vols.; closed stack and storage
 capacity: 1,000. Total volume capacity: 12,250.

Figure 75:   Paradise Hills Branch
                       San Diego Public Library
                         San Diego, Calif.
                      Exterior and entrance view

Cost of site: gift
Cost of Building: $ 84,735
Furniture: $ 5,408
Landscaping by Park Department: $ 3,197
        Total: $ 93,340
Opened: November 2, 1964.
Population served: 11,610.
Book capacity: 20,000 volumes.
Area: 3,875 sq. ft.
Construction: concrete block.
        Floor: rubber tile.
        Furniture: Bro-Dart.
Special features:
        a. Folded plate roof with non-glare light
        b. Reading garden
        c. Parking area for 14 cars

Figure 76. Edwin A. Benjamin Memorial Branch Library
San Diego Public Library
San Diego, Calif.

Cost of site: City-owned.
Cost of building: $ 95,811
Furniture: $ 6,871
Landscaping by Park Department: $ 4,663
     Total: $ 107,345
Opened: March 22, 1965.
Population served: 17,646
Book capacity: 20,000 volumes.
Area: 3,875 sq. ft.
Construction: concrete block.
     Floor: rubber tile.
     Furniture: Bro-Dart.
Special features:
     a.   Reading garden
     b.   Sculpture by Ira Spector
     c.   Parking for 18 cars.

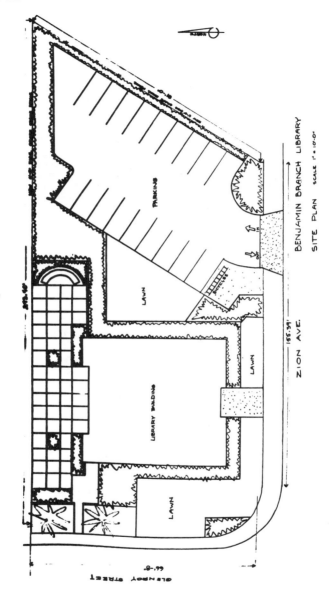

Figure 77. Edwin A. Benjamin Memorial Branch Library
San Diego Public Library
San Diego, Calif.
Site plan

Figure 78.   East San Diego Branch Library
                     San Diego Public Library
                        San Diego, Calif.

Cost of site: City-owned.
Cost of building: $ 86,511
Furniture: $ 6,099
Landscaping by Park Department: $ 3,389
        Total: $ 95,999
Opened: December 14, 1964.
Population served: 26,347
Book capacity: 20,000 volumes.
Area: 3,875 sq. ft.
Construction: concrete block.
        Floor: rubber tile.
        Furniture: Bro-Dart.
Special features:
        a. Outdoor reading garden.
        b. Sandcast sculpture on garden wall by Ira Spector.
        c. Parking for 16 cars.

41st Avenue Branch
Lake County Public Library
Griffith, Indiana

Location: Calumet Township.
Architect: Joseph B. Martin & Associates.
Costs:

Building cost (including built-in equipment):	$	66,480.18
Cost per square foot:	$	16.62
Site:	$	6,792.00
Fees: Architect:	$	2,659.31
Equipment and furniture (other than built-in):	$	10,162.22
Total project cost:	$	86,093.71
Cost per square foot:	$	21.52

Floor area: 4000 square feet.
Lighting: Fluorescent.
Floors: Carpet.
Heating: Gas, air filter.
Shelves and stacks: Case, Myrtle desk.
Library furniture: Charging desk: Myrtle desk.
                          Exhibit cases: Built-in, in building contract.
Books: Open shelf capacity: 17,700 volumes.

Figure 79.   The Forty-First Avenue Library, constructed on the
              basic plan used for seven of the buildings in the Lake
              County Public Library system, is 4,000 sq. ft. with
              a capacity of 17,700 volumes.

Figure 80. <u>Maple Valley Branch</u>
King County Public Library, Seattle, Wash.

This building of unusual design utilizes native wood effectively.

Location: Maple Valley, Washington.
Opened: July 14, 1968.
Architect: Johnston-Campanella-Murakami.
Landscape architect: Glen Hunt.
Building size: 4,000 square feet.
Total cost: $112,000.
Book capacity: 25,000 volumes.
Source of funds:
        Library Services and Construction Act
        Matching Funds $ 47,700.
Site: donated by Joseph Flynn and Ivar Orcutt.
All-purpose meeting room.
Parking: Lot leased from Seattle Water Department.

Figure 81. Maple Valley Branch, King County Public Library.
Interior view-Reading Room
Interesting grill design breaks height of ceiling over charging area.

Schererville Branch
Lake County Public Library
Griffith, Indiana

Location: Schererville, Indiana
Architect: Joseph B. Martin and Associates.
Size: 4,000 square feet.
Costs:
         Building (including built-in equipment):
                                        $ 66,480.18
                 cost per square foot $ 16.62
         Site: $ 11,050.00
         Fees: Architect $ 2,659.31
         Equipment and furniture
                 (other than built-ins): $ 10,162.22
         Total project cost: $ 90,351.71
                 cost per square foot: $ 22.59
Lighting: Fluorescent.
Floors: Carpet.
Heating: Gas.
Air conditioning.
Exhibit cases built-in, included in building contract.
Book capacity: Open shelf capacity: 17,700 volumes.
Ceilings: Acoustical and fireproof.
Glass: Heat absorbing.
Meeting room: Soundproof, multi-purpose type, accommodating
        40 people.   Equipped with kitchenette facilities.

Figure 82.   The Schererville Library, constructed on the basic
              plan used for seven of the buildings in the Lake
              County Public Library system.

Figure 83. Encinitas Branch
San Diego County Library
San Diego, Calif.

Location: 540 Cornish Drive, Encinitas, California
Architect: San Diego County Dept. of Public Works.
Date of completion: Sept. 19, 1965.
Population served: 10,147.
Anticipated yearly circulation: 95,000.
Dimensions of site: 205x211 feet (approximately 1 acre).
Dimension of building: 4100 square feet.
                         Reading room, 63 feet in diameter
Parking spaces: For public, 10; for staff, 2.
Costs:

Site: Owned by county		
Electrical work:	$	10,000
Plumbing:	$	5,100
Heating and cooling:	$	9,400
Built-in furniture:	$	3,850
Other furniture and equipment:	$	6,245
Landscaping and site work (earth work and paving)	$	9,450
Fees: Owner's architect		
Carpet:	$	6,500 (in contract)
Total project:	$	86,738.

Source of funds: Retirement Board.
Building construction: Type: Wood frame.
Lighting: fluorescent in reading room and stacks.
Floor covering: Carpet on pad.
Type of heating and/or cooling: Gas heat and cooling. Completely
    air-conditioned.

Figure 84. Suburban Acres Branch, Tulsa City-County Library System,
Tulsa, Oklahoma. Opened, September, 1963. Browsers' Bench and
Entrance.

Architect: Donald H. Honn.
Consultants: Knoll Associates (interior).
Costs: Building cost (including built-in equipment): $49,872.44
          Cost per square foot: $11.87
          Gross floor area: 4200 square feet
          Site: Gift of Tulsa Public Schools. Landscaping: $558.55
          Fees: Architect: $3,540.86
          Equipment and furniture (other than built-in): $13,634.02.
          Additional costs: Sewer: $1,540.60
          Total project cost: $69,146.47
          Cost per square foot: $16.46
Lighting: Fluorescent. Floors: Vinyl asbestos, Kentile.
Heating: Central, gas.   Air conditioning: Central air-cooled.
Shelves and stacks: Amestack, Oklahoma Seating.
Library furniture: Charging desk: architect designed, Central
                        Mill; Catalog cases: none, book catalog;
                        Exhibit cases: Architect designed, Oklahoma
                        Fixture; Chairs: Knoll; Tables: Steelcase;
                        Lounge furniture: Knoll; Carrels: Central
                        Mill
Books: Open shelf capacity: 15,000 vols.
         Closed stack and storage capacity: 2,000
         Total volume capacity: 17,000.

Figure 85.   Goodlettsville Branch
              Nashville and Davidson County Library
                   Goodlettsville, Tenn.

Building costs:
       Building and landscaping: $ 110,486
       Equipment and furniture: 20,000
Location of building: Goodlettsville, Tennessee.
Building details
       Size of building: 4,255 square feet
       Book shelving capacity: 11,000
       Reading tables: 7
       Seating capacity: 32
       Study tables: 10
Architects: Taylor and Crabtree.

The Goodlettsville Branch of the Public Library of Nashville and Davidson County was designed and built in 1967-1968.

It contains 4,255 square feet, made up of the Reading Room, Librarian's office and work space, a large meeting room, and ample service areas. The building was designed to contain 11,000 volumes.

This library, a contemporary design of brick and glass exterior walls and a heavy exposed concrete fascia, is sited to face on a quiet side street. To overcome the sloping lot, the architect placed the building on a heavily planted, concrete walled base. This ties the building to the ground and harmonizes with the concrete fascia.

The meeting room is designed to be closed off from the rest of the building and easily used when the library is not open to the public.

Figure 86.   <u>Marcy Branch</u>
                Riverside Public Library Riverside, California

Location: 3711 Central Avenue, Riverside, California.
Architect: Herman O. Ruhnau.
Costs:

Building:	$	80,320
Furnishings and equipment	$	5,711
Sprinkling system and land-scape construction:	$	3,475

Size: Total square feet: 4,275
Books: Shelving capacity, 18,750 volumes.
Floors: Vinyl tile throughout.
Ceiling: Acoustical plaster.
Air conditioning: Complete year-around weather conditioning.
Source of funds: Charles Marcy's bequeath of $55,000 supplemented
        by city funds.
Construction: Circular.
Exterior: Peach face brick walls capped with a white plaster
                fascia that is pierced with dark brown beams set the
                contemporary feeling of the building; panels of colored
                glass spark the exterior color scheme.

Interior: Walls, Norman ruffled face brick. Twelve giant beams
                radiate from the eight foot skydome. These dark
                brown laminated wood arms pierce the white plaster
                ceiling and extend beyond the walls of the building.
Conference room: seats 30 to 40 people, and opens to staff room
        for expansion.
Special features: Charging desk, central location for complete visual
        control. Outdoor reading court fenced and landscaped, opens
        off of reading room. Informal stack area with movable
        "A" shaped cases.

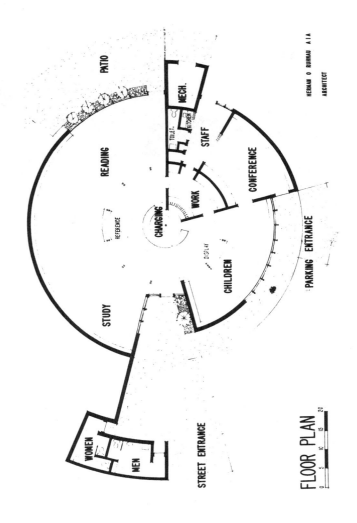

Figure 87. Floor Plan of Marcy Branch
Riverside Public Library, Riverside, Calif.

Figure 88.   <u>Des Moines Branch</u>
                    King County Library, Seattle, Washington.

Location: 22815 - 24th South, Des Moines, Washington.
Opened: December 12, 1965.
Architect: John Kniskern, Des Moines, Washington.
Size of site: 1 acre.
Size of building: 4,584 square feet.
Costs:

Site	$	9,500
Building contract		45,526
Parking lot		1,350
Furnishings		11,042
Landscaping		5,935
Fees, taxes, assessments and misc.		11,147
Total	$	84,500
Total cost per square foot	$	18.43

Source of funds: Donations to site fund $ 9,500
                     City of Des Moines bond issue   35,000
                     Federal Matching Funds   40,000
Book capacity: 25,000 volumes.
Seating capacity: Reading room   26
                      Children's area   14
Lighting: Fluorescent.
Heating: Forced air, gas fired.
Floors: Coir matting.
Ceiling: Acoustic tile.

Figure 89. Des Moines Branch
King County Library, Seattle, Washington. Interior View

Figure 90.   Serra Mesa Branch Library.   San Diego Public Library
                              San Diego, Calif.

Cost of site (74x190): $ 17,962.00
Architect: $ 6,400.00
Cost of building: $ 77,742.00
Engineering costs: $ 2,025.00
Furniture (materials only): $ 5,656.00
Sprinkling system: included in construction contract
Landscaping by Park Department
         (Materials only): $ 12,000.00
         Total $ 121,785.00

Opened: March 14, 1963
Population served: 17,000 in 1960.
Book capacity: 20,000 volumes.
Area: 4,860 sq. ft.
Construction: concrete block and plaster, exposed aggregate
                          panels and expanded glass sun screen.
Floor: vinyl asbestos.
Furniture: Bro-dart.

Special features:
         a. Covered walkway with stained glass panels.
         b. Workroom with formica work tables.
         c. Outside exhibit cases.
         d. Stan guards or rubber boots on doors.
         e. Parking for 14 cars.

Figure 91.   Carthage-Leake County Library.
A unit of the Mid-Mississippi Regional Library System, Carthage,
Mississippi.

The Carthage-Leake County Library, a unit of the Mid-
Mississippi Regional Library System, was built with funds from the
City of Carthage and matching Federal funds from the Library
Services and Construction Act through the Mississippi Library
Commission.

Building costs:
Site	$	8,250
Architect	$	5,243
Construction	$	81,597
Carpeting and drapes	$	5,800
Furniture and equipment	$	21,000
Other costs	$	1,069
Size (square feet) 5,130		
Total cost	$	122,959

Architects: Charles P. McMullan & Associates, Jackson.
General contractor: Roberts Construction Company, Carthage.
Mechanical contractor: Burns Parts and Service, Jackson.
Electrical contractor: J. F. Barnett Plumbing Company, Philadelphia
Consultants:
        Miss Mary Love, Director
        Miss Simmie Roberts, Construction Supervisor
        Mrs. Linda Harwell, Area Consultant
        Miss Mildred Huff, Construction Secretary
        Toney L. Harris, Building Consultant
        Robert L. Grady, Construction Mechanic
Dedicated April 21, 1968.

Figure 92.   Vista Branch Library
                     San Diego County Library
                       San Diego, California
                            Entrance

Location: 325 So. Melrose, Vista, California.
Architect: Lykos and Goldhammer, San Diego, California.
Date of completion: March 25, 1964.
Population served: 14,795.
Anticipated yearly circulation: 160,000.
Site: Irregular. 6.99 acres. Other buildings of the county on this
     site. Library share, if prorated: 1.26 acres.
Dimensions of buildings: 82'2"x56'0".
Area of building: 4809 square feet plus 805 square feet for bookmobile
     area.
Location of site: In San Diego Regional Center.
Parking space: If prorated, about 11 spaces for library.
Costs: Site: Approx. $6,361 (if prorated).
       Construction cost: $101,736 including built-in furniture.
       Other furniture and equipment: $4,743.

These costs are tied in with the total project, a group of county buildings at this location. If prorated the amounts would be approximately
as stated above. The entire project cost $276,000, of which $120,000
was furnished by Federal Funds.

Lighting: Integrated ceiling fixtures. Suspended fluorescent in the
     stacks.
Floor covering: Asphalt tile. Heating and/or cooling: Hot and cold
     water from office building. (In regional center).

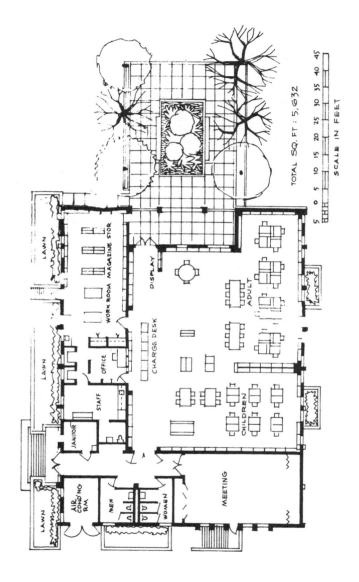

Figure 93. Makawao Library, Maui Public Library
Hawaii State Library System Floor Plan

TOTAL SQ. FT: 5,632

SCALE IN FEET
5 0 5 10 15 20 25 30 35 40 45

WORK ROOM   MAGAZINE STOR

DISPLAY

CHARGE DESK

OFFICE

STAFF

JANITOR

ADULT

CHILDREN

AIR
COND'NG
RM.

MEN

WOMEN

MEETING

LAWN
LAWN
LAWN
LAWN

Figure 94. Makawao Branch
(Hawaii State Library System)

Opened: February 1969.
Size: 5,632 square feet.
Location: Makawao Crossroads, Maui.
Architect: Edwin Murayama.
Roof: Cedar shakes.
Exterior walls: Faced with pahoehoe lava rock from Makena.
Cost of construction: Total $323,000 as follows:
        Building: $219,000
        Equipment: $41,000
        Land: $34,000
        Design and inspection: $29,000
        (Federal funds used: $44,000)
Reader capacity: 60
Meeting room and story-telling room capacity: 70.
Book capacity: 10,000 volumes.
Staff: 5.
Parking spaces: 17 plus 1 reserved for the handicapped.
Special features:
        Carpeted, air-conditioned, equipped with microfilm reader
            and study carrels wired for film strip projection and with
            earphones.
        As part of the Hawaii State Library System it will be linked,
            through the Wailuku Library, by daily phone and teletype
            service with the State Library, Honolulu.
        Designed in Hawaiian style, with cedar shake roof and
            exterior walls of native rock.

Medium-Sized Branches

6, 000-9, 999 Square Feet

Arranged in order of increasing size

Figure 95. <u>St. Albans Public Library</u>, St. Albans, West Virginia
                          6000 sq. feet
Interior view showing skillful use of stone in entryway and on fireplace
                              wall

Location: St. Albans, West Virginia (Population 15,000).
Service area: St. Albans plus parts of adjoining communities.
    Total population, 25,000.
Building completed: 1963 (Became branch of Kanawha County at that
    time).
Size of building: 6000 square feet.
Costs:

Construction:	$	109,394
Architectural and engineering fees:	$	5,823
Legal and administration expenses:	$	300
Site:	$	18,000
Furniture:	$	10,970
Total:	$	144,487

Building design: Built to accommodate a second story if and when
    needed.
Source of funds for building: One half of cost assumed by Area
    Redevelopment Administration and half through local contribution
    in St. Albans and from building funds raised at St. Albans Town
    Fair held each year by St. Albans Library Board. Yearly town
    fair brings together all civic organizations who work together
    raising money for the branch.
Circulation: Approximately 115,000.
Air-conditioning.
Parking: 4 spaces reserved for staff at rear of building. A huge
    supermarket and parking facility is located across the street.
    Their management and the librarian, Nicholas Winowich, agree
    they are good for each other.

Figure 96.   Griffith Branch, Lake County Public Library, opened
             in June of 1967.   Front on east elevation.

Location: Griffith, Indiana.
Architect: Wildermuth and Bone.
Size: 6000 square feet.
Costs:

Building (including built-in equipment) cost per square foot $20.07	$120,420
Site:	12,000
Fees: Architect	7,225
Equipment and furniture (other than built-in)	16,000
Total project cost: cost per square foot $25.94	$155,645

Lighting: Fluorescent recessed.
Floors: Carpet.
Air conditioning with gas heating.
Book capacity: Open shelf capacity, 22,000 volumes.
    Exhibit cases built-in, in building contract.
Ceilings: Acoustical and fireproof.
Glass: Heat absorbing.
Meeting room: Soundproof, multi-purpose type, accommodating
    40-60 people. Equipped with kitchenette facilities.
Unusual feature: This branch uses the same standard floor plan and
    general design as four other new branches.   One architect
    was employed and one contract let for all five structures.

Figure 97. <u>Griffith Branch</u>, Lake County Public Library houses
22,000 volumes within a total of 6,000 sq. ft.   A
glass wall overlooks the outdoor reading patio.

Figure 98. <u>Mariner's Branch</u>, Newport Beach Public Library,
Newport Beach, California.

Figure 99. <u>Mariner's Branch Library</u>, Newport Beach Public Library,
Newport Beach, Calif.

Location: Newport Beach, California
Building features:
  Design: Contemporary, of brick and stucco with laminated beams.
             Two reading courts, flexible spare with minimum of
             fixed walls, particular attention paid to control of sky
             glare.
Architect: Blurock and Ellerbroek.
General Contractor: Warren Crosby.
Building and cost data:
             Building (Design and construction) $ 86,184.00
             Furnishings,equipment (including
                book shelving and charging desk $ 9,575.76
             Total cost $ 94,759.76
             Area of building   sq. ft.   4,950
             Area of covered courts   sq. ft.   1,125
                Total area   sq. ft.   6,075
             Construction price per sq. ft. $ 15.37
             Book Capacity   19,000
             Seating capacity   83
Opened April 2, 1963.

Figure 100. <u>University Heights Branch Library</u>, San Diego Public
Library, San Diego, California--Entrance.

Cost of site (140x50)   City owned
Cost of building (includes architect
    and engineering): $ 135,101
Furniture: $ 6,404
Landscaping by Park Department: $ 1,500
    Total: $ 143,005

Opened: April 19, 1966.
Book capacity: 41,830 volumes
Area: 3,749 sq. ft. on main floor
                                  150 sq. ft. covered walk
                                2,709 sq. ft. lower level
    Total   6,608 sq. ft.

Construction: hollow tile, brick and stucco with
                                   partial redwood siding.
    Floor: Burke 109 marbleized rubber tile, with
                                   asphalt tile downstairs.
    Furniture: card catalogs from Bro-dart.
                                tables and chairs from Sjostrom, walnut
                                   finish, table tops videcor plastic.
    Draperies: Fiberglass Type A, Designer 1D,
                                   pattern "Vertigo", color bronze,
                                   Feneshield Fabrics.

Special features:
    a. Bookmobile headquarters for two vehicles.
    b. Parking for 6 cars can later be expanded with off-street
        parking on Howard Street. Location by Safeway Stores
        parking lot actually provides ample parking.

Figure 101. Glen Innes Branch,
Auckland Public Library, Auckland, New Zealand

Figure 102. <u>Glen Innes Branch</u>, Auckland Public Library, Auckland, New Zealand. Adult Reading Room.

Location: Glen Innes is one of the eastern suburbs of the City of Auckland. The branch site forms part of a 2-acre block set aside for a community center, directly opposite the central axis of the shopping center, immediately adjacent to a large free parking area.

Size: 1 story, low style, 6,870 square feet.

Exterior walls: Precast concrete panels of exposed South Island river schist.

Interior walls: Lined with fibrous plaster.

Floor: Concrete covered with 12-inch square dark gray vinyl tiles, with carpet of yellow tones in adult reading room.

Lighting: 50-foot candles at table-top height over the whole of library area. Tinted glass on the west elevation.

Heating: Underfloor pyrotenax, thermostatically controlled. No fixed partitions except for staff room and kitchen.

Book capacity: 22,000 volumes

Seating capacity: 54 readers

Size of individual areas: Workroom: 300 square feet
                             Children's section: 1200 square feet
                             Lounge area: 400 square feet carpeted.

Staff: Librarian plus 2 assistants. Provision for total of 6.

Hours open: 47 per week

Figure 103. <u>Maplewood Branch,</u> Ramsey County Public Library, Maplewood, Minnesota. Charge-out Desk Area.

Architects: Buetow & Associates
Consultant: Robert H. Rohlf
General Contractor: Larson Building Company - $113,593.89.
Mechanical contractor: Acme Heating, Sheet Metal & Roofing Co.
 $27,735.00.
Electrical contractor: Kehne Electric Company - $15,043.00
Landscaping: Dundee Nursery & Landscaping Company - $1,695.00.
Library furniture & equipment:
 Remington Rand Office Systems $ 18,864.25
 General Office Products $ 3,068.70
 Farnham's $ 1,205.77

Miscellaneous equipment and costs $25,379.54
 (Includes architect and consultant fees)
Site: 2 acres donated by the Village of Maplewood.
Size of building: 7,000 square feet.
Total cost: $206,585.15 (Federal funds, $68,500.00; Library
 Building Fund, $138,085.15)
Dedicated May 21, 1967.

Figure 104.   North End Branch, Boston Public Library, Boston,
              Massachusetts. Children's Area and Atrium.

Dedication date: May 5, 1965.
Architects: Carl Koch and Associates, Cambridge, Mass.
Cost of Building: Over $220,000 plus approximately $30,000 for
          furnishings.
Materials: Brick, glass, ceramics, Philippine mahogany.
Lighting: Softly diffused indirect fluorescent.
Size of building: Approximately 7,200 square feet.
Heating and air-conditioning: Gas heat; air conditioning throughout.
Book capacity: 19,000 volumes.
All-purpose room seating capacity: 100 persons.
Type of design: Simple, one-story red brick in the Roman tradition.
Unusual features:
          This branch is located in a neighborhood with a deep Italian back-
ground and Latinate feeling. Hence the Roman architecture, three pieces
of statuary on Italian subjects; colors of vibrant blues, greens, purple,
orange, red, absinthe green, and yellow in the upholstery and drapes,
all Italianate colors; the furniture in simple, modern walnut in black
and white. There is a colorful children's room with white round tables,
and an informally-furnished browsing area. The all-purpose room is to
the rear of the children's room and separated from it by a handsome
flexidoor.
          Colorful striped area rugs have been used for the first time in
the Boston Public Library branches, having proven themselves of high
durability and low maintenance cost elsewhere.
          All reading rooms have listening apparatus.

Figure 105. North End Branch,
Boston Public Library, Boston, Massachusetts. Browsing Area and Adult Reading Room.

Figure 106.   Sandy Springs Branch, Atlanta and Fulton County
              Libraries, Atlanta, Georgia

Architects: Barker and Cunningham.
Size: 7400 square feet.
Dedicated: Feb. 28, 1965
Cost: Exclusive of landscaping and furnishings: $115,000.
Book capacity:
               15,000 volumes. (Expansion plans call for a balcony
               and a future wing to house additional volumes).
Source of building funds: 1963 Fulton County Bond Issue.
Ceiling: Cathedral type supported by wooden laminated arches.
Walls: Steel, concrete and masonry.
Air-conditioning: Year round.
Assembly room for community meetings.
Location of branch: Vicinity of Atlanta near Sandy Hills
               Shopping Center.
Planned for: Ease of supervision, ease of maintenance, minimum
               staff, simplicity of plan for economy, ease of
               expansion, good heating and air conditioning, in-
               viting appearance of building and grounds.
Special features:
               Pre-cast concrete exterior panels which illustrate
               the history of the graphic arts (see photo) are the
               focal points of the exterior. The panels were
               executed by Fred R. Schoenfeld of Atlanta.
               Fireplace of copper
               Carpeting

Figure 107.   <u>Sandy Springs Branch.</u>

Atlanta and Fulton County Libraries,
Atlanta, Georgia. Exterior Panels.

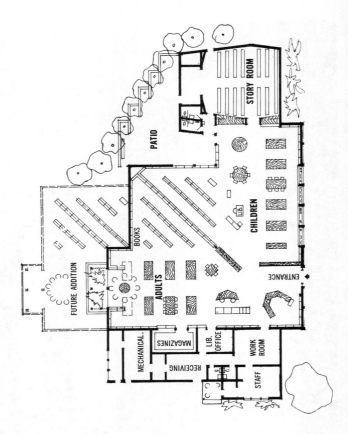

Figure 108. Elva Haskett Branch, Anaheim Public Library, Anaheim, California

Figure 109. <u>Elva L. Haskett Branch</u>, Anaheim Public Library,
Anaheim, California. Exterior.

Dedicated August 12, 1962
Architect: Thomas J. Russell, A.I.A., Long Beach, California.
General contractor: Cal-Grove Builders, Inc., Garden Grove,
California.
Size of building: 7,534 square feet
Present seating capacity:
  Reading area   89
  Auditorium   60
Off street parking spaces: 26
Approximate cost: $170,000
Special features: Outdoor story hour patio, many exhibit cases, ease
of supervision, open modular construction, inviting appearance.

Figure 110.   <u>Elva L. Haskett Branch</u>, Anaheim Public Library,
Anaheim, California. Adult Reading Room.

Figure 111.   Pico Rivera Library, Los Angeles County Public
               Library System.

Location: Pico Rivera, California.
Dedicated: December 18, 1961.
Architect: Harold J. Nicolais.
Size: 7,568 square feet.
Cost of project:

Architect s fee:	$	13,625
Construction	$	196,942
Furniture	$	13,836
Shelving and incidentals	$	15,319
Total Cost	$	239,722.

Book capacity: 42,000 volumes.
General building description: Round contemporary design of brick
    masonry walls, air-conditioning, concrete slab floors.
Lighting: Fluorescent.
Acoustical treatment.
Parking: 38 cars.

Lake Hills Branch, King County Library, Seattle, Washington.
Location: 15230 Lake Hills Blvd. , Bellevue, Wash. 98004
Opened: December 8, 1968.
Architect: John Morse & Associates.
Landscape
  Architect: Glen Hunt & Associates.
Building area: 7,600 square feet.
Costs:

Site preparation	$	34,417
Construction contract		210,161
Furnishings		20,582
Total cost	$	265,160

Site: Donated by Lake Hills Community Club.
Book capacity: 25,000 volumes.
Multi-purpose room.
Floors: Carpeted.
Air conditioned.
Phonograph listening tables.
Source of funds:

Donations by Cascade Library Association	$	10,000
King County Library bond issue, 1966		140,219
Library Services & Construction Act		114,941

Figure 112.   Lake Hills Branch, King County Library, Seattle,
                 Washington. Floor plan.

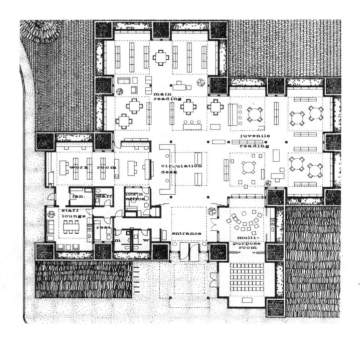

Figure 113.   Lake Hills Branch, King County Library System.
               Bellevue, Washington

Figure 114.   Entrance Detail, Lake Hills Branch of the King County
               Library System, Bellevue, Wash.

Figure 115.   <u>Crenshaw-Imperial Branch,</u> Inglewood Public Library, Inglewood, California.

Location:	11141 So. Crenshaw Blvd. , Inglewood, California, at a signalized intersection adjacent to a shopping center.
Opened:	October 1965.
Architect:	Graham Latta.
Costs:	Not given.
Building area:	7,760 square feet.
Book capacity:	40,000 volumes.
Seating capacity:	100.

Air Conditioning.

Phonograph records and tapes.

Parking:	Adequate parking is provided.
Special features:	Listening tables, art reproductions, individual seating. Typing rooms. Photocopier.

Ballard Branch
Seattle Public Library
Seattle, Washington

Location: 5711 - 24th Avenue, N. W. , Seattle, Washington.
Population served: 46,000.
Date of completion: June 7, 1963.
Architects: Mandeville & Berge, 500 Union Street, Seattle,
                Washington.
Area:
        Dimensions of site: 100' x 200'
        Square feet of floor space: 7,900 square feet
        Dimensions of building   119' x 65' (outside dimensions)
                                    44' x 20' (basement)
            Reading room: 38' x 59'   19' x 16'
            Children's area: 26' x 59'
            Staff room: 12' x 15'
            Work room: 15' x 40'   15' x 6'
            Heating and ventilating: 19' x 22'
            Janitor's room: 7' x 8'   20' x 19'
            Rest rooms: 5' x 8'   5' x 8'   5' x 8'
Costs:
        Cost of site: $ 70,061.00
        Cost of building construction: 167,258.00
        Cost per sq. ft. (building
            construction)   21.18
        Equipment and furnishings: 11,413.00
        Landscaping (included in contract)   7,198.00
        Art work: 2,800.00
        Washington State Sales Tax: 6,471.00
                Total cost $ 297,177.00
        Cost per square foot: $35.78
Financing: 1956 Library Bond Fund.
Building type outside: Rubble stone walls and piers--stucco panels
        with marble chips.
Lighting: Indirect fluorescent - luminous ceiling.
Floor covering: Homogeneous vinyl Corlon sheeting over concrete
        floors.
Heating and ventilating: Gas fired boiler with multi-zoned air handling
        and DX coils for cooling.
Equipment and furnishings: Shelving, Ames catalog cases, Stacor
        chairs, Bella, Knoll tables, Magna charging desk.
Seating capacity: Adult: 55; juvenile: 45.
Book capacity: Open shelves: 27,816; work room and storage:
        4,104; total: 31,920.
Parking: 20 cars.

Exterior walls of marble chip aggregate stucco, ashler stone columns,
a cedar shake room and an unusual ridgepole covered with etched copper are distinguishing characteristics of this branch library.

Figure 116. <u>Ballard Branch</u>, Seattle Public Library, Seattle, <u>Washington</u>. Exterior View.

Figure 117. <u>Ballard Branch</u>, Seattle Public Library, Seattle, <u>Washington</u>. Interior View.

Lake City Branch
Seattle Public Library, Seattle, Washington.

Location: 12501 - 28th Avenue, N.E., Seattle, Washington.
Population served: Approximately 30,000.
Date of completion: October 28, 1965.
Architect: John Morse and Associates, Tower Building,
                 Seattle, Washington.
Art work: Bronze gates by George Tsutakawa.
Area: Dimension of site 300x130.5.   Square feet of floor
                 space 9546.   Adult public area 67x57.   Children's
                 public area 67x31.   Service wing: Circulation
                 lobby 32x15.   Work area behind circulation desk
                 20x27.   Storerooms 12x6 and 11x5.   Toilets
                 6x8, 6x8, and 6x8.   Staff lounge 18x12.   Quiet
                 room 8x8.   Librarian's office 13x10.   Corridors
                 5x9 and 5x19.   Enclosed front courtyard 42x20.
                 Enclosed rear courtyard 42x17.
Costs: Building, $224,068.   Site, $50,000.   Furnishings,
                 $28,365.   Art work, $5,500.   Fees and taxes,
                 $35,108.   Miscellaneous, $1,481.   Total cost,
                 $344,522.
Financing: $44,000 from 1956 Library Bond Fund.
                 Balance from City Cumulative Reserve Fund.
Building type: Reinforced brick masonry walls, steel truss roof,
                 exposed brick and dry wall interior.
Lighting: Fluorescent panels with plastic diffusers.
                 Incandescent high lighting.
Floor covering: Vinyl asbestos and carpet over concrete slab.
Equipment and furnishings:
                 Steel shelving, Ames
                 Card catalog, Union Zeiss
                 Custom desk, shelving and millwork, Soderlund
                 Incidental furniture, Bank and Office Interiors.
Heating and ventilating: Package type gas fired air conditioner
                 mounted on roof.
Seating: Adult 50. Children 50.
Parking: 32 cars.
Book capacity: 32,000 adult.   12,000 juvenile.

Figure 118.   Lake City Branch, Seattle Public Library,
Seattle, Washington. Exterior view.

Figure 119.   Lake City Branch, Seattle Public Library,
Seattle, Washington. Interior View.

Large Branches
10, 000-14, 999 Square Feet
Arranged in order of increasing size

Figure 120.   Donald G. Mitchell Branch, New Haven Free Public
              Library. New Haven, Connecticut.

Architect: Gilbert Switzer.
Consultants: Sylvan R. Shemitz and Associates (lighting).
                Sasaki, Dawson, DeMay Associates (landscaping).
Size: 10,000 square feet.
Costs: Building cost, including built-in equipment $256,321.
                    Cost per square foot: $25.63
                Cost additions:
                    Site: City land, sitework in general contract
                    Landscaping: $2,373
                    Fees: Architect: $21,945
                    Legal: $187
                    Furniture and equipment other than built-ins:
                        $27,851.34
                    Art Work: $200
                Total project cost: $321,000. Cost per sq. ft. $32.10.
Lighting: Fluorescent. Down lights, wall-mounted cylinders;
                    stack lights.
Floors: Carpet; vinyl tile, terrazzo.
Heating and air-conditioning: Oil fired, all-air, multiple zone,
        low velocity, with air-cooled condensers located in roof.
Shelves and stacks: Steel.
Book capacity: 35,000 volumes.
Meeting room seating capacity: 75.
Reader seating capacity: 45 adults, 50 children.

Interior finish maintains the low key used in the overall design. This
branch avoids the use of great quantities of glass. It has no picture
windows.

The Donald G. Mitchell Branch was the first to be built under a plan
recommended by Emerson Greenaway, director of the Free Library
of Philadelphia and library consultant to the City of New Haven.

Figure 121. <u>Raleigh Branch Library</u>, Memphis Public Library,
         Memphis, Tennessee

Opened: 1966
Building area: 10,000 square feet.
Site area: 34,500 square feet.
Population served: 20,000 now (up to 50,000 in near future).
Costs:
         Site: $ 20,000
         Construction: 189,890
         Equipment: 18,704
Book capacity: 37,275.
Reader seats: 92.
Meeting room seats: 100.

Figure 122.   <u>Raleigh Branch Library</u> Interior features blue and gold
         carpet, two information and reference desks side by side.

Figure 123. <u>Greenwood Branch,</u> Corpus Christi Public Libraries,
Corpus Christi, Texas. Unusual square-on-square design.

Completed: September 1966. Architects: Orby G. Roots and James M.
Burnett. Size of building: 10,000 square feet. Plan: Unusual
square-on-square design. Meeting room: Divided by a folding door
allows two meetings simultaneously.

Interesting philosophy underlying square-on-square, and round
shapes. The round feature was conceived by the architect who built the
Parkdale Branch, Corpus Christi's first. He felt that the only way the
proverbial librarian could do all the tasks outlined for her would be for
her to be placed in the exact center of the room, build the multi-purpose desk around her, and surround the desk with the various service
areas and workroom. This plan has proved very workable and the
second branch, Greenwood, retained the round circulation desk and
used the square-on-square effect. Work area is glass enclosed.

Special features:
1. Drive-through night depository for books adjoins the
parking area.
2. Placement of the book stacks on a radial pattern to allow
complete visual control of all parts of the reading room and children's
area from the central focal point of the large circular charge desk.
3. Thirty foot long corkboard mural on one wall of children's
alcove.
4. Automatic sliding glass doors at two main entrances, one
at the street intersection, one at the parking lot.
5. A cork mural which can also serve as a bulletin board,
but looks nice even when seasonal decor does not change the simple
background into the message of the day.
6. Greenwood Branch serves as headquarters for the Community Action Program with a full range of special services for the
disadvantaged.
7. Branch acts as a collection agency for city utility bills--
finds itself involved in being the "answer man" for any questions area
residents want resolved. Serves as a satellite city hall.

Figure 124. Greenwood Branch, Corpus Christi Public Library.
Interior showing round charging area.

Figure 125. Greenwood Branch Library. Floor plan.

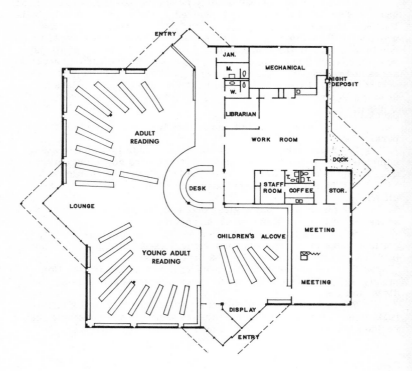

Figure 126. <u>Hobart Library,</u> Member of the Lake County Public
Library System, Indiana. Unusual architecture shown
in this series of eight square forms interconnected to
form one large space of 10,000 square feet.

Location: Hobart, Indiana.
Size: 10,000 square feet.
Costs: Not given.
Book capacity: 38,000 volumes.
Floors: Carpeted.
Air Conditioned.
Multi-purpose meeting room enclosed by movable partitions.
Outside reading and story area.
Walls: Exterior and interior of textured concrete.
Roof and ceiling: Laminated wood beams and timber decking.

Unusual feature:

Building on three levels separated by three steps, each
providing changes of elevation in view of the lake adjoining the site.

Question: Does this not pose a problem for the handicapped and
for book carts going from one level to the other?

Figure 127. <u>Parkdale Branch,</u> Corpus Christi Public Libraries,
            Corpus Christi, Texas.   Interior, showing circular
            charging desk.   Bookstacks are placed like the spokes
            of a wheel in this round building, and there is wall
            shelving between the blue-tiled pillars.   Adult and
            juvenile card catalogs flank the circulation desk to be
            equally accessible to the public and the staff.

Location: 4425 Gollihor Street, Corpus Christi. Prime shopping
              center location.
Dedicated: October 2, 1962.
Architect: Joseph Hans.
Size: 10,000 square feet.
Materials: Concrete and steel.
Book capacity: 80,000 books.
Large lounge with an entrance on the patio was designed both for
              staff use and as a meeting room for the public.
Walls: Interior: Brick with glass panels between circulation
              desk and anteroom.
Cost of building: $173,700. Bond issue for $195,000.
Bookmobile garage with loading dock opening directly into the
              workroom.
Future expansion provided for by a partially finished second floor.
Design: Modern in-the-round structure.
Special Features:
              Glare-free smoked glass window panels approached over a wide
              free-form bridge.
              Comfortable reading and browsing centers are provided both
              near the main entrance and children's door.
              Blue tiled pillars on the walls with wall shelving between.
              Book stacks arranged like the spokes on a wheel.
              Garden patio highlighted with garden sculpture is a pleasant
              location for outside story-telling and reading.

Figure 128.   South Boston Branch, Boston Public Library.

Opened: November 1, 1957.

Location: 646 East Broadway.

Architects: Shepley, Bunfinch, Richardson, and Abbott, Boston.

Book Capacity: 22,000 volumes.

Size: 10,332 square feet.

Construction material: Cinder blocks, brick, steel, and acoustical
        control.

Ceiling: Three-way radiant panel functional provides heating, cool-
        ing, and acoustical control.

Interior design: Open modular type reading room.

All-purpose meeting room has motion picture projection equipment,
        record playing equipment, and sound track.

Special features:

        Landscaping includes a garden with numerous trees to be
        used as an outdoor reading room and story hour gathering
        place.

Figure 129. Sunnyside Branch, 100 Edgewood Road, Linden, New
Jersey. Branch of Linden Free Public Library.
Simplicity of design marks this medium-sized branch.

Completed: June, 1960
Architect: Milton L. Scheingarten, A.I.A. Fee $15,100--6% of
cost.
Size of building: Approximately 10,200 square feet. Includes 1,655
square feet devoted to housing the Recreation
Commission. Library, 8,535 sq. ft.
Type of construction: Long-span steel joists on bearing walls of
brick and block back-up; insulrock roof, concrete
slab on grade; aluminum sash and curtain wall with
tile insulated panels.
Building cost: Cost of site - none - City owned
Construction cost: $ 18.60 per square foot
Building cost: $213,571. including paving
Landscaping   4,385.
Sculpture: 5,300.
Furniture: 28,386.
Total $251,642, plus $22,813
for books and other equipment.
Source of funds: Special appropriation $5,000; special ordinance
1959, $285,000.
Lighting: Luminous acoustic in reading area; other areas recessed
incandescent. Exterior wall brackets and post lights--
Holophane.
Floors: Terrazzo in lobby and toilets; asphalt tile in storage area;
rubber tile in other areas.
Heating and air conditioning: Central oil-fired hot water heating with
heating coils in air-conditioning units and convectors in other
areas. 20 ton AC unit for library, 7-1/2 ton AC unit for
auditorium; 3 ton AC unit for recreation area.
Books: Total volume capacity: 20,000; Linear footage wood shelving:
57'x7' high; 33'x5' high; 190'x4' high.
Seating capacity of auditorium: 125; Seating capacity for readers:
Adult, 68; children, 50. Parking area: 6,508 square feet.

Figure 130. <u>West End Branch,</u> Boston Public Library.

Address: 151 Cambridge Street, Boston, Massachusetts.

Dedication: January 25, 1968.

Architects: Maginnis and Walsh and Kennedy, Boston, Massachusetts.

Cost of building: Over $320,000 plus approximately $22,000 for
    furnishings.

Materials: Red brick, concrete, and insulated glass in aluminum
    frames.

Size: Over 10,600 square feet.

Books: Over 22,000 volumes.

Type of design: Modern hexagonal unit attached to a rectangular unit
    at western boundary.

Lighting: Natural light through window walls. Fluorescent. All-
    purpose room equipped for sound and projection purposes.

Note: One branch librarian administers this branch and the North End
    Branch.

Unusual features: Space is provided for the permanent storage of
    voting equipment which will be in use during elections when
    the all-purpose room will become a polling place.

Figure 131.   <u>Nokomis Branch</u>, Minneapolis Public Library,
              Minneapolis, Minnesota. Stone and glass are
              artistically combined in this 10,600 sq. foot branch.
              A story-telling loft, reached by an open stairway, is
              a unique architectural feature, and in the center of
              the building is a pool in which is set a specially-
              commissioned glass and metal sculpture, a gift of the
              airport area Merchants' Association. It will feature
              the play of light and water over colored glass.

Completed: September 1968.
Size: 10,600 sq. ft. (Ground floor 8,000 square feet.
                   Lower floor, 2,600 square feet).
Architects: Buetow and Associates, Inc., St. Paul.
Meeting room - Capacity 100 people, equipped with sound and
                projection equipment.
Entire building air-conditioned.
Elevator.
Cost: Land $54,950.00
                Building, including architect's fee - $420,078.00.
                Equipment and furnishings - $50,508.00.
                Contingency, appraisal, and condemnation fees -
                   $10,752.00.
                Total cost - $536,288.
Parking: Space provided for approximately 20 cars.
Book capacity: 30,000 volumes.
Fully carpeted in earth tones which are repeated in the furnishings.
Stone walls used on interior. Exterior brick and decorative concrete.

Nokomis Community has an attractive, sound, residential environment. It has the city's largest proportion of single houses, and
educational attainment in 1960 was equal to or above the city's
average. Also, this community showed the second highest median
family income of any community in the city.

Meadow Park Branch
Evansville Public Library, Evansville, Indiana

Opened: December 9, 1968. This is a regional branch.
Location: At the edge of a large shopping center.
Service area: 15,000-25,000 people.
Staff: 6 full time, 3 part time, and a janitor.
Architects: Heronimus-Knapp-Given, Associates.
Book capacity:35,000-50,000 volumes.
Size of building: Approximately 11,070 square feet.
Cost: $350,150.
Source of funds: Local bond issue, $225,000 and site, $22,650.
                   Federal grant, $102,500.
Evansville profited by mistakes made in the building of McCullough
            Branch two years earlier. Meadow Park has less
            glass, does not have two public entrances to the
            reading room.
Special features: All non-library services (public phone, rest
            rooms, drinking fountain, and meeting room) are
            outside the library proper.
            Sound system - ceiling speakers in all areas to pro-
            vide background music, and a public address system
            and ten individual "listening posts" around the wall of
            the reading room. It is all tied in to a console in
            the librarian's office where she can play tapes,
            records, or AM-FM radio over any one of three
            channels. The sound system was a gift from the
            late Marjorie B. Harte, a member of the library
            staff for many years.
Building consultants:
            Donald E. Thompson, Librarian, Wabash College,
                Crawfordsville, Indiana.
            Arthur Harrell, Consultant, Title II, Library
                Services and Construction Act, Indiana State
                Library, Indianapolis, Indiana.

Figure 132.   Meadow Park Branch, Evansville Public Library.

Figure 133. <u>Hampton-Illinois Branch,</u> Dallas Public Library, Dallas,
Texas. Exterior View. Interesting combination of
square and round design.

Opened: April 4, 1964.
Architect: Harold A. Berry.
Size: Floor space, 11,181 square feet.
Costs: Not given.
Book capacity, maximum: 45,000 volumes.
Seating capacity:
               Library, 83.
               Auditorium, 100.
Auditorium: Used for library-sponsored programs and is available
               to educational, civic, cultural and governmental
               organizations.
Exterior: The form of the library develops from the convergence
               of large circular and rectangular masses. Set
               against the arresting lines of the structure, the
               turquoise-tiled roof overhang and the beige building
               stone express a genial contemporary effect,
               emphasized by the metal and ceramic sculpture in
               the lobby, a gift of the architect.
Interior: A clerestory above the lobby adds a soaring dimension.
               The glow of upholstery fabrics and the warmth of
               walnut underline an effervescent decor.

This branch is part of an expanding public library system for
Dallas, initiated by the branch survey of 1957, sponsored by the
Friends of the Dallas Public Library, and supported by bond issues
in 1958 and 1962.

Figure 134. <u>Hampton-Illinois Branch.</u> Young Adult Area.

Figure 135. <u>Hampton-Illinois Branch.</u> Children's Area.

Figure 136. <u>Roslindale Branch</u>, Boston Public Library. Combination
of round and rectangular design to fit an odd-shaped
site.

Courtesy of the Trustees of
The Boston Public Library

Location: Shopping area.
Architects: Isador Richmond and Carney Goldberg, Boston.
Size: 11,600 square feet. Public service area: 7,500
                 square feet.
Costs: Building: $293,650 (architectural fee, $21,666.60;
                 landscaping, $1,000). Furnishings and equipment,
                 approximately $40,000.
Materials: Structural steel, plain and reinforced concrete.
Floors: Vinyl asbestos tile.
Heating: Hot water.
Lighting: Fluorescent supplemented by incandescent.
Book capacity: 26,000 volumes.
Building design:
        An irregularly-shaped pentagon site with a culvert carrying
        an underground brook across one corner posed a problem.
        The architects had to leave this area free of construction or pro-
        vide access to the culvert within the building. The building was
        therefore built semi-circular in shape with a low-flying dome
        surmounting the center. Natural light is admitted through large
        window areas on the facades facing heavily trafficked streets.
All-purpose room (pie-shaped) has kitchenette, cloak room, a platform.
Special features:
        Smoking room 12x19.5 feet. Equal reading room space for
        children and adults, 2000 square feet each. Large storage
        room, 29x25 feet. Control desk for charging has vision of
        entire semi-circular area.

Figure 137. <u>McCollough Branch</u>, Evansville Public Library,
Evansville, Indiana.

Opened: June 1, 1965.
Architect: Jack R. Kinkel.
Staff: 6 full-time, plus 3 part-time and janitor.
Book capacity: 35,000-50,000 volumes.
Size of building:
               11,668 square feet.
       McCollough Branch also serves as the bookmobile head-
       quarters.   A large drive-through garage with an adjacent
       loading dock filled with books, accommodates the mobile
       unit.   There is a workroom for the bookmobile staff. This
       branch is so located on the perimeter of the city that the
       bookmobile can reach the people it is designed to serve on
       the fringes of the city and in the county.   No longer must
       the bookmobile staff fight traffic for one to seven miles
       before reaching the first stop and first borrower.
Special features:
       McCollough has a drive-in window for service. There is no
       front door. Entrances are at either end of the reading room.

       The front wall of the reading room is made entirely of glass.
       This has been found to be a mistake, because it precludes wall
       shelving there and makes the branch too vulnerable to vandalism.

       Two-color carpeting--one color for the main traffic lane and
       around the charging desk, another for the rest of the reading
       room. This permits replacement of the most used carpet with-
       out trying to match the rest. It also provides a psychological
       dividing line between the reading room proper and the charge
       area.

Figure 138. <u>Kahului Branch</u>, Hawaii State Library System. Located
on the Island of Maui, this attractive branch serves a
population of approximately 20,000.

Location: Island of Maui.
Built: 1962.
Population of service area (1967 estimate): 19,400.
Site: 66,556.
Building size: 11,862 square feet.
Book capacity: 30,000 volumes.
Circulation, last fiscal year:
                 86,301.
Off-street parking:
                 30.
Building is expandable.

West Valley Regional Branch
Los Angeles Public Library, Los Angeles, California

Location: 19036 Vanowen Street, Reseda, California.
Opened: November 14, 1960.
Architect: Allison and Rible.
Area served: Designed as regional branch, to be administrative
     headquarters for library service in western portion of San
     Fernando Valley.
Floor space: 12,469 square feet (gross).
Site: Interior lot in West Valley Municipal Center.
Cost: Plans $ 21,200
                    Total construction costs (estimate):   268,038
                    Furnishings including shelving,
                        circulation desk, reading room,
                        office and workroom furniture
                        (estimate):   43,608
                    Total cost (estimate): $332,846
                Total building cost (estimate) $260,617
                Cost per square foot: $20.90.
Book capacity: 65,700
Book stock: 62,000.
Circulation: 666,000 (estimated).
Parking area: 21 parking spaces, plus municipal parking lot in rear.
Style and materials: A contemporary pavilion type structure; structural
     steel columns placed outside the walls of building with porcelain-
     ized aluminum sun screen mounted on the upper part of the
     columns.
Color scheme: Exterior: Blue expanded metal sun screen, dark
     brown steel columns. Exposed pebbles in various tones
     in concrete panels.
               Interior: Walls of colonial blue, antique gold and
     sunlight yellow. Doors of burnt orange provide a pleasant
     accent.
Floor: Rubber tile, desert sand shades.
Lighting: Fluorescent tubes.
Ceiling: Acoustical tile.
Heating and ventilating: Fully air-conditioned.
Seating capacity: 84 adults, 42 children.
Special features:
               Free standing partitions in blue or gold partially
     enclose the charging desk area and tend to separate the
     different areas of the library. The huge column-free space
     is particularly impressive and allows maximum flexibility in
     stack and furniture arrangement. Lounge area between adult
     and children's room.
Furnishings: Tables, chairs, charging desk, shelving: wood, light
     birch; desks and vertical files: steel, desert sage.

Figure 139. West Valley Regional Branch, Los Angeles Public Library.

Loch Raven Community Branch
Baltimore County Public Library
Towson, Maryland

Architect: Fryer and Associates.

Size: Gross floor area: 12,500 square feet.

Costs:	Building cost (includes some built-ins):	$304,100
	Cost per square foot: $24.32.	
	Site:	4,500
	Fees: Architect:	18,246
	Miscellaneous:	3,000
	Equip. and Furn. (other than built-ins):	35,557
	Total project cost:	$382,412
	Cost per square foot: $30.57	

Lighting: Armstrong integrated ceiling (recessed and surface-
mounted fluorescent), recessed incandescent.

Floors: Acrilan carpet (public areas); Pennsylvania bluestone
(lobby); vinyl asbestos tile (lower level non-public
areas and meeting room).

Heating: Gas-fired hot water/hot air.

Air conditioning: Chilled water.

Books: Open shelf capacity: 35,000 volumes; closed stack and
storage, 7,500.

General: The site for the branch library is a steeply sloped,
wooded ravine with a small stream. The branch is located on
one side of the slope and the public parking area on the opposite
slope. A pedestrian bridge crosses the ravine and connects the
parking lot with the main entrance in a court within the building.
Grade level entrances are provided by surfaced walkways through
the woods.

Unconcealed quartz-textured columns rise from the
ground like trees and thrust through the second level to the roof.
Exposed aggregate exterior walls and a lower level patio also
blend the structure into the surrounding foliage and land con-
tours. Three large exterior window areas provide from the
interior a secluded atmosphere despite the fact that the site
adjoins one of four large shopping centers located at a nearby
busy intersection. At night these windows present, through the
trees, a bright and pleasant view of the interior. This effect is
reinforced by a narrow illuminated window strip which circum-
scribes the building at the second floor level.

Inside, the children and adult areas are carpeted, with
teak, walnut and polished chrome furniture. The public service
floor contains a lobby, periodical and book storage room,
clerical and librarians' offices. The lower floor includes a
small staff room, restrooms, some mechanical equipment, and
a meeting room. The floors are paved with a seamless resilient covering. This covering enhances the outdoors feeling of
the meeting room which has two walls of glass.

Figure 140. Loch Raven Branch, 1048 Taylor Ave., Baltimore, Maryland.   Branch of Baltimore County Public Library.   Adult area, upper floor; verandah and meeting room, lower floor.

Figure 141.   <u>Far Rockaway Branch</u>, Queens Borough Public Library,
              New York

Architect: Mr. Robert Bien.
Population served:
                37,344.
Site Size: 12,560 square feet.
Building Size: 8,518 square feet.
Cost: $323,000.
Lighting: Fluorescent.
Floors: Vinyl asbestos.
Heating: Forced air, gas-fired.
Air conditioning:
                Air cooled, 50 tons.
Parking spaces on site:
                6
Dignified simplicity is the tone of this one-story branch with a
    limited construction budget.   The building exterior is of pre-
    cast concrete harmoniously blended with dark brown colored
    brick.
Book capacity:
                Over 33,000 volumes.
Multi-purpose room has separate access.
Special attention has been laid to the traffic flow in relation to the
    the basic layout.
Built under the supervision of the New York City Department of
    Public Works.

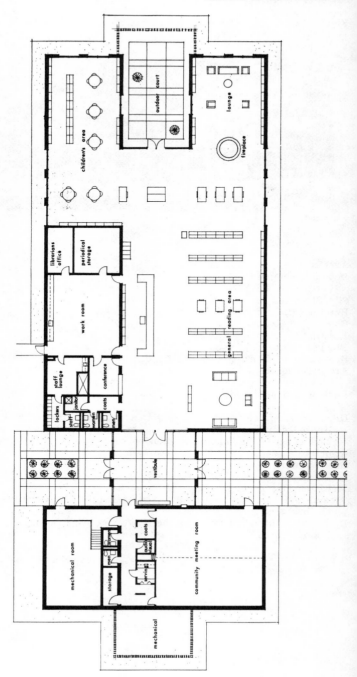

Figure 142. Brooklyn Center Public Library,
Branch of the Hennepin County Library System. Floor plan.

Figure 143. Brooklyn Center Public Library, branch of the
Hennepin County Library System, Minneapolis,
Minnesota.

Location: Village of Brooklyn Center, Minnesota.
Architects: The Cerny Associates, Architects and Engineers.
Size: 12,718 square feet.
Costs:

    Building: $248,888 provided by Federal grant of $60,000
                   and local funds of $188,888 from the Village
                   of Brooklyn Center.

    Furnishings and equipment, $35,000, provided from the
    Hennepin County Library Fund.

Book capacity:
               30,000 volumes, plus periodicals and reference
               materials.
Floors: Carpeting.
Ceilings: Acoustical design integrating heating, cooling, and
                   lighting.
Community room with audio-visual facilities.
Walls: Aesthetically pleasing but low maintenance. Interior,
                   brick.
Open air patio for summer activities.
Comfortable browsing lounges with center fireplace.
Public address system.
Complete air-conditioning.

Figure 144.   <u>Ross-Cherry Creek Branch,</u> Denver Public Library,
              Denver, Colorado.

Photo by Pat Coffey

Opened: July, 1962.
Architect: Paul R. Reddy.
Size: 13,000 square feet (two floors and basement).
Service area: Estimated at 62,600 persons.
Costs:

Architect's fee:	$ 13,377
Site:	47,500
Building:	243,213
Equipment and furniture	25,529
Total:	$329,619

              Cost per square foot: $25.35.

Sources of funds: Funds for the site and building provided by the
    Frederick R. Ross Library Trust Fund. The City and County
    of Denver purchased books and equipment and provided for
    staffing.

Lighting: Fluorescent.
Floors: Vinyl asbestos
Meeting room capacity: 100.
Heating: Hot water and air
    combination.
Children's area seating capacity:
    16
Outside book return.
Parking: 24 cars plus delivery
    area.

Book capacity: 50,000 volumes
    (30,000 of these in basement
    storage area).
Air-conditioning.
Main reading room capacity: 62
Special story hour area seating:
    40.
Second floor suite houses Record-
    ing for the Blind, Inc.

Design: Contemporary structure faced with white precast stone made
    of marble aggregate.

Figure 145.   Southeast Branch, Minneapolis Public Library, Minneapolis, Minnesota.

Architect: Ralph Rapson.
Opened: December 26, 1967.
Approximate service area: 30,000.
Book capacity: 30,000 volumes.
Remodeled from a building that was formerly the University office, State Capitol Credit Union.
Cost: Total cost of land, building, and equipment: $498,000.
Source of funds: City: $452,000; Federal funds under the Library Services and Construction Act, Title II: $46,000.
Size: Approximately 13,000 square feet, as follows:
                 Ground floor: 5,800 sq. ft.
                 Basement floor: 7,200 sq. ft.
                 Garage ramp - deck over: 5,500 sq. ft.
Exterior: Brick and decorative concrete
              Very ornate entry design
              Plate glass windows
Interior: Concrete floors and ceilings
              Tile-brick floor, brick walls
              Hardwood woodwork
              Central air-conditioning
Meeting room to accommodate 100.
Chair lift to bring the handicapped from the garage into the lower level of the building.
Parking on site: Concrete deck at rear of building accommodates 8 to 10 cars. Basement unheated garage accommodates 10 to 12 cars.

Figure 146.   South Oak Cliff Branch, Dallas Public Library,
               Dallas, Texas

Size: 13,110 square feet.
Architect: Harper and Kemp, Dallas, Texas.
Fees paid: Architect $16,077. Soil exploration study $1,000.
               Total $17,077.
Costs: Building, $232,523.50. Building cost per square foot
               $17.73. Site cost $96,500, Furnishings and
               equipment, $40,379.19. Total costs $369,402.69,
               plus architect.
Book capacity: 50,000 volumes. Size of present collection,
               51,000 volumes.
Seating capacity:
               Library - 83; Auditorium - 100.
Size of population, student body, or clientele served: 70,000
Offices: One, size 14x14 feet.
Staff room: Sofa, dining table with chairs, sink, oven, three
               burner stove, refrigerator, cabinets, individual
               staff lockers.
Heating and air conditioning: Heating: forced warm air over hot
               water coils. Air-conditioning: chiller and compressors.
Lighting: Fluorescent (flush) in most areas, to IES Lighting Hand-
               book standards. Incandescent (recessed) in certain areas.
Floors: Vinyl asbestos tile.
Noise control: Acoustical tile in most areas; Plaster, Keenes
               cement, and luminous ceiling in certain areas.
Type of construction: Steel frame. Sand-hued brick and glass with
               vertical accents in white marble.
Parking spaces: 34.   Landscaping: Cost $2,898.02.

Figure 147. West Side Branch, Public Library of Des Moines. Reading Room Layout.

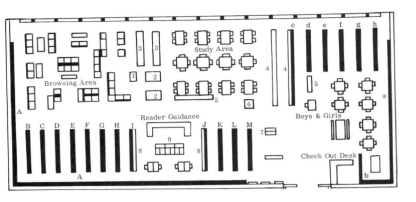

1. Newspaper rack	a. Juvenile fiction
2. Bibliography tables	b. Picture books
3. Unbound magazines	c. Philosophy
4. Bound magazines	d. Science
5. Card index	e. Technology
6. Atlas	f. Arts and literature
7. New books	g. Travel and biography
8. Adult reference materials	h. History
9. Pamphlet files	
	G. Art
A. Adult fiction	H. Literature
B. Philosophy and religion	I. Literature
C. Social science	J. Travel
D. Language	K. Biography
E. Science	L. History
F. Technology	M. History

Figure 148.   West Side Branch, Public Library of Des Moines, Iowa

Location: Adjacent to a shopping center and junior high school.

Service area: Estimated at 100,000. Will be about 116,000 by 1980.

Circulation: 450,000 items of library material.
50,000 professional services annually.

Site size: 84,000 square feet.

Building area:
14,000 square feet
(Reading room, 7,366 square feet, all other areas
6,634 square feet).

Parking Spaces:
70

Design: The library is conceived of as two separate structures
connected by a glass walled entrance foyer.   The two
buildings are set upon a stylobate which raises the floor
line several feet above the existing grade.

Lighting: Combination of natural and artificial.

Ceilings: Low acoustical over bookstack area; high exposed concrete beam ceiling acoustically treated.

Exterior: Brick, glass, some exposed concrete.

Air conditioned on a year-round basis.

Book capacity: 75,000 volumes housed at close of 1968.
(Total capacity not given)

Seating capacity of reading room: 52 reference readers; 38 adult
browsers, 30 children. Total of 120.

Multi-purpose meeting room: Seats 125.

Headquarters for one bookmobile, its staff, and 15,000 books.

Very Large Branches

15, 000 Square Feet and Up

Arranged in order of increasing size

Figure 149. Tesson Ferry Branch, St. Louis County Library,
St. Louis, Missouri. Regional Branch to serve South
St. Louis County.

Figure 150.   Tesson Ferry Branch of St. Louis County Library has
               an area especially for children, with tot-sized furniture
               and an aquarium of colorful tropical fish.

Location:	Concord Village.
Size:	22,000 square feet.
Architects:	Syl G. Schmidt and Associates.
Opened:	June 30, 1958.

Two meeting rooms, wood paneled and separated by a folding
               partition for easy conversion to one large unit.
Basement provides storage space for 50,000 volumes, mechanical
               equipment and staff rooms.
Air conditioning.
Exterior: Brick with brick showing on interior.
               Large windows across front.
               Sun control with traverse draperies of fiberglass.
Lighting: Fluorescent, illuminated ceiling.
Open modular construction.

Special features:
               1. Extrance placed at rear on a cutoff street to avoid
                   danger from heavy traffic on Lindbergh Blvd., a
                   main artery.

               2. Built-in aquarium and planter in children's area.

               3. Library Bureau tables in a variety of shapes.

               4. Informal groupings of tables and chairs at many
                   points.

Catonsville Area Branch
Baltimore County Public Library
Baltimore, Maryland

Architects:	Smith and Veale. Size: 24,210 square feet.
Costs:	Building cost (includes some built-in equipment): $431,700; cost per sq. ft.: $17.83; gross floor area: 24,210 sq. ft. Site: $45,766. Fees: Architect: $28,000; misc. $1,000 Equipment & Furniture (other than built-in): $46,145. Total project cost: $571,087; cost per sq. ft.: $23.59.
Lighting:	Recessed and surface-mounted fluorescent, recessed incandescent.
Floors:	Rubber tile (public areas): vinyl asbestos (staff areas); carpet in lounge (carpet has also been added to adult reading area).
Heating:	Gas-fired hot water/hot air (heat exchanger).

Air conditioning: Chilled water, Carrier.

Shelves & stacks: Bracket; Royalmetal.

Furniture: Charging desk: in general contract; readers' tables and chairs: Steelcase; desks: ASE; meeting room chairs.

Books: Open shelf capacity: 73,000 volumes; closed stack and storage capacity: 10,000; total volume capacity: 83,000.

General description: The building is perceived by pedestrians and motorists as a one-level scheme resting in a landscaped terrace elevated a few feet from the street level. A large expanse of glass punctuated by wide concrete columns emphasizes the main entrance and opens to view the grass and terrace areas. Walls of rusticated colonial brick enclose the main book collection and children's area on either side of the entry. A broad unifying band of textured cast concrete surrounds the building at the roof line. The building is simple in form, rich in texture, and in the variety of interior spaces preserving the quiet dignity of the neighborhood. The main reference and reading area is enclosed by a high vaulted ceiling formed by cantilevered steel "umbrellas" from which the surrounding low roof of the bookstacks is suspended. A clerestory of gray solar glass illuminates the space. The ceiling of the children's area is a series of "sound chambers" to confine noise of the several groups in different areas of the room. One wall of glass looks out under a wide overhang onto a tree-shaded terrace, providing a pleasant atmosphere for reading and story hours. In contrast, the adult reading area is essentially an interior space which concentrates on the main functions of the library. Added functions of the library situated on the lower level include a community auditorium for meetings and library programs, and a Catonsville Room, a comfortably furnished room for quiet reading and small discussion groups. Both areas open up onto a sunken landscaped garden court.

Figure 151. <u>Catonsville Area Branch</u>, Baltimore County Public Library. Entrance.

Figure 152. <u>Catonsville Area Branch</u>, Baltimore County Public Library. Exterior View.

Figure 153.   Plaza Library, Regional branch of the Kansas City
              Public Library, Kansas City, Missouri.

Date opened: October, 1967.
Size: 28,000 square feet.
Architects: Frank P. McArthur, Tanner, Linscott, and Anson.
Cost: $825,000.
Seating capacity:
             180 adults, 87 children.
Book capacity:
             90,000 volumes.
Meeting room capacity:
             95 persons.
Conference room capacity:
             18 persons.
Materials: Precast concrete masony exterior.
             Interior: Marble walls and flooring in entry.
             Light well with fountains inside north window wall
                exposure.
Floor covering: Carpet in public area.
Free parking for patrons. No. of spaces not indicated.
Book return on driveway.

Collection emphasizes current popular titles, with depth in standard
works and classics. The major function of this regional branch is
the provision of a large, carefully-selected collection to meet the
interests and demands of the general adult and juvenile reader.
There is a circulating collection of long-play records.

Randallstown Area Branch, Baltimore County
Public Library, Baltimore, Maryland

Architect: Glenn L. Watkins
Size: 29,000 square feet.
Costs: Building cost (includes some built-in equipment):
$483,000; cost per sq. ft.: $16.65; gross floor area:
29,000 sq. ft.
Site: $10,000.
Fees: Architect & engineer: $30,000; misc.: $28,000.
Equipment & furniture (other than built-in): $67,200
(includes carpet).
Total project cost: $618,000; cost per sq. ft.: $21.32.
Lighting: Recessed fluorescent.
Floors: Acrilan carpet (Public areas); vinyl asbestos (staff
areas).
Heating: Gas-fired hot water/hot air.
Air conditioning: Chilled water, Carrier.
Shelves & stacks: Bracket, Estey.
Library furniture: Charging desk: in general contract; readers'
tables and chairs: Steelcase; desks: Metalstand; meeting
room chairs: Knoll; children's readers' chairs, Crucible;
special library furniture: Weinberg.
Books: Open shelf capacity: 100,000 volumes; closed stack and
storage capacity: 30,000; total volume capacity: 130,000.

General description: This two-floor building rises one and one-half
floors above the grade of the shopping center parking lot in
which the branch is located. The branch is box-shaped with a
medium-brown brick exterior broken by white columns and
tinted glass. The entrance is flanked by glass enclosed areas
which serve as ceiling-to-floor showcases. A short flight of
stairs leads to the spacious lobby with the two reading areas on
the right and left of the charge desk. An open wood screen
separates a periodical and microfilm area from the charge
desk. The main study areas are flanked by bookstacks under a
lowered ceiling and large glassed areas at opposite ends of these
areas enhance the feeling of spaciousness. Librarians' offices
on either side of the lobby, a periodical storage room, and a
workroom complete the first floor. A public meeting room,
staff room, and large storage area are included in the lower
floor.

As anticipated, this facility is the busiest branch with its first
year of circulation projected over 500,000 volumes. (Patron
demand, much evident during the construction period, required
a trailer stocked with books and librarian on the site.) The location of this branch, in its highly library-conscious community,
was not as essential to its use as might be true in other communities, thereby making it less essential for a shopping center
site. However, two shopping centers were eager to have
the library constructed on their sites. Their eagerness,
in fact, allowed for the purchasing of a site, near one of
the centers, at a very reasonable price.

Figure 154. Randallstown Area Branch, Baltimore County Public Library.

Chapter 17

Award-Winning Branches

The branches selected for inclusion in this chapter are mainly award-winners in the Library Buildings Award Program sponsored since 1963 by the American Institute of Architects, the American Library Association, and the National Book Committee. They are chosen for this chapter on the basis of size and type. There are also several other winners of local or regional architectural awards.

Photographs and floor plans are to be found in the annual architectural issues (December 1) of Library Journal. Outstanding libraries are also sometimes written up in the Architectural Record. Any library contemplating a program of branch building will find these periodicals extremely valuable. Also useful are the building institutes held in connection with the American Library Association conferences and some state library association conventions. The literature in the field of library buildings is plentiful, but the institutes and their proceedings, as well as many of the books, mostly emphasize academic and large library buildings. There has been a dearth of material on smaller libraries and branches. Joseph L. Wheeler's The Small Library Building (1963) No. 13 in the A.L.A. Library Administration Division's series of pamphlets in the Small Libraries Project, is one of the few publications to give real emphasis to the needs of libraries planning smaller quarters. Rolf Myller's The Design of the Small Public Library, Bowker, 1966, is another fine and explicit publication in this field.

Visiting branches of the size and type planned is one of the best methods of obtaining information, since a staff that has been working in a new building is usually willing to discuss the good points and the mistakes which have emerged. The state library agency can usually supply a list of new branches recently erected in the area.

Small Branch

Sequoyah Branch
Knoxville Public Library, Knoxville, Tennessee

Merit Award Winner, 1963

Size of Building: 3,528 sq. ft.
Book Shelving Capacity: 12,500.
Tables: 10.
Seating: 46.
Building completely air-conditioned.
Architect: Barber and McMurry, Architects.

Costs:

Building and Parking:	$55,917.00
Equipment and Furniture:	10,856.52
Architect's fee:	3,354.02
Land: City owned	
Landscaping: Gift	
Total Cost	$70,127.54

Figure 155.   Floor plan, Sequoyah Branch.

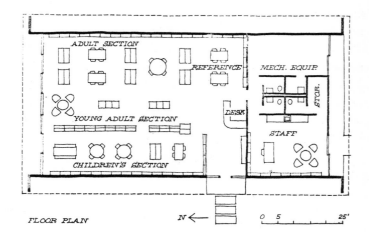

FLOOR PLAN   N ←   O 5   25'

Figure 156. <u>Sequoyah Branch,</u> Knoxville, Public Library, Knoxville, Tennessee.   Built 1961.

Figure 157.   The Sequoyah Branch is an example of a small branch with simple but pleasing exterior lines and a completely functional interior. The heavy supporting beams make interior columns or posts unnecessary yet because of their light color and harmonious relationship to the ceiling they are not oppressive. This is the adult service area as seen from the corner of the charging desk.

Small Branch

Berkeley Public Library, Berkeley, California, South Branch

Merit Award Winner, 1966

This branch, built in 1961, makes imaginative use of low-priced materials. Included in its 4,360 square feet is an 800 square foot patio with benches, reflecting pool, trellis work and paving. Nonpublic functions are efficiently grouped, and exits to street and parking areas are well controlled. The parking area is fenced and landscaped. Patio, paving and parking area cost approximately $5,000 out of the tight budget.

The Berkeley Library system was forced to replace one of its obsolete and crumbling branches and decided, since a bond issue was not possible, to do it with the very minimum of funds. $63,62? was made available to construct a fireproof one-story building containing a reading room for adults and children, separated by a movable partition. Added to it was a workroom and study for the librarian, a storage and heater room, and wash rooms. Better illumination and higher quality materials would have improved the total building, but it represents good results within budgetary restrictions.

Specifications are as follows:

Exterior finish: Concrete block curtain walls, exposed inside and
        out. Best Block and Basalite; redwood trim, Cabot stained.
Structure: Reinforced concrete grade beams on piers, concrete
        columns and laminated wood beams.
Floors: Concrete slab, Conrad Sovig color hardened. Amtico vinyl
        tile in offices.
Roof: Built-up roof, tar and gravel, rising over the adult reading
        room to a height of 16 feet, culminating in an eight feet
        square skylight. Eight foot overhangs protect the building
        against the weather.
Lighting: Pryne, Marco, Lightcraft and United Light and Ceiling
        Co.
Windows: Kelco louvers, operating sash.
Skylight: A. W. Lilly Co.
Heating: Gas fired radiant.
Area: 3,560 sq. ft. plus 800 sq. ft. patio. Book capacity 11,500
        vols.
Cost per sq. ft.: $16.00.   Plumbing: American-Standard.
Insulation: 1-1/2 in. batts.
Cost: $60,000.

All materials were selected to hold upkeep to a minimum. Standard concrete blocks were turned on edge as trim, their voids filled with amber glass. Existing shelves from the old library were reused and refinished. Interior partitions were covered with mahogany plywood and all exposed wood surfaces including the hemlock ceiling were left natural.

An attempt was made to design a public building with a residential character in the Berkeley tradition. Reason for the fairly large patio was the fact that the surrounding neighborhood is relatively unattractive. The branch, with its daylight openings all directed towards self-contained patios, gardens, and the 800 sq. ft. outdoor reading room, provides a pleasing contrast.

Ostwald and Kelly, Berkeley, were the architects.

Figure 158.   Floor Plan, South Branch, Berkeley Public Library

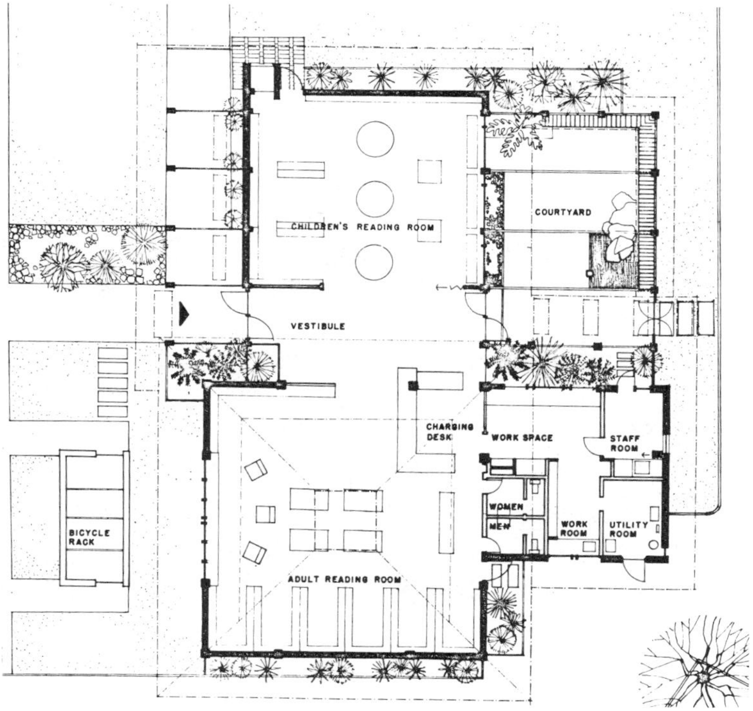

Figure 159. South Branch, Berkeley Public Library, Berkeley, California, makes imaginative use of low-priced materials.

Courtesy of Ostwald and Kelly, Architects
Berkeley, California

Figure 160. Interior view: South Branch, Berkeley Public Library, Berkeley, California. Note the interesting ceiling design with central skylight for natural light.

Courtesy of Ostwald and Kelly, Architects
Berkeley, California

Magnolia Branch
Seattle Public Library, Seattle, Washington

First Honor Award, 1966

A larger branch of 6,523 square feet, the Magnolia Branch of the Seattle Public Library, completed July 1, 1964, and cited for first honors in 1966, is still some 1500 square feet smaller than today's generally recommended minimum.

Roman Mostar, describing the library in the Pacific Northwest Library Association Quarterly (Vol. 30, No. 4, July 1966, p. 251), said:

> The problem facing the architectural firm of Kirk, Wallace, McKinley and Associates of Seattle was to create a library building that would be residential in character, warm to match the madrona trees on the site, and yet as functional inside as a modern library should be. Recognizing the need of enticing people into the new building, they chose to design a low, wooden building with an exterior of cedar shingles. A modern structure of steel and glass of the type so prevalent in this age, they felt, would have been completely out of place in the wooded, residential lot.
>
> Clerestory windows, all facing north, give the library the best possible reading light, and the resulting different ceiling heights inside give variety and relief from the usual flat ceilings. The book shelves are fashioned of teak-grained plastic laminate so like the real wood that the observer even feeling the material can scarcely tell the difference.
>
> Sofas are set upon cinnamon-brown carpets by the windows. Tables and chairs from Nakashima of New Hope, Pennsylvania are solid walnut. They contribute to the warmth of this library so much more than the chrome-legged chairs and tables so commonly called for in today's public buildings.
>
> A community committee raised funds to provide an individual piece of art, a bronze sculpture created by Professor Glenn Alps of the University of Washington School of Art, and mounted on the wall of the north courtyard.

Building data:

Population served: 20,000.
Date of Completion: July 1, 1964.
Architect: Kirk, Wallace, McKinley, AIA, & Associates.
Area:

Dimensions of site:			120x180
Square feet of floor space:			6523
Dimensions of Building:			
Main Floor			119x59
Basement			50x13
Reading Room:			
Adult			42x57
Children			32x46
Staff room:			16x13
Work room:			13x26
Work office:			13x16
Librarian's office:			9x10
Rest rooms:	5x6	5x6	5x9

Costs:

Cost of site:	$35,115.00
Building cost: excluding built-ins and shelving	126,507.00
Cost per square foot:	19.39
Finish carpentry, shelving and cabinets:	21,000.00
Landscaping (included in contract):	4,330.00
Art work (financed by citizens' donations): approximately	2,000.00
Furnishings:	9,956.00

Financing: 1956 Library Bond Fund

Building type: Wood post and beam--exterior walls of red cedar
                 shingles and glass.

Lighting: Indirect fluorescent with incandescent highlights--
                 four north lighted clerestories.

Floor covering: Vinyl tile over concrete.

Heating and ventilating:
                 Gas fired hot air system with air conditioning unit,
                 packaged type.

Equipment and furnishings:
                 Shelving, circulation desk and built-ins by Tacoma
                 Millwork Supply; tables and chairs by Nakashima;
                 and incidental furniture by Morreddi, Magna Design,
                 Shaw-Walker and Remington Rand.

Seating: Adult   50
         Children   35

Book Capacity: 1,425 lineal feet at 9 books per foot   12,825
                   720 lineal feet at 14 books per foot   10,080
Parking: 16 cars

Figure 161. Floor Plan. Magnolia Branch.

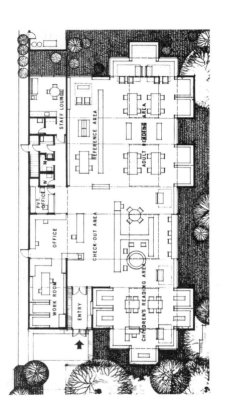

Figure 162. Magnolia Branch, Seattle, Washington. Attractive
    entrance and natural wood exterior harmonize with woodsy
    site and madrona trees. Steps may provide a problem for the
    handicapped.

Figure 163. Magnolia Branch. Architectural model shows complete
    layout in relation to site.

Medium-sized Branch

Southwest Branch
Seattle Public Library, Seattle, Washington
Merit Award Winner, 1964

Building data:

Population served: 23,500 (est.).
Date of completion: July 14, 1961.
Architect: Durham, Anderson and Freed.
Sculptor: Charles W. Smith.

Area:

Dimension of site: 180' x 120'
Sq. ft. of floor space: 6,966 sq. ft. Main floor. 847 sq. ft.
   Basement.
Dimension of building: 93'-6" x 93'-6".

Dimension of various areas in the library:

Reading Room	52' x 60'
Stack Room	20' x 22'
Children's Area	37' x 31'
Heating, Ventilating and storage	38' x 20'
Meeting Room	22' x 14'
Janitorial Room	5' x 9'
Staff Room	15' x 15'
Work Room	23' x 15'
Librarian's Office	9' x 12'
Rest Rooms	10' x 17'
Garden Area	
Rear Court	12' x 77'
Front Garden	26' x 40'

Costs:

Cost of site: $40,952.61
Cost of building construction: $131,449.15 (exclusive of tax
   & Architect's fee).
Cost per sq. ft. (bldg. constr.) $16.85 (enclosed space &
   including site devel.)
Cost of equipment, shelving,
   furnishings and sculpture $22,195.52
Cost of landscaping   6,000.00 (allowed).

Financing: 1956 Library Bond Fund.

Building type (Outside construction): Exposed moduled steel frame
   with aluminum frame windows and S.C.R. brick filler panels.

Lighting: Fluorescent lighting with acrylic plastic diffusers.

Floor covering: Robbins Lifetime Vinyl.

Heating and air conditioning:

> Gas fired boiler with Carrier air conditioning unit.

Equipment and furnishings:

> Stock furniture from Bank and Office Interiors. Steel-
> case tables with Formica tops, chrome legs. Herman
> Miller drapes, plastic chairs. Naugahyde sofas and lounge
> chairs. Knoll upholstered lounge chairs and pedestal
> Formica tables. Custom furniture from Frederick &
> Nelson. Cabinets of walnut and black steel. Jungle table
> Naugahyde, Formica and black steel.

Shelving:

> Ames metal shelving cantilevered from flush wall standards,
> and custom wood shelving.

Color Scheme:

> Exterior: Exposed steel frame and trim painted vanilla
> bean brown. Cascade brick panels, satin
> finished anodized aluminum.
>
> Interior: Metal shelving in almond yellow and tiber gold.
> Walnut finish on doors and millwork. Off-
> white vinyl floor. Doeskin walls in work
> room.

Seating Capacity: 105

Book Capacity: at 8 books per lineal foot   25,320.

Lineal feet of shelving:

> 3,165.

Parking for public (number of cars):

> 21 cars.

Meeting room seating capacity:

> 14 to 18 persons.

Figure 164. <u>Southwest Branch,</u> Seattle Public Library. Floor Plan.

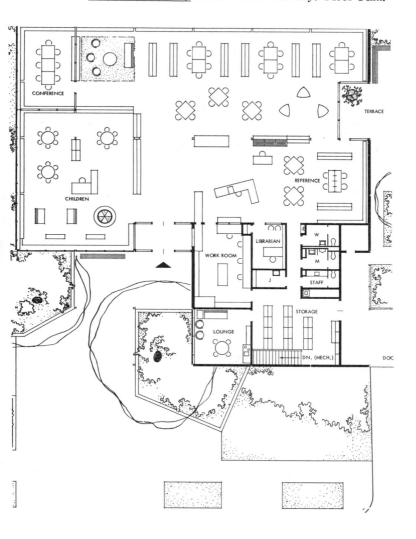

Figure 165.   <u>Southwest Branch</u>, Seattle Public Library,
        Seattle, Washington.

Photo by Werner Longgenhager

Figure 166.   Lounge Area, Southwest Branch.

Medium-Sized Branch

Coconut Grove Branch
Miami Public Library, Miami, Florida

Merit Award Winner, 1964

Size: 6,374 square feet.

Architect: T. Tripp Russell.

Book Capacity: 20,000 volumes.

Cost: $ 102,847.95.

The ground floor contains the children's room, work room, staff lounge, and receiving and storage area. The first floor contains the adult reading room, public toilets, browsing room, and work space behind the circulation desk. Entrance to this raised first floor is up a ramp; however stairs must be used to descend to the children's room from the adult area.

Coconut Grove Branch is among the relatively newer branches in Miami, Florida. Located in an upper class community that felt strongly about old houses and trees, the people were sentimentally attached to the original frame library building. Accordingly, the architect incorporated certain architectural features of the old structure into his design for the new and created a striking hillside library building on three levels.

Architecturally the building is quite a success and has won several awards in addition to the 1964 Award of Merit of the American Institute of Architects and the American Library Association. Functionally this branch presents some problems. The three levels are connected by stairs rather than ramps on the inside and there is no elevator, so that books have to be carried from level to level or shunted down a slide to the basement children's room. An expensive dumb waiter was installed to cope with this, but it takes time to load and unload the books. The children's room cannot be supervised at times from the adult section, which makes a larger staff necessary. Also, a staff member working alone in the children's room in the evenings is apt to feel somewhat uneasy and cut off from the rest of the building. One good feature is that the children's room has its own exit and charging desk. These are used during especially busy times to keep swarms of youngsters from traipsing up and down the stairs to the adult section.

The distinctive, high-peak, wood and stone structure, recalling features of the original village library next door, is planned to fit into the historic background and appearance of its neighborhood.

Figure 167. <u>Coconut Grove Branch,</u> First Floor.

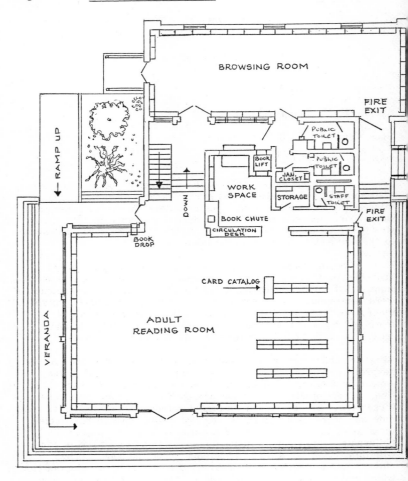

Figure 168. <u>Coconut Grove Branch,</u> Miami Public Library, Miami, Florida

Photo: Miami-Metro News Bureau
Miami, Florida

Figure 169. Children's wing and entrance, Coconut Grove Branch.

Photo: Miami-Metro News Bureau
Miami, Florida

Medium-sized Branch

Flora B. Tenzler Memorial Branch
Pierce County Library System, Tacoma, Washington

First Honor Award Winner, 1964

Size: 8,612 feet.
Cost: $400,000.
Architect: Russel N. Garrison, A.I.A.
Landscape Architect: Chaffee-Zumwait & Associates.

This outstanding branch is divided up as follows:

1. Vestibule - contains entry drafts and provides space for display. Floor areas, 216 square feet.

2. Foyer - provides small waiting area and display space. Floor area, 432 square feet.

3. Control - contains control desk placed to assure visual control over the entire public area. All reference and information material is located in this area. Floor space, 972 square feet.

4. Adults area - has a study area which overlooks the court and a high ceiling section. For lounge type reading. Floor area, 2,772 square feet.

5. Children's area - located adjacent to the court for outside story time and is screened by glass re-lights to contain sound and afford surveillance from both the Control desk and adult area. Floor area, 1,286 square feet.

6. Meeting room - to be used for public gatherings re-lated to educational pursuits. Has a separate en-trance and a sound resisting door. Floor area, 643 square feet.

7. Young adults' area - has a low ceiling study area and a high ceiling lounge reading area similar to the adult area. Contains newspaper and magazine display and is joined to the meeting room for ex-pansion by means of folding doors. Floor area, 1,286 square feet.

8. Storage room - used for storage of chairs and tables in the meeting room. Floor area, 72 square feet.

9. Janitor's room - centrally located to provide maintenance equipment. Floor area, 36 square feet.

10. Men and women's lavatories - accessible from the halls, which can be locked to provide separate access to the library and meeting rooms.

11. Staff - lounge area for off-duty staff members contains wardrobe unit, kitchen unit and lavatory. Floor area, 234 square feet.

12. Librarian's office - used for consultation with patrons and administrative work. Built-in shelving. Floor area, 120 square feet.

13. Workroom - contains equipment for processing and repairing books. Is adjacent to service drive for receiving books from the central library. Floor area, 324 square feet.

14. Basement - contains the furnace, incinerator, water heater, control panels, and storage space for garden equipment. Floor area, 396 square feet.

Specifications:

Floors: Main floor and basement - Concrete slab on grade. Floor area over basement - Reinforced concrete, supports on reinforced concrete beams.

Walls: Masonry. Brick and concrete block cavity with insulation fill.

Window. Color anodized aluminum frames with Glasweld Spandrel panels.

Interior. Metal studs with gypsum lath and plaster.

Roof: Frame. Steel columns, girders, and beams.

Cover. Three-inch thick tectum decking supported on steel bulb "T"'s.

Power: Electrical power is supplied to the building through underground service.

Lighting: Fluorescent light tubes are suspended from the ceiling, over removable plastic panels. The light is conducted and directed through these panels down to the study area.

Incandescent chandelier light fixtures are located over the adult and young adult reading areas.

Exterior lighting is located in the soffits and ground around the building perimeter. These lights are automatically controlled by a timer to switch on at dusk and off in the the morning.

Heating and Ventilating: Electrical heat is supplied to the
    children's area by means of floor cables in the concrete slab.
    This heat is thermostatically controlled with the main heat-
    ing system. The purpose of floor heat in the children's
    area is to allow the children to sit with comfort on the
    floor. Warm air to the remainder of the building is sup-
    plied by a multi-zone gas-fired furnace to three separate
    zones in the building. Zone one is the children's area;
    zone two is the adult area; and zone three is the young
    adult's area and meeting room. The warm air is forced
    through ducts in the floor and is introduced into the room
    through supply registers in the toe space of bookshelves.
    The return air grilles are located in the walls of the high
    ceiling areas. These grilles return the cold air back to the
    furnace for heating and recirculating.

        The amount of warm air in each room is regulated by an
        automatic temperature control unit.

Sprinkler system: The exterior lawn and planting areas receive
    water through an automatic sprinkler system. This system
    is divided into zones which are automatically actuated at
    various times during the day and night. Water is supplied
    to the sprinkler heads through plastic pipes. The various
    seasonal demands for water are controlled from the master
    valve.

Interior finishes:

    Floors: Vinyl tile, selected for its acoustical, light
    reflection, and maintenance qualities.

    Walls: Gypsum plaster over metal studs, selected for fire-
    proof requirements.

    Ceiling: Low ceiling areas are removable plastic panels
        which direct the light downward in a uniform quality and
        permit sound to be absorbed in the acoustical roof deck.
        High ceiling areas are of acoustical plaster and plastic
        skylight. The latter has one-inch air space sandwiched
        between two layers of plastic. This reduces heat loss
        to a minimum.

Exterior finishes:

    Slabs: Painted concrete, pebbled concrete, and quarry
                    tile.
    Walls: Brick cavity and white glasweld panels.
    Soffits: Cement plaster.
    Fascia: Gold anodized aluminum.
    Door and Window Frames:
                    Color anodized aluminum.
    Columns: Ceramic veneer over steel pipe columns.
    Roof: Clay tile.

Figure 170. Floor Plan, Flora B. Tenzler Memorial Library.

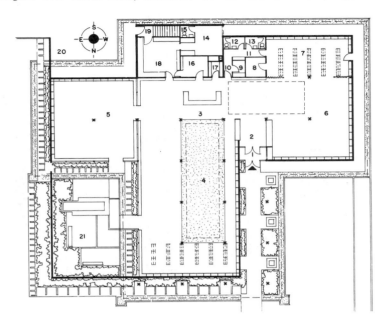

Legend

1	Vestibule	12	Men
2	Foyer	13	Women
3	Control	14	Staff
4	Adults' Area	15	Lavatory
5	Children's Area	16	Office
6	Young Adults' Area	17	Storage
7	Meeting Room	18	Work
8	Storage	19	Entry
9	Janitor	20	Staff Parking
10	Hall	21	Court
11	Hall		

Figure 171. Flora B. Tenzler Memorial Library. The natural beauty
of the site demanded that special care be given to preserve the
existing trees and integrate the architecture so as to achieve
a friendly co-existence with nature. Throughout this project
the architect worked closely with the landscape architect to
achieve a harmonious relationship. Certain geometric patterns
appear in both the architecture and landscaping.

Photo by Hugh N. Stratford,
Mountlake Terrace, Washington

Figure 172. Gracious Interior of the Flora B. Tenzler Memorial
Library.

Photo by Hugh N. Stratford,
Mountlake Terrace, Washington

Medium-sized Branch

Sanger Branch
Fresno County Free Library, Fresno, California

Award of Excellence, 1967.
San Joaquin Chapter
American Institute of Architects

Building Data:

Dedicated: March 19, 1967.

Location: 1812 Seventh Street, Sanger, California.

Population Served: Sanger area: 22,300
                           City of Sanger: 9,650

Architect: Allen Y. Lew, A.I.A.

General Contractor: Robert G. Fisher Co. , Inc.

Cost of Builidng: $228,521
    Furnishings: 24,600

Financing: Site provided by the City of Sanger.
              Building provided by County of Fresno and partially fi-
                 nanced by Federal Library Services & Construction
                 Act funds.

Site: Dimensions of site: 150' x 215'
         Landscape architect: Allen Y. Lew, A.I.A.
         Landscaping: Fresno County Parks and Recreation Department.
         Parking facilities: 30

Building: Wood-frame with pre-cast concrete columns & glu-lam
              beams. Exterior finish of basalt exposed aggregate tile.
         Floor area: 8,994 sq. ft.
         Book Capacity: 40,000 volumes.
         Seating Capacity: 67 in reading room. 75 in meeting room.
         Floors: Kentile vinyl asbestos tile and Berven carpet.
         Lighting: Fluorescent.
         Heating: Gas-fired forced air heating, & self-con-
                                 tained refrigeration.
         Furniture: Bellview Library furniture; Ames shelving;
                                 Art Metal desks; Metalcraft upholstered
                                 chairs; Virco stacking chairs.
         Walls: Vinyl wall covering, teak paneling in foyer,
                                 meeting room, and librarian's office
         Glass: Solarbronz.

Special features: Meeting room, with kitchen facility, which may be
                       reserved by community groups.
                    Built-in screen in meeting room for film showings.
                    Record listening tables.
                    Open patio adjoining children's area.

    Sanger Branch Library is the first Regional Branch of the
Fresno County Free Library and is the headquarters for bookmobile service to the area.

Figure 173. Floor plan. Sanger Branch, Fresno County Free Library.

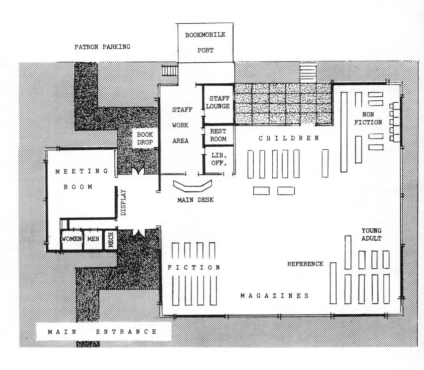

Figure 174. Sanger Branch, Fresno County Library, Built in 1967.

Photo by Rondal Partridge,
Fresno, Calif.

Figure 175. Attractive Approach to the Sanger Branch.

Photo by Rondal Partridge
Fresno, Calif.

Large Branch

Casa View Branch
Dallas Public Library

Award of Merit, 1966

The Casa View Branch Library was completed February 29, 1964. Almost unparalleled biblio-pandemonium marked the branch opening when 9,132 books were circulated in eight hours!

With its broad slashes of pre-cast stone panels and light-washed spaces, the branch is an embodiment of Southwestern elan.

The entranceway, keynoted by piebald sky-lighting and sur-rounded by glass, opens into the quarry-tiled main lobby. The natural effect is carried through in the reading area with earthy shades of brown and tan highlighted by a wall of glass paneling.

The walnut and stone planed auditorium is available for com-munity use. Reservations must be made by contacting the library.

The building, which includes an auditorium and a bookmobile garage, was the recipient in 1966 of an Award of Merit under the program sponsored by the A.I.A., the A.L.A., and the National Book Committee.

Architect: William H. Hidell, A.I.A., Dallas. Architectural fees $16,077.00.

Soil Exploration Study: $1,000.

Cost of Building: $240,600.

Size of Building: 13,820 square feet.

Construction Cost per square foot: $17.40.

Site Cost: $35,131.49.

Library Equipment and Furniture: Remington Rand.

Informal Furniture and Accessories: Stewart Office Supply Company

Total Cost of Equipment and Furnishings: $44,640.41.

Type of Construction: Pre-cast stone and concrete panels, steel, glass.

Noise Control: Acoustical plaster in public areas, workroom and office. Portland plaster in mechanical room and garage.

Wood Finishes: Stacks, fruitwood; auditorium, walnut.

Interior Color Scheme: Stacks, grey shelves with walnut and panels.

Floors: Entranceway, lobby, auditorium - quarry tile; other areas - vinyl tile or asbestos tile.

Heating and Air Conditioning: Direct expansion, Dallas Plumbing Co.

Maximum Shelf Capacity: 64,000 volumes.

Size of present collection: 77,000 volumes.

Staff: 26 (professional, 5; clerical, 7; maintenance, 4; pages, 7; bookmobile, 3).

Seating Capacity: Library, 83; auditorium, 100.

Study Rooms: None.

Offices: No. of them, 1. Size: 10'x11'.

Staff Room: Sofa, dining table with chairs, sink, oven, three burner stove, refrigerator, cabinets, individual staff lockers.

Parking Space: Lot holds 20 cars.

Landscaping: Cost $3,534.26. Richard B. Myrick, landscape
    architect.

Lighting: Recessed fluorescent; in both stacks and reading area
    IES Lighting Handbook standards.

Bookmobile: Gerstenslager (1961), 4,000-book capacity.

Circulation 1965/66 Fiscal Year: Branch, 444,978; bookmobile,
    48,433.

Population served (1966): 150,000.

Adult Department Services:
    Books, reference materials, pamphlets, periodicals,
    selected telephone directories and college catalogs, reading
    guidance, and programs.

Young Adult Department:
    Books and magazines for teenagers' recreational reading,
    personal assistance, and a school program of booktalks.

Children's Department:
    Books and reading materials for boys and girls, story hour
    and kindred activities, and guidance in book selection for
    children and parents.

Bookmobile:
    Operating from the branch is a bookmobile that will make
    regular stops throughout the area.

Figure 176.   Large branch of 13,820 square feet, the Casa View
               Branch of the Dallas Public Library includes an
               auditorium and bookmobile garage.

Figure 177.   Interior view, Casa View Branch.

Photos: C. D. Bayne
Courtesy: City of Dallas

Figure 178.   Activity at Charging Desk, Casa View Branch. Adult
               stacks in background.

Figure 179.   Bringing the outdoors indoors. Interior view, Casa
               View Branch.

Photos: C. D. Bayne
Courtesy: City of Dallas

Large Branch
Wilmot Branch
Tucson Public Library, Tucson, Arizona

Merit Award Winner, 1966

Building Data:

Opened for service: September 21, 1965.
Architect: Nicholas Sakeller and Associates

The Wilmot Branch is a 15,500 square foot building with a book capacity of 84,000. Originally planned as a 4,000 square foot neighborhood unit, the concept, in tune with the times, quickly grew to almost four times this size.

Wilmot Branch is of masonry construction in a modern Southwestern design. Stonework over the front entrance represents a record of man's progress in knowledge and writing.

A large exhibit case in the lobby and paneled cabinets for exhibits in the meeting room provide plenty of display space.

Large black wrought iron gates separate the library from the main lobby. A light, comfortable reading lounge is located in a sunken floor area slightly below the library floor level and is conducive to reading for pleasure. Magazines and newspapers are located here.

For the convenience of the handicapped and persons of limited mobility a ramp leads down to the reading room. A soundproof conference room seating 16 people is furnished for the use of the public and library meetings.

Seating: Library   145
          Meeting Room   100
          Conference Room   16
Parking: 75
Service Area: Approximately 75,000 people on the far east side of the city.
Hours: Tuesday-Friday - 10 a.m. to 9 p.m.
              Saturday   - 10 a.m. to 6 p.m.
              Sunday and Monday-Closed.

Staff: There is a staff of 17 people, including 7 professional librarians.
Services Offered:
  Adult Department: Books, reference materials, framed art prints, phonograph recordings, periodicals, newspapers, pamphlets, reading guidance, and programs.
  Young Adult Department: Books and magazines for teenagers, recreational reading, personal assistance, a program of book talks, and other activities for young people.
  Children's Department: Books and reading material for boys and girls, story hour and kindred activities, personal guidance in book selection for children and parents.
Costs: Site, Architectural Fees, Construction Costs: $ 342,606
        Library Furniture, built-in Miscellaneous
        equipment and landscaping: 64,124
                                        Total $ 406,730

Figure 180.   Floor plan, Wilmot Branch, Tucson Public Library.

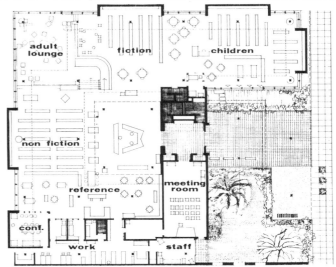

Figure 181.   Entrance area, Wilmot Branch, Tucson Public Library.
Note how well the entrance area blends with the
characteristics of the Southwest.

Photo by: Manley,
Tucson, Arizona

Figure 182.   The sweeping simplicity of design of the Wilmot
               Branch, Tucson Public Library, is both impressive
               and restful.

Figure 183.   Comfort, convenience, and carpeting--the three C's
               that make Tucson Public Library's award-winning
               Wilmot Branch a joy to behold and to use.

Photos by: Manley,
Tucson, Arizona

Large Building--System Member Library

Mill Valley Public Library
Member of North Bay Cooperative System, California

Merit Award Winner, 1968

Size: 18,000 square feet (9,000 square feet on each of two levels).
Note--this approximates the size of some area or regional
branches).

Completed: July, 1966.

Architect: Wurster, Bernardi and Emmons, Inc.

Site: Located a half-mile from the lively center of a vital and
culturally aware community, at the sloping upper end of a city-
owned park. The park, 5.7 acres of towering redwoods, features
the historic remains of the original John Reed sawmill, built in
1836, from which the community takes its name.   Cascade Creek
runs through the park and is flanked by picnic facilities.   The
community's request that none of the redwood trees be removed
determined the placement of the building and limited its dimensions.

Program: A building designed in harmony with the rustic atmosphere of the community, which would preserve and permit enjoyment of the lovely natural site.

        Two percent of the budget was allocated to purchase art
objects, and a significant decision was made to utilize available
local talent in providing unique custom furnishings.

        The original Carnegie library won the Dorothy Canfield
Fisher award for excellence and variety of service (in serving
a community of 10,000 or less) in 1962.   The original circulation figures were four times the average for libraries of com-
parable size.   (Since relocating, there has been an increase of
40% usage.)

Design Solution: A building to enhance the wooded setting, lending
its charm to the landscape and taking character from it in a continuing exchange.   Planned for utmost simplicity, the building is
subordinated to the beauty of the site.

The orientation of the building, without necessitating the removal of any redwoods, allowed an area of 9000 square feet at ground level. Excavation of the downhill slope provided an additional 9000 square feet on a lower level, while retaining a low single-story scale at the front elevation. The horizontal roof line harmonizes with the vertical dominance of the redwoods.

The roof is steeply pitched, with a low, wide overhang slanting down to the 9-foot height of the side walls. Four dormer windows, soaring above the roof line to a 16-foot height, are spaced across the front of the building, punctuating its 168-foot length. Two larger dormers dominate the rear facade.

A wide deck runs the length of the building on the sheltered side, away from the city street, 10 feet above ground. This outdoor reading area offers direct experience with the trees and park landscape.

The brick paving of the entrance plaza leads into the building for a distance of 12 feet, past a redwood-paneled foyer featuring glass display cases, a hand-crafted light fixture and dedication plaque.

The width of the building is 55 feet. The upper level houses the adult reading room, children's reading room, stacks, special display areas, and main desk, which is backed by the librarian's office and a staff workroom. The reading areas seat 60 adults and 40 children.

A gallery, meeting rooms, board room and staff lounge are on the lower level. The gallery accommodates 50 to 60 people, with a built-in screen for film showing. One-third of the lower level is currently for public use.

The visual focus of the interior is a dramatic wood-burning fireplace, of white-painted concrete and natural firebrick, with custom-designed lounge seats and low table grouped before it.

Stacks are metal with redwood end panels, grouped in four ranges of four double-faced stacks, supplemented by four low, free-standing wood stacks. All metal files are encased in oak.

All doors along the south wall open to the reading deck. Predominating expanses of glass bring an unusual amount of natural illumination to the interior, augmented by subdued fluorescent fixtures suspended from the roof beams. A floor-to-roof sheer bay window at the east wall projects over the park. The windows of the west wall (in the children's area) frame Mount Tamalpais.

The furnishings are architect-designed, relaxed and comfortable. Interior furnishings are crafted in walnut and oak; deck furniture in natural redwood. All the art work (ceramic pottery, metalwork, sculpture, etc.) was handcrafted by local artists.

Landscaping: Redwoods, madronas, oaks and bays are indigenous to the site. To these existing trees were added dogwoods, California maples, ivy ground cover, azaleas, rhododendrons, and ferns at the bases of the redwoods. Sonoma stone was used for grading wherever possible, rather than concrete retaining walls.

Materials: Steel frame construction. Tilt-up exposed aggregate panels in a mixture of brown and grey river rock. Red clay tile roof supported by Douglas fir glu-lam columns, stained dark brown, and redwood-stained beams, exposed on the interior. Natural redwood supports and purlins for dormer windows. Windows plate glass with small panes for pleasing design and easy replacement. Black-painted metal sash. Entry plaza and foyer of red brick, laid dry. Interior walls of resawn redwood boards, sealed. Floors steel joist with plywood sub-floor. Floors carpeted with specially-designed and woven 100% wool blend throughout upper level, stairs, gallery, board and staff rooms, for acoustical treatment and low maintenance. Colored troweled concrete in storage and non-public areas on lower level. Reading deck of Douglas fir beams, decking, supports and railings.

Forced-air heat throughout, thermostat-controlled. Auxilliary radiant heating in less frequently used rooms. All mechanical and electrical systems designed for future expansion.

Figure 184.   Mill Valley Public Library. This large building repre-
               sents an informal blend with the existing surroundings,
               using natural materials and intimate scale.

Photo by: Robert Brandwis,
San Francisco, Calif.

Total Costs, by Category of Expenditure:
    Architect and Consultant Fees and Costs: $ 40,019.26
    New Construction: 379,430.56
    Equipment and Furnishings   40,235.43

    Other Costs:
        Site work and landscaping $ 21,397.75
        Moving from old library   2,339.00
        Bond issue costs   2,253.84
        Audit fee   500.00
        Insurance and miscellaneous   602.01
    Total Cost: 486,777.85

Figure 185. Interior view, Mill Valley Public Library, Mill Valley, California. Though not designated as a branch, this library is of branch size and is a member of the North Bay Cooperative System.

Photo by: Alexandre Georges, Pomona, New York

Large Regional or Area Branch

W. Clarke Swanson Regional Branch
Omaha Public Library, Omaha, Nebraska

Merit Award Winner, 1966

Area: 25,510 square feet.
Opened: January 1966
Architect: Leo A. Daly Co.

Community:
1960 Population   34,555
1980 (Estimate--City Planning Dept.)   106,700

The community is well above the median of the city in dollar
income, years of school attended, and home ownership. It is
characterized by rapid residential and commercial development.
Major shipping centers and office buildings draw the public from
all Omaha and vicinity into this area.

There are twenty-four schools in this area, and eleven more are
proposed.

Type of Library: Large library facility to provide full and adequate services to all age groups within its area, with provision
for additional load drawn by shopping centers, new schools and
further residential development west.

Special Services: Auditorium and Conference Room serve as
centers for a variety of library-sponsored and community
activities.

Building Areas (Exterior Dimensions)
Ground Floor   12,550 sq. ft.
First Floor   12,960 sq. ft.
                 Total   25,510 sq. ft.

Building Areas (Interior Dimensions)
First Floor - 177' x 70'   12,390 sq. ft.
    Adult Stack Area   1,742 sq. ft.
    Adult Seating Area   2,686 sq. ft.
    Adult Work Room   680 sq. ft.
    Adult Traffic Area   1,025 sq. ft.   6,133 sq. ft.

    Teen-Age Stack Area   78 sq. ft.
    Teen-Age Seating Area   1,330 sq. ft.   1,408 sq. ft.

    B&G Stack Area   1,326 sq. ft.
    B&G Seating Area   1,496 sq. ft.
    B&G Work Room   500 sq. ft.
    B&G Traffic Area   867 sq. ft.   4,189 sq. ft.

Stairwell	180 sq. ft.	
Vestibule	480 sq. ft.	
Total	12,390 sq. ft.	

Ground Floor - 177' x 70'   12,390 sq. ft.

Tech. Proc.		
Catalog Room	1,920 sq. ft.	
Sound Room	450 sq. ft.	
Order Room	650 sq. ft.	3,020 sq. ft.
Auditorium	851 sq. ft.	
Conference Room	432 sq. ft.	1,283 sq. ft.
Office		198 sq. ft.
Storage Room		999 sq. ft.
Staff Room		576 sq. ft.
Rest Rooms		625 sq. ft.
Janitorial		360 sq. ft.
Mechanical		3,196 sq. ft.
Distribution		222 sq. ft.
Corridors, stairs, etc.		1,921 sq. ft.
		12,390 sq. ft.

Seating Capacity

Area	Sq. Ft. per Reader	Seats
Adult	35	54
Reference	28	24
Teen-Age	33	43
Boys and Girls	29	55
		176
Auditorium		63
Conference Room		15

Book Capacity-Actual

Open Shelves

Area	Books per Standard Shelf	No. of Shelves	No. of Sections	Books
Adult Fiction	25	217	31	5,425
Adult Non-Fiction	25	735	105	18,375
Reference	18	112	16	2,016
Teen-Age	25	77	11	1,925
Boys and Girls	30	812	116	24,360
Boys and Girls (Pict. Bks.)	40	20	10	800
		1,973		52,901

Closed Shelves				
Charge Desk (Adult)	25	12	4	300
Charge Desk (B&G)	25	12	4	300
Work Room (Adult	--	--		
Work Room (B&G)	25	28	4	700
Librarian's Office	25	9	3	225
Shelving Section (Adult)	25	28	4	700
Shelving Section (B&G)	25	28	4	700
				14,175
				17,100

Area	Books per Standard Shelf	No. of Shelves	No. of Sections	Books
Other Shelving				
Magazines (open)		28	7	
Magazines (closed)		147	21	
Phonograph records		425		

Parking Spaces: 92

Special Features:

> Air conditioned.

> Vestibule doors closing off library permits the use of the Auditorium and Conference Room after library hours.

> Two points for the charging of books are provided because of the expected volume of business.

The site of the building, 130,000 square feet, has a valuation of approximately $150,000. It is located at an intersection of prominent visibility on major north-south and east-west thruways midpoint between the two major shopping centers in western Omaha.

Due to the limitation of space in the central building, technical processing has been transferred to the branch. In 1967, Swanson Branch, with a total book stock of 58,685 lent 367,860 books, 4,787 records, 213 pamphlets, 3,486 mounted pictures. Frank E. Gibson, the Director, anticipates an ultimate book circulation of 600,000-700,000 from this branch. In the same year, 1967, 89 library-sponsored meetings were held. Various community groups held 133 meetings.

Figure 186.   Dramatic night shot of the W. Clarke Swanson
               Regional Branch, Omaha Public Library, Omaha,
               Nebraska, 25,510 square feet.

Figure 187.   W. Clarke Swanson Regional Branch. Interior.

Photos: Julius Shulman,
Los Angeles, Calif.

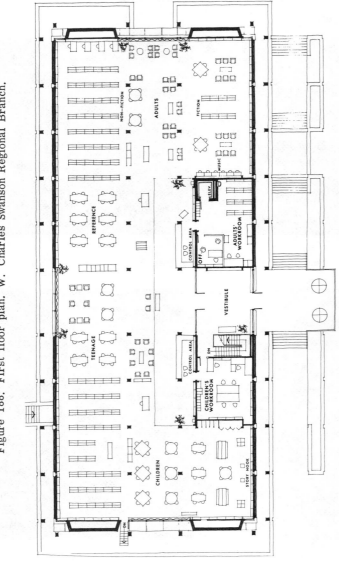

Figure 188. First floor plan. W. Charles Swanson Regional Branch.

Large Branch

New Carrollton Branch
Prince George's County Memorial Library
Hyattsville, Maryland

National First Prize Regents Award,
Society of American Registered Architects

Ground broken:	January 1969.
Architects:	Masiello & Associates, Lantram, Maryland.
Size:	55,669 square feet. Lower level, 27,758 sq. ft. (over half of lower level left unfinished for future expansion). Upper level, 27,911 sq. ft.
Book capacity:	150,000 Volumes.
Site:	4.5 acres. Gift of a developer.
Population Served:	100,000-150,000 (within three mile radius of building).

Cost: General contract - $1,074,785, not including library furniture or carpeting, which will cover all of the upper level except the entrance lobby. Prince George's County Library has found with their other buildings that an amount equal to 15% of the contract price has been adequate for carpeting, furniture, and equipment. In the case of the New Carrollton Branch it will also cover a consultant fee for an interior designer.

Method of financing: County bond, authorized by the State Legislature for counties not having "home rule," of which Prince George's County is one. This is the sixth branch to be constructed under a building program begun in 1963. Architects have been hired for the 7th and 8th buildings, and land is being acquired for four more. None of the projected buildings is to be as large as New Carrollton, however.

Unusual feature: All-electric building. Heat and air-conditioning will both be powered entirely by electricity to keep the place dustless. This is unusual in this part of the country.

Distribution of space:

Lower level:

Meeting room with projection room, kitchenette, and W. P. A. system: 1903 sq. ft.

Conference rooms for public use - 2: one, 407 sq. ft.; the other, 60 sq. ft.

Stack area: 1774 sq. ft.

Shipping room with loading dock: 720 sq. ft.

Staff lounge and locker space: 1524 sq. ft.

Mechanical equipment and maintenance areas: 2015 sq. ft.

Lower lobby: 1893 sq. ft.

Also on the lower level are public toilets, corridors, stairways, cloak room, storage room, elevator, and the switchboard, with one way glass to provide supervision of lower lobby.

Upper level:

Offices and work rooms for Y.A., A., Children and Reference: 1409 sq. ft.
Circulation work room: 828 sq. ft.
Children's room: 4587 sq. ft.
Children's program room: 403 sq. ft.
Adult reading and reference room: 14,641 sq. ft.
YA reading room: 840 sq. ft.
Periodical storage: 682 sq. ft.
Librarian's, assistant librarian's, and secretary's offices: 1,078 sq. ft.
Lobby, circulation desk, stairways, etc. in the remaining space.

Figure 189.   Architect's rendering of the 55,000 square foot new Carrollton Branch of the Prince George's County Memorial Library.   Located in New Carrollton, Maryland.

Large Branch

Sprain Brook Branch
Yonkers Public Library, Yonkers, N. Y.

Award of Merit Winner, 1964

The 2-1/2-million dollar branch of Yonkers Public Library
was dedicated in 1962 and was awarded a citation of merit in 1964
under the joint awards program of A.L.A., the A.I.A. and the
National Book Committee. Eli Rabineau was the architect.

Reinforced concrete is the main material. The branch is
located on one of the busiest thoroughfares of the city. Its strik-
ingly beautiful sun screen of various colored enameled panels, its
graceful vaulted arches of concrete, and its large expanses of glass
cannot fail to catch the eye of passers-by.

The Sprain Brook Branch is so planned that by means of
ramps and elevators, a person may enter and traverse the entire
65,000 square feet without having to use a single stair step. There
is a 147-car parking lot in its tastefully-landscaped five acres,
much appreciated by patrons in heavily-trafficked Westchester
County.

Unique features include a Senior Citizens Center operated
jointly by the library and the Municipal Recreation Commission;
four study carrels like those in college libraries equipped for
manual or electric typewriters, dictaphone, tape recording, etc.
A large fine arts area with soundproof listening booth and specially-
equipped listening tables is a prime attraction. There is a 40-seat
projection room, special display shelving for phono records, a huge
amount of display space, including museum-type panel display equipment, and an acoustically perfect auditorium with a complete professional theatre and lighting equipment for its stage. A 4000-
square feet area houses the project of the Westchester Library
System for centralized purchasing, cataloging, and processing of
books.

There is an outdoor reading area which cannot, of course,
be used the year around in the New York climate, but it is useful
and impressive in the good seasons. This very large branch, one
of the largest, if not the largest in the country, has brought its
borrower registration up well above 50 per cent of its 200,000
population service area and has been producing a circulation well
over 2,000,000 annually.

Figure 190.   Sprain Brook Branch, Yonkers Public Library,
               Yonkers, N. Y. 65,000 sq. ft. - one of the largest,
               if not the largest in the U. S. Lower Level.

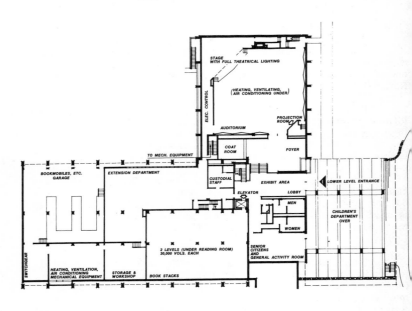

Figure 191.   Sprain Brook Branch. Mezzanine Floor.

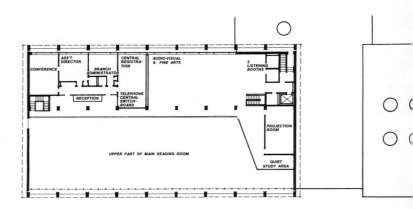

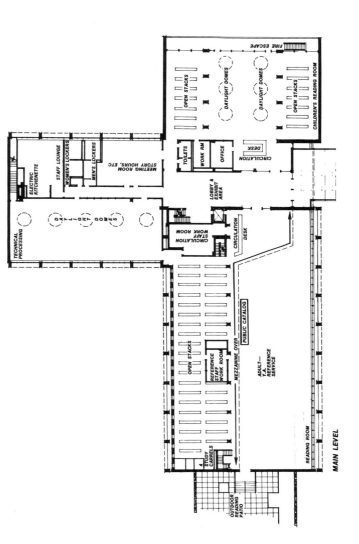

Figure 192. Sprain Brook Branch. Main Floor.

Figure 193.   Probably the largest individual branch in America,
the Sprain Brook Branch of the Yonkers Public
Library.

Figure 194.   Children's Room of the Sprain Brook Branch.

Chapter 18

Branch Furnishings and Equipment

As Martin Van Buren pointed out in a talk before the 1963
Institute on Library Furniture and Equipment sponsored by the
Library Administration Division of A.L.A., the type and color
tone of furniture can make a profound impression on the patron,
creating the atmosphere of the entire library.

The A.L.A. Library Technology Program is currently working on a publication on the selection and purchase of library furniture. As of December, 1968, a draft of the manuscript had been
submitted, but much editorial work remained to be done. Watch
the LTP column in the A.L.A. Bulletin for an announcement of
publication.

Since no comprehensive furniture and equipment guide for
libraries is yet available study the suppliers' catalogs and such
publications as Library Furniture and Equipment, Proceedings of a
three-day institute sponsored by the Library Administration
Division of A.L.A., 1963; The Library Environment; Aspects of
Interior Planning, Proceedings of the Library Equipment Institute
sponsored by the same group in 1965; and American Public Library
Buildings by Wheeler and Githens, A.L.A., 1944, which is out of
print but may be borrowed.

In selecting furniture, if financially possible, employ the
services of a competent interior decorator as consultant. Choose
furnishings for: usefulness; beauty and harmony with building
interior colors, materials, and design; durability of finish and
upholstery; ease of maintenance; comfort; strength through sound
construction and extra bracing; lowest cost that offers all of the
above qualities; avoid sharp corners; all leg tips should have
glides or they should be added.

591

Tables and chairs should be arranged in informal groupings rather than in regimented straight rows. Attempt to use higher pieces around the perimeter of areas and low units in the middle or open areas so that the view remains unobstructed and a feeling of spaciousness is maintained. Tall furniture or standing stacks badly spaced can also interfere with proper supervision of the public service areas from the charging desk.

An angled or radial pattern of arrangement for the book stacks can aid supervision. Stacks should never be placed at right angles to the desk to form hidden pockets. Good supervision is one advantage of the circular type of branch. If the charging desk is located in or near the middle, good visibility is possible down all aisles of the stacks. Reader tables can be located close to the charging area with the standing stacks radiating around the room at the outer perimeter.

One of the prerequisites before ordering furniture and equipment is awarding the contract through a bidding procedure. It should be noted that many a branch has had its scheduled opening held up because furnishings and equipment did not arrive in time. Allow six months or more from the time the contract is let for delivery of the items ordered. All preliminaries should be taken care of well in advance of the building completion, and the specifications of what is needed should be started as soon as erection of the branch becomes a certainty. If there is a long period between inception and submitting of the specifications to bidders, some prices may have to be revised.

The actual procedures involved in preparing bid documents and the taking of bids are not clear to many librarians. Libraries that are publicly supported must, ethically and legally, secure their furniture through competitive bidding. Very exacting requirements for quality and precise regulations must be adhered to if Federal funds are involved. Clear, thorough specifications encourage fair competition among bidders and help to protect the library from firms which may look for loopholes in standards of quality. [1]

Figure 195. Bro-Dart Contemporary Juvenile Furniture in the children's room of the James V. Brown Library, Williamsport, Pennsylvania.

Specifications should describe the product or the work to be done. Included should be details as to size, form, construction, materials, quality, performance, and finish. The contractual and working agreements between the contractor and the city, county, or library board should be clearly defined. The specifications should be brief, in simple language, specific, without duplication, have few cross references, specify stock or standard item, be arranged logically, include all matters that have any application but nothing inapplicable, and should not specify the impossible.[1]

The various sections of the furniture bidding documents are:

1. Advertisement for bids: Duplicate of public ads for the newspapers.

2. Invitation to bidders: A detailed description of the job, time, place and date of bid opening, performance bond requirements, delivery and installation schedules, and eligibility of bidders.

3. General conditions to bidders: Detailed instructions to bidders, legal and contractual terms, and data concerning working arrangements.

4. Construction specifications: General standards of construction and materials, and detailed construction standards of particular items of library technical furniture.

5. Schedule of equipment: A list of furniture selections (shelving, specialized library furniture, miscellaneous furniture, draperies, carpeting, special designs). Unit prices should be requested for all items.

6. Bid opening procedures: Opening of bids may take several hours if numerous items of miscellaneous furniture are involved. With categories requiring lump sum bidding, the procedure is fairly fast.

7. Tabulation of bids: May become complicated because there are always deviations and alternative proposals.

8. Evaluation of bids: A common problem is the 'qualified bid.' If a quotation is submitted with the qualification: 'Quotations are for our standard line, or something similar, all detailed specifications are legally eliminated. If such a bid is accepted, the library is helpless and must accept whatever the bidder proposes as standard. Most designers and architects reject a 'qualified bid.'

9.   Award of contracts: Three to four weeks are allowed
     for tabulation and evaluation of bids and decisions as
     to awards.   Few bidders will guarantee their quota-
     tions for longer than this.

10. Schedule of payments: Contractors are usually paid
     in two steps: about 80% on delivery of goods to the
     site and acceptance, the remainder after installation
     and inspection. [1]

At least two copies of bid documents should be sent to bidders, one for their records, one for submittal.

Various formulae have been suggested for determining costs
of furnishings and equipment before bids.   In the 1967-68 cost survey of public library buildings made by Hoyt Galvin, the average
cost of furnishings for selected branches of from 7,000 to 9,000
square feet was $28,830. [2]   In general, outlay on furnishings and
equipment will be 10 to 15 percent of the cost of the completed
building.

The following furniture and equipment list is adapted from
the lists of several large city and county libraries.   No such list
will fit the exact needs of every branch, but this one considers the
requirements of three sizes of buildings;

Class I: 8,000-26,000 square feet
Class II: 4,000- 8,000 square feet.
Class III: 2,400- 4,000 square feet.

Variations for each of these are indicated on the list, which is
presented merely as a checklist, to be added to or subtracted from
as needs dictate.   The dimensions given throughout the list are
practical and, in many cases, almost standard.

Furniture and Equipment

A.   Book ends: in sufficient number, including plenty of over-
                  size cushioned bottom to prevent marring
                  shelves quantity: Standard_____Oversize_____

B.   Book trucks (carts):
     Class 1 building-10 trucks.
     Class 2 building- 6 trucks.
     Class 3 building- 4 trucks.

C.   Bulletin boards:
     1.   Public: one generous sized bulletin board near entrance
          for local announcements (at least 12 square feet).
          Use best quality cork for backing.

Figure 196.   Individual carrels ranged along a wall afford privacy
               and are being used increasingly in libraries.   Note
               contrasting light and dark tones of these carrels at
               the Suburban Acres Branch, Tulsa City-County Library
               Tulsa, Oklahoma.

   2.   Workroom: Total of approximately 25 square feet
bulletin board area to provide:
- (a)   delivery information.
- (b)   staff assignments (time sheets, schedules, work assignments, staff meeting notes, etc.). Provide trough for pencils, thumb tacks, etc.
- (c)   branch information (location charts, comparative statistics, accident information, etc., placed low enough to be easily reached and read).

   3.   Staff quarters: One bulletin board no smaller than 18" x 24" for housekeeping directions and assignments.

D.   Catalog cases: (all to be 5, 10, or 15-drawer multiples and all to have sliding shelves, except items 5 and 6)

		Class 1 building	Class 2 building	Class 3 building
1.	Adult	60-360 drawers	30-60 drawers	15-30 drawers
2.	Juvenile	70-180 drawers	25-70 drawers	15-25 drawers
	Total	130-540 drawers	55-130 drawers	30-55 drawers
3.	Shelf-list			
	Adult	15-90 drawers	10-15 drawers	5-10 drawers
	Juvenile	25-60 drawers	10-25 drawers	20-40 drawers
	Total	40-150 drawers	20-40 drawers	25-50 drawers

   4.   Registration file: Provide, in counter, at charging desk, space for 4 fifteen-drawer units. Original installation in Class 3 and Class 2 buildings should consist of 3 fifteen drawer units.

   5.   Adult reference desk: 4 drawers.

   6.   Children's librarian's desk: 2 drawers.

E.   Chairs:

   1.   Reading room chairs for adults and children as space allows.

   2.   Posture stools, high--2 for circulation desk.

   3.   Posture chairs, low--1 for each staff desk.

   4.   Easy chairs and/or sofa in reading room if branch design allows.

   5.   Folding or stacked chairs (30-75) for classes and meetings, with portable rack.

   6.   Workroom chairs: 1 posture chair for desk.
                         1 side chair for each work table.

   7.   Staff quarters: 4 chairs for class 3 building.
                         6 chairs for class 2 building.
                        10 chairs for class 1 building.

   8.   Branch librarian's office: 1 desk chair, 2 side chairs.

F.   Desks:

Charging desk (may vary depending upon entrance), but suggested is: U-shaped desk.

Entrance on one side, exit on other for natural flow of traffic and efficiency in service.

Electrical outlet at desk and at counter.

Comment: U-shaped desk in this position is compact and
takes up less floor space than one facing door.
No glare from street.
Drafts from doors more easily controlled.
Good supervision of both adult and children's rooms from
this type of desk.

G.   Display racks:
      1. Book: 2 adult and 1 children's (portable or table
                       style).
                    1 adult and 1 children's (display rack and
                       double-faced with bulletin board, 33" high
                       x 42" wide and 24" deep).
      2. Magazine: 1 magazine display case for current issues in
                       adult area (48" wide x 60" high x 22" deep).

H.   Shelving:
      Adustable shelving throughout.
      Placed to be easily supervised from charging desk.
      As much wall shelving as building design allows.
      Number of floor stacks needed will depend upon the capacity
         of wall shelving in relation to total book stock planned for
         specific branch.
      Shelf capacity for storage: 8 books to 1' shelf space:
         150 books to a section on the average; shelf capacity for
         reading room: 6 books to 1' shelf space: 126 books to a
         section on the average. 7 shelves to a section of adult
         fiction; 6 shelves to a section of non-fiction; 5 shelves
         to a section of juvenile.
      1. Adult:
          Height: 6'10' (7 shelves); counter 42" (3 shelves).
          Width: 3' on centers.
          Depth: 8' generally; 10' for reference books; 12-14"
                       for magazines.
          Magazines: Should consist of 2 sections each containing
                       18 adjustable flat shelves and 1 base shelf.
          Reference: Convenient to charging and reference desk
                       supervision.
      2. Children's:
          Height: 5'1/2' (5 shelves high); counter 42" (3 shelves).
          Width: 3' on centers.
          Depth: 8' generally; 12" for magazines and picture
                       books.
          Magazines: Provide 2 sloping shelves in counter height
                       shelving adjacent to entrance.
          Picture Books: Provide shelving with 4 adjustable
                       dividers per shelf located in counter height
                       shelving adjacent to entrance.
      3. Branch librarian's office:
          Height: 42" (3 shelf). Depth: 12".
      4. Workroom:
          Height: 6'10' (7 shelf). Depth: 12".

5. Magazine storage:
   Located in workroom. Height: 6'10". Depth: 12".
   Quantity: 11   -   Class 3 building
             14   -   Class 2 building
             34   -   Class 1 building

I. <u>Tables</u> (maximum number as space allows):
   1. Reading room:
      (a) Adult - Standard, 36" wide;72" long;   29" high.
                  Reference,48" wide; 90"long;   29" high.
      (b) Children's-
                  Standard   30" wide;60" long; 24" high.
                  Round, 48' diameter;   25" high.
      (c) Catalog Consultation, Class 1 and class 2 buildings
          only: 72" long, 42" high.
   2. Workroom:
      (a) Work tables:
           Class 1 building   -   3 tables.
           Class 2 building   -   2 tables.
           Class 3 building   -   1 table.
           (Each 2'6" x 5'; linoleum top with no ridge on edge
           from metal binding).
      (b) Delivery, incoming (3' x 5' minimum).
           Linoleum top with no ridge on edge from metal
           binding.
      (c) Delivery, outgoing (2'6" x 5').
           Linoleum top with no ridge on edge from metal
           binding.   Plan convenient place for scissors,
           twine, crayon, pencils, clips, envelopes, routing
           slips, delivery tags. Storage space below. Hinged
           doors. Two shelves (delivery bags, mendery bags,
           newspaper, brown paper, bindery paper, poster
           paper, etc. , kept here).
   3. Staff quarters: 1 table.

J. <u>Telephone:</u>
   1. Charging desk: Desk type to ring at this location.
   2. Extensions: Librarian's office - desk type.
                   Reference desk - if separate reference
                   desk is included in plans.

K. <u>Transaction Card Storage Cabinets</u> - if transaction cards are
      used; size dependent on type and size of cards:
   Major storage at Headquarters.
   Storage equipment at branches in six drawers or covered
      trays.

L. <u>Typewriters</u>
   Class 1 building - 5 typewriters.
   Class 2 building - 4 typewriters.
   Class 3 building - 3 typewriters.

M. <u>Typewriter Stands:</u> Provide for each typewriter.

N.   Vertical files (metal, legal size):
     1.   Class 1 building - 2 4-drawer and 1 3-drawer with index
                              file of 4 trays.
          Class 2 building - 4 4-drawer and 1 3-drawer with index
                              file of 4 trays.
          Class 3 building - 5 4-drawer and 1 3-drawer with index
                              file of 4 trays.
     2.   Children's room - 1 4-drawer.
     3.   Office   - 1 4-drawer.

O.   Miscellaneous:
     1.   Atlas case (43" high and 29" wide and 27" deep).
     2.   Dictionary stand (44" high x 24" wide and 14" deep).
     3.   Microfilm reader: Will become a necessity for every
          branch library. Provide table on casters with drawer
          and sliding shelf. Consider area that can be
          darkened for use of film reader.
     4.   One or two photocopying machines, depending on branch
          size and usage.
     5.   Shelf stools with hand-hold: 1 each in adult section,
          children's section and magazine storage.
     6.   Staff room equipment:
          Can opener - wall mounted.
          Cupboard - adequate to hold dishes, pans, etc.
          Cup dispenser.
          Dishes, flatware, pans, etc., as required.
          Refrigerator - apartment size, right or lefthanded.
          Sink - counter type, double compartment with gar-
             bage disposal (or combination stove, sink and
             refrigerator unit).
          Couch area: Couch; Couch cover; Blanket;
                               Pillow; 2 pillow cases.
     7.   Supply cupboard: Locate near center of longest wall.
     8.   Waste baskets: 1 for each desk and work table in
          reading room and workroom.
          1 large and 1 small in staff quarters.
          1 large for each lavatory.

Costs vary so much from year to year that any price list
is likely to be quickly out of date. However, the list of furnishings and equipment proposed in the early stages of planning for an
8,064-square foot branch in Santa Ana, California, is reproduced
on the following pages. Since the average size of new branches
built from July 1, 1968 to July 1, 1969 was over 8,800
square feet, this list may be useful to libraries planning a branch
of that approximate size. Costs listed are taken from furniture and
equipment catalogs issued in 1968 for 1968-69. Since most cities
and counties will require that furnishings and equipment go to bid,
retail prices are of no value for the final costs but serve only to provide a rough guide for preliminary budgetary planning.

Estimated Furniture Costs (1969):
Branch Library of 8,000-10,000 sq. ft.

3 Complete Thirty-tray card catalog cabinets @ $515.00	$	1,545.00
2 Record Racks (Kersting), Natural Birch @ $99.95		199.90
1 Turntable		250.00
8 Reading Tables 72" x 36" x 29" high @ $133.95		1,071.60
56 Straight chairs with padded backs @ $30.00		1,680.00
13 Lounge chairs @ $84.50		1,068.50
1 Oblong coffee table 50" x 21" x 15"		54.00
2 Round coffee tables 42" in diameter 15" high		108.00
1 Wooden executive desk 58" x 32" top, walnut construction		140.80
2 Secretarial posture chairs Naugahyde upholstery		82.10
2 Double face Carrels @ $347.00		694.00
4 Single Carrels @ $174.00		696.00
1 Regiscope		750.00
1 Cash register		300.00
1 Typewriter (Olympia)		300.00
1 Combination Book display case and Bulletin Board		123.85
2 Descending platform book trucks 26" x 22" 29" high at back, 26-3/4 high in front @ $224.00		448.00
3 Steel booktrucks in color @ $47.50		143.50
1 Tall office chair		57.00
1 Visible file for reserves		30.00
1 Wall clock		30.00
- Lees Nylotile (2nd choice, wall-to-wall carpeting 640 sq. ft. @ $8.00 sq. yd.		5,120.00
1 Dictionary stand		95.75
8 wastebaskets @ $4.00		32.00
1 vacuum cleaner		150.00
4 Step stools @ $25.00		100.00

Children's Room

2 Complete thirty-tray card catalog cabinets @ $515.00	1,030.00
5 low 72" x 36" #E-72 Amer. Seating Cat. @ $133.95	669.75
4 Sloping tables for picture books @ $193.00	772.00
4 Benches @ $84.00	336.00
1 Round low table 48" in diameter 23" high	142.00
34 Low reading chairs (4 primary) @ $30.00	1,120.00
1 Wooden Executive desk 58" x 32" top, walnut construction	140.80
1 Waste Basket	4.00
1 Secretarial posture chair Naugahyde Upholstery	25.25

Reference Room

6 Tables 72" x 36" x 29" high @ $133.95	803.70

40 Straight chairs with padded backs @ $30.00   1,200.00
 1 Reader Printer   1,300.00
 2 or 3 Micro readers @ $225.00   675.00
 1 Table (sorting) 36" x 60" x 30" high   59.80
 2 Waste baskets @ $4.00   8.00
 1 Round Table 4' in diameter   138.00

Librarian's Office

 1 Conference desk 75" x 40"   181.65
 1 Executive posture chair, Walnut with pine or
     brown upholstery   57.95
   One man office with safety vault   69.25
 2 Straight arm chairs @ $47.75   95.50
 1 Waste basket   4.00
 1 IBM Wide carriage electric typewriter   475.00
 1 Typewriter table   30.00
 1 Electric clock   30.00

Work Room

 3 Double pedestal desks 54" x 30" x 29" high
     @ $103.65   310.95
 2 Typewriters (Olympias) 1 wide carriage @ $225.00   450.00
 2 Typewriter tables @ $30.00   60.00
 3 Secretarial posture chairs Naugahyde upholstery
     @ $ 41.05   123.15
 2 Side chairs Naugahyde upholstery @ $ 25.25   50.50
 1 Wall clock   30.00
 4 Waste baskets @ $ 4.00   16.00
 1 10-Key adding machine   79.00

All-Purpose Room

 1 Folding table 30" x 72"   53.50
80 Folding chairs (mist green with green upholstery)
     @ $ 4.83   386.40
 1 Folding chair caddy 4 Ft. double   95.38
80 Chair clamps   11.20
 1 Movie projector   (approximate) 149.75
 1 Slide projector   "   "   119.95
 1 Projection screen 70" x 70"   48.95
   Sink, refrigerator, stove combination with
     cupboards above   500.00

Conference Room

 1 Conference table 72" x 36"   137.25
 8 Chairs upholstered seats & backs @ $34.00   272.00
 1 Rental typewriter (leased by Company)

Staff Lounge

1 Sink, stove, refrigerator combination with cupboards above	$	500.00
1 Table (Nordia) 36" x 48"		30.00
4 Chairs (Nordia) @ $25.00		100.00
1 Studio couch or sofa		100.00
1 Lounge Chair		90.00
1 End table		20.00
1 Coffee table		20.00
1 Clock (wall or ?)		30.00
1 Minute Man coat rack single faced		36.75

Shelving

Standing stacks - 249 ft. (double-faced cases, including 16 adult, 7 feet high, and 8 juvenile, 5 feet high. Philippine mahogany). Constructed locally.	6,000.00

Miscellaneous

Drapes for two picture windows, 15 ft. wide, 7 ft. high (estimate)		1,000.00
Bookends, 800 @ $28.50 per 100= $228.00 36 @ .80= $28.80		256.80
Bicycle stand		150.00
Curb return box		360.00
Rubber door mats		10.00
Miscellaneous items		200.00
Total	$	36,636.18

Floor coverings:

Floor coverings, if tile or linoleum, are usually considered with the building specifications. However, carpeting is gaining increasing popularity as a floor covering for libraries, and if used, is often considered with the furnishing bid. Advantages of carpeting are the following:

1. Ease of maintenance. Studies and experience have shown it is also cheaper to maintain than vinyl or other types of tile, battleship linoleum or terrazzo, although original cost is higher than for all but terrazzo.

2. Carpet is a highly efficient heat insulator. Excellent barrier to cold.

3. Beauty.

4. Safety. Fewer slips and falls occur.

5. Sound deadening effect. Absorbs both airborne and impact noises.

6. Gives patrons and staff a sense of pride in their building.

7. Comfort, easy on the feet.

Carpet can be expected to last from 10 to 20 years, depending on the amount of usage. Any type of wall-to-wall carpeting can be laid very easily over concrete. Concrete must be raised from contact with the ground and properly insulated. If this is done there is no danger of carpet deteriorating.

Carpet absorbs light more than waxed or polished tile and linoleum floors and is less likely to cause glare.

A new type of tile carpeting has lately been introduced which comes in 12-inch squares. If the squares can be fastened down flat enough so that there are no loose edges to cause tripping, this type of carpeting offers the advantage of being able to replace worn sections which receive the greatest wear. Cost averages around 70¢ a square foot or $6.30 a square yard. This is much less than a good-grade of library carpeting. Branches should try to purchase all-wool carpeting as it stands up under hard usage much better than nylon, orlon or other materials which tend to pack down. However, 70% wool, 30% nylon, or 15-denier virgin nylon are satisfactory.

If carpeting is impossible for the branch, rubber tile would be the first choice of many. It is, however, the most expensive type of resilient flooring. Vinyl asbestos is a second choice. Asphalt tile should be used only in utility or storage areas where there is very little traffic. For further information, read "Carpeting in Libraries," by William B. Jorgenson, an acoustical evaluation of the effect of carpeting in reducing noise in libraries (Library Journal, Dec. 1, 1967, p. 4344), and "Is Carpeting Practical?" by Martin Van Buren (Library Journal, Dec. 1, 1965, p. 5152-56).

When comparing tile or linoleum floor covering with carpeting the cost of polishing materials must be taken into consideration. Floor wax of good quality is expensive even when purchased in large quantity. Terrazzo floors are even more expensive than carpeting, will require constant polishing, and will develop cracks in ten years or less.

Light-colored floors are to be preferred, and with a minimum of pattern, especially in colors which blend with furniture and walls.

Charging desk:

The central administrative feature in the branch is the charging desk. It is technical equipment with very special requirements, and is often built on a unit principle to suit the needs of libraries of various sizes. If a suitable combination of units cannot be supplied by a library furniture manufacturer, the charging desk will have to be custom made. In the latter case, every detail should be painstakingly planned by the head librarian, staff members who will work at the desk, and the branch supervisor. No single piece of furniture or equipment is more important, for a poorly designed charging desk can waste time and tire staff, and may provide insufficient storage for supply items which are needed daily. This author visited one branch where the charging desk had been built so deep from front to back that the staff members could barely reach the books to charge them out, and short patrons could not reach across the desk to pick them up.

If a charging system is being used which requires filing of book cards in circulation trays, a well should be installed in the desk, large enough to house the number of trays required for current circulation and with extra space for future expansion. A depressed area for the cash register is also desirable. The top of the desk should be as unimpeded and uncluttered as possible. If photocharging or some type of mechanical charging method is used, the camera or machine will probably have to be on top of the desk. Putting in a well for equipment which may vary in size and shape as replacements are made is not advisable.

Every charging desk must provide the usual essentials: a cash drawer for money (if a cash register is not being used); a drawer for pens, pencils, keys and other miscellaneous items; a built-in registration file (if borrowers are still being registered).

Figure 197.   Typical charging desk units sold by library furniture
               suppliers.   They can be combined to form almost any
               size or shape of desk desired.

Charging Desk Units

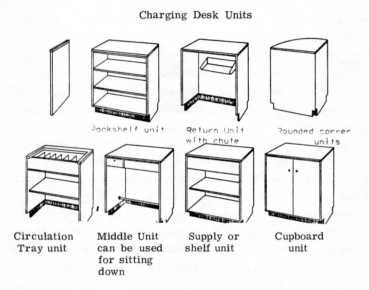

Bookshelf unit   Return Unit   Rounded corner
                    with chute   units

Circulation   Middle Unit   Supply or   Cupboard
Tray unit   can be used   shelf unit   unit
               for sitting
               down

A cupboard for supplies, a well-padded return bin, and shelves for
books needing mending, for snags, and for books on reserve, are
also needed.   Reserve books can sometimes be kept on shelves behind the desk, if that space is not all needed for ready reference
books.   There should be a parking place for several book trucks
next to the desk but out of the line of traffic.   If possible, have a
"lost and found" cupboard or shelf at the main charging desk.

        The most common dimensions among available modular pro-
duction charging units are: 30 inches wide, by 26 inches deep, by
39 inches high.

Tables:

        Recommended table heights are given in the specifications
lists in this chapter.   Tables should be well braced with steel in
the legs or have aprons as bracing.   Veneered construction is adequate and permits some color effects not possible with solid tops.

Figure 198.   Steel, wood, and plastic are combined in modern tables
               and chairs at the Ross-Cherry Creek Branch of the
               Denver Public Library, Denver, Colorado. Note use of
               light and dark on walls, furniture and woodwork. The
               davenport at far left, upholstered in plastic, is the most
               practical type for the hard use received in a branch.

Plastic laminates justify the extra cost by providing a surface that will withstand heat, water, and abrasion. These laminates are available in wood grain finishes or in solid colors. Avoid tables with a high level of light reflectance. Wood tops and metal legs make a good combination. A 36-inch width has been found sufficient to allow two people to work across from each other in comfort. Tables used in outdoor reading rooms should be completely weatherproof and sturdy enough to stand extremely hard use. Outdoor tables should not have to be moved inside at night, since most outdoor reading rooms and patios are fenced or have some sort of enclosure. Metal tables with a durable finish of several coats of exterior enamel are best for such use.

In the conference room a light but sturdy folding banquet table will provide flexibility, since it can be removed if space is needed for more chairs for a group meeting.

Materials in furniture (particularly shelving):

Wood is a warm material. It has beauty and durability and is easier to repair than metal or plastic. However, it is subject to swelling and shrinkage and is also more vulnerable to carving, scratching, gouging, or burning.

Metal can be molded into shapes having much more structural strength than a piece of wood of the same size. Steel shelving, because the uprights can be higher, will accommodate seven shelves rather than the six which are normal with wood shelvings, and thus provide about 17 per cent more book capacity. Steel shelving with wood end penels is both practical and good looking. There is an increasing tendency to combine wood and metal for greater strength and rigidity and a more handsome appearance. Steel shelving costs one-third to one-half as much as wood shelving, although wood end panels increase the cost.

Displaying Phonograph Records:

The conventional display method is on a low table with divided storage bins housing the records with their cases facing outward. These bins facilitate easy browsing, but they occupy

Figure 199. Audio-Visual Section, W. Clarke Swanson Branch,
Omaha Public Library, Omaha, Nebraska. This type
of record holder is sturdy, attractive and easy for
the patron to use. However, it takes up a good deal
of floor space and is more expensive than the bookcase type unit with pull-out racks. The individual
listening units shown at left and right of the record
table are preferred by patrons to the multiple listening tables.

considerable floor space. Another type of record cabinet or con-
tainer is a Quik-See Unit which looks like a deep bookcase but
contains pull-out wire racks the width of 12-inch records. The
racks pull out very easily on ball bearings when the weight of the
records is on them. These units hold up to several hundred long-
play records, and are available in a variety of sizes. They take
up less floor space than browsing bin units, and hold more records
proportionately.

Two listening units with earphones should be sufficient for
the average branch. A very large branch would need two or three
times as many, or perhaps several small listening booths. A number of neat-looking tables equipped with pull-out drawers with
changers, earphones, and surprisingly good tone are available.

Microfilm Readers and Photocopying Equipment:

A microfilm reader-printer is to be preferred over a reader
only, but the cost is from six to seven times greater. A photocopying machine, coin-operated, has been listed as desirable, but
it is rapidly becoming indispensable. Ths use of these machines
in branches has proved to be far heavier than originally expected
and they have helped to reduce vandalism and stealing of materials.
Most machines now available can be set to supply pages at 10¢
each.   There are several good makes on the market ranging from
portable table models costing only a few hundred dollars to large
console machines which are leased or placed in libraries on a
share-the-profit basis. In the latter case a guaranteed monthly
volume of use is normally required, and the library has to pay
the difference if the minimum is not achieved.

Typewriters:

At least one typewriter in the branch should be an electric
machine since the evenness of touch on an electric typewriter produces better stencils and master copies for duplication. A good
arrangement in a workroom is to have a row of several desks
down the middle of the room containing the typewriters and personal drawer space for each staff member, plus several individual
carrels along one wall where a measure of privacy can be secured
when work requiring concentration is to be done.

Work Tables:

A good-sized delivery table and work table should each be
supplied. The delivery table should be near the workroom door to
the parking area, to facilitate transfer of materials from delivery
trucks. The work table is for light mending, poster-making and

Figure 200.   Plan for delivery table developed by David W. Bass
               for Los Angeles Public Library branches.
               Scale: 3/4"= 1 foot.

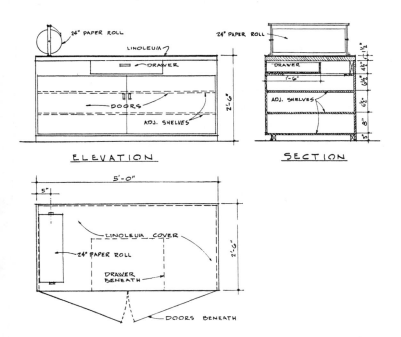

any other work requiring a fairly large surface. It should, therefore, be of generous proportions and should be adjacent to a sink.
It could be a wall counter table suspended so that there is plenty
of knee room under it. There should be a well-divided cupboard,
either built in or standing against one wall, to be used for storage
of supplies. Dividers help to keep items separated and make it possible to assess quickly which are getting low. At least two book trucks
should be available in the workroom for use at all times, for un-
packing new books that come from Central, or for discards, books
to be mended, etc.

Special Equipment:

Special equipment for magnifying print for the reader with
poor eyesight, special shelving for the large-print books, an over-
head ceiling projector, an opaque projector, a filmstrip and slide

projector, a movie projector and screen are among other items of
equipment which may be needed in a branch. If the library budget
does not make such items possible, local groups may sometimes be
persuaded to present such items as gifts.

Meeting or All-purpose Room Equipment:

Folding chairs for the meeting or all-purpose room, a
compact combination refrigerator-range-sink combination, coat racks
or a closet section for wraps, several tables, and kitchen equipment are all useful in a branch providing space for community programs or meetings. A 30-40 cup coffee-maker is almost standard
equipment.

Figure 201.   Dwyer Unit Kitchenettes of this type are placed between
               the meeting room and staff lounge in most branches of
               the Lake County Public Library System, Griffith,
               Indiana. The units are purchased through community
               contributions.

Book trucks:

The most popular type of book trucks today are the smaller
light metal trucks with two or three level or sloping shelves.   These
trucks have large rubber wheels that swivel, and they maneuver
easily and operate quietly.   Bro-Dart, Gaylord, and Demco all
make this type of truck, which costs in the neighborhood of $50.00.

Blinds and drapes:

If large picture windows are used, blinds or draperies are
almost a necessity unless there is a very large overhang on the
outside of the building.   Even if not actually needed for practical
reasons, colorful drapes add much to the interior appearance of
the building.   They should be floor length unless there is book
shelving under the windows, should be of easily-cleaned material,
operate on traverse rods, and harmonize with the color scheme of
the carpeting and furnishings.   As a rule, solid color drapes are
more suitable unless all other interior colors are solid, subdued,
or monotones.   Fabrics should be sturdy, resistant to sun deterioration and fading, and not easily inflammable.   They should be made
by competent workmen and should be properly weighted.

Book drops:

These have been discussed in previous chapters.   Use curb
return boxes with caution and only if the branch neighborhood is
relatively free from vandalism.   A book return slot in the building
wall is preferable.

Magazine and newspaper racks:

Magazine and newspaper racks of the wall-mounted type are
best in a branch, because the free-standing models take up much
more floor space.   Wall racks, of course, reduce wall shelving
space for books, but they are less expensive than free-standing
models, and the latter can make a reference or reading area look
cluttered.   Wall racks can be built in by the contractor if they are
specified in the planning stage.

Dictionary or atlas stands:

    Separate dictionary and atlas stands are available with slop-
ing tops upon which large, heavy books can be opened out. The
dictionary remains open on the stand at all times. The atlas cases
have a number of wide deep shelves which accommodate the large
atlases flat.

Display cases for paperbacks:

    At least two shallow five- or six-shelf book racks, to stand
back to back, should be purchased for display of the paperback collection in a prominent position near the front entrance of the branch.
If two are purchased, one can be used for fiction titles, the other
for non-fiction.

Filing cases:

    Filing cases are needed in the public service area, usually
the reference section, for the pamphlet collection, or for a picture
collection, and for special files such as sheet music, government
documents, etc. Those in the public area may be of wood or
metal (beige or pale green, but not the dark green so often seen in
offices in the past) and should be full suspension for ease of use by
the public. Office file cases, from one to four drawers, may be
any color and type desired. The full suspension files are preferable since they seldom jam and are easy to pull in and out. Non-
suspension files may be used if they will be loaded quite lightly.
Legal-size files are best for the public service area, as they will
hold larger pamphlets and documents, but letter-size may suffice
for office use.

Index tables:

    Special index tables should be purchased for the Readers'
Guide, Education Index, or other heavily-used indexes. The usual
type has a sloping top backed with one or two shelves for the index
volumes. A special table with sliding shelves for wide volumes is
available. The lifting of these heavy volumes is minimized by use
of the sliding shelf or sloping top tables. Carrels placed side by

side or a flat-topped table can be used if special index tables are not available.

<u>Shelving:</u>

Some librarians have had unhappy experiences with shelving constructed on the job or in local shops. The precision and accuracy of machine-made shelving may be lacking, with a consequent loss of flexibility in interchanging shelves, adding or removing sections, or in the future purchase of component parts. If shelving is to be made locally, be sure of the following:

1. That all wood is properly and fully dried by air or kiln and all surfaces sealed against absorbing moisture.

2. The wood is clear and free from knots and defects.

3. The wood members used for uprights and shelves are thick enough to bear the heavy weight of books for years without sagging, buckling or twisting. A finished thickness of one inch is recommended, seven-eighths might be acceptable.

4. Exposed surfaces should not only be sealed but finished with high quality varnish.

5. No unsupported span of shelves should be over three feet.

6. All shelves are adjustable. Metal adjustment strips are easier to install and more precise than holes bored for pins in the uprights. [3]

Book Capacity of Shelving for Various Types of Books[3]

No. of Books per

Types of Books	Foot of Shelving	Linear foot of single-faced wall shelving	Linear foot of double-faced shelving	Recommended width of shelves (inches)
Fiction	8	56	112	8
General non-fiction	7	49	98	8
Technical and scientific	6	42	84	10
Medical	5	35	70	10
Law	4	28	56	8
Bound Periodicals	5	35	70	10-12
General average	7	50	100	--

Notes

1. Van Buren, Martin. "A Guide to the Preparation of Furniture
    and Bidding Documents." Library Journal, v. 91, no. 21.
    Dec. 1, 1966. p. 5845-5850.

2. Galvin, Hoyt R. "Public Library Building in 1968." Library
    Journal, v. 93, no. 21. Dec. 1, 1968, p. 4498-4511.

3. Galvin, Hoyt R. , and Van Buren, Martin. The Small Public
    Library Building. Unesco. 1959. p. 89.

Lists of furnishings taken from lists prepared by the Santa Ana
Public Library Extension Section in March, 1969, and the
Contra Costa County Library, Pleasant Hills, California, as
adapted from the Los Angeles Public Library lists for branch
furnishings and equipment.

Chapter 19

Branch Standards

"Standards are living goals. As goals change for each of us
in our everyday life, so with standards. As new situations and new
challenges arise, existing standards must be re-examined and re-
appraised."[1]

So begins the introduction to <u>Alabama Standards for Alabama</u>
<u>Public Libraries,</u> and it is an excellent statement to bear in mind
in considering branch standards. No set of standards should have
the effect of freezing patterns of library service and administration,
and no one set of standards is likely to prevail very long, for
they must constantly be upgraded to meet new or increasing needs.

Some standards, however, may be so utopian that most libraries see no possibility of attaining them in the foreseeable future.
It is wiser to produce working standards that can be achieved within a reasonable length of time.

The lack of standards for branch libraries has been decried
in the professional journals by a number of librarians, but although
there is no one set of criteria, a surprising number of suggested
standards exist for almost every aspect of branch planning and
operation. They are chiefly to be found in books and general
standards, documents issued by state agencies and associations and
by the American Library Association.

"In developing plans for federal funds and state aid projects
where such funds are available, public libraries have found it
necessary to establish standards of service in branch libraries,"
Roberta Bowler points out.[2] Branch standards should include
population and area to be served, floor area in square feet, book
stock, minimum expected annual circulation, working hours of professional and non-professional employees, average total hours per
week open for public service, and approximate annual current

budget for staff, materials and other items.

In this volume standards gathered from various sources have been included in the chapters where they seemed most applicable: standards for materials in the chapter on the branch collection, standards for buildings in the chapter on housing the branch, staff standards with the chapter on staffing. A few others, in the form of charts, tables or very general statements are included here.

In an overall summary of a medium-sized branch circulating 100,000 or more books, Wheeler and Goldhor state:

> It should have its own building, though sufficient ground area for parking need not be on the same plot. A branch circulating 100,000 or more books per year should have about 8,000 square feet of floor space, of which 7,000 should be on the main floor, at sidewalk level, with about 75 seats for adults and young adults and 50 for children, and a book stock of 25,000 with active discarding and 1,500 books added each year....Such a branch would be open about 8 hours a day at least 5 days a week and have a staff of 5 or 6 full-time employees, other than the custodian, and including two or three professional librarians."[3]

The cost of such a branch at 1961 prices was suggested as $200,000, including equipment and furnishings. In light of price increases since that time the current figure should probably be set at from $250,000 to $300,000. (See chapter on costs.) Certain other of the Wheeler and Goldhor recommendations also seem low today, particularly in the light of the present emphasis upon reference work in branches. The initial book stock, according to more recent suggested standards, should be no less than 30,000, and the staff should be a minimum of 7-8 employees. Wheeler and Goldhor advocate a full range of materials for the branch collection: a wide selection of books, vertical file materials, current and back issues of magazines and newspapers, phonograph records, pictures, and maps. A branch should also be able to borrow promptly any materials in the rest of the system. The reference collection should number several hundred volumes.[4] In addition, many branches today are supplying 8mm. films, filmstrips and art prints.

Wheeler and Goldhor further state that branches should

supply reading guidance for children, high school students and adults
be able to answer at least 10,000 adult reference questions per year
regularly offer book-centered programs for children and adults
tailored to the needs of the neighborhood, and actively cooperate
with schools, social agencies and clubs in the community.[4]

Very detailed standards for branch buildings and equipment
were prepared by the Los Angeles Public Library in connection with
the construction of the 28 branches funded by a 1957 bond issue.
These were revised in 1961 and at this writing were undergoing
another revision. The recommended size of buildings is being increased in the latest revision and the new standards will specify a
multi-purpose community room for each branch, a feature not included in the previous standards. According to Harold Hamill, former
City Librarian, the new standards will recommend that the smallest
agency be 7,500 square feet, with others of 9,000 square feet and
many over 10,500. Regional branches are planned to be 17,500
to 20,000 square feet. The community rooms in the regular branch
will accommodate 75-100 persons and those in the regional branches
will have a larger capacity. This revision should be of great value
to other large systems, since Los Angeles has learned a great deal
from the experience of building many branches in the last 10 to 12
years.

Florida Standards for Public Library Service (1967)[5] state
that urban branch libraries should serve populations of 25,000 to
50,000, contain working collections of 20,000 to 50,000 currently
useful volumes, and be open 48 hours or more each week. The
smallest branch library in a rural area should serve a trade area
population of at least 5,000 and be within 15 minutes driving time
of the citizens using it. It should contain at least 15,000 up-to-
date books on subjects of current interest and be open to the public
25 or more hours each week.

The Florida standards specify that all library systems
should provide a minimum of 2 to 2-1/2 books per capita. Annual
discards should average five per cent of the total book stock and
new books purchased should total at least one-quarter of a book
per capita. A branch library serving a population in excess of

8,000 should be under the supervision of a professional librarian, and any library serving more than 25,000 should have, in addition to the professional head librarian, a full-time professional reference librarian and a professional children's librarian.

A.L.A.'s Minimum Standards for Public Library Systems, 1966 contain statements on "community" libraries which may be applied to federation or cooperative system members and to urban or rural branches. Among these general points are:

1. They should be accessible to every user, connecting him with the total resources of his area, state, and the nation.

2. They should have sufficient resources to provide the most frequently-requested material from their own collections.

3. They should be part of a system of libraries with which they have a clear and official relationship, thus providing access to the widest possible range of services and materials by regular communication within the system.

In contrast with the 15-minute driving time recommended in the Florida standards as a service radius for rural branches, the A.L.A. Statistical Standards[6] recommend: "Maximum travel time to the library: 15 minutes for urban areas and 30 minutes for rural areas." Florida's 15 minutes may be the better recommendation.

Standards for South Carolina Public Libraries, Revised 1969[7] has only a few references to branch libraries as such. They suggest that branches should be open at least five days a week at the hours best suited to the community served, that all branches should have access to the headquarters library reference department by telephone at all open hours, and that staff members in general should participate in community activities, spreading these contacts to encompass the diversified interests of the community. This excellent set of standards is concerned mainly with individual, area resource libraries and county or multi-county libraries. Many of the standards cited, however, could be applied to branches, with variations depending upon the size of the branch unit.

In an article entitled "Better Branch Libraries,"[8] Frederick Wezeman points out that the average branch of a city system,

tending toward larger units with specialized personnel, larger book
collections, and adequate reference and bibliographic resources,
should have 30,000-40,000 volumes, about 100 current periodicals,
and more bibliographies, indexes and reference books than in the
past. Wezeman also recommends a floor area of 8,000-12,000
square feet, week-day opening hours 9 a. m. to 9 p. m. , and 9 to
5 on Saturdays; and a minimum of three professionals, with five
full-time staff for each 100,000 books circulated. Wezeman's
recommendations seem more realistic today than those proposed by
Wheeler and Goldhor.

Fresno County Free Library, Fresno, California, Branch
Standards[9] are presented in three categories: county branch,
metropolitan area branch, and large metropolitan area branch or
county regional headquarters. Although more elastic than some
standards in the ranges provided, the Fresno standards are higher
than many, although not unreasonably so. Although issued five
or six years ago, they appear very applicable today:

County Branch

Population	5,000-10,000
Annual circulation	35,000-60,000
Hours open	66-72
Staff	6 (Librarian II, Librarian I, 2 library assistants, 2 pages)
Building size	8,000-12,000 sq. ft.
Book capacity	20,000-50,000
Reader capacity	50-75
Parking	25-35 cars
Auditorium (optional)	100 seats

Metropolitan Area Branch

Population	10,000-25,000
Annual circulation	60,000-100,000
Hours open	66-72
Staff	6 (Librarian II, Librarian I, 2 library assistants, 2 pages)
Building size	4,000-8,000 sq. ft.
Book capacity	20,000-30,000
Reader capacity	40-60
Parking	20-30 cars
Auditorium (optional)	50 seats

Large Metropolitan Area Branch
or County Regional Headquarters

Population	Over 25,000
Annual circulation	Over 100,000
Hours Open	69-72
Staff	10 (Librarian III, II, I, 3 assistants, 3 pages)
Building Size	6,000-12,000 sq. ft.
Book capacity	30,000-50,000
Reader capacity	60-120
Parking	30-50 cars
Auditorium (optional)	150 seats
Bookmobile garage	

Changing Patterns: a Report to the Cleveland Public Library and Cuyahoga County District Library,[12] by the Regional Planning Commission in 1966 set certain minimum standards to be used in establishing new branches or relocating old ones. These included:

1. Minimum circulation within the public service area-- 50,000-60,000 per year.

2. Minimum registration within the public service area-- 3000 patrons.

3. Building size: 1.4 to 2.6 sq. ft. per registrant; minimum of 6000 square feet.

4. The plan for branch library service in metropolitan Cleveland projects need for two levels of services: a) The present type of branch library service serving a relatively small segment of population; and b) A system of 12 regional branches to be completed by 1980 to provide an intermediate level between the Cleveland public main library and the branches. The regional units would also serve as community libraries for the population immediately surrounding them. These units would stock between 125,000 and 250,000 books, including a comprehensive reference collection, and would be located within 10 minutes driving time from any user's home, excluding parking time.

In a study made in 1959 for the Public Library of Des Moines, Iowa, entitled Neighborhood Library Service,[14] Dr. Frederick Wezeman proposed the following for a branch of at least 8,000 square feet:

1. At least 7,000 square feet should be on the main floor at street level. (Continued on page 628)

Guidelines for Determining Minimum Space Requirements[11]

Population Served	Size of Book Collection	Shelving Space(a) Linear Feet of Shelving(b)	Amount of Floor Space	Reader Space	Staff Work Space	Estimated Additional Space Needed(c)	Total Floor Space
Under 2,499	10,000 vol.	1,300 linear ft.	1,000 sq. ft.	Min. 400 sq. for 13 seats, at 30 sq. ft. per reader space	300 sq. ft.	300 sq. ft.	2,000 sq. ft.
2,500-4,999	10,000 vol. plus 3 books per capita for pop. over 3,500	1,300 linear ft. Add 1 ft. of shelving for every 8 bks. over 10,000	1,000 sq. ft. Add 1 sq. ft. for every 10 bks. over 10,000	Min. 500 sq. ft. for 16 seats. Add 5 seats per M. over 3,500 pop. served, at 30 sq. ft. per reader space	300 sq. ft.	700 sq. ft.	2,500 sq. ft. or 0.7 sq. ft. per capita, whichever is greater
5,000-9,999	15,000 vol. plus 2 books per capita for pop. over 5,000	1.875 linear ft. Add 1 ft. of shelving for every 8 bks. over 15,000	1,500 sq. ft. Add 1 sq. ft. for every 10 bks. over 15,000	Min. 700 sq. ft. for 23 seats. Add 4 seats per M. over 5,000 pop. served, at 30 sq. ft. per reader space	500 sq. ft. Add 150 sq. ft. for each full time staff member over 3	1,000 sq. ft.	3,500 sq. ft. or 0.7 sq. ft. per capita, whichever is greater

| 10,000-24,999 | 20,000 vol. plus 2 books per capita for pop. over 10,000 | 2,500 linear ft. Add 1 ft. of shelving for every 8 bks. over 20,000 | 2,000 sq.ft. Add 1 sq.ft. for every 10 bks. over 20,000 | Min. 1,200 sq.ft. for 40 seats. Add 4 seats per M. over 10,000 pop. served, at 30 sq.ft. per reader space | 1,000 sq. ft. Add 150 sq.ft. for each full time staff member over 7 | 1,800 sq. ft. | 7,000 sq.ft. or 0.7 sq.ft. per capita, whichever is greater |
| 25,000-49,999 | 50,000 vol. plus 2 books per capita for pop. over 25,000 | 6,300 linear ft. Add 1 ft. of shelving for every 8 bks. over 50,000 | 5,000 sq.ft. Add 1 sq.ft. for every 10 bks. over 50,000 | Min. 2,250 sq. ft. for 75 seats Add 3 seats per M. over 25,000 pop. served, at 30 sq.ft. per reader space | 1,500 sq. ft. Add 150 sq.ft. for each full time staff member over 13 | 5,250 sq.ft. | 15,000 sq.ft. or 0.6 sq.ft. per capita, whichever is greater |

(a) Libraries in systems need only to provide shelving for basic collection plus number of books on loan from resource center at ANY ONE TIME.

(b) A standard library shelf equals 3 linear feet.

(c) Space for circulation desk, heating and cooling equipment, multipurpose room, stairways, janitors' supplies, toilets, etc., as required by community needs and the program of library services.

From: Interim Standards for Small Public Libraries: Guidelines toward Achieving the Goals of PUBLIC LIBRARY SERVICE (Public Library Association, American Library Association, 1962). In applying these standards it must be remembered that branches do not ordinarily catalog or process books so workroom space can usually be less than designated.

Experience Formulas for Library Size and Costs[13]

Population Size	Book stock vol. per capita	No. of seats per 1,000 popula.	Circulation vol. per capita	Total sq. ft. per capita	Desirable 1st floor sq. ft. per capita
Under 10,000	3-1/2-5	10	10	.7-.8	.5-.7
10,000-35,000	2-3/4-3	5	9.5	.6-.65	.4-.45
35,000-100,000	2-1/2-2-3/4	3	9	.5-.6	.25-.3
100,000-200,000	1-3/4-2	2	8	.4-.5	.15-.2
200,000-500,000	1-1/2	1-1/4	7	.35-.4	.1-.125
500,000 and up	1-1-1/4	1	6.5	.3	.06-.08

From: Wheeler, Joseph L., and Goldhor, Herbert. Practical Administration of Public Libraries. Harper and Row, c1962. p. 554.

Standards for Location of Public Library Facilities (1963)

The following, quoted by Roberta Bowler in Local Public Library Administration, 10 are from a set of 1963 standards by the City Planning Department of Los Angeles.

Type of Facility	Minimum Land Area	Maximum Service Radius	Population to be Served	Minimum Parking Spaces
Branch libraries (neighborhood, community)	20,000-30,000 sq. ft.	2 miles	25,000-50,000	25-35
Regional Library	50,000 sq. ft.	2 miles, immediate area; regional branches	300,000-350,000	75
Area Library (administrative center for region)	2 acres	2 miles, immediate area; regional branches, entire area	1,000,000-1,500,000	200

2.   There should be about 75 seats for adults and young adults and 50 for children.

3.   The book stock should number at least 25, 000, with active discarding and 1, 500 books added each year.

4.   It may be necessary to pay as much as one-third of the cost of the building for a strategically-located site.

5.   The branch should be open 8 hours a day at least 5 days a week.

6.   The staff should total 5 or 6 full-time employees (other than the custodian) and include two or three professional librarians.

7.   There should be a well-weeded stock of up-to-date, pamphlets on a wide variety of subjects, 5, 000 pictures, 500 recordings.

Dr. Wezeman's recommendations are apparently based upon the Wheeler and Goldhor figures in Practical Administration of Public Libraries.

As an alternative to the use of specific standards to evaluate a branch library, another approach is to use a checklist of facilities, services, and all aspects of branch operation. The library can be rated A, B, C, D, or F, using a common grading procedure, on each item, thus revealing areas which need strengthening or improvement.

The following list is adapted from 100 Tests for a Good Library, devised in 1966 by the Director and Supervisors' Group of the Santa Ana Public Library:[15]

80 Tests for a Good Branch Library

1.   Top-level branch librarian.
2.   Backing of a top-level system director.
3.   Sound administrative policies and procedures based on progressive current practices in other branch libraries.
4.   Progressive approach to new developments.
5.   Good relationships with other library departments in the system.
6.   Written long-range goals and objectives.
7.   Continuing study to increase efficiency.
8.   Participation of branch staff in decisions.

9. Program for encouraging library recruitment.
10. Accurate methods for measuring usage.
11. Use of all available community surveys and studies of the branch service area to improve service.
12. Use of automated equipment when volume of business warrants.
13. Written procedures for handling emergencies.
14. Good cooperation with area schools.
15. Regular staff meetings.
16. In-service training program from the central library or localized for the branch.
17. Well-planned branch budget.
18. Per capita support meeting national standards.
19. Book budget at least 25% of total budget (if branch book budgets are separate from central book budget).
20. Good work equipment.
21. Effective delivery system from central library.

Organization:

22. Written job descriptions for all positions.
23. Not less than 3 to 1 ratio between non-professional and professional employees.
24. Library materials well organized for public use.
25. Efficient, modern book check-out system.
26. Security measures to inhibit loss.

Building:

27. Sufficiently-large, well-planned building.
28. Building easily accessible.
29. Attractive, inviting atmosphere.
30. Attractive, comfortable reading and browsing areas.
31. Adequate parking area.
32. Adequate seating.
33. Good lighting, acoustics, and temperature control.
34. Regular maintenance of building and grounds efficiently performed.
35. Adequate outside sign and lighting.
36. Good directional signs to and within library.

Staffing:

37. Sufficient number of staff to meet A. L. A. standards.
38. Competent staff.
39. High staff morale.
40. Good orientation program for new employees.
41. Good internal communication at all levels within the branch and with the central library and other branches.
42. Enough staff for good supervision of public areas.

43. Staff participation in community affairs.

Book collection:

44. Written adult, young people's, and children's book
     selection policies, usually formulated by the Central
     Library, available to give out to patrons when needed.
45. Aid of subject specialists from central library in book
     selection.
46. Continuing and systematic program of discarding and
     replacing items of continuing value.

47. Good collection of local history material.
48. Books in order on shelves.
49. Books maintained in attractive physical condition.   Use
     of plastic jackets.

Services:

50. Library service program geared to community needs.
51. As wide a range of services as possible.
52. Convenient hours to meet standards.
53. Well-developed reference service.
54. Well-developed program of reader guidance.
55. Strong program of library service to adults.
56. Active program of service to young people.   Intensive
     program for children.
57. Desirable ratio of service to children and adults.
58. Special book collections for special interests.
59. Good collection of audio-visual materials and facilities.
60. Conference room and study carrels.
61. Various convenience services (copying machine, coin-
     operated typewriter, pen dispenser, public telephone
     in foyer, etc.).
62. Meeting room for library sponsored activities and other
     community groups.
63. A smooth-functioning reserve system.
64. Effective inter-library loan program with other libraries.
65. Service to community groups.
66. Participation in cooperative library projects.

Technical services:

67. Well-maintained, usable card or book catalog, usually
     supplied by central.
68. Good arrangement for mending, binding, and preserving
     library materials, usually in cooperation with central
     library.   Light mending often done at individual branch.

<u>Public relations and publicity</u>:

69. Area residents well informed concerning services.
70. Effective and extensive National Library Week and
     Children's Book Week observance.
71. Provision of book talks and speeches to community
     groups.
72. Active display and exhibit program to stimulate reading
     and library use.
73. Strong and active Friends of the Library group.
74. Ideas solicited from patrons through suggestion box and
     questionnaires.
75. Successful promotion program for encouraging gifts and
     memorials.   Written policy regarding acceptance of
     gifts.
76. Staff participation in professional organized activities.
77. Use of news media in the area to promote activities
     and reading.
78. Attractive and useful booklists on popular subjects.
79. Branch represented on radio or TV whenever expedient
     and possible.   Must be correlated with central
     publicity.
80. Arrangement for exhibiting work and crafts of local
     residents.   Cooperation with area organizations on
     this.

Obviously, no one branch will be likely to rate A in all of these tests.   However, the list provides an easy method of self-evaluation and is a good antidote to too much complacency, which, in branch operation as elsewhere, can be a major factor retarding progress.

Since the tests are couched in general terms, reference to specifics will often be necessary.   What is adequate--in staffing, in book and audio-visual materials, in physical equipment and buildings?   We have attempted to answer these questions, at least partially, in this and other chapters.   It is important to remember, however, that standards are constantly changing and that continuing effort is needed to keep abreast of them.   Only a short while ago one full-time staff member per 2, 500 of population served by a library unit was deemed sufficient.   Now one staff member per 2, 000 of population is recommended.   This figure, in the future,

may change again, perhaps to 1,500, or it may be that the effective
use of automation in branches will reverse the trend and result in
a recommendation of one staff member for each 2,500 or
3,000 population.

Branch librarians interested in evaluating their children's
services will find Standards of Service to Children in Public Libraries of California helpful.   This document was worked out by
the Children's and Young People's Section of the California Library
Association and was published in the California Librarian for
October, 1962 (p. 199-204).   Most of these standards can be applied to branch library service for children, with slight modifications to fit smaller units.

The Public Library section of the Louisiana Library Association published in 1964 a set of general standards entitled
Standards Statement for Louisiana Public Libraries,[16] which
contains some specific references to branches:

> For library systems basic branches should have quarters
> of 2,100 or more square feet; a basic collection of
> 10,000 books; a minimum staff of one branch assistant
> plus one or more workers; and should be open 40 or
> more hours six days a week to carry on a program of
> activities meeting local interests and needs.

It is clear that these standards apply to small towns or
parish branches maintained as part of a county or other rural
system, since the square footage is too low to apply to urban
branches.   The Louisiana standards further state:

> Non-urban or rural branches are considered economically
> sound when established in centers of 3,000 or more
> people residing within a mile and a half radius; service
> elsewhere in the area should be given from bookmobiles,
> with one bookmobile operated for each 10,000 to 20,000
> population.

For urban branches Louisiana uses the Wheeler and Goldhor
formulae.

The following set of standards is based on multiples and is
primarily applicable to large branches of 15,000 square feet with
at least 10,000 square feet on the main floor:

Initial book stock = 1-1/2 times population served.

Annual replacement of book stock = 2/10 of a book per person per year for population served.

Staff: 1 staff member for each 15,000 annual circulation.

Circulation standard should be 7-10 times population served.

Hours of Service: 9:00 a.m. to 9:00 p.m. Monday through Friday; 9:00 a.m. to 6:00 p.m. Saturday.

Meeting rooms: 100-150 seating capacity.

Committee room: 10-15 seating capacity.

The Contra Costa County Library, Pleasant Hill, California, in its 1959 Master Plan for Library Service,[17] issued the following standards. These are now being revised and today this system does not favor branches smaller than 12,000 to 14,000 square feet. The policy of the Board of Supervisors is to furnish the staff and book collections to communities which provide suitable quarters. The 1959 standards (high then) were:

	Communities of 7,500-25,000	Communities over 25,000
Size of building	8,000 sq. ft.	9,000-26,000 sq. ft.
Parking	40 cars, minimum	65 cars
Book capacity	15,000-37,000	38,000-150,000
Hours open	40-62 per week	62-84 per week
Estimated annual circulation	75,000-250,000	over 250,000
Forum room (auditorium) optional	80 seats, add 1,164 sq. ft. to building	200 seats, add 2,550 sq. ft. building
Staff (full-time equivalent)	4-7, including 2 professionals	8 or more, including 3 professionals

The Alameda County Library, Hayward, California, proposes the following standards.[18]

Floor space:	4 volumes per sq. ft.
Seating capacity:	3 per 1,000 volumes (1 children's chair for each 1-1/2 adult chairs).
Parking:	1 parking space for every 2 seats in library.

Application of these ratios produces the following numbers for a medium-sized branch of 8,000 square feet.

Book stock:	32,000 volumes.
Seating capacity:	100 (60 adults, 40 children).
Parking	50 spaces

In a recent survey, <u>Study of Branch Libraries for the Lincoln City Library</u>,[20] Dr. Frederick Wezeman suggests the following:

Large Branch: (Minimum of 12,000-14,000 square feet;)

A. Staff
1. At least 3 professional librarians, specialists in children's, young people's, and adult work.

2. Minimum of 5 clerical staff members. Most new large branches produce so much use a larger staff than anticipated is needed.

B. Materials:
1. Minimum collection of 30,000-40,000 volumes to provide an acceptable level of service. Experience has shown librarians must constantly raise the minimum book stock needed for new, large branches.

2. 1000 reference works with plenty of bibliographic tools and indexes. The branch should be able to serve about 80% of the reference needs of its patrons.

3. At least 100 magazines and an adequate back file of many of these.

4. A well-weeded stock of up-to-date pamphlets on a wide variety of subjects. The sale of a selected number of these, particularly government publications, is a worthwhile added service.

C. Hours of service:
    1. A large branch should be open daily from 9:00
        a. m. to 9: 00 p. m.; on Saturdays from 9: 00
        a. m. to 5: 00 p. m. , and on Sunday during the
        school months from 2: 00 p. m. to 5: 00 p. m.

D. Special features:
    1. Drive-up window service and book deposit should
        be provided and designed so it can be manned
        by circulation personnel.

    2. There should be ease of access from the parking
        lot, at the same time providing for pedestrian
        safety and access and also for those coming to
        the library on bicycles.

    3. There should be a multi-purpose room to be used
        as a community meeting room for library pro-
        grams, as a quiet reading room, for story hours,
        and for exhibits and displays.

It is obvious from the foregoing sets of standards that both
the recommendations and approaches or bases upon which figures
are recommended vary considerably. Some more standard basis is
needed, with graduated sets of figures based upon size of the area
to be served. The American Library Association has endeavored
to do this with regard to systems serving a minimum of 100,000
population, but a similar set of standards is needed specifically for
branches.

For the moment, the community wishing to establish branch
service or to become part of a system must at present choose from
among the sets of standards now available that one which best fits
its community and the available funds. The main objective should
be to choose standards which provide potential for improvement and
attainable goals.

Out of this welter of standards, nevertheless certain agreed
minimums seem to emerge. Few experts recommend branches of
less than 6,000 square feet, and 8,000 is more generally accepted
now as a minimum. Five full-time staff, including two professionals, is a basic recommendation. A book collection of 25,000
is considered a minimum for a 6,000-8,000 square foot branch,
but the best measure seems to be a graduated standard of so many
books per capita based on population, with a larger number per
(continued on page 638)

Recommended Standards for Libraries [19]
Serving Populations of 5,000 or more

	5,000 - 15,000	15,000 - 25,000	25,000 - 35,000	35,000 - 60,000+
Populations	5,000 - 15,000	15,000 - 25,000	25,000 - 35,000	35,000 - 60,000+
Physical Size				
Site (1 sq. ft. per capita) less for 1-1/2 stories	5,000 - 15,000	15,000 - 25,000	25,000 - 35,000	35,000 - 60,000
Building (.35 sq. ft. per capita)	1,750 - 5,250	5,250 - 8,750	8,750 - 12,250	12,250 - 21,000
Parking (1.5 sq.ft. for each 1 sq.ft. of building)	2,625 - 7,875	7,875 - 13,125	13,125 - 18,375	18,375 - 31,500
Reader Capacity (seats)	35 - 50	50 - 100	100 - 150	150 - 200
Circulation				
Annual at present 4.1 per capita rate (average branch per capita 1959-50)	20,500 - 61,500	61,500 - 102,500	102,500 - 143,500	143,500 - 246,500
Staff (ALA 1:2,500 population) Total for newly established branches *(minimum 2, with 1 for each additional 3,000 population of area served)	2 - 4.28	4.28 - 7.14	7.14 - 10	10 - 17

	1:15,000 circ.	1:15,000 circ.	1:20,000 circ.	1:20,000 circ.
Staffing formula for established branches *(ratio to circulation) minimum of 2 (ALA 1:25,000 in city systems under 10,000, with minimum of 3; plus 1:20,000 population 10,000-250,000; 1:15,000 over 250,000)	1:15,000 circ.	1:15,000 circ.	1:20,000 circ.	1:20,000 circ.
Book Stock (1.5-2 per capita, under 10,000; 1 per capita over 10,000)	7,500- 15,000			
Total volumes	5,000- 15,000	15,000- 25,000	25,000- 35,000	35,000- 60,000
Shelf capacity in volumes (over 10,000, 2/3 of total)	6,000- 10,000	10,000- 17,000	17,000- 23,000	23,000- 40,000
Hours open (for every added hour open add minimum of 2 hours added to staff - these hours require minimum staffs listed above)	35	35-56	56	56

*exclusive of custodial staff

From: Hawaii Department of Education, State Library Services, Recommended Standards for Libraries Serving Populations of 5,000 or more.

capita for smaller populations.

The following is based on standards used by the Minneapolis Public Library:

Standards and Space Allocation
15,000 sq. ft. branch

Main floor of building:	10,000 square feet
Adult service area	4,000 sq. ft.
Young People's Service area	500 sq. ft.
Adult periodical and book storage area	500 sq. ft.
Children's service area	2,500 sq. ft.
Workroom	1,250 sq. ft.
Circulation area	1,250 sq. ft.
Total	10,000 sq. ft.

Basement of second floor area:	5,000 square feet
Meeting room	1,500 sq. ft.
Conference room	500 sq. ft.
Storage room	1,500 sq. ft.
Utility room	1,000 sq. ft.
Stairs, toilets, etc.	500 sq. ft.
Total	5,000 sq. ft.

Grand total	15,000 sq. ft.

Population served: 20,000-40,000.

Size of land needed: 30,000 sq. ft. or twice area of branch.

Initial book stock: 1-1/2 x population served.

Annual replacement of book stock: 2/10 of a book per person per year for population served.

Circulation estimated: 7-10 times population served.

Hours of service: 9:00 a.m. - 9 p.m. Monday through Friday
9:00 a.m. - 6 p.m. Saturday

Meeting room: 100-150 seating capacity.

Conference room: 10-15 seating capacity.

Notes

1.   Alabama Library Association. Division of Public Libraries, Committee on Standards. Alabama Standards for Alabama Public Libraries. May, 1966. Introduction.

2.   Bowler, Roberta. Local Public Library Administration. Inter-

national City Managers' Association, 1964. p. 259.

3. Wheeler, Joseph L., and Goldhor, Herbert. Practical Administration of Public Libraries. Harper and Row, c. 1962, p. 412-413.

4. Ibid. p. 414.

5. Florida Library Association. Florida Standards for Public Library Services. Florida Library and Historical Commission. 1967. p. 24-28.

6. American Library Association. Public Library Association, Standards Committee and sub-committees. Statistical Standards, Addenda to Minimum Standards for Public Library Systems, 1966. 1967. p. 1.

7. South Carolina Library Association: Public Libraries Section. Standards for South Carolina Public Libraries. 1969. p. 8-9.

8. Wezeman, Frederick. "Better Branch Libraries." Minnesota Libraries. v. XX, No. 6. June, 1962. p. 170-171.

9. Fresno County Free Library, Fresno, California. Branch Standards, 1964. 1 page.

10. Bowler, Roberta. Local Public Library Administration. International City Managers' Association, 1964. p. 268.

11. American Library Association: Public Library Association. Interim Standards for Small Public Libraries: Guidelines toward Achieving the Goals of Public Library Service. American Library Association, 1962.

12. Regional Planning Commission. Cleveland and Cuyahoga County, Ohio. Changing Patterns: a Report to the Cleveland Public Library and Cuyahoga County District Library. Cuyahoga County, Ohio, 1966, p. 13-15.

13. Wheeler, Joseph L., and Goldhor, Herbert. Practical Administration of Public Libraries. Harper and Row, c. 1962. p. 554.

14. Wezeman, Frederick. Neighborhood Library Service: A Survey of the Extension Services of the Public Library of Des Moines. 1959. p. 31-38.

15. Santa Ana Public Library, Santa Ana, California. 100 Tests for a Good Public Library. Director and Supervisors' Group, 1966.

16. Louisiana Library Association: Public Library Section. Standards Statement for Louisiana Public Libraries. 1964.

17. Contra Costa County Library, Pleasant Hill, Calif. Master Plan for Library Service, 1959.

18. Alameda County Library, Hayward, Calif. Branch Standards.

19. Hawaii Department of Education, State Library Services. Recommended Standards for Libraries Serving Populations of 5,000 or more, March, 1963. Mimeographed.

20. Wezeman, Frederick. Study of Branch Libraries for the Lincoln City Library (Lincoln, Nebraska). The Library, 1967. p. 45-47.

Chapter 20

Why Belong to a System?

In this volume, as previously explained, member or affiliated libraries in non-consolidated systems are included because in
many areas they are replacing the older pattern of branches with
closely-knit relationships with strong, centralized administrations.
Member, affiliated, or cooperating libraries were also included in
the April, 1966 issue of Library Trends on current trends in branch
libraries,[1] with the explanation that they possess many of the
characteristics of branches in a unified city system.

Independent community libraries, in areas where a county
or regional system is being formed, may be invited to become a
branch, an affiliate, or a cooperating unit, retaining in the latter
case, a higher degree of local autonomy.   Those systems which
use the "member" or partnership approach have usually been more
successful in persuading independent libraries to join.   This concept presents a more satisfying relationship from the standpoint of
the smaller library.   Small independent libraries in some areas
have held out against the trend toward cooperation, fiercely guard-
ing their independence at all costs.

As a general rule, the smaller the individual town library,
the greater the advantages of belonging to a system, however the
relationship be defined.   We shall examine some of the objections
raised by independent libraries opposed to the system idea and
shall attempt to answer them.

1. Most often voiced is the fear of being "swallowed up" or
integrated into the system to the point where local identity and
local autonomy are severely diminished or lost entirely.   Systems
vary as to the degree of centralization and uniformity of procedures
required, but, in general, past experience has shown such fears
to be unfounded.   Where such qualms are nevertheless hard to

quell, the non-consolidated type of organization may be a possible
solution.

For many libraries, joining a system has resulted in added
services and often a doubling or more of the library resources
available to a community. County or regional boards have usually
arranged for local community board representation on the larger-
area board or have worked closely with existing boards to work out
policies, procedures, and problems. Once the new partnership is
accepted, the operational machinery established, and time allowed
for it to function smoothly, complaints that local identity and control
are lost become less frequent. This is particularly true in the
more flexible and loosely-knit federations and cooperative systems.

2. Where central purchasing and processing are part of the
new system arrangement, a common complaint has been that "books
arrive much more slowly. We receive them ready for the shelves
but much later than we used to when we ordered and catalogued in
our own libraries. "

It is true that a busy central purchasing and processing
center may not always be able to get fully-processed books out to
individual member libraries quite as quickly as they could order
and obtain them directly. These possible delays, however, may be
offset by the following advantages:

a) Books arrive at the participating libraries fully
cataloged and processed ready for the patron. Thus
they are often in his hands as quickly as if they had
arrived sooner but had to await cataloging and processing by overworked local staff members.

b) The classifications are apt to be more accurate, the
catalog cards more complete bibliographically, and the
class numbers more consistent.

c) Through quantity purchasing the cooperative system may
be able to secure a larger discount from jobbers and
thus supply more books for the same money.

d) Local librarians are relieved of a large burden of
routine paper work, cataloging, and processing, thus
releasing more staff time for work with the public.

e) Valuable space does not have to be set aside in local
buildings for technical processing routines. This space
can often be converted to public use.

f) Cost of supplies should be less because of quantity
purchasing.

g) Centralized cataloging will usually cost the individual
library no more than its former cost per book, and
may cost less due to higher volume operations. The
centralized centers are not set up to make a profit but
to serve their members.

3. Some communities believe that joining forces with other
system members in ordering and processing books will result in
their not being able to select their own titles. This is not the
case in most systems. In practically all instances the local library
makes its own selections. An exception might be a very small
rural branch with no qualified staff member capable of selecting
books.

4. Local boards sometimes fear they will be abolished, but
in many cases when an established library has joined a system, the
local board has continued to function. In dealing with this kind of objection, a careful distinction needs to be made between the traditional branch and the cooperating or member library. A regular
branch is usually administered directly by the county or regional
board through a centrally-appointed librarian. In the non-consolidated type of organization, the political structure or pattern of
organization of local units usually does not change. Members
cooperate in the performance of certain functions and services to
the mutual benefit of all, and local boards and officials still
determine policies and procedures. New York, Montana and
California all have successful cooperative systems and the state
agencies in these states can supply further information concerning
their operation.

County and regional library systems grew by trial and error
before today's cooperative patterns were common. These pioneers
did not have the opportunity to learn from the experience of others,
and they sometimes made too many changes too rapidly or imposed

directives rather than working out problems with local boards and
librarians as a team at a conference table.

There is and was, however, nothing wrong with the systems
concept, though its implementation is as subject to human error as
the implementation of any other idea. The motives of those ad-
ministering system centers have sometimes been misinterpreted by
the critics, but there is plentiful evidence by now that belonging to
a system is a decided advantage for any library unable alone to
meet the standards of adequate service in a dynamic society.

Any independent community library too small to meet the
current American Library Association minimum standards should
seriously consider affiliation with, membership in, or at least cooperation with the nearest strong system. "The headquarters unit
of the system may be the main unit of a county, multi-county, or
regional library; one or more libraries designated from a group of
libraries banded together to provide modern library service, or a
unit established and maintained by the state agency. "[2]

Before entering into contractual agreement, the independent
community library board, staff, and local government must be prepared to accept some apparent disadvantages and weigh them against
the potential advantages. The arrangement must be approached with
an open mind and the system headquarters given sufficient time and
opportunity to demonstrate what it can do for the local library. It
is important to remember that the central library or headquarters
must have time to get to know the new affiliate or member library,
its community, resources, staff, board and other officials, and the
tastes and interests of its patrons before it can be expected to do a
good job of providing supplementary help and materials. The local
library's board and staff can help the central agency learn these
things rapidly, but clear lines of communication are necessary
from the outset.

Too often a small library which joins a larger system expects both communication and benefits to flow in only one direction.
The member library must be willing to share its resources with
other members by cooperating on inter-library loans, reciprocal
borrowing, if that is part of the organizational plan, and attendance

at system workshops and conferences. It should be prepared, in the spirit of wanting to improve service, to accept suggestions offered by system specialists; some small library staffs and boards, apparently convinced that their library is about the best there is, are reluctant to consider any change. It is laudable to be proud of one's library but one should be sure that the pride is justified. There are few, if any, libraries that cannot stand improvement.

The library's governing authority, whether a formal library board, a city council, or a city manager, must also be willing to pay the library's fair share of the cost of cooperative projects which will benefit all members of the system, such as teletype, a film pool, central purchasing or processing, or IBM sorting equipment, to mention only a few items. Few community libraries find their expenses increased by membership in a system. On the contrary, government funding of many of the costs, and the savings resulting from volume purchasing and efficient management have often resulted in additional services furnished at little or no cost to the local area.

If both sides approach a system or cooperative arrangement with open minds there is less chance of failure. Among the potential advantages of system membership for the formerly independent small library are:

1. Books from system headquarters, fully processed and ready to go onto the shelves.

2. Many more books available for local borrowers.

3. Monetary savings in the centralizing of routine processes and the larger discounts available if orders are put through the central office.

4. Good in-service training programs for local staff and workshops for library administrators.

5. The advice and help of subject specialists and children's and young people's specialists when needed.

6. Expert book selection help and the availability of a wider range of bibliographic tools.

7. Stronger reference collections and information retrieval systems, teletype, or direct line reference aid.

Figure 202. The TTY (Closed Circuit Teletype), one of many
            advantages of belonging to a system. This communi-
            cation device connects the 14 libraries and administra-
            tion center of the Lake County Public Library in
            Griffith, Indiana.

8. Elimination of expensive duplication of certain valuable
materials, with individual system members perhaps specializing in
certain fields.

9. Through membership in the system, benefits from federal
and state aid programs for which the small library might otherwise
not be eligible.

10. Special programs for the illiterate, the handicapped, the
disadvantaged, the homebound or other special groups, through
central planning and funding.

11. Development of new ideas, systems and services through
sharing knowledge and experience with other libraries in the system.

12. Bookmobile service, through demonstrations or federal
programs, to serve fringe areas in smaller towns not large enough
to have branches.

13. Assistance, when needed, in planning buildings, furnishings and equipment.

14. Financial compensation to libraries whose resources are heavily used in the system or state network. This will offset any possible costs incurred for services rendered or equipment purchased. If most of the advantages flow one way, contractual or other fair-share monetary agreements will be made.

15. Strengthening of audio-visual collections (phonograph records, films, tapes, back files of periodicals on microfilm, and similar non-book materials).

16. Membership in a system may create better salary standards and fringe benefits for staff members, as city officials find other communities in the system raising their standards.

17. The system may be able to furnish help and information in campaigning for higher local library budgets.

18. Certain clerical procedures such as sending overdues, mending, binding, keeping financial records, processing inter-library loans, reproducing catalog cards, ordering and cataloging, when done at system headquarters, allow member libraries to put more of their salary money into providing professional reference and advisory staff to serve the public.

19. Through its larger contacts system headquarters can help a community library solve its personnel problems when they cannot be solved locally. Headquarters can often send substitutes to help out in an emergency.

One example of a successful system is the Vancouver Island Regional Library, Nanaimo, British Columbia, Canada. This consolidated-type system was founded in 1936. By 1968 it consisted of eighteen branches and two bookmobiles with 314 stops. Its policies are set by a Board of Management, made up of representatives from the 5,000 square-mile service area. Residents of Vancouver Island enjoy these benefits from the Vancouver Island Regional Library:

1. Access to a collection of over 175,000 volumes, with 18,000-20,000 new books added annually.

2. Branch libraries established in municipalities whenever density of population warrants one, with the local librarian paid by the Regional Library.

3. Direct professional library service to give reference aid and provide for individual reader requests, as well as those of community groups.

4. Regular calls by a well-stocked bookmobile, in those areas where road conditions permit, giving individualized and direct service to borrowers not close to a branch.

5. Constantly changing and revitalized branch and book-mobile collections, with strong emphasis on children's books where needed.

6. Many periodicals for reference and enjoyment.

7. Shut-in service for readers who cannot get to a branch library.

8. Mail service to borrowers who cannot be reached in any other way.

9. Resources of other libraries available through inter-library loan.[3]

Another example of a successful system is the Mid-Continent Public Library Service, with headquarters in Independence, Missouri. This system serves three counties. According to James A. Leathers, Director, a unique feature of the System's branch library service is an inter-communication system devised in 1966, with each of the 27 branches connected by teletype to the Administrative and Technical Service Headquarters building. Located in the Administrative and Technical Service building is a master shelf list showing the holdings of the entire system. Each morning at 9 o'clock, four distribution trucks leave headquarters and by the time they return in the afternoon they will have visited every branch that is open.

"It is the philosophy of this system," Mr. Leathers says, "that any book is available to any patron regardless of the specific location of that particular book or the branch which the individual patron uses. During the year 1967, over 45,000 items were inter-library loaned within the Mid-Continent System. The various branches have been strategically located so that patrons do not have to travel more than four miles to reach an outlet of their public library. We feel that it should not be necessary for an individual to travel a great distance, regardless of the material which he or she might wish to obtain. "

In <u>Practical Administration of Public Libraries</u>, Wheeler and Goldhor state:

> Two facts have become clear. Independently the small individual libraries can never achieve such full, varied, efficient, and economical service to the public, even when given advisory and book service by the state commission, as they could by joining larger regional units.

After reviewing the advantages of system memberships, Wheeler and Goldhor conclude:

> Each aspect of each small-town and village library would greatly benefit...regional or cooperative systems are now in successful operation in many states and are rapidly increasing, stimulated by supplementary Federal funds.

> The other point: responsibility for internal good management has always to continue inside the small local library, as in the branches of a large city System. The small library cannot profitably go it alone, but it may constantly grow more efficient. The very smallest cannot afford a full-time trained librarian unless the time and salary can be divided among two or three towns. Good appointments are more likely under central direction from a regional head. [4]

But not everyone sees systems in the same way. Karl Nyren of the <u>Library Journal</u> staff, after a day at the Nassau Library System on Long Island, commented:

> Systems in New York are of the federation or membership type with little coercive authority at the top and much freedom allowed to libraries as members. In the Nassau System there are 52 directors, each responsible to his own board of trustees and not to any system authority. It is technically an association of independent libraries banded together to create and share a common service center. The center does book processing, acquisitions work, payrolls, business and maintenance services. [5]

The problems which Mr. Nyren describes are not uncommon in very large systems. Among them are:

1. The system should be the sum of all its parts but the Service Center itself is rapidly becoming the system and Center staff think of themselves as the system rather than as one of its agencies.

2. Rotating book collections and consultant services from

headquarters are less in demand as member libraries
build up their own collections and acquire their own
specialists.

3. Members can withdraw, and if a large number refused
the Service Center could conceivably go out of business.
The Center therefore has to sell its programs but com-
plains that some are ignored by member libraries.

4. The system director, because of the independence of
member libraries, feels he is not in the driver's seat.

5. Vigorous attempts to cooperate with school libraries have
failed. The author believes there has been continual
failure to coordinate library programs at community
levels, especially in service to students.

6. The main sore spot in system relations is the time it
takes to get a book through the system.

7. Some friction exists between the Center professionals and
the member professionals. All want a central reference
facility but the Service Center wants to run it, while
members want it run by an independent staff.

8. Each librarian wants her own collection built up rather
than the collection of the Service Center.

9. Imaginative demonstration projects to serve the disadvantaged were started but member libraries would not
continue funding them after the critical period of system
support.

The central disagreement, Nyren concludes, seems to be
that members of the system want more services to help them
function as local library agencies, whereas the Service Center wants
to build up its own strength. Mr. Nyren believes that in this particular situation there has not been enough centralization to accomplish the declared aim of better and cheaper library service.
For all the money spent, the results have been "pretty small."
Nyren concludes:

> We have evolved a new type of library agency--one sadly
> misrepresented...but one with raw, exciting promise. [5]

That these problems are found by one observer in one situation does not nullify the value of the system concept. One lesson
which may be drawn is perhaps that there is an optimum size
beyond which a system may lose its effectiveness. Where that

optimum lies is a question requiring further research and analysis.

Walter Kaiser, in a comprehensive <u>Library Trends</u> article,[6] accounts for the rapid rise of non-consolidated library systems in recent years as follows:

1. The rapid increase in incorporated municipalities brought about by the movement of population to the fringe cities and particularly to the open land adjacent to the central city. This population's previous experience with good public library service in the central city has generated a demand for similar service in the new environment.

2. The development and acceptance by the profession of the systems concept as exemplified by its endorsement in <u>Public Library Service, 1956.</u> The systems or cooperative approach to library service was strengthened by similar movements in the fields of public health, education, water supply, and sanitation.

3. The successful demonstration of the systems approach as a means of solving many of the problems of the smaller library.

4. The success of the cooperative systems movement in New York State, where adequately-financed, far-reaching plans, and strong professional and lay leadership produced new, exciting and successful developments.[7]

Mr. Kaiser makes a clear distinction between consolidated and non-consolidated systems:

> The consolidated system may be defined as a system where a single library board or other agency or official has responsibility for the total library program including books, personnel, buildings, and finance. In the non-consolidated system, the local library board is responsible for and controls the operation of its library including selection of personnel, books, building maintenance, hours, program, and budget. If the non-consolidated system is a federated system, the library is established and its board appointed by the sponsoring governmental unit such as a county board of supervisors. If it is a non-consolidated cooperative system, the system is formed, and its board of trustees is elected by a vote of the trustees of the member libraries.
>
> Finally, it is important to note that membership in the non-consolidated system is voluntary and that fundamental autonomy is retained by the member library. The numerous examples of cooperative arrangements of an

informal nature and contracts of a limited nature are not
considered to constitute a system in the meaning here
intended. The system, as understood here, should provide a wide range of services from a central source to
affect significantly the quality of service rendered at the
agency level.

The advantages of the non-consolidated system, as Mr.
Kaiser sees them, are:

1. It is a practical governmental structure. The political
    scientist may prefer unification by consolidation, but
    the people and their elected representatives have
    shown little enthusiasm for the method. The forma-
    tion of the non-consolidated system meets less
    resistance.

2. Even if consolidation of all public library agencies in
    a large metropolitan area were possible, the resulting
    monolithic library organization would not likely be
    conducive to the provision of the best library service
    because there is the danger of any large organization,
    particularly a public agency which is free of compe-
    tition, becoming a cumbersome, inefficient
    bureaucracy.

3. The large number of library trustees involved in
    operation of a system increases the number of com-
    munity leaders who have concern for the system and
    its future. Broad representation brings added strength.

4. The non-consolidated system fosters organizational
    tensions which are healthful and which can improve
    staff and institutional performance. One such tension
    is the ever-present possibility of withdrawals from
    the system.

5. Deference to central authority as such is at a mini-
    mum in federations and cooperatives. Non-con-
    solidated systems have numerous checks and balances;
    power is dispersed, and democratic patterns of be-
    havior are encouraged.

Non-consolidated systems also have potential weaknesses,
Mr. Kaiser points out:

1. A unified administrative authority is lacking. Some
    recommendations of the system may be ignored,
    leaving only the authority of persuasion. The very
    flexibility of the cooperative system may, if over-
    indulged, imperil its effectiveness and existence.
    The administration of member libraries in a non-
    consolidated system may be delegated to the central

agency, as is the case with some of the agencies of the Wayne County (Michigan) Public Library. This pattern appears to be the exception but may be increasingly effective in the future.

2. Power is dispersed among many libraries, trustees, and city officials. The larger the measure of freedom the more the incidence of controversy, often over quite minor matters. The consolidated system has not eliminated this type of staff problem but possibly keeps it under better control.

3. The non-consolidated system does not have the simplicity of organization of the consolidated system. Policies and procedures can be developed, adopted and implemented more speedily in a consolidated system. In addition to the usual internal organizational hierarchy, the libraries in a non-consolidated system have library boards, occasionally Friends of the Library groups, legislative bodies, or city managers, any of whom can ruffle the administrative waters.

Not related to the possible structural deficiencies, but a serious disadvantage of some non-consolidated systems is the lack of a large reference collection. The system aiming at full library service requires access to the specialized personnel and extension collection of a reference center. Another potential weakness is the lack of reciprocal borrowing privileges in some non-consolidated systems, although state laws in New York and Michigan insist on this feature.

The trend toward affiliation with a non-consolidated system, nevertheless, is a strong one and should grow if financial and service incentives continue. An increase in state aid and the uncertain future of federal aid, possibly unobtainable except by libraries agreeing to join systems, will affect the trend to membership. The medium-sized library has discovered a comfortable place in the non-consolidated system which permits the retention of fundamental autonomy, is voluntary, and drains off no local funds.

Membership in a system may produce other advantages than those which accrue directly to the library patron. Staff members of a formerly independent library in a small community that has not made provision for certain fringe benefits may also find their situation improved in a number of ways through participation in system benefits.

If a city or county accepts membership in a system, the city or county authorities must be prepared to give local library employees the same benefits enjoyed by others in the system. Often the jurisdictional authorities are forced into raising salaries and increasing benefits when they face the competition afforded by other cities or counties in the same regional system. These factors, of course, may also be stumbling blocks when trying to persuade local, city or county officials to join a system.

Among staff benefits which may be available to staff, in part or in toto, are the following:

Employees Credit union membership

A group retirement plan other than Social Security or combined with Social Security

A group hospital and medical insurance plan, sometimes partially or fully paid by the governing body of the system

A group term life insurance plan

U. S. Savings Bond payroll deduction plan (optional)

A more liberal vacation

Possibly a more liberal sick leave allowance

A shorter work week

More paid holidays

Leaves of absence

Broadened friendships through contact with many more librarians in the area

Opportunity to participate in workshops or conferences at system expense

Advice and encouragement from consultants when problems arise and the solution seems difficult.

Not all of these benefits will necessarily be added through system membership. The system may not offer all of them, or the former city or county government may still hold jurisdiction over the local library. But in many cases added advantages will make the lot of the local librarian and her staff more pleasant.

Notes

1.   Kaiser, Walter. "Libraries in Non-Consolidated Systems.
      Library Trends, v. 14, no. 4. April, 1966, p. 440-441.

2. American Library Association. Minimum Standards for Public Library Systems. American Library Association, 1966. p. 17.

3. White, Fred T. Some Facts About the Vancouver Island Regional Library. Mimeographed. 2 pages. n.d. Vancouver Island Regional Library Headquarters, Nanaimo, British Columbia, Canada.

4. Wheeler, Joseph L. and Goldhor, Herbert. Practical Administration of Public Libraries. Harper and Row, c1962, p. 433-34.

5. Nyren, Karl. "A New Breed of Cat." Library Journal, v. 93, no. 16. Sept. 15, 1968, p. 3091-95.

6. Kaiser, Walter. "Libraries in Non-Consolidated Systems." Library Trends, v. 14, no. 4. April, 1966, p. 440-449.

7. University of the State of New York. A Primer of Public Library Systems in New York State. Albany, the University of the State of New York, 1963.

Chapter 21

Public Relations and Publicity

It hardly seems necessary to repeat the principle that the
best advertising any business or institution can have is the satisfied
customer. Nowhere is the public impression gained across the desk
of more importance than in a branch or small member library
where individual staff members come face to face with patrons
much more often than is likely to occur in a larger library.

The word-of-mouth advertising that results from a pleasant
smile, a gracious manner, infinite patience with a fumbling request,
a friendly but not prying interest in patron's affairs and problems,
and a conscientious effort to use every possible method of securing
what the patron needs is of great value. The branch should provide
in-service training sessions and general discussions on improving
public relations while giving service, whether in person or on the
telephone.

The greatest problem, however, is reaching the non-user,
finding ways to get him into the library and inform him of available
services, and then by friendly treatment to make him want to return
and become a steady borrower. The hardest point to make with
the average non-user is that even the smallest library may hold
something of interest for him.

I like to think of a copying machine, a rental typewriter, a
free film shown in the multi-purpose room, or an exhibit of the art
of neighborhood school children as public relations devices. These
things can draw people into the library who might not come at all
otherwise.

It is this writer's contention, no matter how utopian it may
sound, that every branch of medium size, serving 25,000 or more
people, should have a full-time staff member as a community coordinator whose sole purpose is to get out into the service area and
perform the following duties:

656

1. Try to secure permission to speak, at least once a year, at every organization in the library's service area, to explain the library's services, display books along the lines of the group's interests, and invite those present to become borrowers.

2. Meet informally with small groups such as councils of pastors, school principals, P.T.A. presidents, welfare workers, community leaders, heads of government agencies, to figure out ways to cooperate for better service to the people.

3. Place book and other library exhibits in vacant store windows or windows of going concerns which by the very nature of their business have little use for windows. Such exhibits should, however, be changed frequently.

4. Visit school libraries, recreation centers in local parks, boys' clubs; plan joint programs involving library materials; become aware of their resources.

5. Visit government war-on-poverty programs in the area, such as Community Action Centers, Youth Corps or Job Corps regional offices, confer with officials, involve the library in any programs which seem feasible and desirable in order to encourage use of the branch or member library.

6. Ring doorbells, confer with block leaders and older pioneer residents who know many people and can help publicize the branch. Ask for their comments and criticisms. What should the branch be doing that it is not doing? What should it be offering that it is not offering? Are some of its activities falling short of their mark?

7. Arrange for many more group visits to the library than in the past, being sure to coordinate such visits with the children's and adult staff members concerned.

8. Plan and publicize special activities for Book Week and National Library Week.

9. Plan and supervise special summer activities with the disadvantaged: story hours in parks, in the branch patio or on the lawn; special music, magic, games, puppets and similar programs slanted especially for the non-user.

10. Work with area newspaper editors, radio stations, and T-V stations to publicize branch activities.

Such a person would work closely with the public relations or community coordinator of the central library or system headquarters and with the supervisors of the various services: children's, young people's, and adult. The duties would combine publicity, public relations and community contacts. If there were one such person in each branch or member library, he would meet with the central coordinator or service supervisors and would plan both activities and projects that could be carried out in all branches, and others designed specifically for a particular neighborhood or branch.

Most libraries, and particularly branches, have long lacked the staff time and specialized personnel to arrange these out-of-the-library contacts and then make them effective by subsequent participation and follow-up. Branch staffs often do not live in the branch community and do not meet residents in their clubs, churches, or other local activities. The publicity-community relations person should be required to live in the area and take part in its activities as an individual as well as a staff member. Such a person should be carefully chosen, should possess special qualifications, and should be well paid. Successful experience in public relations or social welfare work may be more valuable than a background of technical library training. The position would require the incumbent to acquaint himself thoroughly with the library's objectives, public services, and problems. He should have a work station or office at the branch and should check in daily for an hour or two to report on the previous day's activities, and leave a memorandum of his planned activities for that day.

At times the publicity-community coordinator might be needed to host some of the inside-library activities he may have generated, but his schedule should remain flexible enough to allow him to accomplish his primary purpose of outside contact work. This type of position was proposed as far back as the 1930's.

Although this plan requires an additional staff member, it may be justified by the new emphasis on work with the disadvantaged. A single public relations or community coordinator at the central library cannot do the intensive work that is needed in every branch area. Some librarians may feel that such an added position is unnecessary because most of today's branches have all the customers they can handle... and more.   But when a library can claim only 25 to 50% of the residents of its service area as borrowers, many of whom are inactive borrowers whose names appear only on the record, it is obvious there are more unserved than served, and the unserved in many cases may have a deeper, if as yet unfelt, need for library service.

Even if it is absolutely impossible to employ a special publicity-community coordinator, the branch librarian can do much to publicize the branch library's services and activities and to try to reach the non-user.   The branch librarian should not, in any case, be tied to a round of routine duties.   She should carry out as many of the following functions as possible:

1. Encourage residents of the service area to bring exhibits of arts and crafts, hobbies, or other special displays, rather than using the multi-purpose room or available wall and exhibit space for national traveling exhibits or non-local displays.   The local material may not have as much cultural value, but it will have far more personal value for patrons and potential patrons.

2. Encourage staff members to live in the neighborhood and take part in its activities.   The branch librarian should set a good example by doing it herself.

3. Try for closer cooperation with nearby schools, and particularly with the school librarians.   Meet with them, encourage class visits on a large scale.

4. Go out into the community as much as possible in the daytime--to service clubs, luncheons, church groups, women's clubs, not as regular participant but as occasional visitor.   Talk about the library when given the chance, formally and informally.

5. Plan occasional "way-out" programs that will attract teenagers, help change the image of the library from that of a formal, somewhat "stodgy" institution.

6. Solicit the cooperation of local Boy Scout officials, through the local area council office, to have Boy Scouts distribute doorknob hangers, branch folders, or other publicity door-to-door in the neighborhood.   Check city ordinances regarding distribution

of such materials. Boys should knock on doors and hand the material to the householder personally, not leave it lying on a porch. The Scouts earn merit badges in public service by doing this sort of thing for public agencies.

7. Study publicity techniques, learn from experts how to produce attractive, dynamic brochures, flyers, bookmarks, programs, if there is no central publicity or art department to do this to branch specifications.

8. Get the cooperation of local newspapers and neighborhood shopping news. The latter will sometimes give a library a free ad as a public service. Tap local radio stations for free public service time for story hours, book reviews, or spot announcements

9. Aim publicity at specific groups and interests, especially the non-users. Do not use vague generalizations.

10. Keep records of satisfactory service (testimonials)--the difficult or unusual reference question answered, the way groups or individuals have been helped by books. Without using names describe these case studies in print, on radio, or before groups.

11. Put publicity materials in the language of the layman. Don't get involved with library terminology and professional jargon.

12. Foster enough extra-curricular adult and juvenile activities to make the branch a true community center. All activities do not have to be "literary" in character.

13. Subscribe, if possible, to a good publicity service like Library Publicity Clippings, P.O. Box 702, Santa Ana, California, 92702, and make use of the news stories, posters, bulletin board ideas, radio spot announcements, and publicity tips received in these packets. The annual cost of Library Publicity Clippings is well within the means of even the smallest community library or branch.

14. Have a good number of clear, directional signs inside the building and a large well-lighted sign on the outside. Some cities permit small signs at various points throughout the city directing people to a community or branch library.

15. Encourage organizations to contribute books, equipment, or flower arrangements for the service desk. Acknowledge such

gifts through the press or by easily-read signs, or both. People who give to a library feel a sense of identification that is stronger than that gained by just being a borrower.

16. Organize and work with a branch Friends of the Library chapter. Use volunteers from this group who have speaking ability to help give book reviews and library talks.

17. Recognize neighborhood achievement by a display or news story of the "happening" on the bulletin board. Include a photo of the person involved if there is one available.

18. Publicize economies in branch operation or simplifications of routines--anything that indicates better service for less money. The neighborhood taxpayers will appreciate it.

19. Do a book review column in the neighborhood newspaper. Short comments on a number of books are much better than one or two long reviews. The more books you mention, the more variety of interests you will include.

20. Ask to put library posters on bulletin boards of local schools, churches, colleges, in windows of any businesses that will permit it. Try to have one permanent poster in all vantage points in the service area.

21. Use vacant store windows on busy streets or store windows not used by the owners to set up displays of books with suitable posters. Change the displays frequently.

22. Since all radio stations and T-V stations, to satisfy the licensing requirements of the Federal Communications Commission, must allocate a certain percentage of time to free public service programs, the library system or branch may be able to secure such free time. Most stations try to pass around the time in rotation to various public agencies in order to be fair. Check with your local stations, after clearing through the central library.

23. Publicize, through displays or newspaper stories, accomplishments of staff that have news value.

24. Keep colorful displays on bulletin boards and change them often.

Figure 203. Branch Publicity Booth. Mrs. Frieda Beitchman, Library Assistant (left), and Miss Frances Lepie, Librarian, Brighton Branch, Boston Public Library, help patrons at outdoor library booth at the Allston-Brighton Community Field Day, Smith Playground, Allston, Massachusetts.

25. Involve as many citizens as possible in library projects and events.

26. Duplicate and distribute directory of clubs and organizations in the area and advertise the library's services on the front and back.

27. Distribute book lists on maternity and baby care, pregnancy, and sex hygiene in hospitals and doctors' offices. Lists on health and dieting would also be picked up in such places. Make up book lists or cooperate with Central to make specialized book lists for distribution as follows (Examples only):

Books on hunting and fishing to sporting goods stores;

Books on cookery to grocery stores;

Home repair to hardware and paint stores;

Crafts to playgrounds and recreation directors.

28. Have attractive posters in city buses advertising the branch locations, services, and hours. Secure permission of bus companies to place them and change them at intervals. Most companies will cooperate if they have any unsold space.

29. Run stories in the newspaper on lists of recent books to fit a special season, with brief comments on each. Get a good lively lead.

30. Have a booth at the State Fair or County Fair advertising the library system. Feature branches. (See Figure 203.)

31. See if you can send out, without charge, library folders or brochures with Chamber of Commerce material, utility bills, or tax bills.

32. Send out booklists on baby care to new mothers or expectant mothers, a welcome letter with application for library card to newcomers in the area, a list of bookbooks and books on housekeeping to newlyweds, all through cooperation with the local welcome wagon or hostess service maintained by the merchants.

33. Celebrate any type of anniversary such as the branch's first, tenth, 25th, etc. Give it good publicity.

34. Send out a letter to local business executives, particularly factory heads, asking if the library can help in any way. Stress invitation to working men to come "just as you are," perhaps on their way home from work.

The branch librarian can initiate or suggest publicity for his branch, Wheeler and Goldhor point out,[1] but as much as possible of the handling and preparation of it should be at the central library. A branch librarian can undertake many publicity enterprises in his own neighborhood where he and the branch staff are acquainted, including phone calls to group heads, book reviews, programs and meetings at the branch. A branch librarian who feels inadequate in the field of publicity should delegate it to an assistant.[1]

One of the best means of getting the public into a branch is to offer a series of programs on topics of branch interest. If the branch has no meeting room it is sometimes possible to secure the use of a nearby room or hall, or to hold the event in the library after closing hours.

Helen Hoeffgen of the Flint (Michigan) Public Library describes such a series of programs sponsored by a Flint branch located in a school building. [2]   After clearing with the Central Library, the branch launched in 1961 a series of three lecture programs on "Community Problems." The programs were publicized by personally presented handouts and by flyers, bookmarks, and notices placed in local school bulletins. Subject experts were invited to speak and coffee was served. The first series was entitled "The Our Town" series. Some of the subjects were "Delinquency and Vandalism--Your Concern," "Preparing Your Child for College," and "Helping Your Child in Science and the Three R's." Time was given for questions from the audience. [2]

In addition to the publicity techniques already mentioned, radio spot announcements and newspaper notices were used, with newspaper writeups following each of the first three programs. The turnout for the series was gratifying. [2]

An estimated audience of 600 turned out in the summer of 1963 to hear a musical program of "Family Favorites" presented on the lawn in front of the library addition to the school. It was presented by the Motor City Concert Band and sponsored by The American Federation of Musicians, Local 542. The band was so located that the audience faced both the musicians and the fully-lighted branch, thus displaying the bookshelves inside. The band concert has been repeated annually and has become almost a tradition at the branch. [2]

Lecture programs were later broadened to include such topics as "Urban Renewal Programs--How they Will Affect You," "Family Estate Planning and Wills," "Wonderful Places to Take Children in Michigan," etc. High quality movies were also offered by this branch, and drew crowds so large that they sometimes had to be moved to the school gymnasium. This branch, the Civic Park Branch of the Flint Public Library, has no meeting room, but this article illustrates what a determined staff can do in public relations despite this handicap. Activities of this type can also offset the disadvantage of being located in a school building.

Branch publicity should always be cleared with the central

library public information officer, or with the library director if there is no special person handling the system publicity. If a central public relations person knows that a branch librarian has the training and experience to produce good publicity, as well as the good judgment to know where and when to release it, he will usually work closely with the branch staff member and encourage such participation, but many branch heads do not have this specialized ability. It is usually inadvisable to release material directly from a branch to communication media. A central public information officer is schooled, as a branch librarian may not be, to think through the possible long-range effects of a news story which may arouse controversy. The average branch librarian, also, is not a commercial artist, and amateur art, unless of unusual quality, is poor publicity. Amateur news writing is also to be avoided. Newspaper editors do not wish to rewrite story after story and will soon stop using poorly-written material. If there is no one available in the entire system to produce professional art work or do professional newswriting, such projects should be contracted out to commercial artists and writers, even though the cost may be higher.

Cooperation with the "Welcome Wagon" was mentioned in our list of publicity techniques. It is a most effective means of making a newcomer feel welcome in a new community or neighborhood. A letter of welcome, in the packet of material taken by the Welcome Wagon hostess, should always include a special invitation to visit the library and should stress that the library, with its pamphlet and book materials about the area, its history, interesting places to visit, institutions, and town politics, is one of the best possible sources to learn about the new community. Welcome Wagon hostesses often visit newlyweds, parents of new babies, and new businesses. The branch should see to it that appropriate library material accompanies each of these packets as well.

Good examples of the kinds of materials to include in the hostess packets are those of the Lake County Public Library, Griffith, Indiana. This library provides the greeters with a map showing the system and all branch locations, a leaflet describing the system and its services, with specific mention of the library in

Figure 204.   Brochure printed for the Welcome Wagon of
                Gastonia, North Carolina. Reverse side contains
                names, addresses, telephone numbers, and hours
                of the branches listed.

GASTON COUNTY
PUBLIC LIBRARY

115 WEST SECOND AVENUE ✦ GASTONIA, NORTH CAROLINA

Telephone: 865-3418

Main Library Open:
   Monday through Friday ....*9:00 a.m. to 9:00 p.m.*
   Saturday............... ....*9:00 a.m. to 6:00 p.m.*

Your Public Library welcomes you and your family and invites
you to visit your library often and take advantage of the many
library services available to you:

BOOKS for Home Reading, both informational and recreational
for all ages; 16 mm EDUCATIONAL FILMS; FILMSTRIPS;
PHONOGRAPH RECORDS; ART REPRODUCTIONS, Prints,
and Art Slides; CURRENT MAGAZINES and newspapers for reading and reference in the library; BUSINESS AND INDUSTRY
informational aids; REFERENCE and Reader-Advisory services
for all ages; LEARNING TO READ BOOKS and Reading Aids
for Adults and children of all ages; LARGE PRINT BOOKS
and recordings of the Bible for the Blind; and STORY-HOUR
and summertime reading programs for children.

These Library Services are made available to you through the Main
Library in Gastonia, the Bookmobile, and the seven Branch
Libraries in the County located at Belmont, Bessemer City, Cherry-
ville, Dallas, Lowell, Mount Holly, and Stanley.

the particular community, and three bookmarks and booklists: for the newcomer, the newlywed, and the new parent. Adult and juvenile registration cards are also included. The library makes up three kinds of packets and has them ready for the hostesses. A good supply is always kept on hand, since it is almost impossible to determine how fast the material will be used.

Nothing makes a better impression upon a branch patron than to receive a postcard in the mail calling his attention to a new book the library has received within the area of his particular interests. To do this successfully the branch librarian must either know her patrons very well or have patrons complete a form or card stating their specific hobbies or interests. These cards or forms may then be filed alphabetically under the interest or hobby named, with cross references if several are listed.

New books are then checked against the subject file to see which patron or patrons should receive cards. If several patrons name the same areas of interest, some system of rotating the notices is necessary so that the same people do not always have first chance.

The smaller the branch the easier it is to carry out such a system. In a very large branch it can become expensive and time consuming, though telephone rather than mail notification may reduce either of these factors. Books needed by several people should be held only for a stated period, with no renewal. A reader-interest card might be set up as follows:

GEMS AND MINERALS (Collecting and craft work)   Phone

Jones, Harry L.	665 W. 5th St.	541-6392
Wheeler, Roscoe	1512 Elm St.	542-6511

The Mobile (Alabama) Public Library uses such a system and mails what it calls a "Red Carpet Reserve." According to Director Hank J. Blasick, the cost of the red carpet reserve system has been minimal, but the application of the system appears to have been fairly limited.

A personal note of welcome from the branch librarian to new

school principals, ministers, store managers, etc., carries even
more impact than the Welcome Wagon hostess as far as the library
is concerned, for this welcome is not mixed in with many others.
Names of new homeowners can be secured from real estate agents.
New appointments in the area may be gleaned from local newspapers.

A continuing concern of many branch librarians, apart from
the time to work up news stories for the local press, is what to
write about. What is important enough to be news? Following is
a list of subjects that can provide good news material if written up
skillfully

> Formation of a new system
>
> New services in the library
>
> Any new convenience equipment such as a copy machine,
> rental typewriter, listening tables for records
>
> Special displays and exhibits for the public
>
> Any special events
>
> Regular events such as story hours, Great Books. Try to
> find something different each time an announcement is
> written. Avoid mechanical repetition
>
> Noteworthy gifts of books or equipment from individuals or
> groups
>
> Special National Library Week or Book Week activities
>
> Activities and social affairs of the Friends of the Library
>
> New staff members
>
> Staff resignations and retirements
>
> Achievements of staff
>
> Special vacation borrowing privileges
>
> Announcement of the summer reading program for children,
> news of its progress, names of those receiving
> certificates or special awards at end of program
>
> Any noteworthy rise in circulation or number of borrowers
>
> Advent of a new charging system
>
> Highlights of the annual report, sometimes of the monthly
> report
>
> Achievements of Library Board members (affiliated
> libraries in a system)
>
> Appointment of new board members (affiliated libraries in
> a system)

Attendance of librarian or staff at workshops, conventions, or special meetings

Election to office of staff or board members

Human interest features on reference questions asked

Human interest features on anything happening in the library

Anniversaries of the library establishment or erection of new building

News of a new branch building to be erected and details as they develop

New books column

Photos of children's activities--any special events such as a doll show, hobby show, magician's show, etc. Accompany with news story

Book sales conducted by the library or Friends of the Library (used books, gifts, or discards)

Branch cooperation with other agencies on any special project

New clubs or interest groups being sponsored by library

Any change in rules which will affect the public, such as amount of fine, term of borrowing, etc.

A prime example of a good publicity device, worked out practically on the spur of the moment, but highly successful, proves that it is only necessary to do something unusual to gain the news spotlight. Remodeling was in progress at the Lakewood Branch of the Dallas Public Library in 1961, and it became apparent towards the end that the reopening date could not be met:

> Lee Brawner, branch head at the time, conferred with Branch Chief Wyman Jones. Mr. Jones conferred with assistant library director Lillian Bradshaw, and she in turn with the chief librarian, James D. Meeks. The staff then took tables, display racks, and book trucks outside the branch and set up a regular sidewalk library like the book stalls in Paris. The book fair booths were borrowed from the Young Adult office. The staff unearthed and donned berets. Checkered table cloths were secured to contribute to the Gallic air. Candles were stuck in coke bottles. A beach umbrella to cover the charging desk lent a festive air. Thin volumes of verse were loaded into a tray with a sign saying, 'Poetry, mes amis?'

> News coverage was sparkling and breezy. Radio stations aired spot announcements; television cameras rolled, and the newspapers carried photos and features about 'Paris

in Dallas.' The Dallas Times-Herald remarked that 'the Lakewood Branch has the only sidewalk cafe going where you can get food for thought that is rare and well done at the same time.'

During the few days circulation totaled almost 5,000.[3]

The following is an example of an invitation to community groups to avail themselves of a branch meeting room:

To: Community Organizations

From: The Librarian--Cleveland Avenue Branch Library, Montgomery (Alabama) Public Library.

Re: Use of Conference Room for Meeting and Other Activities.

DID YOU KNOW?

Your library has a room specially furnished for conferences and meetings; the room is furnished with a conference table and chairs for seating fourteen persons comfortably, other chairs and space in the room are available for thirty or more persons.

This room is rent free, providing it is used during library hours; the hours are as follows: Monday, Wednesday, and Friday, open at 9:00 a.m., close at 6:00 p.m. Tuesday and Thursday, open at 11:00 a.m., close at 8:00 p.m. Saturday, open at 9:00 a.m., close at 5:00 p.m.

For use during non-library hours, please consult the librarian.

This is a community service from your public library. You are invited to use this service as well as other services of the library.

Notes

1. Wheeler, Joseph L. and Goldhor, Herbert. Practical Administration of Public Libraries, Harper and Row, c1962, p. 156.

2. Hoeffgren, Helen. "Branch Library Programs: Operation Shoestring Budget." Wilson Library Bulletin, v. 43, no. 6. Feb., 1969, p. 545-51.

3. Jones, Wyman. "Paris in Dallas." Library Journal. v. 86. no. 17, Oct. 1, 1961, p. 3242-43.

Figure 205:   Los Angeles publicizes its branches.   Reverse side
              lists names and locations of all branch libraries in
              the system.

3 KINDS OF
LIBRARY SERVICE...

You will get the most use and pleasure from the Los
Angeles Public Library if you know something about the
three basic kinds of library facilities in the city. You will
save time and energy by going to the right place the first
time. We hope this guide will aid you.

•

COMMUNITY LIBRARY — There are 54 community
branch libraries in the City of Los Angeles. Each branch has
a small but well-rounded collection, concentrating on the
more popular books and magazines. Collections in these
branches range from 9,000 to 50,000 volumes. Bookmobiles
serve areas without permanent library facilities.

•

REGIONAL LIBRARY — The city is divided into seven
regions for library service. The regional branch has a more
extensive collection in all fields and offers some services not
available at the community branch level. Regional collections range from 40,000 to 80,000 volumes. The regional
branch is also an administrative headquarters for that area.

•

CENTRAL LIBRARY — The most extensive collection of
books, magazines, films, and other material is in the Rufus
B. von KleinSmid Central Library, Los Angeles Public Library,
630 West Fifth Street. More than 1,200,000 volumes are
housed here. The Central Library is divided into departments
staffed by librarians who specialize in particular subjects.

•••

There is a
branch library
NEAR YOU

in the city
of
LOS ANGELES

Figure 206:   Oakland's Latin American Library invites its Spanish-
               speaking residents in their own language.   The same
               information appears on the reverse side in English.

**A LA BIBLIOTECA
LATINOAMERICANA**

CLASES

...EN ESPAÑOL   ...DE ESPAÑOL E INGLÉS
  E INGLÉS...   ...DE CIUDADANÍA

**LIBROS
REVISTAS
PERIÓDICOS
PELÍCULAS
DISCOS**
...CLÁSICOS
...RITMOS LATINOS
...DE ENSEÑANZA

PROGRAMAS
...DE PELÍCULAS!
...FIESTAS ESPECIALES!
...EXHIBICIONES!

Visiten

E. 14th Street   Avenue

Fruitvale

LA BIBLIOTECA

1457 Fruitvale Avenue
Oakland, California 94601
TELÉFONO   532-7882

Oakland's Latin American Library invites its
Spanish-speaking residents in Spanish, on the
reverse side the same information appears in English

¡GRATIS!

Figure 207:   Austin, Texas, provides a map showing location of
               all branches, plus addresses and phone numbers.

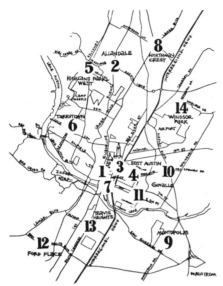

WELCOME TO AUSTIN! AS A NEW RESIDENT OF AUSTIN
      YOU ARE URGED TO USE AND ENJOY

The austin Public Library

EVERY MEMBER OF YOUR FAMILY MAY HAVE A FREE
   LIBRARY CARD. COME IN SOON FOR BOOKS, RECORDINGS,
   FRAMED PRINTS, MAGAZINES, INFORMATION, STORY HOURS.
      SEE THE MAP FOR LIBRARY NEAREST YOU.

1.	Central	472-5433	401 West 9th Street
2.	Allandale Branch	452-1394	5802 Burnet Road
3.	Brackenridge Hospital Station		1400 East Avenue
4.	Carver Branch	472-8954	1165 Angelina
5.	Highland Park Branch	465-6602	3317 Hancock Dr.
6.	Howson Branch	472-3584	2500 Exposition Blvd.
7.	Lakeside Station	476-5406	85 Trinity
8.	Mobile Station	452-3048	7941 N. Lamar Blvd.
9.	Montopolis Station	385-0709	1200 Montopolis Dr.
10.	Oak Springs Branch	926-4453	3101 Oak Springs Dr.
11.	Pan-American Station	476-9193	2100 East 3rd
12.	Southwood Branch	444-2110	1617 W. Ben White Blvd.
13.	Twin Oaks Branch	442-4664	202 East Oltorf
14.	Windsor Village Branch	452-7331	5800 Berkman Dr.

Figure 208.   Summer programs highlighted at Newark, N. J.,
                Public Library Branches by this single-sided sheet
                featuring children's activities.

*What's Going On at
the Library this Summer?*

One thing after another!

story hours •

summer reading club •

film programs •

arts and crafts •

practice in reading aloud •

and MORE!

VISIT YOUR LOCAL LIBRARY FOR MORE INFORMATION

Main Library	5 Washington Street
Branch Brook Library	235 Clifton Avenue
Clinton Branch	739 Bergen Street
North End Branch	722 Summer Avenue
Roseville Branch	99 Fifth Street
Springfield Branch	50 Hayes Street
Vailsburg Branch	75 Alexander Street
Van Buren Branch	140 Van Buren Street
Weequahic Branch	355 Osborne Terrace
Bookmobile	

Children's Department
NEWARK PUBLIC LIBRARY
Newark, New Jersey

Figure 209.   Any branch with a photocopier could use a bookmark
               like this. Sketch should match the type of machine
               owned by the library.

PHOTOCOPYING
SERVICE

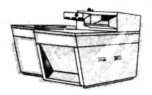

- Fast
- Easy
- Accurate

FOR 10 CENTS A SHEET, YOU
MAY COPY SUCH LIBRARY
MATERIALS AS:

    PAGES FROM BOOKS
    AND MAGAZINES

    PAGES FROM PAMPHLETS

    NEWS CLIPPINGS

    CHARTS AND GRAPHS

    OTHER PRINTED MATERIALS

REFERENCE MEZZANINE

SANTA ANA PUBLIC LIBRARY
8th and Ross Streets
Santa Ana, California

Figure 210.   Venice Branch of the Los Angeles Public Library
appeals to its patrons with slightly psychedelic bookmarks like these two, phrased in contemporary
language.

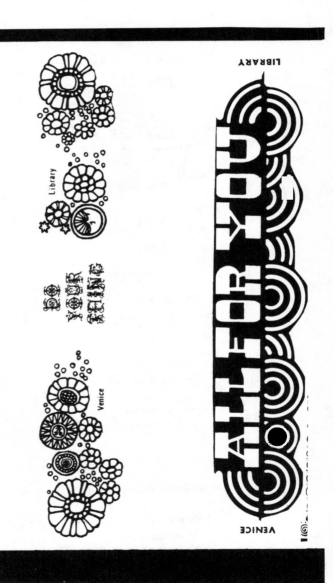

Chapter 22

Today's Trends and Needed Research

Paramount among trends today is the increased building of larger branches, known variously as "regional," "area" or "district" libraries. City systems are finding it expedient to create fewer but better branches. Such branches, with their richer resources, larger staffs, and improved facilities can come much closer to meeting the needs of an ever-increasingly complex society.

Why should larger branches be the order of the day, taking into account the fact that there is also a trend toward groups of satellite branches which are comparatively very small and serve primarily to provide popular reading and reference on a fairly elementary level? Frederick Wezeman, in his Study of Branch Libraries for the Lincoln City Library, Lincoln, Nebraska, 1967, gives a list of excellent reasons: [1]

1. Increased title demand. In the past twelve years there has been more than 100% increase in the number of titles published in the United States. Branches must be larger to house even a significant number of this constantly increasing annual output.

2. More people are attending school for longer periods of time, studying many different subjects. Continuation schools and adult evening classes are on the increase.

3. Increasing variety in the number of occupations and professions. More knowledge is required by workers in a larger number of fields.

4. Routine study needs for young people and adults require larger book collections, periodical files, and pamphlet collections.

5. Increasing demands on the local tax dollar make it impossible to provide a branch library for every neighborhood.

677

6.   In relation to construction and operating costs, better quality service can be provided in larger branches at a lower cost per book circulated. Savings are afforded in staffing, servicing, physical maintenance, branch deliveries, cataloging and processing.

7.   The larger unit can provide a base for bookmobile operation and save the time required to drive the mobile unit back and forth through the heavier central traffic in a city.

8.   Increased use of the automobile lessens the necessity for having branches close together. People are used to using their cars for shopping and will make use of branches wherever there is good parking.

9.   Crime and child molestation are on the increase. Parents are reluctant to let their children walk any distance alone to a branch library. Therefore, the old standard of a library within walking distance of every child loses validity.

10.   The larger branches can share some of the reference responsibilities of the central library, which is usually overloaded in this aspect of service.

11.   The larger branch can provide meeting rooms, story hour facilities, more adult education activities.

12.   Staffing is improved with larger branches. The circulation can justify having more trained specialists for work with children, young people, and adults.

13.   The entire service becomes richer, more complete, more satisfying to patrons.

Paradoxically, the present day trend in libraries throughout the country to reach out to the so-called "disadvantaged" has also stimulated the establishment of small satellite "reading centers" or "neighborhood centers" in a number of city systems. Bookmobiles are also serving metropolitan areas in an effort to reach the residents of "in-between" areas or those cut off from the nearest branch by natural or traffic barriers. They can also serve those who find it difficult to reach the larger branches because of lack of transportation or their own physical condition.

Smaller branches alone are unsatisfactory because with no closer supplementary resources than one central library they are unable to meet the increasingly varied and complex demands of students and teachers, professional men, business men, technicians, and the ordinary citizen. Reading centers make no attempt to be anything but sources of popular reading and limited information. Patrons can be referred to a regional or area branch without making the long trip to the central library. Thus larger regional branches, supplemented with satellite reading centers, may well provide the standard service pattern of the future for city systems.

Dramatic results are often attained when a changeover to larger branches is made. Frederick Wezeman also made a study of the branch libraries in Des Moines, Iowa in 1959.[2] He recommended that the six existing small branches be gradually replaced by four large branches to be located in the four quadrants of the city. In 1965 the West Side Branch was opened, replacing three of the older branches. It was a 14,000 square foot building on an 84,000 square foot site. The main reading room alone had 7,336 square feet. A bookmobile garage and work area were included.

During the first year of operation West Side Branch loaned 334,799 books, 3,464 more than the combined circulation of the three branches it replaced. Reference and reader advisory questions showed an increase of 9,575 over the combined total of the three replaced branches.

Kenneth Shaffer says: "The revolution in private transportation does away with the need for multitudes of costly, small branches of public libraries where service potential is relatively low."[3] Other factors which have helped make small branches impractical include the decline in rural population, the tremendous increase in paperback titles and distribution points for them, coupled with the increasing affluence of American citizens and their willingness to spend money on books, the large increase in distribution of magazines, and improved roads.

Not all librarians agree with the trend toward larger branch units. In a letter to the author dated April 4, 1968, Hoyt Galvin, Director of Libraries, Public Library of Charlotte and Mecklenburg County, Charlotte, North Carolina, said:

> Our seven city branches only average about 4,000 square feet, and these branches depend heavily upon the main library for reference services and supplementary books

delivered daily. It is easy to argue that these branches
would give better service if larger in space, books, and
staff. Still, I doubt that we would reach the people
without putting the branches where the people go frequently in the normal pursuit of their activities. In fact, with
more funds, I would argue to open more branches of the
type we have rather than reduce the number and have
more adequate facilities. We are convinced that people
in depressed areas will not travel far to use libraries.
In fact, it is extremely difficult to get these people to use
libraries at all. It is our conclusion, therefore, that for
this community it is more effective to have a larger number of smaller branches than to seek to develop the
larger, more adequate branches.

Another dissenting opinion is that of Edwin Beckerman,
Director of the Free Public Library of Woodbridge, New Jersey.
In a letter written June 19, 1968, Mr. Beckerman said:

There has been very little written about the desirable
size or kinds of service to be offered by branch libraries.
What has been written is, I feel, open to question. Does
a branch library have to serve 35,000 or 40,000 people
to make it a viable operation? I have one branch library
that probably serves no more than 16,000 or 17,000 people
which circulates 130,000 books a year and in my opinion
provides a valuable service for the community without
meeting some of the standards which have been mentioned
by some library experts. Every study I have done on
branch library operations, and I think this is duplicated
in the work of many other people, would indicate that the
further one goes from places where people live, the lower
the use that results. Larger branches more widely spaced
may be more practical from a library point of view in
terms of the kind of services that can be offered, but is
it really more effective from the user's point of view if
substantially fewer people take advantage of these services?
I suspect some kind of balance has to be struck. Location
is important and so are resources.....

.....I suspect that some city systems require more
rather than fewer branches located closer to the neighborhoods in which people live. People living in depressed
areas, for example, are less likely to use branch
facilities in another neighborhood than they might if
branches were located closer to the places they live.
Some areas, perhaps, should not have branches but
should locate library facilities in multi-service centers.
We have a few examples of this kind of library development in metropolitan areas, but I suspect they lack adequate evaluation.

Emerson Greenaway [4] believes that as time passes more and more emphasis will be placed on extension services, with greater cooperation among libraries the answer to a great many problems. "By 1980," he says, "over 80 per cent of this country's population will be living in some 212 Standard Metropolitan Statistical Areas (as described by the U.S. Census). Cities in densely populated areas are merging into one another. This creates a problem for branches located anywhere near the line between municipalities." [4] Residents of such congested metropolitan areas cannot understand why they cannot use the facilities of any library. Take, for example, the case of Anaheim, Santa Ana, Orange, Tustin, Fountain Valley, Costa Mesa, and Garden Grove, a complex of seven large cities in Southern California, some 30 or so miles south of Los Angeles. It is almost impossible in driving through this area to tell when one goes from one city into another, so closely do they merge and interweave at some points.

Four large libraries serve these seven cities: three city systems and a very large county system, each within the confines of its own tax district. Reciprocal borrowing, at the time of this writing, was possible only through occasional interlibrary loan or by purchase of a non-resident card by the borrower. Some type of reciprocal arrangement will undoubtedly be worked out in time, and may, in fact, have been by the time this appears in print. But it is the considered opinion of Mr. Greenaway and many others that the total resources of contiguous areas should be available to all residents of all of the area, and such arrangements will become increasingly common in the future as systems consolidate or cooperate in regard to certain types of service.

Mr. Greenaway suggests that there be three levels of service in any given area:

Level I - Neighborhood and school library, serving mainly children, housewives, senior citizens, and other interested citizens.

Level II- Regional and academic library, serving high school and college students, business and professional people, industrialists, and other adults.

Level III-   Central or research library, to be a capstone
              to the entire extension system, providing "in
              depth" service of all kinds.

A book catalog should be produced of the holdings of all libraries in the area and there should be a copy of it in each agency.
Greenaway believes there should be wider use of interlibrary loan
and cooperative buying to prevent unnecessary duplication. He also
emphasizes that the lack of professional librarians will increasingly
result in branches being staffed by non-professional personnel, but
with professional supervision. [4]

Among other trends already apparent in branch services or
which will affect branch service in the future are the following:

Expanded reference, informational, advisory and guidance
services to persons of all ages. [5]

Greater recognition of the necessity for helping the out-of-
school adult learn how to use the library in order to be better able
to pursue his own program of continuing education. [5]

Better branch buildings because architects are becoming
more aware of library needs. More emphasis on functional aspects. [5]

More elasticity and liberalism in book selection. [5]

Greater involvement in the programs and problems of the
branch service area. [5]

More effort to cooperate with professional groups and
agencies in planning new programs and in providing library materials and services to support them. [5]

More systematic study of the community and the library's
relationship to it. [5]

Greater use of advanced mechanization in the performance
of certain activities. [5]

More freedom for branch librarians in planning their total
program.

More service and attention to the handicapped, through
greater use of audio-visual equipment and physical design of
buildings for easier use.

Increasing tendency to combine bookmobile operations and
garage with branches rather than with the central library.

Figure 211. Branch Bait to Bring in the Children. Branches nowadays use all sorts of devices to lure children inside the walls and expose them to books. Here the Orange County Public Library's Chee-Chee, whose name is based on one of the animal characters in Hugh Lofting's Doctor Doolittle books, is surrounded by children who participated in the Mesa Verde Branch's summer reading program. Administrative headquarters of the Orange County Library are located in Orange, California.

Figure 212.   Book Delivery to your Door May be Common in the
                future.   A messenger delivers books from the
                <u>Montclair Public Library</u>, Montclair, New Jersey.
                A small fee is charged.

Larger parking areas.

Books delivered by messenger or mailed out from branches. Delivery is made after a telephone call.

More branches located in shopping malls and shopping centers. As malls supplant centers, branches will move into mall locations.

Meeting rooms or all-purpose rooms in every branch.

More unconventional architectural design. There may be a vogue for round, octagonal, even triangular or other atypical shapes of branch buildings.

More library-sponsored activities outside the library walls, as staff members reach out to draw in non-users. This is now being done increasingly in cooperation with government programs.

Many more new modern facilities to replace outmoded and unattractive older buildings, because of state aid construction grants.

More staff subject specialists in larger branches to provide greater depth in reference and research activity.

Extensive use of all media of communication in carrying out the branch informational and educational functions.

Decreasing emphasis on the more casual forms of entertaining reading; more emphasis upon the informational and educational facilities.

Unless the rate of book and periodical loss slows down, greater security measures and more security devices in all libraries.

Provision of more convenience services such as rental typewriters, copying equipment, conference rooms, pen machines, phone booths.

All-modular construction of branches with little or no use of supporting columns. More use of laminated beams.

More participation of staff in community activities and city planning.

Greater use of branches by the public because of increased leisure time (shorter work week), earlier retirement, increased prosperity.

Quick access, even by smaller branches, to the books of the nation, if not the world, through networks of material transfer and communication. [6]

Fewer back files of periodicals in branches and more such files on microfilm with microfilm readers and reader-printers available.

Closer work and communication with minority groups.

Drive-in libraries, which may become as popular as bank drive-ins. [6]

Children's and Youth Libraries will assume increasing importance. [6]

More feedback on how patron's needs are being met, which will result in improved service. [6]

More language material available in branches, reaching down into the children's collection. More attention to Mexican-American and other ethnic groups, with more Spanish-speaking staff members, signs in Spanish, etc., particularly in the Southwest and border states.

Increasing student use of branches as school needs grow. The rise in number of community colleges, often located in branch service areas, has affected branch use in many cities.

Growing emphasis on rapid reading courses in colleges and adult education classes, which will continue to stimulate general library and branch use.

Increasing need for research on the part of scientists, business men, and industrialists which will require more reference sources at branches, even though the bulk of this type of service will be carried on at central libraries set up as research centers. Larger regional and area branches will be expected to provide far more of this kind of service than has been provided by the traditional branch of the past.

A further increase in cooperation.

More specific application of business methods to library management. Work simplication, efficiency studies, surveys, evaluation, much more effort to measure results are a few of the applications. [7]

Figure 213.   Increasing student use at elementary and junior high
              school levels, a present-day trend. <u>Nathan Hale</u>
              <u>Branch</u>, Tulsa, Oklahoma City-County System.

Libraries which will be less and less "book centers" and more and more materials centers for books, periodicals, films, phono records, art prints, tapes, and other types of material. [7]

A change in the type of professional training, and increasing specialization among librarians, even in branches.

Increasing use of bookmobiles, but more careful study to determine the feasibility of bookmobile service versus branches or other methods of extension.

More specialized branches: downtown business branches of city systems, children's or youth libraries in separate buildings, branches aimed at meeting the needs of specific groups such as Mexican-Americans.

More central libraries converting to reference and information centers, leaving branches to carry the main load of recreational and general informational reading requirements.

Increasing problems in the support of library service, created by the move of city dwellers to suburbs, which is likely to continue. With sewers, streets, lighting systems, and transportation to be provided first, suburban areas, usually unincorporated,

cannot finance library buildings and operation.   Urban libraries
must be prepared to extend services to those areas through branches
and by means of contracts or the formation of county systems.

Philip H. Ennis, writing on "The Library Consumer," points
out that these major problems arise from the high-speed development of the suburbs:

1.   The librarian must make an important choice.   Should
he strengthen the central library collection and services or should
he follow his dispersing customers to the city's outskirts and
suburbs?   Providing branches and bookmobile service to these new
concentrations of population can be expensive and often requires a
duplication of purchasing and staffing.   Since branch efficiency is
related to good leadership and the presence of a strong resource
center for materials and assistance, it is difficult to give adequate
branch service in a system in which the central library or headquarters has not been strengthened to meet expanding needs.   But
available funds are rarely sufficient both to expand and strengthen
the central source at the same time.   Which shall come first?

2.   The breaking up of a former population concentration
into autonomous widely dispersed localities makes it difficult, if
not impossible, to consolidate demand for library service and the
resources to meet that demand.   The formation of many small, inadequate branches around a city causes residents to become dis-
couraged when their study and reading needs can be met only
partially.   So they form the habit of purchasing books or obtaining
them in any way possible except through the public library.

3.   The groups slowest to move from the core of the inner
city have in many cases been those of low economic power.
Minority groups such as the Negroes and Mexican-Americans remain in the older residential areas, are hungry for library service
and education, but do not have the tax potential to support either
good libraries or schools.   They need branches and they will support bond elections or referenda to help secure funds for them.
It has been shown in most areas that the greatest affirmative vote
comes from those of the highest educational background and from
areas with a heavy concentration of Negro population.

Needed research:

It is only in the last two or three decades that scientific methods of research have been applied to library operations, but much more research is still necessary. Among the areas which need further study and development are:

a. Accepted sets of standards for the various types of branches, which spell out the area to be served in terms of geography and population, describe the size of the building, scope of book collection, and number of staff required.[7]

b. An acceptable set of definitions and standards for services given beyond those in the central library (e.g. regional branches, community branches, sub-branches, reading centers, stations, etc.)[7]

c. An exhaustive study of nationwide needs for branch library services, based heavily on information from library users.[7]

d. Comparative studies of the effectiveness of city systems with regional branches and satellite branches, as against systems having a larger number of smaller branches.

e. Study of the effectiveness of the new small reading centers.

f. A study bringing the A.L.A. School-housed Branch Survey up to date. There are fewer such branches now; strengthening of school libraries has affected the need for such branches. Opinions have changed in many cases.

g. More study, covering costs and service potential, of leased branches in shopping malls and centers, versus leased branches in other locations.

h. Gathering of data on leasing costs, provisions of leases, factors affecting square foot costs in various types of locations and parts of the country. Advantages and disadvantages of leasing versus building.

i. Study in depth of the social role of branch libraries.

j. Branch work with the disadvantaged.

k. Development of a standardized form for reporting building data and costs.

l. Further study of the relationship between branch service and headquarters, branch staff and headquarters staff.

m. Study of the pros and cons of belonging to a system, based upon interviews with small-town independent libraries which have become members of federations or county or regional branches.

n. Greater application to library operations of such measurement devices as time and motion studies, work analysis, work simplification.

o. More surveys of branch systems by outstanding professional experts, with recommendations for improvement.

p. Salary studies of branch personnel in cities of less than 35,000 population.

q. A bibliography of research studies and surveys specifically of branch operations.

r. Cost studies for various-sized branches. Which size operates best at least cost? Is there an optimum size?

Wheeler and Goldhor[9] note that data for library operations have to be interpreted in the light of cost index changes, of salaries in parallel fields, of time-saving studies and devices in business and public administration, of paperback and periodical sales and the growth of school libraries, of better or poorer location and access to a library or branch. Statistics, they say, can indicate what has happened but often fail to explain why. Psychological factors may be influential. Standards to be promulgated as to per-capitas of budgetary components and costs, or of materials and services, need to be adjusted for population size. A scientific basis needs to be established for standards. Any standard involving cost has to be a somewhat arbitrary compromise among:

a. The average of current performance and costs of various services and materials.

b. Performance and costs for a group of superior libraries, on the ground that what a number of good libraries can do makes a fair standard for others to meet.

c. The constant increase in costs due to the decreasing purchase value of the dollar.

d. The increasing variety, better quality, and intensive character of service being demanded by the public year after year, involving greater expenditure.

In January, 1964, the report by the Library Administration Division of the American Library Association, Review and Evaluation of Access to Public Libraries, stated:

> An extensive, well-supported study of branch library service is an obvious and crying need. This should cover all aspects of the community library service program, including clientele and use, optimum size and location of facilities, hours of service, administration and staffing, selection and maintenance of the book collection, and system relationships. [10]

It should be noted that the San Diego Public Library, San Diego, California, has conducted annual studies of branch staffing and related matters, with the results tabulated by size of cities. These highly useful reports are issued in mimeographed form, usually in February or March.

Edwin Beckerman, Director of the Free Public Library of Woodbridge, New Jersey, in a letter to the author in June, 1968, asks:

> Have we really thought out the implications of the revolution in technology that is now taking place? While some technological changes may not be currently applicable, the chances are that within the next ten years it will be possible to rely more heavily on main libraries to transmit information to branches through closed circuit television, etc. Will the branches we are building today enable us to plug in new systems of transferring information from the library to the patron?

Notes

1. Wezeman, Frederick. A Study of Branch Libraries. Lincoln City Library, Lincoln, Nebraska, 1967. p. 44-45.

2. Wezeman, Frederick. Neighborhood Library Services. Des Moines Public Library, Des Moines, Iowa, 1959.

3. Shaffer, Kenneth. "Library Building Needs in Massachusetts." Bay State Librarian, V. 54, July, 1964, p. 3-4.

4. Greenaway, Emerson. "New Trends in Branch Library Service."
    Library Trends, April, 1966, p. 451-457.

5. Gates, Jean Key. Introduction to Librarianship. McGraw-Hill,
    1968. p. 208-9.

6. Coplan, Kate, and Castagna, Edwin. The Library Reaches Out.
    Oceana, 1965. p. 394.

7. Greenaway, Emerson. "New Trends in Branch Library Service."
    Library Trends, April, 1966, p. 451-52.

8. Ennis, Philip H. "The Library Consumer." In: The Public
    Library and the City. Ralph W. Conant, editor. MIT Press
    (Massachusetts Institute of Technology), c1965, p. 15-31.

9. Wheeler, Joseph L. and Goldhor, Herbert. Practical Admini-
    stration of Public Libraries. Harper and Row, c1962, p.
    130-133.

10. American Library Association, Library Administration Division.
    Review and Evaluation of Access to Public Libraries. The
    Association, 1964. Mimeographed, p. 7.

APPENDICES

Prospectus or Short Building Program
(For a Medium-Large Branch)

Information about East Whittier Branch, Whittier Public Library, Whittier, California

What is a Branch?

A branch library is usually defined as a library in its own building, or in suitable leased quarters, with a substantial and permanent book collection, with paid staff and open to public use on a regular schedule of hours. A branch library is a means of extending certain services of the central library; it is not a means of increasing the level of service available. A branch library allows greater access to books and other library materials; it does not increase the depth and scope of resources. The strength of a branch library is directly dependent upon the strength of the central library.

Where Should it be Located?

Proper location is in or near a shopping center on the ground level, with sufficient off-street parking spaces. It should be located within a mile to a mile and a half radius of the central library and serve a population of 25,000 to 50,000.

What Will a Branch Cost?

East Whittier branch site is to be acquired in 1965.

$80,000 is already earmarked in City's capital fund.

Building   Estimated at $250,000 to 375,000

10,000 to 15,000 square feet at about $25.00 a square foot.

Should probably not be less than 15,000 square feet. If

less, then built so that it can be expanded easily.

Functional, aesthetically pleasing and economical to
operate.

Furnishings   Estimated at $ 40,000 to 50,000

Shelving for initial book collection of 25,000 volumes
expandable to 50,000.

Reading tables and chairs seating at least 50 children and
young adults and 25 adults.

Circulation desk, equipment.

Lounge and story hour room furnishings.

Book collection   at 1964-1965 costs $135,000 to 150,000

25,000 new volumes at a unit cost

of $5.25 to $6.00 fully catalogued,

processed and put on the shelves   _____

Total branch building estimated at

$505,000 to $655,000

The decision about the financing will rest with the City
Council.   The East Whittier Branch could be financed in this way:

Sales tax receipts earmarked for the building as has been
the City's policy and practice with the new Whittier
Public Library and the new Community Building.

Bond issue would require payment of interest on the money
borrowed as well as repayment on the principle with the
result that over the necessary period of time the cost
would increase.

When Will it Open?

It takes two years to plan, build, book and staff a branch
according to the best experience in branch building in Los Angeles,
Santa Monica, Pasadena and elsewhere.

How Much Will the East Whittier Branch be Used?

Borrowers:

Serving a population of nearly 30,000 in a high reading
area at least 50% of the East Whittier residents will
hold borrowers' cards and probably borrow an average

of 25 books a year on each card.

Circulation:

300,000 to 400,000 volumes a year.

Reference Service:

Information and ready-reference use is hard to estimate but it will probably be high. Reference requests of a substantial nature requiring technical reference books and the bound magazines collection will be referred to the central library.

Hours Open:

12 noon to 9 P. M. Monday through Friday, 10 A. M. to 6 P. M. Saturday and closed Sunday.

Staff:

In order to meet the schedule of hours open, handle the volume of circulation and the information and ready-reference requests the branch will need a minimum staff of 8--3 professional and 5 non-professional.

The above information compiled from:

Master Plan for the Whittier Public Library, prepared by the staff, approved by the Board of Library Trustees, November 1962.

The Whittier Public Library, Report of a survey by Harold L. Hamill, City Librarian of Los Angeles, May 1964.

Practical Administration of Public Libraries, by J. L. Wheeler and Herbert Goldhor, p. 410-30, Harper, 1962.

The Small Library Building, by J. L. Wheeler, p. 9-10, American Library Association, 1963.

Appendix B

Detailed Building Program
(Single Branch)

Santa Ana Public Library: (8, 064 ft. Branch)

Service Area:

The branch of the Santa Ana Public Library will serve primarily the residents within a one-mile radius of the location at Fairview and McFadden Streets. Fringe area usage is also to be expected in lesser degree for another 1/4-mile. These figures, therefore, represent the immediate and highest usage areas. Population in this area is estimated at just short of 32,000.

Neighborhood Characteristics:

The characteristics of the neighborhood, according to the latest survey available, 1966, are as follows:

Median income $7,150	Racial origins:
Avg. unemployment 8. 5%	White 78. 5%
Median age 21. 5 years	Negro 9. 0%
Owner occupancy of	Mexican-American 10. 8%
homes 63. 3%	Other 1. 7%

There are two large multiple housing units within two blocks, one housing 542 families, the other 140. Another is planned immediately behind and adjacent to the proposed branch. There are three large trailer courts in the area, catering to adults and senior citizens. A medium-sized shopping center is located at the other end of the block on the corner of McFadden and Sullivan Streets. It includes a large supermarket. Patrons could use this parking area as an overflow if the library parking stalls were filled. They would have to walk only a few hundred feet.

Objectives:

The branch shall be considered as a community library giving service to the fullest possible extent compatible with its budget
and staff. The branch size chosen is based upon the tenet that it
is more efficient and economical to have fewer and larger branches
of 8,000-10,000 square feet serving 30,000 to 35,000 people than
many small branches with limited collections, staff, and other
resources.

Potential Usage:

The community is growing in population through high rise
apartments in particular. The three nearest bookmobile stops--
Jerome Park, Lingan Lane, and Nakoma Drive, and Sullivan and
Willets Streets--rank 2nd, 5th, and 7th in usage in a list of 21
stops, showing heavy patronage. Five elementary schools, a
junior high school and a senior high school are within one mile.
This is an area of homes with very few commercial establishments.
It is believed that a great deal of use will be made of the branch by
students doing study and reference work, especially in the evening
hours; by children in the afternoons and Saturdays, and by family
groups in the evenings for browsing and recreational reading.
Mothers with small children will undoubtedly come in greater numbers in the morning and early afternoon hours. Community use
will grow and the branch will become a center for cultural and
civic activities through use of the multi-purpose room for meetings
and displays.

Service Program:

A service program was worked out and is attached. Upon
this service program the building program is based.

Quantity Factors:

A.   Seating space:

At least 50-75 people will be expected to use the main
reading room in the evenings, perhaps two-thirds of this
number in the afternoon to 6 p.m. It is expected that all

possible seating area will be occupied Monday through
Thursday evenings as use of the branch increases. 15
to 30 children may be in the children's area after school
and on Saturdays at any given time. Seating space, including benches, totals 42. Parents will be with the
children in many cases. Story hour time will attract up
to 50 or 60 children and will require use of the multi-
purpose room. Several dozen cushions will be provided
to avoid setting up folding chairs for story hours and to
add to the informality.

During the busy hours from 3 p.m. on we can expect from
10 to 20 people to be making use of the reference room.
Others will be using reference material and taking it to
the general reading area.

From 10 to 15 persons will be able to use the browsing
area, adult and young adult.

Staff Requirement:

It is estimated that approximately 7-1/2 full-time equivalent
staff will be needed to operate the branch. The staff will ideally
consist of:

Branch librarian (professional). Librarian II	$8500
Professional children's librarian, Librarian I	7200
Library Clerk II	5800
Two Clerk Typist I's at $5400	10,800
Two pages full-time at $4000	8000
100 hours student page help per month	2100
Substitute help	300
Total	$42,700

Hours Open to Public:

The building will be open to the public during the following
hours:

Monday through Friday	10 a.m. to 9 p.m.	55 hrs.
Saturday	10 a.m. to 6 p.m.	8 hrs.
		63 hrs.

It is not planned to offer service on Sunday. Because of wide variations in the use of the library at various times of day, it is desirable that the public areas be so arranged as to permit the required supervision to be carried on by a minimum staff during the hours of light traffic.

Maintenance:

Maintenance of grounds, the building, and the heating equipment will undoubtedly be handled by the city gardeners and custodians. Utilities will probably be paid by the city and included in a rental fee which will include utilities and services of the gardener and custodian. However, should this not be the case, an item of at least $9,000 per year should be included in the operating budget for custodial service and utilities. A branch this size should be able to be handled properly with 4 to 5 hours of custodial and grounds maintenance.

Building--General Type:

A one-story building at ground level with one public entrance is required. It will be 8064 square feet in area. Parking space at the rear of the building and at the west side will accommodate 30 cars. Parking spaces for staff should be marked off adjacent to the back wall of the building, separate from the public area. This can be parallel parking if there is not sufficient room for angle parking.

Book Capacity:

Adult main reading room= 24,000   Reference Area = 2000
Boys and Girls section = 12,000   Adult browsing area= 2500
Young People's Alcove = 1200
            Total book capacity = 41,800 volumes

Exterior Requirements:

1. Rock facing across front of building, full walls and under picture windows.

2. Concrete block or redwood, double construction. Concrete block to be faced with stucco. Architect to help determine most economical and harmonious combination with rock facing.

3. Large picture windows in reference and children's areas to provide passersby a good view into library activity. 15 ft. width to within 3 ft. of ground level. High windows above wall shelving for natural light. Tinted glass or good overhang on roof to avoid glare on west windows.

4. Outside book return--by front entrance. Provide with lock, similar to Master Depository #1112 S.D. with lock. Provide with lighted sign if not located at front entrance.

5. Bicycle rack--inconspicuous but near front entrance.

6. Building sign--prominently displayed, large and artistic, either on post or on building.

7. Flood lights--front and rear, on time clock. Parking area behind must be well-lighted to avoid problems.

8. Delivery entrance at side, to workroom--4 feet wide double doors for ease of delivery and ample size for fire exit.

9. Parking: 30 spaces marked off at side and rear. All parking area concrete or blacktopped.

10. Landscaping--attractive but low maintenance must be a factor. Try for shrubs and plants that require a minimum of watering and replanting each year.

11. Water meter--separate water meter for sprinkling system.

12. Built-in sprinkling system in small landscaped area at front of building, so planned it will not play on building front.

13. Avoid weird or unusual shape or type of roof. Conventional design with long-lasting and low maintenance material used.

Relationships of Interior Areas:

A. Reference area behind and closest to central desk for ease of supervision, control of materials and saving of staff steps when reference books are needed for telephone questions and other requests. Easier for patrons to ask for help.

B. Charging desk placed near entrance to reference room for reasons already given, facing entire open public area, close to front entrance for patron step-saving in returning books, ease of supervision of entrance, close to children's room for ease of checking out children's books and easy supervision of children's room when no children's librarian on duty. Also close to librarian's office so she can man the desk when necessary and also communicate with the clerk on duty there.

C. Magazine room just off reference room for convenience of reference users and saving steps of staff in getting magazines to central desk when no page is on duty and patron is unable to find the magazines for himself.

D. Librarian's office next to desk, as stated, plus answering desk clerk's queries when necessary, for supervision of entire public area through glass on all sides, of workroom, and of rest rooms across the hall. Communication with those in workroom and at desk quicker and easier.

E. Staff workroom is next to rest rooms for staff and kitchen facilities for staff yet remote from public area for quiet for both staff and public. Workroom has outside wide door to parking area for ease of deliveries and orderly flow of materials. No cataloging or processing will be done, but workroom will need built-in wall shelving for supplies and books received from the Central Library and needing minor processing before being put out, desks for staff, and two typewriter tables, plus a work table for simple mending. A sink will be needed.

F. All purpose room at back corner of building allows outside entrance and exit and room can be closed off from main library after its closing hours. Juxtaposition to public rest rooms gives access to same after library is closed. Having the all-purpose room at the opposite end of building from adult reading room helps noise problem at night if there are musical or other programs from which sound could carry. However, the inside walls of the all-purpose room should be sound proof insulated as much as possible to prevent this. The all-purpose room should have kitchen and storage area at end of room partitioned off by folding doors of plastic or wood. There should be special wall surface for hanging pictures.

G. Rest rooms should have double doors, one at each end, so that inner doors can be locked and outer doors left open at night for access to all-purpose room when there is something going on.

H. Young adult browsing area and alcove is in center back, easily supervised from main desk.

I. Adult browsing area is just off adult reading room, likely to be quieter.

J. Adult reading room is at back of building, away from street, thus apt to be quieter. Reader-advisor desk should be at entrance to this area.

K. Book stacks are placed at an angle for ease of supervision from the central check-out desk and to break the monotony of right angle lines. All wall shelving is built in, 8 standing shelves, 9 ft. long, double faced to be in adult reading room, 6-1/2 ft. high. Low shelving to separate adult and children's areas is 4 ft. high, double faced. Lower shelves of all stacks should be tilted for greater ease in reading titles. All shelves should be adjustable. Wood shelving preferably, although steel stacks could be used if birch end panels were used.

L. The card catalog is located directly across from the central desk, handy for both the public and the staff member manning the desk. Also near the Reader Advisor.

M. The book collection is on open shelves.

N. The central charging desk and R.A. desk require phone connections and are fairly close together. A floor connection would be necessary for the R.A. desk.

Interior Requirements (General):

1. Light-colored, birch or maple furniture to lighten up the area.

2. Fire alarm system.

3. Laminated beam construction to avoid load bearing posts in reader open area.

4. Sound-proofing ceiling tile, which combined with carpeted floors should solve the noise problem almost 100%.

5. Direct telephone line to the Central Library reference department.

6. Heating and air conditioning unit should be one combination of adequate size to heat the entire building. A time-tested system that would not ring up heavy repairs, such as Carrier or equivalent. Located as centrally as possible in this plan.

7. All plumbing located as close together as possible for economy.

8. Lighting should be fluorescent throughout with the standard amount of candlepower to give sufficient light but avoid glare. Illuminated ceiling if possible. White light better than soft white or pink tone.

9. Floor covering should be carpeting throughout of the separated tile type if funds warrant; otherwise a good grade of battleship linoleum or tile. Use a color that cleans easily but adds to the color scheme.

10. Built-in shelving around all walls indicated, to be included in contractors bid, also standing shelving.

11. Pastel colors for interior decoration, pleasing to the eye yet giving a live, warm impression. Colors to be determined later. Furniture colors to harmonize.

12. Drinking fountains to be refrigerated type.

13. The building should be both functional and beautiful with function being given top priority. The general impression as one enters should further the emotional, intellectual, and spiritual values the library wishes to emphasize. The outside impression, with its picture windows and pleasing lines should invite all to enter.

Circulation Desk:

To be designed with two work stations at same desk-- chargeout and return. Check-in station closest to main entrance-- equip with cut out for cash register, drawers for transaction cards, p slips, desk supplies, pencils. Lower shelves for "ask-at-desk books." Check-out station cut out to accommodate photocharger, foot rail below. Drawers for supplies and open shelves beneath for books. Bread board type pull out shelf by photocharger

approximately 24' wide. High chair on casters. Low section at
end for registration of new borrowers. Equip with one drawer,
adjustable shelves. Place to get knees under.

Size--approx. 10 feet wide, 3 feet deep at ends, narrowing
to 2 feet. Shape as shown. Should be designed in detail as a
special unit in consultation with the library staff and branch librarian.

Behind circulation desk provide low shelving 4' high to provide space for ready reference material and divide charging desk
from reference area. Provide at least five feet of space between
counter and rear unit for free movement of staff.

Detailed Specifications--Each Area:

Adult Reading Room: Stack Area: Conference Room
Size 52x54' - 2808 square feet.

Initially equipped with 17 standing double-faced stacks, 9
feet in length, 7'6' high, 7 shelves high with adjustable
shelving. Constructed of wood with end paneling to match
furniture. Lower shelf slanted to permit easy reading of
titles but with false back to prevent books sliding to back
of shelves and being hard to see.

Eight reading tables, 2 double carrells, and four single
carrells will provide seating space for 56 persons. Tables
will be 3x6 feet, preferably with colored formica tops for
ease in upkeep and a note of color. Chairs will be of the
padded back straight type, 56 being required for this area.

The conference room should be 8x10 feet, with one 3x6
reading table, with six chairs of the same type as used in
the reading area. It should be sound-proofed and consist
of wood partition up three feet, with glass above that for
four feet. A small typewriter table and chair in the corner
will accommodate a rental typewriter and allow the room to
double as a conference and typing room.

The adult reading area is to be set off from the boys' and
girls' area by low four foot shelving, four shelves high, extending from the east wall in a westerly direction 50 feet.
This shelving should be double faced, used for boys' and
girls' books on the south side, for adult books on the north
side.

The adult card catalog will be located at the entrance to the
adult reading area, across and a few feet north of the charging desk. It will be nine feet long, contain 90 drawers,
accommodate 108,000 cards, enough for some 36,000 books.
As the collection increases to capacity, at least one unit of
15 drawers will have to be added.

A reader's adviser desk with posture chair will be located approximately midway of the opening into the adult reading area. It should be 30x60", face the charging desk and open area in the center from which patrons will approach. A phone connection in the floor will be necessary at this point.

Two lengths of high shelving, one 22 ft. long, one 8 ft. long, 7' 6" high, will be used to form an alcove in the northwest corner of the reading room for a young adult collection of about 1200 volumes. The long section will be double faced to include Y.A. books on one side, adult browsing-room books on the other. The shorter section will also be double-faced and will contain young adult books on one side, adult books on the other; a coffee table and four lounge chairs will complete the furnishings of the Y.A. alcove.

Boys' and Girls' Section:
Size: 36x50' - 1800 sq. ft.

The Boys' and Girls' section should contain separate rest rooms located in the southwest corner of the area, against an outside wall, with a hose bibb on the outside for watering the small landscaped area in front of the building. Each rest room should be 5x5' with the doors opening inward. The boys' room should contain only the conventional fixtures, as there will not be room for a separate urinal. The drinking fountain should be located on the outside wall of the boys' rest room, to connect with the same plumbing pipes and well away from the corner where it could splash on walls, books, or bulletin board.

The drinking fountain should be lower than an adult fountain and should be of the refrigerated type.

The northwest corner of the boys' and girls' area shall be set off by low shelving and a sloping table to form a small alcove for picture books. Shelving in this section should be deeper and higher between shelves, but total height will be 4 feet, the same as the other low shelving used as dividers.

Four or five rectangular tables, 3x6' and 26 inches high, each with six chairs should be provided in this area, plus one or two round tables about 4 ft. in diameter and only 23 inches high. Three sloping tables with benches should be included.

The children's librarian's desk should be 30x60" with a posture chair and should face inward toward the room. In the corner next to the rest rooms, the Head of Children's Services recommends a large bulletin board on the wall with a separate display table below or a built-in counter to keep book marks, folders, and other descriptive literature. It can be used for book display as well.

Standing stacks, double faced, 5-1/2 ft. high, with 5
shelves, adjustable, will be needed at the outset. The
room will accommodate seven of these. Built-in wall
shelving will be around the walls, 6 ft. shelving with five
shelves, adjustable.

24-30 chairs will be needed for the reading tables, in color.
Smaller, lower chairs for the round table.

Carpeting in this area as well as in the remainder of the public area. Could be a different but harmonizing color. The
only problem in having different colors would be if it were
deemed desirable later to decrease the size of the children's
area and increase the size of the adult area by moving the
low stacks. It would be a patchwork problem. Also, if the
reverse were desired, increasing the size of the children's
area and decreasing the size of the adult area.

Adult Browsing Area:
Size: 16x18' - 284 sq. ft.

This browsing area will be created by using the solid partition of the all-purpose room in the northwest section of
the building as one side and the high shelving separating the
young adult area on the other. Book capacity will be approximately 2,500 books, arranged by categories. Two
small coffee tables and eight lounge chairs will present an
inviting appearance as one enters the front door.

Reference Area:
Size: 32x24' minus the small area occupied by the back of the
charging unit.

This area will accommodate approximately 2,000 reference
works, an alcove for microfilm and microfilm viewers, a
magazine rack along the west wall, and magazine storage
on wide shelves below the upper racks. A sorting table
will be necessary, 3x5' for use of the page in returning
magazines to the shelves. As it is hoped to have back issues of magazines on microfilm for five years back, a
great deal of storage space for back issues of magazines
will not be needed. Current magazines will be displayed
and will be kept for approximately one year back.

About five reading tables 3x6' can be accommodated in the
reference area. Six would make it very crowded. One
round table can also be accommodated near the magazine
rack. Built-in wall shelving across the south wall and
beneath the picture window and built-in shelving on the
north wall will be tall--7 ft. and will be divided into six
shelves. The low shelving behind the desk will have a
counter top for use of staff and public in looking over reference volumes.

A counter with room beneath for knees should be constructed along the walls of the alcove for microfilm readers. There will be room for two straight readers and a reader-printer. Film storage will be in a cabinet on the north side of the small alcove. This should be a solid wall, and the cabinets should be deep enough to accommodate the standard microfilm storage boxes. Three chairs will be needed for this area.

Open Area or Corridor down the Middle:

This area should be unobstructed as far as any furniture in the middle of the open sweep of vision is concerned. However, along the west wall separating the public rest rooms from the main corridor, 8 ft. in length, there will be either two Quik-See record units or one single bin, with one listening post for records. If deemed desirable, this listening post can be placed in the northwest corner of the reading room, outside the conference room, but in this case would be at a considerable distance from the record cabinets.

The Workroom:
Size: 12x20' - 240 sq. ft.

This area is large enough to accommodate three staff desks 30x60' and a work table or counter along the west wall. Cabinets and shelving should be built in all around the room wherever there is wall space, leaving room only for a medium-sized bulletin board on one wall with a counter and cabinets beneath. This storage space will hold books in process, supplies, exhibit materials, etc. One cabinet, under the work table should provide shallow and deep shelves for cardboard and other children's exhibit materials. Materials for seasonal decorations, for making signs, for all possible needs, will be provided in this room. The floor covering in this area can be tile. Three posture chairs should be provided for the desks, as well as at least two typewriters and an adding machine.

Staff Room: Staff Rest Room:
Size: 10x17 - 170 sq. ft. including rest room.

This room will contain a studio couch, a dining table and four chairs, preferably in wood grain with plastic top, a combination electric refrigerator and sink unit and equipment (hooks) for hanging wraps in the entry hall to the rest room. The rest room door should not open directly off the staff room proper. The rest room should have the stool in a booth and should have a lavatory placed in a vanity counter with large mirror above it. There should be a small cabinet for medicines, cleaning compound, extra toilet paper and paper towels.

This room should have a wall clock, preferably electric,
tuned in with the other clocks in the building, all of which
should be synchronized.

All Purpose Room:
Size 24x32 - 768 sq. ft.

Will accommodate as high as 80 people with folding chairs
set up. Storage room is set off in the northwest corner of
the room, 4x10 ft. to accommodate these chairs and any
projection equipment. There will be shelves for the latter.
Next to the storage area will be a sink unit with a small
range and oven alongside for use by groups meeting and
wishing to serve refreshments. A folding accordion door of
wood or plastic will shut off this area when not in use. A
large screen for projection should be installed on the wall
at the front of the room, on the west wall. The foyer,
which can be locked off from the library proper at night,
will have a drinking fountain and entrance to the rest rooms.
It will also have an outside entrance that can be used for
entrance and exit. It should have a self-locking door. A
built-in or hanging wall projection screen, preferably electric, should be provided on the west wall. The walls of
the room should have a type of covering that will be convenient for hanging or fastening displays. A plain pine
backing is suggested, covered with some attractive cloth
material similar to burlap. This type of surface should be
used from about 3 feet up to about 7 feet. The floor covering in this room should also be carpet if possible. If
necessary to cut costs, a good-looking fairly resilient tile
could be used. If the building is built on a concrete slab,
asphalt tile may have to be used. Lighting should be artificial, with no outside windows. This will make for uniform
soft lighting in the room, save expense, and provide a safety
measure against break-in and disappearance of valuable items
that might be on display. The room must be adequately
ventilated with the air conditioning or some other system to
provide for a crowd of as many as 80-90 people in the room
at one time. If funds permit, an attractive wall paneling of
birch or mahogany should be used above and below the exhibit area of the walls.

Rest Rooms and Janitor-Utility Areas:

The two public rest rooms for general and meeting-room
use must have doors at both ends, so that the doors leading
into the main library can be locked at night from the outside and still permit ingress from the meeting room foyer.

Size: Each rest room is 5x8', the minimum size that will
accommodate stool, lavatory, and inner partitions around
the stools. The men's rest room should have a urinal in
addition to the regular stool. Plumbing is back to back

whenever possible to save on expense. Rest room doors
should open inward. The walls should be of very durable
material, hard to scratch or mark upon and it would be
highly desirable to sand blast them, a method which helps
to hold down vandalism and wall marking.

The janitor closet is combined with the heating and air
conditioning equipment room and is also 5x8'. Should it
prove that this is not a large enough area for the type of
heating and air conditioning to be installed 2 or 3 extra
feet can be gained in width by cutting down on the staff
rest room and staff room area. The architect would make
this adjustment if necessary. However, it is usually possible to secure combination plants that will not be wider
than 5 feet. If the plant is operated by gas, it should more
than meet all building safety codes and the walls of this
room should be lined with fireproof material such as
asbestos, or be a standard fire wall.

Librarian's Office:

The librarian's office is 10x12' or 120 square feet.

This is slightly larger than most offices in buildings of this
size. However, it will afford more shelf area for professional material, more comfort when conferring with
visitors, room in case another desk needs to be put in for
a typewriter (small typewriter desk). A small work table
and a file will also be housed in the office.

Entrance

Just inside the front door and to right and left two brick or
stone planters, preferably the latter to match the stone
facing on the outside, will enhance the attractiveness of the
first impression. These can be planted with some rather
impressive large plants that do well indoors and with a
south exposure. A drain pipe should be installed at the
bottom of each planter with an opening in the outside wall
so that when the plants are watered there will be an outlet
and the soil will not smell sour.

Parking Area:

Parking stalls should be a generous 10x20'. The area should
be black-topped, as should all of the lot except the area immediately in front of the building. A 6 to 8' setback
is desirable.

Building Program for a Large Branch
(Showing Careful Analysis of Community Characteristics)

OFFICE OF LIBRARY SERVICES
DEPARTMENT OF EDUCATION
HONOLULU, HAWAII

October 24, 1967

McCully-Moiliili Branch Library

Planning the Facilities

1. Determining Library Service Area:

   Since the size of the facility is directly proportional to
   the number of potential clients that may use it, a library
   service area was established to indicate the geographic area
   that the library will serve.

   The service area was determined for the McCully-Moiliili
   Branch Library by considering the following:

   I.   Driving Time

   II. Influence of other libraries

   This service area will include the following: McCully,
   Moiliili, Ala Wai, Bingham and Pawaa.

2. Population Projections:

   The service area of the McCully-Moiliili Branch Library due
   to hotel-apartment zoning has a tremendous potential for population growth. The 1960 population of 30,000 shown in
   Table III was determined from tracts and blocks census.

   1960 Census Tract and block numbers indicating the 1960
   population within this service area is shown in Table III.

   On the basis of these 1960 census figures, the population
   projections of the area to be served by the proposed library
   are as follows:

1960	30,000
1965	33,750
1970	37,500
1975	41,250
1980	45,000

It is anticipated that the population will level off after 1980.

Table I

The 1960 McCully-Moiliili Population by Tracts

Census Tract No.	City Block No.	1960 Population
19	1 (Portion), 5 (Portion), 6-12	2,576
20	16-21, 22 (Portion), 32	664
22	1-3	2,719
23	A11	3,798
24	A11	5,856
25	A11	4,138
26	A11	4,517
27	25-29, 31-43, 47	2,895
34	21, 22	86
35	1, 2, 14-17, 29, 30	839
36	1, 29, 30	1,347
37	8-10, 12, 13, 23	491
	Total	29,926
	Say	30,000

3.   The Size of the Facility:

The size of the structure for the McCully-Moiliili Branch
Library is based on the State General Plan Standard of
0.35 sq. ft. per capita for the building, and the population
projections for the service area given above.

With this data the estimated size of the structure was
developed for several different years and is shown in
Table II.

Table II

Facility Size

Year	Population Projection	Facility Size 0.35 of Population	State Size 0.85 of Population
1960	30,000	10,500 s.f.	25,500 s.f.
1965	34,000	11,900 s.f.	28,920 s.f.
1975	41,000	14,350 s.f.	34,850 s.f.
1980	45,000	15,750 s.f.	38,250 s.f.

Using appropriate criteria it has been established that the user agencies' requirements can be accommodated by the size of buildings indicated in Table II.

4.   Space Allocation:

The building size determined in prior sections has been broken down into a functional space program developed for years 1965, 1975 and 1980.   This is shown in Table III.

5.   Recommended Construction:

In order to reach a decision on the size of library that should be constructed now, it is necessary to consider several factors.   Probably the most important of these is, which scheme will afford the most economy to the State.

Accordingly, an economic comparison was made on whether we should construct the ultimate facility now or whether we should delay the construction until some later date to more nearly coincide with the need.

Since the advantage is so small it may be questioned whether or not it really is economical to construct the total facility now.   However, examination of another factor may solve the dilemma.

A comparison of the space program for year 1975 and 1980 given in Table III will show that the major expansion is planned for the reading room areas.

Since this is the main public service area of the library, during the construction of the additional area which will take from 4 to 6 months will be limited if not altogether restricted.

Although this disruption of library service to the public cannot be measured and entered as a direct factor in the economic comparison, it does lend more support to construction of the total facility now.

Accordingly it is recommended that the facility structure
be constructed with a total area of 15,750 square feet as
indicated in the following space program:

Space Description	Recommended Construction
Charging Desk	400
Adult Reading Room	6,650
Children's Reading Room	3,300
Story-Telling - Meeting Room (w/ 130 Ø Storage Area)	1,750
Work Room	800
Magazine Storage Room	800
General Storage Room	100
Librarian's Office	100
Staff Room	200
Public Toilets	300
Staff Toilet	50
Janitor's Storage	50
Ground Maintenance Room	50
Circulation	800
Entrance - Lobby	400
Total	15,750

Funding for Facility

Act 217/66 (F86)	$	82,000
Act 195/65 (B5)		111,600
Act 52/64 (B3e)		325,000
Act 201/63 (B41)		361,000
Federal Funds (P.L. 89-511)		70,000
Total	$	949,600

Table III

Space Program

Space Description	Recommended Allocation in Sq. Ft.		
Population - Year	34,000- 1965	41,000- 1975	45,000- 1980
Circulation Desk	400	400	400
Adult Reading Room	4,450	5,750	6,650
Children's Reading Room	2,050	2,900	3,300
Story-Telling - Meeting Room (w/130 ∅ Storage Area)	1,750	1,750	1,750
Work Room Area	800	800	800
Magazine Storage Area	600	700	800
General Storage Room	100	100	100
Librarian's Office	100	100	100
Staff Lounge	200	200	200
Public Toilets	300	300	300
Staff Toilet	50	50	50
Janitor's Storage Room	50	50	50
Ground Maintenance Room	50	50	50
Circulation	600	800	800
Entrance & Lobby Area	400	400	400
Total Areas	11,900	14,350	15,750

Summary

The McCully-Moiliili Library will be a quasi-regional library of the Hawaii State Library System. Ultimately it will house 100,000 volumes of library materials including books, microfilm, records, tapes and other materials. It will house a well-developed and in depth reference collection. The facility is expected to contain temperature and humidity control equipment to reduce the noise level, remove dust and acids from the air, and to provide a humidity level for the protection of library materials and equipment. The facility design provides for two levels with the children's room and parking on the first level and the adult, young adult, reference and periodical reading areas on the second level.

Appendix D

The School-Housed Library Branch:
a Bibliography

Ahlers, Eleanor. "School and public library cooperation; Standards, Goals, Now What?" Ohio Library Association Bulletin, 30:15-20 Jan. 1960.

Ahlers, Eleanor. "School and public library relationships: a selected bibliography." ALA Bulletin 53:134 Feb. 1959.

American Library Association. American Association of School Librarians. Board of Directors. "Library services act and school libraries." ALA Bulletin 52:124 Feb. 1958.

American Library Association. American Association of School Librarians. Committee for implementation of standards. Standards for School Library Programs, and a discussion guide.

American Library Association. Public Library Division. "Public Library Service." ALA 1956. 74 p.

Anthony, L. "School library serves the community." Illinois Library. 28:101-2. Jan. 1946.

Batchelder, Mildred L. "Public library influence in school libraries." Library Trends 1:271-85 Jan. 1953.

Beasley, K. E. and Robinson, C. E. "Study and recommendations of library districts for Pennsylvania." Pennsylvania State University Institute of Public Administration. 1962. 85 p.

Bowerman, G. F. "Librarians oppose bipartite boards." Library Journal. 73:688-95. May 1, 1948.

Bowler, Roberta. "Local public library administration." International City Managers' Association. 1964. p. 275-276.

Broderick, Dorothy M. An Introduction to children's work in public libraries. H. W. Wilson, 1965.

Cecil, H. L. and Heaps, W. A. School library service in the United States: An interpretive survey. Wilson, 1940.

City of Los Angeles. Bureau of Budget and Efficiency. "Organization, administration, and management of the Los Angeles Public

Library. Vol. VI. Extension Service Requirements. July, 1949.
p. 84.

Cole, T. J. "Originiand development of School libraries." Peabody
Journal of Education 37:87-92, Sept. 1959.

Fargo, Lucile F. Library in the school. 4th ed. ALA 1947. 374-
375.

Githens, Alfred M. and Munn, Ralph. Program for the public libraries of New York City. New York City Planning Commission,
1945. p. 89, 90.

Hayner, Irene C. A Study of Michigan public libraries administered
by school boards. Library School, University of Michigan,
1955-56. Unpublished report.

Hamill, Harold; Laich, Katherine; Siegel, Ernest; and Bishop,
Edith. Public and school libraries, joint statement issued by the
director and three staff members of the Los Angeles Public
Library.

Henne, Frances. "School libraries and the social order." Library
Trends 1:263-70. Jan. 1953.

Joint Committee of NEA and ALA. Schools and public libraries.
NEA 1941.

Krarup, A. "Portland severs an old bond." Library Journal 71:101-
4, Jan. 15, 1946.

McJenkin, V. "Library service to secondary school students; its
problems and opportunities for school and public libraries. "
National Association of Secondary School Principals Bulletin
50:10-17, Jan. 1966.

Mahar, Mary H. "How do the public library and the school library
supplement and complement each other in providing services for
children, youth, and young adults?" Idaho Librarian 17:no. 1,
Jan. 1965, p. 25-29.

Martin, Lowell. Branch library service for Dallas: a report
sponsored by the Friends of the Dallas Public Library. 1958.
p. 64-65.

Martin, Lowell. "Relation of public and school libraries in serving
youth." ALA Bulletin 53:112-17, Feb. 1959.

Peterson, H. N. "Keep the public library a free agency." Library
Journal 73:521-6+ April 1, 1948.

*Peterson, H. N. "Public library branches in school buildings."
ALA Bulletin March 1960. p. 215+ .

Peterson, H. N. Survey of branch requirements for the Ft. Worth Public Library. 1959, p. 52, 54-55.

Rowell, John. "Report card to Pennsylvania School librarians. The School-public library combination." Pennsylvania Library Association Bulletin Nov. 1963, p. 29-33.

St. Julian, B. A. & Brother, S. "Dialogue of cooperation between school and public libraries." Louisiana Library Association Bulletin 29: 73, Summer 1966.

Sealock, Richard. "K C.: Problems and progress." Library Journal 93: no. 10, May 15, 1968, p 1943-44.

Smith, Hannis S. "The Case for independent school libraries." Minnesota Libraries 19: 220-221, no. 8. Reprinted from The American School Board Journal. Dec. 1959.

Stevenson, Gordon. "The School board that played public library." Library Journal 93: 2434, 2437-8, no. 12, June 15, 1968.

Wezeman, Frederick. Combination school and public libraries in Pennsylvania, 1965. A study with recommendations, sponsored by the Pennsylvania State Library, Harrisburg, Penn. Aug. 1965.

Wheeler, J. L. and Goldhor, H. Practical administration of public libraries. Harper and Row, 1962, chapt. 22.

Wheeler, J. L. Reconsideration of the strategic location for public library buildings. Univ. of Illinois Graduate School of Library Science. 1967. 36 p.

White, Ruth. The School-housed public library: a survey. ALA. 1963.

Wildermuth, Ora. "I prefer the independent library board. ALA Bulletin 35; 443-47 July 1941.

Winslow, Amy & Robinson, Alan. "The Public library and the school library; similar ends but different methods." News Notes of California Libraries, v. 55, no. 3, Summer 1960, p. 323-328.

Wisconsin Dept. of Public Instruction. "Organizational relationship, a policy statement." Wisconsin Library Bulletin. Mar. 1967. 89-94.

Wisconsin. Free Library Commission. Proceedings of the 8th Institute on public library management: Public library - public school relationship. 1961. 64 p.

Appendix E

Building Information Bibliography

American Carpet Institute.
  Cutting costs with carpet. The Institute, n. d.

American Library Association. Library Administration Division.
  Problems in planning library facilities... The Association, 1964

  Library Equipment Institute. The Association, 1965.

American Library Association. Library Technology Project.
  The use of carpeting in libraries, a report. The Association,
    n. d.

American Library Association. Public Library Association.
  Guide lines for determining minimum space requirements...
    The Association, 1962.

"Carpeting for libraries." Library Journal 87: 742-743, F 15 '62.

Contra Costa County Library.
  Branch building size. 1957 (mimeographed).

Eastlick, J. T.
  A library building program. University of the State of New York
    State Education Department, New York State Library,
    Library Extension Division, n. d.

Foothill College Library, Los Altos, California.
  Carpeting, a Report. October 12, 1963 (mimeographed).

Hamill, H. L.
  The Whittier Public Library, report of a survey. Los Angeles,
    the author, 1964.

Los Angeles Public Library.
  Building standards for new branches. The Library, 1960.

California State Library.
  News Notes of California Libraries. Volume 58, No. 3, Summer
    1963, p. 346.

Poole, F. G. ed
  "Library Furniture and Furnishings." Library Trends, April
    1965.

San Francisco Public Library.
Policy on construction of branch libraries. 1963 (mimeographed).

Wheeler, J. L.
The small public library. American Library Association, 1963.

Wheeler, J. L. and Goldhor, Herbert.
Practical administration of public libraries. Harper, 1962.

Whittier Public Library Staff.
Master plan for the Whittier Public Library. The Library, 1962.

Appendix F

General Bibliography

1. Alabama Library Association. Division of Public Libraries. Committee on Standards. Alabama Standards for Alabama Public Libraries. May, 1966. Guidelines for determining Minimum Space Requirements.

2. Alabama, University of. Course Outline in Public Library Administration, n. d.

3. American Library Association. It's Your Library. Branch Library or Bookmobile? Mimeographed. American Library Association, n. d. 3 pages.

4. American Library Association. Review and Evaluation of Access to Public Libraries. (Report of the Directors). American Library Association, 1964. Mimeographed, p. 7.

5. American Library Association. Statistical Standards, addenda to Minimum Standards for Public Library Systems. American Library Association, 1967. p. 4.

6. American Library Association; Library Community Project. Headquarters Staff. Studying the Community; a Basis for Planning Library Adult Education Services. American Library Association, 1960. p. 12-14.

7. American Library Association. Public Libraries Association. Interim Standards for Small Public Libraries: Guidelines toward Achieving the Goals of Public Library Service. American Library Association, 1962.

8. American Library Association. Public Libraries Association. Committee on Standards. Minimum Standards for Public Library Systems. American Library Association, 1966. p. 17 and 54.

9. American Library Association. Small Libraries Project. List: Suggested Reference Books. Adapted from a list prepared by the North Carolina State Library, revised by the South Carolina State Library Board. Rev. 1966.

10. Anderson, John F. Wilmot Branch, Tucson Public, Receives Award of Merit for Distinguished Accomplishment in Library Architecture. Arizona Libraries, Fall, 1966, p. 7-11.

11. Aubrey, Claude B. The Shopping Center Branch Library: a
     Brief Report. Ontario Library Review, Feb. 1961, p. 17.

12. Bailey, J. Russell. Mr. Architect, Listen. Library Journal,
     Dec. 1, 1965, p. 5147-5151.

13. Bard, Harriett E. Reaching the Unreached. Wisconsin
     Library Bulletin, Jan.-Feb., 1966, p. 7-15. Same, in
     Library Occurrent, May, 1966, p. 31-37.

14. Bateman, R. B. The Selection and Display of Books for a
     Small Branch Library. Library World, May, 1957, p.
     175-7, and 683.

15. Benjamin, Selma. How many Blocks to New York? Library
     Journal, Jan. 15, 1968, p. 265-266.

16. Blasik, Hank J. Red Carpet Reserve. Flyer sheet and letter
     sent to author, 1968.

17. Bloss, Meredith. The Branch Collection. Library Trends,
     April, 1966, p. 422-432 (ed. by Andrew Geddes).

18. Bowler, Roberta B., ed. Local Public Library Administration.
     International City Managers Association, 1964, p. 32-34,
     77, 145-146, 259, 260, 263-268, 272-276, 282, 303-304,
     412-413.

19. Bradshaw, Lillian M. Library Lesson Learned, in: City
     Beat, by Jerry McCarty, Staff Writer. The Dallas Times
     Herald, Nov. 25, 1968.

20. Branch Libraries. Library Journal, Dec. 1, 1965, p. 5180-
     5185; Dec. 1, 1966, p. 5869-5879.

21. Branch Libraries Multiply to Meet Popular Demand. Library
     Journal, Dec. 1, 1964, p. 4733-4742.

22. Branch Librarians to be Rotated. Edmonton Public Library
     News Notes, Oct. 1961, p. 54-55.

23. Brooklyn Sets Up District Libraries to Serve as "Family
     Reading Centers." Library Journal, Nov. 1, 1960, p. 3954.

24. Brown, Eleanor Frances. Bookmobiles and Bookmobile
     Service. Scarecrow Press, 1967.

25. Buildings for Books: Are They Obsolete? Architectural
     Forum, May, 1964, p. 81-99.

26. Burson, Phyllis S. Corpus Christi Round Libraries: Parkdale
     Branch Public Library. Texas Library Journal, Winter,
     1964, p. 134-136.

27.   Byam, Milton. History of Branch Libraries. Library Trends,
      April 1966, p. 72.

28.   Campbell, Henry Cummings. Metropolitan Public Library
      Planning Throughout the World. Pergamon Press, 1967,
      p. 64-66, and 68-71.

29.   Carman, Stanley B. Preparing a Program for the Design of
      a Library Building. Minnesota Libraries, June, 1962, p.
      163-165.

30.   Carroll, J. M. Boston Branch. Library Journal, Feb. 15,
      1961, p. 780-781.

31.   Carter, Mary D. , and Bonk, Wallace J. Building Library
      Collections. 2nd ed. Scarecrow Press, 1964, p. 79.

32.   Castagna, Edwin. Library Service of the Future; Guess What's
      Ahead. In: The Library Reaches Out, by Kate Coplan and
      Edwin Castagna. Oceana, 1965, p. 379.

33.   Chappell, Yvonne H. Mobile's Two New Branches. Southeastern
      Librarian, Summer, 1964, p. 125-127.

34.   Charlton, B. M. County Headquarters and Branches; Branch
      Viewpoint. Library Association Record, April, 1961, p.
      128-130.

35.   Chastain, Katherine E. A Community's Cultural Center.
      Pioneer, May-June, 1958, p. 10-11.

36.   Cheek, H. C. Low Budget Planning. Pioneer, May, 1958,
      p. 9.

37.   Cleveland and Cuyahoga County Library Systems; Regional
      Planning Commission. Survey of Reading Habits. Conducted
      by Fuller, Smith & Ross, Inc. , Dec. 1, 1965.

38.   Coburn, M. Children's Branch, Public Library, Opens in
      Toronto. Library Journal, Jan. 15, 1963, p. 282. Same
      in: School Library Journal, Jan. 1963, p. 34.

39.   Contra Costa County Library, Pleasant Hills, California.
      Branch Standards.

40.   Coplan, Kate, and Castagna, Edwin. The Library Reaches
      Out. Oceana, 1965, p. 394.

41.   Davies, J. The Problem of the Decline in Use of New
      Branch Libraries and Some Suggested Remedies. Library
      Association Record, August, 1961, p. 274-276.

42.   Dempsey, F. J. Berkeley's Award-Winning Branch Library. Il.
      plan. California Librarian, April, 1967, p. 75+ .

43. Doms, Keith. Public Library Buildings. In: Bowler, Roberta.
     Local Public Library Administration. International City
     Manager's Association, 1964, p. 301-302.

44. Elks, Hazel, Director, Free Public Library, Elizabeth, New
     Jersey. Letter to author, dated May, 1968.

45. Duthie, R. Glen Innes (Auckland, New Zealand) Branch
     Library. New Zealand Libraries, Aug.-Sept., 1966, p.
     142-150.

46. Enoch Pratt Free Library, Baltimore, Maryland. Book
     Selection Policies. 3rd ed., 1963, p. 7.

47. Farrington, J. B. Patrons Feel at Home at this Branch
     Library. Il. Pioneer, Jan. 1961, p. 7-9.

48. Fickes, Eugene W. Mistakes that Have Been Made in Recent
     Library Buildings. In: Libraries Building for the Future.
     American Library Association, 1967, p. 17-19.

49. Florida Library Association. Florida Standards for Public
     Library Services. Florida Library and Historical Com-
     mission, 1967, p. 24-28.

50. Frantz, John C. Big City Libraries: Strategy and Tactics for
     Change. Library Journal, May 15, 1968, p. 1968-1970.

51. Frantz, John C. County and Regional Library Service Today's
     Reality in America. Minnesota Libraries, June, 1962,
     p. 155-156.

52. Fresno County Free Library, Fresno, California. Branch
     Standards. Fresno County Free Library, 1964, 1 page.

53. Galvin, Hoyt R. Letter written to author, Nov. 4, 1968.

54. Galvin, Hoyt R. Public Library Building in 1968. Library
     Journal, Dec. 1, 1968, p. 4498-4511.

55. Galvin, Hoyt R., and Van Buren, Martin. The Small Public
     Library Building. Unesco, 1959, 1962, p. 48-50, 51, 55,
     and 89.

56. Garrison, Gary. Some Recent Public Library Branch Location
     Studies by City Planners. Library Quarterly. University of
     Chicago Press, April, 1966, p. 151-55.

57. Gates, Jean Key. Introduction to Librarianship. McGraw-Hill,
     1968, p. 208-209.

58. Geddes, Andrew. Leasing Our Way. Library Journal, Dec. 1,
     1961, p. 4088-4090.

59. Goldhor, Herbert. Library Bookateria. Library Journal,
     Nov. 1, 1958, p. 3074.

60. Grafton, Samuel. Danger Stalks Our Parks. Reader's Digest,
     July, 1964, p. 114-117.

61. Graybill, E. S. Ceilings and Sound. Library Journal, Dec. 1,
     1961, p. 4086-4087.

62. Greenaway, Emerson. The Future of Adult Services in the
     Public Library. American Library Association Bulletin,
     Jan. , 1968, p. 49-50.

63. Greenaway, Emerson. New Trends in Branch Library Service.
     Library Trends, April, 1966, p. 451-457.

64. Gregory, Ruth W. Search for Information About Community
     Needs. In: Group Services in Public Libraries. Library
     Trends. July, 1968, p. 15-16.

65. Grundt, Leonard. Branch Library Inadequacies in a Typical
     Large City. Library Journal, Oct. 1, 1965, p. 3397-4001.

66. Hamill, Harold. Reaching Out to a City of 459 Square Miles
     (The Los Angeles Public Library). In: The Library Reaches
     Out, by Kate Coplan and Edwin Castagna. Oceana, 1965,
     p. 82.

67. Hamill, Harold, Director, Los Angeles Public Library, Los
     Angeles, California. Selection, Training, and Staffing for
     Branch Libraries. In: Current Trends in Branch Libraries.
     Library Trends, April, 1966, p. 412.

68. Havens, S. Branches, More or Less? Library Journal, Dec.
     1, 1964, p. 4761.

69. Henderson, W. R. Plant a Library in a Shopping Center?
     Arizona Librarian, Spring, 1967, p. 7-9.

70. Herispe, Mary L. Role of the Public Library in an Under-
     privileged Neighborhood. Thesis. M. A. in Library
     Science, Catholic University of America, 1961, 58 pages.

71. Highlands Branch Library (Edmonton). Il. plan. Edmonton
     Public Library News Notes, Dec. , 1963, p. 90-92.

72. Hoeffgren, Helen. Branch Library Programs: Operation
     Shoestring Budget. Wilson Library Bulletin, Feb. , 1969,
     p. 545-551.

73. Howard, E. A. Ethel F. McCollough Honored in Evansville.
     Focus on Indiana Libraries, August, 1965, p. 54-55.

74. J. C. Hamilton Branch, Shreve Memorial Library. Louisiana Library Association Bulletin, Spring, 1962, p. 33.

75. Jefferson, George. Public Library Administration. Philosophical Library, 1966, p. 39.

76. Jefferson Market Courthouse Will Open in the Fall as a branch library of New York Public. Bookmark, July, 1967, p. 352-353.

77. Jenkins, Joseph H. Programming and Financing Library Buildings. In: Libraries Building for the Future. American Library Association, 1967, p. 35-39.

78. John F. Kennedy Branch. Focus on Indiana Libraries, Aug., 1964, p. 36.

79. Jones, Wyman. A Foursome for Dallas. Library Journal, Dec. 1, 1964, p. 4733-4736.

80. Jones, Wyman. Paris in Dallas. Library Journal, Oct. 1, 1961, p. 3242-3243.

81. Jones, Wyman. Penetrating the Neighborhood of a Community. In: The Library Reaches Out, by Kate Coplan and Edwin Castagna. Oceana, 1965, p. 63-78.

82. Jones, Wyman. That Was the Day That Was. Library Journal, July, 1964, p. 2752+.

83. Jordan, Robert T. Home Delivery Library Service. Wilson Library Bulletin, Dec., 1967, p. 403-405.

84. Kaiser, Walter. Libraries in Non-consolidated Systems. In: Current Trends in Branch Libraries, Andrew Geddes, ed. Library Trends, April, 1966, p. 440-449.

85. Kane, Joseph N. Famous First Facts. H. W. Wilson, 1964, p. 342.

86. Kealty, Francis. An Architect's View of Library Planning. Library Journal, Dec. 1, 1963, p. 4521-4525.

87. Kountz, John C. Charting a Course in Charymaki: a Didactic Tale with Overtones. American Library Association Bulletin, April, 1967, p. 407-408.

88. Kountz, John C. Community Branch, Area Branch. American Library Association Bulletin, April, 1967, p. 407-408.

89. Leaseback Financing for New York Public Library's Riverdale Branch. Bookmark, Nov., 1965, p. 56-58.

90.   Long Beach Public Library, Long Beach, California. The
      Courier, Feb. , 1969, p. 1.

91.   Los Angeles Public Library. Basic Principles of Planning
      Needs of the City of Los Angeles Public Library.
      Mimeographed, n. d.

92.   Louisiana Library Association.   Public Libraries Section.
      Standards Statements for Louisiana Public Libraries.
      Public Libraries Section, Louisiana Library Association,
      1964, p. 10-11, 18-21, and 23.

93.   Lyman, William. Preliminary and Final Drawings, Bidding
      and Construction.   In: Libraries Building for the Future.
      American Library Association, 1967, p. 39-40.

94.   McAdams, Nancy R. Super-Librarian and Sub-Architect.
      Library Journal, Dec. 1, 1966, p. 5827-5831.

95.   McBee Systems, Greenwich, Connecticut.   Field Report. p.
      S-594.   Reprinted from Sales Management, Oct. -Dec. ,
      1961.

96.   McClarren, Robert R. , and Thompson, Donald E. Architectural
      Checklist.   Library Journal, Dec. 1, 1966, p. 5832-5837.

97.   McDormand, Ruth M. Administration of Branch Libraries with
      Special Reference to the Atlantic Region.   Atlantic Pro-
      vinces Library Association Bulletin, May, 1967, p. 49-52.

98.   Maihl, Viola R. Planning the Branch Library. Pioneer, Nov. -
      Dec. , 1960, p. 8-11.

99.   Martin, Lowell A. Branch Library Service for Dallas. Dallas
      Public Library, Jan. 1, 1958, p. 64.

100. Martin, Lowell A. The Purpose and Administrative Organiza-
      tion of Branch Systems in Large Urban Libraries. Paper.
      University of Chicago, Graduate Library School, 1940.

101. Metcalfe, Keyes D. Library Lighting. Library Journal, Dec. ,
      1961, p. 4081-4085.

102. Metcalfe, Keyes D. The Use of Hindsight in Planning Library
      Buildings. In: Libraries Building for the Future. American
      Library Association, 1967, p. 4.

103. Meyer, Edith Patterson.   Meet the Future: People & Ideas
      in the Libraries of Today. Little, Brown, 1964, p. 93-94.

104. Mississippi Library Commission.   A Survey of the Branches'
      Service of a Multi-County Library System.   Mississippi
      Library Commission. Jackson, Mississippi, 15 pages.

105. Mississippi Library Commission. Trustee Manual. Mississippi Library Commission. Jackson, Mississippi.

106. Moreland, George B. Operation Saturation: Using Paperbacks, Branch Libraries in Maryland Conduct an experiment to Equate Book Supply with Patron Demand. Library Journal, May 15, 1968, p. 1975-1979.

107. Mortimore, A. D. Branch Libraries (Great Britain). Deutsch, 1966, 154 pages.

108. Mostar, Roman. Magnolia Branch Library, Seattle. Pacific Northwest Library Association Quarterly, July, 1966, p. 251-252.

109. Mostar, Roman, Seattle: Sensitive and Unagressive (Magnolia Branch 1965). Library Journal, Dec. 1, 1966, p. 5878.

110. Nashville Claims a First for Its Airport Reading Room. Library Journal, Jan. 1, 1963, p. 74.

111. Neutra, Richard J. Centerpiece of a Library. Library Journal, Dec. 1, 1964, p. 4695-4697.

112. Newport Beach, City of. Public Library Standards for Planning Future Growth, 1967-68. Duplicated.

113. Norman, E. K. From Barrymore to Books. Pioneer, March, 1958, p. 3-5.

114. Nyren, Karl. A New Breed of Cat. Library Journal, Sept. 15, 1968, p. 3091-3095.

115. Nyren, Karl. The Transfer of Authority. Editorial. Library Journal, June 1, 1968, p. 2189.

116. Overman, Edward S., and Anders, Mary E. Portrait of a Library System: Country Style. Library Journal, March 15, 1962, p. 1084-1088.

117. Peterson, Harry N. Survey of the Fort Worth Public Library Branch Requirements. Washington, D. C., 1959, p. 52, and 54-55.

118. Philadelphia to Start Regional Library Service. Library Journal, Aug., 1962, p. 2716-2717.

119. Ramsay, Margery C. Location of Branch Libraries in a County Library System. Thesis, M. S. degree in Library Science, University of California, Jan., 1958, chapter IX, p. 120-135.

120. Roanoke, Virginia, Department of City Planning, and Roanoke
     Public Library Board. Branch Libraries, a Long Range
     Development Plan. The Authors, 1963, 25 pages.

121. Roberts, Don. This is My Beat. Library Journal, Jan. 15,
     1968, p. 259-264.

122. Robinson, Charles W. Area Branches for Baltimore. Library
     Journal, Dec. 1, 1965, p. 5183-5185.

123. Rose, Ernestine. The Public Library in American Life.
     Columbia University Press, 1954, p. 110.

124. Rowe, Harry M. , Jr. Hunt Foods Foundation Library
     (Fullerton Public Library). Il. Plan. California Librarian,
     Jan. 1966, p. 7+.

125. Russell, Thomas J. Client-Architect Relationship. Excerpt
     from address given at the California Library Association
     Conference, 1963, San Francisco, California.

126. Russell, Thomas J. Ten Steps for Achieving a Successful
     Library. Mimeographed sheet, 1 page, n. d.

127. Ruffin, Carolyn F. The Not-so-silent Inner City Branch
     Library. No. 1 in a series: Libraries That Care.
     Abridged by permission from The Christian Science
     Monitor, c1968. The Christian Science Publishing Society,
     all rights reserved. Sept. 7, 1968.

128. San Diego Public Library, San Diego, California. Branch
     Library Staffing Manual. Mimeographed. March, 1968,
     9 pages.

129. San Diego Public Library, San Diego, California. Branch
     Library Staffing Pattern. Mimeographed. March, 1969.

130. San Diego Public Library, San Diego, California. Branch
     Library Standards.

131. Santa Ana Public Library, Santa Ana, California. Branch
     Library Objectives. 1965.

132. Santa Ana Public Library, Santa Ana, California. Branch
     Library Service Program. Mimeographed. Nov. , 1968.

133. Santa Ana Public Library, Santa Ana, California. 100 Tests
     for a Good Public Library. Administrators and Supervisors
     Group, 1966.

134. Santa Ana Public Library, Santa Ana, California. The School-
     housed Branch: a Situation Survey. Santa Ana Public
     Library, 1968.

135. Sealock, Richard B. Extending Services. In: Local Public Library Administration, Roberta B. Bowler, ed. International City Manager's Association, 1964, p. 273-274.

136. Shaffer, Kenneth. Design for Tomorrow. Bridgeport Public Library, Bridgeport, Connecticut, 1966, p. 37-38, and 64-65.

137. Shaffer, Kenneth. Library Building Needs in Massachusetts. Bay State Librarian, July, 1964.

138. Shaw, Robt. J. , ed. Libraries Building for the Future. American Library Association, 1967.

139. Sinclair, Dorothy. Administration of the Small Public Library. American Library Association, 1965, p. 90-99, and 162-163.

140. Small Scale Library in Tennessee. Architectural Forum, May, 1964, p. 93.

141. Smith, Geoffrey. County Headquarters & Branches: Headquarter's Viewpoint. Library Association Record, April, 1961, p. 128-130.

142. South Carolina Library Association. Public Libraries Section. Standards for South Carolina Public Libraries. 1964, p. 6.

143. Sprain Brook Branch, Yonkers Public Library. Il. Bookmark, June, 1964, p. 267-268.

144. Stoffel, Lester L. The Large City Library from the Viewpoint of the Suburban Library. In: The Public Library in the Urban Setting, edited by Leon Carnovsky. University of Chicago Press, 1968, p. 92-93.

145. Trim Branch Library for the Suburbs. Architectural Forum, May, 1964, p. 89.

146. Tulsa City-County Library System, Tulsa, Oklahoma. Policy Manual. May, 1967, Sect. 7:3. 1.

147. Two Florida Libraries Named ALA Award Winners. Florida Libraries, Dec. , 1964, p. 15-16.

148. University of the State of New York. A Primer of Public Library Systems in New York State. Albany. The University of the State of New York, 1963.

149. Vainstein, Rose. Study of Branch and Bookmobile Needs for the City of Victoria, Canada. 1962.

150. Van Buren, Martin. A Guide to the Preparation of Furniture Specifications and Bidding Documents. Library Journal, Dec. 1, 1966, p. 5845-5850.

151. Van Buren, Martin. Is Carpet Practical? Library Journal, Dec. 1, 1965, p. 5152-5156.

152. Volin, Larry K. Architectural Barriers. Library Journal, Dec. 1, 1962, p. 4396.

153. Waldron, Jane Francis. Comparison of Branch Library Services in Three Seattle Communities. Thesis. MS in Library Science, University of Washington, 1957, 137 pages.

154. Warncke, Ruth. Library Objectives and Community Needs. In: Group Services in Libraries. Library Trends, July, 1968, p. 8-10.

155. Waters, R. L. Free Space: Can Public Libraries Reserve It? American Library Association Bulletin, March, 1964, p. 232-234.

156. Wezeman, Frederick. Better Branch Libraries. Minnesota Libraries, June, 1962, p. 170-171.

157. Wezeman, Frederick. Combination School and Public Libraries in Pennsylvania: A Study with Recommendations. Pennsylvania State Library, August, 1965.

158. Wezeman, Frederick. Neighborhood Library Service. Des Moines Public Library, 1959, p. 31-38.

159. Wezeman, Frederick. A Study of Branch Libraries. Lincoln City Library, Lincoln, Nebraska, 1967, p. 44-45.

160. Wheeler, Joseph L. The Effective Location of Public Library Buildings. University of Illinois, Urbana, Illinois. Occasional Papers No. 52, July, 1958, p. 2, 5, 8, and 33.

161. Wheeler, Joseph L., and Goldhor, Herbert. Practical Administration of Public Libraries. Harper & Row, 1962, p. 156, 411-412, 413, 414, 417, 419, 420, and 433-434.

162. Wheeler, Joseph L. The Small Library Building. No. 13 in The Small Libraries Project. American Library Association. Library Administration Division, 1963, 36 pages.

163. White, Fred T. Some Facts about the Vancouver Island Regional Library. Vancouver Island Regional Library Headquarters. Mimeographed, n. d., 2 pages.

164. White, Ruth M. The School-housed Public Library: A Survey.
      American Library Association, 1963, 62 pages.

165. Young, Helen A. County Branch for Richfield - Liquor Store
      Profits Finance. Library Journal, Dec. 1, 1961, p. 4112.

Index

736

North End Branch, Boston
(Massachusetts) Public Library, 492-493
North End Branch, San
Bernardino (California)
Public Library, 377
North Point Area Branch,
Baltimore County Public
Library, Towson, Maryland,
54
Nyren, Karl, 649-650

Objectives, branch, 66
Oktibbeha County Library
System, Starkville,
Mississippi, 458-459
Older Americans Act, 406
Omaha (Nebraska) Public
Library
W. Clarke Swanson Branch,
580-584, 609
Orange County Public Library,
Orange, California, 177,
301, 308, 402, 409, 683
Fountain Valley Branch, 314
Mesa Verde Branch, 301,
314, 683
West Garden Grove Branch,
308
Westminster Branch, 402
Organization, types of, 48-50
Organizations, community,
137-138
Outreach programs, 280-281,
299
Overman, Edward, 126

Paperbacks
Display cases for, 614
Increase in, 78
Paradise Hills Branch, San
Diego (California) County
Library, 463
Parents, library programs for,
280, 287
"Paris in Dallas" publicity
project, 669-670
Parkdale Branch, Corpus
Christi (Texas) Public
Library, 509, 512
Parking requirements, 354-356,
361-362, 363
Parks as locations, 338-339

Pennsylvania Avenue Branch,
Enoch Pratt Free Library,
Baltimore, Maryland, 69, 74
Peterson, Harry, 351, 445
Philadelphia Reading Centers,
161, 162
"Phoebe" (film), 280
Phoenix, Arizona, 38
Development plan, 38
Phonograph records, displaying,
608-609
Photocopying equipment, 610
Publicity for, 675
Pico Rivera Branch, Los
Angeles (California)
County Public Library
System, 498
Pierce County Library System,
Tacoma, Washington
Flora B. Tenzler Memorial
Branch, 560-564
Pioneer Library System, New
York, 291
Planning the branch, 361-386
Building program, 423-452
General principles, 382-384
Mistakes in, 377-381
Plaza Library, Regional Branch,
Kansas City (Missouri) Public
Library, 540
Policy and procedure manual,
274-275
Population explosion, effect of,
76
Portable branches. See Mobile
homes as branches, and Railroad car branch
Posters, 660, 661, 663
Pre-school Class, Boston
(Massachusetts) Public
Library, 289
Prince George's County Memorial
Library, Hyattsville,
Maryland
New Carrollton Branch,
584-585
Problems of branch libraries,
29
Procedure manual. See Policy
and procedure manual
Processing, centralized, 642-
643
Programs, lecture, 663-664